Social Problems and the Quality of Life

Second Edition

Social Problems and the Quality of Life

Robert H. Lauer
Southern Illinois University at Edwardsville

ωcb
Wm. C. Brown Company Publishers
Dubuque, Iowa

wcb group

Wm. C. Brown
Chairman of the Board

Mark C. Falb
Executive Vice President

wcb

**Wm. C. Brown Company
Publishers, College Division**

Lawrence E. Cremer
President

Raymond C. Deveaux
Vice President, Product Development

David Wm. Smith
Vice President/Marketing

David A. Corona
Assistant Vice President/Production Development and Design

Janis M. Machala
Director of Marketing Research

William A. Moss
Production Editorial Manager

Marilyn A. Phelps
Manager of Design

Mary M. Heller
Visual Research Manager

Book Team

James L. Romig
Editor

Maxine Kollasch
Production Editor

Lisa Bogle
Designer

Mary M. Heller
Visual Research Editor

Mavis M. Oeth
Permissions Editor

To Jeanette Carol
". . . the greatest of these is love."

Contents

1

Foundations 3

2

Problems of Deviance 75

3

Problems of Inequality 261

Second Edition

Social Problems and the Quality of Life

Robert H. Lauer

Southern Illinois University at Edwardsville

wcb
Wm. C. Brown Company Publishers
Dubuque, Iowa

wcb group

Wm. C. Brown
Chairman of the Board
Mark C. Falb
Executive Vice President

wcb

**Wm. C. Brown Company
Publishers, College Division**

Lawrence E. Cremer
President
Raymond C. Deveaux
Vice President, Product Development
David Wm. Smith
Vice President/Marketing
David A. Corona
Assistant Vice President/Production Development and Design
Janis M. Machala
Director of Marketing Research
William A. Moss
Production Editorial Manager
Marilyn A. Phelps
Manager of Design
Mary M. Heller
Visual Research Manager

Book Team

James L. Romig
Editor
Maxine Kollasch
Production Editor
Lisa Bogle
Designer
Mary M. Heller
Visual Research Editor
Mavis M. Oeth
Permissions Editor

Cover photo by Bob Coyle

Copyright © 1978, 1982 by Wm. C. Brown Company Publishers

Library of Congress Catalog Card Number: 81-67391

ISBN 0-697-07565-6

Second Printing, 1982

Global Social Problems
517

List of Tables

Preface

Someone has said that one of the problems of the modern world is that people know so much and feel so little. This book is based upon a different assumption: that we feel so little because we know too little. One purpose of this book, therefore, is to provide information about social problems that will increase our concern about those problems. In particular, I have explored how each problem considered here influences the quality of life of those affected. I hope that as the reader sees how quality of life of people is adversely affected by social problems, his or her sense of concern about these problems will deepen.

Concern is not enough, though. We must also have insight into the causes of problems. If we understand the roots of our problems, concern can be turned into action. A second purpose of this book, therefore, is to stimulate insights into the causal factors. Each problem is analyzed as a complex phenomenon in which both social structural and social psychological factors are at work. This approach avoids a simplistic and partial view by demanding that we see social problems in the light of the multiple, interrelated factors that combine to cause and perpetuate those problems.

Organization of *Social Problems and the Quality of Life*

This book is organized to answer a set of questions. What is a social problem? How can we gain a sociological understanding of social problems? What kinds of thinking should we avoid in our attempt to understand problems? What is the meaning of and what are the causes of particular problems?

Part 1 lays the foundation by showing how such questions can be approached. In chapter 1 we distinguish between personal and social problems, discuss various theoretical approaches, and make explicit the theoretical approach used in this book.

Chapter 2 examines some common but misleading ways of thinking about social problems. It is important to see how fallacious thinking clouds our understanding. Chapter 2 also describes the various ways of getting valid knowledge about social problems.

The remainder of the book deals with the social problems that most acutely influence our lives. The particular problems we discuss are those most visible or most likely to be a part of our knowledge or experience. There is no relationship between the order in which they are treated and either their seriousness or the intensity of concern that they generate. The headings under which the problems are grouped are useful categories rather than priority labels. Part 2 is "Problems of Deviance"; Part 3, "Problems of Inequality"; and Part 4, "Global Social Problems."

Each problem is discussed in relation to the various social factors that cause and help to perpetuate it. And each problem is examined for its impact on quality of life—of those affected indirectly as well as directly.

Interrelationship of Problems

We should observe that the various problems, while treated separately, are often interrelated. For example, health problems intersect with the problems of aging, the environment, poverty, drugs and alcohol, and race. Poverty intersects with the problems of race, crime, population, health, drug addiction, and aging. As we discuss the effects of various problems on the quality of life, keep in mind that some people are burdened by a number of social problems simultaneously.

While this book must necessarily be organized around problems rather than the people who suffer from them, we must not lose sight of the individuals whose quality of life is depressed by multiple problems. They need more than understanding; they need help. In dealing with each problem, therefore, we give some attention to ways of resolving it.

Special Features of *Social Problems and the Quality of Life*

A number of pedagogical aids are designed to enhance the usefulness of this book. Questions at the beginning of each chapter call attention to some of the important issues or common misconceptions that will be treated. Each chapter begins with a description of its organization and ends with a summary to provide a quick overview and review. Important terms and phrases are italicized or, if they may be unfamiliar to students, set in boldface type and defined in a glossary at the end of each chapter.

Inserted into each chapter is an "Involvement" section that suggests projects that offer students firsthand involvement in the problems discussed in the chapter. The Involvements allow students an opportunity to take the initiative in their own learning. Some Involvements suggest how students can do their own research into a problem. Others suggest how students can participate in some attempt at resolution of a problem. The activities can be individual or group projects. If they are pursued as individual projects, the results can be put together by the instructor or by some of the students and presented to the class. I believe that these Involvement activities offer invaluable learning experiences, for they activate one of the most effective methods of education—self-education.

At the end of each chapter is a list "For Further Reading" for students who want to dig more deeply into a topic. Some of these resources are drawn from the references cited throughout each chapter and accumulated in an alphabetical reference list at the back of the book.

Supplementary Materials

Supplementary materials to this text are available. An *Instructor's Manual* is designed to help the instructor plan class work and presentations. A *Student's Study Guide* is designed to help the student master the material in the text. Both were prepared by Professor Joseph W. Rogers, Department of Sociology and Anthropology, New Mexico State University.

The *Instructor's Manual* includes summaries of the main ideas of each chapter and lists of student learning objectives. Classroom lecture or discussion topics are suggested along with special readings to provide additional background or motivation for each topic. Class activities related to the topics are also suggested. And for each chapter a three-part set of suggested test questions is included—in essay, multiple-choice, and true/false formats.

The *Student's Study Guide* is organized
similarly to highlight the main ideas and key
concepts of each chapter. Lists of learning
objectives for the student are followed by fill-
in and multiple-choice review exercises. An
overall multiple-choice quiz for each chapter
is followed by a set of "Challenge Questions"
requiring essay-type answers. At the end of
each chapter is a key to the quiz and a
"Feedback" section that directs the student's
attention to those pages and concepts in the
text particularly relevant to the Challenge
Questions. Each chapter also includes an
"Application" section that suggests classroom
or individual exercises to reinforce the
student's learning.

Acknowledgments

Many people are important in producing a
book. The personnel at Wm. C. Brown
Company have been most helpful and
supportive. Bob Nash and Elizabeth Munger
did yeoman's service on the first edition. This
second edition, hopefully, has been improved
as well as updated by the comments of
teachers and students who used the first
edition. Finally, my wife, to whom the book is
dedicated, has helped me immeasurably with
both content and form of the materials.

Robert H. Lauer

Social Problems and the Quality of Life

Foundations

A Chinese philosopher once remarked that one should not attempt to open clams with a crowbar. Any task, in other words, demands the proper tools. Part 1 of this book is about the proper tools for the study of social problems. In chapter 1 we will distinguish social from personal problems and discuss the implications of defining a problem as social or as personal. Then we will examine several theoretical perspectives that have been applied to social problems. Finally, we will discuss the perspective used in this book. In chapter 2 we will explore various ways—both appropriate and inappropriate—of getting the information we need to understand social problems. These chapters will lay the foundation for our study. They prepare us to delve into particular problems and to use the proper tools to open our clams.

4

Understanding Social Problems

1 **How do personal problems differ from social problems?**

2 **What difference does it make if we define a problem as personal or as social?**

3 **How do various theories explain social problems?**

4 **How are social problems related to the quality of our lives?**

5 **What kinds of factors cause and help to perpetuate social problems?**

Who would be at fault if you were unemployed and poor? Would you be at fault because of your laziness or your unwillingness to begin at the bottom and work your way up? If so, you would have a **personal problem.** Or, would factors such as the state of the economy be at fault? If so, you would be caught up in a social problem.

The question of "fault" is important because Americans tend to turn **social problems** into personal problems and to deal with them by trying to find out *who is at fault*. In this chapter we deal with what has to be the first task: the distinction between personal and social problems. We will look at the difference defining a particular problem as personal or as social makes.

We will also look at the sociological approach and see why we are justified in calling certain problems social rather than personal.

We will then examine five theories that have been used to explain social problems.

Finally, we will present our own approach and definition of social problems, which will be the framework for our analysis of each problem discussed in this book.

Personal vs. Social Problems

We define a personal problem as one whose causes and solutions lie within the individual and the individual's immediate environment. A social problem, on the other hand, is one whose causes and solutions lie outside the individual and the immediate environment. The distinction is not based on the individual's experience of suffering, because a certain amount of suffering may occur in either case.

C. Wright Mills (1959:8–9) made a similar distinction, calling personal problems the "personal troubles of milieu" and social problems the "public issues of social structure." He offered a number of illustrations of the difference between the two. If one individual in a city is unemployed, that individual has personal trouble. The person may be lazy, or have personality problems, or lack skills, or have family difficulties that consume all of his or her energy. But when the unemployment rate is high and millions of individuals are affected, not just one or a few, we confront a public issue. Such a problem cannot be resolved by dealing with individual personalities or motivations.

Similarly, a man and woman may have personal troubles within their marriage. They may agonize over their troubles and ultimately separate or divorce. If theirs is one of few marriages that experience such problems, we may conclude that they have personal problems and their marriage broke up because of some flaw in their personalities or in their relationship. But when the divorce rate soars and millions of families are broken up, we must look for causes and solutions beyond the personalities of individuals. The question is no longer, What is wrong with those people? but, What has happened to the **institution** of marriage and the family in our society?

In one sense, our defining a particular problem as social, or as personal makes no difference. The person who is poor and out of work will still be so whether the cause is laziness, lack of motivation, or the state of the economy. The couple that breaks up will still experience the pain of divorce whether the cause is their inadequacies as people or developments in the society that resulted in a general disruption of the institution of marriage and the family.

In other ways, our defining a problem as social or as personal is crucial. The distinction determines the *causes of the problem* that we identify, the *consequences of the problem,* and how we attempt to *cope with the problem.*

The Causes of Problems

When asked why there is poverty in affluent America, a 31-year-old female bank teller said the poor themselves are to blame because most of them "are lazy and unreliable . . . and the little money they do make is spent on liquor and nonnecessities rather than for their economic advancement" (Lauer, 1971:8). Such an answer illustrates a common approach to a problem: that it—in this case poverty—is a personal problem. The *victims of the problem are blamed,* and both the origin and the solution of the problem are identified with the victims.

Similarly, the problems black people have are said to be because they don't want to work to advance themselves. Violence is said to be caused by malicious individuals who must be forced by severe punishment to control their aggressiveness. Overpopulation is said to be caused by too many people being stupid, stubborn, and insensitive to the seriousness of having too many children.

As we will see in succeeding chapters, defining these and other problems as social will lead us to identify quite different causes for them. We will look at factors other than the qualities of individuals. Even a problem like mental illness must be understood in terms of factors outside the sick individual.

Figure 1.1 These people are working on their problems in a group therapy session. It will make an important difference whether their problems are defined as personal or social.

A word of caution is in order here. We are not arguing that *all* problems are social problems; nor that personal problems have no social factors involved (as the following pages show, our behavior is always social); nor that all social problems are free of any personal elements. There are certainly psychological and, in some cases, physiological factors at work in mental illness. People who are prone to violence may have an identifiable personality problem. Some of the poor are undoubtedly unwilling to work for a living. The point is that if we stop with such factors we have a distorted view of the causes of the problems.

All problems we will examine in this book affect a significant number of people. Problems are part of the social life of America and, as such, we must search for their causes in social factors. The importance of social factors will be underscored when we examine the sociological approach to understanding human life.

The Consequences of Problems

Just as our viewing a problem as either personal or as social leads us to identify different causes, our choice also leads to very different consequences. Consider, for example, a father who can obtain only occasional work and whose family, therefore, lives in poverty. If the man defines his problem as the result of his own inadequacies, he will probably despise himself to some extent and passively accept his poverty. Sennett and Cobb (1972:96) told of a garbage collector, a man nearly illiterate, who placed the blame for his lowly position entirely on himself: "Look, I know it's nobody's fault but mine that I got stuck here where I am, I mean . . . if I wasn't such a dumb shit . . . no, it ain't that neither

. . . if I'd applied myself, I know I got it in me to be different, can't say anyone did it to me." This man defined his problem as personal and, consequently, viewed himself as inadequate.

The *sense of inadequacy*—blaming or downgrading oneself—is not uncommon among the impoverished. Whiteman and Deutsch (1968: 104–106) measured and **correlated** the amount of deprivation and the self-evaluation of a group of fifth-grade children. They defined deprivation in terms of such things as housing dilapidation; the extent to which the parents had educational aspirations for the children; the presence or absence of dinner conversation; and the number of cultural experiences the children anticipated in the near future. The more deprived the child, the more likely that child had an unfavorable self-evaluation.

If a problem is defined as personal, *individual strategies* will be employed in efforts to cope with the problem. Thus, the victim of the problem will look inward for a solution. Sometimes that solution is found in *an escape mechanism,* such as neurosis, physical illness, heavy drinking, or self-destructive behavior. At other times the solution is sought from specialists such as psychotherapists or religious advisors who help individuals to change. These specialists may enable the individual to adjust to the problem, but not ultimately resolve it. If America's poor became devoutly religious, they might be able to bear their deprivation in peace as they looked forward to the riches of an afterlife. However, their poverty would remain. If America's troubled families sought the help of counselors, they might learn to cope with their troubles, or at least learn to bear up under them. But, troubled families would continue to appear as fast as ever.

Helping individuals deal with personal problems is important; however, it can be only a stop-gap approach to social problems. Nonetheless, many Americans believe that an individual approach is the only appropriate approach, insisting that the locus of the problems is within the individual. America's conservative religions, in particular, have emphasized the personal nature of our problems. As a letter to the editor of a religious magazine put it:

> The Master's plan for reform was to call men—never attempting to change the society but always changing the man. When the hearts of men change, the society in which they live changes. A thousand contemporary Martin Luther Kings, Jr. marching on every city in the world will never change the hearts of men. . . .[1]

Similarly, Hadden (1969:80) reported a study of clergymen that showed that the more conservative the minister, the more likely he was to agree that people in poverty "could do something about their situation if they really wanted to."

Not all those who live in poverty see the problem as personal, and not all the poor see themselves as blameworthy or helpless. Some have defined their poverty as a social problem and have participated in collective action designed to attack the problem. For example:

> A farmers' cooperative that started in a tiny backroom office is helping rural blacks in the Mississippi delta break the chains of economic servitude that have been their lot since the Civil War. Operating with little government aid, the Humphreys County Union for Progress and its cooperative have brought a previously unknown degree of economic security to almost a hundred farm families. They have provided the things that many Mississippi black farmers have been

used to not having—credit, reasonably priced supplies and fertilizers, equipment and machinery, and a more stable market and earnings for their crops. [Washington Consulting Group, Inc., 1974:4].

One of the leaders of the cooperative pointed out that he and some of his fellow farmers wanted to better their lot and decided they might do so through some kind of collective action.

Thus, to see a problem as social is to open the possibility of completely different consequences from those that may occur when the problem is defined as personal. If the man defines his problem as the result of the state of the economy, he may join in collective action such as a social movement or a rent strike group or an organization set up to relieve the plight of the poor. He will probably not despise himself, because he will not blame himself for his poverty. He may feel a certain indignation, but he will not hate himself. He will see that his problem is not only a personal problem but a problem of his society, and that he is a victim rather than a culprit.

In subsequent chapters we will look at various ways of attacking social problems and will cite examples that highlight the difference in coping with a problem when it is defined as social.

For instance, to define poverty as a *social* problem is to recognize the need for *collective action* that attacks factors outside individuals. The following case study illustrates this point (Lauer and Crismon, 1972).

A case study: poverty in Edgeville.   Edgeville (not the real name of the community) was located in an area called the "Valley of Despair" by a metropolitan newspaper in the state. In 1966 there were 13,000 inhabitants in the valley, and they had a higher rate of poverty than the nation as a whole. There was not a single physician, dentist, or lawyer in the area.

Poverty emerged with a vengeance in Edgeville when the coal industry collapsed. Automation and the shift to strip mining eliminated all but ninety jobs in the mining industry. The community deteriorated rapidly. The poverty of the people was evident in such things as lack of water and sewage systems, inadequately maintained roads, poor medical care, and a pervading sense of hopelessness and powerlessness.

In 1967 the situation began to change, however. A number of people, funds, and services began to come into the valley from various sources. For example, a Quaker volunteer teacher helped the residents of Edgeville secure a grant from the Office of Economic Opportunity to build a community center. Two nuns arrived to aid in community development. Various other people came in, and all worked together to generate a sense of *collective responsibility and collective power* to alter the situation. New economic opportunities opened up as a result of various projects, including a new, small factory that manufactured pallets (small wooden frames used for loading and moving cargo in factories, warehouses, and trucks).

How did all this come about? A number of things had to be changed in Edgeville. One was the "company store mentality" of the people themselves. The miners had formerly lived in company-owned houses and purchased their goods at company-owned stores. Their whole lives were encompassed by the mining company. They developed **attitudes** of dependence that eroded their ability to make decisions and their sense of being able to control their own lives. Their feeling of powerlessness was so deep-rooted that it had led them to accept their poverty passively.

But more than attitudes had to be changed. A second aspect of valley life that inhibited people from attacking their poverty was the difficulty of communication. The people were scattered about in the mountains, and the roads were bad. Mistrust was common, tending to characterize all relationships. The outsiders worked at building up both hope and a sense of solidarity among the people.

A third factor in Edgeville was the *power structure*. One family possessed virtually all the power. The family had been linked to the mining company in the past, members having acted as overseers and rent collectors for the company. When the company reduced its operations, the few jobs that remained in mining were mediated through the family. The family also took over the old company store, and through it controlled the food stamp program. Vouchers for food stamps were signed over to the store, forcing the recipients to buy their goods there (this was made possible by political and friendship ties between family members and members of the county Office of Economic Opportunity). Through various means, the family maintained control for a long time. Power and threat were exercised freely.

The family was suspicious of outsiders and resisted efforts at change. When the nuns first came to Edgeville, for example, family members charged that they were trying to build a Catholic church in the area; this played upon the anti-Catholic sentiments among the people.

Other outsiders were said by the family to be hippies or communists.

But the outsiders altered the power structure of the community. With them present, the family was no longer able to exercise power arbitrarily, for the agencies represented by the outsiders could impose various kinds of sanctions. With the family's power diminished, the attitudes of community members began to change, and eventually the outsiders were able to marshal the support of enough members of the community to bring about the changes noted above. Edgeville is not yet prosperous, but it no longer wallows in despair. The bondage of poverty is finally being broken.

The important point for our purposes is that Edgeville's poverty could not have been attacked successfully if it had been regarded as a personal problem. The people were neither lazy nor lacking in ability, but they did lack power and capital, both of which were brought to them from the outside. Moreover, their problem demanded collective action, not simply individual efforts.

There are, then, important differences that result from defining a problem as social rather than personal. This does not mean that everyone who defines a problem as personal will fail to resolve it. Perhaps an alcoholic can find a solution through psychotherapy, but we will still have the national problem of alcoholism. An individual can deal with his or her poverty by migrating to a new area with more opportunities, but this will not solve the national problem of poverty. On the other hand, not everyone who defines a problem as social will find resolution. Even if Edgeville's residents had recognized their poverty as a social problem, they might not have been able to change it without the external help that brought in capital and broke

Figure 1.2 Some possible differences when a problem—poverty in this case—is defined as social or as personal.

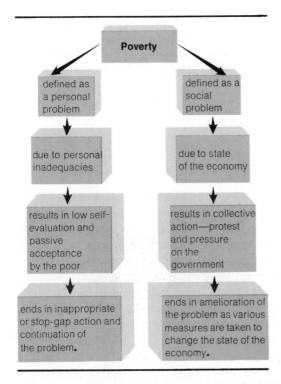

down the local power structure. In other words, unless we define such problems as social, we will fail to locate their causes and will be unable to cope with them.

The Sociological Approach

We have seen that how we define problems makes a difference in the way problems will be handled. This still leaves open the question whether one or the other definition is true. We have been assuming that the sociological approach is the appropriate one, but is that a legitimate assumption? Isn't it a matter of what kind of person one is? Isn't it true that all problems can be reduced to personal problems? One

student remarked after a semester of hearing the sociological approach to problems, "I still think that if any person *really* wanted to, he could get out of poverty." The student still believed that all behavior can be explained by individual factors such as motivation and personality.

The sociological approach requires that even individual factors be explained in social terms. In essence, the sociological approach is the scientific study of human behavior and social life in terms of the *social* factors involved. "Social," in turn, denotes regularities and patterns rather than idiosyncratic or unique factors. We will illustrate the validity of the sociological approach by giving evidence of the *social nature of human life.*

The Social Nature of Attitudes

What is your attitude toward pain? Probably you prefer to avoid it. We would expect most people to have the same attitude. But, as Zborowski (1952) showed there are important differences in people's attitudes toward pain and in their experience of suffering. Zborowski demonstrated that attitudes toward pain and the experience of suffering are social phenomena, and that those attitudes differ in important ways from group to group.

Zborowski's study involved patients in a New York Veterans Hospital who could be classified into three different groups: Jewish, Italian, and "Old American" (English, Scandinavian, and others). He also interviewed healthy representatives of the same three groups. The groups differed significantly in their attitudes toward and experience of pain. The important point here is that the differences were not only between individuals, but between groups as well.

The Jewish and Italian patients appeared to react similarly to pain. Both groups tended to express their feelings freely, reporting their suffering, their groans, and their crying. They had no hesitation admitting they complained about their pain and desired and expected sympathy from others. In spite of the similarities, the two groups expressed quite different attitudes toward pain. The Italian patients were concerned about the immediate experience of pain. When they were given medication to relieve their suffering, they seemed to forget the pain and act normally. The Jewish patients were concerned about the long-range meaning of their pain. They tended to be reluctant to accept medication; if they did accept it, they continued to be worried and depressed about the meaning of the pain even after the pain was relieved.

"Old American" patients were stoic. They said that they saw no point in complaining or crying out. They tried to suffer in silence, or at least wait until they were alone before groaning or crying. Like the Jewish patients, the "Old Americans" were concerned with the long-range meaning of the pain. Unlike the Jewish patients, they tended to be optimistic about the future.

This study illustrates the social nature of our attitudes—the fact that our attitudes tend to come from the groups of which we are a part. An individual might have an attitude of disdain toward pain, not because that individual is particularly brave but because he or she is part of a group that values such an attitude. An individual might be prejudiced against other races, not because of that individual's experience with those races but because of the individual's membership in a group that supports prejudice. Or, an individual might romanticize and support war, not because that individual is genetically programmed to be violent but because he or she belongs to a group that shares such an attitude.

Attitudes are social, and to the extent that problems involve attitudes, those problems are social.

The Social Nature of Norms

Norms are shared expectations about behavior. "Normative behavior" is, therefore, prescribed behavior—the behavior that is expected of each of us by the rest of us. By definition, then, norms are social. However, many people would not accept this definition; they view standards for behavior in either individualistic or near-mystical terms. In the former case, standards are set by an individual who charts his or her own course regardless of what others may think or say. Americans have tended to exalt this fictional individual, the one who refuses to submit to majority opinion. He or she lives according to conscience (so long as that conscience, of course, does not violate traditional American values). In the latter case, the near-mystical view of standards, God or the nation or reason is the source of our norms. In this view, we all "know" what is right or wrong even though we may not always follow the right. Indeed, everyone "knows" right and wrong because everyone has a conscience or reason.

But norms, like attitudes, are social. We learn and abide by norms in accord with the groups of which we are a part. The norms may be widespread in the society, or restricted to a particular area, or found only within a particular, small group. Consider, for example, the following account from the study of a small Missouri town in the 1940s:

> A retired preacher recounted tales of a dozen murders that had occurred within his memory. He and many other people knew the motives and details of each murder, but when officers came into the community to investigate, practically everybody questioned withheld all important information. Part of this unwillingness to cooperate came from fear of reprisals by kinsmen of the guilty, but part of it came from the feeling that men should be allowed to settle disputes in their own way [West, 1945:97–98].

The townspeople including the minister, upheld the "feud law," which gave people the right to settle their conflict even by murder. The norms of the community violated the laws of the land, but the norms were stronger than the laws.

Similarly, a young woman with pierced palms went into a Florida hospital one day in 1967. Initially she said she had fallen on a nail-studded board. Eventually she admitted that she was the girlfriend of a member of a motorcycle gang and that she had been nailed to a tree for violating one of the gang's norms. According to the standards of the gang, a member's "old lady" had to give all money to her man. This young woman had withheld $10. As punishment, she was nailed to a tree for fifteen minutes while the gang sat in a circle and watched her.[2]

Again, the norms of the group violated the law. However outrageous or weird some norms may appear to us, people who follow norms are doing what we all do—abiding by the *standards of the group* or groups of which they are a part.

Our behavior standards are not created by us individually, nor are they mystical phenomena that come directly from God or intuitively through our minds. They are social, and to the extent that problems involve norms, those problems are social.

The Social Nature of Behavior

Why do people behave the way they do? Is it because of the kind of people they are? That is, does an individual engage in a violent act because he or she is an aggressive person by nature or has an aggressive personality? Is a man a homosexual because he is "sick"? Is a woman a prostitute because she is evil or oversexed? As in the case of attitudes and norms, behavior is more than a matter of the kind of people we are dealing with. Behavior is social in the sense that we behave as we do because of our experiences with other people and because of the social context in which we behave. Thus, violence, homosexuality, prostitution, and behavior must be understood in terms of the social factors at work.

A dramatic example of the *impact of social factors on our behavior* is provided by Philip Zimbardo (1972). In an effort to understand the psychological effects of imprisonment, Zimbardo and some associates set up an experiment in which about two dozen young men simulated a prison situation. Half the men were designated prisoners by flipping a coin while the other half acted as guards. The guards worked out their rules for keeping order and respect in the prison. They were also free to develop new rules. They worked on eight-hour, three-man shifts. The men who acted as prisoners were picked up at their homes, searched, handcuffed, and fingerprinted at an actual police station. They were then taken to the experimental jail, where they were put into uniforms and taken to cells where they were to live for two weeks, three

14

Figure 1.3 *Top:* Group norms lead some people to behave in ways that differ from the majority.

Figure 1.4 *Bottom:* The mere presence of others changes the way we act.

B.C.

by johnny hart

prisoners to a cell. The motivation to participate in the experiment was the payment of $15 per day.

The twenty-four men selected had been screened from a group of over seventy who had applied for the experiment. The final group was composed only of those who were physically and emotionally healthy. All were from middle-class homes and were intelligent college students.

After six days, however, the prison had to be closed because the situation got out of control and developed in a way the experimenters had not anticipated:

> In less than a week the experience of imprisonment undid (temporarily) a lifetime of learning; human values were suspended, self-concepts were challenged and the ugliest, most base, pathological side of human nature surfaced. We were horrified because we saw some boys (guards) treat others as if they were despicable animals, taking pleasure in cruelty, while other boys (prisoners) became servile, dehumanized robots who thought only of escape, of their own individual survival and of their mounting hatred for the guards [Zimbardo, 1972:4].

Three prisoners had to be released within four days because of hysterical crying, confused thinking, and serious depression. All but three prisoners were willing to forfeit the money they had earned in exchange for parole. Visitors with experience in prison life indicated that what was happening was exactly the kind of thing that happens in real prisons.

Zimbardo brought the experiment to a halt, he says, because he realized he was no different from the subjects. He could have acted as brutally as the guards or as docilely and filled with hatred as the prisoners. The experiment forcefully and dramatically demonstrated how our behavior is the result of "social forces and environmental contingencies rather than personality traits, character, will power," or other qualities of individuals (Zimbardo, 1972:6).

Human life, then, is social life. An individual's attitudes are not something unique to that individual, something created or developed in isolation from others. Rather, an individual's attitudes develop through interaction with others and are shared with the group or groups of which he or she is a part. Likewise, norms are social and behavior is social in the sense that everything we believe and do is a function of our relationships with others.

The sociological approach to problems is to identify those social factors that account for the problems—attitudes, norms, group memberships, and other factors we will examine in subsequent chapters.

There are personal problems but the problems we will discuss in this book are social problems, and we must search for their causes and their resolutions in social factors.

Theoretical Explanations

The question we must now raise is, How can we explain social problems? To say that a problem is social rather than personal is not to *explain* it.

Sociologists have developed a number of theories. In simplest terms, a *theory is an explanation*. We all use theories to understand the world in which we live. Some people explain poverty in terms of laziness. Their theory involves work, motivation, and innate qualities of individuals: a man is poor because he is the kind of person who is unwilling to work. Others might explain the man's poverty in terms of the economy. Their theory involves work, motivation, and the quality of a social institution: the man is poor because, although he is willing to work, the depressed state of the economy has shut off his job opportunities.

Sociological theories are more complex than these, but they, too, are efforts to explain. Moreover, sociological theories avoid reducing social problems to personal troubles. We will look at five kinds of theory that have been used to explain social problems, and then outline our own approach—social problems as contradictions.

The Social Disorganization Theory

One way to view any society is in terms of a *network of norms* about behavior. In this view, the stability of any society depends upon *consensus* about what is expected of individuals within that society. If people agree on what is appropriate and inappropriate behavior, the society is stable and the people should be well adjusted. But, **when the consensus breaks down for some reason, when the existing rules of behavior no longer hold and are not replaced by new rules, or when the existing rules are challenged by a new set of expectations, the society is said to be in a state of social disorganization.** In other words, social disorganization is a state that signals change in that people for one reason or another no longer share a set of expectations about behavior.

An early text argued that "the dynamic nature of social change inevitably entails a certain amount of disorganization" (Elliott and Merrill, 1934:27). In turn, the text said, disorganization is manifested in such things as poverty, political corruption, vice, and crime. While there is agreement that social disorganization always results from some kind of social change (if B, then A), social change theorists do not agree that change always causes social disorganization (if A, not necessarily then B). Therefore, we will deal with social change as a separate category below.

The consequences of disorganization are *stress for individuals and various problems for the society.* For example, suppose the expectations regarding the **roles** (the behavior associated with particular positions) of husband and wife break down. This would be a state of social disorganization in the institution of marriage. We would expect considerable individual stress (as husbands and wives groped for mutually agreeable expectations) and the social problem of instability in marriages and family life. The individual stress would result because neither mate would know precisely what the other expected, and neither would know precisely what to expect of the other. Human beings are oppressed by too few rules as well as by too many rules. The instability might be seen in increasing numbers of divorces and separations, and it would result from the conflict over role expectations. Such instability would be defined as a problem because people view marriage and the family as the foundation for a healthy social order.

In their study of a maritime province of Canada, Macmillan and Leighton (1952) described a community in which economic change was the primary cause of social disorganization. In turn, social disorganization led to high rates of sexual deviance, crime and delinquency, and alcoholism. The loss of an economic base by the community led to a situation in which there was a "loosened and confused system of values and practices," with the people existing in a "world in which there were two answers to most questions, often contradictory" (Macmillan and Leighton, 1952:240). In time, this social disorganization was linked with the various problems mentioned above, and the community became notorious in the area as a whole group of people who "are just no damn good."

Despite such studies, social disorganization is no longer considered a useful concept by many sociologists. For one thing, it clearly does not apply to all problems. Wars, for example, are much easier to pursue when the societies involved show internal consensus rather than social disorganization. Nazi Germany was a well-organized nation when Hitler led it into World War II in 1939. Poverty in most societies continues because of the highly organized nature of the society; the poor may accept their lot because they support the existing rules. Thus, although the term "disorganization" implies something negative, social "organization" can be as deleterious in its effects. *Approval of the status quo* is implied when the term "disorganization" is used, and many sociologists object to that implication.

Another reason social disorganization as a concept is not considered useful is because the concept itself may require explanation. If the role expectations in marriage and the family break down, the divorce rate may go up, but we need to ask why the rules broke down in the first place. We have not really explained the increased instability of the family until we account for the social disorganization. Similarly, in the 1952 study by Macmillan and Leighton, where the disorganization of the community was the outcome of economic change, we would not understand the root cause of the many social problems in the community without identifying the economic basis for the social disorganization.

The Social Change Theory

Social change refers to alterations in the patterns of interaction or in such aspects of **culture** as norms, values, and technology. Social change may include anything from changed attitudes about something to large-scale processes like urbanization.

Some sociologists identify social change as the primary cause of social problems. In particular, rates of change have been linked with social problems. Some sociologists believe that problems arise because the rates of change vary for different parts of the society. Others think that problems arise because of the rapid rate of change. The view that **conflicting or rapid rates of change cause social problems** is different from the idea that change causes disorganization and thus, problems.

The notion that conflicting rates of change result in social problems was argued by William Ogburn (1938), who coined the term *"cultural lag."* Ogburn said that various parts of modern culture change at different rates. The parts are interdependent, so change in one part demands change in other parts. For example, industry and education work together, with education training people so that they are capable of performing various tasks in industry. If a change in industry occurs, such as the introduction of computers into the production process, a change must occur in education, such as programs to train people in the various aspects of computer programming and data processing. Unfortunately, Ogburn said, there is typically a lag between the changes in the various parts of a culture, and during the lag there is "maladjustment." Social problems arise, then, because of conflicting rates of change and, in particular, because technology is changing more rapidly than other aspects of culture.

Ogburn's thesis is illustrated by modern medical techniques, which preserve and prolong life. When these techniques are introduced into an underdeveloped country, typically they cause an increase in population by reducing the death rate but not the birthrate. The increased population cannot be assimilated by the economy, and problems of poverty are intensified, perhaps with outbreaks of violence within the society. The problems are further intensified if traditional values forbid the use of birth control techniques. Eventually the economy and the values may "catch up" with the medical techniques, but in the meantime there are serious social problems in the society.

The importance of rate of social change was suggested by Sorokin (1942:206), who argued that mental illness and suicide increase measurably as a result of rapid change during periods of cultural transition. In those periods, said Sorokin, the "old sociocultural edifice is crumbling and no new structure has yet been erected," and conflict, including value conflict, is rife among people. The whole society is rapidly changing, and the people are filled with conflict. The result is intense stress, which leads to such things as mental illness and suicide. This idea of the trauma of experiencing too much change in too short a time was popularized by Toffler (1970), who coined the term "future shock" to describe the psychic disruption caused by rapid change.

Rapid change has also been associated with *conflict and dissent* within societies (as Sorokin

noted). For example, rapid change has been said to result in generational conflict as the young grow up in a world entirely different from the world their parents grew up in. They acquire perspectives that do not mesh well with those of their parents, and as a consequence they rebel against the entire older generation. Dissent and political turmoil are associated with rapid change particularly in nations undergoing economic development. Nations whose economies are growing out of a very poor past into greater affluence experience political turmoil in proportion to the rate of change; the higher the rate of socioeconomic change, the higher the level of political turmoil.

While both conflicting and rapid rates of change may generate or facilitate the emergence of social problems, such explanations have limited applications. For one, they imply that change is necessarily disruptive or traumatic. A number of studies show, on the contrary, that a rapid rate of change may be considered desirable by the people experiencing it. It may occur without any evidence of psychic trauma, or, at least, without any substantial increase in psychic trauma. In such cases, the change appears to be conducive to psychic well-being. If stress results, it is among those who do not participate in the change rather than those who experience it (Lauer, 1974:544). Thus, a slow rate of change may be more stressful than a rapid one. Nations may go to war or protest groups may resort to violence because situations do not change rapidly enough.

Change also does not account for the perpetuation of a problem, though it may give insight into how and why a problem appeared. For example, why does poverty persist in the United States when there is general agreement that we have the resources necessary to eliminate it? The theories of conflicting or rapid rates of change are not helpful in trying to answer the question. Change, as an explanatory or causal concept, must be combined with other sociological concepts if we are to understand the rise and persistence of social problems.

The Value Conflict Theory

Are social problems primarily the outcome of the conflicting **values** of different groups in the society? While certain values—ideas about what is desirable—are common to virtually all groups in a society, many values vary from group to group. In other words, in any society there are both *shared and diverse values* among the various groups. In the United States, for example, the National Association for the Advancement of Colored People and some white, segregationist groups (such as the American Nazis) share the values set forth in the Declaration of Independence regarding the right to life, liberty, and the pursuit of happiness. They come into conflict at the point where their values relate to the racial structure of society. The former believe in equality of the races and the latter affirm the need to keep the races separate. Each group holds that its values about racial distinctions, contradictory as they are, are crucial to the pursuit of life, liberty, and happiness. Therefore, conflict is inevitable.

The value conflict perspective was developed in the 1930s (Waller, 1936; Fuller, 1938). The argument in essence, is that **any societal condition becomes a social problem when there are "value clashes" about the condition.** This perspective assumes that there is always a *power struggle*. Each of the contending groups with different values strives to establish social conditions that its values designate as preferable. For example, people who oppose the use of birth control devices often oppose them for everyone and not merely for themselves. People who advocate open housing do not tolerate any exceptions to their cause. People who advocate war against our "enemies" may define peacemakers as traitors. There is inevitably a struggle for power as each group strives to influence the society to act in accord with its values.

The conflict of values with resulting power struggle is well illustrated by the continuing abortion controversy. Those who argue in favor of abortion believe, among other things, that a woman has the right to control her own fertility, and that the physical and emotional well-being of the woman is at least as important as any rights of the unborn child. Those who argue against abortion believe, among other things, that the fetus is a living human being and, therefore, abortion is murder. The unborn child, they say, has the same rights as anyone else. Both groups share a value about human life, but they differ about whether the life of the pregnant woman or the life of the unborn child takes precedence.

The struggle for power between these contending groups moved into the legal arena. Ultimately, a Supreme Court decision in 1973 overturned all state laws that limited a woman's right to abortion during the first three months of pregnancy. The struggle did not end with that decision, however, because anti-abortion groups began to agitate for a constitutional amendment and to support or oppose candidates for Congress in relation to their stand on abortion. The issue continues to be highly charged and bitterly contested.

Figure 1.5 Contradictory values within a society often lead to a power struggle because each group wants to impose its values on the whole society.

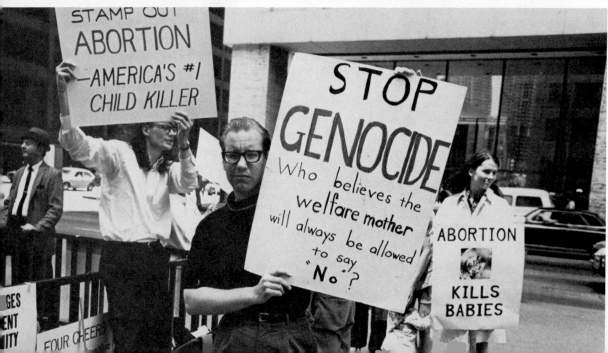

For groups to have different values means that the same conditions may be defined in different ways. Hence, *problems can be defined quite differently by diverse groups.* When the United States was engaged in the Vietnam War, there was general recognition that the war presented us with a social problem, expressed by demonstrations of many groups and by many young men avoiding service in the armed forces in one way or another. For some people the problem was the war itself: their values led them to oppose the war as unjust. For others, whose values led them to support the war, the problem was the cowardice or treason of the large number of Americans who protested the war. Similarly, various groups acknowledge that America has a race problem but define that problem in different ways. For some the problem is outside agitators coming into a community. For others the problem is white racism. Still others view the problem as one of capitalist exploitation.

In some cases there is disagreement about whether a social problem even exists. When a 50-year-old business consultant was asked why poverty exists in affluent America, he responded, "There is no true poverty in America today because there are organizations such as United Fund and the Salvation Army. . . . People can live off of less than $3,000 a year without being a poverty case" (Lauer, 1971:8).

We see that different values can lead people to define the nature of a problem differently, and even to deny that a particular condition is a problem.

There are limitations to the usefulness of interpreting social problems in terms of value conflicts. If a problem is the result of values to which people are deeply committed, can it ever be resolved? Even if one group wins in the power struggle and imposes its own way on others, will not the struggle continue so long as the values are held? In other words, a problem may appear insoluble—unless or until people recognize that values may change over time and that values are affected by the conditions of existence.

A more serious limitation of the value conflict perspective is that some problems may arise out of shared rather than conflicting values. For example, war may be the result of nations having the same values concerning political leadership, economic advantage, scarce natural resources, or territorial control. Racial conflict may be rooted in different groups having shared values about status, power, and privilege more than in their having conflicting values about integration or segregation. Invariably, shared as well as conflicting values are involved, and a particular problem may represent one or the other kind of values, and perhaps both at once.

The Deviance Theories

In the discussion of social disorganization we pointed out that any society consists of a *network of norms* about behavior. The social disorganization point of view sees a social problem as the result of breakdown of the network of norms. The **deviance** approach regards the problem as the **result of particular violations of the norms rather than a general breakdown.** Certain individuals or groups may assert their right to behave in a way that departs from the norms. They act, or assert their right to act, by *standards that conflict with the prevailing expectations* about appropriate behavior.

Obviously, not everyone who violates a norm is a criminal, delinquent, or immoral person. At least since the turn of this century, the time of Émile Durkheim, one of the founders of sociology, we have known that the same behavior (and sometimes the same person) may be considered moral or immoral, healthy or pathological, ingenious or bizarre. The definition depends upon who or which group is defining the behavior. For example, Martin Luther was labeled both a saint and a heretic. And Ignaz Semmelweis, who greatly reduced hospital deaths by his insistence on sterile conditions, and who is regarded today as a pioneer in surgical antisepsis, was driven to insanity by the bitter opposition of his fellow physicians.

Furthermore, certain behavior may be defined, even within the same group, as deviant at one time and normal at another. At one time most Protestants viewed birth control as immoral. Today most Protestants probably would not even view the matter as a moral issue. Some would define the unregulated (rather than planned) conception of children as immoral.

If social problems are seen as violations of norms, the violators themselves may be defined variously as criminals, insane, unethical, freaks, or rugged individualists. Therefore, sociologists who advocate the deviance theory tend to assert or assume that deviants are as human and normal as the rest of us. They believe that *deviant behavior reflects social definitions rather than individual pathology*. In particular, they argue that the distribution of power in society determines which behavior is considered deviant and which is not. Thus, in America, individual thievery may result in a number of years' imprisonment for the offender, but corporate thievery may result in only a fine or an order to change the offensive behavior.

Advocates of the deviance viewpoint may

well be asked, Why do some people choose to break the norms of their society? A number of explanations have been offered. Some have been rejected by sociologists, such as the biological theories of criminality that were developed in the nineteenth century. One such explanation was that there is a criminal type of personality caused by hereditary and degenerative factors rather than social conditions. Later empirical studies disproved the claimed correlations between criminal behavior and particular physical characteristics. More recently, some researchers have tried to explain criminal behavior on the basis of a chromosomal abnormality. Most males have one X and one Y chromosome. Rarely, a tall, white male will have an extra Y chromosome. This XYY pattern has been linked with violent crime and with mental retardation. Obviously, however, it cannot explain crime by women or by blacks. Biological explanations developed in the nineteenth or twentieth century cannot adequately account for crime.

For a sociological view of deviance, we will examine Robert Merton's ideas about anomie; Edwin Sutherland's ideas about differential association; and ideas of the proponents of labeling theory. All three are variations of the deviance perspective.

Anomie: Robert K. Merton. In an early formulation, Merton (1939) argued that *rule breaking* would be normal for some segments of any society. Every society has certain *cultural goals* and certain *legitimate means of reaching those goals,* and every society has individuals or groups who are blocked from the legitimate attainment of the goals. Merton called this situation **"anomie"—a structural breakdown characterized by incompatibility be-**

Figure 1.6 Merton's typology of modes of adaptation.

	Are culturally approved means of reaching goals accepted?		
	Yes	No	No, and new values substituted
Are culturally approved goals accepted? Yes	Conformity	Innovation	
No	Ritualism	Retreatism	
No, and new values substituted			Rebellion

tween the culturally approved norms and goals and the available means to act in accord with those norms and goals. For example, in the United States "success" is generally considered a worthy goal attainable by all. While a few Americans are nonconformists and reject the legitimacy of the goal, most pursue that goal and define it as worthy and attainable. But, in fact, there are not sufficient opportunities for everyone to be successful. For various reasons the rags to riches story (or even the small wealth to great wealth story) will always characterize only a few persons. Thus, we have a social structure that pressures many individuals toward nonconforming behavior as they try to come to terms with the legitimacy of the goal and their own inability to achieve it.

What will an individual do when faced with a culturally legitimate goal and limited possibilities for attaining the goal through legitimate means? Merton suggested a variety of responses, which he called "*modes of adapta-*

tion" (fig. 1.6). One mode is *conformity:* the individual defines both the cultural goal and the culturally appropriate means of achieving the goal as legitimate and desirable. Another mode is *innovation:* the goal is accepted but the means adopted are illegitimate. A third is *ritualism:* the individual compulsively follows the legitimate means even though the goal has been rejected or abandoned. A fourth mode is *retreatism:* rejection of both the goals and the means. A fifth is *rebellion:* not only rejection of both goals and means but also commitment to replace them with a different system. Merton emphasized that these modes of adaptation refer to behavior in specific situations, not to generalized personality traits. A person might alter the mode of adaptation as he or she goes from one social activity to another (say, from economic to religious or political activity).

The scheme is illustrated by the American goal of monetary success and the means available to achieve that success. Obviously, not everyone can become wealthy. There are sufficient opportunities for only a few. People will adapt to this limitation in various ways. Some will conform and "succeed." Others, the innovators, will try to succeed through crime. The ritualists will continue to work hard and press for their children to achieve what they know they cannot achieve. The retreatists will succumb to such deviant behavior as mental illness or drunkenness. And the rebels will become political radicals, pressing for structural changes in what they believe is a debilitating economic system.

Merton did not claim that his modes of adaptation completely explain all deviant behavior. On the contrary, he specifically denied that, for example, all crime is an expression of an innovative adaptation to the social structure and anomie. Furthermore, Merton was careful to point out that he was not talking about value conflict only. The criminal's values do not necessarily differ from the values of other people (recall the point made earlier, that shared rather than different values may explain some problems). The conflict is not one of values, but is a "conflict between culturally accepted values and the socially structured difficulties in living up to these values which exerts pressure toward deviant behavior and disruption of the normative system" (Merton, 1957:191).

In sum, Merton's explanation of deviance involves a social structure in which there are generally accepted cultural goals and generally accepted means of reaching those goals. While the goals are universally attainable in the ideology, only a few are attainable in practice. People adapt to the contradiction between the ideals and the reality in various ways. Some conform, but others deviate by rejecting goals or means

or both. We are still left with the question, of why individuals choose a particular mode of adaptation via one kind of deviance rather than the others that are possible.

Differential association: Edwin Sutherland.
The **differential association** theory was developed with specific reference to crime (Sutherland, 1939). While the theory has been modified over time, the initial formulation argued that criminal behavior is learned in the process of social interaction, particularly in the individual's **primary groups** (those people with whom the individual has frequent intimate, face-to-face interaction, such as parents, spouse, children, and close friends). As Sutherland noted, we are all exposed to various and contradictory ideas of right and wrong behavior. Even those who consider themselves and their acquaintances prime examples of law-abiding citizens share some ideas that are deviant. For example, a "pillar" of the community once informed me how to minimize my personal property tax by making a false declaration of the worth of the property. The procedure was not considered illegal or unethical, however, because "everyone" did it.

Which standard, then, will we choose? Will we follow the official, legal standard or the one "everyone" follows? Sutherland said that **we will tend to accept those definitions of behavior that we encounter most often in our primary group interaction,** even if we are dealing with criminal or noncriminal, conformist or deviant behavior by the official, legal standard. The process is illustrated by the delinquent boy who was asked by an exasperated judge, "Why do you do such things?" Reflecting upon the question later in his life, the boy noted that it made no sense to him at the time, because everyone he knew did the things that incensed the judge. Most of the people with whom he associated, and whose approval he wanted, defined as appropriate behavior the acts that appalled the judge.

Obviously, Sutherland's theory involves *learning.* Individuals learn to be deviant through exposure to more definitions of what behavior is acceptable though illegal than definitions that conform to the law. Yet, simple exposure is not enough. The exposure must be measured in terms of the frequency, duration, priority, and intensity of **interaction** with others significant to that individual (in the sense that their approval is important to the individual). Interaction preponderantly with those who favor illegal behavior increases the tendency toward criminal behavior. Furthermore, the concept of "priority" in this context means that those who learn illegal behavior early in life are more likely to be influenced by it than are those who encounter it later. The "intensity" condition stresses the point that interaction with those to whom we have emotional ties, instead of just anyone, is what counts.

We should note one further point about Sutherland's theory. An individual does not automatically become a criminal because of heavy exposure to definitions favorable to illegal behavior. In later work, Sutherland pointed out that there must also be opportunity for the individual to behave illegally. Even with exposure to a preponderance of definitions favorable to illegal behavior, the individual will not become deviant without opportunities.

We pointed out earlier that Merton's anomie theory does not explain why a person's deviant behavior would be of one kind rather than another. Sutherland's theory could be used to fill that gap. Albert Cohen (1955) sought to synthesize the anomie and differential association theories in his analysis of delinquent **subcultures.** A subculture is a group within a society that shares much of the culture of the larger society while maintaining certain distinctive cultural elements of its own. Cohen argued that working-class boys who have to adapt to anomie do so by creating *a subculture that contradicts middle-class values.* Once the subculture is established in a gang, for instance, others learn its norms through differential association, because a gang is a primary group. Members exhibit illegal behavior in order to *gain status* in the gang. Cohen's formulation was extended by Cloward and Ohlin (1960), who identified different kinds of delinquent subcultures that arise as working-class boys attempt to adapt to anomie. In one subculture boys learn to be thieves; in another they have fights with other gangs; in a third they retreat into things such as drugs.

How useful is the combined Merton and Sutherland deviance theory? The suggestion that illegal behavior may be considered appropriate by some groups may puzzle or outrage some people, but there are good social-psychological grounds for the theory. We all behave with reference to people whom we define as significant to us. We all need social approval. We all adopt and support the viewpoints of groups to which we belong. In these respects, people who are criminal or delinquent are not different from other people. They are different, however, in their *exclusion or isolation* from the conventional segments of society and the conventional channels for attaining approved goals.

A deviance theory lends itself most readily to analysis of crime, delinquency, and other deviant behavior. It does not offer much help for other problems. It does not aid our understanding of war and poverty. Even in areas where a deviance theory is most useful, certain difficulties arise. In a later chapter we will discuss one such area—white-collar crime, the name applied to crimes committed by middle-class people in the course of their work. White-collar crime includes such things as falsified expense accounts, kickback schemes, and false advertising. Such crime clearly violates societal rules, but it may not be legally defined as criminal, and often the offenders are not treated as criminals.

Finally, and unfortunately, the word "deviance" has negative connotations. It implies that the existing social order is desirable. In fact, many social problems arise because the existing order is undesirable for some segments of the population. "Deviance" may in such cases be a healthy reaction against an unjust social order.

Labeling.   Labeling theory has a different emphasis from the variants of deviance just described,[3] although, like them, it identifies social problems as violations of societal expectations. **Labeling theory focuses on the process by which individuals are defined and treated as deviants.** Contradictions in the social structure are not emphasized, nor are the consequences of participating in certain groups. The theory is concerned with how a deviant identity is imposed on certain individuals, who thereby receive certain negative treatment, and perhaps develop a negative image of themselves.

There are a number of assumptions in labeling theory.[4] First, the *reactions of others* are what make the individual aware that his or her behavior is deviant. Behavior is defined as de-

viant not in reference to some universal and absolute moral values, but only in reference to the reactions of other people.

Second, *no behavior is inherently deviant.* The kind of behavior considered deviant varies from one society to another, as cross-cultural studies have illustrated. For example, many Americans typically have considered obscene language less appropriate for females than for males. However, among certain aborigines of Australia, females are expected to use such language, while it is immoral for males to do so. Similarly, while premarital sex typically has been disapproved in America, it has been the norm in certain other societies.

A third assumption of labeling is that the distinction between deviant and conventional behavior is vague, since *what is defined as deviant changes with time and place.* Behavior defined as acceptable at one time may be unacceptable at another time. In colonial America all religious groups allowed drinking in moderation. During the nineteenth century, however, total abstinence emerged as the norm for a number of religious groups.

The labeling theory arose out of the work of Edwin Lemert (1951) and was extended by the work of Howard Becker (1963). Deviance, according to Becker, is not a particular type of behavior but is the consequence of some particular behavior being defined as deviant. The deviant is simply someone who has been successfully labeled an outsider. To say "successfully" labeled implies, among other things, that everyone who behaves in a particular way will not actually be labeled. It also implies that some people may be unfairly labeled, having broken no rules. There are four different outcomes with respect to any particular behavior. (1) The individual may have *violated a rule* and **sanctions** are applied. (2) The individual may have violated a rule but escapes sanctions. (3) The individual may conform to rules but still have sanctions applied. (4) Or the individual may conform to rules and escape sanctions (Becker, 1963:19).

Becker emphasized the impact of labeling upon the individual. He argued that deviance is the result of social interaction after the fact and is not an expression of a flawed personality. When a person first behaves in a deviant fashion, it is described as **primary deviance,** which means that the individual still considers himself or herself to be a conforming member of the society. Once successfully labeled, however, the person is likely to continue in the deviance because others respond to him or her as a deviant. The individual has now entered **secondary deviance** (Lemert, 1951:75–76). The deviant behavior has become incorporated into the individual's *self-concept.* The difference between the two is illustrated by a young woman who first engages in sexual intercourse for money and argues, "I'm not a prostitute, I just had to get the money," and then continues her behavior and soon says, "I am a prostitute."

According to labeling theory, the crucial matter is not the behavior of the deviant, but the *societal reaction*—the fact that the individual is labeled as a deviant by others. A person may be so labeled without breaking any rules, particularly if he or she is relatively powerless and belongs to a minority group or a low socioeconomic class.

The significance of being labeled is illustrated by a study in which applications for employment were sent to various employers (Schwartz and Skolnick, 1964). The applications were of four different kinds. One did not indicate any criminal record. In another, the applicant was said to have been tried for assault and acquitted, and a letter from a judge was enclosed to certify the acquittal. In the third, the applicant was said to have been tried for assault but acquitted. In the fourth, the applicant was said to have been convicted for assault. Other than the information about criminal record, the applications were identical. The researchers found that the proportion of positive responses to the applications decreased from 36 percent for those with no record, to 24 percent for those certified as acquitted, to 12 percent for those acquitted but lacking the letter, to 4 percent for those convicted. An apparent label, even for an acquitted individual, affected such crucial things as the individual's ability to get a job.

If a person cannot get a job, there is pressure to turn, or return, to crime. Once labeled, a person tends to be caught in a vicious circle from which there is no escape: the label is applied; it affects the responses of others to the person; the person is thus forced to behave in a way which reinforces the negative responses; thereby the appropriateness of the negative responses appears to be confirmed.

Labeling theory has been applied to a number of problems besides crime. It has been used to analyze the effects on the handicapped of being stigmatized and to analyze the behavior of check forgers, drug users, the mentally ill, and homosexuals. Like other theories, it is useful for some problems but certainly not for all. Even where labeling theory applies, it may not explain. Labeling theory does not account for those who choose or who are committed to some type of deviant behavior: for them, the label

28

identifies a prior reality. Are there not persons who are already committed to homosexuality before being labeled a homosexual? Are there not persons already committed to an illegal career before the authorities labeled them criminals? Are not some individuals labeled deviant because they have already become deviants? As Rotenberg (1974) argued, labeling theory needs to take into account the process of self-labeling, which is not always the consequence of a societal label.

Labeling theory also fails to explain the reactions of persons who resist the effort to be labeled. There have always been people who were members of groups labeled as inherently inferior or rightfully subordinate but who rejected the label and the behavior it implied. The lower castes in India, the burakumin in Japan, and various ethnic and racial groups in the United States have been labeled as inferior. But, there have always been individuals in those groups who resisted the label and asserted their right to equality with the larger society.

The Social Structure Theories

This is the final type of sociological explanation of social problems to be considered. Finding a descriptive name to cover the *critical and radical theories* included is difficult. The entire society may be considered the problem, including the total institutional network and the dominant ideologies. The fundamental problem may be narrowed to the capitalist system of production and the consequent exploitation and alienation. In any case, these theories share an **underlying rejection of the structure of the society,** in contrast to the other theories, which often support the basic social structure. The solution suggested is also radical: the social order must be restructured if the problem is to be resolved.

The social structural views include Marxist and neo-Marxist theories, although not exclusively. They all have a wholistic viewpoint, insistent that we must look not to individuals or particular groups, but to the structure of the entire society. As Gliner (1973:xiv) said:

> American society itself has become a social problem, not only for its inhabitants, but for millions of other human beings who share this planet . . . the major problems within this society are interdependent; in order to understand any problem, you must consider its relationship to others. If American society is the problem, then you and I are part of the problem, victims of it, responsible for it, and potential agents for doing something about it.

The essence of such a view is that because all parts of the society are interdependent, treating any social problem means treating the whole society.

The structural approach is illustrated in an analysis of America's race problem. Frank Joyce (1969:129) insisted that "racism is a natural product of the history, culture, and socio-politico-economic structure of the United States." He then showed the historical basis for the contemporary racial pattern. Historical development led to the creation of an ideology that justifies the pattern of racism. An ideology of white supremacy has been incorporated into American cultural patterns, resulting in a **caste** system that separates whites and blacks. Furthermore, Joyce argued, this caste system will be maintained because it works to the advantage of the elite who make the important decisions for the society. Racism supports the white **class** structure as well as the white-black caste system, because the struggles between white and black workers deflect the white workers from their struggle against business. As a result, "racism in any multi-racial capitalist society is inevitable and functional" (Joyce, 1969:147).

The social structural view has also been used to explain sexual inequality. As Barbara Deckard (1975:414–26) pointed out, both the socialist and the radical feminists of recent years have explained the inequality between the sexes in terms of the social structure. The socialist feminists follow Engels in attributing the oppression of women to the class system. They argue that men and women were equal in primitive society, because both did work that was necessary for survival. As the primitive social structure gave way to a society marked by social classes, state power, and male-headed families, women lost their position of equality. This change was a consequence of the transition from hunting, gathering, and primitive agriculture to a more developed form of agriculture and animal raising.

In other words, a new economic pattern resulted from increased production. As people began to create a surplus above their own needs for survival, social classes developed, with some producing and some receiving the surplus. Furthermore, the surplus was controlled by a few individuals who were able to build up their private property. The nature of the economy—large-scale agriculture and animal raising—allowed men to assume the dominant roles and control the surplus. Marriage and families became necessary so the accumulated wealth could be transmitted to one's heirs. Marriage allowed a man to own his wife and thus be assured of legitimate sons to inherit his property. The wife's role, no longer that of an equal

in production, was reduced to bearing children for the man who owned her.

Women thus lost their equality and became an oppressed group. They have continued to live in oppression in all societies with social classes.

> In modern capitalism, women are oppressed by their subordinate role in the family and are doubly exploited as workers. Women are still defined in terms of the traditional female role as primarily housewives. . . . Even when women do work at paid jobs, their position in the labor force is not taken seriously—it is not really where they belong. Therefore women serve as a reserve army of labor—to be employed when needed and fired, without political repercussions, when not [Deckard, 1975:415–16].

As this argument suggests, the oppression of women serves useful functions for capitalism. Women provide the system with a cheap reserve labor force, that helps keep profits high.

The socialist feminists emphasize how the entire social structure reflects the economy and maintains the oppression of women. The radical feminists, on the other hand, stress the domination of women by men as historically prior to all other kinds of oppression, whether capitalism, racism, or other. They argue that the basis for male domination is psychological rather than economic. As the New York Radical Feminists state the case:

> the purpose of male chauvinism is primarily to obtain psychological ego satisfaction, and . . . only secondarily does this manifest itself in economic relationships. . . . The political oppression of women has its own class dynamic; and the dynamic must be understood in terms previously called "non-political"—namely the politics of the ego. . . . Man establishes his "manhood" in direct proportion

to his ability to have his ego override woman's, and derives his strength and self-esteem through this process [quoted by Deckard, 1975:420].

According to the radical feminists, the historical domination of woman by man lies in biology. Man has been able to make woman dependent upon him because of woman's biological function of bearing children. Technological advances in birth control—and perhaps soon in artificial methods of reproduction—provide the opportunity for woman to be free of male domination. But that freedom will be gained only through a feminist revolution that will destroy, not merely reform, the social institutions that have perpetuated sexism.

Obviously, the social structural theories are much broader than the others we have examined. They leap over the deficiencies of the others by focusing our attention on some of the larger historical processes and social forces that generate social problems. However, they also have limitations, particularly when used as an explanatory framework for all social problems. For example, if racism is the natural outgrowth of a capitalistic social order, how do we account for race problems in noncapitalistic societies? It is possible to recognize that racism pervades the institutions of American society and works to the advantage of some Americans without concluding that it is the inevitable outgrowth of capitalism.

Theories as Complementary

The several theoretical orientations discussed seem contradictory in that certain problems appear to be more fully explained by one theory rather than another. Yet, these theories are complementary. If we try to explain all social

problems within the frame of a single theory, we are as simplistic as the person who attributes every problem to personal faults of individuals: war results from bad leaders; poverty is due to lazy heads of families; and racism comes from rednecks. The theories offer options to this fault-of-the-individual explanation, but no theory is sufficient by itself.

Together, the theories suggest two things of importance. First, *social problems have multiple causes*. In studying any particular problem, we might find a breakdown of rules, stimulated by social change, facilitated by the institutional structure, and compounded by value conflicts. The different theories are not wrong, but they are inadequate when used separately as complete explanations.

Second, *social problems are manifested at various levels of human organization*. A particular problem may exist at the individual, the group, the societal, and even the global level. These insights represent the viewpoint in this book, which we will now examine in detail.

Social Problems as Contradictions

Our approach will be complex because social life is a complex. Social problems involve multiple causes and are manifested at multiple levels of human life. Our attitudes, our ideas, the expectations we have about people's behavior, the ways we relate to people, the typical practices and policies of various organizations, the exercise of power by political and business leaders—these and other factors enter into social problems.

The concepts that we will use to discuss problems are diagrammed in figure 1.8. The pairs of arrows indicate *mutual influence*. For example,

Involvement

Dear Editor: About This Problem . . .

The letter to the editor of a religious magazine (see footnote 1) illustrates the point that many people define social problems in personal terms. Another example appears in a 1971 newspaper story. The Vice President of the United States, according to the account, spoke to a group of Illinois farmers. He began his speech by turning to the governor, and referring to welfare recipients, said; "Maybe you should send interior decorators over to all those deadbeats' apartments—to paper the ceilings with help-wanted ads."

Many similar examples can be found in magazines and newspapers. Specify the appropriate action to take if we accept such analysis of social problems. In other words, identify the consequences of accepting such a viewpoint.

Read the letters to the editor in recent issues of any national news magazine. Some of those letters will deal with various social problems. Decide to what extent the writers imply that the problems are personal or social. Trace the implications of the letters, noting the personal or collective action the letters urge or imply, and speculate on possible consequences of following the writer's advice. Do the letters give analyses that fit into the sociological theories discussed in this chapter?

As an alternative, assemble a number of other students and lead them in a group project. Each student should interview one or more people outside the university community, asking them whether the grievances expressed by women, racial minorities, and the poor constitute problems. Have your group ask these people what they believe to be the causes of these problems and what can be done about the problems. Have your group record the age, sex, and race of all respondents. Tabulate the results of all group members to see whether answers differ by age, sex, or race. Decide to what extent the respondents give answers that fit into any of the sociological theories discussed in this chapter.

Figure 1.8 A model for analysis of
social problems.

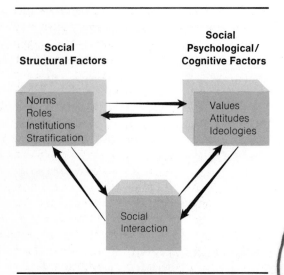

Social
Structural Factors

Social
Psychological/
Cognitive Factors

Norms
Roles
Institutions
Stratification

Values
Attitudes
Ideologies

Social
Interaction

social structural factors affect the way people interact. Norms and roles may lead a white person and a black person to treat each other as equals at the factory but not in other settings. The influence can go both ways: patterns of social interaction can alter the social structural factors, too. In recent years, for instance, women have insisted on interacting with men in ways that have altered the female role. Similarly, blacks have persisted in interacting with whites in ways that have changed traditional roles. An **ideology** of white supremacy can help to create and maintain the subservient role of "nigger." But, as blacks refuse to accept the role and assume instead the same kinds of roles as whites, the ideology will be rejected by increasing numbers of people.

By the very nature of social life, there are numerous *contradictions* between the elements in figure 1.8. When the contradictions are defined as incompatible with the *desired quality*

of life, we have a social problem. For example, the role allowed the aged in our society contradicts our value of human dignity and is incompatible with the desired quality of life of the elderly. The role allowed the elderly thereby constitutes a social problem.

The term **contradiction** here means that opposing phenomena exist within the same social system. The phenomena are opposing in the sense that both cannot be true or operative. This tends to create pressure for change, and ultimately the contradictions may be resolved through change.

Social problems arise when one or more of the opposing phenomena are defined as incompatible with the desired quality of life. This means that not all societal contradictions signal social problems, but only those defined as having implications for the quality of life. For instance, religion tends to be a unifying force, proclaiming a duty to love, to make peace, and to establish brotherhood. However, religious people often have been the staunchest supporters of war. Christian leaders on both sides of the conflict in World War I assured the combatants that "God is on our side." This is a contradiction, but religion is not considered a social problem by most observers.

The opposing social phenomena that are defined as problems may be contradictory sets of *norms,* conflicting *values,* different *rates of change,* a contradiction between *ideology* and *reality,* a contradiction between *values* and *patterns of interaction,* and so forth. In fact, any particular social problem tends to involve a number of contradictions.

Consider the problem of sex inequality. Among the opposing phenomena involved in the problem are:

1. the *ideology* of equal opportunity vs. the *reality* of female opportunities for participation in the economy;
2. our *value* on the pursuit of happiness vs. the narrowness of the traditional female *role;*
3. our *value* on human dignity vs. male-female *interaction* in which females are treated as intellectual inferiors.

Each of these oppositions involves some element incompatible with the desired quality of life of many women.

Quality of Life

What is this *quality of life* that plays so prominent a role in determining whether a contradiction will be defined as a social problem? In recent years, concern about the quality of life has grown in this country. It ranges from concern about safety standards for children's toys to governmental subsidies for the arts. Few people disagree with the desire of Thoreau to avoid discovering, at the point of death, that

> . . . I had not lived. I did not wish to live what was not life, living is so dear; nor did I wish to practise resignation, unless it was quite necessary. I wanted to live deep and suck out all the marrow of life . . . [Thoreau, 1968:113].

Our own desire to "live deep," to maximize the quality of our lives, is reflected in a number of studies made during the 1970s. The Midwest Research Institute evaluated all the states of the union along such dimensions as equality, agriculture, technology, education, and health and welfare.[5] Each state was scored on each dimension, and then ranked according to the resulting overall "quality of life" it offered. This concept of quality of life included things such as economic opportunity, health facilities, an environment conducive to good health, access to recreational and cultural activities, and minimal crime.

Many American cities and counties also have been concerned with the quality of life in their own areas. We get an idea of the meaning of "quality" from their investigations. For example, a 1973 report on a study in Los Angeles County detailed changes in the "well-being of residents of Los Angeles" in terms of seven areas: educational achievement; economic inequality; physical accessibility to things such as job opportunities, public services, and cultural and educational institutions; residential preferences by various racial groups; effects of pollution on elementary school recreation; indicators of health care; and indicators of crime (Stern, 1973).

Newport News, Virginia used a similar set of characteristics to determine the quality of life it offered. Its survey included health conditions; educational attainment and facilities; measures of family and individual adjustment; income, poverty, and employment in the area; equality of opportunity; crime; and condition of and services for the aged (Newport News Community Development Program, 1973).

There is considerable agreement about things that influence the quality of life. Americans desire good economic conditions, meaning job opportunities and financial security. We want good health and access to good health care facilities. We want the opportunity for a good education. We want the facilities and opportunities for participation in cultural activities. We want to live and work in areas where there is minimal crime. We want to have respect from other people. We want to be able to respect ourselves and to have a sense of our own worth. We want to be able to live without fear and with reasonable freedom from stress. These are the conditions that Americans generally believe will enable them to "live deep and suck out all the marrow of life." When a contradiction is incompatible with such conditions—when we are exploited or unjustly restricted in our opportunities, or subjected to unnecessary stress, or treated with ridicule—the quality of our lives is diminished and we define the element as a social problem.

Multiple Levels of Social Problems

Social problems are manifested at *multiple levels of social life*. The factors that cause, facilitate, and help to perpetuate social problems are found at the individual, the group, the societal, and, in some cases, the global levels.

Consider, for example, the race problem. The various theories we have examined all contribute to our understanding of the problem, and they apply at different levels. For instance, the social disorganization theory might locate the breakdown of rules about racial interaction in migration or technological change. If we look at the race problem in terms of social change, we could also point to migration and technological developments. Or we might stress the different rates of change in the society (the legal system has altered interaction patterns, some of which are still resisted by existing norms, values, and attitudes). We could focus on the different values of whites and blacks that lead them to struggle for different aims. Applying the deviance theory, we could emphasize that legitimate means for attaining goals have been

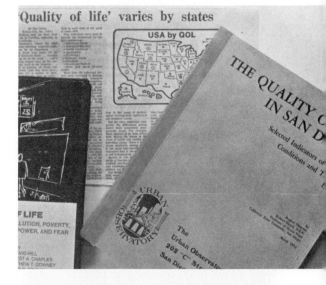

Figure 1.9 During the 1960s and 1970s Americans became concerned about the quality of life throughout the country.

closed to blacks, or that the negative labels applied to blacks have been used to justify discrimination. Finally, in accordance with the social structure theory, we might emphasize the functions of racism in a capitalist economy.

Social interaction patterns, social structural factors, and social psychological factors are all part of the problem, and the factors involved occur at multiple levels. The inclusive approach in this book stresses the need to consider factors at all levels in order to gain a complete understanding.

Consider race again. At one level the problem may be manifested as an attitude of prejudice combined with a value of individualism (meaning that the government should not force us to interact with other races). Add to that an ideology that defines the oppressed race as inferior and therefore deserving of an inferior position. These values, attitudes, and ideology explain and help to perpetuate a structure in which the oppressed race remains in the least desirable roles, institutional positions, and socioeconomic stratum. Furthermore, interaction between the races is restricted, permitting little opportunity for reevaluation and change. However, interaction can never be so confined as to prevent the development of new values, attitudes, and ideologies, and with that development comes changes in interaction patterns and in the social structure.

Diverse ideologies usually are available in any social order to legitimate a change in interaction patterns.

Some members of the oppressed race may perceive a contradiction between an ideology of the free pursuit of happiness and the realities of their situation. They may use the ideology and the contradiction to shape new attitudes and values among the oppressed. They may also create new ideologies, such as a myth of their own superiority. They may restructure their interaction with their oppressors and strive to alter patterns of interaction and elements of the social structure. They may attempt to change the content of education, the power structure of the government, the practices and policies of the economy, and the activities and ideologies of religion.

The race problem appears at multiple levels of human life. It is not only a question of breakdown of norms; or of social change; or of conflicting values of different groups; or of labels applied by one group to another; or of the structure of institutions. The race problem involves all these things.

Social Action for Resolution

Social problems often give rise to *protest groups* and intergroup conflict as expressions of social action. Such groups arise because not everyone in the society will define a particular situation the same way. For example, the contradiction between the ideals of American life and the reality of life for most black Americans is not defined by all Americans as incompatible with the quality of life. Some deny that blacks have less access than whites to desirable aspects of American life. In other words, they deny the existence of a contradiction. Perhaps they deny that the contradiction represents a *social* problem. If blacks have not attained the quality of life that whites have, argue some people, the blacks themselves are at fault; they lack the necessary ambition or the required intelligence.

If all Americans denied the contradiction, there would be no race problem in this country (even though a foreign observer might see the contradiction). On the other hand, if all Americans affirmed the contradiction and demanded change, the problem might be quickly resolved. Because the contradiction is defined differently by different collectivities, intergroup conflict plays a part in resolving social problems.

We use the term "collectivity" here in reference to members of opposing groups in the conflict who agree on particular issues. The race problem, for example, is not simply a white vs. nonwhite matter. The abortion problem is not a case of Catholics vs. Protestants. Sexual inequality is not men vs. women. Poverty is not the rich vs. the poor. In each case there are members of both groups on both sides of the issue.

All social problems are characterized by opposing groups with opposing ideologies and contrary definitions of the contradiction. One side will argue that the contradiction is incompatible with the desired quality of their lives, while the other side will argue that there is no contradiction or that the contradiction is necessary or that the contradiction exists but is not rooted in the social system (in other words, the victims of the contradictions are blamed for their plight). Such conflict is the context in which efforts to resolve problems takes place.

In subsequent chapters we will discuss ways problems may be attacked by social action. There are many reasons why resolution of most social problems through social action will be slow and agonizing: problems are manifested at multiple levels of social reality; numerous factors are involved in causing the perpetuating problems; and intergroup conflict surrounds most problems.

The Changing Nature of Social Problems

One additional factor adds to the difficulty of resolving social problems—both the definition and the objective aspects of a particular problem change over time.

The *changing nature of social problems* is illustrated by poverty. First, we note that definitions of poverty have changed over time. A 1952 edition of a social problems text omitted the two chapters on poverty that had appeared in the original 1942 edition (Reinhardt, Meadows, and Gillette, 1952). The omission reflected the tendency during the 1950s for Americans to believe that poverty was largely a problem of the past. The objective conditions of poverty have also changed over time: the amount of poverty has changed (as measured by some standard such as family income); the composition of the poor has changed (such as the relative proportions of racial and ethnic groups); and the organization of antipoverty efforts has changed (such as the vigor and focus of protest groups and official attitudes and programs).

Our recognizing such changes in problems is important to both our understanding and our action. For example, many people continue to identify poverty as essentially a problem of work—the poor are thought to be unemployed. As we will see, the problem of poverty would be little changed even if every able-bodied person in America had a job. It is true that during the depression of the 1930s a considerable number of the impoverished were unemployed. Many people who lived through that period continue to associate poverty with unemployment, failing to recognize the changed nature of the problem. To continue associating the two is to misunderstand the contemporary problem and thereby fail to take appropriate action. At one time in our history, providing more jobs would have had a greater impact on poverty than it would today. Today, increasing the number of jobs will not significantly alter the poverty problem.

A Definition

Social problems have been defined in various ways. The definition presented now follows directly from the above discussion: *A social problem is a condition or pattern of behavior that (1) contradicts some other condition or pattern of behavior and is defined as incompatible with the desired quality of life; (2) is caused, facilitated, or prolonged by factors that operate at multiple levels of social life; (3) involves intergroup conflict; and (4) requires social action to be resolved.*

This definition applies to all the problems discussed in this book. It might be argued that, for example, the drug addict is engaged in self-destruction but does not harm others, or that prostitution is a "victimless" crime that only involves consent between adults. But, as we will see, these and other problems are defined by people as incompatible with the desired quality of life. We will see that there are good grounds for that definition because all the problems have consequences for a considerable number of people who may not be directly involved. The drug addict's behavior is more than self-destruction; it is a threat to the citizen he may rob to support his habit and an expense to the citizens who pay for (through taxes) the criminal justice system and rehabilitation programs.

The definition enumerated earlier will shape our examination of the particular problems considered in this book. First, we will "get the feel" of the problem by seeing how it affects people's lives: we will examine how the problem involves a contradiction and is defined as incompatible with the desired quality of life. Second, we will analyze the multiple-level factors involved in the problem. We will not be able to relate every factor identified in figure 1.8 to every problem: research has not yet identified the components of each problem. In every problem we will see multiple-level components, which will show how that problem arises and tends to be perpetuated. Third, we will consider social action designed to resolve the problem. Our examination of problem resolution actions will be sketchy; any adequate treatment would require a book in itself. But, we will discuss some kinds of social action for each problem we discuss.

Summary

We need to distinguish between personal and social problems. For the former, the causes and solutions lie within the individual and his or her immediate environment. For the latter, the causes and solutions lie outside the individual and his or her immediate environment. Defining a particular problem as personal or social is important because the definition determines the causes we identify, the consequences of the problem, and how we will cope with the problem.

To understand social problems—problems whose causes lie beyond the individual's qualities—we need a theoretical perspective. Sociologists have developed a number of theories to explain social problems, including social disorganization, social change, value conflict, deviance, and social structure.

The social disorganization theory traces problems to the breakdown of norms, often caused by social change. The consequences of disorganization are stress at the individual level and problems at the societal level.

The social change theory may be linked with the idea of social disorganization, or it may emphasize conflicting or rapid rates of change. Conflicting rates occur when different parts of a culture change at different rates, leading to cultural lag. A rapid rate creates the trauma known as "future shock."

The value conflict theory views social problems as the clash of contrary values of different groups in a society. Within any particular society, different groups have both shared and dissimilar values. The latter leads to the definition of some condition or behavior as a social problem.

The deviance theory includes the anomie theory of Merton, the differential association theory of Sutherland, and the labeling theory developed by Lemert. Anomie theory locates social problems in the denial of culturally valued goals to many people (at least through culturally legitimate means). Differential association theory stresses the importance of the individual's primary relationships in defining different kinds of behavior. Labeling theory posits that the societal reaction to deviant behavior affixes the label to an individual, and the labeling itself becomes the cause of social problems.

The social structure theory identifies the structure of the society as the problem. It may be a capitalist economy or the whole system of interrelated institutions, but all social problems stem from the notion that that structure is debilitating for people.

The theoretical framework we will use considers social problems as contradictions. It emphasizes the view that multiple-level factors cause and help perpetuate problems. We must understand social problems in terms of the mutual influence between social structural factors, social psychological/cognitive factors, and social interaction. Our definition of a social problem, thus, is a condition or pattern of behavior that is a defined contradiction incompatible with the desired quality of life; that is caused, facilitated, or prolonged by multiple-level factors; and that requires social action for its resolution.

Glossary

anomie   literally, normlessness; as used by Merton, it refers to a structural breakdown characterized by incompatibility between cultural goals and the legitimate means of reaching those goals

attitude   a predisposition about something in one's environment

caste   social category of a closed stratification system; that is, an individual's position throughout life is completely determined by his or her father's social rank (caste membership)

class   social category of a relatively open stratification system; that is, in spite of inequalities of property, power, and prestige, individuals have some degree of opportunity to change their class position

contradiction   opposing phenomena within the same social system

correlate   ascertain the degree of relatedness, from 0 to 100 percent, between two events or phenomena

culture   refers to the way of life of a people, including both material products (such as technology) and nonmaterial characteristics (such as values, norms, language, and beliefs)

deviance   behavior that violates norms

differential association   the theory that illegal behavior is due to preponderance of definitions favorable to such behavior

ideology   a set of ideas to explain or justify some aspect of social reality

institution   a collective pattern of dealing with a basic social function; typical institutions identified by sociologists are the government, economy, education, family and marriage, and religion

interaction   reciprocally influenced behavior on the part of two or more people

labeling theory   the theory that deviant behavior is the result of individuals being defined and treated as deviants—a form of self-fulfilling prophecy

norm   shared expectations about behavior

personal problem   a problem that can be explained in terms of the qualities of the individual

primary deviance   deviant behavior of an individual who still considers himself or herself as a conforming member of society

primary group   the people with whom we have intimate, face-to-face interaction on a recurring basis, such as parents, spouse, children, and close friends

role   the behavior associated with a particular position in the social structure

sanctions   mechanism of social control for enforcing a society's standards

secondary deviance   deviant behavior by an individual who regards himself or herself as deviant

social change   alterations in interaction patterns or in such aspects of culture as norms, values, and technology

social disorganization   a state of society in which consensus about norms has broken down

social problem   related to the fact that human beings live together in organized societies; i.e., a condition or pattern of behavior caused by social factors

subculture   a group within a society that shares much of the culture of the larger society while maintaining certain distinctive cultural elements of its own

values   the shared ideas within a group of what is desirable

For Further Reading

Cuber, John F., and Robert A. Harper. *Problems of American Society: Values in Conflict.* New York: Henry Holt and Co., 1948. Adopts the framework laid out by Fuller and analyzes a variety of problems from the value conflict view. Social disorganization is discussed and rejected.

Elliott, Mabel A., and Francis E. Merrill. *Social Disorganization.* New York: Harper & Row, 1961. Originally published in 1934, this work still represents one of the best efforts to analyze social problems from the social disorganization perspective. A wide range of problems is discussed, from prostitution to revolution.

Henslin, James M. *Introducing Sociology.* New York: Free Press, 1975. Chapter 1 discusses the sociological imagination in clear terms and through the use of good illustrations.

Lemert, Edwin M. *Social Pathology.* New York: McGraw-Hill, 1951. A treatment of problems in terms of personal and social deviation; contains the original formulation of labeling theory.

Long, Priscilla, ed. *The New Left.* Boston: Porter Sargent, 1969. A collection of essays by activists, including a number of analyses of social problems from the social structural perspective.

Rubington, Earl, and Martin S. Weinberg. *The Study of Social Problems: Five Perspectives.* New York: Oxford University Press, 1971. Discusses in some detail five types of explanation: social pathology, social disorganization, value conflict, deviant behavior, and labeling.

Notes

1. From a letter to the editor in *The Baptist Program,* February 1969, p. 25.
2. *Newsweek,* December 11, 1967, p. 33.
3. For a more extended discussion of labeling theory, see Robert H. Lauer and Warren H. Handel, *Social Psychology: The Theory and Application of Symbolic Interaction* (Boston: Houghton Mifflin, 1977), chapter 6.
4. William J. Filstead, *An Introduction to Deviance* (Chicago: Markham, 1972), p. 2.
5. Reported in the East St. Louis, Illinois *Metro-East Journal Magazine,* July 1, 1973, p. 11.

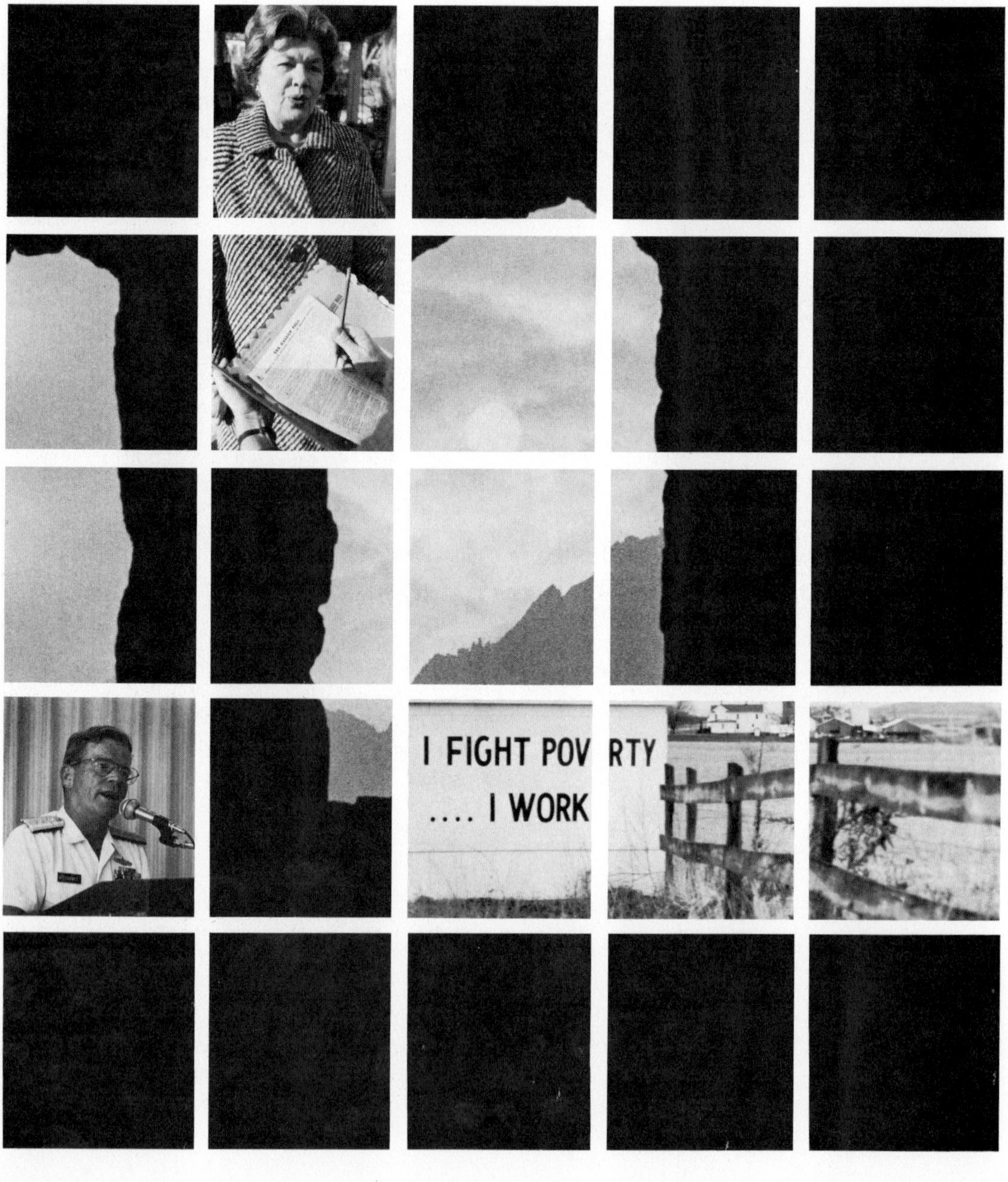
I FIGHT POV RTY
.... I WORK

Myths and Facts: How Do We Know?

1   **Why are there so many myths about social problems?**

2   **What are some wrong ways to think about social problems?**

3   **How can we get valid information about social problems?**

4   **Are all kinds of research equally helpful in getting information?**

What causes juvenile delinquency? A child psychiatrist suggested that a lack of mothering is the main cause. "Mothering" refers to "the source from which the infant gets comfort, from which he develops a 'social tie,' learning the ability to love by being loved."[1] Without mothering, the child can never develop a positive self-image, and this poor opinion of self, combined with a low **socioeconomic status,** is conducive to delinquency.

A different view comes from a youth worker, who laid the blame for delinquency on adults:

> What then is juvenile delinquency? It is but the reflection of adult modes, morals, and methods. Actually, there is no form of juvenile vice, violence, or viciousness that does not have its counterpart on the adult level. . . . So long as adults live the loose, lax and lewd lives that they do, we can hardly expect boys and girls to be different [Fornwalt, 1959:9].

Another view was offered by a Christian minister who suggested that, among other things, we need to recognize the value of "a good sound thrashing," which is of great value in straightening out a child's thinking and behavior. In addition, argued the minister, "serious consideration should be given to laws that will permit the whipping of juvenile delinquents by duly constituted and supervised officers of the law" (Bell, 1958:39).

Finally, a convict gave his opinion on the matter, noting that the problem will not be solved by juvenile courts or probation officers:

> There's only one way to solve it—raise kids the right way. When a kid gets to the point where outsiders have to step in to correct him, he's in a world of trouble and so are his parents. There's no substitute for a Mom and Dad.[2]

To these analyses, we could add others based on the theories discussed in chapter 1. We could say, for instance, that juvenile delinquency results from the breakdown of rules that followed the rapid change in our era; or from the labels applied to young people in lower socioeconomic strata; or from the definitions of appropriate and inappropriate behavior that prevail in juvenile groups.

There are, in other words, myriad explanations for juvenile delinquency—and for all other social problems. The question we raise in this chapter is, How do we know which explanation is correct? All of the above may sound reasonable, but not all are necessarily true. In fact, many myths surround social problems. How do we distinguish myth from fact?

We will answer the question in two ways. First, we will look at various *intellectual cul-de-sacs.* A cul-de-sac is a street with only one outlet—it is a blind alley. An intellectual cul-de-sac is thinking that does not carry us forward but, rather, leaves us in a "blind alley" because our thinking comes to a dead end. The common intellectual cul-de-sacs in discussions of social problems are various *fallacies of thinking.* We will see how these fallacies have been used to analyze social problems, creating myths that lead to a dead end in our thinking.

We will then look at how sociologists *research* social problems by gathering facts to test various explanations. The facts may lead us to revise our explanations or to abandon a particular explanation. In any case, the study of social problems is not an exercise in speculation. We want explanations that are supported by evidence.

The theoretical perspective we have adopted in this book—social problems as contradictions—is based on research and not merely on reason. Subsequent chapters will show that various kinds of research support the argument that social problems involve multiple-level factors, not single or separate causes operating at only one level of social life.

The Source of Myth: Fallacies of Thinking

In this part of the chapter we will look at ten different fallacies that have been used to analyze social problems.[3] A familiarity with the fallacies will help you to logically formulate your own analyses and to evaluate the analyses and arguments of others.

Fallacy of the Dramatic Instance

The fallacy of the **dramatic instance** refers to the tendency to *overgeneralize,* to use one or two or three cases to support an entire argument. This is a common mistake among those who discuss social problems, and it may be difficult to counter because the one or two or three cases often are a part of the *individual's personal experience.* For example, in discussing the race problem of the United States an individual may argue that "blacks in this country can make it just as much as whites. I know a black businessman who is making a million. In fact, he has a better house and a better car than I have." You might counter this argument by pointing out that the successful businessman is an exception. The other person might dismiss your point: "If one guy can make it, they all

Figure 2.1 One or a few dramatic instances of an abuse are often overgeneralized and interpreted as if they were examples of a widespread problem.

47

can." The fallacy of the dramatic instance mistakes one or two or three cases for a general situation.

This fallacy is difficult to deal with because the argument is based partly on fact. There are, after all, black millionaires in America. But, does this mean there is no discrimination, and that any black person, like any white person, can attain success? Many Americans believe that welfare recipients are "ripping off" the rest of us, that we are subsidizing their unwillingness to work and supporting them at a higher standard of living than we ourselves enjoy. Is that true? Yes, in a few cases. Occasionally, newspapers report instances of individuals making fraudulent use of welfare. But does this mean that most welfare recipients are doing the same? Do people on welfare really live better than people who work for a living?

The point is, in studying social problems we must recognize that exceptions always exist. To say that blacks are exploited in America is not to say that *all* blacks are exploited. To say that the poor are victims of a system rather than unwilling workers is not to say that one can't find poor people who are unwilling to work. To say that those on welfare are generally living in oppressive circumstances is not to deny that some welfare recipients are cheating and living fairly well. To use such cases in support of one's argument is to fall into the trap of the fallacy of the dramatic instance, because social problems deal with general situations rather than with individual exceptions.

As this suggests, the fact that someone knows a lazy poor man or a rich black or a cheating welfare recipient may be irrelevant. After all, millions of people are involved in poverty and in the race problem. *Systematic stud-*

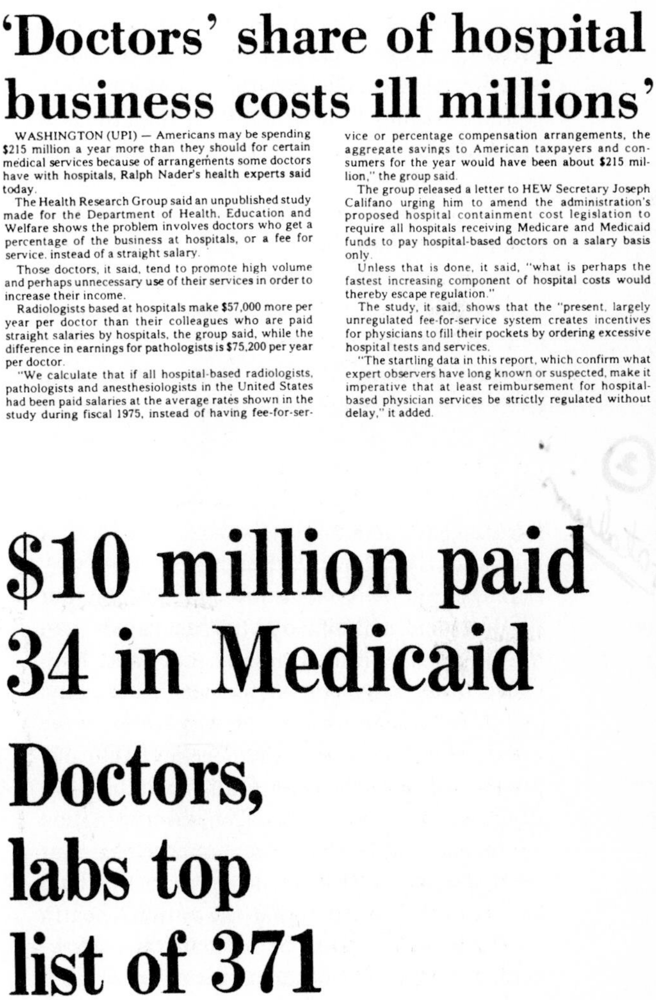

'Doctors' share of hospital business costs ill millions'

WASHINGTON (UPI) — Americans may be spending $215 million a year more than they should for certain medical services because of arrangements some doctors have with hospitals, Ralph Nader's health experts said today.

The Health Research Group said an unpublished study made for the Department of Health, Education and Welfare shows the problem involves doctors who get a percentage of the business at hospitals, or a fee for service, instead of a straight salary.

Those doctors, it said, tend to promote high volume and perhaps unnecessary use of their services in order to increase their income.

Radiologists based at hospitals make $57,000 more per year per doctor than their colleagues who are paid straight salaries by hospitals, the group said, while the difference in earnings for pathologists is $75,200 per year per doctor.

"We calculate that if all hospital-based radiologists, pathologists and anesthesiologists in the United States had been paid salaries at the average rates shown in the study during fiscal 1975, instead of having fee-for-ser-

vice or percentage compensation arrangements, the aggregate savings to American taxpayers and consumers for the year would have been about $215 million," the group said.

The group released a letter to HEW Secretary Joseph Califano urging him to amend the administration's proposed hospital containment cost legislation to require all hospitals receiving Medicare and Medicaid funds to pay hospital-based doctors on a salary basis only.

Unless that is done, it said, "what is perhaps the fastest increasing component of hospital costs would thereby escape regulation."

The study, it said, shows that the "present, largely unregulated fee-for-service system creates incentives for physicians to fill their pockets by ordering excessive hospital tests and services.

"The startling data in this report, which confirm what expert observers have long known or suspected, make it imperative that at least reimbursement for hospital-based physician services be strictly regulated without delay," it added.

$10 million paid 34 in Medicaid Doctors, labs top list of 371

ies are needed to determine whether the one or two or three cases we know represent the norm or the exception. The fact that there are black millionaires may be less important than the fact that in 1977, 35.2 percent of black families had incomes of $6,999 or less, compared with 14.2 percent of white families in the same income group. At the other end of the scale, 23.9 percent of white families, compared with 10.8 percent of black families, had an income in excess of $25,000. Such figures are more pertinent to the race problem than are cases representing exceptions to this general pattern.

②
fatalism

Fallacy of Retrospective Determinism

Retrospective determinism is the argument that things could not have worked out any other way than they did. It is a *deterministic* position, but the determinism is aimed at the past rather than the future. The fallacy asserts that what happened historically *had* to happen historically, and it had to happen just the way it did. If we accept this fallacy, we would believe that our present social problems are all inevitable. We would say that avoiding racial discrimination or poverty has always been impossible; that there were no alternatives to the wars in which we have been involved; that the nation's health could not have been any better than it has. However regrettable any of the problems are or have been, the fallacy of retrospective determinism makes them the unavoidable outcomes of the historical process.

This fallacy is unfortunate for a number of reasons. History is more than a tale of *inevitable tragedies*. History is important in enabling us to understand social problems, but we will not

benefit from history if we think of it merely as a determined process. We cannot fully understand the tensions between America's minority groups and the white majority unless we know about the decades of exploitation and humiliation preceding the emergence of the modern civil rights movement. Our understanding will remain clouded if we regard those decades as nothing more than an inevitable process. Similarly, we cannot fully understand the tension between the People's Republic of China and the West if we view it only as a battle of economic ideologies. We must realize that the tension is based in the pillage and humiliation that China was subjected to by the West. Again, our understanding will not be enhanced by the study of history if we regard the Western oppression of China in the nineteenth century as inevitable.

If we view the past in terms of determinism, we will have little reason to study it, and we will be deprived of an important source of understanding. Furthermore, the fallacy of retrospective determinism is but a small step from the stoic *acceptance of the inevitable.* That is, if things are the way they had to be, why worry about them. Assuming that the future will also be determined by forces beyond our control, we are left in a position of apathy: there is little point in trying to contest the inevitable.

This fallacy is probably less common in discussions about social problems than the fallacy of the dramatic instance, but it does appear in everyday discussions. For example, in responding to the question about the causes of poverty in America, a 64-year-old service station owner said, "To go back through history, it's traditional; there's no special reason, no cause for it. We can't get away from it. It has just always been this way." A similar fatalism cropped up in the response of a young businessman: "I don't actually know the cause of poverty, but it is here to stay and we must learn to live with it. We have to take the good with the bad."[4] Journalists promote this explanation by using phrases like, "It had to happen. . . ." The phrase may be a good lead into a story, but it reinforces the fallacy of retrospective determinism.

An individual might view social problems in deterministic terms for reasons other than intellectual conviction. Determinism can relieve us of responsibility, and can legitimate our lack of concern with efforts to effect changes we do not want. Whatever the basis for affirming determinism, the outcome is the same: we may as well accept the problem and learn to live with it because it is inevitably upon us and inextricably with us.

Whether determinism involves the past, present, future, or all three, thinking about social problems in deterministic terms leads to apathy.

Fallacy of Sequence-Equals-Cause

According to an old story, a rooster once noticed that every morning after he crowed the sun rose. He consequently reasoned it was his crowing that caused the sunrise. This is the **fallacy of sequence-equals-cause** (what philosophers call *post hoc*)—the assumption that if one event follows another, the first is the cause of the second.

It is true that one of the ways to determine *causal relationships* is to establish a temporal sequence, to show that two things are related to each other and that one follows the other in

time. If we would find that a need for achievement is correlated with educational attainment, we can try to determine if the need leads to the education or if the education creates the need (or if something else causes them both). We can learn from a sample of people whether the need or the educational achievement occurred first in their lives.

Social life is complex, and *temporal sequence* is no guarantee of causality. Other factors may be involved. In the example, parental attitudes might lead to both the need for achievement and educational attainment, but further investigation would be necessary to determine the exact relationships.

While temporal sequence is one way to establish causal relationships, we must be careful about drawing conclusions without a thorough study of the situation and an effort to identify all the relevant factors. The point is not to avoid making causal conclusions, but to avoid facile conclusions based on nothing more than a temporal sequence.

Fallacy of Misplaced Concreteness

There is a tendency to explain some social problems by resorting to **reification**—making what is abstract into something concrete. We often hear people assert that something is the fault of "society" or that "society" caused a certain problem. This is the fallacy of **misplaced concreteness.** What is society? In what sense can society "make" or "cause" or "do" anything? To say that society caused a problem leaves us helpless to correct the situation because we haven't the faintest notion where to begin. If, for example, society is the cause of juvenile delinquency, how do we tackle the problem? Must we change society? If so, how?

The point is that "society" is an abstraction, a concept that refers to a group of people who interact in particular ways. To *attribute social problems to an abstraction* like "society" does not help us resolve the problems. Sometimes people who attribute the cause of a particular problem to society intend to *deny individual responsibility*. To say that society causes delinquency may be a way of saying that the delinquent child is not responsible for his or her behavior. Still, we can recognize the social causes of problems without either attributing them to an abstraction like society or relieving the individual of responsibility for his or her behavior.

To deny that "society" is a valid explanation of social problems is not to deny the social causes of problems. We can identify those aspects of any society that facilitate the rise and continuation of social problems. Some societal arrangements may impede certain kinds of problems, while others facilitate the emergence of those problems. If we say society is the cause of a problem, we may overlook the fact that diverse social arrangements have different effects on problems.

Society, in short, does not cause anything. Rather, problems are caused by that which the concept of society represents—people acting in accord with certain social arrangements and within a particular cultural system.

⑤ Fallacy of Personal Attack

A tactic among debaters is to *attack the opponent personally* when one can't support one's

Figure 2.2 Much consumer product advertising uses testimonials or assertions that rely on a post hoc argument, such as: "I started eating 'Health Nuts' and now I'm on the football team." No causal connection is claimed, but it is certainly suggested. The humor of this Ziggy cartoon lies in reversing the implied result to an undesirable one.

position by reason, logic, or facts. This diverts attention from the issue and focuses it on the personality. We will call this the **fallacy of personal attack** (philosophers call it *ad hominem*). It can be remarkably effective in avoiding the application of reason or the consideration of facts in a discussion of a social problem. We will extend the meaning when applying this fallacy to the analysis of social problems; we will use it to mean either attacking the opponent in a debate about a problem, or *attacking the people who are the victims* of the problem.

Historically, the poor have suffered from this approach to their problem. Matza (1966) detailed how the poor of many nations in many different times have been categorized as "disreputable." Instead of offering sympathy or being concerned for the poor, people tend to label the poor as disreputable and, consequently, deserving of or responsible for their plight. This means, of course, that those of us who are not poor are relieved of any responsibility.

That our nation has the resources to eliminate poverty is generally recognized. We could argue effectively that the problem should be resolved, that no individual in the United States should live in poverty. However, the American poor are commonly castigated. Rather than reasoning about the problem, many Americans dismiss it by attacking the poor as a disreputable group. In research referred to previously (Lauer, 1971), the most common response from 1,400 middle-class people to a question about the cause of poverty was that the poor lack motivation. A young businessman said that poverty exists because of the lazy people, those who "think they deserve things handed to them. They have never worked and probably never will

because they expect too much." Similarly, a young woman asserted, "The cause of poverty rests solely on the shoulders of the poverty-stricken people themselves. . . . They have no ambition whatsoever, and it's no one's fault but their own."

A number of problems have been dealt with by attacking the people involved. Ryan (1971) called this "blaming the victim" and said it involves nearly every problem in America:

> The miserable health care of the poor is explained away on the grounds that the victim has poor motivation and lacks health information. The problems of slum housing are traced to the characteristics of tenants who are labeled as "Southern rural migrants" not yet "acculturated" to life in the big city. The "multiproblem" poor, it is claimed, suffer the psychological effects of impoverishment, the "culture of poverty," and the deviant value system of the lower classes; consequently, though unwittingly, they cause their own troubles [Ryan, 1971:5].

The meaning and seriousness of any social problem may be sidestepped by attacking the intelligence or character of the victims of the problem or of those who call attention to the problem. We need only recall a few of the many labels that have been thrown at victims to recognize how common this approach is: deadbeats, draft dodgers, niggers, kikes, bums, traitors, perverts, and so forth ad nauseum.

Appeal To Prejudice

In addition to attacking the opponent, a debater may try to support an unreasonable position by using a technique we will call **appeal to prejudice** (philosophers call it argument *ad populum*). It involves using popular prejudices or passions to convince others of the correctness of one's position. When the topic is social problems, this means using *popular slogans* or *popular myths* to sway people emotionally rather than using reasoning from systematic studies.

For example, a popular slogan that appeared as a car bumper sticker during the early 1970s read, "I fight poverty; I work." This appeal to popular prejudice against "freeloaders" used the popular myth that the poor are those who are unwilling to work. This kind of appeal is doubly unfortunate because it assaults the character of the poor unfairly, and it is based upon and helps to perpetuate a myth. As we will see, the poverty problem is not a problem of work. Jobs for the unemployed will not eliminate poverty from America.

Some slogans or phrases last for decades and are revived to oppose efforts to resolve social problems. "Creeping socialism" has been used to describe many government programs designed to aid the underdogs of our society. The term is not used when the programs are designed to help business or industry, or when the affluent benefit from the programs. It has been remarked, "What the government does for me is progress; what it does for you is socialism."

In some cases, the slogans use general terms that reflect *traditional values*. Thus, the various advances made in civil rights legislation—voting, public accommodations, open housing—have been resisted in the name of "rights of the individual." Such slogans help to perpetuate the myth that legislation that benefits blacks infringes on the constitutional rights of the white majority.

Myths, in turn, help to perpetuate social problems. In the absence of other evidence, we all tend to rely upon popular notions. Many Americans continue to assume that rape is often the woman's fault because she has sexually provoked the male. These Americans either have seen no evidence to the contrary or have dismissed that evidence as invalid. And, unfortunately, myths tend to become so deeply rooted in our thinking that when we are confronted by new evidence, we may have difficulty accepting it. At the end of a sociology course in which social problems were stressed, a student said to me, "I *still* think that if someone wants to work and get ahead, they don't have to be poor. If they want to bad enough, they can get out of their poverty."

Myths are hard to break down. But if we want to understand social problems, we must abandon the popular ideas and assumptions and resist the popular slogans and prejudices that cloud our thinking, and choose instead to make judgments based on evidence.

Circular Reasoning

The ancient Greek physician Galen reportedly praised the healing qualities of a certain clay by pointing out that all who drink the remedy recover quickly—except those whom it does not help. The latter die, and are not helped by any medicine. Obviously, according to Galen, the clay fails only in incurable cases.[5] This is an example of **circular reasoning:** using conclusions to support the assumptions that were necessary to make the conclusions.

Circular reasoning often creeps into analyses of social problems. A person might argue that blacks are inherently inferior and assert that

their inferiority is evident in the fact that they can hold only menial jobs and are not able to do intellectual work. In reply, one might point out that blacks are not doing more intellectual work because of discriminatory hiring practices. The person might then reply that blacks could not be hired for such jobs anyway because they are inferior.

Similarly, one may hear the argument that homosexuals are sex perverts. This assumption is supported by the observation that homosexuals commonly have remained secretive about their sexual preference. But, one might counter, the secrecy is due to the general disapproval of homosexuality. No, comes the retort, homosexuality is kept secret because it is a perversion.

Thus, in circular reasoning we bounce *back and forth between assumptions and conclusions.* Circular reasoning leads nowhere in our search for understanding of social problems.

Fallacy of Authority

Virtually everything we know is based on some *authority.* We know comparatively little from personal experience or personal research. The authority we necessarily rely on is someone else's experience or research or belief. We accept notions of everything from the nature of the universe to the structure of the atom, from the state of international relationships to the doctrines of religion—all on the basis of some authority. Most people accept a war as legitimate on the authority of their political leaders. Many accept the validity of capital punishment on the authority of law enforcement officers. Some accept the belief of religious authority that use of contraceptives is morally wrong in spite of the population problem (they may even deny that there really is a population problem).

This knowledge that we acquire through authority can be inaccurate, and the beliefs can exacerbate rather than resolve or ameliorate social problems. The **fallacy of authority** means an *illegitimate appeal to authority*. Such an appeal obtrudes into thinking about social problems in at least three ways.

First, the *authority may be ambiguous*. Appeal is made to the Bible by both those who support and those who oppose capital punishment, and by both those who castigate and those who advocate help for the poor. Supporters of capital punishment point out that the Bible, particularly the Old Testament, decreed death for certain offenses. Opponents counter that the death penalty contradicts New Testament notions of Christian love. Those who castigate the poor call attention to St. Paul's words, that he who does not work should not eat. Those who advocate help for the poor refer us to Christ's words about ministering to the needy and feeding the hungry. Consequently, an appeal to this kind of authority is really an appeal to a particular interpretation of the authority. Because the interpretations are contradictory, we must find other bases for making our judgments.

Second, the *authority may be irrelevant to the problem*. The fact that a man is a first-rate physicist does not mean he can speak with legitimate authority about race relations. We tend to be impressed with people who have made significant accomplishments in some area, but their accomplishments should not overwhelm us if those people speak about a problem outside their area of achievement or expertise. Nor should we be overwhelmed by the wisdom of our forebears. Benjamin Franklin was a re-markable man, and his advice on how to acquire wealth has been heard, in part at least, by millions of Americans throughout history. But whatever the value of that advice for Franklin's contemporaries, it is of little use for most of America's poor today.

Finally, the *authority may be pursuing a bias* rather than studying a problem. To say that someone is pursuing a bias is not necessarily to disparage that person, because pursuing a bias is part of the job for many people. We would expect military officers to analyze the problem of war from a military rather than a moral, political, or economic perspective. By the same token, decisions about war should not depend solely upon the analysis of military leaders—a point well expressed by the quip, War is too important to be left to the military. From a military point of view, one way to prevent war is to be prepared to counter any enemy attack. If we are militarily strong, this argument goes, nations will hesitate to initiate an attack against us. Consequently, we must not allow another nation to better us in either sophistication or supply of its arms.

That is the military point of view, and who knows more about war than the military? If we accept this line of reasoning and acquiesce to the authority of the military, we will engage in an arms race. Social scientists who have studied this problem point out that the invariable outcome of an arms race is war. In other words, what is necessary, from a military point of view, to prevent war or defend the nation adequately in the event of war is the very thing social scientists find likely to lead to war.

While some people pursue a bias as a normal part of their work, others pursue it because of

vested interests. In 1971 the Secretary of the Interior announced that fewer men were being killed in coal mines than in the past.[6] As of June 13, 1971, ninety-one men had been killed compared to ninety-five the previous year. The Bureau of Mines had not wanted to issue such an optimistic report because up until June 2 the figure was higher for 1971 than for 1970, not lower. Only an accident between June 2 and June 13, 1970, enabled the Secretary to make his report of a significant decline. In other words, it was only during a short period of time that it could be said that the number of mining deaths had decreased; for most other times an increase would have to be reported. A possible reason for the Secretary's action was a considerable amount of adverse publicity and criticism regarding the enforcement of safety standards. Although he was an appointed authority with respect to mining problems, the Secretary's report masked rather than illuminated the problems—perhaps a result of his vested interests.

Authority can be illegitimately or arbitrarily assumed and illegitimately or inaccurately used. Both represent the fallacy of authority.

Fallacy of Composition

That the whole is equal to the sum of its parts appears obvious to many people. That what is true of the part is also true of the whole likewise seems to be a reasonable statement. But the former is debatable, and the latter is the **fallacy of compositon.** As economists have illustrated for us, *what is valid for the part is also valid for the whole* is not necessarily true. Consider, for example, the relationship between work and income. If a particular farmer works hard, and the weather is not adverse, his income may rise.

But if every farmer works hard and the weather is favorable, and a bumper crop results, the total farm income may fall. The latter case is based upon supply and demand, while the former case assumes that a particular farmer outperforms other farmers.

In thinking about social problems, we *cannot assume that what is true for the individual is also true for the group.* An individual may be able to resolve a problem insofar as it affects him or her, but that resolution is not available to all members of the group. For example, a man who is unemployed and living in poverty may find work that enables him to escape poverty by moving or by concentrated effort or by working for less than someone else. As we will see in our discussion of poverty, that solution is not possible for most of the nation's poor. Something may be true for a particular individual or even a few individuals and yet be inapplicable or counterproductive for the entire group of which the individuals are members (as in the example of farmers).

 ## Non Sequitur

A number of the fallacies already discussed involve non sequitur, but we need to look at this way of thinking separately because of its importance. Literally, **non sequitur** means *"it does not follow."* This fallacy is commonly found when people interpret statistical data.

For example, the data may show that the amount of welfare payments by state governments has increased dramatically over the past few decades. Those are the facts, but what is the meaning? We might conclude that the number of those unwilling to work is increasing, that more and more "freeloaders" are putting their hands into the public treasury. But, there are other explanations. The increase may reflect adjustments due to inflation. Or, the increase may reflect efforts to get welfare money to eligible recipients who did not receive money because they were unaware of their rights. Or, the increase may be the consequence of a sudden rise in unemployment due to governmental efforts to control inflation.

Daniel Bell (1960:chapter 8) showed how statistics on crime can be misleading. In New York one year, reported assaults were up 200 percent, robberies were up 400 percent, and burglaries were up 1,300 percent! Those are the "facts," but what is the meaning? Again, we might conclude that a crime wave occurred that year. Actually, the larger figures represented a new method of crime reporting that was much more effective in determining the total amount of crime. An increase in reported crime rates can mean different things, but it does not necessarily signify an actual increase in the amount of crime.

One other example involves studies of the American soldier that were made in World War II.[7] The researchers were asked to investigate the high incidence of venereal disease among black soldiers. They found that black soldiers did have a higher rate of venereal disease than white soldiers. That was the fact, but what did it mean? We might have concluded that the blacks were more promiscuous than the whites. However, the researchers came up with an intriguing and different explanation. For one, black soldiers had a lower average educational level, and venereal disease was higher in general among those with a lower amount of education.

That relationship had nothing to do with race because white soldiers with less education also had higher rates of venereal disease than white soldiers with more education. Still, this was not a sufficient explanation because it could not account for the large difference in rates between the races. Other data showed that 7 of every 1,000 sexual contacts resulted in venereal disease in black soldiers, while the figure for white soldiers was only 4 of every 1,000. These findings led the researchers to conclude that the only basis for the different rates was that a greater proportion of the women available to blacks were infected. In other words, black soldiers were not less moral than white soldiers, rather they were once again the victims of racism—the women who were available to blacks were more diseased than those available to whites.

These illustrations are not meant to discourage anyone from drawing conclusions. Instead, they are another reminder of the need for thorough study and the need to avoid quick conclusions, even when those conclusions seem logical on the surface. Contrary to popular opinion, *"facts" do not necessarily speak for themselves.* They usually must be *interpreted,* and they must be interpreted in the light of the complexity of social life. Furthermore, numerous logical conclusions usually can be drawn from any particular set of data. The perspective of this book—social problems as contradictions—offers explanations of facts that take into account the complexity of social life.

The Source of Facts: Social Research

The various "intellectual blind alleys" we have considered create and help to perpetuate myths about social problems. *Social research* is designed to gain information about social problems, so that we may have a valid understanding and employ a realistic effort at resolution.

Not everything called research *is* research. Some so-called social "research" aims at shaping rather than gaining information, at supporting a preconceived notion of reality rather than discovering social reality. For example, in 1975 a U.S. congressman sent out a letter designed to get a sample of people's attitudes toward labor unions.[8] Actually, the letter attempted to shape information, and the attitude questionnaire that accompanied it was designed to enlist support for the Congressman's anti-union stance. The letter began by asking, "What will happen to your state and local taxes—your family's safety—and our American way of life, if the czars of organized labor have their way in the new Congress?" The Congressman then asked the recipient to respond to the questionnaire and return it immediately. The letter went on to stress the importance of returning the questionnaire by using phrases such as "George Meany and his henchmen," "power hungry union professionals," "rip-offs which enrich the union fat cats at your expense," and "freedom from union tyranny." The questionnaire itself clearly reflected the Congressman's feelings in requesting yes-or-no responses to questions such as, "Do you feel that anyone should be forced to pay a union boss for permission to earn a living?"

Involvement

Fact or Fiction?

The various fallacies discussed in this chapter can be found in both oral discussions and writings about social problems. For example, in a 1970 issue of the publication of a fraternal order, a man expressed some of his gripes:

> Let some guy, blind as a worm from living in a . . . university library, emerge to write idiocy about child raising and large sections of the media will spread his sublime thought everywhere to mislead the simple and the sincere.
>
> Result a generation later: a large and growing crop of juvenile fools, meatballs, self-haters, parent and authority haters, drug addicts and bums of all types, including a fine sprinkling of the female of the species.

What fallacy or fallacies are involved in his complaint?

Find an example of fallacious reasoning about a social problem in a magazine or newspaper (letters to the editor are often useful). Identify the fallacy involved. Using the materials in the second half of this chapter, suggest ways of getting valid information about the problem.

As an alternative, use simple observation to test the accuracy of common (or your own) notions about people involved in social problems. Visit a meeting or gathering of people who are involved in a particular problem. For instance, visit a gay bar or a meeting of gay activists, a feminist group, a meeting of Alcoholics Anonymous, or an ecology group. Ask a number of people to describe the typical member of the group you visit, and compare their responses (and your own preconceptions) with your observations.

If we want to gain information and to discover the nature of social reality, we must use scientific social research. Scientific research is both rational and *empirical*. That is, it is logical and it comes to conclusions on the basis of facts rather than speculation or feelings. The stages of such research typically include: a clear statement of the problem or issue to be researched; formulation of *hypotheses* so that the problem or issue is in researchable form; selection of the appropriate method, including the sample; collection of the data; analysis of the data; and interpretation and reporting of the conclusions. A guiding principle throughout the foregoing stages is our desire to discover the facts, not confirm our preconceptions.

Many different methods can be used in social research. We will look at four methods that have yielded important information about social problems: survey research, the statistical analysis of official records (particularly of government data), experiments, and participant observation.

Survey Research

The **survey** uses interviews and/or questionnaires to get data about some phenomenon. The people from whom the information is gathered are normally a *sample* of some larger *population,* and the data include everything from attitudes about various matters to information such as sex, age, and socioeconomic status. We can learn two important aspects of social reality from surveys. First, we can discover the *distribution of people along some dimension.* For example, we can learn the proportion of people who say they will vote Republican or Demo-

cratic in an election; or the proportion of people who favor, oppose, or are neutral about capital punishment; or the proportion of people who believe that a national health care plan is a step toward socialism. Second, we can discover *relationships among* **variables** (a variable is any trait or characteristic that varies in value or magnitude). For example, we can investigate the relationship between people's position in the stratification system (socioeconomic status) and their attitudes toward the race problem or sexual inequality or the plight of the poor.

We should note that any method of social research has strengths and weaknesses. Gaining valid information is not easy. For instance, in survey research there is always some question whether the respondents are being truthful (knowingly or unknowingly). Those who engage in social research should know the various research problems, as well as the technical matters of setting up and pursuing the research.

Survey research is probably the most common research method used in sociology. Studies of research articles published in the major journals of sociology have revealed that about 90 percent used interviews or questionnaires as the basic source of data (Brown and Gilmartin, 1969; Phillips, 1971). A good deal of information about social problems has been gained through survey research.

We will examine in detail one piece of such research that dealt with the problem of aging. It illustrates both the technique of survey research and the information it can yield about a social problem.

The research involved activities and attitudes among the aging. Its purpose was to inquire into whether or not aging reduces involvement in activities and changes attitudes:

Figure 2.5 Survey research by interview or questionnaire is a widely used method of gathering sociological data. A statistically determined sample of the group concerned can represent the whole group with a high degree of accuracy.

Most cross-sectional surveys agree that it does, but recent longitudinal evidence tends to question the extent of this reduction. Are decreases in activities related to decreases in satisfaction? Disengagement theory maintains that high satisfaction in aging results from acceptance of the "inevitable" reduction in interaction, while "activity theory" maintains that reduction in activity results in reduction of satisfaction. Is there a persistence of life style among the aged? There is evidence that, regardless of the average effects of aging, individual persons tend to maintain relatively high or relatively low levels of activity and satisfaction during their later years. Does aging increase homogeneity or differentiation? Again, theories have been advanced supporting both positions [Palmore, 1976:252].

The sample for the research consisted of 127 volunteers who were ambulatory residents of North Carolina. The research was longitudinal (conducted over time) rather than cross-sectional (conducted at one point in time) in order to identify a process of change or a pattern of stability as people age. The volunteers were first examined and interviewed from 1955 to 1959. They were interviewed at three-year intervals for a total of four *interview sessions* over about a twelve-year period. By the time of the last interview, the mean (average) age of the group was 78, with a range of 70 to 93.

One set of questions in the interview related to activity. The respondents were asked questions such as how many days they spent in bed the previous year and how many club meetings they usually attended each month. In all, activities in five areas were measured: health, family and friends, leisure, economic, and religious. Another set of questions dealt with attitudes. The respondents were asked questions such as the extent to which they felt miserable most of the time, their degree of satisfaction with the work they were doing, and the extent to which they felt their life was meaningless. In all, attitudes about eight different areas were measured: health, friends, work, economic security, religion, usefulness, family, and general happiness.

What did the researcher discover? First, there was no significantly decreased involvement in either activities or attitudes among the men in the sample and only slight decreases among the women. This was contrary to the common belief that the aged "disengage" from activities. The researcher suggested two possible reasons for his findings: (1) aging people may perhaps disengage in some activities only to engage in others. They may retire from work and from some organizations, but increase their activity with friends or with new organizations or with family; (2) the people in this research were relatively healthy. It may be that disengagement is a characteristic of the ill or the disabled rather than of all aging people.

Second, there was a relationship between changes in attitudes and changes in activities. Some of the respondents did decrease their activities, and the researcher found that reduced activity was accompanied by decreased satisfaction with life. In America, the aging must keep active in order to stay happy (this supports "activity" theory and is contrary to "disengagement" theory).

Third, the researcher found that people tend to persist in their activity level as they age. Those who are quite active tend to remain so, and those who have a relatively lower level of activity tend to remain at that lower level. Finally, there was a tendency for activity and attitude scores of men and women to converge over time; Palmore found that the men and women in his sample grew more alike over the period.

In sum, survey research was conducted to test some common ideas about aging and to see which of two contrary theories (activity vs. disengagement) could be supported. There was clear support for one theory over the other, and a number of ideas about the aged were shown to be untrue for this sample. Such research has clear implications for policy, for our efforts to deal with the problem. Those who want to enhance the happiness of the aged will not think of retirement in terms of sitting in the sun but in terms of meaningful activities. Social research gives us insight into the various problems, and it suggests realistic ways of resolving those problems.

Statistical Analysis of Official Records

In the research example there were a number of statistical questions that the researcher asked, and a number of others that could have been asked by subjecting the data gathered to statistical analyses. For instance, the researcher looked at **mean** scores of his respondents for various activities and attitudes. For a particular activity, an individual could score from 0 (inactive) to 10 (highly active). The average score for men on religious activity was 6.3 at the first interview and 6.0 at the fourth interview. We can say that, on the average, little change in religious activity occurred over the time of the research. But, is this statement accurate? Is the change from 6.3 to 6.0 a significant change? If not, how much change in the mean score would be required before we could say the change was significant, that the difference in scores represented a change we could probably find in every other group of aged people we tested?

The researcher answered this question by employing a **test of significance.** A test of significance is a technical way of determining the probability that our findings occurred by chance. Palmore found that some of his results were statistically insignificant: a test of significance showed that the change from 6.3 to 6.0 could have occurred by chance and would probably not represent a decrease among all groups of aged tested. In other words, other groups of aged people could have revealed an increase in the score over time.

We will not examine details of tests of significance; they require greater knowledge of statistics. We should note that many of the findings about social problems discussed in this book, whether gathered through survey research, experiment, or official records, have been subjected to statistical tests. This gives us confidence that the results apply to more groups than the one tested. Thus, we can make general statements about, say, women in America without having surveyed the majority of women in our research.

There are some questions that Palmore might have asked about his sample but did not. For instance, How many men had scores at each level of religious activity? This would have given us a **frequency distribution,** which we will use in subsequent chapters. The frequency distribution gives us information not available in the mean. As table 2.1 shows, quite different frequency distributions of the same number of

Table 2.1   Frequency Distribution of Two Sets of Hypothetical Data

Score	Number In	
	Set A	*Set B*
1	10	3
2	2	10
3	2	7
4	6	0
Mean score	2.2	2.2

cases can give the same mean. If the scores in the table represented thousands of income dollars of women in an organization, we would draw different conclusions about the women's economic well-being in the two cases even though the means were the same.

Another question that can be asked is, What is the **median** score? The median is the score below which fall half the scores and above which fall the other half. This question was not particularly pertinent to Palmore's research, but it gives us important information when we are dealing with things such as income distribution. For instance, if A and B represent two communities in table 2.2, the mean income of the two is quite different. We might conclude that the people in community B are better off than those in community A. Actually, the median income is the same for both A and B, and the higher mean for B is due to the two families with very high incomes. Thus, *extreme figures* will affect the mean but not the median. When we find a big difference between the mean and the median, we know some extremes are involved.

| Table 2.2 | Frequency Distribution, Mean, and Median of Two Sets of Hypothetical Income Data |

Income Level	Number of Families	
	Set A	Set B
$ 1,000	2	1
2,000	1	2
3,000	1	1
4,000	1	0
5,000	2	1
10,000	0	2
Mean	$ 3,000	$ 4,714
Median	3,000	3,000

Statistical analysis is useful for several types of research, especially for official records such as government data. Suppose we wanted to see if women are discriminated against with respect to income. We would want a frequency distribution of male and female incomes, and mean and median income for the two groups. This information can be obtained from government census data: the analysis has already been made, and we need only interpret it. Furthermore, we would not need to make a test of significance because census data involve the entire population; tests of significance are used only when we want to know the probability that our findings about a sample are true for the population.

Not all official records are statistically analyzed, and not all are as complete as census data. Yet, there is much data available that we can use in our efforts to improve our understanding of social problems. For an example of the utility of the statistical analysis of official records, we will look in detail at the study of

Paula Dubeck (1976), which compared male and female state legislators.

Sexual inequality became a matter of intense concern in the 1970s, and Dubeck's study involved one aspect of that inequality—participation in state legislatures. Historically, females have held few elective offices at the state and national levels, despite the fact that roughly 51 percent of all registered voters in the United States are female. Why are they so underrepresented in state legislatures? Why were no more than 7 to 18.5 percent of females sitting in the various state legislatures as of 1973? Are the expectations for females more stringent, or is access to political office made more difficult for females than for males?

Dubeck answered these questions by examining the legislators in a *random sample* of eighteen states. One hundred twenty-six women were in the legislatures in 1971 and 1973. She accumulated background information on the women from *Who's Who in American Women, Who's Who in American Politics* and from state blue books. She was able to secure sufficient information for eighty of the women, and these eighty comprised her female sample. She also took a sample of the males in the legislatures, obtaining information on them from *Who's Who in American Politics* and from state blue books. One hundred twenty-seven male legislators were in the sample. For both males and females, information was obtained on marital status, education, occupation, age at which each legislator first served in his or her position, election mobility (holding an elected position different from the current one in the two years prior to the election for the current position),

Figure 2.6 Lynn Martin, U.S. Congresswoman (Ill.). Through the use of public records and statistical analysis of data gathered from records, Dubeck (1976) showed the characteristics that will most likely gain an individual access to office, and showed that there are sex differences in those characteristics.

party leadership, and whether the legislator was serving in January 1973.

There were a number of statistically significant differences between the male and female legislators. The males had a higher level of educational achievement and were younger when they started their terms. Twice as many males were lawyers. However, the females were more likely to have been active in party leadership prior to their elections. On a number of other variables, there were no statistically significant differences between the sexes.

What do these findings mean for sexual inequality?

> For men, party leadership is only infrequently part of the set of credentials which they carry to the state legislature; for women, however, and more specifically, women who have not attained a four-year college degree or better, party leadership activity is a critical part of this same set of credentials. This suggests that men, as a rule, are judged on promise, or their *potential* for success, while this may be true only for women who have attained a higher level of education; otherwise, women are judged on more proven criteria [Dubeck, 1976:51].

Through the use of public records and statistical analysis of data gathered from those records, Dubeck showed the characteristics that will most likely gain an individual access to political office, and showed the fact that there are sex differences in those characteristics. This kind of research can yield valuable insights, as we will see in succeeding chapters. The research requires no interviewing or questionnaires, only a knowledge of statistics and the imaginative use of public and official records available.

Experiments

In essence, the *experimental method* involves manipulation of one or more variables, control of other variables, and measurement of the consequences in still other variables. The variables that are manipulated are called the **independent variables,** while those that are measured to see how they have been affected are called the **dependent variables.** To ascertain that the independent variables are causing the change in the dependent variables, the experimenter uses both *an experimental and a control group.* Measurements are taken in both groups, but the control group is not exposed to the treatment (the independent variable).

Suppose we want to set up an experiment to test the *hypothesis* that prejudice is increased by negative interpersonal encounters with someone of another race. We might get a group of white volunteers, test them on their level of prejudice, and select twenty of them who score about the same (that is, we control for level of prejudice). We then divide them into two groups, each of which will receive the same brief lecture from a black male. One group is treated kindly by the lecturer, while the other group is treated in an abusive manner. Following the lecture experience, we again test the twenty subjects for their level of prejudice.

If the results of our experiment were according to table 2.3, the hypothesis was supported. All ten of those who heard the abusive lecturer increased in their level of prejudice, while none of those who listened to the kindly lecturer showed an increase. In practice, experiments never come out this neatly. Some people who

Table 2.3   Results of a Hypothetical Experiment on Interracial Contacts and Level of Prejudice

Attitude of Lecturer	Prejudice Level	
	Increased	*Stable*
Abusive	10	0
Kind	0	10

listen to the abusive speaker will not increase in their level of prejudice, and some who listen to the kindly speaker will show more prejudice afterward. In other words, factors other than just the interpersonal contact are at work. The experimenter tries to control the setting and the subjects in order to minimize their effect on any other variables. In practice this is impossible to do. Nevertheless, the findings are often statistically significant, allowing us to make some conclusions about the variables we study.

The nature and usefulness of experiments is illustrated further by a detailed consideration of an experiment by Bandura, Ross, and Ross (1963), which was designed to test the effects of aggressive "models" on aggressive behavior in children. The experiment was inspired in part by the debate over the effects of violence in the mass media on children's behavior, and by reported incidents of violent behavior following exposure to violence in the mass media. In particular, the experiment sought to determine whether and to what extent children would imitate the aggressive behavior they viewed in films.

The experiment used forty-eight boys and forty-eight girls who were enrolled in a nursery school. The mean age of the group was 52 months. There were three experimental groups and one control group, each with twenty-four subjects. One experimental group watched an adult come into their schoolroom and act aggressively toward a five-foot inflated Bobo doll. The model punched the doll; sat on it while punching it in the nose; pounded it on the head with a mallet; and threw it into the air and kicked it around the room. Another experimental group watched a film in which the same model performed the same aggressive acts. The third experimental group saw a cartoon in which a model was costumed like a black cat and performed the same aggressive acts as in the other two cases.

The control group was not subjected to a situation in which they observed aggressive behavior. All groups were then tested for subsequent imitative and nonimitative aggressive behavior. This test was conducted by taking the children to a different room. First they were subjected to mild frustration by being taken to an anteroom in which there were a number of appealing toys. As soon as each child became involved with the toys, the experimenter told the child that those were the best toys in the school, that not everyone could play with them, and that there were different toys in the next room that could be played with. Each child was then taken into the experimental room, where there were toys that could be used for aggressive behavior and toys that would be appropriate for nonaggressive behavior.

The experimenters summarized their findings as follows:

> The results of the present study provide strong evidence that exposure to filmed aggression heightens aggressive reactions in children. Subjects who viewed the aggressive human and cartoon models on film exhibited nearly twice as much aggression as did subjects in the control group who were not exposed to the aggressive film content. . . . Filmed aggression not only facilitated the expression of aggression, it also effectively shaped the form of the subjects' aggressive behavior. The finding that children modeled their behavior to some extent after the film characters suggests that pictorial mass media, particularly television, may serve as an important source of social behavior. . . . The children who participated in the experiment are by no means a deviant sample; nevertheless, 88% of the subjects in the Real-Life and in the Human Film condition, and 79% of the subjects in the Cartoon Film condition, exhibited varying degrees of imitative aggression [Bandura, Ross, and Ross, 1963:9].

The experimental method enabled Bandura, Ross, and Ross to conclude that aggressive behavior, which includes violence, can be stimulated by observing such behavior in the mass media, then experiencing frustration in a subsequent situation. The mass media affected not only those already inclined to interpersonal violence—deviant or delinquent children—but those children we would call normal. The experiment suggests that our reducing the level of violence in society calls for serious attention to the amount of violence portrayed in the *mass media*. We must be cautious about such a conclusion, however. What people do in a laboratory setting does not necessarily predict what they will do outside the laboratory, in that controlling all variables is impossible. For this reason, experimenters often take pains to make their settings as "natural" as possible.

Participant Observation

Participant observation, the last method we will discuss, involves a number of things. As defined by McCall and Simmons (1969:1), participant observation includes "some amount of genuinely social interaction in the field with the subjects of the study, some direct observation of relevant events, some formal and a great deal of informal interviewing, some systematic counting, some collection of documents and artifacts, and open-endedness in the directions the study takes." In participant observation, the researcher *directly participates in and observes* the social reality being studied. The researcher is both a part of and detached from the social reality being studied.

As a participant observer, the researcher can assume a *number of different roles*. Nan Lin (1976:206–08) summarized these as follows:

> First, he can take the role of *complete participant*, while withholding his true identity from the other participants. . . . Second, the observer can take the role of *participant as observer*. In this role, while the observer still participates in the activities, both he and the participants are aware of his true identity as observer. . . . A third role the observer can take is that of an *observer as participant*. In this role, the observer participates only to the extent that is required to make his observations. . . . Finally, the observer can take the role of a *complete observer*, without any participation in the activities or interactions of the observed.

In other words, there are differences in the extent to which the researcher may become involved in the social reality being studied. For instance, if a researcher used observation to study poverty, he might live in an impoverished

community and pretend to be a poor person—"complete participant." If he let his identity as a researcher be known while he participated in community activities, he would be "participant as observer." If he participated in selective community activities that he specifically wanted to observe, he would be "observer as participant." Watching poor children in a school room behind a one-way mirror would make him a "complete observer."

We will get a more complete picture of the procedures and usefulness of participant observation by discussing a study of psychiatric hospitals (Strauss et al., 1964). Strauss and his associates chose participant observation as a method for studying psychiatric hospitals. That decision required a number of other decisions—who, when, where, and what to observe and interview. For example, the timing of observations was important because all organizations have their own rhythms and sequence of events. In a hospital there are different work shifts, and the wards are different at various points in the day and night. The researcher must also recognize the regular routines, "like visiting hours, meal times, weekly staff meetings, and shift changes when reports are given" (Strauss et al., 1964:22). To account for the variations over time, the researchers made observations both continuously and in selected periods of time.

The researchers also had to decide upon where to locate as they recorded their observations. The information one can get will vary from one location, such as the nurses' stations, to another, such as the conference room. The researchers could stay with particular people, who would bring them into contact with diverse situations, or they could observe particular situations such as admissions or staff meetings, or they could observe various status groups from the patients to the administrators. With a team of researchers, all these approaches can be employed.

Having decided who, what, and when to observe, the researchers had to decide *how* to observe. That is, they had to choose one of the four roles discussed earlier. They decided to participate as observers, to participate fully in the activities of the hospitals while making their own identity known. During the course of their research they asked questions and held interviews when appropriate and necessary.

What do we learn about the problem of mental illness from this research? In the first place, the hospital must be understood as a "negotiated order," which means that there are various and even contrary goals among the staff, different amounts of power held by various groups, and a continuing alteration of rules and procedures. The alteration of rules and procedures occurs through negotiation among the various professionals in the hospital. Thus, in one psychiatric hospital the researchers found that "hardly anyone knows all the extant rules, much less exactly what situations they apply to, for whom, and with what sanctions" (Strauss et al., 1963:151). The negotiations in this context are complicated, because the professionals may share nothing more than the single, vague goal of helping the patient to recover. (The goal is vague because the professionals—nurses, physicians, social workers, and psychiatrists—have different ideologies about appropriate treatment and different notions of what is best for a particular patient.) The care received by a mentally ill patient is not based on predetermined and scientifically sound medical knowledge, but is the outcome of negotiation among various professionals on the hospital's staff, who hold different notions of both the causes of and the cures for mental illness.

The treatment of mental illness by professional negotiations is illustrated in a study of a state mental hospital reported by Schatzman and Bucher (1964). Prior to the actual study, which was part of the same participant observation research noted earlier, a new superintendent had assumed office. The new superintendent attracted psychiatrists to the hospital by giving each psychiatrist his own ward with a team of professionals. Each psychiatrist could establish his own preferred method of treatment. Five wards in the hospital were studied, and each had a different treatment philosophy. The philosophies of treatment varied from a radical patient-government system, where each patient was expected to gain self-understanding and assume increasing responsibility for his or her progress, to a medical authority system in which electroshock and drug therapy typically were used. One ward had an "unresolved" system: the psychiatrist viewed himself as the expert whose authority should be unquestioned, the physician was oriented toward the physical bases of mental illness, and the psychologist and the social worker believed in group therapy.

All the heads of the teams were relatively young men, and they had to negotiate with the more experienced professionals on their teams about methods of treatment and assignment of various tasks. In addition, the teams had a certain amount of turnover, with various professionals changing from one team to another. As a result, nearly every task was subject to change or even to denial through negotiation. If a particular professional said that a particular patient should be treated in a certain way, his position might be accepted or rejected, depending on the ideology of the others on the team and his apparent confidence in what he was saying. In other words, the professional who knew, or who could give the appearance of knowing what he was saying was more likely to have his claim accepted.

Participant-observation research in mental hospitals enabled the researchers to show the problematic nature of caring for the mentally ill. The care does not proceed from factual knowledge about mental illness that is shared among professionals. Rather, the care any particular patient receives depends on the outcome of negotiations among professionals with different and even contradictory ideas about both the causes and the cures of mental illness.

Summary

Each social problem has many different explanations. How do we know which explanation is correct? How can we separate myth from fact in our knowledge of social problems? How can we get reasonable explanations that are supported by reliable evidence? There are two important things we can do. One is to recognize the various intellectual cul-de-sacs, or fallacies of thinking, that have been used to analyze social problems and that create and help to perpetuate myths about those problems. The other is to understand the methods of social research, which are designed to get information that will enhance our understanding by suggesting which explanations are valid and which are not. In other words, an adequate understanding of social problems is based on research, and not merely on what seems to be reasonable.

We have examined at least ten different fallacies frequently used to analyze social problems. The fallacy of the dramatic instance refers to the tendency to overgeneralize, to use a single case or a few cases to support an entire argument. The fallacy of retrospective determinism is the argument that things could not have worked out any differently than they did. The fallacy of sequence-equals-cause is the argument that if one event follows another, the first is the cause of the second. The fallacy of misplaced concreteness is the tendency to resort to reification, to make something abstract into something concrete. The fallacy of personal attack is a form of debate or argument in which an attack is made on the opponent rather than on the issues. Appeal to prejudice is the exploitation of popular prejudices or passions. Circular reasoning involves the use of conclusions to support the assumptions that were necessary to make the conclusions. The fallacy of authority is an illegitimate appeal to authority. The fallacy of composition is the idea that what is true of the part is also true of the whole. Finally, non sequitur is the drawing of wrong conclusions from premises, even though the premises themselves are valid.

Social research attempts to gain an understanding of social problems by investigating social reality. Four methods of research that have given us helpful information in our effort to understand social problems are: survey research; statistical analysis of official records; experiment; and participant observation. Survey research employs interviews and questionnaires on a sample of people in order to get data. Statistical analysis of various official, public records may be simple—computing means, medians, and frequency distributions—or rela-

tively complex—computing tests of significance. Experiment involves manipulation of one or more variables, control of other variables, and measurement of consequences in still other variables. Experiments frequently take place in a laboratory setting, where the researcher has a high degree of control over what happens. Finally, participant observation involves both participation and observation on the part of the researcher; the researcher being both a part of and detached from the social reality being studied.

Each method of social research has certain advantages and disadvantages. Each method tends to give us different kinds of information. The extent of our understanding depends on the variety of methods we use to gather information. We can have greater confidence in the information if it is validated by different methods. As Smith (1975:292) argued, it should be a norm of social science that propositions confirmed by only one method should receive the lowest degree of confirmation, and those confirmed by multiple methods should receive the higher degrees of confirmation. Certainly, we should be cautious about conclusions based on only one study that used one method of research. This means that much research is required before we can be confident of our understanding of social problems, but the extra work can save us from accepting myths of our own making.

Glossary

appeal to prejudice   argument by appealing to popular prejudices or passions

circular reasoning   using conclusions to support the assumptions that were necessary to make the conclusions

dependent variable   the variable in an experiment that is influenced by an independent variable

dramatic instance   the fallacy of overgeneralizing

fallacy of authority   argument by an illegitimate appeal to authority

fallacy of composition   the assertion that what is true of the part is necessarily true of the whole

fallacy of personal attack   argument by attacking the opponent personally rather than dealing with the issue

fallacy of sequence-equals-cause   the argument that if one event follows another, the first caused the second

frequency distribution   the organization of data to show the number of times each item occurs

independent variable   the variable in an experiment that is manipulated in order to see how it effects changes in the dependent variable

mean   the average

median   the score below which are half of the scores and above which are the other half

misplaced concreteness   the fallacy of making something abstract into something concrete

non sequitur   something that does not follow logically from what has preceded it

participant observation   a method of research in which one directly participates in and observes the social reality being studied

reification   defining what is abstract as something concrete

retrospective determinism   the argument that things could not have worked out any other way than they did

socioeconomic status   social categories of people based on similar economic resources, power, prestige, and style of life

survey   a method of research in which a sample of people are interviewed or given questionnaires in order to get data on some phenomenon

test of significance   a statistical method for determining the probability that research findings occurred by chance

variable   any trait or characteristic that varies in value or magnitude

For Further Reading

Bacon, Francis. "On the Interpretation of Nature and the Empire of Man." In *The Sociology of Knowledge: A Reader,* James E. Curtis and John W. Petras, eds., pp. 89–96. New York: Praeger, 1970. Bacon's own explanation of his famous "idols of the mind," various social factors that distort our thinking. Numerous other ideas about social influences on our thinking will be found in the introduction and other sections of this book.

Chase, Stuart. *Guides to Straight Thinking.* New York: Harper & Bros., 1956. An excellent presentation, easily read, of stimulating materials on useful thinking and inappropriate modes of thinking.

Hastings, William M. *How to Think About Social Problems.* New York: Oxford University Press, 1979. A valuable aid for developing analytical and interpretive skills and applying them to social problems.

Huff, Darrell. *How to Lie with Statistics.* New York: W. W. Norton, 1954. A readable, fascinating exposition of proper and improper use of statistical data. Shows how statistics as well as myths can be used to impart wrong information.

Labovitz, Sanford, and Robert Hagedorn. *Introduction to Social Research.* New York: McGraw-Hill, 1971. A brief overview of the process of social research, including collection and analysis of data. Has a useful glossary of terms frequently used in research.

Smith, H. W. *Strategies of Social Research.* Englewood Cliffs, N.J.: Prentice-Hall, 1975. A general discussion of the problems and the process of social research. Examples of an interview guide, an interview schedule, a questionnaire, and field notes taken by a participant-observer are included in the appendices.

Notes

1. Quoted in *St. Louis Globe-Democrat,* November 30, 1962.
2. From a letter to the editor in *The PTA Magazine,* November 1962.
3. Many of the fallacies used in this chapter, along with some additional useful materials on clear thinking, may be found in Stuart Chase, *Guide to Straight Thinking* (New York: Harper & Bros., 1956).
4. These quotes come from the research reported in Robert H. Lauer, "The Middle Class Looks at Poverty," *Urban and Social Change Review* 5 (Fall): 8–10.
5. Galen's reasoning is reported in John McLeish, *The Theory of Social Change* (London: Routledge & Kegan Paul).
6. The details noted were reported in the *St. Louis Post-Dispatch,* June 27, 1971.
7. The results of these studies, including those reported in this paragraph, are found in a review by John Madge, *The Origins of Scientific Sociology* (New York: Free Press, 1962).
8. The letter is in the author's files.

Part 2

Problems of Deviance

What do prostitution, drug addiction, mental illness, arson, and child abuse have in common? Like all other problems discussed in this book, they involve social contradictions, they are defined as having adverse effects on quality of life, and they have multilevel causes. More specifically, they all involve behavior that deviates from norms (recall the discussion of deviance in chapter 1), and they all appear to be within the individual's control and responsibility. To have been born female or black or to be old are conditions one lacks control over and so cannot be blamed for. However, many people believe that one does have control over engaging in homosexual behavior, or prostitution, or using drugs, or robbing a store. Consequently, the problems in this section tend to provoke the same kind of reaction from society: the deviant individuals are (1) condemned and punished, or (2) defined as "sick" and given therapy, or (3) both. As we will see, the factors at work in problems of deviance are the same as those that cause and tend to perpetuate the problems discussed later in this book.

Sexual Deviance

3

1   **What are the various kinds of sexual deviance?**

2   **Are homosexuals sick?**

3   **Why does an individual prefer homosexuality?**

4   **Do Americans really want to get rid of prostitution?**

5   **Is prostitution the result of sexism in society?**

Love, according to Freud, is one of the foundations of civilization. One of the forms of love, sexual love,

> has given us our most intense experience of an overwhelming sensation of pleasure and has thus furnished us with a pattern for our search for happiness. What is more natural than that we should persist in looking for happiness along the path on which we first encountered it [Freud, 1961:29]?

We might disagree with Freud on many of his ideas, but few of us would dispute the importance of sex in human life or deny that sexual fulfillment tends to be linked with our happiness.

What is *sexual fulfillment?* That the sex drive is powerful is recognized by nearly everyone, but how do we find gratification for that drive? In our society, we think of sexual gratification in terms of **heterosexual**—male-female—relationships. We think that these relationships normally occur between consenting adults (who, many people believe, should be formally married to each other and live together). Our traditional ideal has been summarized by a famous psychoanalyst as a "utopia of genitality":

1. mutuality of orgasm
2. with a loved partner
3. of the other sex
4. with whom one is able and willing to share a mutual trust
5. and with whom one is able and willing to regulate the cycles of
   a. work
   b. procreation
   c. recreation
6. so as to secure to the offspring, too, all the stages of a satisfactory development [Erikson, 1950:257].

There are, however, a variety of ways to gain sexual gratification that deviate from the ideal. We cannot discuss all kinds of sexual deviance in detail, but a number will be mentioned below before we turn to a fuller discussion of two: **homosexuality** and **prostitution.** Both kinds of sexual behavior *deviate significantly from American norms.*

Varieties of Sexual Deviance

What is sexual deviance? The answer depends on which society you are talking about. All societies regulate sex, but not all regulate it the same way. In their study of 190 different societies, Ford and Beach (1951) concluded that there are wide variations in normative sexual behavior and that there is considerable permissiveness for some kinds of sexual behavior that Americans consider deviant (such as extramarital sex and homosexuality). Of course, people everywhere take their own norms seriously, but the point is that sexual behavior, like all other behavior, is social. No particular type of sexual behavior is "natural" or "normal" in contrast to other types.

We will briefly discuss here two types of sexual behavior that Americans tend to regard as deviant: sexual intercourse by the unmarried, and sexual intercourse by a married individual with someone other than his or her mate. Included in the former type is premarital intercourse. Kinsey found that the proportion of white women who engaged in premarital intercourse by age 20 increased from about 8 percent in 1900 to about 22 percent by the 1920s. Studies in the 1970s indicate that as many as 75 percent of young, unmarried women have premarital sex relations. The norms about premarital intercourse are changing. In a 1969 poll, 23 percent of the respondents agreed that premarital sex was not wrong. By 1978, the proportion who said it wasn't wrong rose to 59 percent.[1]

Other kinds of sexual relationships between the unmarried are less acceptable. **Promiscuity**—undiscriminating, casual relations with many people—is not acceptable to most Americans. The increasing acceptance of premarital sex is not an increasing acceptance of promiscuity. Those who engage in premarital sex tend to have some commitment to their partners (Lewis and Burr, 1975). A survey of 28,000 readers of a magazine showed that only 4 percent agreed that their ideal person of the opposite sex was someone who had "many sexual conquests" (Tavris, 1977:37).

Cohabitation—an unmarried couple living together—is an increasing but still deviant phenomenon. According to census figures, there were 1.3 million "unmarried-couple" households in 1979, more than double the number reported in 1970. Although many people believe that those who cohabit do so to avoid the commitments of marriage, cohabiting couples seem to have as much commitment to each other as those who are engaged or married (Lewis et al., 1977). Some people cohabit because they do not want to get married (though they may still be committed to their partners), while others look upon cohabitation as a prelude to marriage.

Certain kinds of *extramarital behavior* also deviate from American norms. A type that received considerable attention in the 1970s is the *"sexually open" marriage,* including the practice of **"swinging"** (swapping mates with other couples for sexual purposes). Two researchers who made an eighteen-month participant-observation study of 136 swingers tell how a session involving a number of couples might proceed:

> The ideal . . . is for the initiation of sexual interaction to appear to develop naturally—preferably in a nonverbal way. But with four or more people involved and all the signaling and cross-signaling of intentions that must take place, this ideal can only be approached in most cases. The initiation may begin with little or no socializing, much socializing with sex later on as a natural outgrowth of the good feelings thus created, or some mixture in between . . . swingers consider an ideal gathering one in which everyone can express themselves as individuals *and* appreciate others for doing the same [Palson and Palson, 1972:30].

There may be homosexual as well as heterosexual activity at such gatherings. The Palsons found that females are far more likely than males to participate in homosexual relations.

Many studies report that swinging couples improve their relationships with each other, and that swinging may enhance and even save a marriage.

A different view is put forth by Denfeld (1974), who criticized previous research in part because of the failure to study former swingers (those who dropped out of swinging). Denfeld presented evidence from marriage counselors that indicates swinging may create problems instead of solve them. In particular, jealousy tended to develop among the dropouts. Husbands became jealous of the popularity of their wives or their wives' "endurance capabilities." Wives, on the other hand, reported that jealousy was linked with a fear of losing their husbands. Various other reasons were reported for dropping out of swinging: guilt; new emotional attachments (which got in the way of sex for sex's

sake); unfulfilled expectations about the gratification of swinging; boredom and loss of interest; and fear of discovery.

Although some Americans will probably swing for many years, the practice may have reached its peak in the 1970s. By the mid-1970s there was already evidence that the number of participants was declining (Fang, 1976).

One other type of extramarital sexual deviance is *infidelity*. In the open marriage, sexual relations with people other than one's spouse are expected and are not interpreted as infidelity. However, extramarital relations under other circumstances are viewed as a breaking of trust, a violation of expectations. In the survey of the 28,000 magazine readers mentioned earlier (who were, incidentally, younger, more educated, and more liberal than the average), 67 percent of the women and 56 percent of the men said that sexual faithfulness would be a trait of their ideal partner (Tavris, 1977:37). A 1977 poll showed that about 80 percent of Americans consider marital infidelity as morally wrong.[2]

A few of the numerous kinds of sexual behavior that deviate from the norms have been discussed here. We will now discuss two other kinds in some detail: homosexuality—seeking sexual gratification through relationships with someone of the same sex; and prostitution—sex in return for payment. The two categories are not mutually exclusive, however.

Homosexuality

A homosexual is "one who has a sexual preference for persons of the same sex and who privately or overtly considers himself a homosexual" (Weinberg, 1974:43). In other words, not everyone who engages in a homosexual act at some time can be considered a homosexual. Boys commonly engage in homosexual activity during adolescence, but most of them do not become homosexuals. Moreover, some people are **bisexual,** finding gratification with either sex. The term "homosexual" technically refers to both males and females but the term **"lesbian"** is usually used for females, and the term "homosexual" typically connotes males. We will usually use the terms with that distinction. The bulk of studies on homosexuality have dealt with males.

How many homosexuals are in America? The famous Kinsey survey of 1948 found that about 10 percent of the males studied had been homosexuals for at least three years, but only 4 percent reported themselves as exclusively homosexual (Weinberg, 1974:43–44). A number of studies since Kinsey reported somewhat different proportions. The national study by Hunt in the 1970s indicated that 20 to 25 percent of males, 10 to 11 percent of married females, and about 20 percent of unmarried females had had some homosexual experience (Hunt, 1974). However, only 1 to 2 percent of males said they were predominantly or exclusively homosexual.

Because homosexuals have tended to be secretive about their sexual preference (for very good reasons), knowing the exact number of homosexuals is difficult. Probably about 3 to 4 percent of American men and 2 to 3 percent of American women prefer to be exclusively homosexual (Gagnon, 1977:254). In absolute terms, we are talking about 7 to 8 million people or more. What are the consequences of their sexual preference?

Homosexuality and the Quality of Life

Homosexuality is a pattern of behavior involving social contradictions that both homosexuals and nonhomosexuals define as incompatible with the desired quality of life. Homosexuals themselves point to two contradictions: one is that the American ideology of equality contradicts American attitudes and behavior toward homosexuals; the other is that the actual homosexual role contradicts the stereotyped homosexual role, which is condemned by many "straight" (nonhomosexual) Americans. Many nonhomosexuals argue that it is the homosexuality that is incompatible with the desired quality of life in America, because it distorts human sexuality and *threatens our morals and the institution of the family* (which is the basis for social stability). Some nonhomosexuals, particularly those with professional psychotherapeutic training, argue along a different line. They say that homosexuality is, indeed, incompatible with the desired quality of life because the homosexual has suffered from distorted or inadequate psychosexual development.

Homosexuals also argue that their behavior is a problem—not because of anything intrinsically wrong with the behavior, but because of *societal reaction*. Societal reaction, then, is incompatible with the homosexual's desired quality of life.

In the following paragraphs we will look at some ways the quality of life is diminished for the homosexual. Recall that quality of life is diminished whenever we face things such as restricted opportunities, fear for our well-being, and lack of respect from others. As the following sections detail, the quality of life for homosexuals is diminished by just such factors—restricted opportunities, exploitation, ridicule, being labeled sick or perverted, and stress that creates psychological and emotional problems.

Myths about homosexuality.   First, there is a contradiction between our ideal of the *dignity of human beings* and the prevalent ideology about homosexuals. That contradiction is manifested in a number of *myths about homosexuality.* Perhaps the most common myth is that homosexuals have characteristics that are normal for the opposite sex—males are effeminate and females are masculine. Actually, such traits characterize only a small minority of homosexuals. Some male homosexuals despise effeminate mannerisms and exaggerate masculine characteristics in order to be attractive to other homosexuals. Similarly, in a study of twenty-five homosexual and twenty-five heterosexual women, it was found that the "truck driver image" of lesbians is completely fallacious; virtually no differences existed between the two groups of women other than their sexual preference.[3]

A second myth about homosexuals is that they fear, and are even incapable of having heterosexual relationships. Homosexuality is commonly attributed to unsatisfactory heterosexual experiences, which can cause continuing fear of relationships with the opposite sex. As late as 1966 a national news magazine asserted that there is consensus on the cause of homosexuality, namely that homosexuality is caused by a "disabling fear of the opposite sex."[4]

While experiences with those of the opposite sex may be a factor in the development of homosexuality, there does not seem to be any evidence that homosexuals are incapable of relating to the opposite sex. By definition, a homosexual is one with a preference for sexual relations with those of his or her own sex, exclusively. However, homosexuals do make and maintain good relationships with people of the opposite sex. In a study of sixty-five lesbians, Hedblom (1973) found that almost 90 percent had dated males during their lesbian periods and over half had sexual experience with males. In another study of fifty-one lesbians, Chafetz, Sampson, Beck, and West (1974) reported that all but one of the women had straight female friends and nearly 90 percent had straight male friends (40 percent said that straight males were among their closest friends). A more recent study by the Institute for Sex Research, founded by Kinsey, showed that about one-fifth of the homosexuals in the sample had been married at some time, and about half of them had intercourse from two to four times a week during the first year of the marriage (Bell and Weinberg, 1978). Such studies, combined with the fact that many people are homosexuals for only a part of their lives, suggest that homosexuals are capable of all kinds of heterosexual relationships, and that preference rather than fear is the critical factor.

A third myth is that people typically become homosexual by being seduced by a homosexual. No evidence supports this. In fact, Hedblom (1973) found that the first homosexual contacts of the sixty-five lesbians in his sample were not the result of any kind of exploitation. Instead, the women appeared to have been willing and cooperative.

Finally, there is the myth that the homosexual is attracted to anyone of his or her own sex. Thus, all males—children as well as adults—are subject to the advances of the homosexual, and all females—children as well as adults—

Figure 3.1 Many homosexuals are now rejecting the traditional stigma and are demanding acceptance by society.

are subject to the advances of lesbians. Actually, the homosexual is as selective as anyone else. Some are quite choosy, and others are as willing to be promiscuous as are many heterosexuals. Contrary to popular thinking, a homosexual is unlikely to approach someone and make sexual advances "without first getting a clear indication of sexual interest on (the other's) part" (Barnett, 1973:177).

All these myths detract from the homosexual's desired quality of life because all of them assault the dignity of the homosexual as a human being. Any time myths are perpetuated about any of us we are robbed of some of our human dignity. Unfortunately, as we saw in our discussion of deviance, the labels we apply to people may become self-fulfilling prophecies even if they are inaccurate.

Equality of opportunity.   The American ideology of *equality of opportunity* contradicts the norms and laws about the hiring of homosexuals. The homosexual is a criminal wherever there are **sodomy** laws. As Barnett (1973:8) pointed out, this has resulted in a number of legal disabilities. The laws have not always been enforced, and some have been successfully challenged in the courts. But, homosexuals and lesbians have had to contend with a number of legal barriers to equal opportunity within both the government and the business sectors.

The lack of equal opportunity is not based on any lack of ability or inferior performance by homosexuals. In fact, the homosexual may *suffer discrimination in spite of proven superior performance.* In the fall of 1975 the Air Force discharged a sergeant who openly acknowledged his homosexuality and who wanted the Air Force to change its regulations about homo-

sexuals. The man had an outstanding military record, including a decoration for combat duty. Despite this, he was discharged, and the Secretary of the Air Force refused to reinstate him, arguing that the presence of homosexuals in the military "would seriously impair discipline, good order and morale."[5]

Many homosexuals have to choose between making their identity known ("coming out") and thereby risking their jobs, or remaining secretive and retaining their jobs. Unlike others who are defined as criminals, the homosexual poses no threat to life or property. There is, nevertheless, no equality of opportunity for those who openly avow their preference for homosexual relationships.

Exploitation.   In the past, homosexuals were dismissed from government jobs on the grounds that they could be blackmailed and forced to spy or engage in other criminal acts in order to prevent their identity from becoming known. Of course, the blackmail could have occurred only because of the *laws against sodomy.* Homosexuals were caught in a vicious cycle, exploited by the contradiction between sexual preference and the legal system.

How common is blackmail? One survey reported that about 10 percent of homosexuals had been blackmailed.[6] Undoubtedly, not every case of blackmail involved something as serious as treason or a felony. Still, a good deal of crime has been masked because of the blackmail of homosexuals (Mitchell, 1969). Because a stigma is still attached to homosexuality in many American communities, the blackmail of homosexuals is likely to continue. People with stigmatic identities are always vulnerable to exploitation by those who discover their identities.

Negative sanctions. Sanctions are rewards (positive sanctions) or punishments (negative sanctions) designed to influence behavior (though generically the term is used only in its negative connotation). Homosexuals are usually subjected to *numerous negative sanctions,* including ridicule, suppression, and ostracism. This contradicts the American ideology that every citizen has a right to life, liberty, and the pursuit of happiness. All of the sanctions, of course, are aimed at changing the homosexual into a heterosexual.

One negative sanction is likely to be the reaction of family members to disclosure of homosexuality. Whatever the adjustment made by lesbians with their families, according to Simon and Gagnon (1967:269), "the tendency for strain is evident." An extreme example of family reaction was reported by an older lesbian whose lesbianism was discovered when she was in college. She was placed in a private mental institution to be cured of her "nervous breakdown." In the hospital she was chained to the floor and given numerous shock treatments. She developed a deep feeling of guilt about her homosexuality, left the hospital, and soon married. This relieved her parents, but after seventeen years of marriage and two children, she was divorced and again became a lesbian (Chafetz, Sampson, Beck, and West, 1974:721–22).

Many homosexuals have endured being *labeled "pervert" or mentally ill* by their family or by others. Many people who use such labels perhaps feel that they can help the homosexual to change, but generally they only add to the difficulty of the homosexual.

When negative labels do not work, stronger measures may be used against homosexuals. Gay organizations on college campuses have been suppressed or forced to operate without the funds and facilities available to other organizations. Homosexuals have been dismissed from various businesses and government positions when their sexual preference became known. As well, there is always the possibility of *harassment and "entrapment" by the police.* Entrapment is a method for arresting homosexuals and prostitutes especially. A police officer learns to imitate the language, behavior, and dress appropriate to entice the target group, then he or she goes into an area where the group is known to be. The officer tries to elicit a sexual advance by his or her demeanor, and then will use the elicited behavior to arrest, in this case, the homosexual. The homosexual never knows when someone might try to entrap him or her, or when the police might raid a gay bar, or when some other effort at suppression will have to be faced. Among the sample of homosexuals in the Institute for Sex Research study, nearly one-half of the whites and about one-third of the blacks had been arrested or apprehended by police.

Fear. It is little wonder that *homosexuals live with a certain amount of fear.* One of the freedoms cherished by Americans is the freedom from fear. For the homosexual, this ideal is contradicted by the norms and laws that apply to gay people.

In addition to the constant threat of arrest, exposure, or various negative sanctions, there is the lack of support from social institutions. Homosexuals have learned to expect little but condemnation from family, religion, and employers. No wonder, then, that they attempt to conceal their homosexuality. As Barnett (1973:220) put it: "One experience of listening

Figure 3.2 Arresting a homosexual through the use of police decoys (*top*) is the kind of harassment the demonstrators are protesting (*bottom*).

to a group of heterosexuals talking about 'cock-suckers' and 'queers' is enough to convince any male homosexual that he must at all costs conceal his orientation from others." In their study of sixty homosexuals in a Canadian city, Leznoff and Westley (1966:190) found three reasons why many homosexuals feel concealing their preference is necessary. The most common reason was the "desire to avoid social ridicule," closely followed by the fear of loss of a job or of clients, and then by a desire to protect other people such as the homosexual's friends and family.

In other words, the homosexual is subject to constant fear of exposure if he or she decides to remain secretive, and to fear of negative sanctions if he or she decides to openly affirm homosexuality. This is not to say that every homosexual goes around for the greater part of every day haunted by fear. Nevertheless, it is true that all homosexuals must somehow come to terms with the legitimate fears that hang ever near them.

Psychological and emotional problems. We might expect that it is difficult for homosexuals to avoid psychological and emotional problems as they wrestle with the contradictions that impinge upon their lives. In fact, a number of studies have identified certain problems that result from the *stresses of being a homosexual.* In the past, these problems were often used to support the notion that homosexuals are emotionally ill. More recent evidence suggests a different interpretation; the psychological and emotional problems are not concomitants of the "illness" of homosexuality, but are the consequences of the stress generated by the societal reaction to the individual's homosexuality. In 1973 the American Psychiatric Association, which long supported the notion that homosexuality is a form of pathology, accepted a statement that homosexuality per se could not be considered a mental disorder.

Unfortunately, many psychiatrists, and many more lay people, continue to view homosexuals as "sick." As labeling theory suggests, this viewpoint can become a self-fulfilling prophecy. Thus, in Hoffman's (1967:51) terms, the main cause of "unhappiness and psychopathology" among homosexuals is "society's attitude toward homosexuality":

> A well-known fact in the study of oppressed minorities is that they, tragically, adopt toward themselves the degrading view that the larger society has of them. The homosexual accepts this stigma. He views himself as queer, bad, dirty, something a little less than human.

In accepting the labels applied by society, the *homosexual is likely to feel guilty,* and *self-acceptance* may be *a serious problem.* One lesbian expressed her inner conflict thus:

> I just felt it had to be unnatural. I knew how men and women made love. It was present in the very biology. . . . I somehow decided that if God had intended women to love one another, He would have made it more obvious, like He did for men and women in love [Simon and Ganon, 1967:280].

In view of the stresses induced by societal reaction, how prevalent are psychological and emotional problems among homosexuals?

Evidence from various studies is contradictory. Some studies show higher rates of disturbance, some show lower rates, and some show no differences between homosexuals and heterosexuals. Many studies show both positive and negative facets of the psychological functioning of homosexuals. For example, in one study, a comparison of fifty-seven lesbians with forty-three heterosexual women showed that the lesbians had a higher rate of alcoholism and of attempted suicide but that they were, on the whole, able to achieve as much and be as productive citizens as the heterosexuals (Saghir, Robins, Walbran, and Gentry, 1970). Both male and female homosexuals have a greater incidence of depression, attempted suicide, and alcohol abuse than do heterosexuals. There was not a significant difference in the incidence of neurotic disorders, however, and the homosexuals were generally able to function adequately in society (Saghir and Robins, 1971). In another study, the perceived adjustment and psychological well-being of a group of male and female homosexuals was compared with that of a group of heterosexuals who were similar to the homosexuals in things such as sex, age, and education. Again, there was little difference between the groups. The male homosexuals were somewhat less defensive, and less self-confident than male heterosexuals, and the lesbians were more self-confident than the female heterosexuals. The two groups (homosexual and heterosexual) were quite similar otherwise (Thompson, McCandless, and Strickland, 1971). In conclusion,

> the only obvious difference between homosexuals and heterosexuals is in psychosexual object choice. All experienced clinicians and research workers report that the personality differences among individual homosexuals are far more apparent than the similarities [Hooker, 1972:15].

What does all this mean? First, "there is no inherent connection between homosexual orientation and clinical symptoms of mental ill-ness" (Hoffman, 1967:48). Second, the stress induced by societal reaction to the individual's homosexuality produces some emotional and psychological problems. Third, some homosexuals are able to come to terms with the societal reaction, cope with the problems, and lead well-adjusted and productive lives. The ability of some homosexuals to overcome the induced stress may be related to the extent of their commitment to the gay life. A study of 2,497 male homosexuals in the United States, the Netherlands, and Denmark found that psychological adjustment was a function of commitment to the deviant identity (Hammersmith and Weinberg, 1973). Commitment was measured by responses to the statements: "I wish I were not homosexual," and "I would not want to give up my homosexuality even if I could." Perhaps when the homosexual is able to reject the societal labels and commit himself or herself to the gay life, the stress-induced psychological and emotional problems are resolved. At any rate, such problems must still be confronted by anyone who expresses a preference for homosexuality.

Contributing Factors in Homosexuality

In looking at the multiple-level factors that cause, facilitate, and tend to perpetuate the problem of homosexuality, we need to look at two different phenomena. First, we should examine the *factors that lead the individual to a homosexual preference.* Second, we need to examine the *factors that result in the societal reaction to homosexuality.* Without both sets of factors, of course, there would be no problem of homosexuality. In this section, we will look at the first set.

Hooker (1972:14) observed that there are "many combinations of variables, including biological, cultural, psychodynamic, structural, and situational" that result in homosexuality. Many of these are matters of dispute. Some psychiatrists, for instance, still argue that homosexuality is a form of mental illness, while others maintain that if the homosexual has psychopathological characteristics, it is because of societal reaction, not because anything is inherently pathological about homosexuality. On the other hand, there seems to be little question about two things: homosexuality involves a process of learning, and social interaction is crucial in that process. Let us examine these points in more detail.

First, homosexuality is *a learned pattern of behavior*. There is no innate drive, no biological necessity, for either hetero- or homosexuality. Both patterns are learned as the individual develops. Male homosexuals have been found to begin their experiences in early adolescence, while lesbians have been found to begin their homosexual involvement several years later (Saghir and Robins, 1971). Until adolescence, an individual has the capacity for either kind of sexual involvement and may develop into a hetero- or homo- or bisexual. Obviously, most Americans become heterosexuals. Why do some prefer homosexuality? Henslin (1975:192) argued that the first homosexual experience is typically the result of chance, the outcome of adolescent sexual experimenting. What determines, then, whether that first experience will lead to additional experiences and to a preference for homosexuality? The probability that the individual will continue homosexual activities depends, according to Henslin (1975:192) on how pleasurable the first experience was and

how early in life it occurred; how frequently the individual engages in homosexual activities; and the quality of the emotional relationship between the partners.

If those were the only criteria involved, we would expect to find more homosexuals than we do. We must realize that the general societal situation negatively sanctions homosexuality. In fact, the sanctions have been so severe that we might ask why so many people prefer homosexuality in light of the social costs. Why does an individual become homosexual in the face of extremely strong social pressures toward heterosexuality? The question is difficult to answer because the evidence is contradictory and often has been gathered by people holding strong opinions about the causes. For instance, much of the early research was conducted by people who accepted the notion that homosexuality is pathological, and who, therefore, were seeking the causes of the pathology. Some of the more recent research, on the other hand, has been conducted by people who believe that homosexuality is a matter of preference alone. They tend to find that homosexuals are as normal and healthy as any other group in the population. However, as we argued above, homosexuality must be more than just a matter of preference in view of the strong societal pressures toward heterosexuality.

One factor identified as important for some homosexuals is the *quality of the family life* in which the individual developed. At least some homosexuals have had disturbed relationships with their parents. Simon and Gagnon (1967: 257) reported that the lesbians they studied all described some kind of difficulty in their home life. About half came from homes broken by death, divorce, or separation. And "in almost every case there was a strongly expressed preference toward one of the parents, and attitudes toward the other parent or substitute parent ranged from condescending neutrality to open hostility." Quite different results were reported in a survey of 205 lesbians in Illinois (Hogan, Fox, and Kirchner, 1977). Most of the lesbians said they had happy childhoods, and were raised by both parents. A disproportionate number had been the only child in the family. There were few reports of disturbed relationships.

Weinberg (1974:47) pointed to several kinds of relationships between parents and children that may dispose the children to homosexuality. In one kind, a girl is desired but a boy is born. The mother treats the boy as if he were a girl and emphasizes his effeminate qualities. The boy then may be forced into the homosexual role as he interacts with his peers and may, subsequently, accept himself as a homosexual. In another kind of relationship, the mother acts in a "seductive and alluring" manner toward her son, who develops a deep sense of guilt and an inability to relate sexually to women generally. However, no one particular kind of mother-son relationship is typically associated with homosexual development.

Homosexuals have often had bad relationships with their fathers, who did not serve as effective role-models for their sons. While we cannot say that a particular kind of family background facilitates homosexual development, many homosexuals have had a disturbed relationship with one or both parents.

Another factor that is important in homosexual development is the *norms of one's peers during adolescence.* Reiss (1967) found that young male delinquents would engage in homosexual activities with adults to earn money.

It was a purely financial transaction for the boys and was approved by group norms. The same norms, on the other hand, defined the adult homosexuals as "queers."

The boys did not regard themselves as homosexuals, however, and did not continue homosexual activity when they became adults.

By contrast, if an adolescent *participates in a homosexual clique,* homosexuality may be redefined as preferable, and the individual may accept a homosexual identity as he or she internalizes the norms of the group (Hooker, 1972:13).

An interesting aspect of homosexuality is that in many cases individuals engage in it for only a short period of their lives. As Sagarin (1973:6) noted, the Kinsey studies reported that of those who have homosexual relationships for a three-year period, only about half continue to be exclusively homosexual throughout their lives. There are a variety of patterns, with some individuals going in and out of homosexuality and bisexuality. For this reason Sagarin (1973:10) argued that we have fallen into the *fallacy of misplaced concreteness* in our discussions of homosexuality:

> . . . there is no such thing as a *homosexual,* for such a concept is a reification, an artificially created entity that has no basis in reality. What exists are people with erotic desires for their own sex, or who engage in sexual activities with same-sex others, or both.

To say that someone is a homosexual implies a permanent state of being, whereas in reality, homosexual behavior can be unlearned and abandoned as well as learned and accepted.

Homosexual behavior is learned through interaction with others. Individuals who find such behavior gratifying may have had disturbed relationships with one or both parents, and they tend to participate in groups with norms that accept homosexual behavior. Individuals learn homosexual behavior in such groups. This does not mean, however, that the homosexuality is an enduring characteristic. Many people are exclusively homosexual for only a short period of their lives, and many go back and forth between straight, homosexual, and bisexual behavior.

Contributing Factors in the Problem of Homosexuality

Without the societal reaction to homosexuality that we find in America, we could not speak of homosexual behavior as a social problem. In this section we will look at some of the multiple-level factors that account for this societal reaction and that create stress in those who express a preference for homosexuality.

Social structural factors. In the United States, *normative sexual behavior* is heterosexual. The norms of our society define homosexuality as deviant, and nearly all Americans recognize this. But they don't recognize that such norms do not reflect universal standards or innate biological imperatives. The expected sexual behavior varies from one society to another. In at least a few societies, homosexuality appears to be normative and heterosexuality tends to be avoided. For instance, among the Etero of New Guinea, heterosexual relations are considered taboo for 295 days during the year. Among a neighboring group, the Marind-anim, homosexual relations are considered the ideal, and a large number of the group's children are

acquired through raids on neighboring groups rather than through heterosexual intercourse (Kottak, 1974:287–88).

Even if heterosexual relations are dominant, a society does not necessarily disapprove of or *punish homosexuality*. In her study of a variety of primitive societies, Brown (1952) found that thirty of forty-four of the societies for which data were available punished male homosexuality, and four of twelve punished female homosexuality.

Many modern societies refrain from formally punishing homosexual acts that are conducted in private between consenting adults. Such acts are not considered a crime in Japan, Korea, Mexico, Argentina, Uruguay, Egypt, and the Sudan, for example (Barnett, 1973:307).

In the United States, the norms that define homosexuality as deviant are supported by various social institutions. For instance, the norms are incorporated into the legal system and sanctified by religion. The United States is the only large Western nation that allows the punishment of adults who privately engage in consensual homosexual acts. This reflects the English heritage of America, particularly the views of the Puritans, who saw homosexuality as one symptom of the moral corruption of England in the seventeenth century (Mitchell, 1969:14–16). Changes have since occurred in England. In 1967 the House of Commons reformed the laws on homosexuality and removed private, consensual homosexual acts between adults from the criminal statutes. The United States not only allows communities to retain homosexuality as a criminal act, but allows police to actively harass and attempt to apprehend homosexuals as well.

The changes in England were facilitated by the support of prominent Anglican and Catholic clergymen for the decriminalization of homosexuality. In the United States, on the other hand, a minority of the clergy have attempted to establish new views on homosexuality, but the majority continue to insist that homosexuality is aberrant sexual development and is sinful. In 1965 a Council on Religion and the Homosexual was organized to overcome the "heterosexual bias" of the Bible.[7] The council aimed at decriminalizing homosexual behavior and obtaining full civil rights for homosexuals. But the supporters of the council disagreed about the nature of homosexuality. An Episcopal bishop supported the council's aim of decriminalization but also argued that homosexuals cannot maintain healthy interpersonal relationships: ". . . homosexuality is essentially a pastoral problem dealing with brokenness in humanity the same as many other moral maladies."[8]

Similarly, a prominent conservative Christian magazine editorialized that the church should show compassion toward homosexuals without forgetting, however, that homosexual behavior is condemned by the Mosaic law and is listed by St. Paul "as a vice to which God has abandoned mankind as a result of man's general refusal to acknowledge him as Lord."[9] Fundamentalist Christians in general stress that homosexuality is a "vice" condemned by various Biblical teachings.

Numerous less conservative Christian leaders condemn homosexual behavior, and many homosexuals have reported that attending church only intensified their stress and their sense of guilt. Religion, along with other American institutions, usually condemns homosexual behavior.

Social psychological factors.   The homosexual's stressful environment is maintained by social psychological factors that support and reinforce the norms and institutional arrangements. In the first place, attitudes generally are negative toward homosexuality. A 1969 Louis Harris poll reported that 63 percent of Americans view homosexuals as "harmful to American life."[10] This is, of course, a much harsher attitude than dislike or disapproval. The proportion who disapprove has remained fairly high; 78 percent of the respondents in a 1977 poll said homosexuality is always or almost always wrong.[11] Many Americans fear homosexuals in certain positions in society. According to a 1977 Louis Harris poll, if an admitted homosexual were qualified in every way, he or she would not be allowed to hold a position as: a counselor in a camp for young people, by 63 percent of the people; a school principal, by 58 percent; a minister, priest, or rabbi, by 50 percent; or a doctor, by 40 percent.[12]

Although our values concerning heterosexual relations derive from religion, their existence and force are independent of that institution. Both Judaism and Christianity consider homosexuality a sin against God. Even people who do not hold firmly to traditional religious beliefs often place high value on heterosexuality. In other words, some of the values of religion tend to be retained even when the religion itself has lost much of its importance.

The negative societal reaction to homosexuality is also legitimated by the ideology that

Involvement

Stepping Into the Gay World

"Are you gay?" asked an advertisement in a metropolitan newspaper. "Do you think you might be gay? Need some help?" The ad went on to give a "Sex Help-line" telephone number for people to call. "You have to make up your own mind. But the people at the center might be able to help you think more clearly."

"Gay hot lines" have been set up in a number of places to help homosexuals and lesbians who feel oppressed by guilt or by other people. There are also an increasing number of gay organizations—within churches, bars, and liberation groups.

Get in touch with one of the organizations and visit it. Someone there will undoubtedly be willing to discuss with you the problems of being gay in our society. You might also want to discuss with that person his or her understanding of homosexuality—why people become gay, and how many might engage in homosexual behavior if the stigma were removed.

One reason for the rise of gay organizations is the rejection often experienced by homosexuals and lesbians. As an alternative project, you might get in touch with some organizations in your community and inquire whether they have any official or unofficial position on admitting gay members.

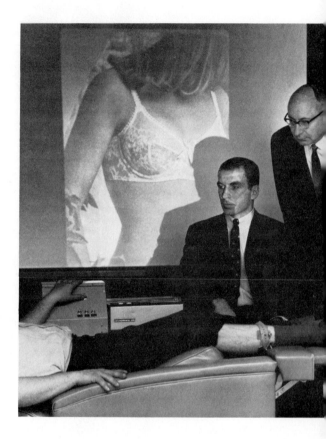

Figure 3.3 A homosexual in therapy. Typically, in our country, homosexuality has been viewed as an illness to be cured.

homosexuals are sick people. For the professional, this means that people who prefer homosexual relations suffer from an emotional disorder and need to be treated in the same way as any other emotionally disturbed individual. One clinician analyzed lesbians as women who can never be happy because heterosexual relations are fundamental to human happiness: "The label 'gay' behind which they hide is a defense mechanism against the emptiness, the coldness, and the futility of their lives" (quoted by Chafetz, Sampson, Beck, and West, 1974:717). This view implies that *those who prefer homosexual relations should be identified, treated, and cured.* It is hard to estimate the number of therapists who continue to view homosexuals as sick despite the 1973 American Psychiatric Association pronouncement, but a 1978 informal poll of 2,500 psychiatrists concluded that the majority still believe homosexuality is pathological.[13]

Many nonprofessionals view homosexuals as *not only sick, but somewhat perverse as well.* Just as many Americans believe that alcoholics could stop drinking "if they only wanted to," they also believe that homosexuals could change their sexual behavior "if they only wanted to." In other words, many Americans view homosexuality as a personal problem, not a social one. They believe that the norms, institutional arrangements, attitudes, values, and ideology that work together to condemn and oppress homosexuals are legitimate.

What Is to be Done?

The position we take about how to deal with the problem of homosexuality will depend on our view of the basic nature of the problem. If we see the problem as the homosexual behavior itself, we might advocate therapy or negative sanctions against homosexuals. If we see the problem as essentially the societal reaction to harmless behavior, we might advocate change in the legal system and in the attitudes that legitimate defining homosexuality as crime. Or, if we view both approaches as valid, we might advocate both a change in the societal reaction and an effort to help everyone learn to be heterosexual. That is, we would believe that we should stop oppressing homosexuals, but we would also believe that homosexuality represents distorted or perhaps aborted sexual development.

There are efforts to change the *legal status of homosexuals*. Some gay activists have challenged the right of anyone to discriminate against homosexuals. In one court case, for instance, homosexual activity by a NASA employee was determined to be insufficient grounds for dismissal.[14] A number of states have decriminalized sexual acts between consenting adults, and dozens of cities have passed ordinances that protect the rights of homosexuals in housing and employment. Many universities have adopted policies of nondiscrimination on the basis of sexual preference. Some courts are now willing to award legal custody of children to a homosexual parent. In general, "the degree of legal progress is truly remarkable" (Vetri, 1979/80:30). Still, there have not been the sweeping reforms necessary to end discrimination. Many legal problem areas remain. Vetri (1979/80:25) listed them: (1) constitutionality of laws that criminalize homosexual behavior; (2) equal opportunity in public and private employment; (3) occupational licensing; (4) family law issues such as marriage, child custody, child

visitation rights, adoption, and financial support after separation; (5) housing; (6) public accommodations access; (7) immigration and naturalization; (8) rights of association and free speech; (9) armed services policies; (10) police harassment; (11) income tax status; and (12) insurance coverage.

Hooker (1961:177–78) suggested three "preventive" steps for dealing with homosexuality. First, we should create "a *climate of opinion* in which homosexuality can be openly and reasonably discussed." Second, we should provide *"healthy sex education,* both of parents and of children and youth." And third, we should provide *family counseling and child guidance services* that will encourage psychologically healthy family life and will also "provide assistance to children with early symptoms of developmental difficulties."

Such suggestions assume that heterosexuality is the ideal. Some gay activists would reject this assumption and would go so far as to assert that homosexuals are the most healthy and most moral people in the society. Both laymen and professionals disagree on whether the problem is the homosexual behavior itself or the societal reaction to it, or both. Consequently, what happens in the future with respect to the problem of homosexuality will depend on the outcome of the conflict between the various positions.

Prostitution

The second type of sexual deviance, prostitution, has been defined as "the granting of nonmarital sexual access, established by mutual agreement of the woman, her client, and/or her employer, for remuneration which provides part or all of her livelihood" (Winick and Kinsie, 1971:3). Prostitutes perform a variety of sexual services, including **fellatio** (oral stimulation of the male genitalia), **cunnilingus** (oral stimulation of the female genitalia), and anal intercourse as well as standard intercourse. A new kind of prostitution appeared in the 1970s—the *"massage parlor."* Bryant and Palmer (1975) conducted an investigation of a number of massage parlors, and found that the services frequently included massage of the genitals. Some of the women who worked in the parlors called themselves "hand whores." In essence, they would massage a male customer to the point of orgasm, although they would not offer standard intercourse. The massage of the genitals was typically done only upon request by the customer. Not all customers want a massage to orgasm (Armstong, 1978). The typical customer, according to data gathered on 183 patrons of a parlor in Illinois, is young (35 years old on the average), married, white, from out of town, has orgasm during the genital massage, and finds the experience sexually satisfying (Simpson and Schill, 1977).

Apart from massage parlors, how much prostitution is in the United States? Because official records depend on arrests and because not all prostitutes get arrested, estimating the number of prostitutes in America is difficult. Winick and Kinsie (1971:4) reported that there were 95,550 arrests for prostitution in 1968, but they thought that number was undoubtedly too low for an estimate of all full-time prostitutes (there are also an unknown number of part-time prostitutes). In an attempt to establish some notion of the amount of prostitution, the authors said:

> The average full-time prostitute today works six
> days a week and has three clients daily, so that

perhaps 286,650 men daily or some 1,719,900 weekly use such services [Winick and Kinsie, 1971:4].

The authors also pointed out that the amount of prostitution is roughly the same as it was in the 1930s, when a study showed that 69 percent of the white males in a community of 100,000 people had been clients of prostitutes.

Other observers place the number of prostitutes at anywhere from 100,000 to 500,000. In rough terms, then, prostitution involves as many as a quarter- to a half-million American women who work full- or part-time. Their clients are perhaps half or more of the adult male population in the country. In looking at the meaning of prostitution for the quality of life, we will concentrate on the prostitute, but we should keep in mind that the widespread use of prostitutes by men suggests that the quality of the American male's sex life falls short of what is desired.

Prostitution and the Quality of Life

Prostitutes typically prefer their profession to options they perceive they had. Contrary to opinions held in the past, it is not true that many prostitutes are coerced into "the life" (as they often call it). This is not so much evidence of the high quality of life for the prostitute as it is testimony to the *low quality of life endured by the women* before they decided to enter "the life." Most have apparently decided that prostitution is better than other choices open to them. This point underscores the undesirability of those other choices, because the quality of life for the prostitute has little to be envied.

Figure 3.4 During the 1970s "massage parlors" sprang up throughout the nation, offering a new kind of prostitution.

Physical problems.   In the first place, *prostitution contradicts our value of physical well-being.* Americans cherish good health and value the youthful physique. Most prostitutes, however, face certain occupational hazards that may leave them with physical problems. In the past, *venereal disease* was a prominent problem. Today it is less frequent because many prostitutes get regular medical checkups themselves and also carefully examine each customer for signs of venereal disease. Another common physical problem "is a chronic pelvic congestion characterized by a copious discharge from the cervix and vaginal lining, and a sensation of tenderness and fullness of the side walls of the pelvis" (Winick and Kinsie, 1971:70). The congestion results from the prostitute's avoidance of orgasm during intercourse. She may try to get relief through narcotic drugs.

A different problem is the *physical abuse that threatens the prostitute.* Such abuse may come from a customer or from the **pimp** (one who earns all or part of his or her living by acting as a manager for the prostitute). The highly paid call girl, who serves a more affluent clientele, is not likely to endure physical abuse, but the streetwalker must be constantly alert. As one former prostitute said to Studs Terkel (1972:98), "I remember having knives pulled on me, broken bottles held over my head, being raped, having my money stolen back from me, having to jump out of a second-story window, having a gun pointed at me."

The constant threat of such abuse is one reason why a prostitute needs a pimp: "If you're gonna whore you need protection: a man's protection from other men. All men are in the protection business. . . . If men didn't beat us up we wouldn't need half the husbands we got" (Millett, 1971:95). At the same time, the pimp himself inflicts physical abuse (though he is not likely to kill the prostitute). Sometimes the pimp will beat a prostitute when he begins his relationship with her. Some pimps beat the woman into a state of unconsciousness in order to establish their dominance and insure the woman's loyalty. If the prostitute does not behave in a way the pimp deems appropriate, he may continue to abuse her. One prostitute explained the pimp's behavior as behavior rooted in the fear of not knowing what will happen when one has a slave. In addition, the pimp may feel compelled to maintain his ideal of masculinity before other men:

> Pimps do rotten things. I guess they have to. That life is kind of bitter. . . . You've got to prove everything all over every day, right? You've got all the guys watching you. What do they do? What kinds of really raunchy things do they do? What are they capable of, these cats? I saw a girl walk into a bar and hand the pimp a $100 bill. He took it and burned it in her face and turned around and knocked her down on the floor and kicked her and said, "I told you, bitch, $200. I want $200, not $100." Now she's gotta go out again and make not another hundred, but two hundred. I know of some pimps who killed a whore with an overdose of heroin and then fucked her dead body. They're sick [Millett, 1971:101–3].

We do not know how frequently prostitutes must endure physical abuse from customers or from their pimps, but the threat of abuse is constant, and it is unlikely that any prostitute can ply her trade for many years without suffering a certain amount of abuse.

Physical problems are acute for the prostitute because she must maintain a certain amount of physical attractiveness in order to stay in the life. However, according to Lemert

(1951), *prostitutes age more quickly* than other people because of irregular habits of eating, sleeping, and travel and the effects of drinking, venereal disease, and abortions. Use of drugs and the physical abuse just discussed also probably accelerate the aging process. We have no concrete evidence that prostitutes actually do age more quickly than other people, but it is unlikely that the physical and psychological strains they are subjected to would fail to leave their mark.

Psychological and emotional problems. A psychological problem reported by prostitutes arises from the contradiction between our value of sexual fulfillment and the role of the prostitute. The problem is a psychological counterpart to the previously mentioned physical ailment that can result from the prostitute's avoidance of orgasm. Far from achieving sexual fulfillment, the prostitute often *becomes virtually asexual* with respect to her own sexual functioning. Sex can become meaningless to her: "Prostitution not only puts down women, but it puts down sex—it really puts down sex. Often I really couldn't understand the customer, couldn't understand what he *got* out of this, because I really felt I was giving nothing" (Millett, 1971:96).

The prostitute might find sex "boring." Comparing prostitution with her former line of work, one woman said, " 'Ever since I turned out, I have regarded the work as being a little more boring than the work I used to do when I was a file clerk' " (Winick and Kinsie, 1971:25–26). The prostitute might become incapable of having orgasm. Some prostitutes have a certain amount of sex with their pimps, and some become lesbians. Ironically, the ideal of sexual fulfillment is contradicted by the prostitute's role.

There is also a contradiction between our value of *human dignity* and the prostitute's role. The former prostitute interviewed by Studs Terkel was first a call girl and, then a streetwalker. Both activities were *dehumanizing:*

> As a streetwalker, I didn't have to act. I let myself show the contempt I felt for the tricks. They weren't paying enough to make it worth performing for them. As a call girl, I pretended I enjoyed it sexually. You have to act as if you had an orgasm. As a streetwalker, I didn't. I used to lie there with my hands behind my head and do mathematics equations in my head or memorize the typewriter keyboard [Terkel, 1972:98].

One of the prostitutes interviewed by Kate Millett (1971:104) said the worst part of the life is that the woman sells her humanity, her human dignity, "Not really so much in bed, but in accepting the agreement—in becoming a bought person."

A sense of alienation and isolation, drug use, and attempted suicide may all express a prostitute's sense of lost dignity and dehumanization. Prostitutes generally do not form a cohesive group among themselves because they are competing for customers. They mainly have contempt for their customers, and cannot establish bonds there. They often cannot form close relationships with nonprostitutes or with people unconnected with the life because of the stigma attached to their role. Prostitutes are thus barred from a sense of community with anyone.

One way prostitutes cope with this problem is to seek *refuge in drugs*. We do not know the extent of drug use among prostitutes, but we can be fairly confident from various reports that drug abuse is high. One prostitute said that most of the call girls she knew were on drugs:

> The fast life, the night hours. At after-hours clubs, if you're not a big drinker, you usually find somebody who has cocaine. . . . You wake up at noon, there's not very much to do till nine or ten that night. Everybody else is at work, so you shoot heroin. . . . The work becomes boring because you're not part of the life. You're the part that's always hidden [Terkel, 1972:97].

The rate of *attempted suicide* is also high among prostitutes. In one study, three-fourths of a sample of call girls were found to have attempted suicide. It has been estimated that as many as 15 percent of suicides brought into public hospitals may be prostitutes (Winick and Kinsie, 1971:76).

There is, then, ample evidence of psychological and emotional problems among prostitutes. Moreover, these problems are built into the role of the prostitute, making escape from the problems difficult. For some women, prostitution seems to be a more desirable option than other options that are available, but the psychological and emotional quality of the life that awaits the prospective prostitute may turn out to be depressingly low.

Exploitation.   Quality of life is further diminished by the contradiction between the roles of the prostitute and people she must deal with and our ideal of "I-Thou" relationships where people relate to each other as person to person and not as person to thing. The prostitute's relating to others in the role of prostitute involves *exploitation.* Many people earn their own living by using prostitutes. Formerly, the *"madam"* (a woman who acted as hostess and manager of a brothel) was a prominent figure for many prostitutes. She might receive as much as half the customer's fee. Today, the pimp is the person more likely to exploit the prostitute, taking perhaps all the fees and returning a small portion to her for her expenses.

Pimps, madams, bellboys, taxi drivers, disreputable medical examiners, abortionists, police officers receiving hush money—the prostitute must deal with them all, and they all treat her as a "thing" rather than as a person by using her to make or to supplement their own living. Because the prostitute typically needs these other people in order to pursue her profession, she often has no choice but to relinquish a substantial portion of her earnings.

This exploitation has roused the ire of feminists, one of whom called the arrest and conviction of a prostitute "the greatest spectacle in the court, every day's choicest entertainment" (Millett, 1971:107). The whole social system, argued this feminist, "bleeds" prostitutes both sexually and economically. The women offer their sexual services to men, pay their fines to men, return to the streets only to be arrested again by men—all to satisfy the public's sense of "decorum." Arresting prostitutes satisfies the public because the appearance of police safeguarding morality is maintained. Thus, the prostitute is exploited by the entire society. She is used for various purposes by various people, who all regard her as an object to serve their own interests.

Contributing Factors

If the quality of life for the prostitute is so low, and if many Americans believe the very presence of prostitutes offends our traditional morals, why does prostitution continue? Again, we find that multiple-level factors operate to maintain prostitution.

Social structural factors.   We must examine the social structure to discover why men seek prostitutes and why women enter into the life. In the first place, American society has traditionally held to the norm of sex only within marriage. In addition, sex has not been openly discussed through much of our history. These two factors—*rejection of nonmarital sex* and *no open discussion of sex*—were set forth by Winick and Kinsie (1971:8) as crucial determinants of the amount of prostitution in a society. They pointed out that among the Tokopia of the Solomon Islands, both nonmarital sex and open discussion of sex are accepted, and there is practically no prostitution. They hypothesize that where social norms forbid either or both of these conditions, there will probably be prostitution. This line of reasoning is supported by the fact that open discussions about sex have become more acceptable, and nonmarital sex (especially premarital) has become more widely accepted in American society. At the same time, while roughly the same number of men visit prostitutes as thirty years ago, fewer are young men, and the number of visits by each man has declined (Winick and Kinsie, 1971:185–86).

In addition to traditional norms about nonmarital sex and discussion of sex, the traditional female role will also influence the probability that a male will go to a prostitute. The majority of clients of prostitutes probably are married, but because of the normative role of the American woman, the *institution of marriage* does not provide sufficient *sexual gratification* for males. Winick and Kinsie (1971:193) suggested that married men go to prostitutes to experience variety, to compensate for a lack of gratification with their mates, or to avoid concern about pregnancy, among other reasons. How does the *normative role of the American wife* inhibit sexual gratification in marriage? For a long time a woman was considered superior to a man because of her *moral purity*. It was believed that women *lacked sexuality*—that the wife engaged in sexual relations just to satisfy her husband's animal passions. In a small Missouri town in the 1940s, West (1945:177) found the majority of couples "would consider it immodest to undress completely before each other in a lighted room; many married couples are said never to have seen each other undressed."

Such modesty is no longer normative, and a wife is no longer believed to lack sexual needs and interests of her own. The normative role of the wife has changed in recent years, but the institution of marriage has not changed sufficiently to allow full gratification of the sexual desires of many males. This, of course, is not the only reason men go to prostitutes, but it contributes to maintaining the institution of prostitution.

In the future an interesting twist may develop. Increasingly, women are asserting their own sexual needs and desires, and a growing number are voicing dissatisfaction with their husband's ability to gratify them. Consequently, more extramarital activity may come about at the instigation of women rather than men. Under such circumstances, if husbands maintain the traditional expectation of fidelity, the demand for male prostitutes may expand.

Another aspect of marriage that supports prostitution is the relatively *late age at which Americans marry;* it is far beyond puberty, and for many it is later than the peak of the male sexual drive. High school and college students are not initiated into sex by prostitutes as frequently as they once were, but in his study of thirty-three brothels in Nevada (in areas where prostitution is legal), Symanski (1974) found that high school and college students were among the major sources of business.

The nature of the economy also facilitates male use of prostitution. Workers such as male truckers and salesmen must spend a considerable amount of time away from home. Symanski (1974:373) reported that tourists, traveling salesmen, and truck drivers were also among the major sources of business for the Nevada brothels. To the extent that the *economy requires travel,* there will always be clientele for the prostitute.

Structural factors help explain why women enter the life. In a study of teenage prostitutes in Seattle, Gray (1973) found that the backgrounds of the girls were characterized by *disturbed family experiences* and by *participation in groups with norms that accepted prostitution.* Social and emotional deprivation alienated the girls from their families, and nearly all of the girls were exposed to prostitution by relatives or peers. Thus, through differential association the girls learned to accept prostitution as normative and came to view prostitution as preferable to the kind of life they had in their families.

Other studies emphasized that prostitutes tend to come from a *low position in the stratification system.* Winick and Kinsie (1971:35–36) pointed out that prostitutes usually have relatively little education, unfavorable family lives, and inadequate income from previous jobs that often required no skills. Symanski (1974:368) observed that money or "quick financial gain was often expressed as the main motive" for entering the life. He also found that 25 to 30 percent of the women in the brothels were black. One of the prostitutes interviewed by Millett (1971:64) said she began her career because she was broke: "I just decided fuck it, man, I'm not going to be poor any more."

In terms of Merton's anomie theory, the women who enter prostitution have the same goals as most people but have failed to attain them through legitimate means. Because their efforts to gain success through legitimate means were stifled by the double impact of their lowly origin and the fact that they are female, these women became *innovators,* turning to illegitimate means to gain the culturally approved goals. As we will see in a later chapter, females suffer considerable discrimination in job opportunities and income. When a female must not only cope with this discrimination, but also begin her quest for success from the lower ranks of the stratification system, she may resort to innovative means. When, in addition, she has learned certain innovative means through differential association and has experienced alienation in her family life, she is ripe for recruitment into prostitution.

Social psychological factors. Although "respectable" people are sometimes thought to abhor prostitution, the bulk of the prostitute's clientele are so-called respectable people. Tolerant *attitudes of officials* and public acceptance of the ideology that male sexuality needs the outlet both help to maintain prostitution.

Figure 3.5 Teenage prostitute and her pimp looking for a customer.

It has often been remarked that prostitution could never continue if the authorities were really determined to eliminate it. While this is an overstatement, it is true that police seldom make a concerted, determined effort to stop all prostitution. Sometimes an official openly acknowledges support of prostitution, as in 1969 when the mayor of Terre Haute, Indiana appeared on local television to deny that he intended to rid the city of prostitution, contrary to an earlier news report. His stand in favor of prostitution was supported by the police chief, who argued that Terre Haute had no cases of rape the previous year because prostitutes were available.[15]

Public opinion polls also show considerable support for prostitution. In a 1937 sample of 3,000 Americans who were asked about controlling prostitution, 50.5 percent said that controlled prostitution should be made legal (Winick and Kinsie, 1971:10). Davis (1976:246) reported that a poll conducted by a woman's magazine found only 7 percent wanting to eliminate prostitution. Many people did not want a brothel in their own neighborhood, nor did they want prostitutes walking their own streets, but at the same time, they did not want to eliminate prostitution.

The *tolerant attitude about prostitution* is rooted in part in our *ideology about male sexuality,* as expressed in the argument of the Terre Haute chief of police. In Nevada towns where prostitution is legal, law enforcement people favor the brothels because "they have fewer complaints of disorderly conduct from the houses than from other establishments which serve alcohol. . . . Brothels are not so much good in and of themselves as they are better than alternative institutions" (Symanski, 1974:

376). Parents have said prostitution kept their sons from having to get married early and kept their daughters from getting into trouble. The Nevada brothels were credited with decreasing the amount of rape and other violent crime. Implicit in such statements is the ideology that male sexuality, in contrast to female sexuality, must find expression, and that traditional values about marriage, the family, and the purity of women are contingent on men having a sexual outlet in the form of prostitution. As long as this ideology is held, public attitudes will be tolerant of prostitution.

What Is to be Done?

The widespread existence of prostitution—in different cultures and throughout history—should make us hesitant about accepting any simple approach to the problem. To argue that the police should enforce the law more vigorously would be naive, because both official and public attitudes give tacit and sometimes open support to prostitution.

In recent years, it has been argued that prostitution, like homosexuality, should be *decriminalized,* that all sex relations between consenting adults should be considered legal. Prostitutes themselves have argued for decriminalization and some have banded together to form their own civil rights organization called Coyote. In 1976 members of Coyote gathered in Washington, D.C. and announced the formation of the Hooker's Lobby, which had the explicit purpose of getting Congress to decriminalize laws against sex relations between consenting adults.[16]

Our discussion of the prostitute's quality of life shows that decriminalization will not completely solve the problem. Because of potential abuse from customers, prostitutes will still need pimps. If the prostitutes work in brothels, avoiding the need for pimps, they will still be treated as objects rather than as people and will confront the various psychological and emotional problems inherent in the life.

Decriminalization could be an initial step in removing some of the harassment and exploitation prostitutes are subjected to. However, the problem will be resolved only when the institution of marriage provides adequate sexual gratification for males; when women from lower socioeconomic positions have opportunities for gaining some measure of success in the economy; when the economy does not force males to spend long periods of time away from their homes; and when our ideology about sexuality no longer provides a basis for tolerance.

Finally, we should be aware that resolving prostitution as a problem would not necessarily mean eliminating prostitution as a fact. Prostitution presently is a problem because of its incompatibility with the desired quality of life. Conceivably some prostitution could exist in a society—prostitution that would offer females a profitable career without physical or psychological risks, and that would, at the same time, offer males a sexual service. This state of affairs would require, among other things, that legitimacy and status be granted the prostitute so that she would be treated as a person and not be exploited as an object.

Summary

Sexual gratification is an important part of American life. Prostitution and homosexuality are two ways of gaining sexual gratification that deviate from the ideal. Both involve contradictions and incompatibility with the desired quality of life, and both are sustained by multiple-level factors.

Homosexuality is the sexual preference of at least 3 to 4 percent of Americans. The quality of life for the homosexual is diminished by certain myths, by the lack of equality of opportunity, by exploitation, by negative sanctions, by fear, and by various psychological and emotional problems. Homosexuality itself is learned behavior. Those who prefer it may have experienced disturbed relationships with one or both parents and may have participated in groups with norms that are accepting of homosexual behavior. Many people are homosexual for only a short portion of their lives.

The negative societal reaction to homosexuality imposes stress on homosexuals. Our norms, supported by social institutions, define homosexuality as deviant and deserving of negative sanctions. Homosexuality is subject to legal sanctions and is viewed by religious teachings as aberrant and sinful. These norms and institutional arrangements are supported by the attitude that homosexuality is harmful to American life, by the value of heterosexuality, and by the ideology that homosexuals are sick people.

Prostitution involves from 100,000 to 500,000 American women and perhaps half or more of the male population. The prostitute's quality of life is diminished by physical problems inherent in the life, as well as by psychological, emotional, and economic problems, including fear, alienation, isolation, and exploitation.

Prostitution is maintained because of: (1) our norms about nonmarital sex and open discussion of sex; (2) the lack of sexual gratification in marriage; (3) the late age at which Americans tend to marry; and (4) characteristics of the economy such as males who are required to travel in their jobs, and women being discriminated against in job opportunities and income. The tolerance of prostitution on the part of both the public and officials is rooted in our ideology about sexuality—the notion that male sexuality, in contrast to female sexuality, must find expression.

Glossary

bisexual   having sex relations with either sex or both together

cunnilingus   oral stimulation of the female genitalia

fellatio   oral stimulation of the male genitalia

heterosexual   having sexual preference for persons of the opposite sex

homosexual   having sexual preference for persons of the same sex; someone who privately or overtly considers himself or herself a homosexual

lesbian   a female homosexual

pimp   one who earns all or part of his living by acting as a manager or procurer for a prostitute

promiscuity   undiscriminating, casual sexual relationships with many people

prostitution   having sexual relations for remuneration, usually to provide part or all of one's livelihood

sodomy   intercourse that is defined as "unnatural"; particularly used to refer to anal intercourse

swinging   exchange of mates among couples for sexual purposes

For Further Reading

Bell, Alan P., and Martin S. Weinberg. *Homosexualities: A Study of Diversity Among Men and Women*. New York: Simon and Schuster, 1978. An important study from the Institute for Sex Research, based on a survey of homosexuals in San Francisco. Provides good information on the meaning of being a homosexual in America today.

Constantine, Larry L., and Joan M. *Group Marriage*. New York: Macmillan, 1973. A study of groups of three or more people who were united in a marriage relationship; discusses the interpersonal problems created by such an arrangement.

Greenwald, Harold. *The Call Girl*. New York: Ballantine Books, 1959. A study of twenty-four call girls, the elites of prostitution, in New York City. Provides the background of the women and indications of their low quality of life.

Karlen, Arno. *Sexuality and Homosexuality: A New View*. New York: W. W. Norton, 1971. A thorough examination of homosexuality by a journalist, including historical, religious, psychiatric, and sociological views. The author did some participant observation of homosexuals.

Lewis, Sasha Gregory. *Sunday's Women: A Report on Lesbian Life Today*, Boston: Beacon Press, 1979. Looks at the public and private aspects of lesbian life today, including a history of lesbian politics.

Pittman, D. J. "The Male House of Prostitution." *Trans-Action 8* (April 1971):21–27. An account of a little-known aspect of homosexuality—the male prostitute.

Sagarin, Edward, and Donal E. J. MacNamara, eds. *Problems of Sex Behavior*. New York: Thomas Y. Crowell, 1968. Has chapters on homosexuality and prostitution, including the famed Wolfenden report on homosexuality. A number of other forms of sexual deviance are also discussed.

Winick, Charles, and Paul M. Kinsie. *The Lively Commerce*. Chicago: Quadrangle Books, 1971. The most complete and up-to-date study of prostitution. Includes materials on virtually every aspect—the prostitute, the madam, the pimp, ways of plying the trade, legal aspects, and so forth.

Notes

1. Reported in *Public Opinion*, December/January 1980, p. 28.
2. Ibid., p. 27.
3. Quoted in *Human Behavior*, January 1976, p. 47.
4. *Time*, January 21, 1966, p. 41.
5. Quoted in the *St. Louis Post-Dispatch*, May 2, 1976.
6. Quoted in *Time*, October 31, 1969, p. 64.
7. *Newsweek*, February 13, 1967, p. 63.
8. Ibid.
9. *Christianity Today*, January 19, 1968, p. 25.
10. Reported in *Time*, October 31, 1969, p. 61.
11. Reported in *Public Opinion*, July/August 1978, p. 38.
12. Ibid.
13. Reported in *Time*, January 8, 1979, p. 48.
14. Reported in the *Georgetown Law Journal* 58 (1970): 632–45.
15. *Time*, February 21, 1969, p. 20.
16. *St. Louis Post-Dispatch*, June 22, 1976.

Drugs and Alcohol

1 **What kinds of drugs present a problem to America?**

2 **What is the difference between abuse and addiction?**

3 **How widespread is the drug problem?**

4 **What are the consequences of abuse and addiction?**

5 **Why do people get hooked?**

Americans have had ambivalent feelings about drugs and alcohol throughout history. In general, alcoholic beverages were regarded by the colonists as one of God's gifts to mankind. As Furnas (1965:18) noted, our forebears "clung long to the late-medieval notion that alcohol deserved its splendid name, *aqua vitae,* water of life. . . ." *Drunkenness* was punished, but drinking was generally considered one of the good things available to people. In the early nineteenth century, however, a New York Temperance Society began to urge its members to *totally abstain* from all alcoholic beverages (Furnas, 1965:67).

Until the beginning of the nineteenth century the use of opium and its derivatives was less offensive to Americans than drinking or smoking cigarettes. After the Civil War, however, some Americans began to warn about the dangers of **addiction,** and by 1962 the problem of drug addiction was considered serious enough to warrant a White House Conference. As reported by the President's Commission on Law Enforcement and Administration of Justice (1967a), the drug problem was widespread and insidious:

> Organized criminals engaged in drug traffic were making high profits. Drug addicts, to support their habits, were stealing millions of dollars worth of property every year and contributing to the public's fear of robbery and burglary. The police, the courts, the mails and prisons, and social-service agencies of all kinds were devoting great amounts of time, money and manpower to attempts to control drug abuse. Worst of all, thousands of human lives were being wasted [p. 211].

Our ambivalence has not yet melted into consensus. Many Americans view alcohol as one of the "good things" of life, while others advocate total abstinence. While most Americans view drugs such as heroin negatively, other drugs are considered a benefit. In 1973 the country produced 538,000 *pounds* of tranquilizers and over 32 million *pounds* of aspirin. Furthermore, an enormous amount of drug usage results from medical care. As Hills (1980:118) said, a good many physicians have "come to view loneliness, anxiety, conflict, or unhappiness as symptoms of 'psychic distress,' an ailment to be corrected, eliminated, or 'cured' with drugs. . . . Physicians and the pharmacological industry have combined to hold out the promise of putting an end to personal distress through chemistry." Ads in medical journals advocate the use of tranquilizers for things such as anxiety experienced by people who have a hard time adjusting to new situations.

Some of the ambivalence is rooted in the distinctions among use, **abuse,** and addiction. It is possible to use drugs and alcohol without debilitating (and sometimes with beneficial) effects. Some people appear to be able to use heroin regularly without sinking into the life of desperation often associated with heroin addiction. These people, called "chippers," may be fairly productive and free of criminal activity over a period of twenty years or more (Zinberg and Jacobson, 1976).

The abuse of drugs or alcohol, not the use, creates the problem. We will define abuse as the *improper use of drugs or alcohol to the degree that the consequences are defined as detrimental to the user and/or the society.* Addiction is a form of abuse. The World Health Organization has defined addiction as

> a state of periodic or chronic intoxication detrimental to the individual and to society, produced by the repeated consumption of a drug

(natural or synthetic). Its characteristics include: (1) an overpowering desire or need (compulsion) to continue taking the drug and to obtain it by any means; (2) a tendency to increase the dose; (3) a psychic (psychological) and, sometimes, a physical dependence upon the effects of the drug [Cole and Miller, 1965:262–63].

Not every case of abuse involves addiction. A man may not be an alcoholic, but may get drunk and kill someone while trying to drive his car. A woman may not be hooked on any drugs, but may be persuaded to try LSD, may have a "bad trip" and commit suicide.

Our focus in this chapter will be on abuse, which includes addiction. We will look first at the *different types of drugs and their effects* (including alcohol, which is a drug itself). We will then examine drugs and alcohol separately, looking at patterns of use, effects on the quality of life, multiple-level factors that create and perpetuate drug and alcohol problems, and ways people have attempted to cope with these problems.

Types and Effects

Drugs

Five main types of drugs and some of their possible effects are summarized in figure 4.1. Possible effects vary considerably. Actually, a number of factors bear upon the effects of any particular drug—chemical composition, amount taken, method of administration, and the social situation in which the drug is administered, to name a few. In other words, we need to know more than the physiological effects of a drug to understand the experience of the individual taking it.

A drug imposes no intrinsic and automatic effects on every individual who takes it. As Howard Becker (1953) argued with respect to marijuana, the *effects vary according to how they are defined.* An individual might define himself or herself as either sick or "high," depending on how others with whom that individual interacts define the physiological effects of the drug. Experimental support for this interpretation was provided by Schachter and Singer (1962), who investigated three hypotheses. First, if an individual has a physiological experience for which there is no immediate explanation, that individual will *label the experience* with whatever information is available. This means that the same physiological effects may be labeled by one person as anger, by another as joy, and by another as fear. Second, if there is a ready explanation for a physiological experience, the individual is not likely to choose other explanations that are available. Third, an emotional label will not be attached to an experience unless there is some kind of physiological arousal.

All the hypotheses were supported by the experiment in which some students received an injection of the hormone epinephrine and others received a **placebo.** Among the physiological effects of epinephrine are palpitation, tremor, and sometimes accelerated breathing and the feeling of being flushed. All the students were told they had received the drug in order to determine its effects on their vision. Some were given no information on any side effects; some were correctly informed of those effects; and others were misinformed about the effects. While waiting for the effects, each student was sent to a room where a student who was an accomplice of the experimenter created a situation of euphoria for some of the students and of anger for others. Students who had been injected with the epinephrine and who had received either no information or misinformation about side effects "gave behavioral and self-report indications that they had been readily manipulable into the disparate feeling states of euphoria and anger" (Schachter and Singer, 1962:395).

Similarly, based on fifty interviews, Becker (1953) found that *defining the effects of marijuana as pleasurable is a learning process.* First, the individual must learn the technique of smoking marijuana. Then the person must learn what the effects of the drug are and must learn to associate those effects with use of the drug. Intense hunger, for example, may be an effect, and the user must learn to define that hunger as a sign of being high. Finally, the individual must learn to define the effects as pleasurable rather than undesirable. Effects such as dizziness, thirst, and tingling of the scalp could be defined as symptoms of illness, or just undesirable, but by interacting with others who define those effects as desirable, as the goal for which all have been striving, an individual could learn to define them as desirable.

An additional point should be made about the effects of drug use. As figure 4.1 shows, the physical and psychological dependence created by the use of any particular drug varies considerably, and the effects of some drugs are not yet fully known. For this reason there is considerable debate about how to define "abuse." Many people argue that marijuana is nothing more than a mild intoxicant and that its inclusion in the list of illicit drugs is absurd. Experts disagree about some other drugs also, and there is no consensus on the meaning of "abuse" and

Figure 4.1 Controlled substances: uses and effects. (Source: U.S. Department of Justice, Drug Enforcement Administration, *Drugs of Abuse* [Washington, D.C.: Government Printing Office, n.d.].)

	Drugs	Often Prescribed Brand Names	Medical Uses	Dependence Physical	Potential: Psychological
Narcotics	Opium	Dover's Powder, Paregoric	Analgesic, antidiarrheal	High	High
	Morphine	Morphine	Analgesic	High	High
	Codeine	Codeine	Analgesic, antitussive	Moderate	Moderate
	Heroin	None	None	High	High
	Meperidine (Pethidine)	Demerol, Pethadol	Analgesic	High	High
	Methadone	Dolophine, Methadone, Methadose	Analgesic, heroin substitute	High	High
	Other narcotics	Dilaudid, Leritine, Numorphan, Percodan	Analgesic, antidiarrheal antitussive	High	High
Depressants	Chloral hydrate	Noctec, Somnos	Hypnotic	Moderate	Moderate
	Barbiturates	Amytal, Butisol, Nembutal, Phenobarbital, Seconal, Tuinal	Anesthetic, anti-convul-sant, sedation, sleep	High	High
	Glutethimide	Doriden	Sedation, sleep	High	High
	Methaqualone	Optimil, Parest, Quaalude, Somnafac, Sopor	Sedation, sleep	High	High
	Tranquilizers	Equanil, Librium, Miltown Serax, Tranxene, Valium	Anti-anxiety, muscle relaxant, sedation	Moderate	Moderate
	Other depressants	Clonopin, Dalmane, Dormate, Noludar, Placydil, Valmid	Anti-anxiety, sedation, sleep	Possible	Possible
Stimulants	Cocaine†	Cocaine	Local anesthetic	Possible	High
	Amphetamines	Benzedrine, Biphetamine, Desoxyn, Dexedrine	Hyperkinesis, narco-lepsy, weight control	Possible	High
	Phenmetrazine	Preludin	Weight control	Possible	High
	Methylphenidate	Ritalin	Hyperkinesis	Possible	High
	Other stimulants	Bacarate, Cylert, Didrex, Ionamin, Plegine, Pondimin, Pre-Sate, Sanorex, Voranil	Weight control	Possible	Possible
Hallucinogens	LSD	None	None	None	Degree unknown
	Mescaline	None	None	None	Degree unknown
	Psilocybin-Psilocyn	None	None	None	Degree unknown
	MDA	None	None	None	Degree unknown
	PCP‡	Sernylan	Veterinary anesthetic	None	Degree unknown
	Other hallucinogens	None	None	None	Degree unknown
Cannabis	Marihuana Hashish Hashish oil	None	None	Degree unknown	Moderate

†Designated a narcotic under the Controlled Substances Act.

‡Designated a depressant under the Controlled Substances Act.

Tolerance	Duration of Effects (in hours)	Usual Methods of Administration	Possible Effects	Effects of Overdose	Withdrawal Syndrome
Yes	3 to 6	Oral, smoked	Euphoria, drowsiness, respiratory depression, constricted pupils, nausea	Slow and shallow breathing, clammy skin, convulsions, coma, possible death	Watery eyes, runny nose, yawning, loss of appetite, irritability, tremors, panic, chills and sweating, cramps, nausea
Yes	3 to 6	Injected, smoked			
Yes	3 to 6	Oral, injected			
Yes	3 to 6	Injected, sniffed			
Yes	3 to 6	Oral, injected			
Yes	12 to 24	Oral, injected			
Yes	3 to 6	Oral, injected			
Probable	5 to 8	Oral	Slurred speech, disorientation, drunken behavior without odor of alcohol	Shallow respiration, cold and clammy skin, dilated pupils, weak and rapid pulse, coma, possible death	Anxiety, insomnia, tremors, delirium, convulsions, possible death
Yes	1 to 16	Oral, injected			
Yes	4 to 8	Oral			
Yes	4 to 8	Oral			
Yes	4 to 8	Oral			
Yes	4 to 8	Oral			
Yes	2	Injected, sniffed	Increased alertness, excitation, euphoria, dilated pupils, increased pulse rate and blood pressure, insomnia, loss of appetite	Agitation, increase in body temperature, convulsions, possible death	Apathy, long periods of sleep, irritability, depression, disorientation
Yes	2 to 4	Oral, injected			
Yes	2 to 4	Oral			
Yes	2 to 4	Oral			
Yes	2 to 4	Oral			
Yes	Variable	Oral	Illusions and hallucinations (with exception of MDA); poor perception of time and distance	Longer, more intense "trip" episodes, psychosis, possible death	Withdrawal syndrome not reported
Yes	Variable	Oral, injected			
Yes	Variable	Oral			
Yes	Variable	Oral, injected, sniffed			
Yes	Variable	Oral, injected, smoked			
Yes	Variable	Oral, injected, sniffed			
Yes	2 to 4	Oral, smoked	Euphoria, relaxed inhibitions, increased appetite, disoriented behavior	Fatigue, paranoia, possible psychosis	Insomnia, hyperactivity, and decreased appetite reported in a limited number of individuals

"physical and psychological dependence." There is consensus about some drugs and strong disagreement about others. However, we should keep in mind that the drugs we will discuss are defined by American law as illicit. The nature of the problem will vary from one society to another, depending upon *legal and social definitions of drugs and drug use*.

Alcohol

All alcoholic beverages contain the same drug, ethyl alcohol or ethanol, but the proportion varies in different beverages. An individual can consume about the same amount of alcohol by drinking a pint of beer, a glass of wine, and a shot (1.5 ounces) of whiskey. What happens when that alcohol is ingested? The alcohol is burned and broken down in the body at a relatively constant rate. If an individual drinks slowly, there will be little or no accumulation of alcohol in the blood. But if an individual consumes alcohol more quickly than it can be burned in the body, the *concentration of alcohol in the blood* increases.

A small amount of alcohol can result in changes in an individual's mood and behavior, and as the concentration of alcohol in the blood increases, there are correspondingly more serious effects (National Institute on Alcohol Abuse and Alcoholism, 1975:7–8). A blood alcohol level of about 0.05 percent (one part alcohol to two thousand parts blood) can make the individual feel a sense of release from tensions and inhibitions. This mild euphoria is the aim of many people who drink moderately. As the alcohol level increases, however, there is an increasing loss of control, because alcohol acts as a depressant on functions of the brain. At the 0.10 percent level, the individual's motor control is affected—hands, arms, and legs become clumsy. At 0.20 percent, both the motor and the emotional functions of the brain are impaired, and the individual staggers and becomes intensely emotional. This is the level at which we define someone as drunk.

At the 0.30 percent, an individual is incapable of adequately perceiving and responding to the environment and may go into a stupor. At a 0.40 or higher percent, the individual lapses into a coma and will possibly die.

The subjective behavior associated with these objective measures of alcohol abuse is usually destructive, especially if one goes to work or drives an automobile while intoxicated.

The damaging effects of alcohol abuse are most obvious in the *alcoholic*—the individual who is addicted to alcohol. Alcoholism is defined in various ways. Some people who have studied alcoholism consider it a disease and others prefer to call it a behavior disorder. Most agree that alcoholism involves drinking to an extent that exceeds the norms of the society and that adversely affects the drinker's health, relationships with others, and economic functioning. Alcoholism is defined in terms of behavior as:

(1) loss of control—the victim finds himself drinking when he intends not to drink, or drinking more than he planned; (2) presence of functional or structural damage—physiological, psychological, domestic, economic, or social; (3) use of alcohol as a kind of universal therapy, as a psychopharmacological substance through which the person tries to keep his life from coming apart [National Institute on Alcohol Abuse and Alcoholism, 1975:15].

Because the effects can be so deleterious, and because the use of alcohol is so widespread in

Table 4.1   Drug Use, by Type of Drug and by Age Group, 1979

[Current users are those who used drugs at least once within month prior to this study. Based on national samples of 1,272 youths, 1,500 young adults, and 1,822 older adults].

Type of Drug	Percent of Youths (12–17 yr.)		Percent of Young Adults (18–25 yr.)		Percent of Adults (26 yr. and older)	
	Ever Used	Current User	Ever Used	Current User	Ever Used	Current User
Marijuana and/or hashish	28.2	16.1	60.1	27.7	15.4	3.2
Inhalants	9.0	.7	11.2	(z)	1.8	(z)
Hallucinogens	4.6	1.6	19.8	2.0	2.6	(z)
Cocaine	4.0	1.0	19.1	3.7	2.6	(z)
Heroin	1.1	(z)	3.6	(z)	.8	(z)
Other opiates	6.1	.6	13.5	1.0	2.8	(z)
Stimulants[1]	5.2	1.3	21.2	2.5	4.7	.6
Sedatives[1]	3.1	.8	18.4	2.8	2.8	(z)
Tranquilizers[1]	3.8	.7	13.4	2.4	2.6	(z)
Alcohol	52.6	31.2	84.2	70.0	77.9	54.9
Cigarettes	47.3	22.3	67.6	47.3	67.0	38.7

Z Less than .5 percent.   [1]Prescription drugs.

Source: U.S. Bureau of the Census, *Statistical Abstract of the United States, 1980* (Washington, D.C., Government Printing Office, 1981), p. 129.

our country, many experts consider alcohol abuse much more serious than the abuse of other drugs. Other drugs often receive more attention and are treated more dramatically in the media, but alcohol abuse is the major drug problem in the United States today.

Drugs

Although alcohol abuse is the major drug problem, the use and abuse of other drugs affect nearly all Americans directly or indirectly. We will begin our examination of the problem by looking at the pattern of use—how much is used and by whom.

Patterns of Use

It is difficult to know the number of drug users in the United States. Not all users are addicts, and not all addicts are known to the authorities. A 1979 national sample showed wide variation in use, depending on the type of drug involved and the age of the users (table 4.1). After alcohol, tobacco and marijuana are the most common drugs used by all age groups. In general, nonnarcotic drugs such as marijuana, hallucinogens, stimulants, and depressants are used much more widely than are narcotics. As well, the drug problem is more intense among younger age groups. A national survey of high school seniors in 1979 reported that 65 percent said they had used an illicit drug at some time (Johnston, Bachman, and O'Malley, 1979:7).

Many researchers have focused on the number of marijuana users. Fort (1974:137) estimated that about 26 million Americans have tried marijuana at least once and that 15 million are steady users. Carr (1976:56) reported a 1974 national survey showing that 29 million Americans tried marijuana at least once and that over 12 million were steady users.

By 1979 (table 4.1) over one-fourth of young adults were current users, and 60 percent had at least tried the drug. The proportions in table 4.1 represent a dramatic increase over the preceding seventeen years. In 1962 the proportion of those who had ever used marijuana was less than 5 percent for all age groups. Such figures have led some observers to claim that marijuana is a permanent aspect of American life. For instance, Carr (1976:56) argued:

> In spite of massive law-enforcement efforts in the last decade to suppress its sale and use, marijuana is gradually taking its place with alcohol as the recreational drug of choice for millions of Americans. Marijuana is readily available to all who seek it, and the indications are that its use will continue to rise with each succeeding generation.

Carr's argument is supported by the results of annual surveys of high school seniors. In 1975, 47.3 percent of the seniors had used marijuana at least once, and by 1979, 60.4 percent had experienced the drug. The proportion of current users rose from 40 percent in 1975 to 50.8 percent in 1979 (Johnston, Bachman, and O'Malley, 1979:23). The 1979 figure was only

0.6 percent higher than 1978, suggesting the possibility that usage may be leveling off somewhere around the 60 percent mark.

A particular question often raised is, Does the use of one drug lead to the use of others? One reason sometimes given for avoiding marijuana is that it will lead the user to experiment with other drugs. A number of studies have investigated the question, and in general they support the conclusion that there is a *tendency for multiple use*. That is, the majority of people who use illicit drugs use, or have used, more than one kind of drug and also consume alcoholic beverages. Let us look at a few of the studies reported in the 1970s that bear upon the question.

Weppner and Agar (1971) studied over 1,000 addicts who were admitted to the National Institute for Mental Health Clinical Research Center. Of those admitted, 738 had been addicted to heroin at some time. Nearly 40 percent of the heroin addicts reported that heroin was the first drug to which they were addicted; the other 60 percent indicated they had first been addicted to a different drug. Of those who said they had been using some other drug prior to becoming addicted to heroin, 35.5 percent named marijuana, nearly 18 percent named alcohol, and the rest identified other drugs ranging from narcotics to cough syrup.

In a study of senior and junior high school students, Wechsler and Thum (1973) found that illicit drug use was much more common among "heavier drinkers" (defined as those who said they used distilled spirits and had been drunk from that use). Single, Kandel, and Faust (1974) examined multiple drug use among secondary school students in New York and found

Figure 4.2 A "pot party" in San Francisco. Drug use is found among all segments of the American population.

that the majority of those who used illicit drugs had used more than one kind of drug. Moreover, illicit drug users also tended to use alcohol and tobacco: 94 percent used beer and wine, and 90 percent used hard liquor. Finally, in a study of students in Detroit area high schools, Shapiro (1975) found that users of illicit drugs reported more frequent use of alcohol and tobacco than did nonusers of illicit drugs.

Clearly, then, multiple use is the pattern. People who use illicit drugs are likely to use more than one kind of drug. They may also drink more than nonusers. Nevertheless, use of one drug or use of alcohol does not *cause* the individual to experiment with another drug. Rather, whatever leads an individual to experiment with one substance will probably lead that individual to experiment with others. There is no evidence that smoking marijuana per se drives an individual to experiment with other drugs. In their sample, Single, Kandel, and Faust (1974:346) reported a smaller proportion of multiple users among the marijuana users than among users of other drugs. In other words, while there is a decided tendency for multiple use, many Americans use only marijuana or only alcohol or only marijuana and alcohol. Narcotics users, in contrast, are much more likely to use a number of different kinds of drugs.

Who are the users of drugs? For many people, drug use and particularly drug addiction conjure up images of skid row and the ghetto. However, the problem goes far beyond such places.

Let us look first at the use of marijuana. Fort (1974:137) noted that the research indicates marijuana use "involves all social classes, economic groups, races and religions, and all ages beyond childhood although it is much more frequent in those between fifteen and thirty." The trend in marijuana use is toward pervasiveness. That is, marijuana, like alcohol, has spread across socioeconomic, regional, sex, and racial lines. There are some small differences in use along those lines, however. The 1979 sample of high school seniors showed that marijuana use was (1) somewhat higher among males than females and daily use was substantially higher for males (12.7 percent vs. 7.3 percent for females); (2) lower on an annual basis for college-bound students (47 percent) than for noncollege-bound students (53 percent); (3) lower in the South (41 percent) than in other regions (52 to 61 percent); and (4) higher in larger urban areas (59 percent) than in nonurban areas (43 percent) (Johnston, Bachman, and O'Malley, 1979:18).

For drugs other than marijuana, we find considerable differences in usage along various sociodemographic lines. For example, physicians have a comparatively high rate of addiction—as much as twenty-five to one hundred times greater than that of the general population, with an estimated 1 or 2 percent of all physicians being addicts (Modlin, 1974:3). This does not mean, of course, that most addicts are physicians or that most physicians can become addicts. It means, rather, that physicians have a greater probability of becoming addicts than various other groups.

The *bulk of drug abusers are young, male, poor, nonwhite, and are addicted to heroin* rather than to some other narcotic.

We will explore later some of the reasons for the disproportionate number of narcotic addicts possessing these characteristics.

Drugs and the Quality of Life

We have seen that drug abuse is a widespread problem in America and that it affects all kinds of people. Some people are affected directly—they are abusers—while other people are affected indirectly by the behavior of the abusers. Because abuse involves a number of contradictions defined as incompatible with the desired quality of life, our concern here will be with the *effects of abuse* on the quality of life.

Physical health.   Drug abuse contradicts our *value of physical well-being.* The use of drugs may be related to what Merton called anomie—the result of institutional arrangements blocking fulfillment of such legitimate values as psychological well-being. A person may experiment with drugs because they seem to hold the promise of fulfillment. But the fulfillment is elusive; greater and greater quantities are consumed, and ultimately the person suffers physical and psychological deterioration.

The *physical consequences of narcotic addiction* have been outlined by Himmelsbach (1974:27):

1. In general, addicts eat poorly (food being less important than drugs) and consequently they often suffer the effects of malnutrition.
2. *Anemia* is common; they're generally underweight.
3. They've generally had a number of *infections* because of their carelessness in administering drugs.
4. Malaria, syphilis, fungus infections, endocarditis, hepatitis, etc., are transferable by the needle.
5. Their *dental health* is usually horrible.
6. The death rate of addicts is higher than the death rate of non-addicts.

Addicts suffer a large number of physical illnesses and they tend to die at an early age. The early death is often associated with an overdose of the drug. Heroin slows the vital functions of the body, and if a sufficient amount of the drug is ingested, those vital functions will completely stop. The addict can never be sure how much of the drug constitutes an overdose, nor can he or she be sure about the purity of the drug. Also, the *addict's tolerance level can vary* from one day to another, depending on how much of the drug has been used. If the addict manages to avoid death by overdose, he or she may still die from any of a number of infections carried by the needle.

Various nonnarcotic drugs also may have serious physical consequences. Tobacco may cause more physiological damage among Americans than any other nonalcoholic drug. Among the known consequences of smoking are: reduced life expectancy; increased probability of lung cancer and other respiratory diseases; increased risk of heart disease; and increased probability of complications during childbirth. The effects of tobacco are long-term. Some drugs may have disastrous effects in the short run. Phencyclidine, known as PCP or "angel dust," is a relative newcomer. PCP did not appear on the illegal drug market until the late 1960s. In the 1970s the popular media reported a series of horror stories connected with the drug, including hundreds of murders, suicides, and accidental deaths. The effects of PCP vary from one individual to another, ranging from intense highs to feelings of illness, to mental and emotional collapse, to bizarre and violent behavior. Most users are young white males.

Some consequences of other drugs are briefly noted in figure 4.1. Let us look more closely, however, at the effects of marijuana. The effects of marijuana use are a matter of considerable controversy. Many people insist that those effects are only slight physiological changes in the user, including some increase in the pulse rate, reddening of the eyes, and dryness of the mouth and throat. The 1971 report on marijuana that the Department of Health, Education, and Welfare submitted to Congress concluded that marijuana is safer than alcohol from the point of view of its physical consequences. In the late 1970s, harsh critics of the drug increasingly voiced their stand in the popular and professional media. Various researchers claimed that marijuana could: damage chromosomes; contribute to bleeding gums and other dental problems; alter the hormonal balance and the menstrual cycles of women; damage the respiratory system; lead to apathy and goallessness; and lower the body's immunity to disease.

In an effort to distinguish fact from fiction, Carr (1978) reviewed the evidence and drew conclusions on eleven points that have been researched. His conclusions relating to physical well-being included:

1. Use during pregnancy is an unnecessary risk, though there is no evidence that genetic defects result.
2. Driving or engaging in other activities that require good mental and physical skills may be hazardous if one is under the influence of marijuana.
3. The bulk of evidence indicates that chronic smoking of marijuana does not lead to brain damage.
4. There is increasing evidence that respiratory problems may develop as a result of continued marijuana use.

Although it appears that marijuana poses a greater threat to physical well-being than we once believed, it also may have more medical uses than we once thought. In the 1970s various researchers found marijuana to be useful in treating patients with glaucoma, in relieving the pain of cancer patients, in ameliorating the side effects of chemotherapy, and in relieving the suffering of asthmatics. Undoubtedly, a good deal of research on the effects of marijuana will continue in the 1980s.

Psychological health.   Americans value psychological as well as physical health. The search for "happiness," "peace of mind," or "contentment" is common. The short-range euphoria that follows drug use is misleading because the long-range effects of drug abuse contradict the *quest for psychological well-being.* In a study of ninety-eight young heroin addicts in methadone treatment or abstinence programs in Washington, D.C., Frederick, Resnik, and Wittlin (1973) found a higher rate of *"self-destructive" behavior* than was prevalent in a number of control groups. Use of control groups made it possible for effects of things such as race and religion to be discounted. The researchers found that the addicts had a greater degree of depression than the nonaddicts, a greater number of attempted suicides, and more "aberrant" attitudes toward life and death.

There is little disagreement about the consequences of the hard drugs on psychological well-being, but what about marijuana? Experts disagree to a considerable extent about the psychological consequences of marijuana usage. The Drug Enforcement Administration claimed that "moderate doses" of the drug can have potentially serious results:

The individual may experience rapidly changing emotions, changing sensory imagery, dulling of attention, more altered thought formation and expression such as fragmented thought, flight of ideas, impaired immediate memory, disturbed associations, altered sense of self-identity and, to some, a perceived feeling of enhanced insight. Such distortions can produce feelings of panic and anxiety in an individual who has little experience with drugs. The panic and anxiety can cause the individual to fear that he is dying or "losing his mind." This panic reaction is transient and usually disappears as the drug's effects wear off [U.S. Department of Justice, Drug Enforcement Administration, 1973:36].

Very high doses of the drug, according to the same report, may result in "distortions of body image, loss of personal identity, fantasies and hallucinations. In addition, toxic psychoses can occur after extremely high doses." These effects also cease when the drug is eliminated from the body. Various researchers agree that marijuana use can be hazardous. Camp (1973) reviewed some of the literature and concluded that marijuana use can result in severe anxiety, delusions, paranoia, and psychotic episodes.

On the other hand, critics of the Drug Enforcement Administration noted deficiencies in the methods of research used to obtain data. Geis (1972:161) argued that when all of the evidence has been considered, marijuana represents no "serious threat to the well-being of American society, certainly in terms of present dosages and, extrapolating from foreign data, in terms of heavier dosages." A number of experts agree with this conclusion and argue that the marijuana issue is social and political rather than medical. They contend that the drug is illegal because of historical and political processes rather than because of its deleterious effects on users. There is some truth in this assertion, and we will discuss it further. However, the long-range effects of marijuana use are not fully known. The evidence is contradictory, and we must withhold firm conclusions until more adequate research is conducted.

Interpersonal difficulties.   For Americans, the desired quality of life demands harmonious relationships with others as well as a sense of physical and psychological well-being for the individual. As attested by the popularity of articles, books, and Dale Carnegie courses, Americans value the ability to "get along well" with others. That value is contradicted by the interaction that tends to result from drug abuse.

An addict who is married typically has a passive role in the home. The ex-addict may *continue to have interpersonal difficulties* in the home because he or she may attempt to compensate for past failures and assume a role of leadership. The outcome may be a power struggle between the ex-addict and his or her mate (Sviland, 1974:67). In other cases, there may be unrealistic expectations about the outcome of treatment. The mate of an ex-addict may expect immediate and dramatic changes, and when such changes do not appear, the result can be disillusionment or bitterness. Also, the ex-addict may find that long-term or permanent damage has been done to his or her relationships. The fear and resentment built up over years of coping with an addicted individual may preclude healthy interpersonal relationships.

Economic costs.   All social problems involve certain *economic costs,* and these affect the quality of life. The more money required to deal with the undesirable effects of a social problem, the less money there is for services and pro-

grams that enhance the quality of life. Social problems have consequences that go far beyond the economic costs, but those costs are an important factor in attaining the desired quality of life.

Determining the exact dollar cost of any social problem is difficult. The costs of drug problems involve things such as lost worktime in business and industry, the cost of maintaining the criminal justice system, the expense of rehabilitation and education programs, and losses due to the criminal activity of addicts trying to support their habits.

Although we cannot be precise about the costs of the drug problem, the rough estimates are staggering. The average addict in 1973 spent about $58 daily for his or her drug supply (U.S. Department of Justice, Drug Enforcement Administration, 1973:16). This amounts to over $20,000 per year. For all addicts combined the daily cost of the heroin supply is over $36 million, and the year's total is over $13 billion!

How do addicts obtain money to purchase their heroin? Usually they resort to crime, particularly theft. Stolen goods cannot be redeemed at their wholesale or retail value: an addict might get $1 for each $3 to $5 worth of goods stolen. To net $58 per day to pay for his or her habit, the addict would have to steal $200 worth of property daily. Some addicts are gainfully employed, and some engage in criminal activities other than theft to support themselves. Even if only 60 percent of the addicts steal in order to purchase heroin, they must steal over $27 billion of property per year.

Education and rehabilitation also involve costs. An estimated $828 million to $1.68 billion would be required to treat all the nation's addicts. In the meantime, the federal government has appropriated money for drug education and information programs. The cost of these programs rose from $2.7 million in 1969 to $40.5 million in 1973 (National Commission on Marihuana and Drug Use, 1973:348). Despite these efforts, the problem has become more serious, which means that the economic costs will continue to grow.

Contributing Factors

The various contributing factors have a double-barreled effect: they maintain demand by encouraging use of drugs, and they guarantee a supply.

Social structural factors.   Group norms are one of the most important factors in the drug problem. We noted before that in certain groups norms that are contrary to the norms and laws of the larger society can develop. Those who are integrated into such groups will accept and abide by the norms. In terms of Sutherland's theory of differential association, the individual in such a group will be exposed to a preponderance of definitions that favor the illegal or deviant behavior. Since such groups also are likely to have access to supplies, there is a high probability that the individual will experiment with drugs and ultimately become a drug abuser.

A number of studies of drug use among youth emphasize the importance of this factor. In one study, Schulz and Wilson (1973) surveyed junior and senior high school students in the state of Delaware. Of the nearly 32,000 students in their sample, about 8 percent said they were using some kind of drug, and another 8 percent said they had used drugs in the past. About 16 percent, then, indicated they had experience with illegal drugs at some point in their lives.

The researchers looked at a number of factors previously suggested as important. The researchers found, for instance, that usage was far more extensive in urban than in rural schools. Certain aspects of family life were not very important in explaining drug use, such as whether the father was in the home and whether the child was the first-born, last-born, or only child. Rather, "the strongest single predictor of drug use is the fact that one's friends are drug users" (Schulz and Wilson, 1973:630). Being *integrated into a group in which drug use is approved* is one of the strongest factors leading youth into taking illegal drugs.

The same finding was reported by Thomas, Petersen, and Zingraff (1975) in a study of college undergraduates. These researchers looked at the possible effects of age, sex, social class background, and various attitudes in explaining drug use among the 433 undergraduates they studied. Some of these factors form part of the explanation (recall that throughout this book we argue that *multiple* factors are involved, though obviously not all are equally important). However, the most important factor was integration into a group whose norms approved drug use. Both the willingness to try drugs and the frequency of use were more strongly related to integration into such a group than to any of the other factors the researchers considered.

Some Americans who regard themselves as respectable citizens find it difficult to imagine following group norms when those norms are illegal. We must recall that we all follow the norms of our groups, and we all follow them for basically the same reasons. The respectable citizen who abides by the norm that the appearance of one's house and yard should be neat and clean derives satisfaction and a sense of acceptance from that normative behavior. Similarly, the youth who uses drugs, particularly marijuana, finds certain *rewards* in that usage when it is the norm of his or her group: "To be admired by those whom one respects, to be sociable, to participate in parties . . . to share in the cool round of life . . ." (Sutter, 1970:83).

Role problems are a second social structural factor in the drug problem. *Role problems create stress* in the individual, who may then use drugs to deal with the problems and the consequent stress. One type of role problem is **role conflict.** Two or more roles may be contradictory—as, for example, when a woman experiences a contradiction between her role as a physician and her role as a wife because she simply does not have time to meet the expectations of both her patients and her husband. Contradictory expectations may impinge upon a single role, as when a physician's patients demand the right of abortion and his or her peers and friends define abortion as illegal and immoral. An individual may define the expectations of a role as somehow unacceptable or excessive, as when a physician feels overwhelmed by the multiple demands made upon his or her time and professional skills.

Physicians have been deliberately used in the examples here because of the high rate of drug addiction already mentioned among doctors. The actual cause of addiction is not known, but the problem may be rooted in the stresses of the role. Drug abuse is a symptom of stress, and role problems do generate stress in the individual. To the extent that particular roles are especially likely to create problems, people who occupy those roles will be particularly vulnerable to stress, and perhaps to using drugs to deal with stress.

An important point here is that role conflict is a social phenomenon, not an individual phenomenon. It is not a particular doctor who is oppressed by the demands of the role; rather, all doctors must come to terms with the role of physician in American society. The expectations attached to the role tend to create the same problems for everyone who occupies the role.

Another role problem that can generate stress and increase the likelihood of drug abuse is a *role change that is defined as undesirable*. Such role change occurs when a spouse dies. Suddenly a person is no longer a husband or a wife—that role has been lost.

After the loss (which may be the result of separation or divorce as well as death), the individual must work through what is called the grief process. A person copes with a significant loss by passing through a series of emotional phases. The process may take as long as two or more years. Typically, the initial phase is shock, followed by a period of numbness or lack of intense emotion. In the next phase, the individual wavers between fantasy and reality, overcomes fantasies, and then experiences the full impact of the loss. A period of increasing adjustment follows, punctuated sporadically by episodes of painful memories. Finally, if the full grief process has been experienced, the individual accepts the loss and reaffirms his or her life. But the grief process is painful, and some individuals may resort to drugs.

Figure 4.4   The victim of alcohol and drug abuse are not just the addicts. Eugene O'Neill's powerful play *Long Day's Journey into Night* concerns addiction within a family situation. He shows how addiction is both a result and a cause of emotional turmoil among family members.

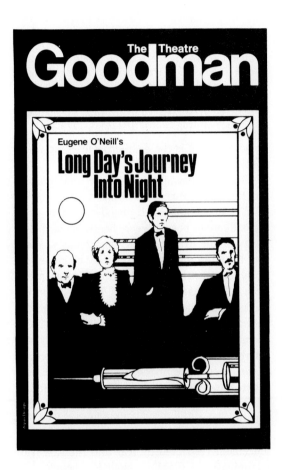

Certain *family experiences* are a third structural factor. In particular, drug use has been associated with patterns of *family use of drugs,* with *broken homes,* and with *flawed family relationships.* We will look at each of these in turn.

First, those who abuse drugs are more likely to come from homes where other members of the family are abusers. A study of drug use in a suburban high school reported that those who used drugs indicated that their behavior was influenced by their parents' habits and use of tranquilizers and sleeping pills (Lawrence and Velleman, 1974). A study of users and nonusers of heroin in Washington, D.C. found that 32 percent of users but only 2 percent of nonusers had members of the immediate family who also used drugs (Craig and Brown, 1975). A pattern of drug use in a family influences the behavior of any particular member of the family.

Second, drug abusers are more likely to come from broken homes than are nonabusers. In the study of heroin use in Washington, D.C., significantly more users had been raised by only one parent when they were in the 6- to 12-year-old age category (Craig and Brown, 1975).

Third, drug abuse is associated with various disturbed relationships within the family. High school drug users have reported a higher rate of parental fighting than have nonusers (Lawrence and Velleman, 1974). More importantly, drug and alcohol use is associated with reported *alienation between youth and their parents* (Wechsler and Thum, 1973). A study of junior and senior high school students revealed that those who had used marijuana, LSD, barbiturates, and amphetamines all reported more hostile relations with parents than did nonusers of drugs (Streit, Halsted, and Pascale, 1974). Young people who use drugs have been found to perceive lack of support from their parents. Bethards (1973) asked a group of high school students whether they could discuss a problem with their parents when they felt worried or troubled by something. Of those who said they could get this support from their parents, only 23 percent used drugs, compared to 42 percent of those who did not perceive they had such support.

Of course, the sense of rejection and alienation from parents can follow from drug use rather than precede it. Even if it is true that, for instance, a young person first uses drugs because of his or her group's norms, then becomes alienated from his or her parents, that alienation is likely to perpetuate the drug use. Thus, although alienation may not be one of the causes of initial use, it is likely to be a cause of continuing use.

A fourth structural factor is the government, and especially the *government's definition of drug use as illegal*. For some drugs, the illegal status is the consequence of social and political processes rather than of scientific evidence. The first national law against marijuana was passed in 1937, when even less was known about its effects than now. The law resulted from scare stories that marijuana use would lead to crime waves. If marijuana use proves harmless, then the "problem" with respect to marijuana will have been nothing more than an unfortunate political decision to make the drug illegal.

Without denying adverse physiological effects of drugs, some people argue that the primary problem in any case is the political stance:

> Since the harms produced by illegal drug use in our society—e.g., crime, disease, death—are almost entirely a consequence of our drug policy rather than the pharmacological effects of such drugs, we must look to the area of social policy as a causal factor in the "drug problem," and those interests involved in creating and shaping a policy of drug control [Reasons, 1974:384].

To what extent is the drug problem affected by political processes?

How illegality affects drug use and abuse in the United States was summed up by Geis (1972:135). First, in an illegal situation, drug use is likely to pose a severe health hazard (the purity of the drug can vary enormously). Second, illegality means that criminal elements are likely to enter the drug traffic in order to profit from black-market dealings. Third, enforcing the law puts the criminal justice system under considerable strain and seems to generate more corruption than does enforcement of other laws. There are many incidents in which narcotics agents keep some of the drugs they have confiscated and later sell them. Fourth, people living in a metropolitan area where there is a high rate of addiction are more likely to become victims of crime and to have their freedom of movement restricted by fear and the threat of victimization. Finally, business people are "bothered by the lack of motivation of the addict . . . and by his unreliability, especially as a likely predator stealing to obtain funds with which to purchase drugs" (Geis, 1972:135).

Essentially, then, the fact that drugs are illegal raises the cost of maintaining the drug habit, deeply involves criminals in the drug traffic, strains the criminal justice system, and leads the addict to undesirable behavior. Criminal involvement results from the potential for high profits, for example, the tremendous profits that may be realized from traffic in heroin. In 1973 a kilogram of heroin cost $60 if purchased from a Turkish farmer's supply of opium. The wholesale price of that heroin in France would have been about $7,000. The wholesale price in New York would have been about $40,000, and the retail price would have been $400,000! (U.S. Department of Justice, Drug Enforcement Administration, 1973:11).

Addiction itself is not a crime. Too often, criminal acts are involved in procuring and distributing drugs and in the behavior of the addict to support his or her habit. Not all drug addicts turn to crime, but only an estimated 7 percent of the funds needed for heroin come from legal sources. Other sources, in the order of probable frequency, are prostitution, shoplifting, burglary, larceny, pickpocketing, confidence games, and robbery (Mushkin, 1975:30). Many of those who become involved in crime to support a drug addiction were already involved in criminal behavior prior to their first use of drugs (Wilson, Moore and Wheat, 1972). As in the case of the youth alienated from their parents, the criminal activity that supports the habit is likely to perpetuate the problem because the person who is a drug addict becomes increasingly estranged from conventional society and increasingly stigmatized as an incorrigible deviant.

Social psychological factors. Marijuana users have *distinctive attitudes* toward society, as various studies show. In one study of college undergraduates, it was found that those who smoked marijuana tended to be *alienated from society* (Knight, Sheposh, and Bryson, 1974). They did not use marijuana because of any personal problems, but they did express dissat-

isfaction with American law, government, marriage patterns, and the work ethic. This dissatisfaction has been described as *the "hangloose" ethic:*

> One of the fundamental characteristics of the hang-loose ethic is that it is irreverent. It repudiates, or at least questions, such cornerstones of conventional society as Christianity, "my country right or wrong," the sanctity of marriage and premarital chastity, . . . the accumulation of wealth; the right, and even competence, of parents, the schools, and the government to head and make decisions for everyone—in sum, the Establishment [Suchman, 1968:147].

These attitudes perhaps followed rather than preceded marijuana use. That is, the young person may have tried marijuana and accepted its legitimacy, then rejected many of the beliefs held by people who define marijuana use as wrong. The young person may have held to the hang-loose ethic and so was willing to try marijuana. In either case, marijuana use is much higher among those who hold the attitudes than among those who reject them (Suchman, 1968).

What about other drugs? What are the attitudes of people who use them? Some indication of motivation may be gained from Project DAWN (Drug Abuse Warning Network), a national program established by the Drug Enforcement Administration to identify drugs abused, patterns of abuse, and to gain various data that might aid in the control of drug use and abuse. The data come from reporting centers throughout the United States; however, keep in mind that the data represent only cases of abuse that have resulted in a crisis. We cannot draw conclusions about all drug users from information about users who have reached a crisis situation. Among those who have reached a crisis, a number of different *motivations for abuse* were reported. Some abusers sought certain psychic effects—euphoria, pleasure, and change of mood. Some were dependent upon the drug, and some intended to commit suicide.

As table 4.2 shows, 38 percent of the cases involved the quest for psychic effects. In other words, 38 percent of those who reached a crisis situation because of drug abuse believed that the drug would have a desirable psychic effect. This attitude was pronounced especially among the younger abusers and among those using marijuana and speed.

Finally, *ideology* is a factor in the drug problem. In fact, positive attitudes, group norms, and ideologies about drug use reinforce each other. Friedenberg (1972:149) summarized the ideology about marijuana as follows:

1. People who are enjoying themselves without harming others have an inalienable right to privacy.
2. A drug whose effect is to turn its users inward upon their own experience, enriching their fantasy life at the expense of their sense of need to achieve or relate to others, is as moral as alcohol, which encourages a false gregariousness and increasingly pugnacious or competitive behavior.
3. Much of the solicitude of the older generation for the welfare of the young merely expresses a desire to dominate and control them for the sake of adult interests and the preservation of adult status and authority.

Table 4.2   Motivation for Drug Abuse by Age, Race, and Sex of Abuser and Selected Drugs
(% of mentions)

	Psychic Effects	Dependence	Self-Destruction	Other
All mentions	38	22	33	7
Age				
15 and under	60	7	22	10
16–19	57	17	20	6
20–29	36	28	30	7
30–39	23	24	46	8
40–49	16	21	53	10
50 and over	13	14	61	12
Race				
White	39	18	35	8
Black	33	35	24	7
Other	41	27	26	6
Sex				
Male	46	29	19	6
Female	31	15	45	9
Drug				
Diazepam	20	9	60	11
Marijuana	82	11	3	4
Heroin	19	76	3	2
Secobarbital	38	21	36	5
d-Propoxyphene	22	6	59	12
Flurazepam	17	4	68	11
Speed	65	28	4	3

Source: U.S. Department of Justice, Drug Enforcement Administration, *Drug Abuse Warning Network, Phase II Report, July 1973—March, 1974* (Washington, D.C.: Government Printing Office), p. 289.

This ideology, like all ideologies, serves the purpose of explaining and validating certain behavior, thereby reinforcing the behavior. It affirms the right of people to engage in behavior that is harmless to others, insists that marijuana use is harmless to others and beneficial to the user, and explains the attitudes of those who oppose marijuana use. Thus, the individual whose group has norms that approve marijuana use has a ready set of beliefs to defend and encourage his or her own use.

Feldman (1970) described the ideology involved in heroin addiction. He noted that the individual who decides to use drugs for the first time "must fit the act into some set of existing beliefs so that his first step toward highly censured behavior can be justified to himself and to important others in his life" (Feldman, 1970:88). In slum neighborhoods these beliefs about heroin involve

> the ideals of toughness, strength, daring, and the willingness to challenge the bleak fate of being poor. Some youths achieve high status reputations built on these qualities. Some do not. . . . Those youths who energetically thrust themselves into the slum neighborhood ideology seek to establish their reputations according to an ideal type: the *stand-up cat*. Puerto Ricans call him a "maucho." Negroes may refer to him as "a bad-ass nigger." And Italians call him a "guy with a pair of balls." But across the boards, he is a stand-up cat [Feldman, 1970:89].

This ideology says that by using heroin *the individual will gain status* in the eyes of those with whom he must continually interact and who are important to him; that drug use will demonstrate those qualities most admired by the group. In other words, the ideology legitimates drug use.

Ideologies can also *inhibit realistic approaches to resolving a problem*. The debate over marijuana has been complicated by contradictory conclusions, even by scientists who have tried to conduct scientific research on marijuana. As a result, opposing ideologies which have no necessary basis in any evidence have developed. As Erich Goode (1970:176) said:

> A man is not opposed to the use or the legalization of marijuana *because* (he thinks) it "leads to" the use of more dangerous drugs, because it "causes" crime, because it "produces" insanity and brain damage, because it "makes" a person unsafe behind the wheel, because it "creates" an unwillingness to work. *He believes these things because he thinks the drug is evil.*

The ideology that makes use of the drug illegitimate is rooted in a negative attitude rather than in evidence. Since the evidence we have contains some contradictions, the ideology cannot be attacked easily.

An important point here is that the political process has been influenced by ideology. Reasons, (1974:389) showed that early in the twentieth century the image of the drug problem reflected the image of the user, who was typically labeled a "drug fiend" or a "dope fiend." Articles warned about the "drug evil," and eventually legislation was passed in an effort to cope with the problem. However, the legislation made the problem a criminal one, and with *criminalization* came the compounding of the problem. For a long time the "criminal approach" meant that the medical approach—or other possible approaches to coping with the drug problem—would be neglected. The ideology defined the problem in terms that led to political action, and the political action may have increased rather than diminished the seriousness of the problem. At least, defining the problem as one to be handled by the criminal justice system has inhibited other approaches that might prove more beneficial.

What Is to be Done?

Many efforts to deal with drug abuse have focused on the individual abuser. The focus on the individual rather than on the social roots leads to an emphasis on treatment rather than prevention. Both treatment and prevention programs, of course, are needed. The drug problem has become increasingly serious despite intensive efforts to resolve it. Our failure to reverse the growing seriousness of the drug problem raises the question of whether eliminating or at least minimizing drug abuse is possible for a society. China resolved its drug problem shortly after the Communist revolution (Rubinstein, 1973). The government forbade the planting of opium, destroyed existing opium crops and equipment used to manufacture the drug, and closed the opium dens. Dealers were sentenced to capital punishment or long-term imprisonment. Local pushers and addicts were given amnesty if they surrendered their supplies, and support if they were subsequently unable to find employment. A massive educational program was initiated, including public rallies at which former addicts related their experiences. The educational program stressed the relationship between the anti-drug program and the war for liberation that had just been won. Addicts were given free treatment, and if they had not broken the habit within a certain period of time they were imprisoned.

Thus, the Chinese made a massive, multiple-level attack on the problem. They treated individual addicts and they attacked the social bases. Their methods were often harsh, but they effectively answered the question of the possibility of resolving an entire nation's drug problem. We would not want to duplicate the brutality of the Chinese approach, but China illustrates the point that we must attack the social bases as well as treat individual addicts. How have we attempted to do that?

Treating addicts.   The basic problem in treating an addict is to reduce or eliminate his or her dependence upon the drug. **Detoxification,** the *elimination of dependence* through supervised withdrawal, is one approach for heroin addicts; *methadone maintenance* is another. In methadone maintenance, the addict orally ingests the drug methadone, which is considered less dangerous than heroin and which has a number of properties that allow the addict to lead a more normal life than would be possible with heroin. Methadone may be used in the detoxification program also, but detoxification involves the elimination of all drug use—including the methadone that is used to help mitigate withdrawal symptoms.

There is evidence that methadone maintenance programs enable the addict to break the heroin habit. Vaillant (1973) reported a twenty-year follow-up study of New York addicts who had been hospitalized in Lexington, Kentucky. Over the twenty years, neither voluntary hospitalization nor imprisonment produced abstinence, but methadone maintenance and compulsory community supervision were fairly effective.

Figure 4.5 A heroin addict gets treatment at a clinic in New York City. The methadone maintenance program has both strong supporters and strong critics.

The use of a narcotic drug on a regular, long-term basis may appear a puzzling way to treat an addict and, indeed, the methadone maintenance program has been criticized. Some people claim the use of methadone assumes that the addict is irreversibly dependent upon drugs and that human problems can be solved by drugs rather than by human relationships (Lennard, Epstein, and Rosenthal, 1972). There is evidence that some addicts simply switch to methadone as their preferred addictive drug, while others continue to use heroin or other drugs while on methadone maintenance. The program, in other words, does not have as high a success rate as originally expected. One five-year study reported that 60 percent of the clients who entered a program discontinued it before the end of the second year; that many of those in treatment failed to take their methadone regularly; and that the decrease in crime among the clients was less than had been expected (Kleinman, Lukoff, and Kail, 1977). Finally, methadone maintenance clinics are criticized for the attitudes of those who staff them, attitudes that range from indifference to contempt, and for the lack of services such as counseling and aid in finding employment.

The latter criticism points to a particularly serious deficiency. As we have seen, drug addiction is a social problem as well as a personal problem. It involves relationships, as well as an individual's physiological dependence upon a drug. Consequently, successful treatment of addicts is treatment that helps them cope with the conditions that led them to use drugs in the first place.

Two well-known residential arrangements for rehabilitation are called *Synanon* and *Daytop Village*. Synanon was started by an ex-alcoholic as a group where other alcoholics could come and discuss their problems. The effort mushroomed into a nationwide organization with thousands of members, primarily drug addicts. The basic approach of Synanon was described by Sviland (1974:75) as a "full-time educational process within a total environment setting," operating on the assumption that the addict is stupid rather than ill. The purpose, therefore is to remove obstacles that cause the addict to behave stupidly. A new member is given food and shelter, but he must withdraw without the benefit of methadone—that is, detoxification occurs "cold turkey." Once detoxified, the addict learns to function without drugs by daily participation in the "Game," a kind of encounter group session in which an individual may attack or be attacked, ridicule or be the subject of ridicule. The outcome is self-discovery and a new psychic security. As well, each addict must work for the community.

Unfortunately, Synanon, which began in 1958, took an unusual turn in the late 1970s. The organization accumulated considerable wealth and property. Members became suspicious of all outsiders. Various accidents occurred to people who challenged Synanon in court. However, such developments do not negate the value of the program that characterized earlier years of the organization.

At Daytop Village, which also takes *a communal approach to the drug problem,* the addict is seen as one who needs a new self-concept in order to cope with life. Like Alcoholics Anonymous, Daytop Village is composed mainly of addicts and ex-addicts, the latter serving as staff members. New members are encouraged first to be detoxified, then to come into the community.

Each member works for the community, but addicts are encouraged to become independent and return to their own communities.

Attacking the social bases.   Treatment of individual addicts is important, yet it is only part of the overall attack on the problem. What can be done in America to attack the social bases of the problem? We could strengthen efforts to reduce the demand for drugs rather than focus on cutting off supplies (this was a major part of the effort in China). The demand for heroin is so intense that efforts to cut off supplies tend to only enhance the potential profit of dealers and waste an enormous amount of effort and money. Demand can be reduced through educational programs and through the detoxification or methadone-maintenance of addicts. However, the group norms that support heroin use probably will not be changed without change in the socioeconomic status of those groups also. In other words, the problem of drug abuse intersects with the problem of poverty and discrimination. In fact, in an examination of four strategies for reducing heroin demand, Brotman and Suffet (1975:64) concluded that coercion, education, correction, and the use of alternative drugs will all fail to eliminate drug use: "Perhaps the time has come to adjust our goals and focus our preventive efforts primarily on high-risk patterns of use—on those patterns . . . where drug involvement demonstrably and significantly increases the chances of self-harm."

Decriminalization of drug use is one additional step that could be taken to attack the social bases of the problem. Decriminalization

Figure 4.6 A trained detector dog finds narcotics. Major efforts have been directed toward cutting off the supply rather than decreasing the demand.

is a controversial issue. Advocates claim that decriminalization would resolve many aspects of the problem—drug traffic would no longer be profitable; the courts would not be required to handle cases of drug violators; addicts would not be required to engage in criminal activity in order to support their habit. Some state laws regarding marijuana have already been revised. Rockwell (1973) argued that marijuana use cannot be suppressed; that the history of marijuana use up to this time is similar to that of alcohol use in the eighteenth and nineteenth centuries, and that the only sensible approach is to regulate rather than suppress usage, as we do with alcohol. This position assumes that marijuana has no long-term deleterious effects, a point still debated. Despite possible long-term effects, however, there is still the question of whether the government should suppress the right of people to use the drug. Both cigarette smoking and heavy alcohol use have demonstrable long-term effects that are destructive, but the use of these drugs is regulated rather than suppressed. Why should marijuana be treated differently?

Decriminalization frightens many people. They believe that decriminalization is an open door to epidemic drug abuse. However, evidence from two states that have decriminalized marijuana, Oregon and California, indicates that only small increases in the number of users followed enactment of the more lenient laws (Cuskey, Berger, and Richardson, 1978).

Regarding heroin use, let us look to England, where the addict is treated as *sick rather than criminal*. Physicians are legally allowed to prescribe heroin (or methadone) for addicts. The addict can obtain the drug at a relatively low

cost. The whole process is carefully regulated and monitored so that addicts are not given unlimited supplies. The system has not eliminated heroin addiction, but it has kept it under control. Furthermore, fewer English than American addicts are arrested for crime, and more English addicts maintain jobs and have a relatively normal life.

This does not imply that the English system would be successful in America; some modifications would be needed. Such a system conflicts with certain American attitudes and values. As Richard Severo (quoted in Geis, 1972:138) said:

> What effect will tens of thousands of addicts, euphoric on government drugs and existing on public welfare (most would not work—the recent British experience shows this), have on the rest of society? Should society subsidize an individual in his own destruction?

Gallup polls show that less than 10 percent of Americans prefer "no penalty" for heroin users, that over half would put users into prison for two years to life, and that over half would put pushers into prison for ten years to life (Geis, 1972:140). In other words, most Americans define the drug problem in criminal terms. We face the choice of altering our definition of the problem or of continuing futile efforts to resolve it through expensive police action.

Alcohol

Because alcohol is a drug, we will find its impact on quality of life and its contributing factors to be similar to other drugs. There are some differences, however, in patterns of use.

Patterns of Use

As in the case of other drugs, we need to know the extent of usage and who the users are.

As reported by the National Institute on Alcohol Abuse and Alcoholism (1975:4):

> For 1970, the projected total number of drinkers in the United States 15 years of age and over was 95,648,000. . . . About one in three adults in the United States are nondrinkers at the present time. The tax-paid alcoholic beverages—distilled spirits, wines, and beers— apparently consumed in 1970 by the average person in the drinking-age population . . . allows for each drinker, about 44 fifths of whiskey; or 98 bottles of fortified wine; or 157 bottles of table wine; or 928 bottles of beer.

Thus, about two-thirds of the adult population drink to some extent. Furthermore, an estimated 30 percent of adults are moderate to heavy drinkers (Wilkinson, 1974:147). Alcohol is much more extensively used than drugs.

In a 1978 Gallup poll, nearly one-fourth of the respondents said liquor had been a cause of trouble in their families at some time. By 1979, an estimated 11 million Americans had drinking and alcoholism problems. Alcohol is also much more extensively abused than other drugs.

What are the *trends in use and abuse?* Periodic efforts are made in the mass media to educate the public on the problem of alcohol. One such effort took place in the late 1960s when the government launched a number of anti-drug programs. Nevertheless, evidence in the 1970s indicated that the problem is growing. The per capita consumption of alcohol increased considerably from 1960 to the late 1970s. This increasing use is reflected in national surveys of high school students. In 1969 the proportion of senior boys who reported trying alcohol was 81 percent. By 1979 the figure had risen to 93 percent, and nearly 7 percent reported daily use of alcohol (Johnston, Bachman, and O'Malley, 1979). We should note that the per capita consumption of alcohol is higher in some other nations than in the United States and that consumption probably was at its peak in this country around 1830 (Rorabaugh, 1979:8–9). Nevertheless, alcoholism is the major drug problem in the nation today.

Who are the abusers of alcohol? In contrast to other drug abusers, the alcohol abusers appear to be pillars of their communities, because most of them are

> employed or employable, family-centered people. More than 70 percent of them live in respectable neighborhoods, with their husbands and wives, send their children to school, belong to clubs, attend church, pay taxes, and continue to perform more or less effectively as businessmen, executives, housewives, farmers, salesmen, industrial workers, clerical workers, teachers, clergymen, and physicians [National Institute on Alcohol Abuse and Alcoholism, 1975:15–16].

The skid row image of the alcoholic is false; alcoholics on skid row comprise less than 5 percent of the total number.

Probably four or five times as many males as females are alcoholics (although the proportion of females may be increasing). In other words, *alcoholism is predominantly a male problem*. In a survey of problem drinking in the United States, about 72 percent of the men interviewed reported that they had at least one serious problem resulting from their drinking. The survey also showed that drinking problems were most frequent among younger men (20 to 24 years old) and resulted in more serious consequences among men in the lower socioeconomic strata (Cahalan, 1970; Cahalan and Room, 1974).

Alcohol and the Quality of Life

We will focus here on the *effects of abuse*. Alcohol, like other drugs, has some medical benefits when used in moderation. In fact, there is evidence that moderate drinkers, compared to both abstainers and heavy drinkers, have a lower rate of coronary heart disease, less likelihood of a heart attack, and a longer life expectancy (Darby, 1978). Alcohol abuse, on the other hand, is highly deleterious to the quality of life.

Physical health.   The physical consequences of alcohol abuse are akin to those of heroin. They contradict our *value of physical well-being*. As mentioned earlier, the immediate effects of intoxicating levels of alcohol include impaired motor performance. The long-range effects of heavy drinking involve impairment of the major organs of the body, including the heart, brain, and liver (National Institute on Alcohol Abuse and Alcoholism, 1975:13). Severe alcoholism can damage some of the higher brain functions resulting in deterioration of mental processes (Blusewicz, Dustman, Schenkenberg, and Beck, 1977). Cirrhosis of the liver, one of the more widely-known effects of heavy drinking, is an occupational disease of the alcoholic.

Heavy drinking may also result in certain muscle diseases and tremors. The function of the vital muscle, the heart, may be impaired by prolonged, heavy drinking. The gastrointestinal and respiratory systems are likewise subject to

Figure 4.7 Overuse of alcohol has long been a stock subject for jokes—perhaps because it is such a widespread problem.

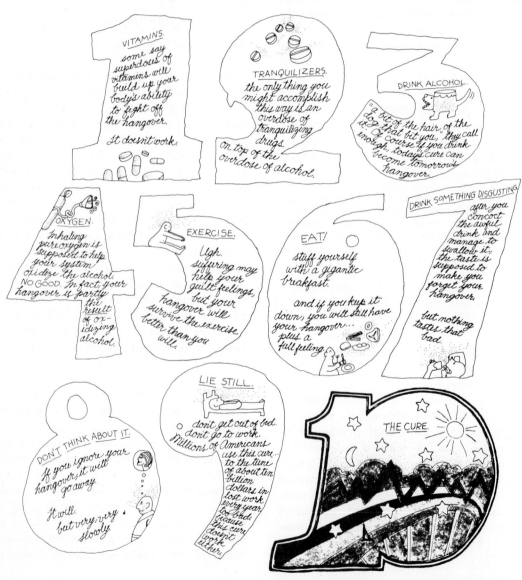

The only way to cure a hangover is before it happens. If you don't drink too much, you don't get a hangover.

impairment by heavy drinking. The ills of the gastrointestinal system can range from nausea, vomiting, and diarrhea to gastritis, ulcers, and pancreatitis. Problems of the respiratory system can include lowered resistance to pneumonia and other infectious diseases.

Heavy drinking, like heroin abuse, may lead to early death. In a study of 261 sudden deaths from disease that occurred in Dade County, Florida, Davis (1975) found that nearly one-third were caused by alcoholic fatty liver. That death is often a violent one for the alcoholic. Davis also examined the records of the county medical examiner and found that 516 drivers were killed in one-car accidents from 1956 to 1974. The alcohol test was positive for 66 percent of the drivers, and 77 percent of those had a concentration of at least 0.10 percent.

In another study, Haberman and Baden (1974) examined the incidence of alcoholism and of drinking in 1,000 cases of death in New York City in a two-month period in 1972. The deaths had been recorded and identified at the Office of the Chief Medical Examiner. Nearly 30 percent of the deceased were alcoholics. Moreover, alcoholics accounted for a high proportion of those who died violently—25 percent of those dying in accidents, 8.6 percent of the suicides, 26 percent of the homicides, and 25 percent of those dying of narcotics.

Unfortunately, the physical impairments and violent deaths associated with the abuse of alcohol are not confined to abusers. Alcohol is involved in more than single-car accidents on the streets and highways. In fact, alcohol is a factor in about half of all highway deaths, and in many of the half-million or more cases involving people who are injured in automobile accidents. The drinking driver is clearly a threat to the quality of life for others and for himself or herself. Furthermore, an estimated half or more of all homicides, nearly one-third of suicides, and half or more of sex offenses involve drinking prior to the act. The use and abuse of alcohol is a factor in an enormous number of incidents involving violence and death.

Psychological health. Our *desire for psychological well-being* is contradicted by the various degrees of impairment that result from alcohol abuse. Even a small amount of alcohol can reduce the individual's sensitivity to taste and smell and pain. Vision can be affected by large amounts of alcohol (one factor in the dangers of driving while drinking). One popular belief is that alcohol "releases inhibitions," so that the person who drinks "loosens up" and may, for example, be more motivated toward sexual activity. Actually, heavy drinking inhibits sexual performance, and alcoholics report a deficient sex life or even impotence. Another belief is that a drink in the evening helps the individual to relax and thereby to sleep better. Whatever the value of *a* drink, several drinks before going to sleep decrease the amount of dreaming, with consequences for the individual's concentration and memory. Moreover, people who are deprived of dreaming during sleep experience increased anxiety, irritability, and sense of tiredness.

The psychological problems of the problem drinker are perhaps best captured in the cry of despair of a noted writer who experienced a personal hell in alcoholism:

> ". . . I had been begging, pleading, demanding toward the last, to be locked up . . . shut up . . . chained up . . . anything . . . and had begun to curse and blame my dearest friends for

what seemed to me their failure to realize how desperately, how stupidly, I needed to be shut up where I couldn't get out and where I couldn't get my hands on a bottle. I had become a confirmed, habitual drunkard, without any of the stock alibis, or excuses" [quoted in Sinclair, 1956:105].

Interpersonal problems.   Alcohol abuse leads to *problems of interaction* both inside and outside the family. When the abuser is married, *stress* is invariably created in the family situation. Mates and children of alcoholics tend to develop various physical and psychological problems of their own. The children are likely to develop behavior disorders or to become alcoholics themselves (Jacob, Favorini, Meisel, and Anderson, 1978). A number of studies have been focused on the problems of the wives of male alcoholics. As commented earlier, the sex life of the alcoholic tends to deteriorate. Wives of alcoholics have been found to suffer some personality dysfunctions as they attempt to cope with their husband's behavior (Edwards, Harvey, and Whitehead, 1970); these dysfunctions diminish if the husband stops drinking.

In a study of eighty-five wives of alcoholics, James and Goldman (1971) discovered a number of ways the women coped with their husbands. The majority used withdrawal within the marriage, and about half used it even when the husband was abstinent. Those whose husbands became violent and aggressive used either withdrawal or attack. One of the more effective measures used by wives to alter their husbands' drinking patterns was the threat to leave (few of the marriages actually broke up, however). These instances show that the undesirable consequences of abuse are felt by a far greater number of people than the abusers themselves. Interaction difficulties of the abuser create psychological and perhaps physical (psychosomatic) problems in those with whom the abuser interacts. The mate of a deceased alcoholic wrote in a letter to a columnist that she was the happiest person alive because her husband had finally drunk himself to death and thereby set her and her children free.

Economic costs.   Alcohol abuse is costly to the nation in a number of ways. A considerable amount of money is involved in the arrest, trial, and imprisonment of those who are drunk. In cities such as Washington, D.C. and St. Louis, Missouri, where drunkenness statutes are strictly enforced, over half of all arrests involve drunkenness (The President's Commission on Law Enforcement and Administration of Justice, 1967a:234).

The costs of alcoholism for industry are considerable. People with drinking problems are absent from work about two and a half times as often as others. Moreover, when they are on the job, they may have problems of interaction. Industry may lose as much as $10 billion a year because of lost worktime and lowered productivity of alcoholic employees.

Of course, these figures are estimates, and all may be challenged. The actual figures might be lower—but they might also be higher. In any case, the economic costs to the nation for drug and alcohol problems are exceedingly high. Those costs represent resources that could be channeled into activities and programs that enhance the nation's quality of life.

Contributing Factors

As with other drugs, the factors that contribute to the alcohol problem both maintain demand and guarantee supply. The problem is embedded in our society.

Social structural factors.   *Group norms* are as important in the use and abuse of alcohol as they are in the use and abuse of other drugs. In a study of over 3,000 adolescents in three midwestern states, the most important factor in explaining alcohol use was the "differential peer association scale" (Akers, Krohn, Lanza-Kaduce, and Radosevich, 1979). The scale measured how many of the respondents' best friends, friends most often associated with, and friends known the longest time used alcohol. The greater an adolescent's involvement with friends who used alcohol, the greater the likelihood the adolescent would use alcohol.

Integration into a group in which use of alcohol is approved does not mean the individual will abuse it. Many people use alcohol without becoming addicted. In fact, groups that use alcohol freely have some interesting differences in rates of alcoholism. A lower rate of alcoholism is correlated with the following characteristics (National Institute on Alcohol Abuse and Alcoholism, 1975:21–22):

1. Children are given alcohol early in life in the context of strong family life or religious orientation.
2. Low alcohol content beverages—wines and beers—are most commonly used.
3. The alcoholic beverage is ordinarily consumed at meal time.
4. Parents typically provide an example of moderation in drinking.
5. Drinking is not a moral question, merely one of custom.
6. Drinking is not defined as a symbol of manhood or adulthood.
7. Abstinence is as acceptable as drinking.
8. Drunkenness is not socially acceptable.
9. Alcohol is not a central element in activities (like a cocktail party).
10. There is general agreement on what is proper and what is improper in drinking.

Under such conditions, a group or an entire society could have high per capita rates of alcohol consumption and relatively low rates of alcoholism. Group norms are an important factor in alcohol use and abuse, but those norms need not demand abstinence to prevent abuse. Both Jews and Italians in the United States use alcohol as part of a traditional way of life, but alcoholism in those groups is extremely low. The norms that approve this use also define the use in a way that makes abuse unlikely.

The *role problems* that can lead to use or abuse of other drugs can also lead to alcohol abuse. People trying to cope with role conflict may resort to alcohol for relief. Undesirable role change may also result in alcohol abuse. One researcher estimated that at least one of every five people admitted to an alcoholism treatment program in a Denver mental health center had started drinking heavily after a major loss or separation (Bellwood, 1975). They had either become fixated at a particular stage of the grief process or had skipped a part of the process. In either case, they sought refuge from their grief in alcohol. Had they been able to work through their grief by other means, they may have avoided a drinking problem in their lives.

The three kinds of *family experiences* noted earlier as contributing to the drug problem are also involved in alcohol abuse. An alcoholic in a family increases the likelihood of children becoming alcoholics. In an early study, Jellinek found that 52 percent of alcoholics had been raised by one or two alcoholic parents (Martindale and Martindale, 1971:229). Broken homes are frequently a part of the background of alcoholics. A study of drinking among junior and senior high school students reported that young people from broken homes indicated heavy alcohol use more frequently than did those whose homes were intact (Wechsler and Thum, 1973). Disturbed relationships within the family are associated with alcohol abuse. "Disturbed" may mean alienation, but it may also mean conflict and disruption. The children of alcoholics are more likely to become alcoholics themselves if family rituals surrounding events such as dinner, holidays, vacations, and visitors are disrupted frequently because parents are engaged in their heaviest drinking (Wolin, Bennett, Noonan, and Teitelbaum, 1980).

Finally, any social structural factors that increase the stress level are likely to increase the prevalence of alcoholism. Horton (1943) looked at various primitive societies and found a positive correlation between anxiety level and drunkenness. He concluded that alcoholic beverages function primarily to *reduce anxiety*. In the United States, a *rapidly changing structure* has been associated with increased alcoholism. Both the recent increase in consumption and the high rate around 1830 have been associated with stresses induced by a rapidly changing society (Strauss, 1976; Rorabaugh, 1979:125f).

Social psychological factors. *Attitudes* toward drinking and drunkenness tend to be different than attitudes toward use and abuse of other drugs. Although alcoholism is a major factor in death and disease, there is little public outcry. Drunks in the movies are frequently portrayed as comic figures instead of tragic figures. Parents who would be horrified to find their children smoking marijuana have allowed them to drink spiked punch or other alcoholic beverages at parties. Such attitudes are inconsistent with the seriousness of the problem and render ineffective any attack on the problem.

The problem of alcoholism is further complicated by *an ideology that essentially transforms it into a personal rather than a social problem.* Many Americans believe the alcoholic can reform if he or she "really wants to change." In other words, they believe alcoholism is basically a problem of the individual's self-control. Beauchamp (1975) called this assumption the *"myth of alcoholism,"* and has argued that accepting it means ignoring various social factors that contribute to the problem. Consequently, instead of attempting to identify and deal with the social factors and resolve the problem, "we spend our time and research trying to find out what causes a minority of drinkers to suffer from a disease which makes them 'unable' to control their drinking" (Beauchamp, 1975:14).

What is to be Done?

Drug therapies, group therapy, behavior therapy, and various programs and facilities are among the ways of helping alcoholics. Drug therapies involve administration of a nausea-producing agent along with an alcoholic beverage, or a "deterrent agent" that causes intense headaches and nausea when alcohol is consumed. Obviously, drug therapy requires close supervision by a physician.

In group therapy, the alcoholic is in a group with other alcoholics and with a therapist who takes charge of the group. The task of the group members is to attain insight into their individual reasons for drinking and to get control over drinking. The task is achieved by frank and open discussion of each alcoholic's life and feelings and thoughts. A form of group therapy that is quite successful and that does not utilize a professional therapist is Alcoholics Anonymous (AA). AA was started by alcoholics. Members gather regularly in small groups to share their experiences and to sustain each other in sobriety. Each member is available to every other member at any time help is needed—when, for example, a member needs to talk to someone in order to resist the urge to drink. Those who join AA begin by admitting they are powerless over alcohol and lack control of their own lives. This is a significant admission because it opposes the ideology discussed earlier (an ideology, incidentally, held by alcoholics as well as by others). New members also agree to submit to God (as they understand God), to make amends to those harmed by their drinking, and to help other alcoholics become sober.

Thousands of alcoholics have sought help through AA. One survey of over 11,000 members reported that 38 percent had abstained from drinking for one year or less, but 25 percent had abstained for six to twenty years or more (Leach, 1973). For many alcoholics, AA has been an effective recovery program.

Behavior therapy is based on the principles of behavioristic psychology, which stresses the rewarding of desired behavior in order to reinforce and continue that behavior. Bassin (1975) has described the use of behavior therapy by some AA groups. A new member of the group is given a red poker chip to keep in his or her pocket or purse. The chip is kept with the individual's change, and serves as a reminder to abstain. If the member cannot abstain, however, ths chip is to be broken and thrown away. If the member resists the urge to drink, the red chip is exchanged for a white chip after one month, and the white chip is exchanged for a blue one after three additional months. After twelve months, the new member celebrates the first anniversary of abstinence and receives a silver dollar. The "reward" is primarily *social recognition*—a group of people lauding a particular kind of behavior and expressing their approval with a token gift.

Alcoholism has been attacked through various other programs and facilities, also. Among these are *community-care programs,* which allow the alcoholic to remain in the home and the community while undergoing treatment. Other programs remove the alcoholic from the community or the home. In 1973 there were approximately 600 *halfway houses* for alcoholics (Ozarin and Witkin, 1975), places where they can function in a relatively normal way while receiving therapy. Most of these are made available to the alcoholics, Alcoholics Anonymous groups, counseling, and various other services. Alcoholics who are acutely ill may have to be hospitalized for a period of time before going to a halfway house or returning to their homes.

Ultimately to resolve the problem of alcoholism the social bases must be attacked. Treating alcoholism as a social problem is considerably more difficult than treating it as an individual problem, because group norms and alternative means of coping with stress are involved. Educational programs must be aimed at

Involvement

"I'd Kill Before I'd Drink"

The author once attended a meeting of Alcoholics Anonymous with a friend who had been "dry" for a short time. As we drove through the countryside to the small town where the group met, the friend kept commenting on the beauty of the scenery. He was enchanted by what I thought was a fairly common view on a warm spring evening. But his years as an alcoholic had been a living hell, and in the course of rediscovering what life can be like when one is free of addiction, he was finding beauty in the commonplace. "I really think," he told me, "that if someone tried to force me to take a drink I would kill them." The thought of ever returning to alcohol terrified him.

One of the best ways to understand the impact of addiction on an individual is to talk with an ex-addict. If you do not know an ex-alcoholic, contact Alcoholics Anonymous and attend one of their meetings. All members are ex-alcoholics. Discuss with one or two members their understanding of why they became addicted, what their life was like when they were addicted, and what finally led them to seek the help of A.A.

List the adverse effects on quality of life discussed in this chapter that apply to your informants. Based on your interviews, make a report, oral or written, of your recommendations for dealing with the problem of alcoholism.

you've got to know when to say when

NATIONAL INSTITUTE ON ALCOHOL ABUSE AND ALCOHOLISM NATIONAL INSTITUTE OF MENTAL HEALTH U.S. DEPARTMENT OF HEALTH, EDUCATION, AND WELFARE

The typical alcoholic American

young   old   male   female

black   white   rich   poor

employed   unemployed   executive   laborer

student   doctor   immigrant   native born

**There's no such thing as typical.
We have all kinds. Nine million alcoholic Americans.
It's our number one drug problem.**

alcoholism, at the responsible use of alcohol, and at helping the public to understand the effects of alcohol use. It is also possible to establish certain "early warning systems," particularly in industry, where the problem of alcoholism may first be manifested. That is, troubles at work are often one of the first overt signs that an individual is facing a drinking problem. "Occupational programming" has been set up in a number of public and private institutions to monitor the performance of employees and identify problem drinking in an early stage (Roman, 1975). Such programs promise to mitigate the misery of alcoholism by early detection.

Summary

The problem of drugs and alcohol is one of abuse and not merely of use. Various drugs have various effects, and the effects depend on the method of administration, the amount taken, and the social situation as well as the chemical composition of the drug. Alcohol, too, has different effects depending on how much is consumed in a given period of time. Alcohol is widely used, and its effects can be extremely deleterious. Many experts consider alcohol abuse much more serious than abuse of other drugs.

A considerable number of Americans use drugs and alcohol. Over half of young adults (18–25 years) surveyed in 1979 reported they had tried alcohol, tobacco, and marijuana, and over half of high school seniors said they were current users of marijuana. Alcohol is more frequently used and abused than other drugs. About two-thirds of all Americans drink, and as many as 30 percent drink moderately to heavily. Both drug and alcohol use and abuse appear to be increasing, and there is a tendency toward multiple use. Most drug addicts are young, male, poor, and nonwhite, while most alcohol abusers are young and male, but nonpoor.

The meaning of the drug and alcohol problem for the quality of life is seen in the consequences for physical health, psychological health, interpersonal relationships, and economic costs. Abusers suffer various undesirable effects in the first three areas, and they inflict suffering on others. The nation as a whole suffers great economic cost because billions of dollars per year are involved in lost services and in efforts to combat the deleterious effects of abuse.

Various structural factors contribute to the problem. An important one is group norms. Integration into a group that approves drug and alcohol use is one of the most reliable predictors of use. Role problems, including role conflict and undesirable role change, create stress in the individual, and that stress can lead to drug and alcohol abuse. A third structural factor is the individual's family. Abusers are more likely to come from homes where family members are abusers, or from broken homes, or from homes where there are disturbed relationships. Finally, political processes affect the problem because our government has defined the problem in criminal terms. The fact that drugs are illegal has several implications: more people are classified as criminal; previously classified criminals become deeply involved in the drug traffic; the criminal justice system is strained; and users and abusers are led into various kinds of undesirable behavior.

Among social psychological factors is the distinctive set of attitudes known as the "hang-loose ethic" found among marijuana users. Many people believe drug use will produce desirable psychic effects. These positive attitudes toward drug use combine with group norms and various ideologies that develop in groups. The ideologies explain and validate drug use. Other ideologies about drug use that develop among officials and the public inhibit realistic approaches to the problem.

The major approach to the problem has been treatment rather than prevention. Efforts to help the individual abuser or reduce the supply available to users have far exceeded efforts to get at the social roots of the problem. If the problem is to be dealt with effectively, both approaches are needed—attacks on the social factors involved as well as treatment of individual abusers.

Glossary

abuse   improper use of drugs or alcohol to the degree that the consequences are defined as detrimental to the user and/or the society

addiction   repeated use of a drug or alcohol to the point of periodic or chronic intoxication that is detrimental to the user and/or the society

detoxification   supervised withdrawal from dependence on a drug

placebo   any substance having no physiological effect that is given to a subject who believes it to be a drug that does have effect

role conflict   a person's perception that two or more of his or her roles are contradictory, or that the same role has contradictory expectations, or that the expectations of the role are unacceptable or excessive

For Further Reading

Brown, Claude. *Manchild in the Promised Land.* New York: Norton, New American Library, 1971. A young black man raised in New York City tells how drugs damaged and often destroyed the lives of a large proportion of the Harlem population.

Jellinek, E. *The Disease Concept of Alcoholism.* New Haven: Yale Center of Alcohol Studies, 1960. A work by a recognized authority; includes one of the best known and most widely used categorizations of alcohol abuse.

Johnson, Bruce D. *Marihuana Users and Drug Subcultures.* New York: John Wiley & Sons, 1973. Based on a survey of 3,500 college and university students, this work provides numerous insights into marijuana use by students and makes a case for the decriminalization of marijuana laws.

National Commission on Marijuana and Drug Abuse. *Marijuana: A Signal of Misunderstanding,* 1972, and *Drug Use in America,* 1973. Washington, D.C.: Government Printing Office. These two volumes of reports are quite readable. They summarize a considerable amount of research on drugs and offer suggestions for reform of laws.

Reasons, Charles. "The Politics of Drugs: An Inquiry in the Sociology of Social Problems." *The Sociological Quarterly* 15 (Summer 1974):381–404. A readable, interesting account of the history of drug laws in the United States with an emphasis on how that problem is shaped by political processes.

Rubington, Earl. *Alcohol Problems and Social Control.* Columbus, Ohio: Charles E. Merrill, 1973. A collection of articles on alcoholism from a social psychological perspective. Includes many interesting materials on skid row alcoholics.

Waldorf, Dan. *Careers in Dope.* Englewood Cliffs, N.J.: Prentice-Hall, 1973. Based on roughly 700 interviews with addicts, this book is an interesting and informative analysis of the lives of drug addicts. Includes both quantitative and qualitative data.

Health Care and Illness: Physical and Mental

1 Why is health a social rather than a strictly medical problem?

2 How much illness is in America?

3 Does everyone have an equal chance for good health?

4 Why do women have more mental illness than men?

5 Why is cancer a social and political issue?

If you were living before 1910, were sick, and randomly chose a doctor, your chances of benefiting from that doctor's ministrations were less than 50 percent, according to one estimate. Your chances today are much better, of course, but they vary in relation to whether you are physically or mentally ill, living in the city or a rural area, poor or well-to-do, among other factors. The unequal probabilities of all Americans having good health and good health care contradict our value of equality. Inequality, then, is one reason why health care is a social problem.

Another reason why health care and illness are social problems is that both physical and mental illness may be induced by the social environment or by the physical environment in which a person must live because of social factors. For instance, poverty may force an individual to live in an unhealthy physical environment. Social factors are prominent especially in mental illness. Some people argue that mental illness is primarily a matter of societal reactions to certain kinds of behavior. We will return to that argument when we discuss labeling and mental illness.

Our *value of good health* is reflected in various surveys. A national sample taken in 1959 attempted to identify the concerns of the American people. Health was the most frequently mentioned personal concern, and the most frequently mentioned factor involved in "the worst possible life" was the health of the individual and his or her family (Cantril, 1965:35). Similarly, in a 1971 national sample, good health was rated the most important factor in a person's quality of life. Seventy percent ranked good health as extremely important, and an-

other 24 percent said health is "very important" (Campbell, Converse, and Rodgers, 1976:377).

When communities attempt to assess the quality of life, health is always a prime criteria: "The maintenance of a healthy environment and a healthy society of people is one of the most essential and desirable states of man" (Newport News Community Development Program, 1973:4). Affluent nations expend enormous sums of money to try to secure good health. Unfortunately, this expenditure includes billions of dollars per year on "worthless, useless, and dangerous products" (Cornacchia, 1976:8). For instance, 6 million arthritics spend hundreds of millions of dollars per year and cancer victims spend at least $50 million per year on various treatments that are largely, if not completely, worthless.

In this chapter, we will examine health care and illness by first drawing the distinction between physical and mental illnesses and then discussing their **prevalence** in American society. (Prevalence, the number of cases of a disease that exist at any particular time, should be distinguished from **incidence,** the number of new cases that occur during a particular period of time.) Next we will see how the problem affects the quality of life. Then we will examine the **epidemiology** of physical and mental illness—the factors that affect the incidence, prevalence, and distribution of illnesses. Finally, we will discuss how the problem has been handled and how it can be attacked.

Nature of the Problem: Health Care and Illness

Are Americans unnecessarily concerned about their health and health care system? After all, do we not have the world's best medical care? Just how serious a problem is illness in our country?

Although in this section we will consider physical and mental illness separately in relation to these questions, the separation is artificial. Physical illness can cause emotional problems. Mental illness can be manifested in physical distress. Both physical and mental illness can have social causes. However, the methods used to assess the extent of each kind of illness are different and must be discussed separately.

Physical Illness

Some indicators suggest that we have made important advances in health matters. For instance, *life expectancy* has increased dramatically (table 5.1). At the turn of the century the average life expectancy of a person was only 47.3 years: by 1978 the figure increased to 73.3. In part, this increase reflects important advances in medicine and public health measures. Sanitation, better diet, and reduced fertility combined with medical knowledge and technology have greatly reduced the prevalence and seriousness of infectious diseases:

> In the old days, people who died from diseases contracted them quickly, reached crisis shortly thereafter, and either died or pulled through. Modern medical researchers have changed this dramatic pattern by taming many once-devastating ailments. Improved conditions of living, along with effective medical skills and technology, have altered the nature of illness in scientifically advanced societies. While patients suffering from communicable diseases once filled most hospitals, treatment centers now serve mainly those afflicted with chronic ailments [Strauss, 1973:33].

Table 5.1   Expectation of Life at Birth, 1900–1978

Year	Total	Male	Female
1900	47.3	46.3	48.3
1910	50.0	48.4	51.8
1920	54.1	53.6	54.6
1930	59.7	58.1	61.6
1940	62.9	60.8	65.2
1950	68.2	65.6	71.1
1955	69.6	66.7	72.8
1960	69.7	66.6	73.1
1965	70.2	66.8	73.7
1970	70.9	67.1	74.8
1971	71.1	67.4	75.0
1973	71.3	67.6	75.3
1975	72.5	68.7	76.5
1978	73.3	69.5	77.2

Source: U.S. Bureau of the Census, *Statistical Abstract of the United States, 1980* (Washington, D.C.: Government Office, 1981), p. 72; and *Historical Statistics of the United States: Colonial Times to 1970*, part 1 (Washington, D.C.: Government Printing Office), p. 55.

Which diseases primarily afflict us today? As shown in table 5.2, cardiovascular diseases ranked at the top in 1978, as they have every year since at least 1960. While the death rate due to heart disease has dramatically declined (figure 5.2), heart disease remains the most frequent cause of death. The second most frequent cause of death has been various malignancies. Millions of Americans have had some form of disease of the circulatory system. A large portion of Americans suffer from hypertension (high blood pressure), and a considerable number have had coronary heart disease, rheumatic heart disease, or stroke.

150

Figure 5.2 Death rates for selected causes, 1940 to 1975, adjusted to age distribution of the 1940 population. (Source: Executive Office of the President, Office of Management and Budget, *Social Indicators, 1976* [Washington, D.C.: Government Printing Office, 1977], p. 6.)

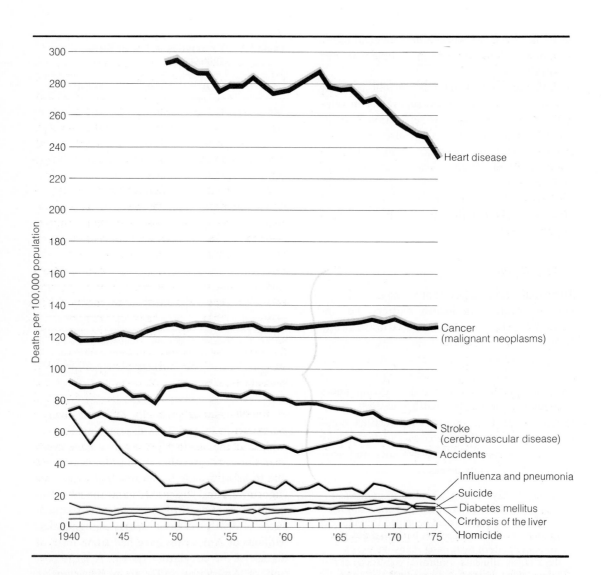

Chronic rather than infectious diseases are our main problem, so although more of us will live to a "ripe old age," we must endure certain limitations. In one national survey in 1971, about 11 percent of the respondents 18 years old or older said their state of health kept them from doing a "lot of things" (Campbell, Converse, and Rodgers, 1976:354).

Various acute illnesses, chronic illnesses, and injuries result in restricted activity and lost days at work for millions of Americans. In 1978, Americans reported an average of 18.8 re-

**Table 5.2.   Death Rates From Selected
Causes, 1978**

Cause	Death Per 100,000
Major cardiovascular diseases	442.7
Malignancies	181.9
Accidents	48.4
Influenza and pneumonia	26.7
Diabetes mellitus	15.5
Cirrhosis of liver	13.8
Bronchitis, emphysema, and asthma	10.0
Nephritis and nephrosis	4.1
Peptic ulcer	2.5

Source: Adapted from U.S. Bureau of the Census, *Statistical Abstract of the United States, 1980* (Washington, D.C.: Government Printing Office, 1981), p. 78.

stricted-activity days per person (that is, days when the individual must reduce his or her usual activities because of illness or injury). In the same year, 30.3 million people had some limitation of activity because of chronic conditions (heart conditions, arthritis, hypertension, etc.).[1] The fact that we are living longer does not mean we all have a better quality of life. Millions of Americans suffer the effects of acute and chronic illnesses.

Mental Illness

Types of mental illness. It is more difficult to get meaningful figures on the prevalence of mental illness than of physical illness. One reason is that even experts disagree on precise *definitions of mental illness.* However, there is considerable agreement about *classification of mental disorders.* First we will distinguish *or-*

ganic disorders from *functional disorders.* Organic disorders involve brain tissue damage and include certain conditions that tend to afflict the aged—senility and cerebral arteriosclerosis. Our concern will be with the functional disorders, which do not involve brain tissue damage. They are separated into three broad categories: **psychoses, neuroses,** and **psychosomatic disorders.**

The functional psychoses (there are also organic psychoses) are the most severe and the most common of the disorders that result in hospitalization. A functionally psychotic person is unable to distinguish between internal and external stimuli. The individual's perceptions and thinking are disordered; in everyday terms, he or she has "lost touch with reality." The individual may have hallucinations or may think in terms of fantasies that have no relationship to the real world in which the individual is living. The individual may experience chronic perplexity and uncertainty. Emotions may vacillate between extreme elation and depression, and behavior may involve either hyperactivity or extreme inactivity.

The most common psychosis among young adults is **schizophrenia,** which typically involves disordered thinking. The schizophrenic individual may have hallucinations and live in a fantasy world, thinking in a way that bears no relation to logic. The schizophrenic may believe that he or she is controlled by external voices or forces. Schizophrenics have problems relating to others and tend to be withdrawn.

Another common psychosis is the **manic-depressive** reaction, which involves fluctuation between emotional extremes. The individual experiences mood swings from periods of high excitement and elation to periods of extreme depression and withdrawal. The disorder is particularly common for the 30- to 55-year age group.

The neuroses are disorders involving anxiety sufficiently intense to impair the individual's functioning in some way. The anxiety, which is the "dynamic center of neuroses," has been described by Horney (1937:61) as "the feeling of an imminent powerful danger and an attitude of helplessness toward it." Because the individual attempts to *cope with anxiety* in various ways, *neurotic symptoms* are of different kinds. There may be a loss of control over parts of the body, manifested in paralysis, tics, or trembling. The individual may battle impulses to behave in ways he or she considers wrong or repugnant. The individual may feel a sense of terror in certain situations, such as a small room, a crowded place, or a high place. The individual's reaction to certain needs may be distorted. Horney (1937:113) described the neurotic need for affection among some of her patients:

> . . . any affection offered meets with distrust, and it will immediately be assumed that it is offered from ulterior motives . . . such patients feel that the analyst wants to help them only for the sake of his own ambition, or that he makes appreciative or encouraging remarks only for therapeutical reasons. One patient of mine considered it a positive humiliation that I offered to see her during the weekend, at a time when she was emotionally upset.

The neuroses vary greatly. In their most severe forms they may be difficult to distinguish from psychoses, even for the expert.

Psychosomatic disorders, the third category, are *impairments in physiological functioning that result from the individual's emotional state.* Certain phrases in our language express the reality of psychosomatic disorders, such as someone who is a "pain in the neck" or who "gives me a headache." Such expressions can be literally true. Our *emotional reactions to others* can result in pains and aches of various kinds. In one such case, a woman complained of severe, frequent headaches for which the doctor could find no organic cause. Later came the discovery that the headaches began when the woman's sister-in-law moved in with her. The woman had never openly expressed her hostility toward her sister-in-law, and her emotional reaction manifested itself in headaches.

The more severe forms of psychosomatic disorders can threaten a person's life. Clausen (1976:112) identifies some as

> severe asthma, ulcerative colitis, hypertension and a good many disorders that we think of as primarily physical. Body and mind are not separable; they are aspects of a functioning person. . . . Thus, while the psychosomatic disorders are readily defined as belonging in the medical context, personality and social situations must be considered in dealing with them.

Clausen's observation bears upon a common misunderstanding about psychosomatic disorders, namely, the idea that the pain is imaginary, that "it's all in your head." Not only is the pain real, but the disorder may even threaten a person's life. The statement might also mean that the sufferer will overcome the physical impairment only if he or she starts thinking properly. However, the individual's real need may be a need for insight or an altered situation *or a restructuring* of relationships.

Extent of mental illness. How prevalent are mental disorders? Obviously, it is difficult to estimate the extent of mental disorders such as psychosomatic disorders. Some physicians judge that as many as half of their patients are suffering from psychosomatic disorders. We all tend to suffer from them to some extent, but we are not all affected to the point of impairment. Many studies have attempted to estimate the prevalence of the psychoses and neuroses, and we will look at these later. First, however, we will address the widespread myth that mental illness is a disease peculiar to modern civilization.

Mental disorders have been linked with social change and with the stresses of a modern, industrial society. This does not mean that such disorders are absent from preindustrial societies. In her studies of the Eskimos in northwestern Alaska and the Yorubas of Nigeria, Murphy (1976) found that many types of behavior considered symptomatic of mental illness in Western society were similarly labeled as evidence of "craziness" in the two preindustrial societies. In both societies, behavior such as talking to oneself, laughing at inappropriate times, regarding oneself as an animal, refusing to eat, and engaging in violence were believed to be symptoms of insanity. In both societies, efforts were made to care for or control the behavior of such people. Moreover, the prevalence of mental illness, 19 percent among the Eskimos and 15 percent among the Yorubas, was comparable to some Western societies.

Studies of mental illness among small, well-integrated groups also point out the pervasiveness of the problem. The Hutterites, a religious group living in villages in Montana and the Dakotas, are an example (Eaton and Weil: 1955). They tend to live in large, closely-knit families, to maintain strong community involve-

ment and religious commitment, and to avoid urban areas. Researchers found the prevalence of mental illness was lower for the Hutterites than for people in urban areas. Nevertheless, the prevalence for the Hutterites was high enough to cause the researchers to reject the notion that urban life in an industrial society is the primary cause of mental disorders. In fact, the rate of severe mental disorders among the Hutterites was about the same as the rate of hospitalization for mental illness in New York State.

Mental illness is a problem of all societies, and its prevalence is not strikingly low in any society. How many Americans suffer from mental disorders? There are two ways to get estimates. We could examine the data on *hospitalization rates,* or we could research communities to get estimates of *"true"* prevalence ("true" because only a minority of people with mental disorders are hospitalized).

Rates of hospitalization must be interpreted cautiously because they reflect changing styles of treatment as well as changing levels of prevalence. Therapy with new drugs became common in the late 1950s, and since then the number of patients in hospitals has decreased, although the number of admissions has increased. In other words, more people are being admitted today than in the 1950s, but they are staying a shorter time, so the total population in hospitals is actually less (figure 5.3). The increasing number of admissions suggests the prevalence is increasing. However, to be sure of this rising prevalence, we must know whether the *rate* (and not just the absolute number) is increasing. Data on patients cared for (table 5.3) support the notion that mental illness is becoming more serious in our society. The rate

Involvement

Rx: Faith

An eight-year-old boy was near death from a disease called encephalomyelitis. He was unconscious in a hospital, paralyzed from the neck down, and experiencing frequent convulsions. A team of doctors agreed that they could do no more, that the boy would likely not live, and that if he did live he would be totally paralyzed and probably imbecilic for the rest of his life. Another physician was called in, one who believed in faith healing. He prayed and laid his hands upon the boy, and repeated the procedure for a number of days. In a period of weeks the boy had completely recovered and had no residual disabilities. Ten years later he was reported still free of any of the symptoms of the disease.

The above account is one of many given by Will Oursler in his book *The Healing Power of Faith.* It illustrates the fact that many aspects of the healing process are unknown and or uncertain. Neither the physician nor the psychiatrist works with an exact science.

Explore alternative forms of healing by reading Oursler's book and also Jerome Frank's book *Persuasion and Healing,* which examines healing methods in primitive societies, in religion, in Communist groups, and in various kinds of psychotherapy. As an alternative, get in touch with one who believes in (and preferably practices) faith healing—a Pentecostal or charismatic (Full Gospel Businessmen's Fellowship) or Christian Scientist—and discuss the nature of health, illness, and healing. What conclusions do you draw from your investigation?

For a different project, investigate a problem dealt with later in this chapter— the medical care available to the poor in your community or in a poor section of your city. A variety of sources for information are available, including census data, telephone directories, interviews with residents, and local medical organizations. How adequate does the medical care appear to you?

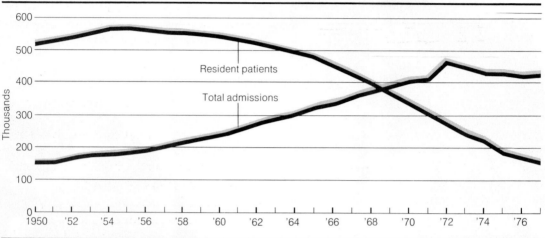

Figure 5.3 Resident patients and total admissions in state and county mental hospitals, 1950 to 1976. (Source: Executive Office of the President, Office of Management and Budget, *Social Indicators, 1973* [Washington, D.C.: Government Printing Office, 1973], p. 12; and U.S. Bureau of the Census, *Statistical Abstract of the United States, 1980* [Washington, D.C.: Government Printing Office, 1981], p. 122.)

for 1975 was nearly three times that for 1955. If we judge the prevalence of mental illness only by the data in table 5.3, we would use the figure of 3 percent.

Community studies put the problem of estimating prevalence in a different light. In the famous Midtown Manhattan study, nearly 1,700 individuals living in New York City were interviewed, and data were secured on things such as psychological symptoms, history of psychiatric care, and childhood and demographic factors (Srole, et al., 1962). The data were organized and given to psychiatrists so each respondent could be evaluated and classified into one of six categories ranging from well (no important symptoms) to incapacitated. Those who could function relatively well in everyday matters were defined as "unimpaired." They comprised 76.6 percent of the total. Thus, 23.4 percent of the sample had psychiatric symptoms that ranged from "marked" to "incapacitation." The fact that nearly one-fourth of the sample (which was representative of the popu-

lation of the area) had serious psychiatric symptoms was startling to professionals and laymen alike. Only 18.5 percent of the people were defined as "well," free of any symptoms. As we will see, however, psychiatric diagnoses are questionable. The figures tell us *how many people psychiatrists would define as mentally ill,* not how many people really are mentally ill.

Other community studies have arrived at different figures for the true prevalence of mental illness. We expect some differences among communities, but perhaps not the spread found: rates that range from 1 to 64 percent. In reviewing many of these studies, Dohrenwend and Dohrenwend (1969) found a median value of 15.6 percent in those studies published since 1950. This extent of mental illness seems greater than hospitalization rates suggest.

By conservative estimate, then, a minimum of 30 to 55 million Americans are defined as suffering from some degree of mental disorder, and perhaps 80 percent of the population have at least mild psychiatric symptoms. How does this affect the quality of their lives?

Table 5.3   Patients Cared For in Mental Health Facilities,* by Type of Treatment Facility, 1955–1977

Year	All Facilities	Total Inpatient Services	Total Outpatient Services
Patients (in thousands)			
1955	1,675	1,296	379
1965	2,637	1,566	1,071
1969	3,573	1,678	1,894
1971	4,038	1,721	2,317
1973	4,749	1,680	3,070
1977	6,640	1,817	4,823
Rates per 100,000 Population			
1955	1,032	799	234
1965	1,374	816	558
1969	1,798	850	948
1971	1,982	847	1,134
1973	2,282	807	1,475
1977	3,079	842	2,236

*Defined as the number of residents in inpatient facilities at the beginning of the year (or the number of persons on the rolls of noninpatient facilities) plus the total additions to these facilities during the year.

Source: Adapted from U.S. Bureau of the Census, *Statistical Abstract of the United States, 1976* (Washington, D.C.: Government Printing Office, 1977), p 86; and *1981* (Washington, D.C.: Government Printing Office, 1981), p. 121.

Health Care, Illness, and the Quality of Life

One effect illness has on the quality of life is this—people must endure considerable stress and suffering because of illness, which is a contradiction to our value of good health. In addition, illness has an impact on interpersonal relationships, it involves a number of Americans in inadequate health care, it interferes with individual freedom, and it involves the individual and the nation in economic costs.

Stress and Suffering

The obvious impact of illness on the quality of life is the *stress and suffering* that illness imposes on people. Mental disorders involve suffering, and something of the feel of that suffering is captured in Anton Boisen's (1936:3) account of his psychotic episode:

. . . there came surging in upon me with overpowering force a terrifying idea about a coming world catastrophe. Although I had never before given serious thought to such a subject, there came flashing into my mind, as though from a source without myself, the idea that this little planet of ours, which has existed for we know not how many millions of years, was about to undergo some sort of metamorphosis. It was like a seed or an egg. In it were stored up a quantity of food materials, represented by our natural resources. But now we were like a seed in the process of germinating or an egg that had just been fertilized. We were starting to grow. Just within the short space of a hundred years we had begun to draw upon our resources to such an extent that the timber and the gas and the oil were likely soon to be exhausted. In the wake of this idea followed others. I myself was more important than I had ever dreamed of being; I was also a zero quantity. Strange and mysterious forces of evil of which before I had not had the slightest suspicion were also revealed. I was terrified beyond measure and in terror I talked. . . . I soon found myself in a psychopathic hospital. There followed three weeks of violent delirium which remain indelibly burned into my memory. . . . It seemed as if I were living thousands of years within that time. Then I came out of it much as one awakens out of a bad dream.

Boisen's account dramatically illustrates the suffering involved in psychosis, in losing touch with reality.

Physical illness also involves *stressful disruptions* in a person's life. If the person's work is disrupted, he or she may be subjected to economic anxiety. The family routine is disrupted in any serious illness. If the illness is protracted, the marital relationship can suffer. The sick person's spouse may become suspicious (Are you really sick?) or depressed or behave in ways designed to gain attention (most attention having been focused on the sick partner). Because illness makes people more dependent than they had been or would like to be, the ill person may have problems with self-concept. The dependent state may lead them to childlike behavior, including tantrums.

Certain kinds of illness generate *long-term fears*. Heart attack victims and cancer patients may have problems of readjustment to normal routines. Such individuals often experience depression and anxiety even when the prognosis for the future is good, and they may have serious reservations about returning to a normal routine. The seriousness and frequency of such problems prompted the establishment of special programs that help patients return to normalcy. For instance, a program at a New York hospital begins with extensive physical and psychological examinations, followed by vocational evaluation and efforts to place the patients in jobs. The programs have scored some successes, though fears generated are so severe that some patients were frightened of the program and expressed a desire to drop out.[2]

Sometimes, serious *emotional problems* are involved in cases of *organ transplants*. One psychiatrist claimed that his studies show that the transplant may be followed by severe depression and even psychosis.[3] For instance, a man who receives a kidney from a woman may fear that his character will be altered or that he will be feminized. One man who received a new kidney came to believe that God had come inside him and that he was being called to help the poor. Heart transplant patients also have suffered various kinds of fantasies, "as the heart assumes a symbolic, human character becoming either malevolent and hostile, or life-giving and enriching."[4]

The disabled also endure stress and suffering. Coe (1970:72) pointed out two critical problems of adjustment to physical disability: "*social devaluation* of the disabled," and a sense of *psychological insecurity*. Social devaluation is particularly acute when the disability is visible. The visibly disabled individual may be treated as inferior and may be subject to serious disadvantages in job opportunities. Such experiences result, in turn, in the second problem—insecurity: "The impact of being in a social status which is devalued, of encountering prejudice and discrimination, and of experiencing characteristic responses to illness results in . . . insecurity, anxiety, and maladjustment" (Coe, 1970:73).

These findings show the close relationship of physical and mental illness. In psychosomatic disorders, emotional states produce impairments of physiological functioning. On the other hand, physical illness can result in psychiatric symptoms. Dohrenwend (1974:303–04) reported a study of 500 individuals in which "those respondents reporting physical illness or injury were considerably more likely to show psychiatric disorder than those respondents reporting other objective loss events whose occurrence was outside their control." To some extent, the problem can become a vicious circle for the individual, who may become entangled in the interaction between physical and mental disorders.

Interpersonal Relationships

There is a contradiction between _the sick role_ and our attitudes and values about desirable behavior, and the result may be disrupted interpersonal relationships. Although we recognize the inevitability of illness, we tend to be reluctant to allow illnesses of others to disturb our own routines.

The _strain on interpersonal relationships_ when one of the interactants is ill is seen in patterns of family relationships. Both physical and mental illness can lead to disruption in the family. Anthony (1969; 1970) studied families in St. Louis in which one member was ill. His associates visited the families at times when all members were together; sometimes they lived with families for a week; they met with family members individually; and they also studied the families in a research center. In other words, the family as a group and individual family members were interviewed and observed in a variety of settings.

Anthony found that families who have a member with chronic illness develop a kind of _subculture_, with the _ill member_ becoming something of _a focal point_ of family life. If the mother is ill, the husband and children may

experience an emotional void in their lives. If the father is ill, there is a likelihood of economic problems, a lowered standard of living. Moreover, the father may tend to monopolize the attention of his wife, leaving the children with feelings of neglect. If the family develops a subculture of illness, they withdraw into themselves, isolating themselves from outsiders. Suspicion, disorganization, and a state of virtual anomie may develop. Abnormal behavior on the part of family members may be not only tolerated but encouraged.

Not all families respond to serious illness in this way, of course. Some families become more integrated and the members experience a greater richness of family life. Others experience a temporary breakdown but recover and return to normal. Still others disintegrate in the face of the challenge, especially if the family was weakly integrated in the past. In all cases, illness presents a serious challenge to the family.

One reason serious illness tends to disrupt family life is that it _precludes proper role functioning_. For example, a woman who is physically or emotionally ill may be incapable of fulfilling her role as mother or her role as wife. This is illustrated in studies of severely depressed women (Weissman, 1972; Weissman, Paykel, and Klerman, 1972). A group of forty depressed women in the 25-to-60 age group were compared with forty normal women to determine the effects of the illness on marital and parental functioning. The depression adversely affected both roles.

The depressed women reported little satisfaction from the marriage (including sex relations), considerable resentment toward their husbands, and an unwillingness to discuss their feelings with their husbands. In the maternal role, the depressed women were less emotionally involved than the normal women with their children. Between the children and the depressed mothers there was less communication, less affection, and more conflict. The mothers also said they felt a good deal of resentment and guilt toward their children. Moreover, these problems of relating were typical at all stages of the family life cycle. Depressed women with newborn children tended to be overindulgent or overprotective or compulsive in caring for the infants. When the children were older, the mothers were incapable of getting sufficiently involved with them to enable the children to learn various kinds of social skills. When the children were grown and had left home, the women were unable to cope with the loss.

As in the case of the interplay between mental and physical illness, the relationship between interpersonal relations and illness can become a vicious circle. Poor interpersonal relationships can be a factor in the onset of a mental disorder (Berkman, 1971), and mental disorders adversely affect interpersonal relationships. On the other hand, *good interpersonal relationships are associated with better health*. Pratt (1972) reported a study in which equalitarian marriages were found to be characterized by better health and health behavior than were nonequalitarian marriages. Equalitarianism was defined as shared power, flexibility in the division of labor in the home, and a high degree of companionship. Compared to their counterparts in nonequalitarian marriages, the women in equalitarian marriages scored higher on a number of health variables, and the men scored higher on total use of health services and on health knowledge.

In sum, there is a relationship between patterns of interaction and health. Illness, whether physical or mental, tends to be associated with disturbed interpersonal relationships. The relation between interaction and illness may be a vicious circle—bad interpersonal relationships being a factor in the onset of illness, and illness being a factor in causing disturbed relationships.

Inadequate Care

Our value of good health is contradicted by the stratification of health care in the United States that is manifested in *inadequate care* for many Americans. Our value of good health is also contradicted by the actual state of the science of medicine. Contrary to the expectations and attitudes of many Americans, *medicine is an inexact science*. Psychiatry, in particular, is a field of *competing ideologies* rather than a science of mental therapy. In other words, our health care is inadequate in two senses: some Americans do not receive the quality of care that is available, and the care many people expect is impossible in view of the present state of knowledge.

Neither the physician nor the psychiatrist works within the framework of an exact science, despite the enormous advances made in medicine since the turn of the century, when the probability of a person being helped by a visit to a physician was less than 50 percent. Nevertheless, a physician may still have difficulty diagnosing an illness correctly, and even with a correct diagnosis the physician may be unable to help. A dramatic illustration is the 1976 outbreak of "Legionnaires' Disease," which af-

Figure 5.4 Acupuncture in China. Medicine is still an inexact science, and many different methods of healing appear to work.

161

flicted a number of people who attended an American Legion convention in Philadelphia. Those who caught the disease experienced chest pains, high fever, and difficulty in breathing. A month after the convention, over twenty people had died from the disease and numerous others had caught it but recovered. Doctors were baffled. They understood neither its cause nor how to help those afflicted. Ultimately, the disease was traced to a bacterium that can evade the immune system of the body. Even when such a cause is found, physicians may be able to do little beyond try to relieve the symptoms and protect against secondary infections.

Psychiatric care is more problematic. There are various schools of therapy, with quite different ideologies of health and illness and different views about diagnostic categories. A psychiatrist's diagnosis of a case will depend partly on *which school of therapy* he or she follows, but even within a particular ideology, diagnosis of mental disorder is difficult. In a noted experiment, Rosenhan (1973) and some assistants pretended to be hearing voices and had themselves hospitalized. The hospitals included private as well as public, underfinanced and well-financed institutions. Once admitted, each of the researchers behaved normally and told the staff the symptoms had disappeared. Nevertheless, their normalcy was undetected by the staffs (although nearly one-third of the other patients seemed to suspect the researchers were not really ill), and the researchers were kept in the hospitals for periods ranging from seven to fifty-two days.

A psychiatric diagnosis may also be influenced by stereotyped thinking. Seventeen first-year psychiatric residents in three New York hospitals were given materials on the case of a young woman who complained of recurrent nightmares. To some of the psychiatrists the woman was described as black, to others she was described as white. The residents tended to diagnose the "white patient" as obsessive compulsive and the "black patient" as schizophrenic or borderline, even though all materials except for race were identical (Blake, 1973).

Apart from the difficulties of diagnosis, there is some question about the *efficacy of therapy*. In a classic review of evidence, Eysenck (1952) reported that there was no evidence that therapy was helpful to neurotics. About two-thirds of neurotics improve within two years whether or not they have psychiatric help. (*Behavior therapy,* developed since Eysenck's report, seems to offer some help with neuroses, however.) A 60 percent success rate with all mental disorders is independent of the particular school of therapy used (Pizer and Travers, 1975:12–13). Thus, many psychotic and severely neurotic individuals are helped regardless of the *type* of therapy administered. Nonetheless, psychiatric therapy is an inexact affair, and as many as 40 percent of those seeking help are not receiving what they need.

Aside from inadequate care because of the inexactness of medical science, *many Americans fail to receive the quality of care that is available.* There are at least two reasons for this: incompetence, and *maldistribution of medical care.*

Incompetence is found in every profession, not only in medicine, and incompetence in medicine is not a problem of physicians alone. One observer contended that as many as 80 percent of all malpractice cases are rooted in problems of hospital functioning—"usually because of a failure to observe fail-safe standards that are on the books."[5]

However, a good deal of evidence suggests that many physicians are incompetent, or are performing their work incompetently. One estimate reveals that about one-third of all hysterectomies performed nationally in 1975 were unnecessary, and that as many as 60 to 70 percent of tonsillectomies could not be medically justified. In all, as many as 2 million unnecessary operations were performed in 1975, with about 11,900 of them resulting in the death of the patient.[6] Despite advances made in medicine, a person can still experience more harm than help from a physician. Ivan Illich (1976) argued that the danger from physicians has outstripped the danger from bacteria, that one of every five people who enter a research hospital will develop *iatrogenic disease* (caused by the physician). Illich overstated his case, but the point that visiting a physician carries risk is valid.

Sometimes the incompetence involves both the physician and other medical personnel responsible for patient care. An investigation of six abortion clinics in Chicago showed that four of them were like assembly lines, with a basic purpose of maximizing profit. As a result, some abortions were performed on women who were not even pregnant, and some of the procedures were performed by unqualified or inexperienced people. Some of the patients developed serious infections and internal damage that might later require a hysterectomy.[7]

Maldistribution of medical care for economic and geographic reasons leaves many Americans without the quality care that could otherwise be available. The expense of medical care means that the aged, young couples with small children, and poor people are likely to have less care than others (Coe, 1970:350–51). *Maldistribution of doctors* means that people in certain areas have less access to doctors than those in other areas. For instance, in the early 1970s, 12 percent of physicians and 18 percent of nurses were in rural areas, but 30 percent of the population lived in those areas (Carlson, 1972). In 1978 the number of physicians per 100,000 population varied among the states from a low of 109 in South Dakota and Mississippi to a high of 585 in Washington, D.C. For dentists, the figures ranged from 31 per 100,000 people in Mississippi to 83 per 100,000 people for Washington, D.C.[8]

Maldistribution of care also involves *variations among health care facilities.* Hospitals differ in the quality of care they offer. Even in the same hospital, patients may experience unequal treatment. A study of 141 emergency room patients in a Baltimore hospital indicated that 60 percent had received ineffective care, while the rest had received either effective care or care that could not be labeled effective or ineffective (Carlson, 1972). Unequal treatment in the same facility is sometimes related to the patient's socioeconomic status.

Variations in quality of care may be most pronounced in mental hospitals. The poorer people, who must use state or municipal facilities are much more likely to get inferior care than those who can afford private hospitals. While state hospitals are not uniformly bad, two investigators remarked that state hospitals' quality of care "sometimes can be so bad that it's hard to tell the difference between the MDs and the patients" (LeBlanc and LeBlanc, 1979:43). They tell of one psychiatrist at a state hospital who told outlandish stories about himself, his wealth, and his connections with the CIA. When he was arrested for attempted murder, he was replaced with a psychiatrist who suffered from depression and was prone to violent behavior. The second doctor quit after murdering his wife. We should not assume that the two psychiatrists are typical. Rather, they serve to dramatize the point that because state hospitals are often desperate for help, they may hire people who are incapable of helping others.

Individual Freedom

Americans are an individualistic people. We cherish the *freedom of the individual* and tend to react strongly to anything that threatens the freedom. However, there is sometimes a contradiction between our value of individual freedom and our value of good health. In essence, we face a trade-off between health and freedom in certain areas. Some religious groups have resisted medical procedures such as blood transfusions and vaccinations on the grounds that their religious beliefs would be violated. If they are forced to undergo such medical treatment despite their beliefs, their religious convictions and freedom of choice are violated. The counterargument is that they may jeopardize the health or the lives of others by their refusal. Their freedom, therefore, does not extend to the point where it affects the well-being of others.

The issue seems to be resolved for many people, yet, consider a similar problem raised by recent advances in biological engineering (Waltz and Thigpen, 1973). The 1972 National Sickle Cell Anemia Control Act required people to submit to a screening blood test to determine the likelihood of their producing children with sickle cell anemia. Many people felt this was a clear invasion of privacy. Many more would probably consider it an invasion of privacy if the next step was taken—preventing people with certain genetic deficiencies from having children, or even from marrying. Certain genetic diseases can be controlled only by forbidding certain couples to have children. Loss of freedom is unquestionably involved, but it can be argued that only by this loss can public health and welfare be safeguarded and human suffering reduced.

The history of medicine is marked by ongoing conflict between the advocates of medical advance and those who defend the freedom of the individual. Greater advances in medicine will intensify the conflict and compound the problems.

Economic Costs

An increasing amount of the nation's *economic resources* are channelled into the effort to combat illness and promote good health. Figure 5.5 traces the dramatic increase in that amount from 1950 to 1979 in both absolute terms and proportion of the gross national product. Total dollars expended on national health increased more than seventeenfold, while the proportion of the gross national product represented by those dollars doubled. Another way to observe the increasing cost is to note that *medical care has been a growing portion of the consumer price index*—three times as large in 1975 as it was in 1950.[9] Since 1950 the economic cost of health and illness has risen much faster than the economic cost of most other things.

The amounts in figure 5.5 represent only expenditures; actual cost is more. Cooper and Rice (1976:21) attempted to determine the actual cost by measuring "the direct outlays for prevention, detection, and treatment and the indirect costs or loss in output due to disability (**morbidity**) and premature death (mortality)." They estimated the *total actual cost of illness* in 1972 at $188 billion—$42 billion of which was the cost of morbidity, and $71 billion the cost of mortality. That is nearly $100 billion more than the $92.7 billion expenditure shown in figure 5.5. The morbidity cost includes lost productivity:

> In 1972, employed men and women lost the equivalent of 1.7 million years of work because of ill health—a loss to our economy of $17.6 billion. . . . Colds, influenza, and other diseases of the respiratory system resulted in by far the greatest losses—about three-tenths for both the years and the dollar amount. Accidents were next with about 17 percent of the losses [Cooper and Rice, 1976:25].

The greatest mortality losses were for circulatory diseases, which accounted for over half the deaths and almost one-third the lost years of work and earnings.

We see here that illness involves a *societal cost,* not just a personal cost. A sick person's expenses may be heavy or minimal—as for colds, influenza and other respiratory problems—but the costs to the nation of millions of individuals with such problems are enormous.

For the individual, burdensome costs often result from long-term chronic diseases and from diseases requiring the use of *sophisticated medical technology.* Consider, for instance, the cost of chronic kidney disease. A young man who

Figure 5.5 National health expenditures, 1950 to 1979. (Source: U.S. Bureau of the Census, *Statistical Abstract of the United States, 1980* [Washington, D.C.: Government Printing Office, 1981], p. 104.)

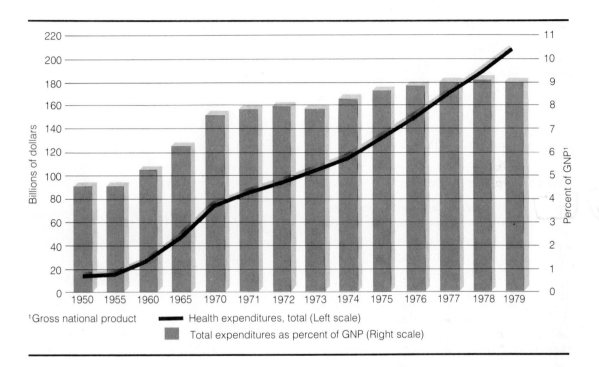

¹Gross national product ▬▬▬ Health expenditures, total (Left scale)

▨ Total expenditures as percent of GNP (Right scale)

had nearly completed a Ph.D. degree suddenly found himself "perennially pauperized," without any hope of either completing the degree or obtaining a job, when he was afflicted by an incurable kidney disease that required removal of the organ. He had to report to a hospital three times a week for kidney dialysis while waiting for a transplant. He lived on $178 a month welfare while the State of California paid for most of his medical expenses—$3,000 per month![10] In 1971 the average annual cost per patient for dialysis was around $25,000.

Even with health insurance, an individual or a family may *find the cost of illness oppressive.* Why the dramatic increase in costs? According to the Department of Health, Education and Welfare, the increase in expenditures on medi-

cal care since 1950 can be accounted for by three broad factors:[11] inflation caused 46 percent; population growth accounted for 15 percent; and 39 percent was attributable to technological developments and increasing use of medical services.

The problem of health and illness involves both the individual or family and the nation in high costs. An increasing portion of economic resources have been consumed by medical care over the past twenty-five years. The situation raises an interesting question. Despite our high value on good health, is there a point where the trade-off between economic resources and health will lead us to sacrifice some health in order to retain more of our economic resources?

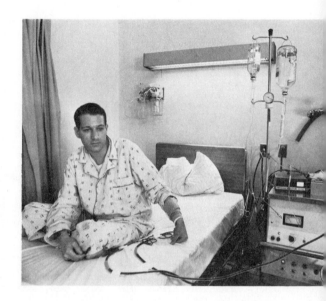

Contributing Factors

We have seen that illness can come about from sociocultural factors and not only from bacteria. In this section, we will examine some of those factors in detail. Furthermore, we will find that sociocultural factors are involved not only in the **etiology** (causes of diseases), but also in inadequate care and maldistribution of care.

Social Structural Factors

Roles. Many studies have shown that *stress* leads to a variety of physical and mental disorders. Stress has been related to cardiovascular disease, digestive problems, heightened susceptibility to infection, problems of the skeletal-muscular system, and mental disorders (Selye, 1956; Levine and Scotch, 1970; McQuade and Aikman, 1974). People who must cope with stress are more likely to get ill than people with little stress. Certain roles are so demanding or so contradictory or so restrictive that the individuals in the roles are subjected to continual stress. However, not everyone who occupies a particular role will experience the same amount of stress, nor will everyone who occupies a particular role get sick. Nonetheless, *certain roles are considered stress-inducing* because they have been associated with a disproportionate amount of illness. In particular, the female role and certain occupational roles in American society induce stress and lead to relatively high rates of illness.

Women seem to have more health problems than do men. Nathanson (1975:57) observed that "one of the most consistent observations in health survey research is that women report symptoms of both physical and mental illness and utilize physician and hospital services for these conditions at higher rates than men."

Women have higher rates of physical illness than do men on nearly all the indices of morbidity and health care utilization, including: "incidence of acute conditions; number of acute conditions; restricted activity, bed disability and days lost from primary activity due to acute conditions; overall days of bed disability; physician visits; and discharges from short-stay hospitals" (Nathanson, 1975:57). The higher rates apply only to women 16 years and older.

Women have a higher overall rate of mental disorder than men, but they do not have higher rates of every kind of mental disorder. As for their higher rate of certain mental disorders, Dohrenwend (1975:369) summarized the numerous studies that have been made and drew the following conclusions:

1. There are no consistent sex differences in rates of functional psychoses in general (34 studies) or one of the two major subtypes, schizophrenia, in particular (26 studies); rates of the other, manic-depressive psychosis, are generally higher among women (18 out of 24 studies).
2. Rates of neurosis are consistently higher for women regardless of time or place (28 out of 32 studies).
3. By contrast, rates of personality disorder are consistently higher for men regardless of time or place (22 out of 26 studies). The "time or place" refers to pre- vs. post-World War II and urban vs. rural settings.

Why do women suffer more physical and mental ailments than men do? There are a number of possible reasons. Perhaps women report their illnesses more than men report theirs because it is more acceptable for a woman than for a man to be sick. Another reason could be biological differences. Yet another reason could be that something in the female role increases the probability of women becoming sick: this reason is supported by recent research.

Gove (1972) reviewed a number of studies and argued that the *sex role of married women results in the higher rate of mental disorders among women.* Married women have higher rates of mental disorders than married men, but single, divorced, or widowed women tend to have lower rates than their counterparts among men. (Among both sexes, married people have lower rates than unmarried.) Thus, according to Gove, it is not the female role per se but the married woman's role in particular that leads to high rates of mental illness.

A slightly different explanation, though still related to role, has been set forth by Nathanson (1975). She notes that women with pre-school children have lower rates of illness than those with older or no children, and that women who are employed have lower rates than those who are housewives. She interprets these findings to mean that women with many role obligations are less likely to become ill than women with fewer obligations.

From these studies we may conclude the *restrictive nature of the traditional role of the married woman* creates stress and leads to high rates of illness. This conclusion is supported by Rosenfield's finding (1980), that when men and women have nontraditional relationships, males tend to have higher levels of depressive symptoms than females. For traditional females, women whose "place is in the home," the role may become increasingly oppressive as their children mature and leave home, taking away what has been the focal meaning of their lives. Many women are expanding into new roles after their children are grown. Those who do not are more prone to lapse into depression in their middle years. The mental disorders that afflict married women, then, are due to the stress of insufficient stimulation; *under*stimulation as well as excessive demands can be stressful (Seidenberg, 1972).

Certain occupational roles illustrate the stress of excessive demands and the consequent tendency toward illness, just as married women illustrate the stress of the restrictive role and the consequent tendency toward illness. Coronary heart disease, in particular, has been linked to certain occupational roles and to the *individual's adjustment to his or her occupational role*. Some jobs involve considerable pressure, which means that they tend to generate considerable stress. The pressures may come from work overload, deadlines, excessive responsibilities, and role conflict, all of which increase the risk of coronary heart disease (House, 1974:19–20).

The relationship between the stress associated with a particular role and the prevalence of coronary heart disease is seen in a comparison of various professional groups. A panel of physicians, dentists, and lawyers rated the stress involved in various specialties within their professions (Kagan, 1971:41). Their ratings of most stressful to least stressful were as follows: the medical specialties of general practitioner, anesthesiologist, pathologist, and dermatologist; the dental specialties of general practitioner, oral surgeon, orthodondist, and periodontist; and the legal specialties of general practice lawyer, trial lawyer, other specialties, and patent lawyer. The prevalence of coronary heart disease correlated perfectly with the amount of stress, with the single exception that coronary heart disease was equally prevalent among medical general practitioners and anesthesiologists. In other words, lawyers in general practice had higher rates than trial lawyers, who had higher rates than those in other specialties, who had higher rates than patent lawyers.

Individuals' adjustments to the roles, as well as the demands of particular roles, are important in disease. Some individuals thrive in a role that others find oppressive. A certain role does not have the same effect on every individual. Rather, how the individual *defines the meaning* of his or her role is what makes that role stressful. (Of course, roles with heavy demands are more likely to be defined as oppressive by individuals who must fulfill those demands). Occupational roles defined as unsatisfying are more likely to be correlated with illness than roles not defined as such.

People with coronary heart disease have been found to be significantly more dissatisfied with their jobs than are people who do not have the disease. The dissatisfaction may be rooted in factors such as tedious details, failure to receive recognition, and conflict with co-workers. In a wide range of occupations, House (1974:18) found correlations between job satisfaction and various heart disease risk factors (smoking, overweight, high cholesterol levels, high blood pressure, and high levels of blood sugar).

Clearly, people with *serious role problems* are more likely to develop illness than are people without such problems. Certain roles are more likely than others to disturb people and thereby lead to illness, notably the role of the married woman and certain occupational roles. Such roles induce stress, because they involve understimulation or they make excessive demands or they conflict with the individual's perceived needs.

The family context of illness.   Among the institutional arrangements that contribute to illness are family patterns of interaction and **socialization** (the process by which an individual learns to participate in a group). The *quality of the relationship between a child and the parents* is crucial for the child's mental health. It has been argued that the relationship with the mother is particularly important:

> With some regularity it turns out that a child's character and mental health depend to a considerable degree upon his relationship with his mother in early years. Adverse relationships seem often to create insuperable obstacles to effective therapeutic treatment at later periods of life [Allport, 1955:31].

However, the child's relationship with the mother cannot be separated from the total family environment. It is not only the child's relationship with the mother, but the overall experience in the family as well that can lead to mental disorders. Sanua (1961) reviewed a number of studies and found they consistently reported that mothers of schizophrenics tended to be overprotective or rejecting or domineering, while the fathers tended to be weak or indifferent or negligent. In other words, the total dynamics of family life, not just one relationship, differentiated the experience of the schizophrenic.

Other mental disorders have been related to family experiences. Berkman (1971) surveyed adults in a California community and found that certain family experiences created the kind of stress in children that can result in mental disorders. Particularly subject to stress that enhanced the risk of mental illness were children in broken homes, in homes where parents quarreled frequently, in homes where parents were in poor physical health, and in homes where the character of the parent or parents was defined in negative terms. A survey of nearly 2,300 adults concluded that marital strains and the problems of parenting were more closely related to depression than were either work or financial stresses (Ilfield, 1977).

A disorganized family is also associated with physical illness. In comparing forty-two families of children hospitalized for acute illness with a group of families with well children, Mutter and Schleifer (1969) found that the sick children had disturbed relations with their parents; that the families of the sick children were less cohesive; and that the mothers of the sick children were not functioning well in their roles. The child who lives in a disorganized family runs a greater risk of physical and mental illness than does a child in other families.

Physical health practices also seem to reflect family patterns. Children reared in accord with a "developmental pattern" tend to have better health care practices than those reared by a "disciplinary" pattern (Pratt, 1973). The developmental pattern implies emphasis on use of reason and information, rewards for good behavior, and autonomy for the child (in the sense that the child does a number of things without the parents' help or reminder). In matters such as sleep, exercise, elimination, dental care, cleanliness, nutrition, and smoking, children reared by the developmental pattern have somewhat better health practices than those reared by a disciplinary pattern, which stresses "unquestioning obedience" to the parents.

Table 5.4   Common Occupational Carcinogens

Agent	Organ Affected	Occupation
Wood	Nasal cavity and sinuses	Woodworkers
Leather	Nasal cavity and sinuses; urinary bladder	Leather and shoe workers
Iron oxide	Lung; larynx	Iron ore miners; metal grinders and polishers; silver finishers; iron foundry workers
Nickel	Nasal sinuses; lung	Nickel smelters, mixers, and roasters; electrolysis workers
Arsenic	Skin; lung; liver	Miners; smelters; insecticide makers and sprayers; tanners; chemical workers; oil refiners; vintners
Chromium	Nasal cavity and sinuses; lung; larynx	Chromium producers, processors, and users; acetylene and aniline workers; bleachers, glass, pottery, and linoleum workers; battery makers
Asbestos	Lung (pleural and peritoneal mesothelioma)	Miners; millers; textile, insulation, and shipyard workers
Petroleum, petroleum coke, wax, creosote, shale, and mineral oils	Nasal cavity; larynx; lung; skin; scrotum	Contact with lubricating, cooling, paraffin or wax fuel oils or coke; rubber fillers; retort workers; textile weavers; diesel jet testers
Mustard gas	Larynx; lung; trachea; bronchi	Mustard gas workers
Vinyl chloride	Liver; brain	Plastic workers
Bis-chloromethyl ether, chloromethyl methyl either	Lung	Chemical workers
Isopropyl oil	Nasal cavity	Isopropyl oil producers
Coal soot, coal tar, other products of coal combustion	Lung; larynx; skin; scrotum; urinary bladder	Gashouse workers, stokers, and producers; asphalt, coal tar, and pitch workers; coke oven workers; miners; still cleaners
Benzene	Bone marrow	Explosives, benzene, or rubber cement workers; distillers; dye users; painters; shoemakers
Auramine, benzidine, alpha-Naphthylamine, magenta, 4-Aminodiphenyl, 4-Nitrodiphenyl	Urinary bladder	Dyestuffs manufacturers and users; rubber workers (pressmen, filtermen, laborers); textile dyers; paint manufacturers

Source: American Public Health Association, *Health and Work in America: A Chart Book* (Washington, D.C.: Government Printing Office, 1975), p. 71.

The industrial economy. Certain aspects of our economy are important factors in the onset of illness. An industrial economy exposes numerous workers to materials that are **carcinogenic** (causing cancer). Some common occupational carcinogens are shown in table 5.4.

People who work in industries using carcinogenic materials are more likely to get cancer than are others.

An industrial economy exposes the citizenry to various illnesses through *different kinds of pollution* also. A number of studies have shown the disastrous effects lead poisoning can have on children—mental retardation, behavioral difficulties, perceptual problems, and emotional instability (Berg and Zappella, 1964). Lead poisoning is most common among ghetto children, who ingest chips of paint from flaking walls or other substances containing lead. Use of lead in paint was discontinued for the most part by 1950, but leaded paint may still exist in some older buildings. Craving for such unnatural substances—a condition called **"pica"**—is frequently associated with impoverished living.

The most familiar pollutant to many Americans is automobile exhaust, which contains carbon monoxide. Carbon monoxide poisoning can lead to apathy, headaches, perceptual problems, retardation, and even psychosis. However, the precise effects of carbon monoxide poisoning are unclear. The amount of carbon monoxide released into the air from automobile exhaust varies considerably from one area to another. We will discuss chemical pollutants further in the last chapter, which deals with ecology and population.

Noise is another kind of pollution that is linked with an industrial economy and that can have deleterious effects.[12] The noise level endured by some workers can create mental stress, as can the noise associated with living near an airport. Noise combined with other sources of stress generates considerable annoyance and may cause mental disorder.

In the late 1970s some Americans became concerned about yet another form of pollution—*electromagnetic radiation.* The amount of electromagnetic radiation, particularly microwaves, in the air has increased enormously over the past decades. Many kinds of electric and electronic equipment emit radiation. High levels of radiation have a variety of effects on rats, including stunted growth, altered reaction time, and abnormal brainwave patterns. In humans, the effects of high levels of electromagnetic radiation may range from stress to serious illnesses such as cataracts and cancer, and from headaches and loss of memory to serious psychiatric problems, according to some researchers. This is all still a matter of dispute, but some scientists and some laypeople feel that electromagnetic pollution is one of the more serious hazards to human health in the future.[13]

Fluctuations in the state of the economy have also been identified as adversely affecting people's health. Brenner (1973) examined admissions to all mental hospitals in New York over a 127-year period, 1841 to 1967, and concluded that economic instability is the prime source of stress in an industrial society. He found that the prevalence of mental illness is inversely related to the state of the economy:

> First, it is clear that instabilities in the national economy have been the single most important source of fluctuation in mental-hospital admissions or admission rates. Second, this relation is so consistent for certain segments of the society that virtually no major factor other than economic instability appears to influence variation in their mental hospitalization rates. Third, the relation has been basically stable for at least 127 years and there is considerable evidence that it has had greater impact in the last two decades [Brenner, 1973:ix].

Complicated statistical methods were used to investigate this relationship, with economic changes being measured by the rate of employment in manufacturing industries. Because of the difficulties in drawing conclusions from such statistical methods, Brenner's conclusions will not be accepted without some further study (see Clausen, 1976:122–23). Nevertheless, Brenner's work is careful and thorough, and it is congruent with the idea that economic problems are a source of stress, and stress generated by things such as economic problems is a source of mental illness.

The politics of illness. We do not usually think of illness as a political issue, but *government policy* is a crucial factor in certain kinds of illness. For example, when political leaders refuse to act against certain economic interests and control chemical pollutants, illness is not only a medical issue, but a political issue as well. The battles against infant mortality rates and cancer illustrate the political nature of illness.

Infant mortality rates are higher in the U.S. than in a number of other nations. The rates vary among American communities: the rate in Washington, D.C. is double that in Utah. Infant mortality rates can be reduced by making medical resources available to communities.

What determines whether or not a particular community will get those medical resources? Unfortunately, it is not need but various other factors (Friedman, 1973). Communities differ in their medical resources because physicians tend to cluster near medical schools; medical schools, in turn, tend to be in large metropolitan areas where national organizations are headquartered. Such concentrations of medical resources have a direct effect on infant mortality rates. They also have an indirect effect on infant mortality rates by influencing the likelihood of

obtaining federal funds for infant health programs. In other words, areas already advantaged by concentrations of medical resources are likely to become even more advantaged by securing federal funds. Programs such as the Maternal and Infant Care Projects could reduce infant mortality rates, but their distribution—a political decision—is unrelated to prior infant mortality rates. Federally-funded infant care programs tend to go to areas with medical schools and headquarters of national organizations. Political influence rather than maximum need dictates the distribution of funds.

Epstein (1976) argued that cancer is now primarily a political and economic issue. He pointed out that cancer is one of the few causes of death that have increased significantly in recent decades, with much of the increase due to lung cancer. Cancer rates show a definite geographical pattern, being particularly high in heavily industrialized areas. An estimated 5 to 15 percent of all cancer deaths are the result of the individual's occupation. In some occupations, the rate is extremely high: 50 percent of long-term asbestos-insulation workers die from cancer. Carcinogenic materials also affect people who are not industrial workers. From 70 to 90 percent of all cancer is estimated to be "environmental in origin, and thus ultimately preventable" (Epstein, 1976:36). It is preventable by regulating the industrial chemicals in the environment. Epstein claimed that such regulation has not been forthcoming, largely because of intense lobbying by the chemical industry, which emphasizes that regulation would have adverse economic impact.

Some people argue that we do not know enough about the effects of various chemicals on human beings to enact meaningful legislation. Epstein (1976:36) disagreed:

> . . . every chemical known to be carcinogenic to humans, with the possible exception of tri-valent arsenic, is also carcinogenic to animals. Many chemicals now recognized as carcinogenic to humans were first identified by animal testing. . . . There can be no possible justification, scientific or otherwise, for leading industrial representatives' or regulatory agency officials' continued insistence that animal data must be validated by human experience before regulatory action can be taken.

Thus, with respect to carcinogens, the government is swayed more by economic arguments than by appeals based on the human costs of our policies. Governmental decisions reflect business interests, and the populace bears the cost in the form of high cancer rates. Ironically, we are uncertain of the economic impact of regulation. There would be some short-term adverse effects in some industries, and it is these industries that have exercised power in the decision-making process. The speculations of industry spokesmen have outweighed the increasing prevalence of cancer. It appears, then, that cancer will continue to be a political and economic issue.

The stratification of illness. We speak of the stratification of illness in two senses: *different patterns of illness* is one sense; and *variations in health care among the socioeconomic strata* is the other. People in the lower strata use health care services less because of the cost of the services, because of their lack of belief in preventive checkups, and because of the inadequacies of the delivery system most available to them (mainly hospital outpatient and emergency rooms or public clinics) (Dutton, 1978).

The National Health Interview Survey showed, among other things: that a smaller proportion of those in the lower socioeconomic strata had hospital or surgical insurance; people in the lower strata made fewer visits to physicians during the year; and those in the lower strata spent less per person on health care.[14] Although poor people spend less per person on health care than do those in the middle- and upper-income brackets, their expenditures are a greater proportion of their total income.

Some socioeconomic differences in health care show a consistency over a considerable period of time. Ro (1964) compared four different surveys conducted at various times between 1928 and 1963. He found a number of relationships between family income and medical care. The lower income families: (1) spent less for medical services and saw a dentist a third as often as higher income families; (2) had a higher proportion of individuals reporting illness without receiving any care; (3) had a lower proportion of persons reporting "no illness"; (4) had a lower average stay in the hospital for maternity care; and (5) had fewer physician visits for prenatal care.

By the 1970s the poor were still using medical services less than would be appropriate for their symptoms (Taylor, Aday, and Andersen, 1975), and they still had more, not fewer, problems of physical health. Low income families tend to have more chronic illness, more days of restricted activity, a higher prevalence of disability, and more days lost from work than do higher income families (Bergner and Yerby, 1968).

The pattern for physical illness, then, is more problems and less help as we descend the socioeconomic ladder. There are a number of reasons

Figure 5.7 The rate of mental disorder may reflect socioeconomic differences more than age, race, or any other single criterion.

for this. Poor people lack information; they cannot afford to pay for adequate medical services; and medical services are concentrated outside the areas where they live.

The pattern for mental illness is similar. In general, the rates of psychiatric disorders are higher in the lower strata, particularly in urban areas. This is true for schizophrenia and personality disorders but not for neuroses or manic-depressive psychosis (Dohrenwend, 1975:370).

One well-known investigation of the relationship between social class and mental illness was conducted by Hollingshead and Redlich (1958) in New Haven, Connecticut. The researchers obtained information on people treated at hospitals and clinics in the New Haven area. They also surveyed the community to establish the overall socioeconomic distribution. They found that 1 percent of the patients and 3 percent of the population were in the upper class; 7 percent of the patients and 8.4 percent of the population were in the upper-middle class; 13.7 percent of the patients and 20.4 percent of the population were in the middle-middle class; 40.1 percent of the patients and 49.8 percent of the population were in the lower-middle class; and 38.2 percent of the patients and 18.4 percent of the population were in the lower class. Clearly, the lower class contributed a disproportionate number of patients.

Many studies confirm the relationship between socioeconomic status and mental illness. The type of mental disorder prevalent in a stratum varies, but the rate of general mental disorder is higher for the lower strata. In fact, some of the reported differences in rate between age and racial groups may actually reflect socioeconomic differences. A random sample of 1,645 adults in a southeastern county of the

U.S. was studied for prevalence of depression. The researchers defined the depressive symptomatology (which is different from manic-depressive psychosis) in terms of five dimensions: "(1) affective symptoms related to lowered mood; (2) a variety of somatic symptoms; (3) altered patterns of psychobiologic reactivity, such as sleep, appetite, etc.; (4) negative self-evaluation . . .; and (5) an existential dimension typified by pessimism, despair, and a gloomy outlook on the future" (Warheit, Holzer, and Schwab, 1973:293). They found that these symptoms of depression were strongly related to socioeconomic status (as measured by education, occupation, and income). Neither age nor race was related to depression. Females had higher levels of depression than males, but the correlation with socioeconomic status was stronger.

The reasons for the higher rates in the lower strata have not been precisely identified. A reasonable assumption, however, is that they relate to factors we have already discussed: more role problems, a greater degree of family disorganization, more economic stress in the lower strata, and less adequate care. In New Haven, Hollingshead and Redlich (1958) found upper- and upper-middle-class patients were likely to receive psychotherapy, while lower-class patients were likely to be given custodial care. Organic types of therapy such as electro-shock were used more frequently among the lower-strata patients. Similarly, Grey (1969:142) reported that lower-class patients in a Veterans Hospital in the Midwest "are less often given psychotherapy and, when given, it involves fewer contacts and results in less improvement as judged by hospital staff." For mental and physical illness, the lower the socioeconomic status of the ill person, the lower the availability of help.

Changing structure: the future shock thesis.

That social change is inherently traumatic for humans has often been assumed—that both the nature of the structure and the *rate of change of the structure* influence health and illness. When norms, roles, institutional arrangements, and the stratification system are in rapid flux, the individual will endure considerable stress, and stress can result in illness. The individual may be so overwhelmed by the lack of stability in the world that he or she may succumb to *"future shock"* (Toffler, 1970).

One effort to determine the effects of change on illness involves the use of the Social Readjustment Rating Scale. A respondent indicates which of the forty-three events comprising the scale have occurred to him or her within the last year. The events include role changes (death of spouse, divorce or marriage, beginning or stopping work, etc.) and changes in institutional participation (school, church activities, financial status). Each event is scaled in terms of how much adjustment it requires. The most stressful event is death of a spouse, which has a score of 100; the least stressful is a minor violation of the law, which has a score of 11. A person's total score thus reflects the number and kind of events that have occurred in his or her life during the previous year. In one study, 79 percent of those scoring 300 or above, 51 percent of those scoring between 200 and 299, and 37 percent of those scoring between 150 and 199 had changes in their health in the year following the changes in their lives (Holmes and Masuda, 1974:61).

On the other hand, there are a number of cases where change is either welcomed or deliberately initiated by people, and where the stress of rapid change seems to be minimal. While a rapid rate of change does increase stress, the stress may be moderated if the people perceive the changes as desirable (Lauer, 1974; Vinokur and Selzer, 1975). People may function in a context of very rapid change with minimal effects on their physical and mental health so long as they desire the changes that are occurring (and, perhaps, so long as they have some areas of stability in the midst of the change).

Social Psychological Factors

Attitudes and values. Certain attitudes and values of those who are ill, of the public, and of medical personnel affect rates of illness and the nature of health care. Coburn (1975) studied a group of Canadian working men and found that those who defined their work as excessively complex had more problems with physical and mental health. Those who defined their work as excessively simple also had more health problems, though their problems tended to be psychological rather than physical. Thus, negative attitudes toward one's work can increase the risk of illness. This is congruent with the value placed on work in Western society—an individual's worth, including his or her sense of self-worth, is closely tied to work. An individual's work is a focal point of his or her existence as well as one of the most time-consuming areas of life. If that significant, time-consuming area of life is defined in negative terms, the risk of illness is increased.

A particular personality type, identified by way of a cluster of attitudes and values, has an increased probability of coronary heart disease. Men who are ambitious, highly competitive, self-driving, and who impose frequent deadlines on themselves have a higher incidence of coronary heart disease than do men with opposite characteristics (Kagan, 1971:41). All of these characteristics are admired in American society. They are long-standing American values. Unfortunately, when accepted and followed diligently, they are also the precursors of illness.

Once a person is ill, the attitudes of others can have an important effect on the ill person's ability to cope. As mentioned earlier, one of the problems of adjusting to disability is social devaluation—the *negative attitudes* people have toward the disabled. Negative attitudes are particularly disturbing in the case of mental illness. A number of surveys report that people react negatively to the mentally ill. People tend to reject a hypothetical person with symptoms of a mental disorder by expressing unwillingness to interact closely with the person. The degree of rejection varies, depending on background characteristics. Males and people in low socioeconomic strata are likely to be rejected more strongly than are females and those in higher socioeconomic strata (Clausen and Huffine, 1975).

That this negative evaluation can be reflected in the *quality of relationships of a mentally ill person* is suggested by an experiment in which college students were asked to interact with a student partner who, they were told, had a history of mental illness (Farina and Ring, 1965). In a control group, the students had to interact with a partner who had no such history. In both cases, the partners were confederates of the experimenter, and in both cases their behavior was perfectly normal. Nevertheless,

Thomas Scheff — labeling theory

those who thought they were interacting with someone with a history of mental illness rated their partner in more negative terms. They described him as one who hindered more than he helped, as an undesirable partner, as someone difficult to get along with, and as unpredictable. *Labeling* the partner as someone with a history of mental illness made an obvious difference in the reactions and evaluations of the students. While the experiment did not investigate whether the "mentally ill" partner perceived the negative evaluation of the other, we can be sure from other studies that many of the negative attitudes were perceived. When negative attitudes are perceived the relationship is negatively affected; that kind of relationship will not help the mentally ill individual.

People's negative reactions to the mentally ill may be changing, however. A sample of students tested in 1971 did not rate "ex-mental patient" in the same negative terms as did a 1962 sample (Olmsted and Durham, 1976). Whether or not a long-term, positive shift in attitudes toward the mentally ill is occurring remains to be seen. Meanwhile, the mentally ill and ex-mental patients must function in an environment of rejection. As suggested by labeling theory, this may tend to perpetuate the illness.

The most thorough use of labeling theory in the analysis of mental illness was made by Thomas Scheff (1966). According to Scheff, the mentally ill are *rule breakers,* though the rules they break are different from the rules criminals break. The mentally ill break rules that govern normal social interaction, rules that define "common decency" and that indicate an acceptance of social reality as defined by the group. All of us occasionally break such rules with impunity. We may, for example, overreact to an

insult, or refuse to talk to someone who has angered us, or talk too loudly or softly. The person who consistently breaks the rules of conventional interaction will at some point be labeled mentally ill.

Scheff offered a series of propositions that explain mental illness in terms of the labeling theory. First, he noted that rule-breaking may be due to a number of different factors, including psychological or organic causes. Some people break rules because of external stress or because of intentional defiance. Why the rules are broken is not Scheff's concern. His explanation started at the point of the actual violation; he merely noted that the violation can arise from various sources.

Not everyone who breaks the rules is labeled mentally ill. In fact, most rule-breaking is "denied and is of transitory significance" (Scheff, 1966:51). A certain amount of rule-breaking always goes unnoticed or unpunished. The response of others varies in accord with, among other things, the kinds of rules that are broken. Loud speech, for example, is less likely to be negatively sanctioned than the refusal to speak at all.

How do we know when to label someone as mentally ill when there are various kinds of behavior that break rules? Scheff points out that *stereotyped imagery of mental illness* is learned early in life, and that these stereotypes are reinforced in normal interaction. We avoid behavior that is a stereotype of mental illness and thereby reinforce the image of that behavior as a symptom of mental illness. Furthermore, we evaluate others in relation to the stereotype.

If an individual behaves within the stereotypical pattern of mental illness, that individual may be labeled mentally ill and rewarded for

(?)

playing out the stereotyped role. Moreover, the individual may be punished for any attempt to abandon the role and adopt more conventional behavior. This sounds contrary to what we think of as the usual way of treating the mentally ill, namely, working with them to restore them to normalcy as quickly as possible. Scheff argued that a mentally ill person will follow a predictable line of behavior. We have a *predictable social order* with mentally ill people because we know how they will behave even if we do not define their behavior as desirable. When an apparently normal person is suspected of mental illness, or an apparently ill person is suspected of regaining normalcy, the normative order is disrupted—we no longer have a stable order of predictable behavior patterns. Consider, for instance, the suspicion that greets a criminal who avows he is beginning a new, law-abiding life; or the anxiety that greets the physically ill person who seems to be recovering too quickly and doing too much too soon. Norm-breaking always generates a certain amount of anxiety. The aged woman who wears short shorts, the college student who is too well groomed in class, the mentally ill person who decides to find a job and lead a normal life all disturb us and are likely to be negatively sanctioned for their behavior. The aged woman and the college student may be shunned, and the mentally ill individual may be told by his relatives that he is not yet ready for such a step.

In other words, once an individual is labeled in a particular way, the responses of others tend to perpetuate the behavior involved. An individual labeled as mentally ill will be treated in a way deemed appropriate, and that treatment will tend to maintain the individual in the men-

tally ill role. Scheff denied that his is a complete explanation of mental illness. His aim was not to supplant psychiatric approaches, but to supplement them and to stimulate new thinking about mental illness. While it is true that mental illness is a medical and psychiatric problem, it is also true that *therapists are susceptible to suggestions in their diagnoses* and may be influenced by labels. In one study, a number of graduate students in clinical psychology, practicing clinical psychologists, and psychiatrists diagnosed an interview (Temerlin, 1968). Five different conditions were created. One group was given no prior suggestion. Another group was told that the interviewee was mentally healthy. A third group was told that the interview was part of a program to select scientists for industrial research. The fourth group was told that the interview was part of a sanity hearing. To the fifth group the suggestion was made that the interviewee was psychotic. The bulk of those in the first four groups diagnosed the interviewee as mentally healthy. However, in the fifth group only three out of fifty made a diagnosis of mental health. The interviews were essentially the same for all five groups.

Thus, the same individual may be labeled as normal or as emotionally ill by qualified therapists, depending on the circumstances of the diagnosis. The label of mental illness—even by a qualified therapist—is not the result of an objective, infallible, scientific diagnosis alone.

Labeling theory has been criticized. Clausen and Huffine (1975:414) pointed out that presuming someone mentally ill and relating to the person in those terms can have undesirable consequences for the person, but there is no evidence that labeling leads to a stabilization of symptoms. In fact, deciding that an individual is mentally ill and taking that individual to psychiatric help more often leads to a reduction rather than a stabilization of symptoms. The labeling issue is debatable, then. We may tentatively conclude that labeling someone mentally ill will adversely affect the person's relationships and may delay return to normalcy. (Recall the experiment of Rosenhan (1973) in which sane people were kept in mental hospitals despite their normal behavior.)

Attitudes and values can influence medical care. The *distribution of physicians* in the United States reflects economic opportunity rather than medical need. Physicians cluster in those areas where they are likely to maximize their income: "In one medical office building in Chicago's affluent North Side there are more doctors than in the entire West Side ghetto of 300,000 people" (Myers, 1971:28). This pattern has been characteristic for some time (Rimlinger and Steele, 1963), and it implicitly means that many Americans are receiving inadequate medical care. Apparently, physicians' attitudes toward working with the less affluent and the value physicians place on income outweigh their commitment to good medical care for all.

The attitudes and values of physicians have inhibited development of governmental programs that would reduce the maldistribution of medical care. Although most physicians now accept and even support Medicare, the American Medical Association vigorously opposed the program when it was first proposed. At the 1965 convention of the AMA "there were hysterical discussions of Medicare ('we would be zombies stepping into involuntary servitude if we accept such fascist control') and intense debate about

a doctors' strike ('. . . it is ethical, proper, desirable, moral and legal not to participate in such socialistic schemes')" (Langer, 1975:336). Earlier, organized medicine had opposed Blue Cross plans for many of the same reasons. In both cases the resultant financial benefits to physicians have been enormous. The programs have also given more Americans better medical care, although this result has been in spite of, rather than because of, the attitudes and values of physicians.

The ideology of free enterprise. The attitudes and values of physicians just described are legitimated by the *ideology of free enterprise.* The physician believes that he or she is perfectly justified in opposing a plan that will bring better health care to more Americans if that plan appears to be "socialistic." We are a nation committed to the free enterprise system, which emphasizes private efforts and free competition:

> . . . the medical profession has largely maintained the nineteenth-century myth that health is a private entrepreneurial matter between physician and patient—modified only by the physician's philosophical and professional humanism. As late as 1967, a newly elected president of the American Medical Association, Dr. Milford O. Rouse, in his inaugural address, responded to reform pressures by reiterating the official and traditional association position that health care was "a privilege"; and by clear inference continued the stance that it was the physician's prerogative to control those social policy decisions that determine whether that privilege would be extended or withheld [Levin, 1974:3].

The ideology of free enterprise combines with a value of high income and negative attitudes toward the underprivileged to justify a continuing fight against programs that could bring

Figure 5.8 A dance therapy session in a hospital. There is ongoing search for new modes of treatment for mental disorders.

better health care to more Americans. From 1949 to 1951 the AMA waged a multimillion dollar crusade against a national health insurance system proposed by the Truman administration.

> All the stops were pulled out in a naked appeal to emotion. Rational discussion of the issues was evaded, and advantage was taken throughout of the doctor's role as one who deals with frightened people at what may be critical moments of their lives. Physicians' offices, well stocked with literature warning of the horrors of government medicine and proclaiming that "the voluntary way is the American way," became the bulwarks of the crusade [Greenberg, 1965:332].

The crusade was partially successful. The government program was defeated, but the AMA was willing to accept voluntary health insurance (which it had once rejected as socialistic).

Many doctors do not hold the attitudes, values, and ideology we have described. Unfortunately, they are not in the majority nor in positions of power in organized medicine. Consequently, the official stance of organized medicine is intended mainly to inhibit efforts to correct the maldistribution of medical care.

What Is to be Done?

As in the case of drug and alcohol abuse, more money and effort have been expended on treatment of ill health than on prevention. The treatment of mental disorders, however, has been of doubtful value. As we have seen, psychiatry is a field of competing ideologies rather than an exact science. The major approaches to psychiatric care are *organic therapy* (including use of electroshock and drugs); *psychotherapy* (emphasizing the relationship between therapist and patient or patients); *milieu therapy* (emphasizing the role of the total environment of the patient); and *behavior therapy* (conditioning the patient through reward and punishment techniques to learn desired behavior and unlearn behavior not desired. (Behavior therapy is used mainly for neuroses.)

Further research aims at making treatment of physical and mental illnesses more effective.

Maldistribution of care within the existing system is a problem that seems simple to solve, but it demands some *innovative programs*. One innovation that has brought better medical care to previously deprived groups is the neighborhood health center. Poor people, minority groups, and residents of rural areas have benefited from the centers, which have been funded by the federal government. The centers provide places "in which care is financially and physically accessible to all members of the community" and in which the services offered are "attractive and sensitive to the special difficulties the poor have in attaining better health" (Reynolds, 1976:47). The centers have a problem maintaining a stable professional staff and they have to cope with the additional problem of declining federal support.

A second innovation is the Health Maintenance Organization (HMO), which now serves millions of Americans. In essence, the HMO is a comprehensive, prepaid plan of health care. The individual pays an annual fee regardless of the state of his or her health during the year (the individual may use nothing more than a check-up). For the fee the individual receives total medical care, including any hospitalization and surgery that is necessary.

Some Americans advocate a third innovative program to correct the maldistribution of care, national health insurance. The United States is the only modern nation that does not have some kind of federally-financed medical program for the entire population. Proposals range from the AMA's plan for comprehensive but private health insurance to a variety of federally-supported or subsidized plans. Many observers feel that some form of national health insurance is inevitable, although the issue has been debated and little acted on since the 1920s.

Innovations in the treatment of mental disorders are also being developed in an effort to achieve quicker, more effective results. In Denver a system of "*community treatment*" offers an alternative to hospitalization (Polak and Kirby, 1976). The system functions with citizen participation and community control in the form of a board of directors for the Southwest Denver Mental Health Services. Many volunteers are used in the program. They may stay with a severely psychotic patient to provide twenty-four hour supervision. An emphasis on treating the patient in his or her own environment means visitation and treatment at the patient's home in some cases. If a patient has an acute problem that typically would have required hospitalization, he or she may be placed in one of six homes in the community. These are homes of healthy families who agree to take one or two patients at a time and who are trained to provide supervision and support for the patients. The program has other features, including the use of tranquilization, but these features are all designed to emphasize and enhance the notion of community treatment. A comparison of patients who participated in this program with patients who were hospitalized indicates that the community treatment was more effective.

Some innovations aim at *prevention*. Neighborhood or community health centers attempt to provide check-ups for early detection or prevention of physical illness. Similarly, "preventive psychiatry" has emerged as an effort at early detection of mental disorders. Any realistic effort at prevention will have to address the sources of stress in our society. Stress-inducing roles must be changed (the Women's Movement is effecting some changes in the female role). Help must be provided for troubled families. Economic deprivation must be eliminated. Government policy and its agencies must be responsive to health needs rather than to business interests. If we are serious about grappling with the problem of health care and illness, we must be prepared to make some difficult changes in our society.

Finally, increasing numbers of Americans are heeding the call to prevention through diet and exercise. According to the Health Interview Survey, nearly half of all Americans 20 years and older exercise regularly (at least weekly).[15] Many people respond to physicians' advice to reduce our consumption of fats (particularly unsaturated fats), cholesterol, sugar, and salt, and increase our consumption of starches and fresh fruits and vegetables. The health food movement has grown throughout the nation "like an alfalfa sprout" (Keen, 1978). The proportion of adults who smoke cigarettes declined from 1966 to 1980. Obviously, the bulk of Americans highly value good health, and many are willing to follow the advice of those who point the way through diet and exercise.

Summary

Good health is a primary value of Americans. Some advances have been made, as indicated by the increasing life expectancy. The main problem of physical health today is chronic diseases rather than the infectious diseases that plagued society in earlier times. Millions of Americans are limited in their activities because of chronic conditions. Estimating the seriousness of mental illness is difficult because it is hard to define and is often hard to diagnose. There is general agreement, however, about classification and diagnosis of three broad categories of functional disorders—psychoses, neuroses, and psychosomatic disorders—which do not involve brain tissue damage. Mental disorders are found in all societies. In the United States probably 15.6 percent of the population suffer from some kind of mental disorder.

Illness affects the quality of life in many ways. The illness itself and the inadequate care received by many Americans cause stress and suffering. Interpersonal relationships are affected. Individual freedom is threatened by certain medical advances. Often, heavy economic costs are involved for the nation and for individuals. Both physical and mental illnesses cause fears, anxiety, and emotional problems. There is, in fact, a close relationship between physical and mental illness; each can be a factor in bringing about the other, so that the individual can be caught in a vicious circle.

Structural factors contribute to the problem. Certain stress-inducing roles, for instance, have been associated with illness, especially the female role and certain occupational roles. Patterns of interaction and socialization in the family can promote or inhibit good physical and mental health. Our industrial economy exposes us to carcinogenic materials and to various pollutants. Fluctuations in the economy generate stress. Political decisions reflect economic interests rather than health needs.

Health care problems are more serious for those in the lower socioeconomic strata than for those in the higher strata. They suffer higher rates of mental and physical illness and receive less adequate care for both. Also, different kinds of illness characterize the various socioeconomic strata.

One other important structural factor is the rate of change of the structure itself. There is evidence that rapid change can, but does not necessarily, result in illness. A crucial factor in the effects of a changing structure is whether or not the people define the changes as desirable.

Among social psychological factors, attitudes and values have been related to illness. Negative attitudes toward one's work and certain attitudes rooted in traditional American values increase the probability of illness. Once a person is ill, negative attitudes of others can inhibit recovery—a problem stressed by labeling theory. The attitudes and values of physicians contributed to the maldistribution of care and delayed federal programs designed to correct that maldistribution. These attitudes and values are supported by the ideology of free enterprise, which stresses governmental noninterference in medical care.

iatrogenic factors

Glossary

carcinogenic   causing cancer

epidemiology   study of the factors that affect the incidence, prevalence, and distribution of illnesses

etiology   causes of a disease

incidence   the number of new cases of an illness that occur during a particular period of time

manic-depressive reaction   a disorder involving fluctuation between emotional extremes

morbidity   the prevalence of a specified illness in a specified area

neurosis   a disorder that involves anxiety which is sufficiently intense to impair the individual's functioning in some way

pica   a craving for unnatural substances

prevalence   the number of cases of an illness that exists at any particular time

psychosis   a disorder in which the individual fails to distinguish between internal and external stimuli

psychosomatic disorder   an impairment in physiological functioning that results from the individual's emotional state

schizophrenia   a psychosis that involves a thinking disorder, particularly hallucinations and fantasies

socialization   the process by which an individual learns to participate in a group

For Further Reading

Bergen, Bernard J., and Caudewell S. Thomas, eds. *Issues and Problems in Social Psychiatry*. Springfield, Ill.: Charles C Thomas, 1966. Contains various writings that relate sociocultural factors to mental disorders, including the impact of social change on mental health.

Berlant, Jeffery Lionel. *Profession and Monopoly: A Study of Medicine in the United States and Great Britain*. Berkeley: University of California Press, 1975. A comparison of two rather different medical systems, focusing on the ways physicians attempt to monopolize control of medical care.

Frank, Jerome D. *Persuasion and Healing: A Comparative Study of Psychology*, rev. ed. New York: Schocken Books, 1974. A psychiatrist examines healing methods in primitive societies, in religion, in Communist groups, and in various kinds of psychotherapy.

Goffman, Erving. *Asylums: Essays on the Social Situation of Mental Patients and Other Inmates*. Garden City: Doubleday, Anchor Books 1961. A participant-observer study of life in a mental hospital, including how hospitalization affects the patient's relationships and the place of the staff in institutional processes.

Greenberg, Selig. *The Troubled Calling*. New York: Macmillan, 1965. A somewhat dated but very readable work on problems in the medical profession and in health care throughout the country.

Illich, Ivan. *Medical Nemesis: The Expropriation of Health*. New York: Pantheon, 1976. A stinging indictment of the medical profession today, which, the author maintains, is now more a hindrance than a help to our health.

Mintz, Morton. *The Therapeutic Nightmare*. Boston: Houghton Mifflin Co., 1965. An account of the drug industry, criticizing its policies and practices and showing the conflict between financial interests and health needs.

Van Den Berg, Jan Hendrick. *Medical Power and Medical Ethics*. New York: W. W. Norton, 1978. A provocative discussion of the contradictions and dilemmas created at the intersection of modern medical technology with the physician's calling and the patient's interests.

Notes

1. Figures from U.S. Bureau of the Census, *Statistical Abstract of the United States, 1980* (Washington, D.C.: Government Printing Office, 1981) pp. 123, 127.

2. Reported in the *St. Louis Post-Dispatch,* August 1, 1976.

3. Reported in *Human Behavior,* November/December, 1972, pp. 36–37.

4. Ibid., p. 36.

5. *Time,* July 26, 1976, p. 79.

6. Reported in the *Saturday Review,* March 20, 1976, p. 4.

7. *Time,* November 27, 1978, p. 52.

8. Figures from U.S. Bureau of the Census, *Statistical Abstract of the United States, 1980* (Washington, D.C.: Government Printing Office, 1981), p. 111.

9. *Social Security Bulletin,* 39 (May 1976), p. 64.

10. *Time,* December 20, 1971, p. 57.

11. Reported in the booklet, *The Size and Shape of the Medical Care Dollar,* DHEW Publication No. (SSA) 76–11910, 1975, p. 6.

12. Various studies on noise pollution are summarized in National Institute of Mental Health, *Pollution: Its Impact on Mental Health* (Rockville, Md.: National Institute of Mental Health, 1972), pp. 7ff.

13. See, e.g., "Are Americans Being Zapped?" *Time,* August 28, 1978; and Susan Schiefelbein, "The Invisible Threat," *Saturday Review,* September 15, 1979; and "Electricity in Your Body," *Science Digest,* Summer 1980.

14. Reported in *Vital and Health Statistics,* Series 10 (9), May 1964.

15. U.S. Bureau of the Census, *Statistical Abstract of the United States, 1980* (Washington, D.C.: Government Printing Office, 1981), p. 125.

Crime and Delinquency

1 **Who are the criminals in our society?**

2 **How much crime is in America?**

3 **Is crime necessary?**

4 **How do respectable citizens contribute to the crime problem?**

5 **Is a "get tough" policy the answer to crime?**

From time to time, Americans are told they face a crisis due to rampaging crime. In 1971 a New York lawyer whose brother was murdered wrote:

> A man is killed in broad daylight in his street-floor office on a main roadway in the city. . . . Murder has become commonplace. . . . Our No. 1 . . . problem in the city is crime in the streets. Our homes have become fortresses, our defenses pickproof locks, barred windows and burglar-alarm systems.[1]

The man expressed a feeling that became widespread during the 1960s—America was a land besieged by a serious and growing crime problem. Richard Nixon made a campaign issue out of the need for "law and order" in 1968. FBI statistics on the rising crime rate were frightening. By 1978 the FBI reported a serious crime in the nation every three seconds and a violent crime every thirty seconds (figure 6.1). A 1975 Gallup poll reported that when people in the largest cities of the nation were asked to identify the biggest problem in their communities they named crime. Crime was mentioned almost twice as often as the next most frequently mentioned problem, unemployment. This survey is in striking contrast to a similar one of 1949, when poor housing, transportation, unsanitary conditions, taxes, and corrupt politics were all named more frequently than was crime.

Another perspective on crime, one different from the concern with murder, robbery, and theft, is provided by a noted historian, Herbert Butterfield. He wrote that a society can be destroyed by crimes of another kind:

> A civilization may be wrecked without any spectacular crimes or criminals but by constant petty breaches of faith and minor complicities on the part of men generally considered very nice people [Butterfield, 1949:54].

Figure 6.1   The FBI "Crime Clocks" dramatize the extensiveness of crime in the United States. (Source: U.S. Federal Bureau of Investigation, *Crime in the United States, 1978 Uniform Crime Reports* [Washington, D.C.: Government Printing Office, 1979].)

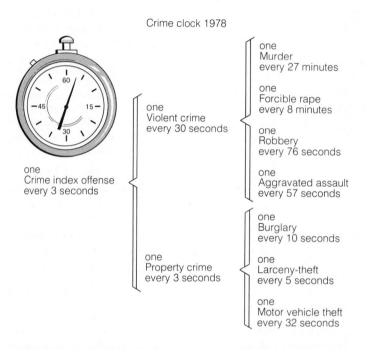

Crime clock 1978

one
Crime index offense
every 3 seconds

one
Violent crime
every 30 seconds

one
Property crime
every 3 seconds

one
Murder
every 27 minutes

one
Forcible rape
every 8 minutes

one
Robbery
every 76 seconds

one
Aggravated assault
every 57 seconds

one
Burglary
every 10 seconds

one
Larceny-theft
every 5 seconds

one
Motor vehicle theft
every 32 seconds

These two contrasting points of view form the theme of this chapter—that crime is a social problem that pervades our society, and it includes both respectable and nonrespectable citizens. As we will see, the problem of race cannot be understood without reference to both whites and nonwhites; the problem of poverty cannot be understood without reference to the nonpoor; and the problem of crime cannot be understood without looking at *"respectable" citizens.* They not only commit crime themselves, but they participate directly and indirectly in the crimes of others as well.

First we will look at the varieties of crime and define crime and delinquency. We will then examine the extent of crime in the United States. We will see how crime and delinquency affect the quality of life, what kinds of sociocultural factors contribute to the problem, and what measures can be taken and have been taken to resolve the problem.

The Varieties of Crime

Technically, crime is any *violation of the criminal law.* That this definition is inadequate will become apparent when we examine "white-collar" crime. Nevertheless, in beginning with this definition, we will speak of crime as those acts that are defined as threatening to the state or to citizens whom the state is obligated to protect. These are the kinds of acts embodied in the criminal law.

What the criminal law defines as crime and delinquency varies over time, but Glaser (1969) argued that we can put virtually all criminal acts into four broad categories; (1) predatory crimes; (2) illegal service crimes; (3) public disorder crimes; and (4) crimes of negligence. We will briefly examine each of these types and then discuss white-collar crime and delinquency.

Predatory Crime

What we generally think of when the word "crime" is mentioned are **predatory crimes**— *acts that have victims who suffer loss of property or some kind of physical harm.* Property crimes are more common, but the public generally defines crimes against persons as more serious. Less than 10 percent of all crime involves acts such as murder or rape, but those violent acts are the ones that arouse the greatest public apprehension.

The most commonly used measure of *crime rates*—the *Federal Bureau of Investigation Crime Index*—covers seven major felonies, all serious violations of the criminal law, and all predatory crimes. (1) *Murder and nonnegligent manslaughter* are willful killing of a person.[2] Not included are deaths by negligence, suicide, accident, or justifiable homicide. (2) *Aggravated assault,* "an unlawful attack by one person upon another for the purpose of inflicting severe bodily injury," usually involves a weapon. (3) *Forcible rape* is defined as actual or attempted sexual intercourse "through the use of force or the threat of force." (4) *Robbery* is the use of force or threat of force to take something

of value from a person. (5) *Burglary*—by definition the "unlawful entry of a structure to commit a felony or theft"—does not necessarily mean force was used to gain entry. (6) *Larceny-theft* is the "unlawful taking or stealing of property or articles without the use of force, violence, or fraud," includes shoplifting, picking pockets, purse-snatching, and the like. The last crime in the FBI Index is (7) *auto theft.*

Because not all predatory crimes are included in the FBI Index, the Index cannot be used as an indication of the total amount of crime in the society. Fraud, for example, is not counted. The omission of fraud is interesting because some of the ingenious crimes of recent times involved fraud through use of computers. Some of the possibilities for computer crime were outlined by Graham (1976:173):

> More and more banks are keeping their accounts on computer files. Someone who knows how to change the numbers in the files can transfer funds at will. . . . A company that uses the computer heavily in all areas of its operations offers many opportunities to the dishonest employee or even the clever outsider. The thief can have the computer ship the company's products to addresses of his own choosing, for instance. Or he can have it send checks to him or his confederates in payment for nonexistent supplies. . . . Much personal information about individuals is now stored in computer files. An unauthorized person who could get to this information could use it for extortion or political blackmail. Also, confidential information about a company's operations or products could be stolen and sold to an unscrupulous competitor.

Some of these possibilities have already become realities. A young man posed as a magazine reporter, toured a telephone company's computer installation, secured as much information as he could, and put a number of discarded punch cards in his pocket. Later he was able to key into the telephone company's inventory-and-supply computer and he began selling a lot of its equipment.[3]

In the first half of 1974 at least $27 million was lost to companies through computer crime, and at least two cases involved the Mafia. A California computer programmer who piled up large gambling debts was forced to provide information to Mafia members and to cooperate with them in theft. In another case the FBI discovered that an important bookmaker in the Midwest was using unauthorized computer time at a local university to calculate his handicaps.[4] Thus, predatory crimes do not necessarily involve face-to-face confrontation with an individual who is determined to take what he or she wants by force. In the computer age, predatory crimes may take on a whole new face and require law enforcement officials to learn a sophisticated new set of techniques.

Illegal Service Crimes

Illegal service crimes do not involve a definite victim but rather "a *relationship between a criminal and his customer*" (Glaser, 1969: 407). The illegal service rendered might be drugs, gambling, prostitution, or high-interest loans. While these relationships violate the law, they are not likely to be reported because the criminal and the customer probably prefer to have the service available.

Public Disorder Crimes

Public disorder crimes also have no definite victim. They are behavior that is *treated as crim-inal only when it occurs before some audience that will be offended*. These crimes include behavior such as disorderly conduct, drunkenness, and indecent exposure. Public disorder crimes are more common than predatory or illegal service crimes, according to arrest figures.

Crimes of Negligence

Crimes of negligence involve an *unintended victim or potential victim*. They include things such as reckless driving and other infractions of the law by automobile drivers. The "criminal" in this case is not deemed to be deliberately trying to harm anyone. Rather, the behavior is a threat or a nuisance from which the public should be protected. Negligence crimes and public disorder crimes comprise the bulk of police work in our nation.

White-Collar Crime

Glaser treats **white-collar crime** as a form of predatory crime, but we will consider it separately. It is the crime of "respectable" people. The term was coined by Edwin Sutherland (Sutherland and Cressy, 1955), who said that white-collar crimes are *committed by respectable people in the course of their work*. However, white-collar crime may not be prosecuted or even defined as criminal because of the problem of obtaining sufficient evidence if the offender is a corporation. Corporations have been known to violate laws relating to restraint of trade. They have engaged in false advertising. They have infringed on patents, trademarks, and copyrights. They have developed systems of rebates in order to maximize their share of

Figure 6.2 White-collar crime touches all levels of the society. Armand Hammer, multimillionaire chairman of Occidental Petroleum Corp., on his way to court in Los Angeles to plead guilty from a wheelchair to charges of illegal campaign contributions, March 4, 1976. He was fined $3,000 and placed on a year's probation.

a market. Individual white-collar crime may not be prosecuted, or even defined as crime because of the offender's high status. A particularly common fraud committed by high-status individuals is to underreport income and other financial assets for tax purposes. White-collar crime also involves police who break the law, including the law pertaining to arrest.

Some of the practices of respectable people are not defined as crimes by the law, but they should be treated as crimes, Sutherland argued. He asserted that businessmen were more criminalistic than people of the ghettoes. A major difference is that criminal law distinguishes between the two groups, so that some acts that logically could be defined as crime are not in the criminal law. Furthermore, some acts involving businesses and corporations are handled by governmental commissions rather than the criminal justice system. We can reasonably argue that when a company advertises a 6 percent interest rate on installment payments and actually collects 11.5 percent, it is committing fraud. The executives of the company will not be charged with fraud; the company will merely be ordered by the Federal Trade Commission to stop advertising the false rate.

A few examples illustrate the diverse acts included in white-collar crime, and also will suggest how pervasive that crime is in America. One example comes from a speech by the Commissioner of Internal Revenue, who told how businesses circumvent the law to avoid taxes and to conceal political contributions.[5] He cited incidents where a manufacturer made payoffs to buyers of his products and then charged the payoffs to the sales, returns, and allowances account. Another manufacturing company billed customers for an amount less than the cost of the products, then made further billings for various engineering and management "expenses." This enabled the company to steal several million dollars in excise taxes because the company paid taxes only on the original amount billed, not on the actual price. The Commissioner also pointed out various ways of making illegal contributions to political campaigns by payments to advertising firms, public relations firms, and fictitious trade associations. Such payments enabled companies to make the political contributions and, at the same time, charge them off as business expenses and deduct them from their taxable income.

Many cases of white-collar crime involve both business and government people, as our second example illustrates. In 1977 the Chicago *Sun-Times* allowed some of its reporters to set up a tavern in order to investigate numerous complaints about corruption. During the time they operated the tavern the reporters had the following experiences: payoffs to city inspectors who then ignored certain health and safety hazards; shakedowns by state liquor inspectors who then ignored liquor violations; tax fraud by accountants who regularly worked with tavern owners to cheat on state and federal taxes; demands by public employees for under-the-table cash for services that should have been rendered for free by the city; and various illegal maneuvers from jukebox and pinball machine operators.[6]

Finally, there is the example of *police crime,* which Sutherland (1939) argued was widespread. An analysis of materials written about police corruption over a twelve-year period was made by Roebuck and Barker (1974), who categorized the corruption into eight areas.

(1) *Corruption of authority* occurs when an officer receives material gain because of his position—free meals, liquor, sex, discounts, and the like. These gifts are not illegal but they are corrupting. (2) Officers receive *kickbacks* of money or other rewards for referring customers to towing companies, ambulances, undertakers, moving companies, and other businesses. (3) *Opportunistic theft* is stealing from helpless victims of other crimes or from stores where the officer is investigating a burglary. (4) *Shakedowns* occur when an officer accepts a bribe for not arresting an offender in a criminal act. (5) *Protection of illegal activities*—such as gambling, prostitution, and liquor violations—is particularly common where "victimless" crimes are involved; activities may be both known to and protected by police. (6) The *fix* occurs when an officer is rewarded either for withdrawing prosecution after an arrest has been made or for "taking care of" a traffic ticket. (7) *Direct criminal activities* include the kind of crime that the police are supposed to stop—burglary and robbery, for example. (8) *Internal payoffs* involve only police officers, specifically those who make assignments, control promotions, or handle other valued things may collect fees from their fellow officers in exchange for preferential treatment.

In a widely publicized case of police corruption in New York City in 1971, a man who had been an officer for fourteen years told an investigating commission that he and other officers "had taken graft as casually as they had handed out parking tickets":

In order to avoid receiving summonses for petty violations, foremen on construction sites pay $5 to $10 per cop per week. When the city marshal evicts tenants, he ordinarily treats the patrolman who assists him to a few bucks. The cop who makes the day's assignments in the station house may get $5 a day from a patrolman looking for profitable work. This is the petty graft that is taken for granted. . . . A cop who is greedy enough can go on to the big money to be made from gambling, prostitution and narcotics. . . . A plainclothesman can make from $400 to $1,500 a month for protecting the rackets.[7]

Other white-collar crimes involve embezzlement, real estate swindles, false advertising, fraudulent repairs by various kinds of servicemen, deception of consumers, investment swindles, unnecessary surgery, and a host of other practices that have been inflicted on the American public. The problem of crime is not just a problem of the person with a gun. The problem of crime involves respectable and nonrespectable citizens, and sometimes even those who supposedly are the guardians of law and order in the nation (as in the Watergate scandal of the Nixon administration).

Juvenile Delinquency

The concept of juvenile delinquency is a modern one. Until the late nineteenth century juvenile offenders were defined as incapable of certain crimes or were treated as adults in the criminal justice system. A child under 7 years of age was considered incapable of acting with criminal intent. A child over 7 who gave no evidence of immaturity could be treated as an adult criminal. This concept began to change in the nineteenth century when a group of reformers set out to redeem the nation's wayward youth (Platt, 1969). These "child savers" helped to establish the juvenile court system in the United States, with the result that juveniles were treated differently from adults, and certain behavior that was once ignored or handled in an informal way came under the jurisdiction of a government agency. Thus, the *concept of delinquency was "invented"* in America in the nineteenth century.

The nation's first *juvenile court* was established in 1899 in Illinois. All states now have a juvenile court system. The court's primary responsibility is to protect the welfare of youth, and its secondary task is to safeguard the community from the youthful offender. This orientation has given judges in such courts considerable discretion. Judges make whatever decision is necessary for the juvenile's protection and rehabilitation.

Three types of juveniles come under the court's jurisdiction (a juvenile is typically defined as someone from the age of 7 through the age of 17). *Youthful offenders* are those who engage in behavior that adults can be tried for in a criminal court. All predatory crimes are included here. *Status offenders* are those who violate the juvenile court code rather than the criminal code. Behavior such as truancy, running away from home, and breaking the curfew is included here. Finally, the court deals with *minors in need of care*—those who are neglected or abused and in need of the court's care. These juveniles do not fall into the category of delinquent, but they are the responsibility of the juvenile court.

The range of behavior defined as delinquent tends to be broad. According to The President's Commission [on Law Enforcement and Administration of Justice] (1967a:55), self-report studies indicate that as many as 90 percent of all young people have engaged in behavior that would fall under the jurisdiction of a juvenile court. Much of this behavior is trivial, including things such as fighting, truancy, and running away from home. In some states, statutes define delinquency so broadly that virtually all juveniles could be categorized as delinquent. Delinquency, then, includes a much greater range of behavior than does crime.

The Extent of Crime and Delinquency

How widespread are crime and delinquency? The question is difficult to answer because of certain problems with official statistics. We will look at ways to gather data, at the problems with official records, and then see what conclusions we can draw about the extent of crime and delinquency.

Sources of Data

The three basic sources of data on crime are *official records, victimization studies,* and *self-reports.* A frequently used official record is the *Uniform Crime Reports* published annually by the FBI. As noted previously, the *Reports* and Crime Index include only seven major felonies. A great deal of crime—indeed, most crime— does not appear in this annual report. Other official sources include municipal police records and the records of juvenile courts. The latter enable us to estimate the number of delinquency cases processed annually, but there is no uniform system of reporting among juvenile courts.

Victimization studies represent a new approach to the gathering of crime data because they attempt to secure those data from the victims of crime rather than from officials or of-

ficial records. A victimization study usually involves interviews at a representative sample of homes. People in those homes are asked whether they or members of their families have been the victims of a crime or crimes during the previous year.

Self-reports are usually used with youth. The youth are asked whether or not they engaged in any of a number of different kinds of criminal activity. Various techniques are used to try to insure honesty and accuracy, and there is some evidence that self-reported crime by young people is fairly accurate.

Problems with Official Records

If we attempt to estimate the crime rate from official records, we encounter a number of problems. Since official records are the most frequently used measure, it is important to recognize those problems. First, quite a number of crimes are *undetected.* In a survey of American adults, 26 percent of the males reported that they had committed automobile theft, 17 percent had committed burglary, 13 percent had committed grand larceny, and 11 percent had committed robbery. In all, 64 percent of the men and 29 percent of the women said that they had committed at least one felony, but none of them had been convicted as a criminal (Wallerstein and Wyle, 1947).

Second, many crimes are *unreported.* In a study of 2,077 cases of victims of crimes, Ennis (1967) noted that only 49 percent notified the police, and 23 percent of those reported that the police never came after being notified. Of the 1,024 cases in which the police came, 25 percent were defined as noncriminal. Ultimately, only

Figure 6.3 Teenage gang members. Crime and delinquency among the young range from trivial offenses to the heavily armed gangs that threaten people in city streets and schools.

fifty people in the 2,077 cases came to trial. Victimization studies consistently show a much higher rate of crime than that indicated by official records. Table 6.1 compares the results of a victimization study by the National Opinion Research Center with official rates of the FBI. Almost four times as many rapes, one and a

half times as many robberies, over twice as many cases of aggravated assault, over three times as many burglaries, and over twice as many larcenies were reported by people than by the FBI statistics. These discrepancies suggest that many victims of crimes never report them to the police. A 1975 Gallup poll supported this conclusion. It showed the percentages of victims of the following crimes who actually reported those crimes: assaults and muggings, 50 percent; vandalization of property, 70 percent; money or property stolen, 64 percent; and home break-in or attempted break-in, 63 percent.[8] Official figures, therefore, underreport nearly every kind of crime.

A third problem with official records is that *definitions of crime change* and the *methods of reporting crime change*. Because a crime is a violation of the criminal law, any change in the law results in changes in the amount of crime. In the early 1930s a considerable number of inmates in federal prisons were there for crimes that would not have been crimes a few years earlier. They were serving time for violating laws related to the Eighteenth Amendment to the Constitution, which brought in Prohibition. Changes in the method of reporting crime can result in an apparent crime wave. As Daniel Bell (1960:138–39) pointed out, some crime waves may really be "crime reporting" waves. For example, some years ago the FBI discovered that police were reporting only about half the number of property crimes that insurance companies were reporting. A new system was implemented, and during the next year there was an enormous increase in the police-reported rate of assaults, robberies, and burglaries. The rates reflected the new reporting methods but not necessarily any increase in the actual rate of crime. Similarly, when the classification rules for aggravated assault were revised in the District of Columbia, the number of cases declined from 4,550 in 1955 to 2,824 in 1956 (The President's Commission, 1967b:24). The change reflected the new classification rules rather than any decline in the crime.

Table 6.1.   Crime Rates: NORC Survey vs. FBI Index
(per 100,000 inhabitants)

Crime	NORC Survey 1965–1966	FBI Rate for Individuals 1965
Willful homicide	3.0	5.1
Forcible rape	42.5	11.6
Robbery	94.0	61.4
Aggravated assault	218.3	106.6
Total violence	357.8	184.7
Burglary	949.1	299.6
Larceny ($50 and over)	606.5	267.4
Motor vehicle theft	206.2	226.0
Total property	1,761.8	793.0

Source: Adapted from The President's Commission on Law Enforcement and Administration of Justice. *The Challenge of Crime in a Free Society* (Washington, D.C.: Government Printing Office, 1967).

The idea behind the Uniform Crime Reports of the FBI is to standardize the definitions of the various felonies so that meaningful comparisons can be made. However, the standardized procedures have not always been followed. For instance, in the FBI Index, "burglary" does not include things such as theft from phone booths. Yet, the President's Commission (1967b:24) reported:

One of the Nation's largest police jurisdictions with one of the most capable police statistical sections has nevertheless regularly reported phone booth thefts in all recent years as burglaries, including more than 900 in 1965.

A fourth problem with official records involves *police procedures*. As mentioned earlier,

Ennis found that one-fourth of the cases investigated by police were not defined by them as crimes. In a study of police procedures in three cities, Black (1970) found that the following factors influenced the decision of police to *define an incident as a crime:* the seriousness of the offense; the extent to which the complainant wanted police action; the "relational distance" between the suspect and the complainant (whether they are family, friends, or strangers); and the complainant's attitude toward the police. In other words, whether or not some behavior is defined officially by the police as criminal depends on factors other than the behavior itself. The President's Commission noted additional factors that influenced crime reporting. It pointed out that police procedures may be affected by things such as political pressure or the desire of the police themselves to make crime rates appear lower than they actually are. This, in turn, is expected to make an area more attractive to business and to residents (The President's Commission, 1967b:24).

A final problem with official records relates to *changing expectations* in our society:

> Not long ago there was a tendency to dismiss reports of all but the most serious offenses in slum areas and segregated minority group districts. The poor and the segregated minority groups were left to take care of their own problems . . . whatever the past pattern was, these areas now have a strong feeling of need for adequate police protection. Crimes that were once unknown to the police, or ignored when complaints were received, are now much more likely to be reported and recorded as part of the regular statistical procedure [The President's Commission, 1967b:22].

Thus, although a great many crimes are never reported, there is evidence that more are being reported now than in the past, which makes the rate of crime appear to be increasing.

These qualifications to the reliability of official records suggest that the amount of crime in the nation is considerably greater than official records indicate. They also suggest that we must be cautious about comparing rates across time and drawing a quick conclusion that a "crime wave" is in process. However, when official records are used in conjunction with victimization studies and other evidence, the increase in seriousness of the crime problem is indisputable.

The Amount of Crime and Delinquency

What do the data tell us about the amount of crime and delinquency in America? In 1967 the President's Commission on Law Enforcement and Administration of Justice published the results of the most extensive study of crime ever conducted by the federal government. Its conclusions were disturbing. For one, the report noted that most Americans think the criminal element represents a relatively small proportion of the population. However, "about 40 percent of all male children now living in the United States will be arrested for a nontraffic offense during their lives" (The President's Commission, 1967a:v).

Not only is the number of criminals large and the absolute number of crimes increasing, but the rate of crime is increasing also. The report traced the increase in crime from 1933 to 1965 and pointed out that the rates of virtually all crimes on the FBI Index have been increasing since the end of World War II, and the rates of increase were greater between 1960

Table 6.2   Crimes and Crime Rates by Type, 1960–1979

Item and Year	Total	Violent Crime					Property Crime			Motor Vehicle Theft
		Total	Murder*	Forcible Rape	Robbery	Aggravated Assault	Total	Burglary	Larceny/ Theft	
Number of offenses										
1960 . . . 1,000	3,384	288	9.1	17.2	108	154	3,096	912	1,855	328
1965 . . . 1,000	4,739	387	10.0	23.4	139	215	4,352	1,283	2,573	497
1968 . . . 1,000	6,720	595	13.8	31.7	263	287	6,125	1,859	3,483	784
1970 . . . 1,000	8,098	739	16.0	38.0	350	335	7,359	2,205	4,226	928
1973 . . . 1,000	8,718	876	19.6	51.4	384	421	7,842	2,566	4,348	929
1975 . . . 1,000	11,257	1,026	20.5	56.1	465	485	10,230	3,252	5,978	1,001
1979 . . . 1,000	12,153	1,179	21.5	76.0	467	614	10,974	3,299	6,578	1,097
Rate per 100,000 inhabitants										
1960	1,887	161	5.1	9.6	60	86	1,726	509	1,035	183
1965	2,449	200	5.1	12.1	72	111	2,249	663	1,329	257
1968	3,370	298	6.9	15.9	132	144	3,072	932	1,747	393
1970	3,985	364	7.9	18.7	172	165	3,621	1,085	2,079	457
1973	4,154	417	9.4	24.5	183	201	3,737	1,223	2,072	443
1975	5,282	482	9.6	26.3	218	227	4,800	1,526	2,805	469
1979	5,521	535	9.7	34.5	212	279	4,986	1,499	2,988	498

*Includes nonnegligent manslaughter.

Source: U.S. Bureau of the Census, *Statistical Abstract of the United States, 1976* (Washington, D.C.: Government Printing Office, 1977), p. 153; and *1980* (Washington, D.C.: Government Printing Office, 1981), p. 182.

and 1965 than between 1940 and 1960. In other words, the increases themselves increased. More crimes were committed per 100,000 people, and the crime rates were increasing at an accelerating rate.

More recent data underscore the *rapid increase in rate of reported crime.* Table 6.2 shows both the absolute numbers and the rates of the seven crimes on the FBI Index from 1960 to 1979. In general, both numbers and rates have continually increased, with violent crimes having increased more rapidly than crimes against property. Some numbers and rates decreased from 1976 to 1977, leading to speculation that the tide turned against rising crime. But, both the rates and the numbers increased again from 1977 to 1979. From 1978 to 1979, the rate of violent crime increased 10 percent and the rate of property crime increased 7.9 percent. Despite the problems with official records described previously, there is agreement that these data represent real increases in the numbers and rates of crime.

Table 6.3   Victimization Rates, Personal and Household Crimes, 1978
(per 1,000 population age 12 and over)

Sector and Type of Crime	Rate	Number
Personal sector		
Crimes of violence	33.7	5,941,000
Rape	1.0	171,000
Robbery	5.9	1,038,000
Assault	26.9	4,732,000
Aggravated assault	9.7	1,708,000
Simple assault	17.2	3,024,000
Crimes of theft	96.8	17,050,000
Personal larceny with contact	3.1	549,000
Personal larceny without contact	93.6	16,501,000
Household sector		
Household burglary	86.0	6,704,000
Household larceny	119.9	9,351,900
Motor vehicle theft	17.5	1,365,100

Source: National Criminal Justice Information and Statistics Service, *Criminal Victimization in the United States: Summary Findings of 1977–78 Changes in Crime and of Trends Since 1973* (Washington, D.C.: Government Printing Office, 1979).

Victimization studies provide additional evidence of the extensiveness of crime in the United States. Table 6.3 shows the victimization rate for various crimes in 1978. The figures represent increased rates (since 1973) of rape, assault, crimes of theft, and household larceny, and decreased rates of robbery, household burglary, and motor vehicle theft. The data in table 6.3 are rates per 1,000 (compared to rates per 100,000 in table 6.2) of people age 12 and over (compared to the total population in table 6.2).

To compare the two sets of data, the figures in table 6.3 must be multiplied by 100, and then decreased by roughly 20 percent. In our comparison, we find that the victimization studies show far more crime than the FBI Index. For instance, in 1978 the rate of aggravated assault was 256 per 100,000 in the FBI report, and about 776 per 100,000 in the victimization study!

Gallup polls on victimization rates have also been taken. A 1979 poll reported that one of every five American households were victimized in the twelve months prior to the poll. Clearly, crime touches the lives of millions of Americans in a very direct way.

Getting information about white-collar crime is difficult, but scattered evidence suggests that such crime is widespread (The President's Commission, 1967b:103). Congressional investigations have uncovered a good deal of *unethical and illegal behavior in business and industry.* Popular magazines carry stories of such behavior in the professions as well as in small businesses and large corporations. Occasionally, experiments are conducted to see how honest repairmen are. The staff of a national magazine disconnected an automobile coil wire, then took the car to 347 garages in forty-eight states. Some immediately diagnosed the problem and corrected it for little or no charge, but 63 percent of the garages "overcharged, inserted unnecessary parts, charged for work not done or for parts not needed, or took other similar action" (The President's Commission, 1967b:103). The evidence is not systematic, but it points to pervasive white-collar crime in the nation.

Finally, there is a huge amount of delinquency in the nation, although we must keep in mind that delinquency by definition includes some relatively trivial kinds of behavior. An estimated one of every six male youths will be referred to a juvenile court because of some delinquent act (not including traffic offenses) before he is 18 years old (The President's Commission, 1967a:55). Data from juvenile courts show that nearly 1.36 million cases of delinquency were processed in 1978, representing 4.6 percent of the population in the 10-to-17 age group.[9] Of all arrests of males in 1979, 39 percent of those for the seven felonies were under 18 years of age.[10] As the commission report said, "America's best hope for reducing crime is to reduce juvenile delinquency and youth crime" (The President's Commission, 1967a:55).

The Distribution of Crime

Crime is unequally distributed in the United States. There are certain regional variations. For example, in 1979 the murder rate for the entire nation was 9.7 per 100,000 inhabitants; yet, the rate by states varied from 1.4 in Vermont to 17.5 in Nevada. Metropolitan areas generally have higher rates of crime than other areas. The rates for metropolitan areas varied from 4.0 in cities with less than 10,000 population to 23.1 in cities with populations of 250,000 or more.[11]

Other crimes show similar variations, both in official records and in victimization studies. In general, the probability of being a victim of a crime is lower in small cities than in large ones, and lower in rural areas than urban areas. A radio broadcast in the fall of 1974 reported that some mathematicians calculated that a male baby born in an American city had a better chance of being murdered than an American soldier in World War II had of being killed.

One's chances of being a victim depend upon the type of crime involved. Murder rates are generally highest in the South, rates of auto theft are highest in the Northeast, and forcible rape rates are highest in the West. An individual is not necessarily safer in the West than in the East, or in Cleveland than in New York City, or in a rural area than in a small city. It depends on what one is safe *from*. Your likelihood of being a victim of a crime depends on the kind of crime, where you live, your sex and race and age, and your education and income.

The data we have presented indicate that, in general, your chances of being a victim are fairly high and they seem to be getting higher each year.

Crime, Delinquency, and the Quality of Life

Widespread crime contradicts our values of freedom from fear, of well-being, and of the right to keep one's personal property. Crime, by definition, often involves exploitive or violent relationships and thereby *contradicts both our values and our ideology* about our nation being a land of opportunity for all. The "land of opportunity" notion loses a lot of its appeal for people who gain some measure of success in it but live in fear that their very success will victimize them by attracting criminal activity; that what they have gained can easily be taken away by someone with a weapon.

For the criminals, according to Merton's anomie theory, the opportunities of this land are

Figure 6.4 A victim of a holdup. This sixty-year-old man was permanently blinded by a gunshot from a teenage thief.

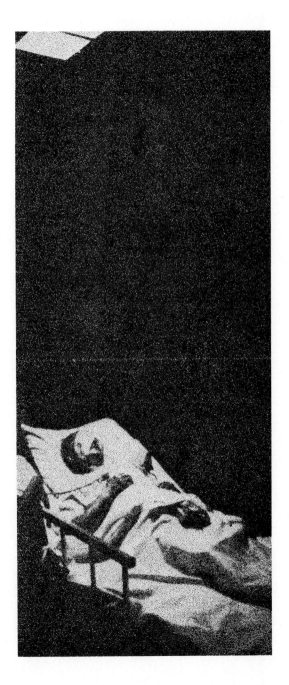

more myth than reality. There is a contradiction between the "land of opportunity" ideology and actual institutional arrangements, and they are blocked from legitimately sharing in the benefits of our society. They therefore use an illegitimate route, crime, to get their share. In brief, crime is an effect of anomie.

In any event, crime diminishes the quality of life for everyone by exacting high physical, psychological, and economic costs.

Physical and Psychological Costs of Crime

Crime causes physical or psychological suffering, or both. The physical and psychological costs of such suffering are difficult to assess, but there is evidence that they are considerable. To get some idea of the physical and psychological costs, we will examine the relationship of crime to physical and emotional health, to fear, and to alienation and anomie.

Physical and mental health. The victim of a crime experiences some **trauma.** The victim may be permanently injured in some way (either physically or emotionally) or even killed. Or, the victim may suffer from mild emotional trauma such as anxiety or depression. People who are robbed, assaulted, raped, or swindled can never measure the cost merely in financial or physical terms; there is psychological damage also—the *emotional trauma* of shame or humiliation or despair.

In the next chapter we will discuss a study of the emotional crises of rape victims. Similar studies of other crimes identify various kinds of emotional trauma among victims. Unfortunately, the victim has been relatively neglected as a focus of study, so we must rely on scattered, descriptive reports for the most part.

Victims of crime may suffer *physical harm* as well as emotional harm. Even crimes that do not, by definition, involve physical harm often result in some physical consequences. For example, a survey of nearly 300 robberies in Washington, D.C. found that roughly one-fourth of the victims suffered some injury. The likelihood of injury was greater in the case of muggings (unarmed robbery of an individual from the rear) than in the case of armed robbery (The President's Commission, 1967a:19).

Fear and its consequences.   Widespread crime can mean *pervasive fear* in a society. The President's Commission (1967a:v) studied two high-crime areas in two diferent cities and found that fear was widespread. Specifically, 43 percent of those questioned reported that they stay off the streets at night; 35 percent said they do not speak to strangers; 21 percent said they use cars or cabs at night; and 20 percent indicated they would like to move to another neighborhood—all because of fear of crime in the area.

A series of Gallup polls from 1965 to 1979 showed that the proportion of people saying they were afraid to walk alone at night increased from 34 to 42 percent during the fourteen-year period. The respondents in the polls were not residents of high-crime areas only, unlike the two studies mentioned just previously. Thus, the fear of being a victim of a crime is widespread in American society. There are certain differences among people and places. In the Gallup polls, females (57 percent) were more afraid in 1979 than were males (25 percent), and people in cities of 500,000 and over were

more afraid (52 percent) than were people in communities of less than 2,500 (25 percent).

Fear may combine with disgust to the point where some people seek to escape. Consider the following account by a former resident of New York City:

> I don't want to live in a city where a woman advertises for a lost dog and receives dozens of telephone calls from a variety of people saying they are torturing the animal and will continue to do so unless she pays large sums of money; or in a city where I am told I must always have $10 in my wallet for a possible mugger because without that I will surely be stabbed. . . . I recall the lady who was buying a magazine in the Port Authority Bus Terminal one evening when a stranger walked up and disemboweled her with a butcher knife. Later arrested, he told police that he didn't know the lady, but "just felt like killing somebody." It's impossible to protect oneself from such madness, and I think it is the fool in New York who is not a coward at heart.[12]

Not everyone who fears crime will leave the community—indeed, not everyone has that option. People who do not leave may *restrict their activities* in various ways. For instance, a person may avoid activities that require him or her to go out at night to public places, or decline what might otherwise be an attractive job. Many kinds of pleasure and cultural enrichment may be missed because of fear of being out at night.

A report to the National Commission on the Causes and Prevention of Violence (Mulvihill and Tumin, 1969:405) mentioned a proposal of Columbia University in New York to construct a new gymnasium in nearby Morningside Park. A controversy that developed over the proposal was said by one witness to be largely irrelevant because "everyone in the community knows that unless one wished to be mugged or knifed, no sane person would go near the park—night or day." The report comments on similar problems of fear and restriction of activities in other urban areas:

> Parks and other facilities in many cities are greatly under-utilized due to their undesirable location. Other community facilities, particularly entertainment centers, also suffer because of location. Attendance at sports arenas in Chicago and Newark, for example, are adversely affected by fear of attack. It has become increasingly difficult for theaters and orchestras to sustain adequate support because of their central city location. Retail outlets complain of high insurance costs and increased theft in downtown locations. Central city violence has greatly increased overall property insurance rates in most areas. These costs are, in turn, charged to the people least able to pay—the ghetto residents. The results are increased hostility and racial discord [Mulvihill and Tumin, 1969:405].

Thus, high crime rates cause a chain of consequences, all undesirable. The fear generated by crime means that everyone loses—victims, people who are afraid they might be victims, and residents and businessmen in high-crime areas.

Alienation and anomie.   White-collar crime also has a psychological impact that cannot be measured in monetary terms alone, Sutherland (1968:153) argued. He pointed out that such crimes create an atmosphere of distrust in a society, lowering social morale and creating widespread social disorganization. People become cynical about social institutions (illustrated by the common belief that all politicians are crooked), and there is a tendency to develop a social Darwinist approach to life (it's a dog-eat-dog world and each of us has to look out for

himself or herself above all else). In a sense, then, white-collar crime may be more damaging to a society than predatory crime. Predatory crime can actually have the positive effect of giving people a sense of the stability and rightness of their institutions and the need to protect those institutions from criminals. White-collar crime, on the other hand, indicates that the whole society is corrupt, that fraud and theft and exploitation pervade the paneled offices of professionals as well as the littered streets of the slums.

While the psychological effects of most crime include various kinds of emotional trauma, the *psychological effects of white-collar crime* in particular include a pervasive sense of *distrust, anomie,* and **alienation.** One type of crime shows that the society has flaws, but the other indicates that the society is sick. As The President's Commission (1967b:104) pointed out, white-collar crime can lead to physical illness and death, as, for example, when the Pure Food and Drug Act or building codes are violated. There is also the potential damage to "our social and economic institutions."

> More broadly, white-collar crime affects the whole moral climate of our society. Derelictions by corporations and their managers, who usually occupy leadership positions in their communities, establish an example which tends to erode the moral base of the law and provide an opportunity for other kinds of offenders to rationalize their misconduct [The President's Commission, 1967b:104].

A judge who sentenced some corporate executives in a price-fixing case noted that the case was "a shocking indictment of a vast section of our economy" and a possible harbinger of doom for the free enterprise system.

To the extent that the public becomes convinced of the pervasiveness of white-collar crime, our whole society can slip into a state of distrust, alienation, and anomie.

Economic Costs of Crime

A great many factors must be taken into account when we try to assess the *economic losses* due to crime. Among the elements that must be included are personal losses of property; the expenses of insurance; costs of loan sharks, false advertising, and shoddy workmanship on consumer goods; lost wages due to lost work time in cases of physical and emotional trauma; the costs of maintaining security systems and other crime prevention measures; and the costs of maintaining the criminal justice system. The criminal justice system alone (including local, state, and federal levels of government) cost over $24 billion in 1978, a 129.1 percent increase since 1971.[13]

We must recognize that it is difficult to put a price tag on crime. The President's Commission (1967b:45) noted that the economic costs must include "ultimate costs to society":

> Criminal acts causing property destruction or injury to persons not only result in serious losses to the victims or their families but also in the withdrawal of wealth or productive capacity from the economy as a whole. Theft on the other hand does not destroy wealth but merely transfers it involuntarily from the victim, or perhaps his insurance company, to the thief. The bettor purchasing illegal betting services from organized crime may easily absorb the loss of a 10¢, or even $10, bet. But from the point of view of society, gambling leaves much less

> wealth available for legitimate business . . . it is the proceeds of this crime tariff . . . that form the major source of income that organized crime requires to achieve and exercise economic and political power.

In other words, some economic costs are difficult to determine, so our estimates are likely to be conservative, and some costs that seem relatively minor may be important factors in the overall problem of crime.

Keeping in mind these cautions, let us try to find out how much crime does cost us in dollar terms. The President's Commission (1967a:31–35) estimated that the economic impact of crimes against persons (including things such as loss of earnings) amounted to about $815 million annually, while crimes against property amounted to nearly $4 billion. Other crimes of that time, such as driving under the influence of alcohol, tax fraud, and abortion, added $2 billion, and another $8 billion was added by the impact of various illegal goods and services (narcotics, loan sharking, prostitution, alcohol, gambling).

More recent figures on losses to business are provided by the government pamphlet *Crime in Retailing* (U.S. Dept. of Commerce, 1975). The report estimated the losses to retail merchants in 1974 at $5.8 billion. Small businesses suffered proportionately more losses than did large firms, and the losses varied somewhat by type of merchandise. For instance, in department stores, the most frequent losses occurred in jewelry and junior and subteen clothing. Drug stores averaged losses in 1974 of around 3 percent of sales. Crime-related losses in food stores were about $1.2 billion on sales of $119 billion. Cigarettes and meat were the two primary targets for thieves in food stores.

Since crime rates are increasing, we expect the economic costs to be increasing also. Public expenditures to maintain the criminal justice system increased from $4.57 billion in 1965 to over $24 billion in 1978, an increase that was reflected at all levels of government from local to federal. Each year the federal government spends billions of dollars for crime-reduction programs, the bulk of the money going to law enforcement and lesser amounts to things such as crime prevention services and rehabilitation of offenders. Figures of such magnitude are difficult to comprehend; we get a better idea of the cost by knowing that in 1978 about $110 for every man, woman, and child in the United States was spent just to maintain the criminal justice system.

The increasing costs of crime can also be seen in the increasing losses to businesses. From 1970 to 1974, total retail sales increased from $201 billion to $284 billion, while crime-related losses of retail stores increased from $3.99 billion to $5.77 billion (U.S. Department of Commerce, 1975:2). Thus, sales increased by 41.3 percent while crime-related losses increased by 44.6 percent. This may not seem like a serious increase in the rate of loss, but we must keep in mind that in some cases businesses are operating near the limit of their capacity to absorb the losses. The 3 percent loss rate for drug stores in 1974 was near the limit, since the profit margin for retail drug stores is not much larger than 3 percent. Furthermore, the increase in losses due to crime means that the business must either increase volume or raise prices. The increase in volume would have to be considerable: in a business operating on a profit margin of 2 percent of sales, each $50 loss through theft would require an additional $2,500 of sales. If increased volume is not feasible, increasing losses inevitably mean increased costs to the consumers.

Contributing Factors

Before looking at specific sociocultural factors that contribute to the problem of crime, we need to discuss an interesting theory proposed to explain crime. The theory states that *crime is a natural, expected aspect of any society*.

Crime as Normal and Necessary

The notion of the normality of crime was set forth by Emile Durkheim (1951:362):

> Now there is no society known where a more or less developed criminality is not found under different forms. No people exists whose morality is not daily infringed upon. We must therefore call crime necessary and declare that it cannot be nonexistent, that the fundamental conditions of social organization, as they are understood, logically imply it. Consequently, it is normal.

Durkheim elaborated the basis for this blunt statement in earlier work. He argued that normal and pathological kinds of behavior are not intrinsically different, they simply represent different collective definitions. That is, any given society defines some behavior as normal and other behavior as pathological. What is normal and what is pathological varies among societies, so the definitions of normal vs. pathological behavior represent collective views of the social group rather than anything inherent in human life or consciousness.

A society exempt from crime is impossible. Crime offends strong collective sentiments, and the absence of crime would mean that every member of the society shared exactly the same strong sentiments, which is impossible (Durkheim, 1938:67). Durkheim argued that crime is necessary, that it serves some useful purposes, because if there is total conformity in a society, there could be no progress. Crime indicates "not only that the way remains open to necessary changes but that in certain cases it directly prepares these changes" (Durkheim, 1938:71). What is criminal in one generation may become the norm in another generation. Durkheim illustrated his point by noting that Socrates was defined as a criminal, but his criminality was actually the new morality and faith of the future—namely, the right of people to independent thought.

Other people followed Durkheim in this line of thought and set forth a theory of crime that emphasizes its normality and necessity. The theory argued that the values of a community establish social "boundaries" on behavior, which, in turn, define crime. The particular kind of boundary creates the pattern of crime. In some societies the boundaries are religious, and crime takes the form of religious aberrations. For example, a strict Protestant sect in the U.S. punishes aberrants by subjecting them to social isolation, which they call "shunning." At the same time, crime helps to sharpen the community boundaries in one way by defining what the community's identity is *not*. A parent who says to a child, "We do not do that sort of thing," is defining the kind of family it is in terms of boundaries to behavior. Similarly, a community that says certain behavior is beyond its moral bounds is saying what kind of community it is. In this way, crime clarifies the values of the community. When the community responds to crime with sanctions, it is asserting its *moral primacy* over the individual and enhancing the *solidarity* of its members. Thus, crime is useful to society.

No victim of crime would find much comfort in this theory. Nevertheless, it is useful in that it reminds us that crime is indeed a matter of *social definition*. Socrates was a criminal in Athens, and black youths who set fire to a Ku Klux Klan hangout were defined as criminals in contemporary America. If we define exploitation, tyranny, and oppression as crimes, then those who hounded Socrates, those who "shunned" a member of their community, and those who oppressed the black youths were all guilty of crimes. The implication here is that certain groups in a society are more likely to be criminals because of their powerlessness. We will discuss later that point: that one of the "causes" of crime is that certain behavior is defined as criminal by those who have the power to set the standards, make the laws, and then enforce them. Unequal enforcement has the same effect as different definitions of what constitutes a crime being applied to different groups. While we agree with the correctness of many definitions of crime, as in the cases of murder, rape, and theft, we should insist that they be applied equally to all citizens, and that acts such as corporate theft be no less serious than individual theft.

Social Structural Factors

Norms.   The *differential association theory* of crime and delinquency described in chapter 1 emphasizes the importance of *norms*. The theory stresses that potential or actual criminals or delinquents have their significant interactions with people whose norms violate the criminal law. The President's Commission (1967a:60–61) presented a sketch of the kind of life a ghetto delinquent has, showing how the delinquent's interaction experiences can lead him or her to accept antisocial norms.

> . . . the delinquent is a child of the slums, from a neighborhood that is low on the socioeconomic scale of the community and harsh in many ways for those who live there. He is 15 or 16 years old . . . one of numerous children—perhaps representing several different fathers—who live with their mother in a home that the sociologists call female-centered. It may be broken; it may never have had a resident father; it may have a nominal male head who is often drunk or in jail or in and out of the house. . . . He may never have known a grownup man well enough to identify with or imagine emulating him. From the adults and older children in charge of him he has had leniency, sternness, affection, perhaps indifference, in erratic and unpredictable succession. All his life he has had considerable independence, and by now his mother has little control over his comings and goings, little way of knowing what he is up to until a policeman brings him home or a summons from court comes in the mail.
>
> He may well have dropped out of school. He is probably unemployed, and has little to offer an employer. The offenses he and his friends commit are much more frequently thefts than crimes of personal violence, and they rarely commit them alone. Indeed, they rarely do anything alone, preferring to congregate and operate in a group, staking out their own "turf"—a special street corner or candy store or poolroom—and adopting their own flamboyant title and distinctive hair style or way of dressing or talking or walking, to signal their membership in the group and show that they

are "tough" and not to be meddled with. Their clear belligerence toward authority does indeed earn them the fearful deference of both adult and child, as well as the watchful suspicion of the neighborhood policeman. Although the common conception of the gang member is of a teenager, in fact the lower class juvenile begins his gang career much earlier, and usually in search not of coconspirators in crime but of companionship. But it is all too easy for them to drift into minor and then major violations of the law.

> That is not to suggest that his mother has not tried to guide him, or his father if he has one or an uncle or older brother. But their influence is diluted and undermined by the endless task of making ends meet in the face of debilitating poverty; by the constant presence of temptation—drugs, drinking, gambling, petty thievery, prostitution; by the visible contrast of relative affluence on the other side of town.

Thus, the lower-class delinquent has few or no experiences with people who would lead him or her to accept the norms of the larger society. The delinquent is drawn to a group because of the need for companionship, and the group develops norms that violate the law. Because the *group membership* is more meaningful to the youth than anything else he or she has experienced, those norms are accepted and followed.

Norms are involved in white-collar crime also. Certain practices in business and industry may be justified on the basis that everyone does them, or that they are necessary for continuing one's enterprise, or that they are acceptable by those in authority. News accounts have reported corporate executives justifying illegal behavior on the grounds that their competitors engaged in the behavior, and if their own corporation did not, they would lose business and profits. In the mid-1970s, newspapers carried accounts of the "scandal" of American businessmen paying off

Involvement

When Is a Crime Not a Crime?

In February 1977 a man was sentenced in an Ohio court to seven to twenty-five years in prison and fined $10,000 for engaging in organized crime; he was sentenced an additional six months in prison and fined another $1,000 for pandering obscenity. The man's crime was publishing a magazine that was defined as obscene literature by the Ohio court. In some other countries where there are no laws against obscenity the man would not be a criminal. This is an example of a point made in this chapter—the fact that crime is a matter of social definition.

Investigate different definitions of crime in several societies by researching anthropological literature or by talking to foreign students at your school. What kinds of behavior are not crimes in the United States but are crimes elsewhere? What kinds of behavior are crimes in our country but are not defined as criminal elsewhere? (One example is the difference in treatment of drug addicts in the United States compared to England, which we mentioned in the text.) Why do you think the differences exist?

influential foreigners in order to secure contracts for business. Such practices were shrugged off by one executive, who pointed out that the alternative was to not do business in the foreign countries.

White-collar crime can become pervasive in an organization or institution, as evidenced by the disclosure of extensive theft and fraud in a state government in the 1950s. One woman who had written checks to nonexistent employees said, "Everyone around me was stealing—bigshot officials and little office people like me. So I did, too" (Velie, 1960:108). Theft and fraud became normative behavior. In other words, norms can influence respectable people to engage in crime because they are the norms of other respectable people.

The politics of control: the prison. How should society respond to crime? The nature of the response is a political decision, and in the 1970s, government was pressed to abandon the notion of **rehabilitation** and put criminals into prisons for *punishment* and *isolation from society*. We will discuss these distinctions further when we look at ways to handle the problem of crime. In essence, the new approach says that "prisons are first for punishment, an essential means for upholding the law; second, they offer rehabilitation for those prisoners who seek it."[14] Advocates of the new approach contend that rehabilitation programs have failed. In this section we will examine the nation's prisons and jails. (A jail is a locally administered institution that has authority to retain adults for forty-eight hours or longer. A prison is a state or federally administered facility for correction only.) We will see that the very nature of these institutions virtually guarantees little or no rehabilitation.

Not all prisoners have *access to rehabilitation programs*. This is particularly true in the nation's 3,921 jails, where only a fraction of the total jail population have access to any programs other than religious services.[15] Only 51 percent of large jails (those with 250 or more inmates) have a rehabilitation program funded by the federal government. Basic adult education is the most common program, followed by vocational training. A much smaller proportion of the smaller jails have programs. Thus, most people who spend time in a jail will not have access to a rehabilitation program.

Some prison inmates may not have elemental physical amenities to which most people are accustomed. As late as the 1960s the nation's only federal prison for women lacked toilets in a number of units. The women were forced to use jars. Such conditions do not apply to all prisons. In fact, minimum security prisons can give the appearance of a "home-away-from-home" when contrasted with other prisons. However, many prisons and county or city jails are unfit for human beings for other reasons, as we will see. If we had deliberately created a system to guarantee continuation of criminal activity, we probably could not have devised anything better than the prison.

The *nature of prison life* makes rehabilitation unlikely. Far from serving as a deterrent to further crime or as a place of rehabilitation, the jail or prison is more likely to be a *training ground* for making criminals more competent and more committed to a life of crime. If the abnormal circumstances of the prison, including extended, close association with hardened offenders, does not assure continued criminal behavior, the **stigma** of having been in prison probably will. The prison itself is a *dehumanizing institution,* and those who enter it are unlikely to escape being brutalized, hardened, and better trained in criminal behavior. A man who spent fifteen months in a federal prison in Pennsylvania for attempted arson said, "I didn't think God could make hell on earth, but I don't see how it could be anywhere else."[16] He had experienced gang rapes, beatings, and threats on his life, and he was certain that he would be executed by other prisoners because he had broken their rules by talking with prison guards.

Similar reports have come from many sources. A 1967 investigation of the Cook County (Illinois) jail revealed a "stomach-turning catalogue of depravity."[17] There were at least three possible murders. In one, an inmate had been strapped to his cot and burned to death. In another, a man was found hanged with his belt. The third case was a fatal beating. A middle-aged woman who chose to go to jail rather than have a bank appraise her home (a question of principle, she said) left the jail after seven days and allowed the appraisal to take place. She was overwhelmed by the overt lesbianism, and reported that one woman was so tormented by lesbians that she tried to commit suicide.

Homosexuality, including *homosexual attacks,* may be common in prisons. One of the more startling reports of such activity comes from research in Philadelphia:

> . . . we found that sexual assaults in the Philadelphia prison system are epidemic . . . virtually every slightly-built young man committed by the courts is sexually approached within a day or two after his admission to prison. Many of these young men are repeatedly raped by gangs of inmates. Others, because of the threat of gang rape, seek protection by entering into a homosexual relationship with an individual tormentor [Davis, 1968:9].

The same research reported that guards do not help much. Many guards do not want to be bothered. One victim screamed for an hour while he was being gang-raped in his cell. The guard simply laughed at the incident. The prisoners who reported it passed a lie detector test; the guard refused to take the test. One conclusion of the research was that such behavior does not appear to reflect true homosexuality. The rapists do not consider themselves homosexuals; rather, the rape seems to be a means of conquering and degrading the victim (see the discussion of rape in the next chapter).

Some of the worst aspects of our society may continue unabated in prisons. Jacobs (1974) spent a number of months in an Illinois penitentiary and found that imprisoned members of four gangs, each of which was operating in Chicago, were continuing gang activities in the prison. Those who did not belong to one of the gangs were subjected to periodic sexual and monetary exploitation. Gang members, on the other hand, fit fairly well into the prison life, and could even enhance their status by "proving" themselves to their fellow gang members while in prison.

Normal behavior and feelings are impossible in prisons. The prison is a *"total institution,"* a place where the totality of the individual's existence is controlled by various external forces. Those who enter the maximum security prison are immediately deprived of various things we value: liberty, goods and services, heterosexual relationships, autonomy, and security (from attacks of other prisoners) (Sykes, 1958:65–78). The constraints of prison life are so severe that an individual must focus on *survival* rather than personal development or change. A prison psychiatrist pointed out that the combination of the inmate code and the demands of the authorities virtually eliminate any possibility of individual growth or personal lifestyle.[18] There is a popular notion that "stone walls do not a prison make," and that even in a cell the individual's mind is free to roam and explore. The prison psychiatrist argued that only a rare individual can transcend the forces that impinge upon him or her and thereby avoid the **dehumanization** of the prison.

The *inmate code* contributes to the dehumanization. The code requires that an inmate must never report infractions of rules by another inmate and must never notice anything. For example, an inmate walking down a prison corridor saw a fellow inmate lying on the floor, bleeding. He had an impulse to help the man on the floor but went to his cell instead. Other inmates who discussed the incident with the prison psychiatrist agreed with the behavior. They pointed out that if the man had called a guard, the guard would suspect him of having struck the man on the floor, or would have intensely questioned him. Furthermore, any other inmate who saw him call the guard would accuse him of "snitching." Had he stopped to personally help the fallen man, he might have been beaten by the man's attacker. Also, to personally help would suggest a homosexual relationship between the two inmates.

At best, humane impulses tend to be suppressed by the realities of prison life. At worst, those impulses may be obliterated. The experiment of Zimbardo (1972), discussed in chapter 1, showed that "mature, emotionally stable, normal," and intelligent young men who participated in the prison experiment were thoroughly dehumanized by the pathology of imprisonment. In an earlier study of 500 psychotic prison inmates, Silverman (1943) found that although only a small number were psychotic prior to imprisonment, 80 percent were psychotic by the end of their first year in prison.

Prison inmates learn not only to *suppress feelings of concern or sympathy* (if they have not learned to do so before entering prison), but also learn more criminal skills. Gresham Sykes (1961) called this process the *"corruption of authority and rehabilitation."* The process occurs naturally, Sykes argued, as a result of confining criminals for an extended period of time under a *situation of deprivation*. The "corruption of authority" refers to a closing of the gap between prisoners and cellblock guards in a maximum security prison. For example, guards fail to report rule infractions, or they transmit forbidden information to prisoners, or they neglect certain security procedures, or they share in the prisoners' criticisms of prison officials. This corruption is due to a number of factors. Friendships may develop because guards and prisoners are in close, continual contact, and Americans value the notion of being a "good Joe." There is also a system of reciprocity. The guard, expected by his superiors to run a tight but smooth ship, may grant certain concessions to inmates in return for their good behavior. Corruption may also result from default of responsibility: guards give certain minor tasks to trusted inmates, and their authority erodes as more and more tasks are yielded.

The corruption of authority leads to a corruption of rehabilitation because the corruption of authority makes the inmate "still more unresponsive to legitimate social controls by encouraging the criminal in patterns of conniving, deception, and counterattacks against the normative order" (Sykes, 1961:197). In effect, the prisoner improves the criminal skills that equip him or her to continue a criminal career upon release from prison, with an eventual return to prison the probable result.

The family of the delinquent. Because *the family plays a significant role in the socialization of children,* much attention is focused on the family background to try to discover why young people become delinquents. Many popular and professional statements link delinquency with broken homes. More recent research, however, questions the impact of broken homes on delinquency, for although delinquents are more likely to come from disrupted homes (Chilton and Markle, 1972), it is not the disruption so much as it is the *quality of the relationship between parents and children* that is a factor in delinquency.

The importance of the quality of family relationships was stressed by the President's Commission, which noted "the principle that whatever in the organization of the family, the contacts among its members, or its relationships to the surrounding community diminishes the moral and emotional authority of the family in the life of the young person also increases the likelihood of delinquency" (The President's Commission, 1967a:63). The homes of delinquent children are more likely to have *antisocial parents,* or to *lack warm, loving, supportive relationships* between parents and children, or to have a *minimum of parental involvement* with the children (Yahraes, 1978; Smith and Walters, 1978). The greater the number of families with such characteristics, the greater the number of delinquents.

Social stratification and crime. Crime and delinquency are related to the social stratification system in three ways. (1) The kind of behavior considered criminal is defined by those who have power within the system. (2) Different kinds of crime tend to be committed within different strata of the system. (3) Disproportionate numbers of criminals come from different socioeconomic levels.

A good deal of the behavior of relatively powerless people is defined as criminal, although behavior of more powerful people that is logically the same is not defined as criminal. This is true especially when the behavior involves monetary exploitation. A corporate executive might support the definition of employee theft as criminal but would not define false advertising and exploitation of consumers as theft or crime. A physician might deplore abuses of the welfare system, labeling them criminal fraud, but think little about prescribing expensive brand-name drugs rather than less expensive generic counterparts because, in part, his or her retirement plan rests on investments in the pharmaceutical industry. In both cases, those who influence the defining process are the *holders or wielders of power in the society,* and they *do not define their own behavior as criminal.*

Among the lower socioeconomic strata, delinquency and violent crimes are prevalent, while white-collar crime is commonly associated with the middle and upper strata. This assessment is independent from the predisposition of the police to define the behavior of a

lower-status individual as criminal. The nature of ghetto life invariably results in high rates of delinquency:

> The inner city has always been hard on whoever is living in it . . . it is in the inner city that delinquency rates have traditionally been highest, decade after decade and regardless of what population group is there. . . . As the members of each population group gain greater access to the city's legitimate social and economic opportunities and the group moves outward . . . the rates of disease and dependency—and delinquency—drop. But in the inner city, now occupied by a different group, the rate of delinquency remains roughly the same, regardless of race, religion, or nationality [The President's Commission, 1967a:59].

Many studies support the conclusion that delinquency rates are highest among the low socio-economic strata in the inner cities, regardless of the race or religion or nationality of the people. Similarly, violent crime, its offenders, and its victims are most common in urban areas where there is

> low income, physical deterioration, dependency, racial and ethnic concentrations, broken homes, working mothers, low levels of education and vocational skill, high unemployment, high proportions of single males, overcrowded and substandard housing, high rates of tuberculosis and infant mortality, low rates of home ownership or single family dwellings, mixed land use, and high population density [The President's Commission, 1967a:35].

No one of the factors quoted can be taken in isolation. Rather, they form a cluster of characteristics associated with the bottom levels of the stratification system, and they work together to produce a high rate of violent crime.

The third way the stratification system is related to crime is in the disproportionate number of criminals who come from the lower socioeconomic strata. As suggested earlier, part of the reason is that the powerless and deprived are more likely to be defined as criminals. Several studies over the last few decades have revealed many consistencies in the characteristics of people *labeled as criminals*. Their general *powerlessness* and their location in the stratification system are clear. Criminals are more likely to: (1) lack *social anchorage* in the sense of growing up in a stable family that is integrated into the community; (2) come from a lower-income family; (3) be young, particularly for certain kinds of crimes (in 1973, individuals under 18 accounted for over one-fourth of all arrests); (4) be male (nearly 85 percent of all those arrested in 1973 were males); (5) come disproportionately from a minority group (in 1973, 28.6 percent of all arrests were nonwhites).

These figures refer to arrests, not to numbers brought to trial or convicted. As a study of crime in Florida shows, the *powerless are more likely to be defined as criminals throughout the criminal justice system* (Chiricos, Jackson, and Waldo, 1972). The study involved 2,419 individuals who were accused of a felony. Florida law gives judges the option of withholding **adjudication** of guilt from people placed on probation. The judge's decision, then, determines whether or not the individual will carry the *stigma of being a "convicted felon."* Who is most likely to have "adjudication withheld"? Who is most likely to be labeled a "convicted felon"? Those most likely to be labeled felons were older, black, poorly educated, previously arrested, and defended by a court-appointed rather than a personal attorney. In other words, people with the least amount of power and the fewest resources are most likely to be required to carry the stigma of convicted felon. This is not to say they are innocent of the crime. Rather, it is to point out that the criminal justice system does not treat equally people who commit the same kinds of crime; those in the lower strata are likely to be treated more severely.

Social Psychological Factors

The attitudes that prison conditions generate in inmates help to perpetuate the problem of crime. Attitudes of so-called respectable people contribute to the crime problem, also.

Attitudes of respectable people provide the necessary support for a good deal of officially defined crime, even though these poeple do not view themselves as culpable or as contributing to crime. The assertion has been made that prostitution could not continue anywhere without official support. Certainly, it could not continue without the support of the respectable clientele it serves. Neither could it continue without the overt or covert support of the police. Automobile theft in New York City offers another example of such respectable support. Upwardly mobile young men in business and the professions buy Porsches at a fraction of their retail cost. The cars fit their aspirations but not their current incomes. They "know that the cars are stolen, but they do not care."[19] Such crime would have no payoff without the customers, and the customers are respectable people who may not view their behavior as criminal or as contributing to criminal behavior in any significant way (after all, one can reason, if I do not buy it someone else will).

Attitudes of respectable people that stigmatize criminals thereby contribute to continuation of the criminal careers. Often, the very people who decry crime resist providing any help to the criminal. The experience of an arsonist (Johnson, 1973:392–93) is an illustration. The man found a job in a hospital and hoped to become a respectable citizen. The questionnaire he filled out to get the job asked if he had a criminal record, and he wrote "no." After six weeks of training as a surgical technician, he was called in and told that his criminal record had been discovered and that he would have to resign. Among other reasons, they told him that people like judges and lawyers would resent an ex-convict dealing with them in the operating room. The man was stunned, got drunk, got arrested for a fire in an old apartment house, and was returned to prison (although he may have been innocent, but he didn't know because he was drunk at the time.)

Attitudes toward white-collar criminals are ambivalent. Generally, unless the acts are flagrant, overt violations of our standards of right, white-collar criminals may be only mildly sanctioned for their behavior.

Finally, in looking at the social psychology of *committed criminals or delinquents*—that is, those who have entered into what labeling theorists call *secondary deviance*—we find a distinctive set of attitudes, values, and other attributes. For these individuals, delinquency or crime has become a *way of life*. They have a *"subterranean" set of values*—hedonism, a focus on immediate gratification, and the ability to outwit and "con" others. They appear to be untouched by punishment, and they continue their deviant ways and account for much of the crime in the nation. For them, deviance is a way of life (Schmalleger, 1979; Cernkovich, 1978; Horwitz and Wasserman, 1979). This is illustrated by studies that have examined the *self-concepts of delinquents.* Typically, the studies reveal congruence between attitudes toward the self and behavior. Clinard and Fannin (1965) looked at both middle-class and lower-class delinquents. In all cases the behavior was congruent with the attitudes toward the self. The middle-class delinquents saw themselves as clever, smart, smooth, bad and loyal. The lower-class delinquents saw themselves as tough, fearless, powerful, fierce, and dangerous. The lower-class delinquents also committed more violent offenses and generally behaved more violently.

What Is to be Done?

The study of social problems could be a thoroughly depressing enterprise if we did not remind ourselves that there are some victories in the struggle to enhance the quality of our lives. Overall, crime and delinquency are not yet under control, much less vanquished; however, there are some victories that give us hope. Many individual programs and efforts have been quite successful,[20] and yet, a realistic attack on crime will require action at various levels of social life. The President's Commission (1967a:279–91) suggested that crime could be significantly reduced if a number of programs were undertaken. These include: (1) insuring that all Americans have equal access to the benefits available in our society; (2) revising the criminal justice system to eliminate inequities; (3) intensifying research into the problem; (4) increasing the financial commitment to po-

lice, courts, and correctional agencies; and (5) inducing all segments of the society to accept responsibility for planning and implementing the necessary changes. We will look at a few specific steps that have been and can be taken, but first we need to discuss the issue of punishment vs. rehabilitation.

Punishment or Rehabilitation?

Earlier we mentioned that during the 1970s pressure arose to abandon rehabilitative programs as useless and to focus on isolating and punishing criminals. Conservatives have long argued for a *"get tough" policy.* To "get tough" means intensified punishment: "There is only one way to stop the continuing spiral of serious crime in this country: concentrate on putting career criminals and crime repeaters in prison for long terms with virtually no parole or probation."[21] In addition, went the argument, the death penalty must be imposed for certain crimes.

One advocate of punishment and isolation is James Wilson (1975), who argued that rehabilitative programs are useless and that criminals must be separated from society by imprisonment. Prisons will not eliminate the causes of crime and they will not rehabilitate many criminals, Wilson argued, but they will punish and isolate the criminal. A society must be able to protect itself from criminals and to make criminal behavior costly.

In contrast, Chaneles (1976) argued that we should construct some realistic programs of rehabilitation because reform works better than punishment. He pointed out that a 1970 Task Force on Prisoner Rehabilitation concluded unanimously that rehabilitative programs were effective and that they should become the focus of prison policy. The task force report said that if rehabilitation—particularly *job training*—were available to more prisoners, a substantial reduction in crime could be realized.

The arguments about the effectiveness of punishment vs. rehabilitation go on. The advocates of punishment and isolation are correct when they contend that prisons do not rehabilitate; there is ample evidence of that. This is not to say that rehabilitation programs cannot be effective. In fact, rehabilitative efforts may need to be combined with punishment. There is strong evidence that punishment is a deterrent to crime (Tullock, 1974), but it is not so much the harshness as the *certainty of punishment* that seems to deter.

Thus, the criminal justice system in the United States should be revamped in accord with a twofold thrust. First, punishment for crime must be made more certain; second, rehabilitation programs must be extended and made more effective. Certainty of punishment will act as a deterrent for some and will remove others from society, while rehabilitation will change some of those who have been removed from society and restore them to socially useful lives.

Community Action and Involvement

Crime prevention is not just a matter of official action. Communities can become involved and act to reduce crime. Conklin (1975:9) argued that informal social control in the community is even more effective in preventing crime than the formal methods of the government:

> In a closely knit community, there is surveillance of public and private places. If surveillance is reinforced by willingness to report suspicious events to the police or by willingness to intervene in order to stop a crime, crime can be reduced by increasing the risk to the offender.

There are a variety of other ways citizens of a community can help reduce crime. Some of the ways detailed by the National Advisory Commission on Criminal Justice Standards and Goals (1973:66–67) are: citizen patrols; campaigns to improve streetlighting; volunteer work in probation departments or correctional institutions; providing employment and training for ex-offenders; counseling young people on various problems; and reporting crime to the police. Hundreds of cases throughout the nation testify to how successful local citizen action can be in reducing crime.

Aid to Victims

A relatively recent effort to deal with some of the effects of crime involves *aid to the victims*. In 1972 Congress passed legislation that allocated $5 million to victims of federal crimes and $10 million to help states set up their own programs of help. This effort was designed to correct a long-standing injustice, as expressed by an attorney:

> . . . a victim is twice victimized—once by the criminal and once by the criminal-justice system. . . . As a society, we've ignored the victim. Offenders get all kinds of attention—counseling, job services, lawyers—while most victims get no assistance whatsoever. This is not only wrong. It's ludicrous.[22]

Figure 6.6 Citizen participation is an important part of the fight against crime. *Left:* As part of a community crime-control effort in Chicago, Hyde Park citizens carry whistles to blow whenever the police are needed. Anyone who hears a whistle immediately reports the location to the police by telephone. *Right:* The mayor of a large city views pictures that were part of an anti-crime comic book project.

Some of the problems faced by the victim of a crime may be a lack of transportation to court, difficulty in retrieving stolen property from the police, threats by defendants if the victim testifies, and the amount of time consumed by the various procedures in the criminal justice system. An aid program can compensate for some of the losses incurred by the victims.

Summary

Crime is one of the problems of most concern to Americans. Technically, crime is any violation of the criminal law. Therefore, the acts defined by law as crime vary over time. We classify crime into four broad types. (1) Predatory crime, which includes white-collar crime, is an act that causes a victim to suffer loss of property or physical harm. (2) Illegal service crimes involve things such as drugs or prostitution. (3) Public disorder crimes have no definite victim but are acts that offend the public. (4) Crimes of negligence involve an unintended victim or potential victim. The term "juvenile delinquency" covers a broad range of behavior, frequently including trivial behavior such as fighting, truancy, and running away from home.

Crime and delinquency are widespread and growing, as measured by various indexes—official records, victimization studies, or self-reports. One-fourth or more of Americans may have been the victim, or intended victim, of a crime in any one year. Crime is not uniformly distributed, however; the likelihood of being a victim depends on the kind of crime, where the person lives, and his or her sex, race, age, education, and income.

Crime diminishes the quality of life and exacts physical, psychological, and economic costs. Crime threatens physical and mental health. It generates fear, which restricts the activities of people. White-collar crime can lead to pervasive cynicism, alienation, and anomie. Crime costs the nation billions of dollars each year, and the costs are increasing because the amount of crime is increasing.

Durkheim and others set forth a theory of crime in which they argued that crime in any society is both normal and useful because it helps to establish an identity for the community and to enhance the solidarity of members of the community. The theory itself reminds us that crime is a matter of social definition; that one of the "causes" of crime is that certain behavior is defined as criminal by those with the power to set standards and make laws.

Norms are an important sociocultural factor contributing to the problem of crime and delinquency because they encourage members of certain groups to engage in criminal behavior. In particular, norms that are counter to the law have developed among lower-class youth and groups of businessmen and professionals.

The political aspects of crime control contribute to the problem, especially through our country's prison system. Prisons make rehabilitation unlikely because they tend to dehumanize offenders, removing them further from noncriminal social control, and to make them more competent in criminal activity.

The family may be a factor in juvenile delinquency. Delinquents come disproportionately from families with poor relationships between parents and children.

The stratification system also relates to crime. Monetary exploitation of others is more likely to be defined as crime among lower-class people than among middle- and upper-class people. The lower class has a greater proportion of violent crime and delinquency, while the middle and upper classes have more white-collar crime. A lower-class individual is more likely to be defined as a criminal by the processes of the criminal justice system.

Many attitudes tend to perpetuate crime. Crimes are facilitated by the attitude of respectable people about their own behavior—especially their use of the services of criminals. The attitude of respectable people that stigmatizes criminals tends to keep them in criminal careers. The attitude toward white-collar crime that tends to minimize its seriousness also encourages it. Finally, the attitudes, values, and other social psychological characteristics of some criminals and delinquents form a consistent set that makes for a way of life. Having deviant values and attitudes, and thinking of themselves as people who engage in criminal or delinquent behavior, they tend to maintain their way of life even when they are punished for doing so.

Glossary

adjudication   making a judgment; settling a judicial matter

alienation   a sense of estrangement from one's social environment, typically measured by one's feelings of powerlessness, normlessness, isolation, meaninglessness, and self-estrangement

dehumanization   the process by which an individual is deprived of qualities or traits of a human being

predatory crime   acts that have victims who suffer loss of property or some kind of physical harm

rehabilitation   resocializing a criminal and returning him or her to full participation in society

stigma   that which symbolizes disrepute or disgrace

trauma   physical or emotional injury

white-collar crime   crimes committed by respectable citizens in the course of their work

For Further Reading

Chambliss, William J. *On the Take: From Petty Crooks to Presidents*. Bloomington, Ind.: Indiana University Press, 1978. Shows how respectable business people and politicians help perpetuate crime, particularly organized crime.

"Combating Organized Crime." *The Annals of the American Academy of Political and Social Science* 347 (May 1963). A whole volume of the journal given over to articles dealing with the theory, practice, and prevention of organized crime (as distinguished from individual crime).

Haskell, Martin R., and Lewis Yablonsky. *Juvenile Delinquency*. 2nd ed. Chicago: Rand McNally, 1978. A comprehensive text by two experts with both academic and practical experience. Includes the nature of delinquency, the causes, and various efforts at resolving the problem.

Letkemann, Peter. *Crime as Work*. Englewood Cliffs, N.J.: Prentice-Hall, 1973. Examines the criminal career in terms of things such as the skills demanded if the criminal is to successfully pursue his or her line of work.

Rice, Robert. *The Business of Crime*. Westport, Conn.: Greenwood Press, 1956. Case studies of businessmen who planned and performed arson, narcotic sales, counterfeiting, smuggling, and gambling.

Sutherland, Edwin H., and Donald R. Cressey. *Principles of Criminology*. Philadelphia: J. B. Lippincott, 1960. A widely used, standard text on the various aspects of crime.

Tompkins, Dorothy Campbell. *White-Collar Crime—A Bibliography*. Berkeley: University of California Press, 1967. A bibliography with some annotation and commentary useful for those wishing to study white-collar crime in depth.

Notes

1. Quoted in Robert A. Dentler, *Major Social Problems*, 2nd ed. (Chicago: Rand-McNally, 1972), p. 502.
2. All the definitions of crimes in the FBI Crime Index are taken from *Uniform Crime Reports for the United States*, 1975 ed. (U.S. Federal Bureau of Investigation, 1976).
3. *Saturday Review*, November 15, 1975, p. 10.
4. Ibid.
5. *St. Louis Post-Dispatch*, August 5, 1969.
6. Ibid., January 8, 1978.
7. *Time*, November 1, 1971, p. 26.
8. *The Gallup Opinion Index*, No. 124, October 1975, p. 15.
9. U.S. Bureau of the Census, *Statistical Abstract of the United States, 1980* (Washington, D.C.: Government Printing Office, 1981), p. 199.
10. Ibid., p. 191.
11. Ibid., pp. 183–84.
12. Caskie Stinnett, "Farewell, My Unlovely," *The Atlantic*, August 1976, pp. 23–24.
13. U.S. Department of Justice, *Expenditure and Employment Data for the Criminal Justice System 1978: Preliminary Report* (Washington, D.C.: Government Printing Office, 1980).
14. *St. Louis Post-Dispatch*, April 11, 1976.
15. U.S. Department of Justice, *The Nation's Jails* (Washington, D.C.: Government Printing Office, 1975), p. 12.
16. *St. Louis Post-Dispatch*, June 3, 1976.
17. *Time*, December 15, 1967, pp. 75–76.
18. *St. Louis Post-Dispatch*, August 5, 1969.
19. *Time*, December 20, 1971, p. 12.
20. See, e.g., the cases in *We Can Prevent Crime*, a publication of the U.S. Department of Justice, 1979.
21. *St. Louis Globe-Democrat*, February 21, 1975.
22. Richard P. Lynch, as reported in *U.S. News and World Report*, December 8, 1975, p. 42.

Violence

1 **How much violence is in America?**

2 **Why do people choose violence when nonviolent alternatives are available?**

3 **What are the effects of television on violence?**

4 **Is rape an act of violence or of sexual passion?**

5 **Do women provoke rape by their dress or behavior?**

What would you do if, looking through the window of a building, you saw a human limb hanging up? Your reaction would probably depend on the kind of building. If it would be a bank, you might call the police. If it would be a hospital, you might think the scene crude but would probably do nothing more. In 1788, however, when some boys spotted a limb through the window of a New York City hospital, the result was a riot (Hofstadter and Wallace, 1970:445). A crowd of people came to the hospital, destroyed part of the hospital, and removed and buried some corpses. The doctors were put into a jail for protection from the mob. Four people were killed and several wounded when the mob tried to force their way into the jail to attack the doctors.

Why the violence? The incident occurred before the dissection of bodies was legal. Medical schools found subjects for anatomy lessons by robbing graves. A number of riots occurred as a protest against "body snatching." Still, why the violence? Why didn't people try to reason with the doctors, or bargain with them, or work through the courts? Obviously, there are alternatives to violence. The question we deal with in this chapter is, Why do people choose violent rather than nonviolent forms of behavior? Some kinds of violent behavior were discussed in the last chapter. We will deal with other kinds, including child abuse, in the chapters on family problems and war. In this chapter we will look at violence separately because it enters into nearly every social problem at some point.

To understand why violence enters into other social problems, we need only to recall that social problems involve *intergroup conflict*. The conflict often becomes violent, as illustrated by gangs of straight youths who beat up homosexuals; by race riots; by murders when a drug dealer tries to move in on someone else's market; and by the numerous violent incidents generated by the busing of school children.

Americans have expressed a great deal of *concern* about the problem of violence. In a survey of a national sample of men, over 65 percent spontaneously mentioned some kind of violence when questioned about things happening in the United States that bothered them (Blumenthal, Kahn, Andrews, and Head, 1972:39). In this chapter, we will deal with various kinds of interpersonal and intergroup violence, all of which concern Americans and all of which are widely believed to detract from the quality of life.

We will begin by discussing the meaning, the kinds, and the amount of violence in the nation. We will show how that violence detracts from the quality of life, and we will identify the various sociocultural factors that contribute to the problem. We will discuss ways in which violence can be minimized or eliminated from human life.

We will then discuss rape. We will deal with rape separately for three reasons. First, it is a unique problem. Second, it is a predatory crime, one of the seven on the FBI Crime Index (it may be the most underreported of all crimes on that Index). Some people have treated rape as a form of sexual deviance. However, increasing evidence supports the notion that rape is essentially an act of violence. Third, we will treat rape separately is because it has emerged as an important issue as the women's movement has progressed during the 1970s. In a unique way, the victim of this violent act is typically further victimized by the reaction of all levels of the legal structure—from police officers to male juries.

What Is Violence?

In general, **violence** implies *use of force to kill, injure, or abuse others*. It occurs between two or more individuals as *interpersonal violence,* or it involves identifiable groups in the society and erupts as *intergroup violence* between two or more different races, religions, or political groups. In intergroup situations the violence ultimately means confrontation between individuals, but the individuals behave violently because of their group affiliation rather than because of some interpersonal difficulty. Much of the interpersonal violence that occurs is between people who knew each other prior to the violent confrontation. Intergroup violence, on the other hand, is likely to involve people who were strangers prior to the confrontation.

Violence takes many forms. In American life it may arise as murder within families; assault on victims by thieves; riots between groups or between citizens and authorities; confrontations between labor and management; assassinations and terrorist activities; or the actions of vigilantes.

How Much Violence Is There?

It is difficult to estimate the amount of some kinds of violent behavior. Much is never reported, and for some kinds of violence—riots and terrorist activities—there is no systematic effort to record all incidents. The evidence we do have indicates that there always has been a considerable amount of violence in America. One effort to estimate the amount of interpersonal violence was reported by the National Commission on the Causes and Prevention of Violence (Mulvihill and Tumin, 1969:115–17).

Figure 7.1 The 1960s saw many violent confrontations between students and police or national guard troops.

In a national public opinion survey sponsored by the commission, people were asked whether they had ever been the object of, had observed, or had instigated any of six identified acts of violence. The six violent acts the respondents were asked to respond to were: spanking a child; slapping or kicking; punching or beating; choking; threatening or cutting with a knife; and threatening or shooting at with a gun. (The questions about instigating use of a knife or gun were phrased to make the act one of self-defense.) The results showed 93 percent of the respondents were spanked as children, which is not surprising, but also, 55 percent were slapped or kicked, 31 percent were punched or beaten, 8 percent were choked, 14 percent were threatened or cut with a knife, and 12 percent were threatened or shot at with a gun. The percentages were even higher for those who reported observing acts of violence.

The commission concluded that the incidence of violence is "impressively high." A national crime survey corroborates that conclusion. According to the survey, about 3.8 million incidents of violence among intimates (relatives, friends, neighbors, or work associates) occurred during the survey period, 1973 through 1976. About 40 percent of those incidents resulted in injury, and 13 percent were serious enough to require some form of medical care (U.S. Department of Justice, Bureau of Justice Statistics, 1980:1).

We should also note that the homicide rate in the United States is far higher than in other developed countries such as England, France, Germany, Canada, Italy, and Japan (United Nations, 1973). Additional evidence of the amount of interpersonal violence will be given later in this chapter, in the discussion of rape and in chapter 14, "Family Problems." Evidence suggests that a large number of Americans are involved in some kind of interpersonal violence as participants or observers.

How much intergroup violence is there? Ted Gurr (1969:576) attempted to estimate the amount of civil strife in the United States from June 1963 through May 1968. He identified hundreds of events that involved a total of over 2 million participants and over 9,400 reported casualties. The most common type of violence was interracial. Gurr found over 800 events that were civil rights demonstrations, or black riots and disturbances, or white terrorism against blacks and civil rights workers.

Looking at intergroup violence in historical perspective, we find that the amount of violence fluctuates. Levy (1969:84–100) used newspapers to identify "political violence" in the United States from 1819 to 1968. Political violence was defined as events that involved an official or group of officials being attacked or an individual or group being attacked for political or social reasons. Levy found that the absolute number of violent events increased dramatically from about 1950 on. Given the population growth and the increasing size of newspapers (and hence coverage), recent decades probably have not had a higher rate of internal political violence than have some previous periods (the rate of violence in the decades after the Civil War was quite high). Moreover, fewer deaths have resulted from political violence in recent decades than in earlier periods of our history, and the reasons for political violence have shifted over time. The period from 1939 to 1968 saw a marked increase in the number of incidents motivated by the effort to gain political advantage, by responses to undesirable social conditions, by protest against war, and by racial antagonism. Overall, the study revealed a considerable amount of violence throughout American history, the amount fluctuating from one period to another, and the reasons changing somewhat.

A large number of Americans directly experience some kind of violence. Virtually all Americans are indirectly exposed to violence; those who do not observe it directly are unlikely to miss observing it indirectly through the *mass media:*

> Numerous studies from both commercial and academic research centers clearly support what has long been the contention of many concerned citizens about these elementary points: (1) the menu offered by the mass media is heavily saturated with violent content, including incidents of persons intentionally doing physical harm to one another; (2) more and more people have ready access to the media, with the average American spending between one-quarter and one-half of his waking day attending to the mass media; and (3) for most persons, but particularly for the poor in American society, television is perceived as the most credible and believable source of information on the reality of the world [Baker and Ball, 1969:237].

In one study of television programs during prime evening time and Saturday mornings in October of 1967 and 1968, violence was found in 81 percent of all 1967 programs and 82 percent of all 1968 programs (Baker and Ball, 1969:333). About 66 percent of comedies had violence. In 1976 an average American child between the ages of 5 and 15 could see around 13,000 violent deaths on television.[1] Since then, the TV industry and advertisers have worked to

reduce the amount of violence that is shown. However, the level is still high.

Violence and the Quality of Life

To fully capture the impact of violence in writing is probably impossible. But, we will attempt to get the "feel" of how violence detracts from the quality of life by looking at both objective and subjective evidence. We will see that the impact of violence on the quality of life can be severe and long-term.

Human Injury and Destruction

Violence results in *human destruction* and is, therefore, a *contradiction* to our values of well-being and freedom from fear. Violent crime, riots, and other forms of interpersonal and intergroup violence can lead to both injury and death. During the steel strikes of 1937, violence erupted at the South Chicago shop of the Republic Steel Company. Police moved in to halt picketing, and when the workers threw objects at them, the police opened fire. Ten workers were killed and over 100 were injured (Dulles, 1966:301). Labor-management and interracial confrontations are the kinds of intergroup conflict most likely to result in deaths and serious injuries.

The injured or killed may not have been participating in the conflict. Sometimes people are killed or injured while watching or trying to get through an area where violence is occurring. During the 1965 riots in the Watts section of Los Angeles, a young man was killed by a police bullet while he was standing on a corner. The police fired warning shots over the heads of rioters and one struck the bystander. Several

230

Figure 7.2   A teacher beaten in New Jersey. Strikes have often resulted in violence in American history.

deaths and injuries to innocent bystanders occurred in other cities and on college campuses during the 1960s.

Psychological Disruption and Dehumanization

Previously we discussed the *psychological trauma* endured by the victims of violent crime. Interpersonal violence not only traumatizes the victim, it also forms a link in a chain that perpetuates the violence. Parents who abuse their children were, typically, beaten themselves when they were children. Thus, the *dehumanization process* tends to be continued.

Intergroup violence is no less disruptive and dehumanizing than interpersonal violence. The conflict between Catholics and Protestants in Northern Ireland has been particularly violent. What has been the effect of that violence on the people? Fields (1975) attempted to answer the question with respect to the children of the nation. Beginning in 1971, she studied Protestant and Catholic children in the 6-to-15-year age group. In her first study she found the children to be obsessed with the ideas of death and destruction. On projective tests the children seemed unable to conceive of happy endings to stories they created. During successive years of study some of the children were killed and some joined radical groups. As the children grew older, their stories increasingly reflected an obsession with using violence to establish justice. They seemed unable to conceive of law and order coming to their nation without further killing and bombing.

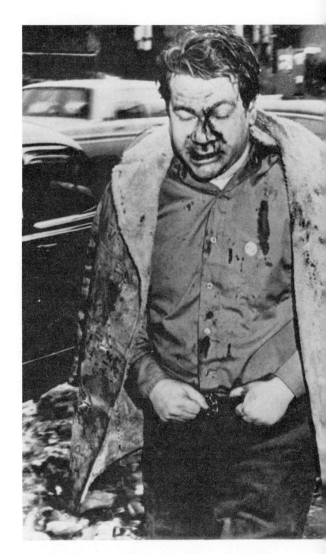

Violence as Seductive Self-Destruction

Throughout our history, groups of Americans have resorted to violence either to bring about certain changes or to try to maintain the status quo. In either case, violence has often been defined as the "only way" to reach the desired goals but has turned out instead to facilitate the victory of the opposition. Because expectations and outcome often have been contradictory, violence has frequently been a kind of *seductive self-destruction.*

A survey of violence associated with the labor movement concluded that when laborers resorted to violence, it was almost always harmful to the union (Taft and Ross, 1969:382). In general, violence did not bring the advantages hoped for by the workers. Noted historian Richard Hofstadter (Hofstadter and Wallace, 1970:37) agreed with this line of reasoning, pointing out that one of the more effective tactics of labor was the series of sitdown strikes of the 1930s. These strikes were designed to avoid rather than instigate violence.

Hofstadter also made the point that violence has seemed more effective in maintaining the status quo than in bringing about change, at least in the short run. The long history of violence by whites against blacks to maintain blacks in a subordinate status has been seductively self-destructive. Whites have not kept blacks subjected, just as management, which employed violence far more than workers ever did, has not prevented unionization of workers. Still, in the short run, violence can be effective in maintaining the status quo. In Wilmington, North Carolina, blacks were making progress in the latter part of the nineteenth century (Nash, 1973). Poor whites grew hostile, believing that blacks threatened them in the labor market. A vigilante group called the Red Shirts was formed and many poor whites were attracted into membership. During the 1898 election, newspaper articles overstated the extent of the blacks political power in order to gain support for the Democratic party. When the election was over, whites were told to overturn "rule by Negroes" and take away the jobs held by blacks. Tension grew and a riot broke out. Nineteen blacks were killed. The violence so terrorized the black community that it retreated into a passive, subordinate condition for more than a generation.

In the long run, blacks were not kept out of the labor market, just as workers were not to be kept out of unions. Those who resort to violence to achieve their ends fail in the long run. Sometimes they fail in the short run. Young members of the New Left in the 1960s helped bring about the demise of the movement by the *indiscriminate use of violence.* The use of violence quickly became counter-productive. As summarized by a radical writer:

> Disruption and confrontation tactics are inevitable where other means fail to get positive response, whether from corporation, educational institution, or the State. But these must be mass actions in this sense: that they articulate real grievances, set realizable objectives, and win the participation and/or the understanding and sympathy of large masses of people. Under no circumstances can they appear to be the artificially contrived gimmicks of confrontation for the sake of confrontation [Green, 1971:97].

The author later pointed out that a sit-in at Columbia University was effective in preventing the school from building a gymnasium on a park site. But, when the leaders of the radical student group on campus "took this to mean that it should organize confrontation as a permanent way of life, and sought constant disruption for the sake of disruption, it soon lost sympathy and support and shrank into a sect" (Green, 1971:97).

Violence, in sum, can appeal to people as a means to bring about certain changes or to resist certain changes. But, violence typically turns out to be counter-productive. Not only does the group using violence fail to achieve its goals, it may also insure victory for its opponents.

Economic Costs

Certain economic costs are involved in violence. The costs of interpersonal violence include, among other things, maintaining the criminal justice system and family service agencies. The costs of intergroup violence include treating those injured and repairing damaged property. There are less obvious costs also. The 1967 Detroit riot severely damaged at least a hundred dwellings and numerous stores. The losses sustained and the costs of cleaning up the damage must both be counted. In addition, "hundreds of businesses lost revenue by complying with a curfew, and thousands of citizens lost wages because businesses were closed" (U.S. Riot Commission, 1968:358).

Contributing Factors

Violence has been linked with a *human need to be aggressive*. Early psychologists said that human beings are aggressive animals by nature. More recent psychologists argue that **aggression** is related to *frustration*. Aggression is the common way to deal with frustration, and since frustration is virtually inevitable, we can expect a considerable amount of aggression in social life.

While frustration can produce aggression, this does not adequately explain violence. Aggression need not take the form of violence. It can be channeled into many outlets, such as competitive sports, business, or hard physical work. Aggression is neither innate nor a necessary outcome of frustration. Rather, aggression is linked with *cultural values and patterns*. Some people emphasize cooperation as strongly as we emphasize competition. To fully explain violence, we must look at various sociocultural factors that contribute to the problem.

Social Structural Factors

Norms.   We noted in our discussion of delinquency that *norms legitimate antisocial behavior* of various kinds, including violent behavior, among some groups. Different groups within a society have different norms with respect to violence, just as different societies have different norms. In a study of child-rearing patterns in six societies, including both Western and non-Western nations, Minturn and Lambert (1964) found variations within and between the nations in the way mothers responded to aggressive behavior of their children.

Mothers in some societies were very likely to punish aggressive behavior, while mothers in other societies were less prone to do so. A group of American mothers (living in New England) in the sample were least likely to retaliate to a child's mother-directed aggression and most likely to reward a child for retaliating in aggressive behavior with the child's peers. The mothers did not want their children to initiate fighting, but as "part of their child training" they encouraged their children to "stand up for their rights" and to fight back, when necessary, if attacked. "The extent to which these parents encourage such aggression is unusual, compared to other samples" (Minturn and Lambert, 1964:198).

The study concluded that American children were encouraged to fight to a much greater degree than were children of the other societies studied. The researchers pointed out that the American children were expected to be "fair" in their fighting, with the result that they were seldom hurt (as were children in some of the other societies studied). Nevertheless, fighting was more acceptable and more common among the Americans than among some other groups. The American way may minimize injuries to the young, but it may also contribute to the high level of violence in the society as the young mature with the expectation that a certain amount of aggressive behavior will occur.

Historically, American norms have legitimated official violence—against radicals, striking laborers, and students, for instance. As we will see later, this official violence is supported by attitudes that approve use of violence for social control. Throughout our history any group defined as radical or as a threat to social order has been defined also as a legitimate object of suppression by violence.

For example, in 1874 unemployed workers gathered in Tompkins Square in New York City to demonstrate their need for help. The group that organized the demonstration had requested a permit, but the police did not inform them that their request was denied until the morning the meeting was scheduled. Over 7,000 people gathered at Tompkins Square on a bitterly cold January morning. At 10:30 the police came to forcefully break up the gathering. Noted labor leader Samuel Gompers, who was there, later described the incident as "an orgy of brutality" with numerous incidents of "police brutality inflicted on the sick, the lame, the innocent bystander" (Hofstadter and Wallace, 1970:347). The police justified their violence by labeling the gathering as "communistic." Newspaper editors throughout the country approved the action. One said that if the "communistic spirit" should rise again, the city officials should "club it to death at the hands of the police or shoot it to death at the hands of the militia" (Hofstadter and Wallace, 1970:345).

A more recent example is the violence of the Chicago police against young anti-war demonstrators during the Democratic Convention of 1968. The committee that investigated the situation called it a "police riot." Many innocent bystanders were injured by the police, including some reporters and news photographers. One reporter described what he saw this way:

> ". . . when the police managed to break up groups of protestors they pursued individuals and beat them with clubs. . . . In many cases it appeared to me that when police had finished beating the protestors they were pursuing, they then attacked, indiscriminately, any civilian who happened to be standing nearby. Many of these were not involved in the demonstrations" [Hofstadter and Wallace, 1970:382].

Another witness said the police acted like "mad dogs" looking for something to attack. Many people were horrified by the brutality of the police, but public opinion polls showed that the majority of people supported the police. This support came not only because some of the

Figure 7.3 Throughout our history, when any group was defined as radical or as a threat to social order, it was defined also as a legitimate object of suppression by violence, such as when: shirtwaist workers in New York City went on strike in 1910 (*top left*); Brooklyn mounted police escorted "scabs" and provisions to the transport company stables during a "street railway" strike (*bottom left*); National Guard troops fired into a mob during the 1894 Pullman strike in Chicago (*top right*); and jobless men during the Great Depression of the 1930s joined together to make demands (*bottom right*).

young people had baited the police by taunting them with obscenities, but because Americans tend to expect and approve violence in the name of social order.

Political arrangements.   Certain political factors affect the level of violence in our society. The history of America is characterized by the *exclusion of racial minorities from the core benefits of and participation in American life.* That exclusion was maintained, and continues to exist to some extent, because of political action or inaction. There is evidence that the exclusion has been an important factor in riots and other interracial violence. "Exclusion" here means both lack of access to economic opportunities and denial of access to the political power by which grievances can be redressed.

Various studies support the conclusion that *political arrangements* have contributed to the urban riots and interracial violence in American history. Lieberson and Silverman (1965) examined interracial riots that occurred between 1913 and 1963. They found seventy-six riots in which violence occurred and the immediate precipitants and underlying conditions could be identified. They concluded that the following factors did *not* appear to affect the likelihood of a riot: rapid population change; high rates of white or black unemployment; low black income or a large gap between black and white income. Factors that did increase the probability of a riot were: "encroachment of Negroes in the white occupational world"; a police force with a small proportion of blacks; a governmental structure unlikely to be responsive to blacks (such as city councilmen elected by city-wide votes rather than by district votes).

In a study of black male heads of households in Los Angeles, Ransford (1968) found a greater willingness to use violence when the man was relatively *isolated* from whites, felt *powerless* over events, and felt *mistreated because of his race.* While Ransford did not measure the sense of inability to effect change through normal political means, the three variables he used suggest that his respondents felt excluded from the political process. More direct evidence comes from Paige (1971), who examined the relationships between *political trust, political efficacy,* and riot participation among 237 black males in Newark, New Jersey. Political trust was measured by a direct question: "How much do you think you can trust the government in Newark to do what is right—just about always, most of the time, some of the time, or almost never?" Political efficacy was measured by the amount of information the respondents had about local and national political figures. Riot participation was measured by asking the respondents whether they had been "active" in the 1967 riot in Newark and what they had done.

Paige found that those respondents who scored high on political information and low on political trust were most likely to have participated in the riot, while those who scored low on information and low on trust were least likely to have participated. In other words, rioters had information about the government; they were not alienated to the point of apathy; and they did not trust the government to be responsive to their needs. This sense of exclusion from the political process was identified by the U.S. Riot Commission Report (1968:205) as one of the important factors in the urban riots of the 1960s:

Table 7.1   Murder Victims, by Weapons Used, 1965–1979

Year	Total Murder Victims	Guns Total	Percent	Cutting or Stabbing	Blunt Object*	Strangu- lations, Beatings	Drownings, Arson, Etc.	All Other**
				Weapons Used or Cause of Death				
1965	8,773	5,015	57.2	2,021	505	894	226	112
1966	9,552	5,660	59.3	2,134	516	896	203	143
1967	11,114	6,998	63.0	2,200	589	957	211	159
1968	12,503	8,105	64.8	2,317	713	936	294	138
1969	13,575	8,876	65.4	2,534	613	1,039	322	191
1970	13,649	9,039	66.2	2,424	604	1,031	353	198
1971	16,183	10,712	66.2	3,017	645	1,295	314	200
1972	15,832	10,379	65.6	2,974	672	1,291	331	185
1973	17,123	11,249	65.7	2,985	848	1,445	173†	423
1974	18,632	12,474	66.9	3,228	976	1,417	153†	384
1975	18,642	12,061	64.7	3,245	1,001	1,646	193†	496
1979	20,591	13,040	63.3	3,954	997	1,557	276	767

*Refers to club, hammer, etc. **Includes poison, explosives, unknown, and not stated; for 1973 to 1975, includes drowning. †Arson only.

Source: U.S. Bureau of the Census, *Statistical Abstract of the United States, 1980* (Washington, D.C.: Government Printing Office, 1981), p. 188.

. . . many Negroes have come to believe that they are being exploited politically and economically by the white "power structure." Negroes, like people in poverty everywhere, in fact lack the channels of communication, influence and appeal that traditionally have been available to ethnic minorities within the city and which enabled them—unburdened by color—to scale the walls of the white ghettos in an earlier era. The frustrations of powerlessness have led some to the conviction that there is no effective alternative to violence as a means of expression and redress, as a way of "moving the system."

The politics of gun control. Government policy on *gun control* bears upon violence in America. America is a land full of guns. In 1974 nearly 7 million guns were manufactured in the United Sates or were imported from other countries. In a 1975 Gallup poll, 44 percent of the respondents said they had some kind of gun in their home, and many had more than one gun.[2] Nationally, 26 percent of the people said they had a rifle, 26 percent said they had a shotgun, and 18 percent said they had a pistol.

Guns are used more than any other weapon in murder, and the proportion of all murders in the United States that involve the use of guns has increased. As table 7.1 shows, the proportion of murders in which a gun was used increased from 57.2 percent in 1965 to 66.2 percent in 1971, and dropped back to 63.3 percent in 1979. Guns are used in other kinds of violence besides murder; assaults and robberies often involve a gun.

Does the widespread existence of guns contribute to the amount of violence in the nation? After all, goes one argument, it is people, not guns, that kill, and if a gun is not available a person will find a different weapon. Professionals dispute the relationship between the number of guns and the amount of violence. Don Kates, a professor of law, said criminological studies show that "peaceful societies do not need handgun prohibition, and violent societies do not benefit from it."[3] Kates argued that ours is a violent society, that violence will not be reduced by trying to control the sale and possession of guns, and that such efforts at control would be largely frustrating and of little social benefit. Many Americans agree that the effort would be frustrating or, worse, it would be counterproductive. A popular slogan puts it, when guns are outlawed, only outlaws will have guns.

Such arguments are reasonable. We pointed out earlier that societal norms are important factors in the amount of aggressive behavior in a society. If parental punishment has little effect on such behavior, why should we believe that laws on gun control will be of any use? Despite such reasoning, the weight of the evidence is in favor of gun control, and we will review some of that evidence here. Societal norms are not the only factors involved in violence. Moreover, American norms make aggressive behavior likely, but they do not necessarily make violent behavior likely. Violence is only one kind of aggression. What, then, is the evidence that favors gun control?

The case for control is well summarized in the staff report to the National Commission on the Causes and Prevention of Violence (Mulvihill and Tumin, 1969:239–40). First, guns are the most frequently used weapon in homicides. They are also the most versatile of weapons:

> Firearms make some attacks possible that simply would not occur without firearms. They permit attacks at greater range and from positions of better concealment than other weapons. They also permit attacks by persons physically or psychologically unable to overpower their victim through violent physical contact [Mulvihill and Tumin, 1969:239].

The gun is also the deadliest of weapons, with a fatality rate about five times as high as the rate for knives.

A second aspect of the argument for control is that guns are the most frequent weapon in armed robbery. The gun is almost essential for armed robbery in many cases because without it the offender is unable to produce the necessary threat of force. The fatality rate in armed robberies involving guns is about four times as high as the rate for other weapons.

Some citizens believe firearms are necessary for defense of the home. This argument has little substance. Many murders occur in homes, but seldom do they involve strangers. A survey of criminal homicide in seventeen American cities in 1967 found that 15.8 percent involved husbands and wives; 8.9 percent involved other kinds of family relationships; 38.8 percent involved friends, neighbors, or other acquaintances; and 15.6 percent involved strangers (Mulvihill and Tumin, 1969:217). In 20.9 percent of the cases the relationship was unknown. Most murders, then, occur between individuals who know each other, and they frequently occur during some emotionally charged encounter. In such cases the gun may be used because it is readily available; if not available, the murder may not occur. Thus, "in the heat of an alter-cation, family quarrel, or jealous rage, guns stored for protection against strangers can be used on friends and loved ones" (Mulvihill and Tumin, 1969:240). There is also the possibility of accidental injury or death because of a gun in the home. More people are probably killed accidentally by guns in homes than are killed by intruders. Ironically, the citizen may face greater danger from the weapon purchased for defense against intruders than from an actual intruder.

The evidence suggests that gun control could reduce some kinds of violence (armed robbery) and minimize the destructiveness of other kinds (assaults and arguments). Public opinion polls show that most Americans favor the *registration of firearms*. Why, then, is there political inaction? Some of the evidence is ambiguous; legislators are not convinced of the value of control; *the lobbying efforts* of the National Rifle Association are strong—to mention just a few reasons. There was no organized effort to counter the persuasion of the National Rifle Association until the mid-1970s, when the National Gun Control Center was formed to mobilize needed counter-offensive both in Congress and in the American public:

> The National Rifle Association, with one million members, has distorted or suppressed the truth about handgun control for years. Its annual, tax-exempt income of over $7 million finances massive educational campaigns to defeat handgun controls . . . the N.R.A. has stepped up its efforts to recruit children in recent years. . . . For only $1.00, a youngster can become a Junior Member and start being indoctrinated in the N.R.A. philosophy that guns are just good, clean, All-American fun.[4]

These statements show that the National Gun Control Center does not intend to mince words in its efforts to convince the people and the Congress that handguns are a "menace" to American society. The organization is too young, however, to have marked effects on either the people or the Congress, and as of this writing the political power of the National Rifle Association prevails.

The stratification system.   In an effort to put violence in America in historical perspective, Graham and Gurr (1969:794–97) identified certain *political and economic inequalities* between various groups that had been associated with violence. The early Anglo-Saxon immigrants to America "effectively preempted the crucial levers of economic and political power in government, commerce, and the professions. This elite group has tenaciously resisted the upward strivings of successive 'ethnic' immigrant waves" (Graham and Gurr, 1969:794). The result was a "competitive hierarchy of immigrants," which is conducive to violence in varying forms. Much of the violence was inflicted by the dominant group on the subordinate groups in an effort to maintain the existing power distribution. Violence between subordinate groups was also common, as in cases where workers out on strike clashed with strike-breakers who were willing to cross a picket line.

Inequalities have also been identified as factors in the urban riots of the 1960s. As the U.S. Riot Commission Report (1968:203) put it, one of the "most bitter fruits" of white racism was

> the continuing exclusion of great numbers of Negroes from the benefits of economic progress through discrimination in employment and education, and their enforced confinement in

segregated housing and schools. The corrosive and degrading effects of this condition and the attitudes that underlie it are the source of the deepest bitterness and at the center of the problem of racial disorder.

The importance of inequality as a cause of violence is underscored by a study of forty-two American cities undertaken by Morgan and Clark (1973). Disorders occurred in twenty-three of the cities in 1967. The researchers measured the *severity* and the *frequency* of the disorders. Severity was measured by things such as the number of arrests and injuries, the amount of property damage, and the duration of the disorder. Frequency was found to be directly related to size of the nonwhite population and size of the police force. They interpreted this to mean that cities with large numbers of nonwhites and police had a greater probability of confrontation—"more opportunities exist for social contacts that could precipitate a disorder" (Morgan and Clark, 1973:616). Severity was directly related to housing inequality (as measured by the percent of each race in substandard housing). Interestingly, a high degree of job inequality (measured by the percent of each race in low-status jobs) was negatively correlated to disorders (recall the finding of Lieberson and Silverman [1965] that low black income and a large white-black income gap did not contribute to rioting).

Clearly, some kinds of inequality are related to violence, and when these inequalities cannot, in the eyes of the oppressed, be resolved through existing political channels, the probability of violence is greatly increased. In terms of *Merton's anomie theory,* people who cannot reach culturally legitimate goals by culturally legitimate means may switch to illegitimate means.

Is There a Subculture of Violence?

We will pause at this point to discuss a prominent theory of violence that combines structural and social psychological factors. Set forth by Wolfgang and Ferracuti (1967), the theory is known as the *"subculture of violence" theory:*

> We have said that overt use of force or violence, either in interpersonal relationships or in group interaction, is generally viewed as a reflection of basic values that stand apart from the dominant, the central, or the parent culture. Our hypothesis is that this overt (and often illicit) expression of violence . . . is part of a subcultural normative system, and that this system is reflected in the psychological traits of the subculture participants [Wolfgang and Ferracuti, 1967:158].

We pointed out earlier that societies differ in the extent to which violence is normative. It seems reasonable that groups within the society could also differ. However, while there are particular groups such as juvenile gangs in which violence is normative, there is no evidence of a subculture of violence running through any broad social categories such as race or socioeconomic strata. Because of the higher homicide rates, some observers argue that the South forms a regional subculture of violence. But, if there ever was such a subculture it no longer exists, as evidenced by the failure of recent studies to find the divergent value system necessary for a subculture of violence in the South (Doerner, 1978; O'Connor and Lizotte, 1978). Most Americans seem to dislike violence, whether they are white, black, poor, or affluent (Erlanger, 1974). There appears to be little difference in values between males who report no participation in interpersonal violence and those who

240

Figure 7.4 Urban guerrilla manuals that have been circulated in the U.S. Such manuals advocate violence as the only way to bring about necessary changes.

report moderate or high participation in interpersonal violence (Ball-Rokeach, 1973).

In other words, in particular groups violence is normative, but we cannot say that whole segments of American society such as a race or the poor constitute a subculture of violence. Those who are oppressed may resort to violence, but there is no evidence that as a group they value and encourage violence.

Social Psychological Factors

Attitudes.   People often *support violence because of attitudes that legitimate it.* A national sample of the attitudes of American men (Blumenthal, Kahn, Andrews, and Head, 1972:243–50) found that violence was justifiable to reach certain goals. Some believed violence was the only way to maintain **social control,** while others believed violence was the only way to achieve *social change.* The proportion who justified violence in the name of such goals was surprising to the researchers:

> We hardly expected that half to two-thirds of American men would justify shooting in the situations described as requiring social control. Neither did we expect that 20 to 30 percent would advise the police to shoot to kill under the circumstances described. . . . The fact that almost 50 percent of American men felt that shooting was a good way of handling campus disturbances "almost always" or at least "sometimes" is particularly disturbing. Most campus disturbances have not involved violence to persons or major damage to property. . . . That 20 percent of American men considered it appropriate for the police to kill in these circumstances indicates the ease with which many people will accept violence to maintain order even when force so used is entirely out of

proportion to the precipitating incidents. The data imply that willingness to reach for a gun is easily evoked [Blumenthal, Kahn, Andrews, and Head, 1972:243].

The proportion of men who believed violence was justifiable to bring about social change was far less. Although more than 90 percent of the men agreed that the kinds of changes demanded by blacks and by students may be needed, most also indicated that they believed the changes (which usually involved some kind of inequality) could come about quickly enough without the use of violence. Less than 10 percent believed that protests involving death and extensive property damage were necessary to bring about the desired changes. About 20 percent believed that protests involving personal injuries and some property damage are necessary for change.

A frequent explanation for violence involves the notion of **relative deprivation,** which means that people have a *sense of deprivation in relation to some standard.* Here, the attitudes of people toward their deprivation rather than any objective assessment of that deprivation is important. This observation goes back at least as far as de Tocqueville (1955:175–77), who pointed out that the French were experiencing real economic gains prior to the Revolution:

> In 1780, there could no longer be any talk of France's being on the downgrade; on the contrary, it seemed that no limit could be set to her advance. . . . Moreover, those parts of France in which the improvement in the standard of living was most pronounced were the centers of the revolutionary movement.

An observer could have told the French that, objectively, they were surely better off at the time of their revolt than they were at other times in the past. But, what if the people used a different standard than their past to measure their deprivation? They might then perceive themselves to be worse off and rebel, which is precisely the idea contained in the concept of relative deprivation.

Davies (1962) used the notion of relative deprivation to explain revolutions. He constructed a *"J-curve" theory of revolution*. In essence, the theory states that *a widening gap between what people want and what they get* leads to a revolutionary situation. People do not revolt when the society is generally impoverished. Rather, a revolutionary state of mind develops when a threat to the expectation of greater opportunities to satisfy needs develops.

There is always a gap between our expectations and the satisfaction of our needs. Some degree of gap is tolerable, and over time both our satisfactions and our expectations tend to increase. Sometimes, however, something happens in a society to suddenly increase the gap between expectations and satisfactions. Our expectations continue to rise while our actual need satisfactions remain level or suddenly fall. The gap then becomes intolerable, and a revolutionary situation is created.

According to Davies's theory, the deprivation of people in a revolutionary situation is relative. Actual satisfaction of their needs may be higher at the time of a revolution than earlier, but their expectations are also higher. The people may be better off in terms of their past, but worse off in terms of their expectations. Their attitudes rather than their objective condition make the situation revolutionary.

Relative deprivation has been identified as a factor in racial militancy and the approval of violent protest by northern blacks. Interviews with 107 riot area residents of Detroit in 1967 showed that those who were most militant in their attitudes and who believed the riots helped the black cause were those who felt relatively deprived rather than relatively satisfied (Crawford and Naditch, 1970). As other studies showed, the rioters were not among the poorest and least educated people in Detroit. They were better off financially and educationally than some others, but they defined their situation as one of deprivation. Their standard of comparison was not blacks who were worse off, but whites who were better off.

Values.   Attitudes that justify violence are often reinforced by certain values. The previously mentioned study of the attitudes of American men toward violence (Blumenthal, Kahn, Andrews and Head, 1972:97–133) shows considerable agreement among American men on two *values that support violence for social control*—**retributiveness** and *self-defense*.

Retributiveness, or retributive justice, is summarized by the notion of "an eye for an eye and a tooth for a tooth." It is a value of punishment, of paying people back for their antisocial behavior. Self-defense is also valued in American society (as well as in other societies):

Defense of self and family is a traditional masculine value in many cultures, including the American, where it is also the redundant and seemingly eternal theme of the western films that play some substantial role in the socialization of boys. . . . The overwhelming majority of American men agreed strongly to the right to kill in defense of self or family, and the majority agreed (though less strongly) that the right exists as well for the defense of one's house (Blumenthal, Kahn, Andrews, and Head, 1972:108).

This quotation makes the point that values supporting violence are internalized, in part, through the mass media. We previously pointed out that American societal norms result in a high level of aggressive behavior. To what extent are the norms, attitudes, and values that underlie violence and the approval of violence learned through the mass media? It is an important, controversial question.

Role of the mass media.   We noted earlier that the *mass media* expose us to an enormous amount of violence. Historically, this has been true of newspapers, just as it is true of all media today, especially television. In fact, violence has often been glamorized in the mass media. In 1872 three men committed armed robbery at a Kansas City fair, wounding a small girl in the process. In reporting the incident, the *Kansas City Times* commented that the deed was "so diabolically daring and so utterly in contempt of fear that we are bound to admire it and revere its perpetrators" (Frantz, 1969:128). We can find many similar examples, in the past and in the present. Stories, plays, movies, and television programs make heroes out of violent criminals and romanticize violent revolutions.

What effect does this glamorizing of violence by the mass media have on society? Some observers argued that the effect is an increased amount of violent behavior. Others argued that people who watch violence on television experience a kind of **catharsis,** a *discharging of aggressive emotions* through vicarious participation of violence. They argue that hostility is neutralized by emotional participation in mass media violence. For example, a man who has become extremely hostile toward his wife can discharge his aggression by abusing his co-workers or kicking his dog or breaking dishes. However, will watching someone else's violent behavior enable him to vicariously discharge his own aggressions?

The answer to this question appears to be no. Displacement of aggression and vicarious discharge of aggression are, after all, not the same thing. On the contrary, portrayal of violence in motion pictures and on television has the effect of increasing the level of violence in our society. Let us look at some evidence for this position.

In one of the reports to the National Commission on the Causes and Prevention of Violence, the following conclusions were drawn with respect to the effects of mass media portrayals of violence (Baker and Ball, 1969:375–79). First, portrayals of violence do affect the audience. That effect "is to extend the behavioral and attitudinal boundaries of acceptable violence beyond legal and social norms currently espoused by a majority of Americans" (Baker and Ball, 1969:375). Portrayals of violence have both short-term and long-term effects. A short-term effect is that the individuals exposed to mass-media violence learn how to perform violent acts and are likely to do so under certain conditions (when the violence in the mass media appears to be justified, for example, and when the individual is in a situation similar to that portrayed). A long-term effect is the *socialization* of people into the norms, attitudes, and values for violence. The probability of such socialization increases as:

1. The duration of exposure increases.
2. The intensity of exposure increases (e.g., number of hours per day).
3. The age of the viewer decreases.
4. The number of other sources of socialization into violence decreases.

244

Jensen/The Spectator/London

5. The number of senses stimulated by the medium increases (e.g., sight or sound).
6. The primacy of the part played by violence in media presentations increases [Baker and Ball, 1969:376].

The report goes into more detail on both short-term and long-term effects, but the circumstances quoted make the point that mass-media violence increases the level of violent behavior in our society.

A similar conclusion was reached by the controversial report of the Surgeon General, which was based on numerous studies and released in 1972 under the title *Television and Social Behavior*. Specifically, the sixth volume, which was a summary prepared by the Scientific Advisory Committee of twelve people, was the source of controversy. According to Rothenberg (1975:1044), the committee was to have been selected from a list of forty social and behavioral scientists. Before selecting the twelve, television representatives blackballed seven of the scientists with "the most outstanding reputations and work in the field of violence research" and replaced them with five television network executives. The resulting committee was then under political pressure to produce a document of unanimity.

As a result, the summary, while it concludes that a causal relationship between violence viewing and aggression by the young was found, is worded so as to lead to misunderstanding. And the *summary* of the summary is flatly misleading, repeatedly using words such as "preliminary," "tentative," and "however" as qualifiers for statements concerning this causal relationship . . . 146 published papers representing 50 studies—laboratory studies, correlational field studies, and naturalistic experiments—involving 10,000 children and adolescents from every conceivable background all show that violence viewing produces increased aggressive behavior in the young and that immediate remedial action in terms of television programming is warranted [Rothenberg, 1975:1044–45].

What kinds of studies formed the basis for the conclusions of the Surgeon General's report? As Rothenberg notes, they used different methods. One example shows how the studies were conducted in this difficult area of assessing the effects of television on people (Lefkowitz, Eron, Walder and Huesmann, 1972:35–135). The researchers made a longitudinal study of aggressive behavior in children. They began in 1959 with 875 school children, the entire third grade of a school in New York. Initially they found that boys who watched a lot of violence on television were likely to be nominated by their peers as aggressive individuals.

The children were studied over a ten-year period. In the thirteenth grade, peer nomination and other measures of aggressive behavior were used. A diet of television violence was again associated with aggressive behavior, as measured by peer nominations, self-ratings, and psychological tests. There was continuity over the period, with those who were aggressive at the earlier age tending to be the same ones who were aggressive at the later age.

An interesting extension of the research was provided by Drabman and Thomas (1977), who compared viewing aggression alone with viewing it in pairs. They found that boys who watched in pairs were significantly more aggressive afterward than those who watched alone. This finding suggests that past research, which monitored children individually, may have underestimated the effects of viewing violence on TV (since many children watch with others rather than alone).

Some evidence shows that violence on television affects adult viewers also. One researcher secured 260 couples as volunteers and had the men watch particular kinds of programs each night for a week. The wives reported on the behavior of their husbands, and the participants filled out a checklist that measured their attitudes, values, self-concepts, and moods. Some programs raised helpful or pro-social feelings, but the programs with large amounts of violence tended to create an aggressive mood level in men throughout the week.[5]

Admittedly, it is difficult to state unequivocally that exposure to the mass media leads to specific effects because of the many other factors that operate within our lives. However, the evidence is growing, and it overwhelmingly supports the position that mass media violence is associated with aggressive attitudes and behavior. The evidence suggests that violent tendencies in people are encouraged and supported and that mass media violence teaches people how to be violent and tends to create violent behavior in viewers.

What Is To Be Done?

We have already discussed some steps for reducing violence in that whatever effectively deals with the problem of crime will also help reduce the level of violence.

First, we have indicated that *gun control measures* may reduce the violence in our society. The National Advisory Commission on Criminal Justice Standards and Goals (1973:214) suggested the following:

The Commission believes that the violence, fear, suffering, and loss caused by the use of handguns must be stopped by firm and decisive action. The Commission therefore recommends that, no later than January 1, 1983, each State take the following action.

—The private possession of handguns be prohibited for all persons other than law enforcement and military personnel.
—Manufacture and sale of handguns should be terminated.
—Existing handguns should be acquired by States.
—Handguns held by private citizens as collector's items should be modified and rendered inoperable.

Such steps will be vigorously resisted by various groups, but without these factors an important factor in interpersonal violence will not be dealt with.

Second, we suggested that violence in the mass media should be reduced. The National Commission on the Causes and Prevention of Violence made four recommendations to the television industry:

The broadcasting of children's cartoons containing serious, non-comic violence should be abandoned. . . . The amount of time devoted to the broadcast of crime, western and action-adventure programs containing violent episodes should be reduced. . . . More effective efforts should be made to alter the basic context in which violence is presented in television dramas. When the resort to violence is depicted as an unusual and undesirable outcome, the context is sharply different from the world of contemporary television in which violence has been the routine method by which people solve problems. . . . The members of the television industry should become more actively and seriously involved in research on the effects of violent television programs, and their future

policies, standards, and practices with regard to entertainment programs should be more responsive to the best evidence provided by social scientists, psychologists, and communications researchers.[6]

While the industry has responded somewhat to the demand to reduce the level of violence, a good deal more needs to be done before violence is significantly reduced. Federal action or large-scale pressure by citizens' groups will probably be needed.

Finally, violence will lessen as we deal with some of the inequalities in our society. We will discuss this further when we consider the problem of wealth and poverty and other problems in Part 3.

The Violence of Rape

Our legal code distinguishes between two kinds of rape—forcible and statutory. **Forcible rape** is defined as actual or attempted sexual intercourse "through the use of force or the threat of force" (U.S. National Criminal Justice Information and Statistics Service, 1975:44). **Statutory rape** refers to sexual intercourse with a female who is below the legal age for consenting. In the past, statutory rape was involved in many cases of questionable justice, such as the following account illustrates. The decision in this case was later reversed.

. . . the defendant was convicted of rape as a result of sexual intercourse with a girl by the name of Liddie. The latter, though not quite 16 years of age, was married, but was being prostituted by her husband. The defendant was one of several men who had visited and had sexual intercourse with her. Neither Liddie's marriage, nor her lack of chastity, nor the fact that the sexual intercourse grew out of a prostitutional situation, sufficed to save the defendant from a long prison sentence [Ploscowe, 1968:220].

Because of the potential for injustice, statutory-rape cases are often not prosecuted. Nevertheless, men are subject to arrest, conviction, and sentencing to prison terms if they have consensual intercourse with an under-age female where there are statutory-rape laws.

Our concern here, however, is with forcible rape, which is one of the seven major felonies in the FBI Crime Index. Forcible rape is an extremely *traumatic experience* for women, the victims. For the perpetrators, rape is typically an expression of violent aggression against women, not an act of sexual passion. The evidence for this view is accumulating.

Number and Characteristics of Victims

How much rape is in the U.S.? It is difficult to say because an unknown number of rapes are never reported to the police (we will discuss some reasons for this below). According to the FBI's *Uniform Crime Reports,* there were over 67,000 instances of forcible rape in 1978, an increase of over 66 percent from 1970. Victimization studies continue to show much higher numbers—154,000 in 1977 (U.S. Department of Justice, Law Enforcement Administration, 1979a:20). The victimization surveys also show that 40 to 50 percent of rape victims do not report the crime to the police. Fear is the major reason. The victims fear the treatment of police or prosecutors. They fear trial procedures, and they fear publicity and embarrassment (National Institute of Law Enforcement and Criminal Justice, 1978:15).

Not every woman is equally likely to be a rape victim. As table 7.2 shows, rape victims are likely to be black, under 20 years of age, and living in families with relatively low income. In other words, they are women of lower socioeconomic status. These findings are in accord with the earlier work of Amir (1971), who studied all the cases of forcible rape in the city of Philadelphia during 1958 and 1960. Amir found that 80.5 percent of the victims were black. The highest rate was in the 15–19 age group, and the second highest in the 10–14 age group. Women in low-status and low-income occupations were at greater risk of being victims than others (Amir, 1971:44, 51, 69). He pointed out that, contrary to popular belief, there was little interracial rape. Blacks tended to rape blacks and whites tended to rape whites:

In 646 rape events, 77 percent involved a Negro victim and a Negro offender, while in 16 percent of the cases the victim and offender were white. The situations in which the offender was a Negro and the victim white, and those in which the Negro victim was raped by a white offender constitute 3 and 4 percent of the total, respectively [Amir, 1971:44].

Also in contrast to popular belief is the fact that a substantial number of rapes involve nonstrangers. In one major study, the researchers found that about half of all the rapes involved strangers, about one-fourth involved "acquaintances," and the remainder involved friends or, in a few cases, relatives (National Institute of Law Enforcement and Criminal Justice, 1978:18). Rapes by "friends" tended to occur in dating situations or other kinds of social interaction. Finally, there is the case of wife rape.

Table 7.2   Rape Victimization Rates, 1977
(per 1,000 population age 12 and over)

Race	Rate
White	0.9
Black	1.0
Age	
12–15	1.6
16–19	2.7
20–24	1.7
25–34	0.9
35–49	0.4
50 and over	0.1
Family Income	
Under $3,000	1.8
$3,000–7,499	1.5
$7,500–9,999	1.2
$10,000–14,999	0.5
$15,000–24,999	0.5
$25,000 and over	0.6

Source: Adapted from U.S. Department of Justice, Law Enforcement Administration, *Rape Victimization in 26 American Cities* (Washington, D.C.: Government Printing Office, 1979), pp. 23, 24, 28.

A long-standing rule of law was that a man who forced his wife to have sexual relations could not be convicted of rape. In 1979, however, a Massachusetts man became the first American to be convicted of wife rape. We do not know how often wife rape occurs. A 1975 survey of twelve rape-crisis centers found that 0.3 percent of the calls dealt with marital rape (Gelles, 1977). As the reporting of wife rape becomes increasingly acceptable, the number and proportion of cases of marital rape will increase.

Rape and the Quality of Life

Regardless of the background characteristics of the victim, the consequences for the quality of life are similar: rape is a highly traumatic experience, and fear of rape probably causes uneasiness in most women at some time.

Much of the *meaning of rape* is captured in the following account of a victim, a twenty-year-old woman who was raped while walking to the parking lot of a college.[7]

It happened about 10 P.M. I had been doing some research at the library and I was in a hurry to get home because I wanted to see a movie on TV. . . . I was standing next to my car, looking in my purse for my keys. I didn't see the man or hear him until all of a sudden he grabbed me from behind and had me on the ground before I knew what had happened. He held a knife to my throat and told me to do what he said and I wouldn't get hurt. I was too scared to move anyway because I could feel the knife pressing against my neck. He was disgusted that I had on jeans and made a derogatory remark about the way girls dress today. He made me take off my pants and perform oral sex on him. Then he raped me. He kept asking me if I liked it, but I was too scared to answer him. He got angry because I wouldn't answer him and he hit me in the breast with his fist. I started crying and he got off of me and let me get dressed. He told me if I told anyone he would come back and rape me again. He said that he knew who I was and where I lived. I started crying harder and shaking all over. He patted me and told me to grow up, that he'd done me a favor and that I was old enough to enjoy sex with a man. He finally left me standing there and I got into my car and went home.

Figure 7.6 Rape is a form of violence that frequently threatens women.

I felt so dirty I took a shower and scrubbed myself all over and got into bed. At 12:30 my roommate came home and I told her what had happened. She insisted I call the police, so I did. Two policemen came to our apartment. . . . They asked such things as where did it happen, and what did he look like, and what time did it happen. They acted like I made it up when they found out it happened two hours ago. The young cop asked me if I had an orgasm and if he had ejaculated. I didn't know what to say as I didn't know, since this was my first encounter with sex. I don't think they believed that either. They told me to come down to the station the next day if I wanted to press charges, but that since I had taken a shower and waited so long I probably didn't have a case. No one told me to go to the hospital to be treated for V.D. or that they could give me something to prevent pregnancy until I talked to a friend the next day. She went with me to the emergency room of a hospital not far from where I live and they told me they didn't treat rape victims. I started crying and she took me home. I was pretty shook-up. For three or four days I stayed in bed. I cut all my classes. Finally, I went back to school and everything seemed to be fine until I saw a story about rape on T.V. I got so upset my roommate called the Rape Crisis Center and had me talk to them about my feelings. I called them eight or nine times in all.

I felt guilty, I thought it was my fault because my mother had been against my leaving home to go to college and against my having an apartment. She had also warned me never to go out alone at night. . . . I didn't tell her I had been raped because I was afraid she'd make me leave school and come back home. So instead of blaming the guy, who incidentally they never caught, I blamed myself for being so dumb and naive. It took about three months to get my head together. I feel I have now, but I still am uneasy if a guy comes on too strong, or stops to talk to me in an isolated place, or even if he gets too close in an elevator. I haven't dated since it happened. I guess I shut everyone out and went on my own head trip, but I've started going places with my girl friends lately and I think I have it together now.

Emotional Trauma

The account illustrates that a rape victim suffers intense *emotional trauma*. Rape contradicts our ideals about healthy, voluntary, and nonviolent relationships. The resulting emotional trauma is incompatible with the desired quality of life. This trauma was systematically described by Burgess and Holmstrom (1974) on the basis of studies of ninety-two adult women victims of forcible rape who entered the emergency ward of the Boston City Hospital during 1972 and 1973.

What Burgess and Holmstrom called the *"rape trauma syndrome"* involves two phases of reaction of the victim: an *initial, acute phase of disorganization* and a *long-term phase of reorganization*. The acute phase, which lasts for a few weeks after the incident, involves both physical and emotional reactions. The *physical reactions* included soreness and bruises resulting from the violence of the offender; tension headaches, fatigue, and disturbance of sleep; various gastrointestinal disturbances such as nausea, stomach pains, and lack of appetite; and genitourinary problems such as vaginal itching and pain. The *emotional reaction* during the acute phase "ranged from fear, humiliation, and embarrassment to anger, revenge, and self-blame. Fear of physical violence and death was the primary feeling described" (Burgess and Holmstrom, 1974:983). Although it may seem surprising that victims should feel guilty or blame themselves, such feelings are apparently common. The girl in the account felt blame-worthy because her mother had opposed her move into the apartment. In another case, a young woman reported strong guilt feelings in these terms:

> I'm single but I'm not a virgin and I was raised a Catholic. So I thought this might be some kind of punishment to warn me I was doing something against the Church or God.[8]

Another victim remarked, "My father always said whatever a man did to a woman, she pro-voked it" (Burgess and Holmstrom, 1974:983).

In the long-term phase of reorganization there were *"motor" and emotional conse-quences.* Common "motor consequences" in-cluded things such as changing residence, changing telephone numbers, and visiting fam-ily and friends to gain support. Among the emotional consequences were nightmares; the development of various phobias, such as the fear of being indoors, outdoors, alone, in a crowd, hearing but not seeing people walking behind one; and sexual fears. One victim reported that five months after the incident she could still get hysterical with her boyfriend: "I don't want him near me; I get panicked. Sex is OK, but I still feel like screaming" (Burgess and Holmstrom, 1974:984).

An unfortunate part of the emotional trauma of rape is the *manner in which many victims are handled by the police and the courts.* In the earlier account the police gave the girl nei-ther sympathy nor help. Only twenty-three of the sixty women who answered the rape ques-tionnaire reported by Medea and Thompson (1974:143) indicated a sympathetic reaction from the police. An Oregon woman said that when her case came to court she felt as if she

were on trial rather than the offender. The de-fense lawyer asked her questions such as whether or not she wore a bra, if she had see-through blouses, if she experienced orgasm dur-ing the rape, and whether she enjoyed the rape.[9] She concluded that if she were raped again she might not be willing to go through another trial. The rape victim is not only abused by the of-fender, she may be victimized again by the legal procedures which are supposed to redress her grievance!

Physical Abuse

The rapist may harm his victim with a weapon, may beat her, choke her, overcome her with brute strength, attempt to make her submissive by threats, and he may murder her. Amir (1971:155) found that 85.1 percent of the rapes he studied involved some kind of force, most commonly "roughness" and beating.

Other studies confirm the frequency of phys-ical harm. In a study of rape victimization in twenty-six American cities, researchers found that 91 percent of rape victims and 63 percent of attempted rape victims were injured. The in-juries ranged from bruises, cuts, and black eyes to internal injuries, broken bones, or wounds (though the proportion receiving the more serious injuries was small) (U.S. Department of Justice, Law Enforcement Administration, 1979b:36).

The *force and brutality so commonly in-volved in rapes* leads us to conclude that we are dealing with an act of violence rather than of sexual passion. The rapist is not someone with

Involvement

Was the Rapist Seduced?

In 1977 in a Wisconsin city, a 15-year-old boy convicted of rape stood before a judge for sentencing. The boy had attacked a 16-year-old girl in a high school stairwell. When the judge put the boy on probation, the immediate reaction of numerous local citizens was outrage, and the case received nationwide publicity. The judge explained his decision as follows:

> "I'm trying to say to women stop teasing. There should be a restoration of modesty in dress and elimination from the community of sexual gratification businesses," declared Dane County Judge. . . . "Whether women like it or not they are sex objects. Are we supposed to take an impressionable person 15 or 16 years of age and punish that person severely because they react to it normally?"*

The judge's decision was based on exactly the kind of attitude we have described—that women are often to blame for rape because they dress and behave in a sexually provocative way.

Many women in the Wisconsin city disagreed with the judge's reasoning and picketed the courthouse. Over 35,000 people signed petitions demanding the judge's removal. Ultimately the judge lost his place on the bench in a special election.

Some citizens in the judge's area of jurisdiction agreed with him. They said they believed there has been a general decline in morality and that it may be difficult to define justice in such a case in a time of sexual freedom. Perhaps one of the more significant comments was made by an attorney who pointed out that a few years earlier the judge's remarks would have "passed without notice." Other people, however, pointed out that rape is an act of violence and represents aggression toward women rather than attraction.

Investigate to what extent attitudes about rape have changed in your community. What proportion of people, particularly men, believe that rape is provoked by the female? To find out, describe the Wisconsin case to about ten people. Ask whether they agree or disagree with the judge's decision, and why. If they agree, or if they appear sympathetic with the rapist, tell them some of the things you have learned in this chapter about rape as an act of violence and about the rape trauma syndrome. Then determine if the additional information makes any difference in their attitudes toward the problem of rape.

*Time, September 12, 1977, p. 41.

an overwhelming sex drive; he is, typically, a man who feels compelled to assault and humiliate women. He uses rape as a weapon to express his hatred of all females. Physical abuse, therefore, is an inevitable consequence for the female victim.

Contributing Factors

Most of the factors discussed earlier that contribute to other kinds of violence probably contribute to rape as a particular form of violence. There are also some factors distinctively associated with the rape problem that tend to *encourage offenders* and to *oppress the victims*.

Social Structural Factors

Certain *traditional norms about sex roles* are factors in some rape cases. The norm that a woman should be "pure" doubly victimizes a sexually active unmarried woman who has been raped. Juries are prone to dismiss rape charges when the woman has deviated from that traditional norm. In a case of a woman being gang-raped by four men, the defense argued that the woman was known by one of the defendants and was, in fact, one of his sexual "conquests." Furthermore, the victim was portrayed as a sexual libertine who had been a cocktail waitress and who was living with a man to whom she was not married. The defendant was acquitted.[10]

The traditional norm that males should be aggressive also is a factor in rape in a number of ways. First, the counterpart to male aggressiveness is female submissiveness. For some men, it may be acceptable to rape an "uppity" woman; such a woman may "need" to be raped so that she learns her proper place (Barlow,

1978:350). Second, in American society, as in others, the male is expected to show his dominance and superiority over the female. It is possible that where these expectations are quite strong, and where various other factors that facilitate violence are present—such as deprivation and inequalities of different kinds—the rape rate will be high.

A little twist to this norm further victimizes females. The male aggressiveness is supposed to be under her control to some extent in that she has traditionally been expected to resist it and to avoid provoking the aggressive male. Thus, males often tend to view rape as something provoked by the female. This view has been so incorporated into the legal system that all-male or male-dominated juries have been known to acquit offenders when a defense attorney could convince them that the woman's behavior was provocative or known to be sexually free. The *burden of proof in rape cases is on the victim,* who must show that she did not precipitate the offense. Even when the offender admits the offense, he may be acquitted if the victim can be blamed for provoking or enticing him. As few as 2 percent of rape offenders are actually convicted and incarcerated according to some estimates.[11]

Social Psychological Factors

"We have to change the attitudes on juries," the executive director of the National Organization for the Prevention of Rape and Assault argued.[12] The humiliating treatment a rape victim is often subjected to during a trial follows from the *attitude that the victim was somehow to blame* for provoking the offender. Although logic is not a powerful tool for changing attitudes, it should be pointed out that "the victim was asking for it" attitude ignores three things. First, women are expected to make themselves attractive to men by their dress and mannerisms. Second, provocative dress cannot be considered sufficient justification for inflicting the physical and emotional brutality of rape upon a woman. As Horos (1974:12) argued:

> Does a woman's dress or mannerisms give any man the right to rape her? Because you carry money in your pocket, does it mean that you're asking to be robbed? Perhaps this myth arose because rape is the only violent crime in which women are never the perpetrators, but always the victims.

Third, provocative dress is not even involved in all rapes. The victim may be an elderly woman in a long robe or a woman wearing a coat or a young girl in modest school clothes. In any case, to focus on dress is simply another way of *blaming a victim for an injustice.*

The *attitude that a healthy woman can always prevent rape* is another attitude that may acquit an offender and oppress the victim—if the woman was fortunate enough not to be killed in the encounter. Ploscowe (1968:210) noted that a number of experts in legal medicine argued that one man would be unable to rape a healthy and vigorous woman if the latter really resisted; thus, the accusation of rape by such a woman may be viewed as false. This attitude ignores at least two things—the *paralyzing fear* that can grip a woman and neutralize her ability to resist, and the *amount of force* used by males in rapes. In the Amir (1971:154) study, one-fifth or more of the rape victims were intimidated with a weapon. In the victimization study of twenty-six cities, two-thirds of the victims said a weapon was used (U.S. Department of Justice, Law Enforcement Administration, 1979b:20). Furthermore, beating, choking, and the threat of death may be effective even though no weapon is visible.

We have already pointed out the lack of sympathy and help a victim often experiences in encounters with the police. The *attitude of the police* may also be that the woman provokes the attack and that a healthy woman cannot be raped against her will. In addition, the police may suspect the woman is merely using the charge of rape to punish a man or get attention for herself. There are cases where a woman uses the charge of rape to retaliate against a man or to fulfill some pathological need.

Furthermore, the police know that not all victims of rape are respectable citizens with backgrounds free of suspicious behavior. Amir (1971:336) found that about one-fifth of the reported rape victims in his study had a police record, with sexual misconduct a frequent cause, and another one-fifth had "bad" reputations.

In part, then, the attitudes of the police reflect a genuine need for caution. Nevertheless, a past police record, provocative clothing, or minimal resistance do not give a man license to forcibly rape a woman. Forcible rape is a physically and emotionally traumatic experience for a woman, and the attitudes we have decribed can only encourage offenders and oppress victims further.

Finally, we must raise the question of the social psychology of the offender. What kind of man is a rapist? Is he mentally ill? Unquestionably, he has a very high level of aggression, particularly toward women. Some psychiatrists say that rapists may be motivated by sadistic

Figure 7.7 A woman learns to defend herself against rape.

impulses and the desire to plunder (Gutt-macher, 1951). This emphasizes the intense aggression in rape, and there is general agreement that every rape involves aggression (Groth, 1979:13). Beyond that, Groth (1979:109) found in his study of over 500 offenders that

> neurotic reactions appear to be underrepresented, accounting for only about 3 percent of the offenders we worked with. Clinical evidence of some psychotic process operating at the time of the offense was apparent in 10 percent. The majority of offenders (56 percent) were diagnosed as belonging to various types of personality disorders (inadequate, antisocial, passive-aggressive, borderline, and the like).

What Is To Be Done?

Three lines of attack can be pursued in dealing with the rape problem. First, the *sex-role norms, legal processes,* and *attitudes* need to be changed. Some of the change will occur only through a painfully slow process of education, for even knowledgeable and well-educated people can be deeply ignorant about rape. A graduate psychology student told the author: "There is a simple way for women to avoid the trauma of rape. They should just decide to relax and enjoy it." Such attitudes encourage offenders and oppress the victims. The fact that a student in graduate school could hold the attitude illustrates the point that changing such attitudes is going to be a painfully slow process.

Second, *rapists need treatment.* Some feminists have argued that rape is a weapon traditionally used by males to establish and maintain their dominance over females. Consequently, the rapist is not a disturbed individual, but may be the man next door

(Brownmiller, 1975). As we have seen, however, rapists tend to be psychologically disturbed in some way. As such, they need therapy, some kind of rehabilitation, and not simply punishment.

The third line of attack is to provide *help for the victims and the potential victims* of rape. In recent years a number of *rape crisis centers* have been established in urban areas to help victims. The centers offer services such as assistance in dealing with (often unsympathetic) authorities, information about available legal and medical care, counseling to facilitate recovery from the emotional trauma, and information and instruction on preventing rape. Some centers offer courses in self-defense.

The attitudes of authorities seem to be changing somewhat in the direction of greater sympathy for the victims of rape. A number of cities have established *rape squads* of male-female police teams with the specific responsibility of dealing with rape cases. The female member of the team interviews the victim while the male helps gather evidence. At least fifteen states have reformed their laws on rape, and hospitals are beginning to open rape reception centers instead of refusing to treat victims.[13] Ultimately, the aim is prevention rather than sympathetic treatment of victims. Meanwhile, the new types of services for the victims and potential victims are a welcome help for women. They suggest that men may be finally realizing that the rape victim should be helped and not oppressed further by humiliating encounters with the authorities.

Summary

Violence is a problem that concerns most Americans. Generally, violence refers to the use of force in order to kill, injure, or abuse others. Interpersonal violence occurs between individuals or a number of individuals. Intergroup violence involves identifiable groups, such as different races or religions.

In estimating the amount of violence, we find an impressive amount based on self-reports, including 14 percent who say they have been threatened or cut with a knife and 12 percent who report having been threatened or shot at with a gun. The U.S. has one of the highest homicide rates in the world. Virtually all Americans are exposed to a vast amount of violence in the mass media.

The meaning of violence can be summed up in terms of human destruction and injury, psychological disruption and dehumanization, economic costs, and "seductive self-destruction." These all diminish the quality of life, and their impact upon that quality can be both severe and long-term.

Violence has been linked with a human need for aggression, yet this is not a sufficient explanation. Various sociocultural factors contribute to the problem. One structural factor is group and societal norms, which make violence more likely among certain peoples. An important factor in intergroup violence is exclusion from the political process. Those who are unable to exert power through legitimate political means may resort to violence. An important factor in interpersonal violence is the lack of gun control. Inequality is related to violence; political and economic inequalities between groups in a society increase the likelihood of violence.

Among the social psychological factors in violence are a number of attitudes that legitimate violence and war, making people more willing to support violence and war. American men justify a considerable amount of violence, particularly when that violence is used to maintain social control. A smaller number justify violence when used to bring about change. A frequent explanation of violence involves the notion of relative deprivation, which means that attitudes toward deprivation rather than the objective condition are the critical factor.

Certain values support violence. Among American men, two values particularly support violence for social control—retributiveness and self-defense. Such values can be internalized, along with attitudes, through exposure to the mass media. The extent to which the mass media socialize people into violent attitudes and behavior is a matter of controversy. However, the bulk of the evidence indicates that violence portrayed and conveyed in the mass media is related to aggressive attitudes and behavior.

Rape is a form of interpersonal violence. As of 1977, at least 154,000 women per year are victims of rape. A victim is likely to be a young, black female in the lower socioeconomic strata. Fear of rape diminishes the quality of life for women. An actual rape may involve the murder of the victim. Perhaps 90 percent or more of rape victims are physically abused, and probably 100 percent suffer emotional trauma. The rape trauma syndrome involves several weeks of acute symptoms and disorganization and a long period of painful emotional readjustment.

Traditional norms and attitudes have the effect of encouraging rape and oppressing the victims: (1) norms about the purity of women and the aggressiveness of males; (2) a traditional attitude that females are supposed to resist male aggressiveness; (3) a belief of many males that women provoke rape and that a healthy woman cannot be raped against her will. These conditions act to put the victim herself on trial in legal proceedings. The police may suspect a victim of making a false accusation, whether or not the victim has a police record or bad reputation as is sometimes the case. But, most victims are innocent, and frequently they are victimized further by the traditional norms and attitudes described.

Studies of offenders show that they are psychologically disturbed to some extent. All have extremely high levels of aggression.

Glossary

aggression   forceful, offensive, or hostile behavior toward another person or society

catharsis   discharging socially unacceptable emotions in a socially acceptable way

forcible rape   actual or attempted sexual intercourse through the use of force or the threat of force

relative deprivation   a sense of deprivation based on some standard used by the individual who feels deprived

retributiveness   paying people back for their socially unacceptable behavior

social control   regulation of people's behavior, feelings, and beliefs in any society by any means acceptable in that society

statutory rape   sexual intercourse with a female who is below the legal age for consenting

violence   use of force to kill, injure, or abuse others

For Further Reading

Bondurant, Joan V. *Conquest of Violence: The Gandhian Philosophy of Conflict.* Berkeley and Los Angeles: University of California Press, 1969. A thorough discussion of the philosophy and methods of nonviolent action for social change, showing how nonviolence has been successful in India.

Brickman, Philip, ed. *Social Conflict: Readings in Rule Structures and Conflict Relationships.* Lexington, Mass.: D. C. Heath, 1974. A large number of readings on conflict in general, with specific readings on violence. Provides a good overview of the problem of conflict in social life.

Brownmiller, Susan. *Against Our Will.* New York: Simon & Schuster, 1975. Presents the feminist argument that rape is a political act of humiliation through which males maintain their dominance over females. Also contains a social and legal history of rape.

Groth, A. Nicholas. *Men Who Rape: The Psychology of the Offender.* New York: Plenum Press, 1979. One of the most thorough psychological analyses of rape offenders available.

Hilberman, Elaine. *The Rape Victim.* Washington, D.C.: The American Psychiatric Association, 1976. The meaning of rape from the point of view of a psychiatrist. Sees rape as an act of violence and humiliation and includes information on ways to deal with the problem.

Hofstadter, Richard, and Michael Wallace, eds. *American Violence: A Documentary History.* New York: Vintage Books, 1970. Provides a wealth of primary materials (original documents) describing various kinds of violence throughout American history.

U.S. National Commission on the Causes and Prevention of Violence. *To Establish Justice, To Insure Domestic Tranquility: The Final Report.* New York: Bantam Books, 1970. A summary of the monumental study and report of the National Commission, including information and analyses of all kinds of interpersonal and intergroup violence.

Notes

1. *Time,* June 7, 1976, p. 63.
2. *The Gallup Opinion Index,* No. 123, September 1975, p. 11.
3. *St. Louis Post-Dispatch,* November 22, 1976.
4. From a pamphlet produced by the National Gun Control Center.
5. From research by David Loye, as reported in *Human Behavior,* March 1976, pp. 32–33.
6. *To Establish Justice, To Insure Domestic Tranquility: The Final Report of the National Commission on the Causes and Prevention of Violence* (New York: Bantam Books, 1970), pp. 172–173.
7. Rape account supplied to the author by a volunteer worker at a rape crisis center.
8. Reported in the *St. Louis Post-Dispatch,* June 20, 1976.
9. Ibid., March 30, 1975.
10. *San Francisco Chronicle,* March 12, 1972.
11. *Time,* October 13, 1975, p. 48.
12. Ibid., p. 54.
13. *U.S. News and World Report,* December 8, 1975, p. 44.

PROCLAIM
IN PHILAD^A BY ORDER OF
PASS AND STOW
PHILAD^A
MDCCLIII

Problems of Inequality

The next seven chapters are concerned with inequalities in distribution of things we value. The inequalities are so great that major segments of our population suffer from serious deprivations.

We will look first at the unequal distribution of wealth in our country and discuss the problems of poor people in some detail. Next we will explore the implications of inequalities in the world of work. Then we will examine how three major categories of our population—the aged, women, and racial minorities—are deprived of an equitable share of the things we value. Finally, we will consider how inequalities affect two valued institutions of our society: education and the family.

All the people whose quality of life is diminished because of these inequalities suffer as a direct cause of circumstances of their birth—in the case of the aged, that being the year when they were born. Although such circumstances often may be indirectly related to the kind of problems discussed in part 2 of this book, the direct cause for those problems is people's deviant behavior. An implication of this distinction is that perhaps our society could more easily or more quickly apply remedies to the problems of inequality.

Wealth and Poverty

1 How widespread is poverty in the United States?

2 Would the poverty problem be solved if everyone were required to work?

3 What do the poor lack besides money?

4 How do government policies contribute to the poverty problem?

5 Do the poor perpetuate their problem by their own attitudes and values?

Someone once pointed out that a man who stores money is like the squirrel who stores acorns; both are trying to provide for basic needs. But, the squirrel is superior to the man in one respect—he seems to know when he has enough acorns, while the man never seems to know when he has enough money. Indeed, studies have shown that the majority of Americans feel that they need more money, regardless of their income. Even if most people do need more, some people are clearly far more needy than others. The truly needy spend their entire lives at the edge of desperation, barely able to gather sufficient money to continue to exist.

In this chapter we will examine that segment of the population for whom the American dream has been most elusive, and we will see how the difficulties of the poor are related to the behavior of the nonpoor. To understand why the poor are poor, we must understand why the rich are rich.

We will discuss what is meant by poverty, and we will try to identify who the poor are, and how many there are. We will see how poverty affects the quality of life. After we identify the structural and social psychological factors that contribute to poverty, we will look at what has been done and what might be done to address the problem.

What Is Poverty?

Poverty in America is old and new. It is old in the sense that it has always existed, and it is new in the sense that it was not commonly *defined as a problem* until recently. As late as the 1950s economists assumed that economically we were consistently improving. We were producing more, people's incomes were increasing, and the question about poverty was not whether, but when it would be eliminated. Although sociologists have always identified poverty as a problem, the Gallup poll showed that not until 1965 did the public begin to identify poverty as one of America's serious problems (Lauer, 1976). An influential factor in spreading awareness of the problem was a book by Michael Harrington (1962), *The Other America*. Harrington identified the poor and portrayed the plight of millions of impoverished people in our country.

Why did Americans generally fail to identify poverty as a social problem until the 1960s? One reason is the poor were largely invisible to many Americans. Another reason is many people insisted that even our lowest income groups were not really poor—because even the poorest in our nation fared better than the starving Asian peasants.

Many of America's poor do have more food, more clothing, and more possessions than the poor in other nations, but the standard for evaluating America's poor cannot be the starving Asian peasant. Rather, we must evaluate poverty in the United States in terms of the *standard of living* attained by the majority of Americans. *Deprivation is relative,* as we saw in the last chapter. America's poor define themselves as deprived relative to other Americans. To tell a person whose family suffers from malnutrition that there are Asians who are starving to death is not consoling, especially when he or she knows that millions of Americans throw away more food every day than that person's family consumes.

In discussing poverty in the United States, then, we are talking about people who are better off than some others in the world, but who have much less than most Americans. But, less of what? How much less? The federal government tried to answer those questions in terms of *income.* The first attempt, in 1964, defined as poor any nonfarm family of four with an income below $3,000 per year. This figure was adjusted up or down for more or fewer people in the family, and it was continually revised to account for inflation. By 1979, an urban family of four with an annual income of $7,412 or less was officially classified as at the **poverty level.**

How are such figures determined? The poverty level is a statistical yardstick developed by the Social Security Administration in 1961. It was based on Department of Agriculture calculations of the cost of a basic diet they called the "economy food plan." The food needs and the costs vary, depending on the size of the family, its sex and age composition, and place of residence (rural vs. urban). In 1964 a nonfarm family of four had to spend about $1,000 per year to purchase the food in the economy plan, according to some estimates. Since the food costs of the poor were estimated to use up about one-third of the total family budget, the poverty line was officially set at three times the current cost of the Department of Agriculture's "economy food plan." Hence the $3,000 a year dividing line between "poor" and "nonpoor."

This income threshold, which by definition separates the poor from the nonpoor, is so low because the "economy food plan" diet on which it was based was originally designed for temporary or emergency use when a family's financial resources were minimal. In addition, to be able to buy the kinds of food the plan specified at the prices used in the calculations required the homemaker to have marketing and planning skills that are rare at any level of income. Few of the families that spent only the amount of money indicated by the plan actually had a nutritionally adequate diet (Pruger and Wilder, 1974:6). Thus, the official definition of poverty is based upon a barely adequate budget for a barely adequate diet.

This way of defining poverty is challenged as anything from inadequate to absurd. Most people agree that the official level is quite low. As we will see later, the lot of impoverished people is wretched (not merely bad) when compared to most Americans. In other words, the official definition excludes many people who define themselves, and whom most of us would define; as poor.

It is interesting to contrast the official definition of "poverty level" with the U.S. Department of Labor's assessment of budgets for urban living. By the official definition, a family of four living in an urban area in 1979 was not poor if they had an income just over $7,412 for the year. But, how well did they live? According to the Department of Labor, an urban family of four in 1979 required $20,517 per year to live moderately well! A low budget was figured at $12,585 annually, and $30,317 was defined as the budget necessary to be a home-owner, to eat out occasionally, and to buy a new car every four years.[1] Families on the low budget were at the bottom of what most Americans would consider an acceptable standard of living. Yet, the official poverty level was only about 58 percent of the low budget. A family with an income a little more than half the low budget was not counted as poor!

Michael Harrington (1962:175) argued that the official definition of poverty leaves out many people who are unable to secure "the minimal levels of health, housing, food, and education that our present stage of scientific knowledge specifies as necessary for life as it is now lived in the United States." If we did account for such people, the official number of the poor would be much higher, and the problem would be far more extensive than it appears to be now. Keep this in mind when we discuss the extent of poverty in the United States in the next section. Many people consider the problem to be more extensive than official figures indicate.

The official definition of poverty is challenged on other grounds, too. Some observers assert that it minimizes the proportion of the poor family's budget that must go to food. This may be true, at least for those in the lowest income bracket. Their food budget was 37 percent of their income in 1960, and since then the **consumer price index** for food has risen faster than the overall price index. The official definition of poverty is challenged also on the grounds that more than money income should be considered; too many important variables (such as tax rates and changing standards) are overlooked when only income level is used.

Any definition is open to challenge, and income is a convenient measure. Our quarrel is not with using an income figure, but with how low the level of income must be before the official definitions acknowledge that there is poverty. If we use the Department of Labor's low-budget income figure instead of the figure based on the Department of Agriculture's "economy food plan" to define the poverty threshold, the number of poor in the country doubles. The level chosen by the federal government makes the problem appear smaller than many of us think it is.

Figure 8.1 The number and proportion of the poor, 1959 to 1978. (The break in the number line, indicated by an "r" is because a new method of calculation was begun.) (Source: U.S. Office of Economic Opportunity, *The Poor 1970: A Chartbook* [Washington, D.C.: Government Printing Office, 1972], p. 63; and U.S. Bureau of the Census,

Current Population Reports, series P–60, no. 120, "Money Income and Poverty Status of Families and Persons in the United States: 1978" [Washington, D.C.: Government Printing Office, 1979], p. 28.)

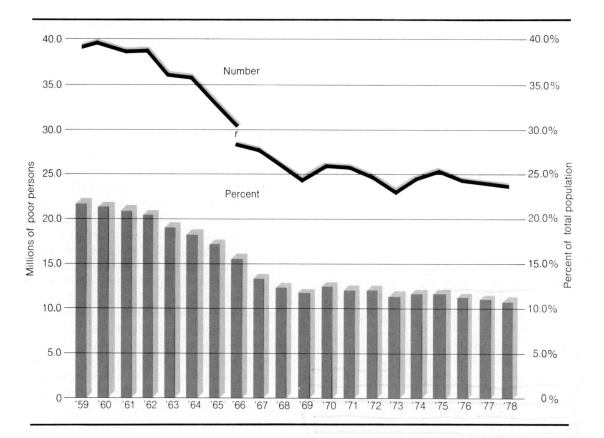

Let us now address three questions concerning the *extent of poverty* in the United States. How many poor are there? Who are the poor? Are the majority of the poor better off or worse off now than they were in the past?

Extent of Poverty

The proportion of Americans officially defined as poor is declining (figure 8.1). By 1978 about 24.5 million Americans, representing 11.4 percent of the population, were categorized as poor.[2] Despite some fluctuations, the general trend is a *fairly steady decrease in both numbers and proportion of those in poverty.*

As Pruger and Wilder (1974:5–6) pointed out, however, we cannot assume the trend will continue. Moreover, as the proportion of the population who are poor shrinks, dealing with their poverty will be increasingly difficult. The public may become weary of antipoverty programs and resentful of financing those programs. People who continue to be poor may be more difficult to help for some reason. They are the ones, after all, who were not helped by previous programs.

Figure 8.2 A poor home in Kentucky. Most of America's poor are white.

A second caution—one dealt with in the last section—is that the official figures minimize the number of the poor. Many of us would probably consider ourselves poor if our income were just above the official poverty level. In addition, there are people who are not now poor but will be, and people who are not now poor but have been. In other words, there is always movement into and out of poverty, so the number of poor at any given time does not tell us the total number of people who will be affected by the problem during their lifetimes.

Even by the official definition, then, we are dealing with a problem that involves millions of Americans—over 11 percent of the population. Depending upon one's view of the level of income necessary for a minimum standard of living, the figure could be one-fifth to one-fourth of the population.

Who Are the Poor?

Wealth and poverty are *not distributed equally* among various social groups. Most Americans are neither wealthy nor impoverished, but the chances of being in one of those categories are greater for certain social groups. For example, the probability of being poor is greater for a family headed by a female, for a nonwhite, and for an old or an unrelated individual. Figure 8.3 shows the proportion of various groups that were poor in 1978. Although the rates of whites are low, as figure 8.3 shows, the majority of the poor are white. In 1978, there were about 16.3 million poor whites and 7.6 million poor blacks. Those numbers represent 30.6 percent of all blacks and 8.7 percent of all whites. Thus, the *number* of poor whites is more than double that

Figure 8.3 Proportion of poverty for different kinds of people, 1978. (Source: U.S. Bureau of the Census, *Current Population Reports,* "Money Income and Poverty Status of Families and Persons in the United States: 1978" [Washington, D.C.: Government Printing Office, 1979], pp. 25–26.)

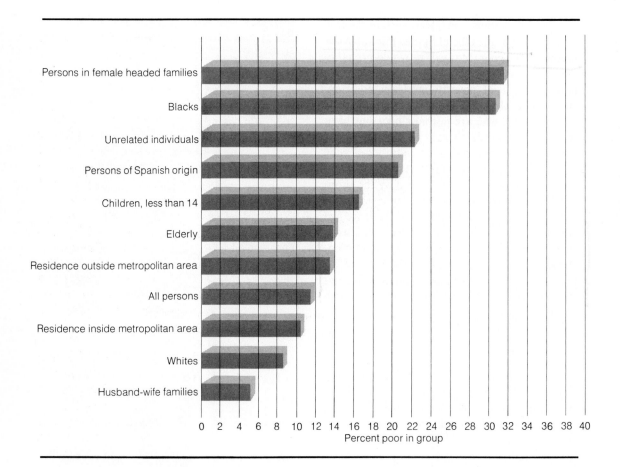

of poor blacks, but the *rate of poverty* among whites is less than one-third of that among blacks.

Figure 8.3 also shows that the rate of poverty is higher outside than inside metropolitan areas. In fact, *rural poverty* is one reason why many Americans are unaware of the seriousness of the problem. To most of us, the rural poor are even less visible than those in urban **ghettoes.** However, about 38 percent of the poor lived in nonmetropolitan areas in 1978, while only about one-fourth of the total population was in those areas.

An additional fact about the identity of the poor is important: contrary to popular opinion, people are not poor primarily because of their *unwillingness to work.* The unemployed do not make up the bulk of America's poor. In fact, in 1978, over 57 percent of the male heads of poor families worked, and 46.3 percent worked full time (table 8.1). Of those who did not work,

Table 8.1   Work Experience of Family Heads Below the Poverty Level, by Sex, 1979
(in thousands, except percent; families as of March 1979)

Work Experience	Male	Female
Total	2626	2654
Worked	1512	1077
Percent worked year-round full time	46.3	13.8
Did not work	1080	1577
Ill or disabled	533	286
Keeping house	18	1024
In school	25	62
Unable to find work	59	123

Source: U.S. Bureau of the Census, *Statistical Abstract of the United States, 1980* (Washington, D.C.: Government Printing Office, 1981), p. 469.

most were unable to hold a job because of illness or age. Poverty is not only a matter of peoples' willingness to work.

The Changing Nature of Poverty

How has the lot of the poor changed over time in our country? Certainly there are fewer poor people than in the past, but are those who remain poor in better or worse condition than the poor of other generations? Although we have no systematic evidence on the question, it seems reasonable that poverty is more difficult to bear as the proportion of the poor grows smaller. It is one thing to be poor when the majority of the people, or even a substantial minority, share your poverty, but it is another thing to be poor when most people are living comfortably or in affluence.

Still, if the poor are making gains relative to the rich, poverty in the 1980s might be less stressful than in the past. Unfortunately, this is not the case. Table 8.2 shows the percentage of national *personal income* received by each **decile** of the population. That is, the population is divided into ten groups, ranked according to income. The "highest tenth" is that 10 percent of the population that received the largest amount of income. The numbers in the columns are the actual proportions of income received by each group in each year. For 1910, the 10 percent receiving the largest amount of income got 34 percent of the total, while the 10 percent receiving the lowest amount got only 3 percent of the total. If income were completely equal among the various groups, each would receive 10 percent of the total. In 1910 the highest group received over three times what they would have received under a situation of perfect equality, while the lowest group's share was less than a third of what it would have been under a situation of equality.

An interesting trend is revealed in table 8.2. The wealthiest are receiving a progressively smaller share of the total income. (Keep in mind the distinction between wealth and income. Although the richest are now getting a smaller proportion of income, their control of wealth has not diminished. Moreover, the impact of a smaller proportion of income is far greater on the bottom than it is on the top.) The redistribution does not benefit the poor; instead, the middle- and upper-middle income groups are the beneficiaries. The 10 percent of the families in the highest income bracket got 34 percent of the income in 1910, but they received only 27 percent in 1970. The next four categories all increased their share. The lowest 30 percent lost ground over the sixty-year period. They improved their position somewhat since 1937, and

Table 8.2   Percent of National Personal Income

Year	Highest Tenth	2nd Tenth	3rd Tenth	4th Tenth	5th Tenth	6th Tenth	7th Tenth	8th Tenth	9th Tenth	Lowest Tenth
1910	34%	12%	10%	9%	8%	7%	6%	6%	5%	3%
1918	35	13	10	9	8	7	7	6	4	2
1929	39	12	10	9	8	7	6	5	4	2
1937	34	14	12	10	9	7	6	4	3	1
1950	29	15	13	11	9	8	6	5	3	1
1958	27	16	13	11	9	8	6	5	3	1
1964	30	15	13	11	9	8	6	4	3	1
1970	27	17	13	11	9	7	6	5	3	2

Source: Data from 1910 through 1937 are from *Studies in Enterprise and Social Progress;* those from 1959 through 1970 come from various editions of *Survey of Consumer Finances.*

especially since 1964, but in 1970 they were still getting a smaller share of the total than those at the lowest levels got in 1910.

When we try to assess the extent of poverty in the United States, we must recognize that while the proportion of the poor is decreasing, the lot of the poor is worsening when compared with the rest of the society. Those who are poor in the 1970s may have more possessions than the poor of 1910 had, but they have a smaller proportion of the total income than the poor received in 1910. Relative to others in the society, the poor in the 1970s are doing worse than their counterparts in 1910.

Poverty and the Quality of Life

A reporter visited with an impoverished family in a Harlem apartment:

Roaches were everywhere. The bathroom floor was continually wet because of a leak below the basin, and the toilet had to be flushed by reaching down into the tank and pulling the stopper. The heat often went off at night, but when the mother complained no one came until the following day, and by then the heat had been turned back on. While the reporter was there, the mother sent one of her sons to the store with 13 cents to buy candy. The candy and some pork and beans was to be the evening meal. The kitchen cabinet contained a box of surplus cheese and some surplus butter, peas, and beans. Coffee, salt and pepper were the only other foods of any kind in the house.[3]

The poor get less of everything we consider important and necessary for a decent life (less money, less food, clothing, and shelter). The *deprivation of the poor is pervasive.* Compared to the nonpoor, infants of the poor are more likely to die. Their children are more likely to fail in school even when they are intelligent. Their children are more likely to drop out of school. They are more likely to become mentally ill. They are more likely to lose their jobs and to drop out of the labor force. They are more likely to experience hostility and distrust rather than neighborliness with those around them.

They are less likely to participate in meaningful groups and associations. They are more likely to get chronic illnesses. In the face of more health problems, they are less likely to own health insurance (a problem only partly relieved by Medicaid). As the ultimate deprivation, they are likely to die at a younger age. In other words, poverty diminishes the quality of a person's life in many ways.

The Right to Life and Happiness

The position of the poor in the economy contradicts our value of the right to life and the pursuit of happiness. The inadequacy of their financial resources deprives the poor of freedom to pursue a full and happy life. Some people argue that lack of money should not be equated with lack of happiness, that many of the poor are carefree, spontaneous, and even better off without the worries that accompany possession of money. Generally, only people who have money use that argument. Actually, there is a positive correlation between income and *perceived happiness.* Surveys of attitudes show that the proportion of people who describe themselves as very happy fluctuated between 1957 and 1972, but the proportion is consistently lower in the lower income group than in the middle and upper income groups (Campbell, Converse, and Rodgers, 1976:27–28). Poverty brings more *despair* than happiness and more *fear* than fullness of life.

Discontent and despair. When deprivation was widespread during the Great Depression of the 1930s, unrest was also widespread. People marched and demonstrated, demanding food and expressing a willingness to fight rather than starve. In a 1932 Chicago demonstration there were "no bands" and "no quickstep," only "rank after rank of sodden men, their worn coat collars turned up, their caps . . . pulled down to give as much protection as possible" as they marched in driving rain.[4]

Despair was also evident in an impoverished group studied by Cornell researchers in 1949 (Beiser, 1965). They found a high rate of broken marriages, family strife, and neglect of children among 118 people living on low and erratic incomes. The people lived close together but did not form a community. Rather, there was pervasive *indifference* and *hostility.* A mental health survey conducted among the people in 1952 showed a high rate of *psychiatric symptoms* such as depression, anxiety, and psychosomatic complaints.

Despair is not the lot of all the poor, but it is much more frequent among the poor than among the nonpoor. When the despair comes, it is devastating. As expressed by an impoverished man in Appalachia:

> We have no money, and no welfare payments, and we're expected to scrape by like dogs. It gets to your mind after a while. You feel as low as can be, and nervous about everything. That's what a depression does, makes you dead broke, with a lot of bills and the lowest spirits you can ever picture a man having. Sometimes I get up and I'm ready to go over to an undertaker and tell him to do something with me real fast [Coles, 1968:25–26].

The despair that always threatens to overcome the poor is manifested in what Rainwater (1967) called *"survival" strategies*—ways of living that enable the poor to adapt to their "punishing and depriving milieu." The *"expressive strategy"* involves manipulating others

Figure 8.4 Contrasting styles of American life.

and making oneself appealing, through means such as bettering someone in a rap session, gaining the affection of a female, wearing dramatic clothes, or winning a gambling bet. The "expressive strategy" leads some nonpoor to define the poor as natural, spontaneous, and carefree. But, as Rainwater pointed out, this strategy, like the others, enables the individual to gain some measure of status and retain some degree of stability and sanity in the midst of an oppressive situation. The *"violent strategy"* involves things such as fighting, shoplifting, or making threats. It is a dangerous strategy for everyone, and not many of the poor adopt it. The *"depressive strategy"* which involves withdrawal and isolation, characterizes a great number of the poor as they grow older. An individual may alternate among the strategies as he or she grows older, but all three strategies have the same purpose—to enable the individual to cope with a punitive situation. As such, they dramatize the despair that always hovers near the poor.

Freedom from fear.   We mentioned in the last chapter that freedom from fear is a condition of the right to life and the pursuit of happiness. The poor live in a *capricious world*. The chronic uncertainty of their lives means they have much to fear. We will discuss this topic further under the subheading "Dilemmas of Poverty." Here we will look at a specific fear that affects the poor more than others—the *fear of being the victim of a crime.*

The poor are more likely than other people to be victims of certain kinds of crime. Table 8.3 contrasts the poorest with the richest Americans in terms of victimization. The poor are far more likely to be victims of rape, robbery, assault, personal larceny, and burglary than are the rich. These *higher victimization rates* are reflected in fear of walking alone at night. A 1979 Gallup poll showed that 55 percent of those with incomes under $5,000, but only 32 percent of those with incomes of $25,000 or more, expressed such fear. For the intervening income categories, each progressive increase in income bracket correlated with a progressive decline in the proportion expressing fear.

The fears and victimization rates are consistent with each other, and both are related to place as well as to people. Because of the inadequate financial resources of the poor, the poor are unable to leave the neighborhoods where they must cope with the fear and the reality of crime.

The Right to Dignity as a Human Being

For the poor, the *right to dignity as human beings* is violated by the *contradiction between our ideal of the worth of every individual and the pattern of interaction between the poor and the nonpoor*. At best, the poor tend to be treated paternalistically. At worst, they tend to be subjected to contempt and rejection. The loss of dignity is manifested in a number of myths about the poor.

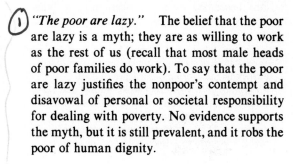

"The poor are lazy."   The belief that the poor are lazy is a myth; they are as willing to work as the rest of us (recall that most male heads of poor families do work). To say that the poor are lazy justifies the nonpoor's contempt and disavowal of personal or societal responsibility for dealing with poverty. No evidence supports the myth, but it is still prevalent, and it robs the poor of human dignity.

Table 8.3   Victimization Rates, by Income, 1977
(per 1000 population age 12 and over)

Crime	Family Income	
	Under $3,000	$25,000 or more
Forcible rape	1.8	0.6
Robbery with injury	5.6	1.0
Robbery without injury	8.1	2.7
Assault	38.5	24.1
Personal larceny with contact	4.6	2.0
Burglary	114.4	96.3
Household larceny	98.7	140.2
Motor vehicle theft	7.5	24.3

Source: Adapted from U.S. Department of Justice, Law Enforcement Administration, *Criminal Victimization in the United States, 1977* (Washington, D.C.: Government Printing Office, 1979), p. 28, 34.

"People on welfare have it good."   The expressive style of coping which we discussed earlier may have helped create the myth that those on welfare often live at higher standards than do people who work. A few "con artists" may manage to earn a substantial living out of *welfare fraud,* but the bulk of people on welfare (and the bulk of the poor generally) live in circumstances that would be repugnant to most Americans. What dignity is in the living conditions described by some women in a New York City ghetto? How "good" do they have it?

> Well, we were sleeping and it was two or three o'clock in the morning and I heard a rat scratching on my bed so I woke up my mother. Then the rat runned away over my sister's arm and my sister woke up and started screaming and screaming. . . . You couldn't sleep at night. I let my baby sleep with me 'cause we

were afraid to let her sleep in the crib. . . . Rats, big rats. I see them. I told Mr. Gonzalez the landlord. He put poison. But I didn't put it because then the rat dies and smells no good. I can't eat and long time smells no good in my apartment. It smells, smells, smells. . . . And every night you hear the rats fighting. . . .

> The kids play in that lot. You see my kid. He got something in the back of his neck, a rash. I think maybe it was from playing in that garbage down here. The children use that lot as their playground. . . . Every night there is a fire in the lot. . . . So I can't sleep. I'm afraid that the building will burn down while I'm sleeping [Goro, 1970:42, 44].

"Welfare is draining us."   One of the more humiliating myths to the poor is that they are social leeches. This myth asserts that the cost of maintaining the poor is depriving the nonpoor by raising taxes and reducing the standard of living. This myth generally includes the assertion or the assumption that people on welfare could be working and earning their own way. Thus, the term "welfare bums" is applied by those who argue for the elimination of welfare programs.

Are people on welfare really "bums" or "freeloaders" or "frauds"? Are they draining the economy and depriving the nonpoor by their refusal to earn their own way? A study by the Department of Health, Education, and Welfare found that less than 1 percent of welfare recipients were able-bodied men. Rather, of the 99.2 percent of recipients accounted for: 24 percent were aged; 8 percent were permanently and totally disabled; 13 percent were mothers (some of whom worked); 1 percent were blind; 2.9 percent were incapacitated parents; and 50.3 percent were children.[5] Another study reported that less than 2 percent of all welfare cases involved cheating.[6] Contrary to the myth, the recipients of welfare are not freeloading. With few exceptions, they are *powerless*, and most are *unable to work*. Among those who are able-bodied, some are pushed out of the labor market by discriminatory practices. A black pastor described such a case at a meeting the author attended. One of his young male parishioners applied for a job and was told he had to be a member of the union in order to work. He went to the union and applied for membership. They told him that he couldn't join unless he had a job. For the able-bodied in rural areas, the problem is not so much discriminatory practices as unavailability of work.

There is no evidence that the poor are freeloading, and there is no evidence that the poor desire handouts. A 1969 Gallup poll asked people if they supported the idea of the government guaranteeing enough work so that each family would be assured an annual income of at least $3,200. Of those earning less than $3,000 annually, 77 percent supported the idea, 11 percent opposed it, and 12 percent had no opinion. Clearly, the majority of the poor do not oppose the idea of working for their income. Another question dealt with a guaranteed minimum income that was not based on work, and only 43 percent of those earning less than $3,000 annually supported that proposal. The poor themselves resist the notion of a handout. They express a preference for working for their livelihood.

Poverty and Health

The circumstances under which the poor are required to live cause higher rates of mental and physical illness among the poor than among the rest of the population. As noted in chapter 5,

people in the lower socioeconomic strata have higher rates and different kinds of illnesses than do people in the middle and upper strata, and the poor make less use of health care services because of problems of accessibility and cost. Clearly, then, poverty contradicts our value of good health.

The relationship between poverty and health is another of the *vicious circles* that often characterize social problems. Because health problems put additional strains on a family's meager financial resources, illness can be perpetuated as a result. Poverty can generate stress that leads to illness that intensifies the stress, and the circle continues. The plight of a family of four—father, mother, and two adolescent girls—illustrates such a situation (Richardson, 1970). The girls suffered from slight malnutrition, heart disease, and chest and back pains. The mother was overweight and bothered by indigestion, and the father had cancer of the stomach. The family had lived in poverty for fifteen years. Interviews with each member in a social service clinic indicated a clear relationship between the various ailments and the feelings of insecurity that were rooted in family troubles. The family obviously required medical attention. Just as obviously, medical attention alone would not resolve their health problems.

The *health difficulties of the poor begin in childhood*. Children in the lower socioeconomic strata have more than twice the chance of becoming psychiatrically impaired than do children in the middle and upper strata (Langner et al., 1970:194). The physical health problems of poor children include some diseases that Americans believe were eliminated from our country. In 1969 a U.S. senator admitted he had found the malnutrition diseases pellagra,

276

rickets, and scurvy in South Carolina. He reported a high rate of parasitic worms among the rural poor in the state and noted that children were apparently suffering from mental retardation as a result of prolonged **malnutrition.** Officials who studied the problem examined 177 children in Beaufort County and found 98 with intestinal worms. Many of the children were existing on 800 calories a day (we need at least 1,500 to 1,800 per day).[7] Similar reports came from doctors who toured Mississippi in 1967 and reported "shocking" conditions among children, with evidence of severe malnutrition and resulting injury to body tissues. Robert Coles (1969) described the conditions in detail. Among other things, he found that most of the children of the poor were in a state of "negative nitrogen balance," a condition of dietary inadequacy in which the body consumes its own protein tissue. The condition results in a wasting of muscles, enlargement of the heart, weakened bones, spontaneous bleeding from the mouth or nose, and other symptoms. Coles also found numerous children who needed surgery for things such as hernia, improperly healed fractures, heart disease, and illnesses of the ear and eye. The physicians were particularly appalled by the fact that a number of the health problems could have been easily corrected had they been treated at the proper time.

Whether we are talking about the rural poor of the South or the urban poor of the North, we find the same problems of ill health directly related to poverty—both the higher prevalence of illness and the less adequate care. In 1966, 618 Boston children from low-income families were examined to determine the state of their health (Salisbury and Berg, 1969). Nearly half the children had physical abnormalities, including some that were major (poor vision, heart murmur, and hypertension) and a larger number of minor ones (overweight and hearing deficiencies). Over half the major and one-third of the minor problems had not been adequately treated. Twenty-nine percent of the children needed extensive dental care. Health is an area in which the poor clearly have a diminished quality of life, and their health problems begin in childhood.

Dilemmas of Poverty

Americans *value* **autonomy** *and equal opportunity*. We want to control our own destinies and we want opportunities for advancement. These values are *contradicted* by the realities of the situation of the poor. People at the lower end of the stratification system have little control over their lives and have few if any opportunities compared to people at the upper end. Poverty is an ongoing series of *dilemmas*. Even when a poor person can choose between options, all of the options may have undesirable aspects.

Consider the problem of existing on a poverty budget. Orshansky (1965:10) pointed out that in 1965 a homemaker had to provide meals at a cost of about $.70 a day for each person (the equivalent figure for 1978 was about $1.52 per day per person). This expenditure provided no more than one small serving of meat, poultry, or fish per day and less than one egg per person per day. If the children bought milk at school or the husband bought coffee at work, the money had to come out of the same small amount or out of the limited funds available for rent, clothing, medical care, or other necessities. Another way to look at it is that the poor person's food budget for a whole day is roughly the

Involvement

From Riches to Rags

In a now-famous experiment, a reporter had his skin darkened and his hair shaved close, and then he began traveling through four Southern states to see what it was like to be a black man. It was a revelation to him; he discovered that he had no idea of what it was like to live as a black person. Some nights, he reported, he was so upset by the way people treated him that he cried himself to sleep. Sometimes the only way to understand what a social problem means for the victims of the problem is to "walk a mile in their shoes." This project will involve you in a personal experience of poverty, but you will need to work with someone else.

First, try to live for two weeks on a poverty-level food budget. From the latest edition of the *Statistical Abstract of the United States,* find the current poverty-level income threshold. (Remember, this is the *most* you could have to be classified in poverty.) Use the figure given for a nonfarm family of four and divide it by three to get a yearly food budget comparable to the way the poverty level was originally defined. Divide the figure by twenty-six to get the two-week budget, and then divide that figure by two to reduce it from four to two people. For example, in 1975 the poverty level for four was $5,500—roughly $1,833 for food; for two weeks, that would be about $70.50. And since there are two of you rather than four, divide by two again. That would allow $35.25 for the two-week period for two people.

As a second part of your experiment, dress in some shabby clothing. Try to achieve a poor though clean look. Then, go to a public place and ask directions. Also go into a department store and ask for help in finding some relatively expensive clothes.

Record your experiences. Describe in detail your experiences and feelings about grocery shopping, cooking, and eating on a poverty budget. Discuss the reactions you received when asking for directions and when seeking to look at some expensive clothing. Discuss the way people related to you with the way you normally experience relationships.

The problem of poverty received less attention from the mass media in the 1970s than in the 1960s. As a final part of your project, you might share your experience by writing an article that reminds people of the great numbers of poor in our nation. Submit it to the features editor of a local newspaper or a general magazine.

cost of one small meal at a fast-food hamburger restaurant. For some of the poor, the choice may be adequate nutrition *or* new clothes, adequate nutrition *or* medical care. Most of us do not face such limited choices.

 One of the key dilemmas of the poor is the choice between security and change. Should a poor individual maintain whatever security he or she has or take some risks in order to change his or her lot? For instance, the ghetto child might be told that the only way to escape poverty is to stay in school and use the education to get a good job. But, the only security the child's family may have against utter deprivation is for the child to drop out of school and earn money to add to the family income. At the same time, perhaps the only way the child can be *psychologically secure* is to accept the negative judgments of his or her peers about school. The low value on intellectualism among many of the poor threatens ostracism to any young person who is serious about education. Furthermore, the child has grown up in an unpredictable world where he or she has felt the powerlessness of the individual to change his or her lot in life. Why should one risk years of schooling (which involves a loss of income) when the payoff is vague and uncertain?

 Adults face dilemmas and the *frustrations of powerlessness,* also. A woman who grew up in a ghetto related an incident in her life: "When I was a girl, I was given a part in the school play. I was as happy as I could be, and proud to think of my parents watching me perform. But on the night of the play my father got drunk instead of coming to school. I was terribly upset at the time, but later on I realized why he had gotten drunk. He was ashamed to come to the play in the clothes he had, and he didn't have

enough money to buy anything new. He didn't know what to do; so he got drunk."

It is easy enough to condemn the man, but we must remember that the poor live with an agonizing mixture of ambition and powerlessness, of the need for security and the need for change. The security is meager, but the risk of change may appear to be great.

Contributing Factors

It is true that there have always been poor people. It is also true that poverty is a global problem and that the poor of other nations are worse off in absolute terms than are the poor of America. Many Africans and Asians die of starvation; few Americans do. But, why is there any poverty at all in affluent America? The United States has sufficient resources to eliminate poverty. Why, then, do millions of Americans continue to suffer an impoverished existence? Part of the answer is that a number of structural and social psychological factors that operate to create poverty also tend to perpetuate it.

Social Structural Factors

The structural factors that bear upon the problem of poverty are the institutional arrangements of government, the economy, the family, and education. We will examine each in turn.

Religion, too, can be a factor, but religion's record on poverty is mixed. It can help perpetuate poverty by sanctioning negative attitudes to the poor or by channeling the energies of the poor away from protest movements into purely religious activities. On the other hand, some of the leaders of the fight against poverty come from strongly religious backgrounds and some are religious leaders. However, in this section we will focus on the other institutions mentioned and examine how they contribute to the problem of poverty.

The politics of poverty. The problem of poverty is the problem of wealth turned inside out. Poverty continues in America, in great part, because of the *distribution of power.* Those who control the wealth are among the most powerful, while the poor are among the most powerless in America. Governmental decisions typically reflect the interests of the well-to-do rather than of the poor.

Two aspects of structure particularly detrimental to the poor are the *multiple decision-making centers* and the *middle-class composition of our bureaucracy.* James (1972:118–19) showed how multiple decision-making centers adversely affect the poor. The term "multiple decision-making centers" refers to the federal, state, and local governmental levels and also multiple branches—executive, legislative, and judicial—at each level. All these facets of government have certain decision-making powers, and all have different constituencies. This means that most categories or organizations of citizens can exercise influence at some point, but it also means that there are many points at which a program or a policy initiative can be stopped. However, some categories of our population have little influence at any point in this complex, and one such category is the poor.

An important aspect of the "poor people's march" on Washington in 1968 was that it was a dramatic attempt to influence all branches of the federal decision-making level. An early organizer was Dr. Martin Luther King, Jr., who was assassinated before the march actually began. The Reverend Ralph Abernathy succeeded King and led an advance guard of leaders into Washington on April 29. They visited Cabinet members and other officials and presented them with the "demands" of the poor. One of the basic demands was for a guaranteed annual income. Thousands of poor people came to Washington and stayed in temporary shelters in a park. Their camp was called "Resurrection City." Some changes occurred as a result of the march and encampment (additional funds were allocated for the food-stamp program, for example), but the people drifted back to their homes before significant gains could be made.

Multiple decision-making centers, therefore, mean that programs designed to help the poor are particularly vulnerable to veto or sabotage or atrophy by neglect. One such example is the 1967 Medicaid program which was intended to insure adequate health care for the poor. The program was to be operated by the states, which would set up their own schedules of benefits and their own definitions of eligibility. The federal government would pay half or more of the costs of the program. States had the option of providing fewer benefits than some other states or of not participating at all. Some states were unwilling to assume any financial responsibility for health care of the poor, so they did not participate. Others set up programs with limited benefits.

The middle-class composition of the bureaucracy also works to the detriment of the poor because the middle-class bureaucrats are prone to act in the interests of their peers rather than of the poor. A striking example of this is the case of the sugar cane workers in Louisiana (Schuck, 1972). Work in the fields is seasonal

Figure 8.6 The "poor people's march" on Washington in 1968 was a dramatic attempt to influence all branches of the federal decision-making level.

and tends to be concentrated in the period of December to mid-January. As of 1972 the workers averaged about $2,635 annually. The growers argued that the figure is misleading, because the workers were also given free housing and were allowed to stay in the homes after they became too old or sick to work. A 1970 survey revealed the nature of the free housing: three-fourths of the houses were infested with rats and had no toilets; half had leaking roofs and no running water.

Because of their meager income, the cane workers often found themselves in overwhelming debt. Their medical expenses were sometimes billed to the growers and deducted from their paychecks. They were sometimes charged for the utilities in their houses. They sometimes purchased their food at a store on the plantation that charged exceptionally high prices and extracted high interest rates for food obtained on credit. A worker might have found himself getting nothing on payday except a slip telling him that he is deeper in debt than he was the last time he got paid.

Why do the workers tolerate the situation? Why don't they find employment elsewhere? The area offers limited types of employment and the workers have little schooling with which to compete for the few jobs available. If a job becomes available somewhere, the worker might not be hired until he has housing off the plantation; however, he cannot leave the plantation without a job! Evidence indicates that the workers would leave immediately if they could find employment elsewhere.

Why does the government tolerate the situation? This is an interesting question in that the growers insist the responsibility for any deficiencies in the workers' situation lies with the

federal government. The U.S. Department of Agriculture is required to see that the workers receive fair and reasonable wages in exchange for massive federal **subsidies** to the sugar growers. The department fulfills this responsibility by annually setting the wage rates of the workers. The department has not acted in the interests of the workers, but of the growers. Each year the workers are given a token increase by the department in order to satisfy the requirement of "fair and reasonable wages," and each year the growers receive their hundreds of millions of dollars worth of subsidies. The middle-class bureaucrats who determine the poverty wages of the workers also support the massive federal gifts to the growers.

Regardless of the intentions of various programs and policies, the work of various interest groups and the middle-class composition of the government make it unlikely that the poor will greatly benefit or that the middle strata will be greatly hurt by governmental action. If various groups do not protect their interests at one decision-making center, they can often find another. In the midst of it all, the poor continue to come out on the short end, as was shown in table 8.2. This is not to say that *no* benefits come to the poor. The poor *have* made some gains in areas such as medical care and job training programs; the proportion of the population officially classified as poor has declined; and there are government people from middle- and upper-class backgrounds who labor in behalf of the poor.

Nevertheless, the nonpoor generally benefit as much from programs designed to help the poor as the poor themselves do. Programs that would help the poor at the expense of other groups are unlikely to be implemented or even

proposed. Medicaid helps some of the poor, but it also makes a number of physicians wealthy. Job-training programs helped some of the poor, but they also provided high-salaried positions for a number of middle-class administrators.

Some benefits do filter down to the poor, but the primary beneficiaries of governmental decisions are (and always have been) the well-to-do. It is ironic that the people on welfare are castigated as "freeloaders" when the well-to-do have used their power since the beginning of the Republic to secure handouts from the federal government. But when the well-to-do secure them, they are called things such as subsidies, or tax benefits to stimulate business. From extensive gifts of land to the railroads to guaranteed prices for various farm products to tax concessions and research money for industry, the federal government has been engaged in a long history of acts that have benefited the well-to-do. In many cases the benefits received by the well-to-do are not as obvious as those given to the poor. For example, airline subsidies, highway construction funds, and money for higher education are among those things the poor contribute to through their taxes but from which they benefit less than the nonpoor.

Few people in the middle class are probably aware of how many benefits they themselves receive from government programs.[8] For example, a young man typically attends a public school, perhaps rides on a free school bus and eats a free or subsidized (and therefore cheap) lunch. If he spends some time in the armed forces, he may pursue a subsidized college education. He may then buy a farm or a home with a loan that is subsidized and guaranteed by the federal government. He may go into business for himself with a low-interest loan from

stinking on men! from the feet!

the Small Business Administration. The young man may marry and have children, who are born in a good hospital that was built in part with federal funds. His aged parents may have serious and expensive health problems, which are largely covered by the federal Medicare program. That program enables him to save his own money, which he banks in an institution protected and insured by the federal government. His community may benefit economically from some industrial project underwritten by the government, and his children may be able to go to college because of financial assistance from the government. Then the man, like many good Americans, may rebel against federal programs and high taxes and assert that this country was built on rugged individualism, unaware that his whole existence is enriched and subsidized by various government programs.

Ironically, through the structure and functioning of government, the well-to-do and powerful give to each other that which they say is immoral to give to the poor. There are some blatant examples of freeloading by the wealthy, in some cases by the very people who castigate the poor. A U.S. Representative from a southern district opposed antipoverty programs in his county even though the median income in 1969 was $1,588 per year. The Representative argued that there was no hunger in his district except the hunger that was due to drunk or mentally ill parents. But, he led a move to get the Department of Agriculture to subsidize a private golf club in his county. The government's share of the cost was estimated at $270,000, while the club members contributed about $70,000.[9] Another example of this "upside-down welfare," as it has been called, was

the case of the U.S. Senator who received over $100,000 in payment from the federal government in one year for not planting crops on his farm land while a welfare child in his state got less than $175 for the year (Walz and Askerooth, 1973:5).

The question raised is, Why is it immoral to feed the hungry and moral to pay for private golf clubs? Is the president of an airline, whose high salary is possible partly because of government subsidies, more moral and American than the child who has no father and receives paltry sums of money through welfare? If the government can pay millions of dollars to rescue a corporation from bankruptcy, why is it wrong to rescue people from poverty? The answer is that the poor are powerless to secure what the well-to-do secure with relatively little difficulty. The decisions of the government reflect the interests of the well-to-do, not the interests of the poor.

The interests of the middle and upper strata that are reflected in government action are also seen in the *tax structure.* Presumably, our tax structure is an equalizing mechanism that takes disproportionately from the rich in order to benefit the poor.

Certain taxes, such as the sales tax, clearly work to the detriment of the poor. Adding 3 to 6 percent to the cost of purchases is considerably more burdensome to the family whose income is only $5,000 per year or less than to the family with an $18,000 or more per year income.

Income tax is not the equalizer it appears to be at first. The "progressive" income tax was intended to take progressively larger proportions as income increased, but in practice this is not the result. We find that the government, in effect, subsidizes the well-to-do through benefits such as investment credits, dividend exclusions, and exemptions of taxes on half of capital gains. These benefits are reductions in taxes for various kinds of investments. None are likely to benefit the poor because the poor have no money invested. These benefits amount to the government giving billions of dollars per year to the well-to-do.

Reports of wealthy people who pay no income taxes tend to rouse the ire of taxpayers. Each year a few millionaires and hundreds of people with incomes of $100,000 or more escape paying federal income tax. Corporations as well as wealthy individuals can sometimes take advantage of loopholes or particular laws and pay no tax in a particular year. In fact, the share of taxes assumed by corporations declined from 23 percent in 1960 to 16 percent in 1975.[10] The public and some Congressmen periodically demand changes to resolve such inequities. While we may argue that justice demands changes, we should also realize that getting the few wealthy individuals and corporations that avoid taxes to pay their proportionate share will not alleviate the burden on the taxpayers nor provide the means to eliminate poverty.

Some people argue that the federal income tax has a negligible effect on the distribution of wealth, but that argument overstates the case. Most of the wealthy do, in fact, pay a considerable amount in taxes. The question is, Do they pay a proportionately larger amount of their income than nonwealthy people? The answer is generally in the negative. In a 1969 report, Barr (1969:23) showed that those with amended gross incomes under $3,000 paid income tax of anywhere from 0 to 20 percent, with the majority paying from 0 to 5 percent. People with incomes of $1,000,000 or more paid from 0 to

between 65 and 70 percent, with the majority paying between 20 and 30 percent. The percentage of income the majority of millionaires paid in income taxes was about the same as the percentage paid by the majority of those in the $500,000 to $1 million bracket; somewhat smaller than by those in the $50,000 to $500,000 bracket; and only slightly higher than by those in the $3,000 to $50,000 bracket.

A Brookings Institution study reported that almost 90 percent of Americans pay the same proportion of their income in taxes of all kinds (federal, state, and local)—roughly 20 to 25 percent.[11] Ironically, the only families paying more than 25 percent were those at the very top and those at the very bottom of the income scale. In other words, when all taxes are considered, the poor pay a higher proportion of their income than do the broad middle strata.

Thus, with respect to some taxes, the proportion of income the poor pay is greater than the proportion paid by the rich. With respect to income taxes, the poor pay a smaller proportion. The large middle groups pay on the average at about the same rate.

The poor have made gains, and they have their advocates in positions of power, but the middle strata have made far more gains. In the 1970s many Americans believed that people in the middle were being squeezed between the rich, who did not carry their share of the fiscal burden of the country, and the poor, who were being given all kinds of benefits paid for by the middle strata. Actually, the United States spends a lower proportion of its gross national product on welfare for the poor than do most other Western nations (Wilensky, 1976).

Poverty and the economy. Our economy works for the rich and against the poor in various ways. A capitalist economy, which is supported by government policies, allows *concentration of wealth.* The fact that the share of income of the richest Americans has declined during this century (table 8.2) is misleading unless we recognize that a good part of the wealth of the very rich does not come from personal income. James Smith (1969) studied the assets of people he called the "super rich"— about 4 percent of the population age 20 and over. The super rich, he found, owned 33 percent of the total net worth of all Americans. Breaking down the total into specifics, the super rich owned 93.6 percent of all state and local bonds; 66.7 percent of corporate stock; 97.6 percent of federal bonds (excluding savings bonds); and nearly 30 percent of all real estate. Clearly, the wealth of the nation is concentrated in relatively few hands.

The economy works against the poor by entrapping them in a vicious circle. Consider, for example, a man whose job pays him only poverty-level wages. He cannot get a better-paying job because he lacks the education or skills. He cannot afford to quit his job to gain the skills or advance his education because he has a family. There is no union, and he is unwilling to risk his job and perhaps his physical well-being to try to organize his fellow workers or even to support a move to unionization. Meanwhile, his debts mount, he may accumulate medical bills, and the rate of inflation may far surpass any wage increase he gets. As he sinks more deeply into debt, he is less and less able to risk the loss of the income he has. Ultimately, he may reach the point of despair we described earlier. Perhaps he will cling to the hope that at least some

of his children can escape the poverty that has wrung the vigor out of his own life.

Are there such jobs? Yes indeed. A pioneering study by Bluestone (1969) showed that 8.5 million Americans were working full time and living in poverty. The basic problem was *low wages in certain industries.* The wages were not wholly due to greedy employers. Most of the low-wage industries were fiercely competitive, and profits were small despite the low wages. In some of the industries, average hourly earnings were as low as $1.25, and as many as 88 percent of the workers were in the low-wage category (southern sawmills and planing mills). Higher wages were available in industries with products for which the demand was fairly stable or increasing—in industries with unionized workers covered by minimum-wage laws, and in industries with relatively large profits. But, hundreds of thousands of Americans had to make do with the low-wage jobs. That the problem has not been resolved is illustrated by the fact that 46.3 percent of all the heads of poor families in 1978 worked full time year-round.

One way to deal with low-paying jobs is to *unionize* the workers. A recent notable example is the attempt to unionize the farm workers. The need for improvement in their economic status is dramatically illustrated in Jacobs's account of his work in California tomato fields in 1964 (Jacobs, 1966). When he posed as a migrant worker and applied at the farm labor office, he was told to report the next day at 5:00 A.M. After waiting awhile at the office the next morning, Jacobs and the other workers were transported by bus to the fields. With a short-handled hoe, fifteen inches long, the plants were to be thinned and the weeds chopped out. The work was backbreaking: "The furrows extend into an eternity of tiny tomato plants and dirt, and the short-handled hoe is an instrument of torture" (Jacobs, 1966:124). The pay was $1.00 per hour. Jacobs concluded the description of his experience by pointing out that a man with the physical stamina to make it could go into the fields six days a week for the eight or nine months such work is available during the year, and earn as much as $1,700 for the year. Would increasing the workers' pay result in much higher prices for tomatoes? Some estimates indicate that doubling the wages of the workers would increase the retail price of tomatoes by only about a penny a can or pound.

The same economy that allows such low-paying labor furthers the disadvantage of the poor in regard to the purchase of consumer goods. Caplovitz (1967) showed that the *poor pay more* for many kinds of consumer goods than do the well-to-do. For example, in his survey he found that 46 percent of the families with an annual income under $3,500 paid a high price for their television sets, while only 37 percent of those with incomes over $3,500 paid a high price. Similarly, 49 percent of low-income families paid over $230 for their washing machines, while only 35 percent of higher-income families paid that amount.

We might assume that the poor were buying merchandise of a quality higher than what the nonpoor were buying. However, Caplovitz found that the goods purchased by the poor were generally lower in quality. Why, then, did the poor pay more for the merchandise? One reason is that the poor often do not know how to shop around. In some cases, they may lack the money and the mobility to shop around even if they have the skill to do so. The mechanisms by which high prices are exacted from the poor are sometimes subtle, and are sometimes the result of a businessman exploiting ignorance. Conot (1970) described some of the practices of a "slum merchant." In one case, the merchant's bill of sale for a television set included a $15 charge for a 90-day warranty on the new set (which, said the merchant, was "pure gold" for himself since there was little likelihood of problems with a new set within 90 days). The same bill of sale deducted a 10 percent down payment before adding the carrying charges and recording a "grand total." The merchant said that this was a "really fine gimmick" because otherwise the customer would realize the set actually cost over $400 rather than the $368.42 shown on the "grand total."

A more frequent reason why the poor pay more is that they do not have enough money to use cash, and when they obtain credit they often pay high interest. The same merchant mentioned previously admitted the following:

> I have this woman, and she comes to me and she still owes me $100, and she tells me that they have cut her check, and she cannot afford to pay $20 a month. So I tell her, "Okay, you're a good woman, I trust you. Just pay me the interest. Five dollars a month." So she has paid me now $5 a month for two years, and she still owes me $100. I can't complain! [Conot, 1970:414].

Attempts to justify the practice of charging poor people higher prices and higher rates of interest usually rest on arguments that the poor are greater risks, and that doing business in ghetto neighborhoods is more costly than elsewhere because of greater losses through theft and higher insurance premiums. However legitimate such practices may be from the viewpoint of the businessman, they do contribute to keeping the poor impoverished.

Patterns of family life.   Education is crucial to the *upward mobility* of better-paying and higher-prestige jobs. If the working poor could get better-paying jobs, they would be able to lift themselves out of poverty. (Keep in mind, however, that this still would not solve the poverty problem because a large number of the poor are not in the labor force.) The better-paying jobs typically demand more education than the poor have, and factors in the family life of the poor make securing that necessary education unlikely.

One aspect of family life that tends to perpetuate poverty is the *size of the family.* In 1978, 37.4 percent of families with five or more children were poor; in contrast, only 8.6 percent with four or fewer children were poor. How the large family perpetuates poverty was described by Orshansky and Bretz (1976:21):

> We have long known that childhood in a large family as opposed to a small one could often be synonymous with growing up poor. Evidence now suggests that any such disadvantage persists into adulthood and even into old age. Unlike the only child or one with just one brother or sister, a youngster from a family with four or more brothers and sisters is apt to leave school early, have less chance to become a professional, face raising a family on an inadequate income, and stand a greater chance of a poverty-stricken old age. Such patterns of fate suggest themselves, in varying degree, for white and black alike, for both men and women, and for natives of large cities as well as those born on farms or in small towns.

Even in small families, however, the family is likely to perpetuate its own poverty by discouraging intellectual achievement. Considerable research shows that the influence of the family is crucially important to a child's intellectual development, and influence is transmitted socially, not genetically. Freeberg and Payne (1967) identified six factors that are important for a child's intellectual growth: willingness to give time to the child; parental guidance; parental aspirations for the child's achievement; acceptance of the child's behavior; providing intellectual stimulation; and using external resources (such as sending the child to nursery school or seeking advice or help in teaching new things to the child). Similarly, Whiteman and Deutsch (1968) found significant correlations between scores on intelligence tests and what they called their "Deprivation Index." The index consisted of six variables: extent of housing dilapidation; parental educational aspiration for the child; number of children in the home under 18 years of age; dinner conversation; number of cultural experiences the child anticipates for the coming weekend; and child's attendance in kindergarten.

In both studies, some of the factors that contribute to intellectual development are not likely to be available to the poor. Therefore, there is a direct relationship between socioeconomic position and scores on intelligence tests plus general academic performance. The lower the position, the lower the scores tend to be.

How disadvantaged are the poor? Surely poor parents can exercise control over some of the factors, such as spending time with their children, or having high aspirations for them. Unfortunately, even these influences tend to be absent. *Interaction with adults tends to be minimal* in poor families. Riessman (1962:37) described the home of the culturally deprived child as a "crowded, busy, active, noisy place where no child is focused upon. There are too many children for this, and the parents have too little time." Keller (1963) found that the poor children she studied watched television, played, listened to music on the radio, and saw many films. But, they did little reading and lacked sustained interaction with adult members of their families. For example, only about half of the children regularly ate one meal with a parent; the rest ate alone or with brothers and sisters.

There is evidence that consistent mothering by one person facilitates development of a child's ability to express himself vocally. Children in poor families are less likely to have such a relationship in their early years. Instead, responsibility for child care tends to be assumed by a number of people, both adults and other children (Jensen, 1968:117).

The interaction that does occur may hinder rather than facilitate intellectual growth. Among the poor there is a *greater proportion of nonverbal compared to verbal interaction*; in fact, verbal interaction tends to be minimal (Hess and Shipman, 1965; Beiser, 1965). This orientation of the poor toward nonverbal rather than verbal, and toward physical rather than mental behavior is manifested in other ways, too. The child is likely to do better on motoric than on verbal tests, and may use fingers while counting and move his or her lips while reading (Reissman, 1962:67).

Because the verbal ability of poor adults is generally low, trying to increase the amount of verbal interaction between adults and children would not help. In fact, many language differences have been found between the lower and the middle and upper socioeconomic strata. These language differences involve things such as grammatical distinctions; pronunciation, stress, and intonation; richness of vocabulary; and style and taste in the selection and use of words and phrases. Differences in these linguistic features mean differences in how the world is experienced and communicated (Hertzler, 1965:368–69). In general, poor parents are equipped with neither the financial resources nor the intellectual tools necessary to maximize the intellectual growth of their children. The parents' own opportunities to acquire these resources and tools are minimal, and hence the family environment they provide will tend to perpetuate the limitations in their children.

The education of the poor.   In general, the lower the income, the less the education. The poor have, on the average, the least amount of education. Our earlier discussion about the vicious circle shows how poverty and limited education reinforce each other. We must extend that discussion to show how the educational environment itself interacts with students to perpetuate the problem. Chapter 13, Education, considers the problems of inequitable distribution of quality education—how schools in poor neighborhoods tend to have meager facilities and inexperienced or inadequate teachers. Here we will focus on how *school personnel affect poverty-level students* at the interpersonal level.

Where children of poor families attend school with children of nonpoor families, there may be **discrimination** against the former. In a classic study, Hollingshead (1949) found that high school students in a small Midwestern town were treated differently by teachers and administrators, depending on the social class level of the students' parents. Students from the lower levels received less consideration and harsher punishments. Then Becker (1952) identified social class variations in aspects of the teacher-pupil relationship such as teaching techniques, discipline, and moral acceptability of the pupils.

Other studies corroborated these findings and extended them to show that *teachers have different expectations for students from different socioeconomic backgrounds* (Kozol, 1967; Fader, 1971). Expectations can significantly retard or stimulate intellectual growth (Rosenthal and Jacobson, 1968). Hence, when middle-class teachers expect students from poor families not to perform well, that expectation can lead the children to perform below their capabilities (Wylie, 1963).

In essence, the poor are less likely than the nonpoor to have gratifying and encouraging experiences in school. They are, therefore, more likely to drop out. One study of high school seniors reported that children from lower socioeconomic levels, compared to those from the middle and upper strata, were more dissatisfied with school, reported more interpersonal problems (such as not being popular), felt more difficulty in expressing themselves well, and were more likely to express difficulties with concentrating and studying (James, 1972:79). It is not surprising, then, that the majority of school dropouts are from the lower strata.

Data from the Educational Testing Service for 1967 showed that in the highest ability grouping of students who took the School and College Ability Test, 91.6 percent from the highest socioeconomic level went to college, but only 76.7 percent from the lowest socioeconomic level went to college.[12] This kind of difference showed up at all ability levels of the group of students. Among students in the lowest ability level, 46.2 percent from the highest socioeco-

nomic level and 21.6 percent from the lowest socioeconomic level went to college.

In sum, the poor are less likely than the nonpoor to perform well in school or to seek more than minimal education—not necessarily because of innate ability, but because of sociocultural factors. Even when ability levels of poor and nonpoor are equated, the poor are less likely to pursue higher education.

Social Psychological Factors

Some attitudes and values held by the poor and the nonpoor help to perpetuate poverty. A good deal of debate has been expended on whether or not certain attitudes and values among the poor combine to create a "culture of poverty." We will review that debate and then consider how the attitudes and values of the nonpoor disparage and discriminate against the poor.

The "culture of poverty."   The concept of a *culture of poverty* was formulated by the anthropologist Oscar Lewis. He identified over sixty characteristics of people who are part of a culture of poverty. Essentially, the characteristics are economic, social, and psychological attitudes and values that arose out of the people's efforts to adapt to their impoverishment. In turn, these attitudes and values tend to perpetuate that impoverishment because they are not conducive to the behavior necessary to get out of poverty (Lewis, 1966:xiv). Combined with "feelings of not belonging, marginality, unworthiness, inferiority, and the feeling that the institutions of the larger society are not there to serve the interests of these people" (Lewis, 1969:149, 151) are attitudes of resignation and fatalism and valuing present over deferred future gratification. Such attitudes and values inhibit a person from sacrificing and striving to advance himself or herself.

The culture of poverty thesis has been vigorously debated on both an empirical and a theoretical level. Empirically, various aspects of the thesis have been shown to be untrue for the majority of the poor. Theoretically, the thesis has been attacked as an inadequate explanatory tool and as a subtle way of oppressing the poor. Valentine (1968:144) concluded his appraisal with these words:

> . . . the main weight and prevailing direction of available evidence are inconsistent with it. . . . When it is presented as a total picture of the culture of the lower class, in my considered judgment this portrayal is absurd. In this form it is little more than a middle-class intellectual rationale for blaming poverty on the poor and thus avoiding recognition of the need for radical change in our society.

For a more balanced assessment of the thesis, we need to keep two points in mind. First, Lewis (1969:153) did not argue that all poor can be characterized by the traits he identified. Rather, he estimated that about one-third of the poor fall into the category of the culture of poverty. Second, some of the attitudes and values identified by Lewis do tend to characterize the poor, although a portion of those attitudes and values might be quickly altered under the proper circumstances.

Among the *attitudes and values* of the poor that work to their detriment are those which *inhibit education* and promote a sense of *fatalism* and *resignation*. Furthermore, people in the lower strata tend to be more concerned with the *appearance of respectability* in their children than with *achievement*. Kohn (1959:340) found clear class differences in the kinds of *qualities*

that parents value in their children. Working-class mothers were likely to value obedience. They wanted their children to recognize parental authority. Middle-class mothers, on the other hand, were likely to value consideration and self-control. Middle-class mothers also wanted their children to have a sense of curiosity. Working-class mothers seemed more concerned about their children's neatness and cleanliness than about their curiosity. It was not as important to them that the child be intellectually active as that the child be presentable. Even among "upper-lower-class" families, Pavenstedt (1965:92) found that parents were more concerned that their children conform to the teacher's expectations than that their children were learning.

On the other hand, some of the fatalism and resignation and skepticism about the possibility for advancement is a *psychological adaptation to the situation of poverty.* To be highly ambitious in the face of no opportunities, to aspire to something high when there is no possibility of reaching it, is to face only bitter frustration. If the poor believe they are powerless, it is because, in part, they are correctly assessing their situation. If they adopt a sense of fatalism toward life, it may be a way of minimizing the agony of powerlessness.

However, there is evidence that if realistic opportunities are presented to the poor, they may shift their attitudes and values and become highly motivated. We already mentioned the Gallup poll that showed a majority desiring work rather than an unconditionally guaranteed income. A study by Reissman (1969) of about 1,500 heads of households in New Orleans showed that the poor, and particularly the black poor, were willing to do virtually anything to get a better job—learn new skills, leave the city, or give up some of their leisure time. Similarly, Davidson and Gaitz (1974) found that poor Mexican Americans were as work-oriented as nonpoor white Americans.

The poor may have a sense of alienation, powerlessness, and fatalism, but no evidence indicates that their attitudes to work are negative or that they are unwilling to earn their own way.

Disparagement and discrimination. As we saw earlier, *the nonpoor tend to disparage the poor.* Through history, and in virtually all societies, the poor have been considered disreputable in some sense. Such attitudes seriously undermine self-respect among the poor and at the same time help perpetuate the political and economic processes that maintain poverty.

Even the clergy have often lacked sympathy for the poor and have blamed them for their condition. The famous nineteenth century preacher Henry Ward Beecher told workers they should be content with receiving a dollar a day to support a family of eight, because water cost them nothing, and if a worker could not live on bread he wasn't fit to live anyway. The modern clergy, particularly the theologically conservative, are also prone to blame the poor. Hadden (1969:80) asked clergy of a number of denominations to respond to the statement "Most people who live in poverty could do something about their situation if they really wanted to." He found that 50 percent or more of those who identified themselves as fundamentalists (extremely conservative) agreed with the statement; agreement of less conservative denominations ranged from 11 to 23 percent.

The net effect of *attitudes that define the poor as blameworthy* is to help perpetuate poverty by justifying discrimination against the poor and denying them help. Political decisions and economic processes that benefit primarily the well-to-do are legitimated and continued. These discriminatory attitudes are particularly strong with respect to those on welfare. Williamson (1974) surveyed 375 people living in the Greater Boston area during 1972 on their attitudes toward welfare recipients. He found a number of negative attitudes, including the ideas that welfare recipients are more idle, more dishonest, and more fertile than they really are. The respondents also believed that the poor have little motivation to work. These beliefs are not supported by the evidence, but they justify opposition to helping the poor and thereby help to maintain the problem.

Negative attitudes toward the poor may become **self-fulfilling prophecies.** If a man is poor because he is out of work, he may find that when he secures work hostility is directed toward him because he comes from an impoverished background. In 1969 a St. Louis area manufacturing company placed a full-page advertisement in the local newspaper, pointing out that a program to bus inner-city workers to the plant had failed. The ad asked what was wrong with the workers. Why were the jobs still open? The company implied that what many people think is actually true—the poor are too lazy to work and will not accept an opportunity even if it is offered to them. A subsequent investigation showed that the hard-core unemployed, who were all black, were unwilling to work because of pressures, hostility, and racial bias.

Similar results were obtained in a study of eighteen hard-core unemployed who were brought into a Midwestern chemical plant as

Figure 8.7 Appalachian poverty. Many of the people in the region resist or refuse welfare, even though they have little opportunity to get out of poverty.

trainees (Lauer, 1972). Managers and workers alike expected the men to fail, and hostility was overt. The men were subjected to various kinds of humiliation. They were closely questioned when they were sick, and one was accused of being on drugs rather than being sick. Arrest records were to be kept confidential by company executives, but a number of the records were common knowledge among foremen and other workers. Two years after the program had begun, only two of the men remained on the job. The failure of the program rested not on the unwillingness of the poor to work, but on the unwillingness of the nonpoor to accept the poor and to treat them as fellow human beings.

Such attitudes toward the poor and treatment of the poor are legitimated by the American value of individualism (that people ought to help themselves rather than depend upon others, particularly the government) and the ideology of equal opportunity for all. Therefore, a widely held belief is that those who don't make it in America are somehow flawed and are blameworthy.

The ideology of wealth and poverty. The American *ideology of wealth and poverty* has two elements: a belief that there are *opportunities for advancement* for all, and a belief that particular characteristics enable someone to seize the opportunity. Huber and Form (1973:91) found that a large majority of their sample from a Michigan community believed that America offers plenty of opportunities. Huber and Form (1973:100) also found the belief that wealth is the result of "hard work, ability, motivation, and other favorable personal traits," while poverty is due to "laziness, stupidity, and other unfavorable personal traits."

The ideology is far more acceptable to the well-to-do than to the poor. The researchers found that the poor tended to attribute their problem to the social structure, knowing that they have worked as hard as everyone else even though they have not reaped the rewards of hard work (Huber and Form, 1973:116). The poor are a minority, and the ideology advocated by the majority legitimates blaming the poor and resisting programs to alleviate poverty. Williamson (1974) found that those among his respondents who believed in this ideology were also those most opposed to increased welfare payments.

Some of the poor also accept the majority ideology. How do they react to their failure? One response found in Appalachian men and welfare women is illness (Ransdell and Roche, 1969; Cole and Lejeune, 1972), which provides the individual with a ready reason for having failed in the land of opportunity. Illness, in turn, tends to perpetuate the poverty because the individual is incapable of behaving in a way necessary to alter the impoverished state. Thus, the American ideology of wealth and poverty inhibits the nonpoor and at least some of the poor from action that could alleviate poverty.

What Is To Be Done?

We might consider what has already been done to resolve the problem of poverty. The so-called *"war on poverty"* initiated in the 1960s was a multi-faceted attack on the problem. The Economic Opportunity Act of 1964 set up several programs intended to benefit the poor, including the Job Corps (to train young people who have little education or skills), the College Work

Figure 8.8 Poor people probably know much more about the lives of the nonpoor than vice versa.

Study Program (to help college students from low-income families), and the Community Action Program. The last was the largest and most controversial aspect of the war on poverty. It was supposed to involve "maximum feasible participation" by the poor so they could help to plan and carry out programs from which they would benefit. Unfortunately, the war on poverty received more publicity than support from the federal and state governments, particularly as the costs of the war in Vietnam mounted and the nation faced recession in the late 1960s and early 1970s. Poverty, though reduced, was still widespread.

To eliminate poverty some attitudes and ideologies among the political leadership must be altered. At the same time, changes in government and the economy must be made so the interests of the poor can be expressed. The commitment of the federal government is essential. Past programs of the federal government have been inadequate, and a commitment to new policies and programs is needed.

Among the past programs, now considered miserable failures by most people, is the *welfare system*. Marmor (1971:33–34) identified six aspects of the welfare system that have brought it to the point of "crisis":

1. The financial aid is inadequate.
2. The amount of aid varies from place to place and from one kind of recipient to another.
3. Administrators in the system follow unjust and arbitrary practices including stigmatizing a recipient.
4. The cost of trying to raise the amount of aid is high.
5. The program discourages family solidarity and undercuts the incentive to work.
6. Certain of the poor—particularly the working poor—are excluded from benefits.

"Pappy, will Lonnie and I ever see international celebrities wearing kicky knits and deep-vented shaped suits in an environment of chrome, smoky plastic, and mirrors?"

With regard to point 5, the welfare system makes family solidarity difficult because aid may be denied when a nonworking, able-bodied man is in the home. The incentive to work is undercut because those who receive help through the Aid to Families with Dependent Children program can keep only a portion of any money they earn if they wish to remain in the program.

What are the options to the welfare system? Some kind of *income maintenance program* offers the best hope. Levine (1970:201–202) suggested a number of points that should be incorporated into such a program. First, income maintenance should mean that everyone will have a "decent level of support." Second, people should be eligible solely on the basis of need— that is, on the basis of family income. Third, recipients should be motivated to work and to get out of the program. This can best be done if they are allowed to keep a large portion of the income maintenance payments as their own earnings increase up to some breakeven point. Fourth, payments should be made regardless of whether the home includes one or two parents and regardless of whether a male head is working. Fifth, the income maintenance program should operate independently of any services provided by social workers. A family should not be required to accept certain services in order to receive the income payments. Finally, the program should be uniform throughout the nation, with no great disparities from one region to another (except, of course, disparities due to different costs of living in various places).

A program similar to that suggested by Levine was proposed by the President's Commission on Income Maintenance Programs in 1969. The commission issued a report that recommended a *"negative income tax"* (NIT) system that would eliminate financial poverty; in essence, "a direct Federal cash transfer program offering payments to all, in proportion to their need" (Marmor, 1971:183–203). The payments would vary by size of family and would be reduced by only fifty cents on the dollar as the family increased its earnings from work (a provision that maintains the incentive to work). When the family income reached $5,000, payments would cease.

Would such a program actually maintain the motivation to work? In view of the attitudes of many Americans toward the poor, probably a considerable number of people would react to the NIT proposal with the argument that "handouts" inevitably take away the incentive to work. Evidence from an experiment in New Jersey showed that an income maintenance program can achieve precisely what it aims to achieve—motivate people to work out of their poverty (Watts and Rees, 1977). The Office of Economic Opportunity found that among 1,300 families in the experiment, a guaranteed income payment tended to motivate the workers to get higher-paying jobs. In other words, rather than lose incentive the workers actually developed more incentive. They had the needed financial base to escape the vicious circle of poverty and the needed realistic opportunity to become motivated.

An income maintenance program must also address the problem of those who are unable to work (the aged and disabled) and those who have responsibilities and commitments that are more important to them than being in the labor force (mothers of preschool children). In other words, not all participants will work themselves out of an income maintenance program. The goal of the program would not be to eliminate all government payments but to eliminate poverty.

In the absence of an income maintenance program, the poor have to *organize* in order to articulate their interests in the institutions of society. A number of organized efforts appear in various parts of the nation already. In the *conflict* between the poor and landlords, for example, rent strikes have been organized. On a national level, only one organization has captured attention—the National Welfare Rights Organization. The NWRO has focused on deficiencies of the welfare system, such as inadequate payment levels and restrictions on eligibility. Correcting the deficiencies will help the poor, but ultimately a commitment to an alternative system like income maintenance is needed.

Summary

Poverty may not be as bad in America as it is in some parts of the world, but America's poverty must be evaluated in terms of the standard of living attained by the majority of Americans. The government's definition of poverty is based on the cost of a basic diet called the "economy food plan." It is revised to account for inflation and varies according to the location (farm or nonfarm), size of the family, and sex and age of the head of the family. In 1979, a nonfarm family of four with an annual income of $7,412 or less was officially poor. This official definition is challenged as inadequate or as unrealistic because it sets the poverty level quite low.

The proportion of the poor is declining in America, but their share of the income is lower than in the past. In 1978 about 24.5 million Americans (11.4 percent of the population) were poor by the official definition. Poverty is not equally distributed among the population, however. Your chances of being poor are greater if you are nonwhite, or aged, or in a female-headed family, or living in a rural area. Contrary to popular opinion, poverty is not basically a problem of unemployment. Many of the poor work, and some work full time.

The quality of life for the poor can be characterized as pervasive deprivation—the poor get less of everything that is valued in our society, including rights to life and the pursuit of happiness. Poverty brings despair and fear, including the fear of being victimized by crime. Various myths that disparage the poor diminish their dignity as human beings. Their health is poorer than that of most Americans, and their poverty and ill health can become a vicious circle. The individual living in poverty is forced to choose between limited, undesirable alternatives.

Among the structural factors that contribute to poverty, the distribution of power is of prime importance. Those who control the wealth are the most powerful, and their interests are typically reflected in governmental decisions. Both the structure and functioning of American government tend to work to the detriment of the poor. Multiple decision-making centers and the middle-class composition of the bureaucracy work to the detriment of the poor. Ironically, the well-to-do and powerful give to each other through government actions what they say is immoral to give to the poor. The economy works for the rich by allowing the concentration of wealth. On the other hand, the economy works against the poor in two ways: they get the jobs with the lowest wages, and they pay the highest

298

prices for consumer goods. The family environment tends to perpetuate poverty when five or more children are in the family. Even when there are few children, poor families tend to transmit poverty by anti-intellectual attitudes and patterns of interaction that inhibit intellectual development. Educational arrangements themselves contribute to the problem because quality education is much less likely to be available to poor children than to nonpoor children. Also, poor children tend not to have gratifying and encouraging experiences in school or to pursue higher education even when they have the ability to do so.

Attitudes and values of both the poor and the nonpoor contribute to the poverty problem. The "culture of poverty" theory asserts that certain economic, social, and psychological characteristics make poverty self-perpetuating. While the "culture of poverty" concept applies to only a minority of the poor, some of the predisposing characteristics are common among them. Given realistic opportunities, however, characteristics such as fatalism and resignation can quickly disappear. The attitudes and values of the nonpoor legitimate their disparagement of and discrimination against the poor. The American value of individualism and ideology of equal opportunity combine to justify negative attitudes toward the poor and programs designed to help them.

Finally, the ideology of wealth and poverty asserts that opportunities are available to all and that certain personal qualities such as hard work and ability enable the individual to seize opportunities. This ideology legitimates blaming the poor for their problem and resisting programs designed to alleviate poverty. While most of the poor themselves do not fully accept the ideology, some do, and they justify their failure as a result of illness.

Glossary

autonomy   the ability or opportunity to govern oneself

consumer price index   a measure of the average change in prices of all types of consumer goods and services purchased by urban wage earners and clerical workers

decile   one of ten equal categories of some variable

discrimination   arbitrary, unfavorable treatment of the members of some social group

ghetto   an area in which a certain group is segregated from the rest of society; often used today to refer to the impoverished area of the inner city

malnutrition   inadequate food, in amount and/or type

poverty level   defined as the minimum income level at which Americans should have to live, it is based on the Department of Agriculture's calculations of the cost of a basic diet they called the "economy food plan"

self-fulfilling prophecy   a belief that has consequences (and may become true) simply because it is believed

subsidy   a government grant to a private person or company to assist an enterprise deemed advantageous to the public

For Further Reading

Goro, Herb. *The Block*. New York: Random House, 1970. Pictures and text combine to present a graphic description of a New York City ghetto and its destructive consequences for human beings.

Gronbjerg, Kirsten, David Street, and Gerald D. Suttles. *Poverty and Social Change*. Chicago: University of Chicago Press, 1978. Shows the historical development of the poverty problem and attempts to deal with it through welfare. Shows how understandings of poverty and views about welfare have changed, and how the ideology of laissez-faire capitalism has guided antipoverty programs.

Harrington, Michael. *The Other America*. Baltimore: Penguin Books, 1962. An important, pioneering work; contains both hard data and illustrative materials on the poor.

James, Dorothy B. *Poverty, Politics, and Change*. Englewood Cliffs, N.J.: Prentice-Hall, Inc., 1972. Excellent discussion of how structural factors tend to perpetuate poverty, including how those factors reflect some basic American values.

Meissner, Hanna H., ed. *Poverty in the Affluent Society*. New York: Harper & Row, 1966. A collection of materials from a wide variety of sources, covering historical perspective, good illustrative materials, and discussions of the relationship between poverty and education, housing, justice, and health.

Miller, S. A., and Pamela Roby. *The Future of Inequality*. New York: Basic Books, Inc., 1970. Insight concerning a national policy for resolving the problem of poverty, along with materials that dramatize the nature of poverty in America.

Piven, Francis Fox, and Richard A. Cloward. *Regulating the Poor: The Functions of Public Relief*. New York: Random House, 1971. A convincing argument that welfare is designed not so much to help the poor as to regulate them and prevent them from erupting into violence.

Spectorsky, A. C. *The Exurbanites*. Philadelphia: J. B. Lippincott Company, 1955. An old but readable and still useful work that describes the life-style of the affluent. Any consideration of poverty should take account of such studies of the nonpoor and the wealthy.

Notes

1. Figures from U.S. Bureau of the Census, *Statistical Abstract of the United States, 1980* (Washington, D.C.: Government Printing Office, 1981), p. 490.

2. U.S. Bureau of the Census, *Current Population Reports,* series P–60, no. 120, "Money Income and Poverty Status of Families in the United States: 1978 (Advance Report)" (Washington, D.C.: Government Printing Office, 1979), p. 3.

3. *St. Louis Post-Dispatch,* April 7, 1968, p. 1G.

4. Described by Paul Hutchinson in Harold E. Fey and Margaret Frankes, eds., *The Christian Century Reader* (New York: Assn. Press, 1962), p. 275.

5. *St. Louis Post-Dispatch,* April 23, 1971.

6. *The Socioeconomic Newsletter,* September 1977.

7. *Time,* February 28, 1969, p. 25.

8. The following account from Senator Stephen Young of Ohio, as reported in Dorothy B. James, *Poverty, Politics, and Change* (Englewood Cliffs, N.J.: Prentice-Hall, 1972), pp. 108–109.

9. *St. Louis Post-Dispatch,* March 15 and August 8, 1969.

10. Ibid., February 23, 1975.

11. Ibid., April 14, 1974.

12. *Social Indicators, 1973,* p. 106.

Work

1 How has the nature of work changed?

2 Does anyone really like work?

3 Will work make you sick or keep you well?

4 How have technology and bureaucracies affected work?

5 How can you maximize your satisfaction with work?

A good many Americans fantasize about becoming independently wealthy so they could do whatever they please. If this fantasy suddenly came true for you, what would you do? Would you work? When the author posed this question to a social problems class, only one male said that he would not work. The rest of the class apparently was committed to the **work ethic.** The work ethic involves the notion that our *sense of worth* and the *satisfaction of our needs* are intricately related to the kind of work we do.

Is work satisfying? When a group of ministers and Christian laymen toured an auto plant, a worker asked one minister if he knew where he was going. The minister said no, and the worker responded, "You are going through hell."[1] On the other hand, many people insist that their work is the essence of their lives. Artists, writers, and others gladly embrace their work throughout their lives and look upon the absence of work with horror.

In this chapter we will explore the diverse meanings people attach to their work and we will look at the changing nature of work and the work force in America. We will consider the kinds of problems associated with work and discuss how they affect the quality of life. We will then note the factors that contribute to and help to perpetuate work problems. Finally, we will outline a few approaches to resolving the problems.

Work and the Workforce in America

Both the *nature of work* and the *nature of the workforce* change over time. One change is an enormous increase in the size of the **labor force** (defined as all civilians who are employed or

304

Figure 9.1 U.S. total labor force, 1800 to 1980. (Source: U.S. Department of Labor, Bureau of Labor Statistics, *Bulletin 1919* [Washington, D.C.: Government Printing Office, 1980], p. 217.)

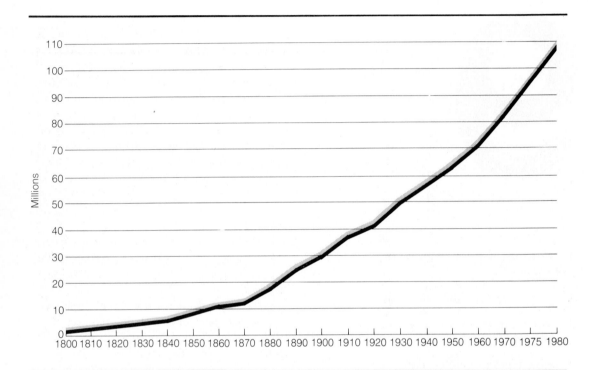

unemployed but able and wanting to work). It was this rapid increase since the beginning of the nineteenth century (figure 9.1) that made possible the nation's swift industrial growth. Since at least 1940 the labor force has been growing faster than the population (age 16 and over). The total number of jobs is even higher than the number of people employed because nearly 5 percent of all employed workers hold a second job (U.S. Department of Labor, 1980:298).

Important changes in the *occupational structure,* in the *composition of the labor force,* and in the *meaning of work* will be discussed first.

The Changing Occupational Structure

"What do you want to be when you grow up?" is a question asked most American children. There are now over 30,000 different answers possible because one characteristic of the American occupational structure is an increasing **division of labor,** or *specialization.*

Not all kinds of jobs have proliferated. If we look at the broad categories of occupations used by the census bureau, we find that since the beginning of the twentieth century the proportion of workers in professional, technical, managerial, clerical, and service jobs has increased greatly. The proportion of workers classified as

Figure 9.2 Technological improvements in farming have greatly reduced the proportion of farmers in the American labor force.

306

Figure 9.3 Percent change in employment by occupation, 1972 to 1979. (Source: U.S. Bureau of the Census, *Current Population Reports*, "Population Profile of the United States: 1979," series P–20, no. 350 [Washington, D.C.: Government Printing Office, 1980], p. 32.)

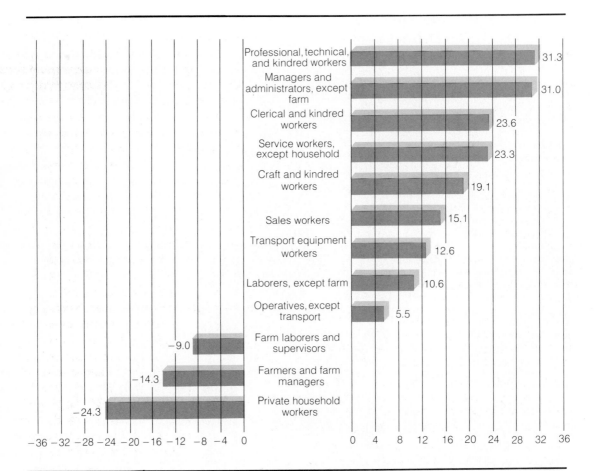

farmers and laborers, on the other hand, has declined dramatically. In other words, there has been a general upgrading of the occupational structure. As technological developments and industrialization continued, the need for farmers and unskilled workmen diminished while the need for various skills and for clerical and other white-collar workers increased. These trends have not abated, as evidenced by the occupational changes in employment during the 1970s (figure 9.3.).

The Changing Composition of the Labor Force

As the general skill level increases, the *educational level of the work force* also increases. In 1952 the median amount of education of the labor force was 10.9 years; about 43 percent had completed high school. By 1977 the median attainment was 12.6 years; nearly 73 percent had completed high school (U.S. Department of Labor, Bureau of Labor Statistics, 1979:60).

Another substantial change in the labor force involves the *proportion of women workers.* About 50 percent of all women age 16 and over were in the labor force in 1978, compared to only 31.8 percent in 1947 (U.S. Department of Labor, Bureau of Labor Statistics, 1979:26). At the same time, the proportion of men declined slightly, so that women comprised 42 percent of the total labor force in 1978.

The labor force also became more *unionized* over time, although the proportion of workers who were members of unions leveled off and declined somewhat during the 1970s (figure 9.4). The kind of workers who are unionized also changed. Public service employees and white-collar workers have been organized in a number of places in the nation.

The Changing Meaning of Work

When we try to determine the *meaning of work* to Americans and how that meaning changes over time, we find ourselves in a morass of contradictions. Some people argue that "a man's work is one of the most important (if not the most important) activities in his life. Those who do not have satisfying jobs rarely have fully satisfying lives" (Sayles and Strauss, 1966:28). Some writers argue that work is purely instrumental toward the goal of *maximum consumption* (Bell, 1960:244–46). Some observers say that most Americans hate their work (Reich, 1970:8), while others find a good deal of *job satisfaction* among Americans (LeMasters, 1975:20). Many observers argue that the *work ethic* has declined. Indeed, surveys and studies show that the bulk of Americans no longer believe hard work necessarily pays off; that unemployment is no longer necessarily viewed with alarm or experienced traumatically; that many people decided to stop working altogether because work is not as meaningful to them as not working is (Lefkowitz, 1979). On the other hand, increasing numbers of Americans are coming into the labor force. A 1978 Gallup poll reported that only one-fourth of the respondents said they would welcome less emphasis on working hard.

What do these apparent contradictions mean? We should recognize that there is some truth to each of the above positions. Some people do hate their jobs, some love them. Although there is a *decline in the work ethic,* the commitment to work is not necessarily declining. In a survey of 366 blue-collar and white-collar workers, Buchholz (1978) found that beliefs about the work ethic were ranked lowest, after humanistic, Marxist, organizational, and leisure beliefs. Workers generally gave highest priority to *humanistic concerns,* but they also believed *work should be a basic form of personal satisfaction.*

Figure 9.4 U.S. membership in labor unions and membership as a proportion of the labor force, 1930 to 1978. (Source: U.S. Department of Labor, Bureau of Labor Statistics, *Bulletin 1919* [Washington, D.C.: Government Printing Office, 1980].)

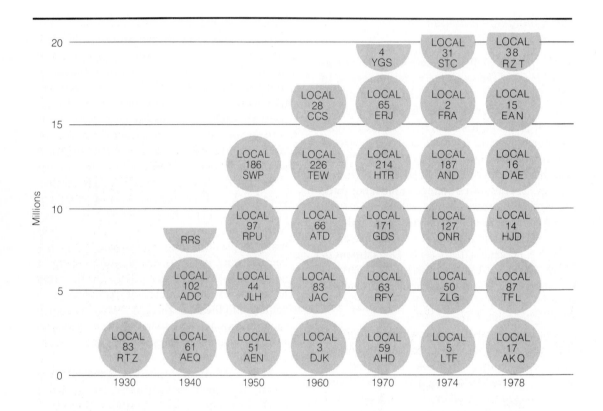

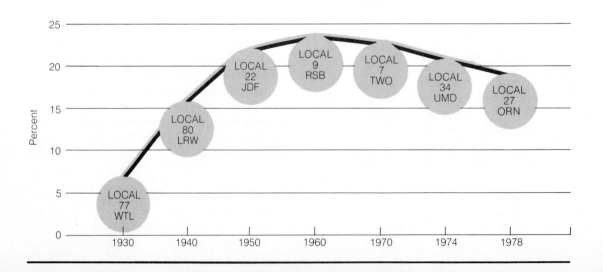

Figure 9.5 Men returning home from work in 1937. Americans are increasingly demanding something more from their work than a paycheck; they expect some degree of personal fulfillment.

It appears that an increasing number of Americans no longer accept the notion that their worth is tied in with their work, or that they have a moral duty to work. Rather, Americans expect their work to have some *meaning,* to be emotionally and intellectually *stimulating,* and to offer them an *opportunity to feel good about themselves and the products of their labor.* Income is no longer the most important facet of an individual's work. Kanter (1978:53–54) summed up the new views well:

Two themes can be said to characterize the ambience of work in America. . . . One theme can be called cultural or expressive: the concern for work as a source of self-respect and nonmaterial reward—challenge, growth, personal fulfillment, interesting and meaningful work, the opportunity to advance and to accumulate, and the chance to lead a safe, healthy life. The other can be called political: the concern for individual rights and power, for a further extension of principles of equity and justice into the workplace and into the industrial order, for equality and participation both in their general symbolic manifestations and in the form of concrete legal rights.

Given the option of working or not working, most Americans would continue to work. However, most would prefer a different job than the one they have. A 1977 survey conducted for the U.S. Department of Labor reported that 38 percent would keep their present job if they had the option; 2 percent would retire and not work at all (down from 6 percent in 1969); and 60 percent would prefer some other job to the one they have.[2] With over 50 million of the 90 million working Americans preferring a different job, and with another 10 to 20 million Americans trying to find employment, the problems of work obviously involve an enormous number of people. Let us look more closely at what those problems are.

Work as a Social Problem

Because most Americans want to work and expect their work to provide some degree of personal fulfillment, there are three basic problems associated with work in America today. First, unemployment and **underemployment** constitute a problem. People are underemployed if they work full-time for poverty wages, or work part-time when they desire full-time work, or work at jobs that are below their skill levels. Second, *dissatisfaction and alienation* constitute a problem. Third, various kinds of *work hazards* constitute a problem.

Unemployment and Underemployment

Underemployment is perhaps as serious as unemployment for those who look to work for meaningful activity. We do not know the extent

Table 9.1   **Unemployment Rates, 1948–1979**
(persons 16 years and over)

Year	Total	White	Black and Other
1948	3.8	3.5	5.9
1950	5.3	4.9	9.0
1955	4.4	3.9	8.7
1960	5.5	4.9	10.2
1965	4.5	4.1	8.1
1970	4.9	4.5	8.2
1979	5.8	5.1	11.3

Source: U.S. Department of Labor, *Employment and Training Report of the President* (Washington, D.C.: Government Printing Office, 1980), p. 249.

of underemployment, but a considerable number of those who would like to shift jobs probably feel their present jobs underutilize their skills. Also, at any one time between 3 and 4 million Americans are working part-time because of slack work, job changing, material shortages, or inability to find full-time work (U.S. Department of Labor, 1980:270).

We have fairly good data on the **unemployment rate.** This rate is the proportion of the labor force that is not working but is available for work and has made specific efforts to find work. The unemployment rate fluctuates considerably (table 9.1). In the late 1970s the rate meant that from 6 to 7.8 million Americans were unemployed in any particular year.

As table 9.1 shows for race, unemployment does not strike all groups the same. Typically, the rates are higher for women than for men, higher for blacks and other non whites than for whites, and higher for the young workers. In 1977 the unemployment rate for workers 16 to

19 years of age was 17.7, more than double the figure for the work force as a whole. The rate for black youth was 38.3, about 2.5 times the 15.4 rate for white youth.

Unemployment also varies by occupational category. In 1979, when the total unemployment rate was 5.8, the rate for white-collar workers was 3.3 and the rate for blue-collar workers was 6.9. Managers and administrators had the lowest rate, 2.1; nonfarm laborers had the highest rate, 10.8 (U.S. Department of Labor, 1980:257). The job categories that are expanding (figure 9.3) are also the ones least likely to have high unemployment rates.

Dissatisfaction and Alienation

We previously defined *alienation* as a sense of estrangement that is usually measured by the individual's feelings of powerlessness, normlessness, isolation, and meaninglessness. This is a subjective approach to alienation. Alienation is an objective phenomenon, according to Karl Marx. In a capitalist society the worker is *estranged from his or her own labor* (because work is something that is coerced and external to the worker rather than a fulfillment of the worker's needs), from other people, and from his or her own humanity. The worker "sinks to the level of a commodity and becomes indeed the most wretched of commodities" (Freedman, 1968:67). Because capitalism wrenches the means of production from the control of those intimately involved in production, workers are necessarily alienated whether or not they feel any sense of alienation.

The amount of alienation in the workplace, therefore, depends on whether a Marxist or a social psychological approach to the question is taken. For Marxists, all workers in a capitalist society are alienated by definition. For social psychologists, workers are alienated to the extent that they perceive themselves as powerless and isolated. Studies that are social psychological in nature indicate some American workers are alienated, but by no means the majority. In fact, a cross-cultural survey of industrial workers—workers most often considered alienated by researchers—showed that the majority would rather continue working in factory jobs than receive their wages for not working (Form, 1973).

Studies of *job satisfaction,* in contrast to those of perceived alienation, also show the bulk of workers as satisfied. Polls taken from 1963 to 1978 show some variations, but between 85 and 93 percent of workers said they were satisfied with their work.[3] How does this square with the fact that well over half of all workers would prefer a different job? In line with the discussion about the changing meaning of work, many workers appear to be reasonably satisfied under the circumstances but feel that their jobs are not maximizing their personal fulfillment. Although they derive some satisfaction from their work, given the chance they would like a different, more fulfilling job.

Who is likely to find his or her job fulfilling? In a survey that asked people what kind of work they would try to do if they could start all over, 93 percent of urban university professors said they would choose similar work; 16 percent of unskilled auto workers said they would choose the same kind of work again (Kahn, 1972:182). In general, far more professional and white-collar workers than blue-collar workers said they would select similar work.

Work Hazards

In 1975 there were about 9 cases of occupational injury and illness for every 100 workers in the nation (U.S. Department of Labor, Bureau of Labor Statistics, 1979:554). There are, in addition, an unknown number of unreported minor accidents. The bare figures do not convey a sense of the ongoing work hazards for some Americans.

We will use the term "work hazards" broadly to include *work-induced stress* as well as *work-related injuries and illnesses*. For example, a spot welder on an auto assembly line told about some of the hazards to which he is daily exposed:

> I pulled a muscle in my neck, straining. This gun, when you grab this thing from the ceiling, cable, weight, I mean you're pulling everything. . . . This whole edge here is sharp. I go through a shirt every two weeks, it just goes right through. My overalls catch on fire. I've had gloves catch on fire. (Indicates arms) See them little holes? That's what sparks do. I've got burns across here from last night [Terkel, 1972:224].

Some taxi drivers work under the continual threat of robbery. Some salespeople endure continual harassment from customers. Some people work under continual pressure, or where there is built-in interpersonal conflict. Stress is probably associated with most jobs at times, but with some jobs, the stress is constant.

Work and the Quality of Life

A professor discussed the problems of working people with one of his university's administrators. "Personally, I would not quit working even if I could," said the professor, "because I basically enjoy what I am doing." The administrator responded with a touch of despair in his voice, "You are lucky. And you are unusual. Apart from you, I don't know anyone who is *really* enjoying his work." For some people, the effect of working is a kind of *emotional and spiritual malaise*. They do not despise their work, but they are not excited by it. At best, they are apathetic or resigned. At worst, they sense an uneasiness or mild but chronic frustration. For some people the job may be a part of the cost of life, but for other people, work has an impact on the quality of life that is more severe and more measurable. One important area that work affects is the mental and physical health of the worker.

Work, Unemployment, and Health

In chapter 5 we noted some of the *physical risks of various work settings*—particularly exposure to carcinogenic materials. Work hazards include much more than exposure to carcinogens, as we will see. We will also look at the health risks of unemployment for those who are out of work but want to work.

Work and health. *Work-induced stress* may lead to physical health problems such as coronary heart disease, migraine, peptic ulcers, and hypertension (Kasl, 1978:18; House et al., 1979). People who are satisfied with their work, on the other hand, tend to have fewer of these health problems and even seem to live longer (Palmore, 1969).

Figure 9.6 Construction workers have higher rates of illness and injuries than other workers in the nation.

The *impact of work on the mental and emotional health of workers* has received a good deal of attention. A special and controversial study conducted for the Department of Health, Education, and Welfare in 1972 had a good deal to say about *"blue-collar blues"* and *"white-collar woes"* and the many problems of mental health related to *job dissatisfaction.* According to the report, things such as low self-esteem, anxiety, tension, and worry are all associated with job dissatisfaction (U.S. Department of Health, Education, and Welfare, 1973:82). Kornhauser (1965:261) related poor mental health specifically to various undesirable working conditions. He pointed out that the higher the occupation (in respect to skill and associated attributes of variety, responsibility, and pay), the better the average mental health.

Perhaps the most extreme consequence of work-induced stress is *suicide.* Various kinds of work-related problems may be associated with suicide or attempted suicide (Brodsky, 1977). Again, the incidence varies by occupation. Policemen, sheriffs, and marshals, for instance, have a rate twice as high or greater than the rate for teachers, judges, and lawyers (Kasl, 1978:8).

A Protestant minister described his own health problems caused by stress at work. The stresses he experienced could occur in virtually any kind of job, and his story shows that no one is immune.[4]

I arrived at my new church with an intense anticipation of a rewarding and fruitful ministry. I brought the enthusiasm and recklessness of youth to a job that demanded the caution and wisdom of age. For about a year, the enthusiasm was sufficient. It carried me through some discouragements and minimized any overt criticism. Then I made the mistake of criticizing an older member of the church. The criticism was neither harsh nor malicious, but the member was quite sensitive and quite influential. I also plunged ahead and pushed programs and began projects without first consulting the officers. At the beginning of my second year, criticism erupted and quickly mushroomed.

For about the next five years, I had problems with various people in the church. And I had a series of things go wrong with myself, both emotionally and physically. At one point, it seemed that everything was coming to a head and there would be a final all-out struggle to see whose way would prevail—mine or those that felt I was taking the church down the wrong road. Just before this culminating battle, I lost about twenty pounds from my slender physique. One week I broke out in a rash. I had severe sinus problems. Worst of all, I nearly developed a phobia about being in an enclosed area with a lot of people. I found it torturous to go to a crowded restaurant. One day I had to leave a church conference because my heart was pounding and I felt intense panic. Sometimes I even felt serious anxiety when I led the worship service.

As it turned out, the "final" battle was not really the final one after all. It had only served to trigger the various physical and mental ailments that I endured for the next few years. Ultimately, we were able to work out the differences we had. I think I gained some in wisdom and lost some of my recklessness. The church began to stabilize and then grow, and some of those with whom I had fought became my best friends. After about eight years or so, I finally lost my fear of crowded places. In a way, I suppose you could say it all had a happy ending. But I wouldn't go through that again for anything. It was the only time of my life when the thought of suicide entered my mind as an appealing option.

Figure 9.7 A tent squatter during the Great Depression. Unemployment has numerous undesirable consequences for Americans.

Unemployment and health. The stress of being forcibly unemployed can be as serious as the stress of working in undesirable conditions or in an unfulfilling job. With the decline of the work ethic and the availability of financial help for the unemployed, some workers do not suffer debilitating consequences, particularly if they were unhappy with their job in the first place (Little, 1973). For most people, however, *unemployment is a traumatic experience.* Even the anticipation of unemployment can increase illness among workers (Kasl, Gore, and Cobb, 1975).

In their study of the impact of chronic unemployment on Appalachian males, Ransdell and Roche (1969) discussed how "idleness and misery" brought about a "deterioration in the mind and body." The men they studied suffered from a great variety of *psychosomatic complaints,* including backaches, headaches, sleeplessness, shortness of breath, chest pains, upset stomachs, and nervousness. Other studies have also found a relationship between psychosomatic illness and unemployment (Fried, 1966:373).

Brenner (1973) examined the relationship between mental illness and the state of the economy over a 125-year period and concluded that instabilities in the nation's economy are the most important variable correlated with rates of admission to mental hospitals. The rate of admission went up during economic depressions and subsided during times of economic prosperity. Another historical study found that unemployment rates between 1920 and 1969 were "the most important and stable predictor of short- and long-term variations in suicide rates" (Vigderhous and Fishman, 1978:239).

Table 9.2   Impact of a Sustained 1 Percent Rise In Unemployment

Stress Indicator	Percent Increase
Suicide	4.1
State mental hospital admissions	3.4
State prison admissions	4.0
Cirrhosis of the liver mortality	1.9
Cardiovascular-renal disease mortality	1.9

Source: M. Harvey Brenner, "The Social Costs of Economic Distress," *Consultation on the Social Impact of Economic Distress* (New York: Amer. Jewish Committee, Institute of Human Relations, 1978), pp. 3–6.

Brenner (1978:6A) calculated the impact of a sustained one percent rise in unemployment in the United States from about 1940 to the early 1970s. The results are shown in table 9.2. While some Americans may no longer find unemployment a traumatic experience, most Americans still suffer emotional and physical repercussions from unemployment.

Interpersonal Relationships

The author once read in a newspaper about a bus driver who always appeared to be cheerful. One day while he was in the midst of heavy traffic with a crowded bus, a passenger asked him if he ever got angry. "Yes," he admitted, "but when I do, I go home and take it out on my wife."

Many people are unaware that work-induced stress affects their relationships with others. (Of course, few people are so crass as to consciously take out their frustrations on their mates.) A number of studies support the notion that the stress of unemployment and work-related stress *can adversely affect interpersonal relationships*.

Unemployment tends to place considerable strain on an individual's relationships, including relationships within the family. During the Great Depression, when the unemployment rate went as high as one-fourth of the labor force, many workers blamed themselves for their unemployment, became disillusioned with themselves, and began to have troubles within their homes (Komarovsky, 1940). A 1960 study showed that the same kinds of problems emerged in less serious economic recessions. Workers were embarrassed by being unemployed, began to withdraw from various social contacts, developed feelings of despair and hostility, and directed some of that hostility toward their families as well as themselves (Wilcock and Franke, 1963).

The interpersonal problems do not appear immediately. They develop slowly and seem to come into full play when a person feels emotionally battered and unable to cope with additional stresses. A welder who lost his job in 1979 tells about the financial stresses, the embarrassment, the feelings of powerlessness, the frustrations of not knowing what to do with his time, and the ultimate deterioration of his total life:

And pretty soon you start creating your own problems. I drank a little heavy. . . . And the wife and I had problems. We started to have little arguments. It wouldn't have happened if I'd been working. They were senseless. They were over little or nothing. We'd just bitch at each other for nothing. We had nothing else to do, just bitch at each other. I constantly raised hell because I was unhappy. She left me at one time for three or four weeks. In fact, it still affects our marriage. We see a shrink regularly.[5]

The unemployed are not the only ones whose interpersonal relationships are affected. Job dissatisfaction is associated with problems in getting along with people (U.S. Department of Health, Education, and Welfare, 1973) and with having less trust in others (Sheppard and Herrick, 1972). One researcher argued that many of the interpersonal problems in the workplace can be traced to the nature of the work: "Give any person a dead-end career ladder, a sense of powerlessness, and a feeling that boss and co-workers are always watching, and he or she will go rigid and mean" (Kanter, 1976:56).

The Nation's Economy

In the 1970s a good deal of concern about the *productivity* of the American worker was expressed. Productivity is measured in terms of output per worker-hour. The continually increasing productivity prior to the 1960s was *a major factor in the nation's rising prosperity.* Productivity slowed in the 1960s, then leveled off and even decreased in the 1970s. The Council of Economic Advisers of the President issued a report in 1979 in which the members said that "one of the most discouraging developments of 1978 was the very slow growth of productivity," which "did much to exacerbate inflation."[6]

While the actual causes of the productivity problem are debatable, some evidence indicates that *alienation is related to work performance.*

Based on their study of blue-collar workers in a forging plant, Cummings and Manring (1977) concluded that powerlessness, normlessness, and meaninglessness result in less self-rated effort and performance, and are associated with increased tardiness.

Thus, when productivity in the workplace declines, the nation's economy suffers, and that means additional problems for a great proportion of Americans.

Contributing Factors

The factors that contribute to unemployment are generally different from the factors involved in work dissatisfaction, alienation, and work hazards. Most of our attention will be devoted to the latter factors, but we will also examine the political economy of unemployment.

Social Structural Factors

The political economy of unemployment. Let us first distinguish between *structural and discriminatory unemployment.* Discriminatory unemployment involves high unemployment rates among particular groups, such as women and racial minorities, and is discussed in the chapters that deal with those groups. Structural unemployment is the *result of the functioning of the politico-economic system itself.* The high unemployment rates that certain groups such as aeronautical engineers or recent college graduates may have at a particular time are due to the functioning of the system, not to a past history of discrimination and prejudice.

Structural unemployment takes various forms. Since the Great Depression, the American economy has been regulated basically in accord with the theories of John Maynard Keynes. In Keynes's view, governments can *control the swings of the economy,* greatly moderating the inflationary and deflationary trends, by means such as spending programs and taxation. There is an *inverse relationship between unemployment and inflation.* When the rate of inflation is high, the government may take steps that will result in an increase in unemployment. Some unemployment is necessary, and some fluctuations are inevitable, but, because of the moderating impact of government intervention, the fluctuations need not be as severe as they were earlier in our history.

The unemployment rates shown in table 9.1 reflect in large part the government's efforts to regulate the economy. There will always be some unemployment in a capitalist economy. The amount can be controlled and perhaps lessened by government intervention, but unemployment cannot be eliminated.

Keynesian theory worked quite well until the 1970s when, contrary to the theory, both high unemployment and inflation struck Americans (and other industrialized nations as well). Americans had to deal with the problem of **stagflation,** a combination of economic stagnation (including high unemployment rates) and inflation. Economists were perplexed, politicians were frustrated, and people groaned under the new burden. Some people believed stagflation was caused by escalation of the price of crude oil by the OPEC countries. Other people cited economic concentration in industry as the cause of the problem. If a small number of huge firms can gain control of an industry, they can continue to raise prices and keep profits high even though unemployment has lowered the demand (Olsen and Parker, 1977). Whatever the cause, a frightening new situation in the world of work confronted people in the 1970s and 1980s. Controlling unemployment seems to be a more difficult task at present than it was prior to the 1970s.

In addition to the overall rate of unemployment, the functioning of the politico-economic system contributes to high rates of unemployment in particular areas or in particular occupations at certain times. *Technological change* such as automation or the introduction of computers into a business can displace many workers and lessen the need for them in the future (recall the problems of Edgeville, discussed in chapter 1). *Government spending priorities* can create many jobs, then eliminate those jobs when the priorities change. For instance, the massive federal funding of the space program in the 1960s created many jobs, some of which then vanished when the priorities changed in the 1970s.

Another factor that contributes to the unemployment rate is the *growth of multinational corporations.* American corporations have established operations in foreign countries because of cheap labor and access to raw naterials. In effect, the corporations have exported jobs to other nations. The unemployment rate also depends on the size of the labor force—that is, the number of people who want to work. In the 1970s the children of the "baby boom" of the 1950s and great numbers of married women were entering the labor force. The demand for jobs rapidly outstripped the available supply.

Contradictory values. Americans have traditionally placed a *high value on hard work,* believing that by working hard an individual can achieve the *American dream of success.* Work has also been considered a *moral virtue.* Americans have also valued education. The educational level of the population, including the work force, has steadily increased. Unfortunately, by the 1970s the values of education and work began to be contradictory. A certain number of college graduates were either unable to find work or they had to settle for jobs that were insufficiently challenging in relation to their educational and skill levels. A 1979 survey of high school seniors showed that over 65 percent rated "finding steady work" as extremely important. When asked what characteristics of their future jobs would be very important, about 90 percent said that the jobs should be interesting, and over 70 percent said that the jobs should utilize their skills and abilities (Bachman and Johnston, 1979). Unfortunately, the job market cannot deliver interesting jobs that fully utilize the skills and abilities of our highly educated labor force.

Contemporary work roles. Even if the labor force did not have a high level of education, there would still be problems with job dissatisfaction and alienation because of the *nature of the work roles* in contemporary society. Our work roles, which were *created by our technology and by the bureaucratization of work,* affect a worker's relationship with the work and with fellow workers.

At least three consequences of technological developments bear upon the meaningfulness of our work. First, along with developing technology came a tendency to develop *highly specialized tasks:* this is the increasing division of labor we noted earlier. In a classic piece of research, James Worthy (1950:174) said, "One has the feeling of division of labor having gone wild, far beyond any degree necessary for efficient production." Basing his conclusions on a long-term study of over 100,000 employees, Worthy found that when jobs become too narrowly defined, both productivity and worker morale suffer.

Second, and associated with the intense specialization, a considerable number of *extremely repetitious, routine tasks* have been created. Donald Roy (1959–60:160) described the work of a group of machine operators in one factory:

> This was standing all day in one spot beside three old codgers in a dingy room looking out through barred windows at the bare walls of a brick warehouse, leg movements largely restricted to the shifting of body weight from one foot to the other, hand and arm movements confined, for the most part, to a simple repetitive sequence of place the die,—punch the clicker,—place the die,—punch the clicker, and intellectual activity reduced to computing the hours to quitting time.

Roy went on to describe various games the workers played to keep from "going nuts" from the monotony.

Barbara Garson (1975) also described the *coping mechanisms* utilized by people who work in routine jobs ranging from typists, to keypunchers, to workers who stack ping-pong paddles all day, to tuna cleaners in a seafood plant.

The deadly routine of many jobs is portrayed in the account of Cindy, a girl who worked for a time in the ping-pong factory:

> My job was stacking the ping-pong paddles into piles of fifty. Actually I didn't have to count all the way up to fifty. To make it a little easier they told me to stack 'em in circles of four with the first handle facing me. When there got to be thirteen handles on the second one from the front, then I'd know I had fifty . . . As soon as I'd stack 'em, they'd unstack 'em. Maybe it wouldn't have been so bad if I could have seen all the piles I stacked at the end of the day. But they were taking them down as fast as I was piling them up. That was the worst part of the job [Garson, 1975:1–2].

Such jobs are stressful to people. A number of studies of blue-collar workers who have machine-paced, repetitive jobs show that these workers have poorer mental health than workers in nonrepetitive jobs. (Kasl, 1978:28). The games that workers create in order to cope with repetitive jobs enable workers to endure their work but do not totally insulate them from debilitating effects.

Third, technological developments are associated with a certain amount of *depersonalization* within the workplace. Workers tend to be *isolated* in certain kinds of jobs. Computerization may result in a degree of isolation. Whisler (1970:76) quoted an Air Force officer who told about the impact of computers on a command-and-control center:

> One of the queerest observations that I have made concerns this mass of engineers, technicians, machine operators, and operations people milling around and working almost unaware that anyone else exists. That is to say, there doesn't seem to be any interaction between the individuals. All of the interaction seems to be with the electronic system. This is quite a change from the old squadron where communication and interaction between individuals were a must to accomplish the mission.

Whisler described how similar isolation occurred in an insurance company when computers were introduced. The new computer system increased the amount of time the clerks worked alone and resulted in a striking drop in communication between clerks. Similar effects have been reported following the introduction of *automation* into automobile plants. The workers in an automated plant in contrast to those in a nonautomated plant, had to pay closer, continual attention to their work, worked at greater distances from each other, and had fewer tasks that involved teamwork; the net effect was less social interaction on the job (Faunce, 1958).

Work roles are also affected by *bureaucratization of work*. Perhaps the majority of Americans work in bureaucratic organizations, which tend to be *authoritarian*. One of the defining characteristics of a bureaucracy is the hierarchy of authority. Workers in an authoritarian organization are likely to experience negative emotions and attitudes ranging from job dissatisfaction to alienation. Rothman (1974:173) surveyed numerous studies in the literature and set forth his conclusion: "Increased hierarchy of authority (centralization and lower degree of worker participation in decision making) is correlated with greater job dissatisfaction and work alienation. Hierarchy of authority is also correlated with expressive alienation." Rothman defined alienation from work as a sense of powerlessness and isolation from the decision-making process, and defined expressive alienation as dissatisfaction with relationships at work. In other words, people prefer to be *involved in decisions that affect them and their work.* People are unlikely to have the opportunity for involvement in bureaucratic organizations. Lacking the opportunity, they are likely to have lower levels of job satisfaction, lower team spirit, lower morale, and less motivation to be productive (Mott, 1972:85–97). A study of salesmen in three different organizations showed that the more centralized the authority, (1) the less likely the salesmen were to be satisfied in terms of self-actualization, (2) the more likely they were to perceive higher amounts of anxiety and stress, and (3) the less efficiently they worked (Ivancevich and Donnelly, 1975).

Other studies show that the mental health of workers in authoritarian situations may suffer. In one study, poor mental health was associated with close supervision and the workers' lack of autonomy (Cooper and Marshall, 1978:93). In another study, various stress symptoms were related to the frustrations of working in a bureaucracy, including a sense of powerlessness (Zaleznik, de Vries, and Howard, 1977).

In addition to the frustrations of working in an authoritarian organization, workers must deal with a certain amount of *built-in conflict that bureaucracies* tend to have. In theory, such conflict is unnecessary because the chain of command is clear—all workers are experts in their own jobs, and there are rules to cover all tasks and any problems. In reality, a certain amount of conflict is invariably built into the roles. There may be *role ambiguity* (a lack of clear information about a particular work role), which results in lower job satisfaction and higher stress levels. There may be *role conflict,* because different groups in the workplace have different expectations for a particular work role, or because the role expectations are excessive. Role conflict, like role ambiguity, leads to lower satisfaction and higher stress levels. (Cooper and Marshall, 1978:85–87). The important point is that these problems are not the result of the individual worker's cantankerous nature, but of contradictions that are part of the work role itself. The individual falls victim to the role and suffers the consequences of lowered satisfaction and higher stress levels.

The political economy of work hazards.

Some jobs necessarily entail more risk than others, and some jobs entail more risk than necessary. Some work-related illnesses and injuries could be prevented or at least minimized if the health and well-being of workers took priority over the profit of the enterprise. Historically, untold numbers of American workers have died in the name of profit and with the approval or apathy of the government. As Berman (1977) pointed out, it has often been cheaper for companies to lose workers through death or injuries than to improve their working conditions. Tragically, many companies choose the cheaper option. Berman cited the example of the construction of the Gauley Bridge in West Virginia during the Great Depression. The workers were forced to dig in a tunnel that had dust so thick that visibility was limited to about ten feet or less. When workers died, their bodies were buried in holes in a nearby field. About 470 workers died, and another 1,500 were disabled by the project. The tragedy of this and similar incidents is not just that they happened, but that so many were preventable. However, it is cheaper for companies to hire new laborers than to take the necessary safety measures.

Involvement

Fun and Games At Work

As various studies in this chapter indicate, many Americans find little pleasure in their jobs, though most expect their work to be enjoyable and fulfilling. By young adulthood, most people have worked at some job. Consider how much enjoyment and fulfillment you have received from your own work experiences. Think about your feelings, the impact on your life, the problems and the satisfactions with respect to any job or jobs you have had. Imagine that someone is interviewing you about your experiences. Write out your answers to the following questions about a job you have had or now have:

What did you most like about the job?

What did you most dislike about the job?

How would you feel about working at the job for all or the major portion of your life? Why?

How were you treated by others in your work role?

Did the job make any difference in the way you feel about yourself? Why or why not?

How could the job be made more meaningful to workers?

Gather with other class members working on this project and summarize the results. What do the results say about the amount of worker dissatisfaction and alienation in America? If the only jobs available were the kind discussed by the class, would most Americans prefer *not* to work? Could all of the jobs be made into meaningful and fulfilling experiences?

Social Psychological Factors

Attitudes.   Certain attitudes about particular kinds of workers and about unions enter into the various problems of work. One attitude that may portend increasing problems is the declining public support for unions. A 1979 Gallup poll showed that only 55 percent of the respondents approved of labor unions, down from a high of 76 percent in 1957. The increasing power of labor unions, along with government intervention, has helped to eliminate some incidents like Gauley Bridge and has greatly improved the conditions of labor. Without the support of public opinion, labor unions will find themselves increasingly unable to bring about further benefits for their members and for labor as a whole. Public opinion is volatile, of course, and may shift again in a more favorable direction. However, the decline since the 1950s in public approval of labor unions is an unwelcome sign to those who strive to improve the lot of workers.

Another attitude that enters into work problems is the sense of superiority people might have toward certain workers. The attitudes of some Americans toward service workers or manual laborers or clerical workers range from patronizing to contemptuous. If some Americans are dissatisfied or alienated, it is, in part, because other Americans *treat them with little or no respect because of their jobs.* Consider the secretary who was working on a rush project when a young executive asked her to fill out a purchase order. She told him he could handle the job, that it would take only a couple of minutes.

"I don't know how to type," he said.
"Well, you should learn," she said. "An Ivy League education and you can't type four words."

"It's not my job," he said. "And besides, my time is worth five times as much as yours."
"Who do you think you are?" she shouted. "I quit. I've had enough of this superiority crap. Just because you're paid five times as much doesn't mean you're worth five times as much" [Bengis, 1977:47].

The incident was the culmination of many experiences in which the secretary was treated poorly by those who regarded her as inferior because of her position in the company.

The ideology and reality of work.   A final factor in work problems is the incongruity of our ideology about work and the reality of work. One line of thought, which dates back to the first Protestants, insists on the *value of all work.* One of the classic devotional writers, William Law (1906:32), said, "Worldly business is to be made holy unto the Lord, by being done as a service to Him, and in conformity to His Divine will." This ideology poses work as a sacred obligation and implies that all work is equally good. The same ideology was expressed by President Richard Nixon in the 1970s, when he said that his mother had emptied bed pans in a hospital as part of her work and that such work was as valuable as his work as president.

Although our ideology emphasizes the value of work and the equal value of all work, we do not, in practice, place equal value on all work. As the incident of the secretary illustrates, some kinds of work are disparaged by people with higher prestige jobs. Many Americans accept the ideology that work of any kind is intrinsically superior to nonwork, only to find themselves disparaged by other Americans who have "better" jobs. The same ideology compounds the problems of the unemployed, who tend to define a social problem as personal and blame themselves for their plight. In addition, the work ideology may make the unemployed feel guilty about not working, even though they are the victims of a politico-economic system rather than blameworthy violators of the American way.

What is to be Done?

The problems of work can be attacked in a number of different ways. First, with regard to unemployment, we could modify our capitalist system and adopt some of the ways of a social democratic nation such as Sweden. Or, our firms could pattern themselves after the paternalistic Japanese firms that do not lay off workers during a recession. Unemployment still exists in these nations, but it is far less than the unemployment of the United States. From 1960 to 1977, U.S. unemployment ranged from 3.5 to 8.5 percent, whereas the range was 1.2 to 2.7 percent in Sweden and 1.1 to 2.0 percent in Japan (U.S. Department of Labor, Bureau of Labor Statistics, 1979:581).

It is unlikely that Americans will want to follow the route of these other nations, however, at least in the near future. Other options include the use of government programs and government spending to minimize unemployment and resolve the high unemployment among particular groups. During the high unemployment periods of the 1970s, some people advocated public work projects similar to those inaugurated during the Great Depression. One step taken was the passage of the Comprehensive Employment and Training Act of 1973, which provided job training and employment opportunities for economically disadvantaged, unemployed, and underemployed people. Although many Americans were helped by the Act, overall unemployment was not reduced. Unless the nation is willing to consider more radical means of reducing unemployment, the rate probably will remain relatively high.

Regarding the problem of work hazards, both government and union power have significantly reduced the incidence of occupational injuries and illnesses in many industries. However, the overall rate remains high, and additional measures must be taken. Companies must be required to spend the necessary funds to provide a safe, clean working environment. In cases such as exposure to carcinogenic materials, research may be needed to develop ways of minimizing the danger.

A variety of measures can address the problems of job dissatisfaction and alienation. From our discussion of the causes of the problems, we can deduce what is needed to resolve them: things such as more challenging work, greater worker participation and control, and more worker autonomy. A number of programs that provide such conditions are already operating, but they are not yet widespread.

Problems of dissatisfaction and alienation can be addressed through *job enrichment,* which involves more worker responsibility and less direct control of the worker, upgrading the skills required for a job, and enlargement of the work so that the worker is not confined to a single, highly specialized task (Herzberg, 1968). A number of job enrichment programs have resulted in higher job satisfaction and worker morale, fewer grievances, and less absenteeism and turnover (U.S. Department of Health, Education, and Welfare, 1973).

A second measure for dealing with dissatisfaction and alienation is *flexitime,* which made

its debut in America in 1970 after being successfully used in Europe. There are at least three different types of flexitime systems, varying by the amount of choice given to the worker. In one type, the employer lets the workers choose from a range of times at which to start their eight-hour work day. A second type allows employees to choose their own schedules. Once chosen and approved, the schedules must be followed for a specified length of time. In a third type, employees can vary their own schedules on a daily basis without prior approval of supervisors. All types do have limits within which employees must function. Millions of Americans now work under flexitime, and the results seem to be greater satisfaction, higher morale, and, in some cases, increased productivity.

A third measure is *participatory management or organizational democracy,* which involves *worker participation in the decision-making process.* At a minimum, the workers participate in decisions about various working conditions. In more extreme forms of involvement, workers may participate in decisions about hiring and firing, about company goals, and even about their own wages and benefits (Lawler, 1977). The value of participation is demonstrated by events at the General Motors plant in Tarrytown, New York. In the early 1970s the plant was noted for its poor labor-management relations and quality of output. The plant had high rates of absenteeism and employee grievances. Then, a decision was made to involve both workers and managers in changing the situation. Proposed changes in the assembly line were first shown to the workers, who were invited to evaluate them. Information was shared and problems were discussed openly. The net effect of worker participation was in-

creased quality of output, significantly less absenteeism and fewer grievances, and much lower rates of employee turnover and breakage.[7]

A final measure, which is unlikely to be widely adopted in America, is *employee takeover of a company.* In a number of instances, employees have either assumed ownership and full responsibility for a company or have been allowed to work without supervisory personnel. The results again tend to be uniformly desirable—higher productivity, lower costs, greater worker satisfaction and morale.[8]

The measures we have discussed draw skepticism and resistance from some Americans, including those in management. However, these measures are successful, practical ways to deal with America's work problems.

Summary

Both the nature of work and the nature of the workforce change over time in America. There have been substantial increases in the size of the labor force and in the division of labor. The labor force is now more educated, more unionized, and proportionately more female. There is some decline in the work ethic, though not necessarily in the commitment to work. Workers now insist that their jobs be a source of fulfillment and not solely a source of income.

Work is a social problem because of unemployment and underemployment, work hazards, and dissatisfaction and alienation. Each year, millions of Americans are unemployed, though the rate varies for different groups and different occupations. Most Americans are not deeply dissatisfied or alienated from work, but the majority of Americans still desire a job different from the one they have. Among the hazards of work are work-induced stress and work-related injuries and illnesses.

Work is intimately related to the quality of life because it involves the worker's health. Work-induced stress, injuries and illnesses, and job dissatisfaction all can adversely affect the worker's health. Unemployment tends to be a traumatic, stressful experience that adversely affects the worker's interpersonal relationships and health. The nation's economy may be negatively affected by worker dissatisfaction, which leads to a lower quality of life for all Americans.

Among the factors that contribute to work problems, the politico-economic system itself is paramount. Structural unemployment is the result of the functioning of that system, which includes the natural swings of the economy, technological change, government spending priorities, and the growth of multinational corporations. The contradiction between our value on work and our value on education means that many workers are underemployed. The nature of work roles in our technological, bureaucratic society produces much dissatisfaction, stress, and conflict. Work hazards frequently are more common than necessary because companies give priority to profit, not to worker health and safety.

Among social psychological factors that add to the problems of work are the attitudes of Americans toward unions and toward other Americans who hold jobs they regard as inferior to their jobs. The contradiction between the ideology and reality of work is another contributing factor. The ideology glorifies work and working and places an equal value on all work. The reality is disparagement of some work and a politico-economic system that guarantees a certain amount of unemployment.

Glossary

division of labor   the separation of work into specialized tasks

labor force   all civilians who are employed or unemployed but able and desirous of work

productivity   output per worker-hour

stagflation   a combination of economic stagnation, including high unemployment rates, and inflation

underemployment   working full time for poverty wages, or working part time when full time work is desired, or working at a job below the worker's skill level

unemployment rate   proportion of the labor force that is not working but is available for work and has made specific efforts to find work

work ethic   notion that our sense of worth and the satisfaction of our needs are intricately related to the kind of work we do

For Further Reading

Brooks, Thomas R. *Toil and Trouble: A History of American Labor*. New York: Delta Books, 1971. A historical overview of the American labor movement from colonial times to the 1970s, including the various struggles and problems that one needs to know to fully understand work as a social problem in America.

Garson, Barbara. *All the Livelong Day: The Meaning and Demeaning of Routine Work*. New York: Penguin Books, 1975. A very readable and illuminating account of routine work, based on interviews and observation, showing how workers cope with the routine.

Perry, Stewart E. *San Francisco Scavengers: Dirty Work and the Pride of Ownership*. Berkeley: University of California Press, 1978. A discussion of the relationship between "dirty work" such as garbage collection and the feelings of the workers, including the way in which worker control can address the problems of "dirty work."

Ritzer, George. *Working: Conflict and Change*. 2nd ed. Englewood Cliffs, N.J.: Prentice-Hall, 1977. A thorough sociological discussion of various aspects of work and working by a sociologist with corporate work experience.

Terkel, Studs. *Working*. New York: Avon Books, 1974. An indispensable book for understanding the meaning of work in America. Includes interview details from a variety of workers, ranging from prostitutes to farm women, to blue-collar and white-collar workers, to professionals and managers.

Whyte, William H. *The Organization Man*. New York: Simon & Schuster, 1956. An old, but classic account of work in the context of large corporations. Whyte shows how workers, particularly managerial workers, can be totally absorbed by the organization.

Notes

1. *Time,* September 29, 1961, p. 61.
2. Reported in *Public Opinion,* December/January 1980, p. 36.
3. Ibid.
4. This account was supplied to the author by the minister.
5. *The Nation,* February 9, 1980, p. 140 (excerpt from Harry Maurer, *Not Working: An Oral History of the Unemployed*).
6. *St. Louis Post-Dispatch,* May 25, 1980.
7. *Time,* May 5, 1980, p. 87.
8. See *Time,* October 4, 1976, p. 80; and *Human Behavior,* December 1975, p. 70.

The Aged

10

1 **Why is age 65 considered old?**

2 **In what sense is old age a social rather than a strictly biological condition?**

3 **Why do some people dread retirement?**

4 **Why are many of the elderly poor?**

5 **What do older people hope to gain through protest?**

At what age does life start going "downhill" as far as enjoyment and excitement are concerned? At 30? 50? 60? 70? The thought of old age makes many Americans shudder because they believe aging means losing all the good things in life. Contrast that view with the view held in traditional China:

> The Chinese lived in anticipation of old age, for growing old was pleasant. There was no superior over the aged except the dead ancestors, who rarely spoke. The aged were supported and not requested to support anyone else. There were only two periods in the life of a Chinese male when he possessed maximum security and minimal responsibility—infancy and old age. Of the two, old age was the better because one was conscious of the pleasure to be derived from such an almost perfect period [Welty, 1970:204].

Unlike the United States, some societies do not consider old age to be a problem. What we consider the problem of the aged involves more than the problem of aging. That is, old age does not arise as a social problem merely because of the biological consequences of growing old. True, certain physical problems inevitably accompany growing old, as we will see, but socio-cultural factors that make the biological process a social problem are also involved.

In this chapter we will consider first the present number and projected number of aged in the United States. Second, we will examine what aging is, biologically and psychologically, in relation to the whole span of a person's life. We will then discuss contradictions that impinge upon aged individuals and diminish their quality of life. We will identify the structural and social psychological factors that make aging a social problem and, finally, suggest approaches for resolving the problem.

How Many Aged?

Before we can estimate the number of aged in America we must decide *who is old*. The decision is arbitrary, a matter of societal norms. From a biological point of view, aging begins at birth and continues to death. In everyday interaction, we may describe as old someone who looks old to us. The meaning of "old" also varies by occupation. A Protestant minister once remarked that he was considered too old at 45 by most of the churches he applied to for service. In other professions an individual may be young at 60; philosophers are not expected to make their major contribution before that time. In other words, the chronological age we define as the beginning point of being "old" is *arbitrary*.

The commonly accepted age of 65 is the one we will use in this chapter. Its arbitrariness is clear when we realize how it became the standard in 1935, when the federal Social Security program was established. Why was 65 chosen? Woodring (1976:18–19) supplies us with some of the historical details. Prior to 1935, employers had no uniform standard for retirement age. Some had no particular age at which retirement was mandatory for all employees. The proposed Social Security program had to specify an age at which an individual could start drawing benefits. The choice of 65 was made by a group of youthful New Dealers (advisers to President Franklin D. Roosevelt) who were charged with the task of drafting the Social Security legislation to be presented to the Congress.

At the time 65 was chosen, there was massive unemployment in the nation. Removing older workers would open opportunities for at least some of the unemployed (about one-fourth of the labor force was out of work). Clearly, the nation could benefit by the retirement of men at 65 from industry (the new program was primarily aimed at industrial workers).

A number of factors were not considered in the decision. One was *individual differences in aging*. People do not age at the same rate. All 65-year-olds do not have the same physical and mental capacities, the same needs, or the same potentials for productive work. Moreover, different occupations have various demands; for some kinds of work, the 65-year-old may be more competent and productive than he or she was at 45, or than his or her younger counterparts are.

Another factor not considered was the attitudes of people affected by the program. No one attempted to determine whether workers preferred to quit at age 65 or whether a different age (either younger or older) was preferred. Nothing in American history suggested 65 as an optimal age; there was no evidence of a need for retirement or of a sudden decline in productivity at that age.

Nevertheless, the *Social Security Act* was passed, and it "had the effect of establishing age sixty-five in the minds of employers and the general public as the one at which workers *ought* to retire" (Woodring, 1976:19). The same age is now used to define the elderly in America. Government data gathered on the aged are gathered for those 65 and older.

How many of these aged, 65 and older, are in America? By 1979 nearly 24.7 million aged (about 11.2 percent of the population) lived in America (U.S. Bureau of the Census, 1980:12). That is a dramatic increase since the turn of the century, when there were just over 3 million aged, or about 4 percent of the total population

Figure 10.1 When she was 67, Lillian Carter, mother of former President Jimmy Carter, joined the Peace Corps and spent two years in India. We should not think of 65 as the age when an individual's usefulness stops.

Figure 10.2   Population, by age and sex, 1900 to 1970. (Source: Executive Office of the President, Office of Management and Budget, *Social Indicators, 1973* [Washington, D.C.: Government Printing Office, 1973], p. 238.)

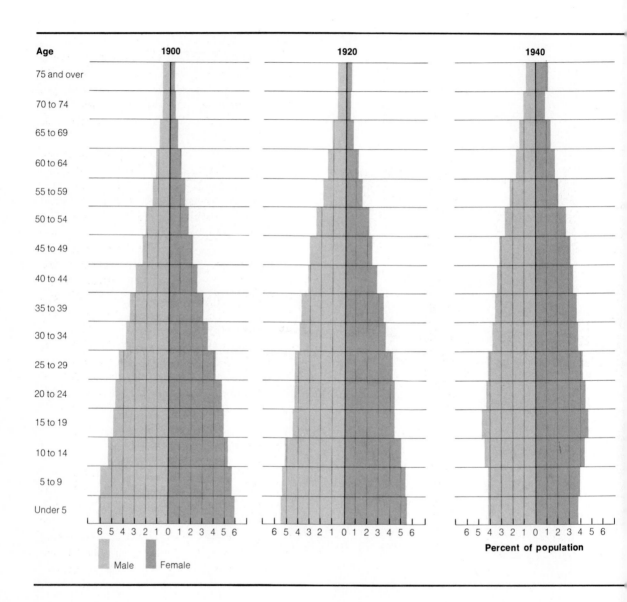

Figure 10.2   Population, by age and sex, 1900 to 1970.

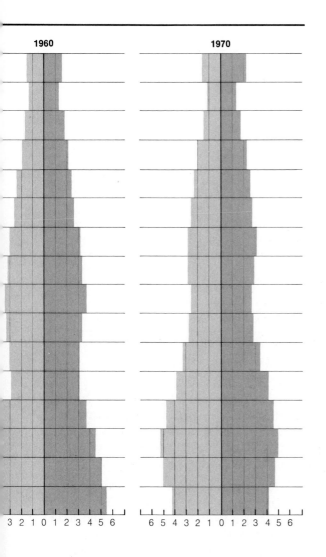

1960
1970

3 2 1 0 1 2 3 4 5 6   6 5 4 3 2 1 0 1 2 3 4 5 6

(figure 10.2). The number and *proportion of the aged are increasing* because the life expectancy of Americans is increasing. Furthermore, a greater number and proportion of the aged are reaching the 70-and-above groups (table 10.1). By 1970 nearly one-fifth of all the aged were 80 years old or older.

Since 1900 the number of aged has increased sevenfold and their proportion of the total population has more than doubled. By the year 2020, when the post-World War II baby boom will be reflected in the numbers, there will be about 43 million aged Americans, who will compose about 15 percent of the population.[1]

Figure 10.2 shows another important fact about the aged—*an increasing proportion is female*. In both the over-65 and over-75 age groups, the proportion of men to women has been declining since 1900 (table 10.2). This trend is expected to continue, so that by 1990 there may be fewer than 68 aged men for every 100 aged women. As we will see later, this difference has implications for the quality of life of the aged.

What is Aging?

Aging is a stage of the human life span most of us hope to live long enough to experience. At the same time, the aging process, which few people look forward to experiencing, usually reminds us of our inevitable death. While aging does not discontinue life, it does bring characteristic biological and developmental changes.

Table 10.1   Percent Distribution of the Elderly in Age Groups, 1900–1990*

Age Group	1900	1930	1960	1970	Projection 1990
65 through 69 years	42.3%	41.7%	37.6%	33.9%	34.2%
70 through 74 years	28.7	29.3	28.6	28	26.8
75 through 79 years ⎫	29	29	⎧ 18.5	18.6	19.5
80 years and over ⎭			⎩ 15.3	19.6	19.5

*Estimated as of July 1.

Source: *Population Bulletin* 30, no. 3 (1975), p. 10. Courtesy of the Population Reference Bureau, Inc., Washington, D.C.

Table 10.2   Number of Men per 100 Women, by Age, 1900–1990

Age	1900	1930	1960	1970	Projection 1990
Over 65	102	100.4	82.6	72.1	67.5
Over 75	96.3	91.8	75.1	63.7	57.8

Source: *Population Bulletin* 30, no. 3 (1975), p. 9. Courtesy of the Population Reference Bureau, Inc., Washington, D.C.

Biology of Aging

Senescence is biological aging. Senescence occurs in all people. It is rooted in our physiological makeup and it does involve certain deteriorations. The causes of senescence are unclear, but the characteristics are identifiable. These characteristics do not appear at the same ages in all people, however, for we age at different rates. Although the characteristics of senescence are rooted in our physiological makeup, various sociocultural factors combine with the biological factors to produce those characteristics.

What are the *characteristics of senescence?* Kart (1976:181–83) lists eight different systems of the body that are affected by aging: (1) the skin, (2) the skeletal-muscular system, (3) the senses and reflexes, (4) the nervous system, (5) the circulatory system, (6) the respiratory system, (7) the digestive system, and (8) "other" systems. Let us study the effects of aging that he notes in each of these categories.

1. The skin tends to become wrinkled, rough, and mottled (marked by spots or blotches). The skin is broken more easily but heals more slowly.
2. The skeletal-muscular system is marked by some stiffening of the joints, height reduction, and a reduction in the total mass of muscle tissue. Muscular strength and coordination decline.
3. The senses and reflexes generally are dulled by age. The sense of touch becomes less

acute, and the sense of vision is affected by various changes in the structure and functioning of the eye. There is a diminished ability to detect the pitch and intensity of sound (incidentally, loss of hearing begins about the age of 20). The older person reacts more slowly, although reaction time may be due to decreased exercise. In one study, the reaction times of a group of men whose ages ranged from 68 to 86 were compared with two groups of men whose ages ranged from 18 to 25—one a group of athletes, the other nonathletes (Botwinick and Thompson, 1970:186–93). Men in the elderly group were significantly slower than the athletes but were not significantly slower than the nonathletes. The extent to which some of the characteristics of senescence are due to sociocultural rather than biological factors is still unclear.

4. The nervous system undergoes some specific changes, including a loss of substance and weight of the brain, and a reduction of the speed of impulses to nerve tissues.
5. Similarly, the circulatory system is characterized by reduced cardiac output, resulting from hardening of the arteries.
6. In the respiratory system, there is a diminishing capacity of the lungs.
7. The digestive system is hampered somewhat by reduced muscular functioning, though many of the digestive problems of the aged may be traced to other causes.
8. Finally, there is a decline in the functioning of other systems, including the reproductive, temperature control, and kidney filtration. Normally, the decline in other systems does not result in any serious problems for the aged.

Aging as Development

Human life is a *process*. A number of psychologists have attempted to identify the particular tasks that must be accomplished at each stage of development. Successful completion of tasks at one stage means that the individual normally proceeds to the next stage and a new set of tasks. It is not always recognized, however, that there are new tasks for the aged as well as for those who are younger. Aging, in other words, is a *new stage in the developmental process* of life.

What are the *developmental tasks* faced by the aged? Some tasks are similar to the tasks of other generations, and some are unique. Some are similar to those of other age groups, and some are peculiar to the elderly. In the nineteenth century, for instance, most men had no transition to retirement. Typically, a man worked until disability or death. Few people had to deal with the "empty nest" problem, since children either did not leave the family house, or they returned there to live with their elderly parents (Chudacoff and Hareven, 1979).

For today's world, Clark and Anderson (1967:398f) identified five adaptive tasks for the elderly. First, the aged must come to terms with the physical limitations inherent in their stage of life. They will no longer be able to engage in certain activites as often or as successfully as they once could. Second, having come to terms with the limitations, the older person must redefine the scope of his or her activities. Third, the older person must find new sources of satisfying his or her needs. This may be particularly acute at the time of retirement for those who hold to the *work ethic*.

A fourth task is to reassess the criteria for self-evaluation. Again, the loss of work is involved, for many Americans define themselves as worthwhile because they have a full-time job. The question the elderly person must face is, "Am I a worthwhile person because of the kind of individual I am, because of the various qualities I possess, or am I worthwhile only as long as I can function in some kind of job?"

Finally, the aged face the task of finding ways to give meaning and purpose to their lives. This task arises throughout the individual's life and must be faced in different contexts in the various stages of development. No longer available to the older person are some of the activities that give meaning and purpose to the younger person—education for a career, the responsibility of rearing children, and productive work.

As in every other stage of life, then, aging presents the individual with certain developmental tasks that must be resolved. Old age is not—or at least need not be—a time of stagnation. Many elderly people find challenges, struggles, and gratifications just as they did in their earlier years.

Continuity and Diversity

There is continuity in an individual's life in at least two senses. First, as we discussed earlier, old age confronts the individual with developmental tasks. Second, research shows that the elderly tend to think and behave and interact with others much as they did when they were younger. Becoming 65 or 70 or 75 does not result in a sudden change of personal style. An individual who turns 65 will certainly face problems of adjustment, but most will not suddenly become different people. In one study that was conducted over a thirty-year period, it was found that there is *considerable continuity in an individual's approach to life:*

> Women who were depressed, fearful and unsure of themselves at 70 were similarly afflicted at 30. Those who were outgoing, busy and cheerful in early adulthood were happy, active septogenarians . . . the best predictor of an elderly man's lifestyle was his lifestyle as a young man. . . . The central features in the lives of [the] . . . "unwell disengaged" was their poor health and social withdrawal. At 30, they tended to be irritable men who fought with their wives over religion and leisure activities. They were tense, nervous and explosive. And they were sickly. They were much the same at 70.[2]

This study does not imply that no changes occurred or that some individuals did not change radically. But, there is considerable continuity, and we tend to carry our style of living into our old age. If we prefer a good deal of privacy when we are 30, we will probably prefer the same when we are 70. If we are difficult to relate to when we are 30, we will probably be the same at 70. If we are outgoing and genial at 30, we will probably be the same at 70.

This continuity was one of the findings of the Duke Longitudinal Study of Aging, which was "initiated to investigate processes of aging among a panel of noninstitutionalized males and females 60 years of age and over from the time of initial observation to death" (Busse, 1970:3). The 256 subjects of the study resided in Durham, North Carolina. Among the findings of the study, which lasted from 1955 to 1967, was that continuity of lifestyle characterized the subjects.

Related to a continuity of lifestyle is a continuity in activity level. We reviewed the research of Palmore (1976) on this topic in chapter 3. That research was part of the Duke Longitudinal Study. It challenged a well-known theory that runs counter to the notion of continuity—the *disengagement theory* of Cumming and Henry (1961), which argued that the elderly maintain life satisfaction by reducing their interaction with their social environment. In essence, according to the theory of disengagement, normal aging is a process of "mutual withdrawal or 'disengagement' between the aging person and others in the social system to which he belongs" (Cumming, 1976:20). According to the theory, this withdrawal may be initiated either by the individual or by others. In either case, the result is a "new equilibrium" between the individual and his social environment, the individual is more detached and less involved than he or she was in middle age. A considerable amount of research refutes the theory, but one group of the aged to whom the theory may apply is the very old who are in poor health.

If aging involves considerable continuity for individuals, it also involves considerable *diversity* between individuals. We have called attention to this fact in noting that people age at different rates. In addition, we should keep in mind that the developmental tasks of the aged are solved relatively easily by some but are traumatic experiences for others. Some of the aged are happier after retirement, particularly those who did not find a great deal of gratification from their work and who developed other interests that retirement gives them the freedom to pursue. Other elderly people confront mandatory retirement with resentment:

Like most people, I never gave much thought to all this when I was younger. I just assumed that all people over 65 were eager to retire and wanted nothing more than the right to go fishing 365 days a year. But when I found myself approaching 65—without feeling particularly "aged" and while still enjoying my work—I began wondering who had decided that everyone became "old" at this fixed chronological age. I began asking who had decided that 65 is the proper age for forced retirement. By whose authority was the decision made [Woodring, 1976:18]?

People for whom work has been the focal point of life may struggle with serious emotional and physical problems when trying to cope with mandatory retirement. Those who developed other interests may greet retirement with anticipation. Some people strike out in new directions. A friend of the author began a small truck farming operation after retirement, learned the real estate business and secured a license, and learned Portuguese prior to taking a trip to Brazil. Others among the elderly use retirement to indulge in a greater amount of privacy.

Aging and the Quality of Life

Thus far old age seems to be little different from any other stage of life. What is our basis for identifying the aged as a social problem? In the next sections we will see that they are caught up in a number of contradictions which do not affect people at earlier stages of life. Because circumstances that cause these contradictions are incompatible with the desired quality of life, we must define aging as a social problem in our nation.

Aloneness

There is a *contradiction between the need of the aged for relationships and the position of the aged in American society*. This is manifested in *aloneness* or in the threat of aloneness. Only a few of America's elderly are actually in the state of aloneness, but all face the threat of it.

We are social animals, unlikely to thrive where we are deprived of relationships. Isolation is literally inhuman. The elderly, like everyone else, need meaningful relationships. As pointed out by pioneer American psychologist William James (1890:293–94), "no more fiendish punishment" could be imagined than to treat an individual as though he or she did not exist:

> If no one turned round when we entered, answered when we spoke, or minded what we did, but if every person "cut us dead," and acted as if we were nonexisting things, a kind of rage and impotent despair would ere long well up in us, from which the cruellest bodily tortures would be a relief; for these would make us feel that, however bad might be our plight, we had not sunk to such a depth as to be unworthy of attention at all.

One of the consistent findings of research investigating happiness or *life satisfaction* among the aged is that relationships are crucial. Medley (1976) asked 301 elderly people about their satisfaction with life as a whole. He also obtained information on financial situation, satisfaction with health, satisfaction with standard of living, and satisfaction with family life. The last was measured by responses to the question, "All things considered, how satisfied are you with your family life—the time you spend and the things you do with members of your family?" Although each of the variables was important, the satisfaction with family life "made

the greatest single impact on satisfaction with life, for each sex" (Medley, 1976:454).

Those with whom the elderly relate need not be family members, however. The important thing is *meaningful interaction* with either friends or family. Tobin and Neugarten (1961) interviewed 187 people who were divided into two different age groups; 50 to 69 years, and 70 years and above. Information was obtained from the subjects on the amount of interaction they had each day; the number of different people with whom they interacted each month; the number of roles in which they interacted with others; their perception of their interaction rate as compared with that rate when they were 45 years old; and a measure of psychological well-being. The researchers found that interaction was quite important to life satisfaction (contrary to the disengagement theory), and that it increased in importance as the age of the subjects increased.

The elderly need relationships, and they need a variety of relationships in order to maximize the quality of their lives (Moriwaki, 1973). Moreover, interaction has no substitute. Activities that do not involve other people are likely to fail as sources of basic gratification. Graney (1975) conducted a four-year study of sixty elderly women, securing information on their activities and their happiness. He found that

> . . . happiness is positively related to social participation in old age. The degree of activity in radio use, visiting friends and relatives, telephone use, attending religious services, attending meetings of voluntary associations, and maintaining memberships in voluntary associations was significantly related to happiness. Participation in two relatively passive activities, watching television and reading, was *not* related to happiness in these data [Graney, 1975:705].

Clearly, social interaction is important to the quality of life of the elderly. Just as clearly, aloneness has deleterious consequences. We should keep in mind the diversity among the elderly. What is "aloneness" for one individual is a desirable level of interaction for another. We have different levels of need for interaction, depending in part on the pattern established earlier in our lives. But, we all need interaction, and when we begin to perceive ourselves in a state of aloneness or as approaching that state, we are likely to suffer some mental and physical problems.

Sometimes the effects of aloneness are subtle and not easily recognized by others. Consider, for instances, the problem of nutrition and eating for those who are alone:

> Eating alone may intensify feelings of loneliness when formerly there was always someone present with whom to eat, or for whom to prepare food. Some may overeat, but often incentive to eat is diminished and interest in eating is at a low ebb when lonely. . . . Also emotions may bring about metabolic changes . . . an alert, energetic woman, 75 years of age, was leading a busy life although she lived alone. She ate well, but metabolic studies showed her to be in severe negative nitrogen balance. She was observed two years later; a marked change in nitrogen metabolism had taken place and she was now retaining nitrogen. Her grandson had come to live with her. Someone to cook for and to share meals with had played a role in maintaining nutrition for this woman [Marble and Patterson, 1975:202–203].

Loneliness, then, can affect some basic physiological processes in the human body. It also affects our sense of well-being, our sense of satisfaction with life. As we have seen, there is a direct relationship between social interaction and life satisfaction among the elderly. Both physically and mentally, the quality of life is diminished by the state of aloneness.

How many of America's elderly are in this state of aloneness? It is difficult to say. As table 10.3 shows, a considerable proportion of the elderly, particularly the women, live alone. The proportion of those living alone increases among the older age groups. Two things should be noted here. First, living alone does not necessarily mean that the person is in a state of aloneness. As we have seen, friends as well as family can provide meaningful interaction. Second, living with someone does not necessarily mean that an individual is *not* in a state of aloneness. As the quote of William James indicates, an individual can be treated as nonexistent while in the presence of others. There is, of course, a greater probability of aloneness if one is living alone, and a lesser probability if one is living with someone else. In any case, aloneness is frequently noted as one of the problems of the aged. And, the threat of aloneness seems to always hover near the elderly individual, since most, if not all of his or her friends are also elderly and may die at any point. Some elderly people prefer to have younger people among their friends, but our society often makes this difficult. As Cottrell (1974:50) noted, "Not even wealth can assure one that he will live out his years among friends and neighbors who care about him."

The Struggle for Autonomy

Americans greatly *value individual autonomy,* the right and the capacity to direct one's own existence. Many Americans would define freedom in terms of the individual's ability to do whatever he or she pleases so long as it does not

Table 10.3   Persons Living Alone, By Sex and Age, 1978
(number in thousands)

Sex and Age	Number	Percent
Both Sexes		
Total, 14 years and over	16,715	100.0
14 to 24 years	1,611	9.6
25 to 44 years	3,976	23.8
45 to 64 years	4,328	25.9
65 years and over	6,801	40.7
Male		
Total, 14 years and over	6,352	38.0
14 to 24 years	870	5.2
25 to 44 years	2,500	15.0
45 to 64 years	1,543	9.2
65 years and over	1,439	8.6
Female		
Total, 14 years and over	10,363	62.0
14 to 24 years	741	4.4
25 to 44 years	1,477	8.8
45 to 64 years	2,784	16.7
65 years and over	5,362	32.1

Source: U.S. Bureau of the Census, *Current Population Reports,* Series P-20, no. 340, "Household and Family Characteristics: March 1978" (Washington, D.C.: Government Printing Office, 1979), p. 3.

harm someone else. This value, however, tends to be *contradicted* more for the aged than for other adults—contradicted by their economic status, by their opportunities for meaningful activity, and by institutionalization (or the threat of it). We will further look at each of these limitations.

Economic status. We value the ability to do what we please, but what we please to do usually requires certain financial resources. While the elderly may not have as wide a range of

desires as younger people, what they would like to do is often stifled by their lack of money.

In 1978 the median income of all households in the nation was $15,064. The median for households headed by someone age 65 and over was $7,081; about one-third of all those households had incomes of less than $5,000 for the year.[3] A *considerable proportion of the aged live in poverty or near-poverty.* The proportion of the elderly who are below the poverty level has been decreasing (table 10.4), but in 1978 over 3 million elderly people still lived in poverty. The female elderly and the black elderly are more likely to be impoverished than are white males. That means that the problems of sexual and racial inequality intersect with the problem of aging to compound the difficulties of the black and female elderly.

The 1971 White House Conference on Aging reported that "the income of elderly people in the past left the greater number of them with insufficient means for decent, dignified living."[4] This still holds true for millions of America's aged. In a sample of 266 elderly in California who had applied for Old Age Assistance, 64 percent said that money was their biggest problem (Tissue, 1972). Similarly, elderly residents in housing projects for the aged were more dissatisfied with life when constrained by lack of money and physical incapacity (both of which bear upon an individual's autonomy) (Smith and Lipman, 1972). A probability sample of the adult population of the nation showed that perceived health and financial adequacy were important predictors of life satisfaction (Spreitzer and Snyder, 1974).

Often the elderly person cannot purchase what he or she would like (or even what is necessary) and may have to seek help from others

Table 10.4   Number and Proportion of Aged Below the Poverty Level, 1959–1978
(number in thousands)

Family Status	Number Below Poverty Level*					Percent Below Poverty Level				
	1959	1970	1972	1973	1978†	1959	1970	1972	1973	1978†
Persons 65 and older	5,481	4,793	3,738	3,354	3,233	35.2	24.6	18.6	16.3	14.0
In families	3,187	2,013	1,444	1,340	1,180	26.9	14.8	10.4	9.4	7.6
Unrelated individuals	2,294	2,779	2,295	2,014	2,053	61.9	47.2	37.1	32.0	27.0

*Figures do not necessarily add due to rounding.
†Not strictly comparable to earlier years because of revised procedure.

Source: Adapted from U.S. Bureau of the Census, *Statistical Abstract of the United States, 1975* (Washington, D.C.: Government Printing Office, 1975), p. 403; and *1980* (Washington, D.C.: Government Printing Office, 1981), p. 466.

in order to pay basic bills. While it may be true that money cannot buy happiness, it is also true that poverty tends to suppress happiness. To the extent that the aged are harassed by financial problems, their autonomy is threatened and the quality of their lives is diminished.

We will discuss the reasons for the impoverished state of the elderly later. Here we want to emphasize that a disproportionate number of the aged are poor, and that financial problems often constitute a serious threat to the autonomy of the elderly.

Opportunities for meaningful activities. We have mentioned that the aged generally maintain continuity in their lifestyles, contrary to the theory of disengagement. The Duke Longitudinal Study (Busse, 1970), which confirmed this point, also found that the elderly subjects who maintained or increased their activities tended to have corresponding satisfaction with life. Reduced activities tended to result in correspondingly reduced satisfaction. One study of small-town residents reported that life satisfac-

tion among the elderly was dependent more on participation in formal groups, such as with a church, than on association with friends or family (Pihlblad and Adams, 1972). The aged need activity along with interaction, and participating in organizations provides both.

How many opportunities to participate in meaningful activity does the elderly person have? Depending on the community, there are probably voluntary associations as well as churches, and a number of leisure activities may be available.

Generally, mandatory retirement removes one of the more important meaningful activities available to people—work. This is especially true for those who found considerable gratification in their work (likely to be those in higher status occupations). This American emphasis on work and the tendency to justify one's existence by work make leisure activities something of a problem. With our ethic of "work before play," how can the aged individual enjoy leisure that is not justified by work?

A career of leisure (play) is characteristic of the socially immature (children) or the socially **superannuated.** For the aging individual, it can only serve to add to his social loss, negating any social benefits that might be derived from remaining active by serving to reinforce a definition of him as superannuated [Miller, 1976:271].

So long as the worth of the individual is tied with work, and so long as leisure must be justified by work done first, the aged will find it difficult to conceive of leisure activities in meaningful terms.

Some of the elderly will be able to come to terms with this problem and find gratification in leisure activities. Others may prefer other kinds of activities but find few opportunities. One of the recommendations of the 1971 White House Conference on Aging was that *older people need greater involvement in community and civic affairs*:

> Public policy should encourage and promote opportunities for greater involvement of older people in community and civic affairs, and for their participation in formulating goals and policies on their own behalf as a basis for making the transition from work to leisure roles. Society should reappraise the current life style sequence of student/worker/retiree roles, and promote role flexibility.[5]

The more opportunities older people have to participate in public affairs and in the decisions that affect their lives, the more individual autonomy they will maintain.

Institutionalization. One of the fears of the aged is being unable to care for oneself and being *placed in an institution*. Studies show that no more than 5 percent of the elderly are in institutions at any particular time (including nursing homes and other kinds of extended care facilities). This figure can be misleading because it tells us nothing about the number of people who will be in an extended care facility at some point in their lives. In a study of death certificates in Detroit for the year 1971, Kastenbaum and Candy (1976) found that 23.7 percent of the deaths occurred in extended care facilities; about 20 percent of those deaths occurred in nursing homes. A considerable number of America's aged—more than previously thought—possibly spend their last days in an extended care facility.

What is it like to be placed in a nursing home? Even a home an outsider might define as a good one is likely to have negative consequences for those who go there. A survey of one hundred patients admitted to a Jewish home and hospital for the aged found that thirty-three made a smooth adjustment with no medical changes; seventeen made a smooth adjustment but had significant medical changes; thirty-one had severe adjustment problems though no significant medical changes, and nineteen had both severe adjustment problems and significant medical changes (Rodstein, Savitsky and Starkman, 1976). In another piece of research, Gubrium (1975) studied a nonprofit church-connected nursing home in which at least two-thirds of the clientele paid for their own care. Many of the elderly residents told the researcher the home was a "nice" place, but they also reported the difficulties they had with their loss of autonomy. An elderly man, for instance, said:

> Well, this isn't home! This is an institution! You come and you go. And well . . . it just isn't there. They're wonderful to you and the surroundings are nice. They're good to you, but it's still an institution. It isn't my home regardless of how nice it is. They ring a bell when you come in. They ring a bell and you sit down. (Sarcastically) You haven't got a home. You have no place to go. So you have to accept it [Gubrium, 1975:88].

The clientele also struggled with the meaninglessness of their daily routines. They considered all days to be alike. They continually emphasized the fact that "each day is the same old routine," which means that "you eat, sleep, and sit around." One woman described the problem this way:

> Oh here, I do practically nothing. I'd rather do a little something. But I wipe off the stuff that I think looks dusty. . . . Now what do I do in the afternoon? That's a big question. What should I do? There's nothing to do. So I take myself a nap and think over this big mistake that I made. What is there to do here? [Gubrium, 1975:163].

Problems of autonomy and the meaning of existence arise in even the best of institutions, and other kinds of problems also are found in many institutions. In 1968 the federal government sponsored a survey of 19,533 nursing homes in the nation to determine the kind of *rehabilitation services*, medical care, and recreational activities available.[6] Such services are important because of the high prevalence of health problems among nursing home residents. Only 32 percent of the nursing homes offered rehabilitation services (these homes had about half of all the residents). Some of the homes that did not have the services sent patients to outpatient clinics. A full-time physician was available in 7 percent of the homes, and 34 percent had regularly scheduled visits by physicians. Recreational activities were offered in 79 percent of the homes, arts and crafts in only 39 percent, and trips were available in only about 25 percent.

There are, then, considerable differences among extended care facilities. The *quality of care* is far better where the residents are more affluent. In nursing homes in the Detroit area, for example, better care was found where residents had their own possessions, were in a nonprofit home or were primarily private-paying, were white, and were visited by outsiders at least once a month (Kosberg, 1973). Outside visitors, of course, mean that the home is more likely to be accountable for the treatment of the elderly.

At best, living in such an institution means that the elderly person loses some autonomy and is subject to a number of constraints. At worst, it may mean neglect and even abuse. Abuse has been observed where aides work closely with residents, where there is little supervision by nurses, and where the nurses feel compelled to defend the institution (Stannard, 1973). In such cases, aides who have little understanding of and little patience with the behavior of the elderly may verbally and physically mistreat their charges. We do not know how common abuse of elderly nursing home residents is, but we know that it does happen. The fact that it happens at all means America's aged must face yet another threat to the quality of their lives.

Figure 10.4 Even in a nursing home with good facilities there is some loss of autonomy for those who are cared for.

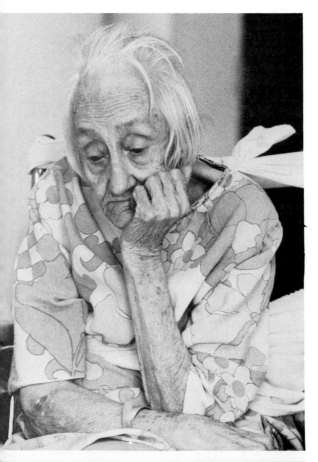

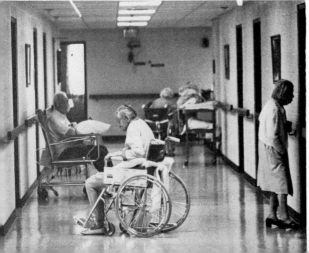

Myths about the Aged

The **stereotype** of an older person was expressed well by Robert Butler. Like all stereotypes, it combines partial truths and myths.

> An older person thinks and moves slowly. He does not think of himself as well as he used to nor as creatively. He is bound to himself and to his past and can neither change nor grow. He can neither learn well nor swiftly and even if he could . . . he would not wish to. Tied to his personal traditions and growing conservatism, he dislikes innovations. . . . Not only can he not move forward, but he often moves backward, he enters a second childhood. . . . Indeed, he is a study in decline; . . . the picture of mental and physical failure. He has lost and cannot replace friends, spouse, job, status, power, influence, income. He is often stricken by diseases. . . His body shrinks and so does the flow of blood to his brain . . . enfeebled, uninteresting, he awaits his death, a burden to society, to his family, and to himself [Saul, 1974:20–21].

In this section we will look at two common myths about the aged that are embodied in the stereotypical portrait. Their effect is to diminish the quality of life of the elderly by a two-step process. First, these myths *imply a negative evaluation*. Notice that in the quotation about stereotypes all the qualities and conditions attributed to the aged are negative. In a second step, these negative evaluations can become *self-fulfilling prophecies*. In other words, the older person who accepts the stereotype can become someone who thinks and moves slowly, who is a study in decline, and so forth, even though he or she has the capacity for vigorous activity.

The *two specific myths that we will examine are that the aged (1) have greatly diminishing intellectual and creative powers, and (2) have few or no sexual needs. These myths actually contradict the needs and the capacities of the aged.*

Intellectual functioning in old age. Most of us know about individuals who were creative in their older as well as younger years. Many philosophers, political figures, and writers and artists continue to function creatively throughout their lives. Nevertheless, the stereotype of the older person is someone who has largely lost the ability to think quickly and deeply and to be creative. Aristotle, William Gladstone, and Pablo Picasso were creative in their old age, but how many Aristotles, Gladstones, and Picassos are there in the world? In other words, the stereotype implies that older people who think well and work creatively are exceptions.

Refuting an idea that can be a self-fulfilling prophecy is difficult; thus it is fortunate that most of the elderly do not accept the idea that their intellectual and creative powers are gone. In a 1974 survey conducted by Louis Harris and Associates, a nationwide sample was asked about the characteristics of people over 65. Two characteristics concerned intellectual functioning. Respondents over 65 tended to agree that the elderly are "very bright and alert" (68 percent) and "very open-minded and adaptable" (63 percent). As for respondents under 65, only 29 percent agreed that the elderly are very bright and alert, and only 21 percent agreed the elderly are open-minded and adaptable (Riley and Waring, 1976:398). Still, as many as one-third of the elderly agree that intellectual sharpness diminishes in old age. Such people can easily become victims of the self-fulfilling prophecy.

There is another problem in trying to determine whether or not intellectual functioning declines in old age. If test differences are found between older and younger people, we cannot know whether the differences show something other than decline with age—such as educational or other generational differences. The median educational level has risen for a number of generations, and the better educated are likely to score higher on the tests. This problem can be handled by testing the same group when they are young and again after they have passed the age of 65. This is expensive and difficult, but it has been done. Gilbert (1973) reported a thirty-five-year follow-up of fourteen individuals who were first tested on mental efficiency when they were in their 20s or early 30s (we must, of course, be very cautious about any conclusions based on only fourteen subjects). There was a decrease in efficiency scores and a slight (not statistically significant) increase in vocabulary level. There were also sizable individual differences in the amount of decline. Some who had dropped from their peak of efficiency could still function as well as the average young person.

In another study, a group of college students was tested in 1919, in 1950, and again in 1960 (Owens, 1966). The test included a verbal factor, a number factor, and a relations factor. There was a gain in the verbal factor and small declines in the number and relations factors. Again, there was *no striking reduction in intellectual functioning.* Rather, there seemed to be slight gains in some and slight losses in other intellectual processes. At this point we do not know how much of the gains or the losses is due to the biological process of aging and how much is due to various sociocultural factors such as education, changing cultural conditions, and motivation of the subjects.

A conservative bias is another aspect of intellectual functioning often attributed to the aged (as in the stereotype description quoted above). This is exaggerated, according to the evidence. While the aged are probably more cautious and less willing to change attitudes, surveys show that in recent years the aged have tended to be more liberal in certain matters, following general social trends (Glenn, 1974).

In conclusion, there is no evidence that people become intellectual fossils when they grow old. There appear to be some gains and some losses in intellectual functioning. Many people who have studied the matter are ready to declare that the notion of intellectual decline is largely a myth.

Sexual functioning in old age. Comics have defined old age as the time when a man flirts with women but no longer remembers why he is doing it. Any number of jokes make the point that sexual functioning has largely vanished by the time a man is old (women are not usually included in this myth). Again, such an attitude can become a self-fulfilling prophecy if believed. Furthermore, religious notions—such as that sex is only for procreation—may intrude also to insure that the older person will no longer function sexually.

This myth, argued Dean (1974), is unfortunate, because sex in our society is equated with life. To maintain one's sexual functioning is to affirm life and to maintain one's morale. However, can the aged maintain their sexual functioning? The Harris poll mentioned in the previous section showed that only 5 percent of the public perceived the aged as "very sexually active," and only 11 percent of the respondents over 65 agreed that the aged are very sexually active. The key word there may be "very." The elderly generally do not function sexually as often as they did in their younger days, but many continue to be active, and some are quite active.

The Duke Longitudinal Study reported that 70 percent of the men continued to be sexually active at 68, and about 25 percent were active at 78 (Pfeiffer, 1974). The study suggested that an individual's life shows considerable continuity in sexual drive and that, given good health, an individual may continue to be sexually active into his or her 80s (Newman and Nichols, 1970). In fact, one study found an increasing amount of interest and activity in about one-fourth of the men surveyed, regardless of age (Verwoerdt, Pfeiffer, and Wang, 1970).

Health and Satisfaction

We saw in chapter 5 that modern medicine has largely conquered the infectious diseases, so more of us will reach a "ripe old age" than did past generations. That also means more of us will have to deal with various chronic illnesses and with consequent limitations in our activity. Table 10.5 shows that a far greater proportion of the elderly than of any other age group are limited by chronic illness. But the majority of us—even the poorest, who have the highest rates of illness—will not be limited by chronic illness, because not everyone who has a chronic condition suffers subsequent limitation of activity. Most people over 60 have at least one chronic condition, but most—at least those

Table 10.5   **Percent of Persons Limited in Major Activity Due to Chronic Conditions, by Selected Characteristics, 1973**

| Characteristic | Unable to Carry on Major Activity | Total | Limited in Major Activity Family Income | | | | | |
			Under $3,000	$3,000 to $4,999	$5,000 to $6,999	$7,000 to $9,999	$10,000 to $14,999	$15,000 to more
Total population	3.1	13.5						
Male	4.7	13.5						
Female	1.6	13.4	(NA*)	(NA)	(NA)	(NA)	(NA)	(NA)
White	3.0	13.4						
Black	4.1	13.8						
Total, all ages			(NA)	(NA)	(NA)	(NA)	(NA)	(NA)
Under 17 years			2.8	2.6	2.4	2.0	1.8	1.3
17 to 44 years	(NA)	(NA)	10.4	9.9	7.2	5.3	4.4	3.6
45 to 64 years			47.4	34.6	24.6	18.5	14.1	9.0
65 years and over			44.5	40.7	37.5	33.4	29.9	29.6

*NA Not available.

Source: Executive Office of the President, Office of Management and Budget, *Social Indicators,* 1976 (Washington, D.C.: Government Printing Office, 1977), p. 201.

under 75—also consider themselves to have relatively good health. The point is not that the elderly inevitably or most likely suffer from ill health and limitations of activity, but that health problems and limitations are more prevalent among the elderly than among any other group.

The greater prevalence of health problems among the aged means a diminished quality of life. At first, this may appear to be only a biological problem, not a social one. Old age inevitably brings certain health problems. We have mentioned that an individual's satisfaction with health is very important in his or her satisfaction with life, but the problem is more than

biological. There is a *contradiction between our medical advances and the role of the aged* (we will discuss role further below). More people are allowed to live to old age thanks to advanced medical knowledge, but they are allowed only a *devalued role.* Moreover, while we have conquered the illnesses that prevented many people from reaching old age, we have not conquered those that afflict old age.

We have here a case of *cultural lag.* Advances in technology (medical science) have outstripped other aspects of the culture (changes in the role of the aged), with the result that there is maladjustment (more people are thrust into a devalued role). To be old is to be devalued. To be old and sick is to be doubly devalued. Ironically, the likelihood that a person will become old and sick is far greater today than it was in the past.

Contributing Factors

We must identify the structural and social psychological factors that devalue old age before we can do anything about revaluing this part of our lives. Most of the problem is created and compounded by these factors, not by the biological aspect of old age. Such problems of the elderly as finances and aloneness are clearly related to social factors. In identifying those factors, we prepare the ground for a brief discussion of what to do about the problem of the aged.

Social Structural Factors

Role problems. In chapter 5 we pointed out that *certain kinds of roles induce stress* because they are too restrictive. Old age is one of those roles. At best, the elderly often have an ambiguous place in American society, and at worst, they are restricted to activities that are meaningless or have limited social value (such as hobbies and other leisure pursuits).

Americans, in other words, generally view the elderly as people who have already made their contribution to society and have retired from productive activity. The old person is expected to "take it easy" and to enjoy himself or herself. This ignores the fact that one of the more important ways we all "enjoy" ourselves is by being involved in *activity that is socially valued.*

Socially valued activity does not necessarily mean work. In some societies the elderly do continue to work. In observing the amazing **longevity** of peasants in the Soviet Republic of Abkhasia, Benet (1976:219) discovered that retirement is unknown:

> From the beginning of life until its end, he does what he is capable of doing because both he and those around him consider work vital to life. He makes the demands on himself that he can meet, and as those demands diminish with age, his status in the community nevertheless increases.

The work load for the peasants decreased between the ages of 80 and 90 for some and between 90 and 100 for others. But, they continued to work for 100 or more years, and their *status increased with age even though their work load decreased.*

In other societies, there is increasing status with age even though work largely ceases. This is the case in traditional China. The point is that the role of the aged must include socially valued activities if they are to experience their time of life as a meaningful stage rather than a loss. In America, few socially valued activities are included in the role of the elderly.

The role problems of the aged were dramatically illustrated to a magazine editor who faced retirement and began "practicing" for it. He sat around his house on weekends and pretended he was retired. One day he decided to go to the supermarket with his wife and push the shopping cart for her. As he wheeled the cart down an aisle, he saw an elderly man pushing another cart. The man was bent down over the handle.

> He was standing on the ground but his head was darn near in the food. I looked at him and I thought, *Thank God I'm not him.* That old man—he wasn't much older than me—he had arthritis of the back so bad he was bent double. That shopping trip hadn't been much up to that point, but now it was important. It made me mighty thankful. I might be pretty old but I could still stand up straight. The old man swiveled his head out of the food. His eye caught mine. . . . All of a sudden he got embarrassed. And he straightened up! He straightened right up. As straight as I was standing. You know something? There wasn't a thing wrong with him. He was just so bored and fed up he couldn't think of anything else to do but lean over something. . . . I got hold of my wife and we finished up that shopping trip in a hurry, checked out, and I haven't been back shopping since [McCracken, 1976:23].

Pushing a shopping cart is not a socially valued activity for a male in American society, but the role of the aged does not include many alternatives.

We cannot emphasize too strongly that it is the social value of the activities associated with the role of old age that is important. Allowing old people to continue working would resolve the role problems for some of them, because work is highly valued in America and is tied with our *sense of self-worth.* Some observers think our work ethic is changing, that Americans are beginning to value people for matters other than the work they do. If so, future generations of the elderly may find it easier to adapt

to the role of old age. At this point, retirement still generally means transition from a valued to a devalued role.

A basic problem of the elderly, then, is that their role is ambiguous, devalued, and therefore stressful. Their role may be further devalued if, as is likely, the elderly person must make the transition from well to sick and from spouse to widow or widower. The role of a spouse still carries with it the socially valued activity of caring for someone else. The widow or widower has lost that activity. With advancing age comes a tendency for one's role to grow increasingly restrictive (which can mean increasingly less meaningful and more stressful). More of us will live to be old than ever before in history. Unfortunately, we do not know what to do with the extra years we have gained.

Norms.   Role problems are reinforced by various norms. *Certain norms narrow the range of activities available to the elderly.* There is certainly no biological reason for requiring people to retire at a particular age. A 1978 law prohibited *mandatory retirement* before age 70 in the private sector and abolished it for most federal employees. But why require people to retire even at 70? Most will retire before that anyway. In 1978 only one-fifth of the men 65 years and over continued to participate in the labor force (U.S. Department of Labor, 1979:236). Why compel those preferring to continue their work to stop their work? Mandatory retirement forces some people to live on an inadequate income and adversely affects the health of those who find the experience traumatic (Givens, 1978:52).

Figure 10.5 It is the social value of
the activities associated with the role
of old age that is important.

Formal and informal norms can keep the elderly out of the labor force. As Cottrell (1974:31) noted, employers may be compelled by law to interview older men, but

> they most often choose the younger man who presumably can be trained at less expense and who will have a longer period of productive employment after training. In other words, employers frequently disregard the facts that show older workers as being more steady, more reliable, more loyal to their employers, and often as skilled and productive as younger men are.

Although the crucial area of work tends to be closed to the elderly, other norms, which concern education and travel for instance, have become less restrictive in recent years. The elderly are now encouraged to enroll in adult education courses or in college for the first time. Organizations offer tours for groups of the elderly, including trips to various foreign countries. Whether such activities are gratifying to the elderly may depend on the extent to which the elderly, when they were younger, defined the activities as valuable in themselves. That is, if when they were younger, they viewed education primarily as a means to a good job rather than a worthwhile pursuit for its own sake, they may not find satisfaction in education when they are older. Or, if they defined travel as a necessary respite in order to be able to plunge back into work with greater vigor, they may not enjoy travel when there is no work to return to. Again, the traditional emphasis on work as the basis for one's worth devalues the satisfaction of all other activities of old age. Broadening the norms of other activities, therefore, will not automatically resolve the problem of old age.

Norms have also tended to reinforce the problem of aloneness for the aged. Although most older people have living children whom they see fairly frequently, there is now a norm that defines *separate residences as ideal.* The older person frequently feels that the children "have their own lives to lead" and should not be burdened by the presence of a parent in the home. Like the norm relating to labor force participation, this is another case of a norm changing to the detriment of the aged. In the past, it was acceptable for three generations to live in the same home. Grandparents, parents, and children who shared a dwelling were regarded as one family. Today, separate residences are believed to be better for all concerned, although this arrangement may compound the problem of aloneness of the elderly, particularly of the widowed. Even if the children live nearby, separate residences mean that the elderly are cut off from the intensive, extensive interaction of the two- and three-generation family.

Institutional poverty.   *Political and economic arrangements* in America have helped to create and perpetuate the disproportionate amount of poverty among the elderly. In 1978, 13.9 percent of elderly people were below the poverty level. In the same year, only about 11 percent of those under 65 were below the poverty level. Why is the rate of poverty higher for the elderly than for other groups?

Part of the answer lies in various political and economic arrangements. One, which we have mentioned already, is the arbitrary decision made in the Franklin Roosevelt administration to set retirement at 65. The 1978 law

Figure 10.6 The norm of separate residences means that the problem of aloneness is compounded for elderly Americans.

that raised the mandatory retirement age to 70 will perhaps help some of the aged. Ironically, the Social Security system itself helps to create poverty among the aged. The aged are not able to get much income from employment, even if they can find work. If an elderly individual earns more than a certain amount, he or she is penalized by reductions in Social Security benefits (Butler, 1973). In other words, the Social Security program discourages the elderly from working. Mandatory retirement plus the provisions of the Social Security program plus norms that discriminate against the aged all work together to effectively minimize the participation of the elderly in the economy. The major source of income for the aged is from Social Security retirement and survivor benefits. In 1967, 89 percent of the elderly had income from retirement and survivor benefits, 50 percent received income from assets, 27 percent had earnings from work, and 12 percent received public assistance (Fitzpatrick, 1975:110).

If the major source of income is retirement benefits, the question of the adequacy of those benefits is raised. Social Security benefits are notoriously low by any standard. In fact, the average benefit received annually by retired workers automatically places an elderly couple below the poverty level, if the couple has nothing but Social Security. The government's provision for the elderly is less than the government's own definition of the poverty level!

We previously pointed out that financial problems among the aged are one aspect of a diminished quality of life. Inadequate income reduces the individual's autonomy. Low income can also aggravate other aspects of the elderly person's life, causing a *chain of negative con-*

sequences to flow from poverty, as Atchley (1975) reported in his study of 233 widows in the 70 to 79 age group. He compared the widows with women of the same age group who were married. He found that widowhood, particularly among working-class women, tended to be associated with inadequate income. The widows who had too little income also suffered, in turn, a series of negative consequences:

> Income inadequacy . . . affects car driving and social participation (which also influence each other). Because American society is spatially structured on the assumption that everyone can get around by private car, widowed people with inadequate incomes become socially isolated and lonely. Income inadequacy and social isolation combine to produce anxiety [Atchley, 1975:178].

In sum, institutional poverty means that many of the aged are poor because of political programs and discriminatory practices in the economy. In turn, their poverty may lead to a series of negative consequence, including isolation and anxiety. The elderly person cannot cope with the isolation and anxiety without first resolving the problem of income. And he or she cannot cope with the problem of income because it is rooted in social institutions.

Stratification and aging.   We can add another comment to our statements about the devalued status of the old. To be old is to be devalued. To be old and sick or old and alone is to be doubly devalued. To be old and in the *lower socioeconomic strata* is to be further devalued. The problem of aging, like other problems, is compounded for people in the lower strata.

The Social Security benefits for the aged were supposed to lessen the income differential

- Poverty increases the likelihood of stress & illness
- Stress (and illness) increase the probability of premature aging
chronically → Premature aging can lead to unemployment problems
- Unemployment problems lead to poverty.
→ - Poverty increases the likelihood of stress and ∴ illness
                                                          etc —

among the aged by giving low-income workers a greater proportion of preretirement earnings than higher-income workers received. This purpose has been thwarted by the fact that the higher-income worker is more likely to have supplemental sources of income. Thus, people who labor throughout their lives in low-income jobs are likely to find themselves more disadvantaged after retirement than before.

One other aspect of stratification and aging is that people in the lower strata actually age faster than people in the middle and upper strata. Here we confront another of the *vicious circles* that we frequently see embedded in social problems. Poverty increases the likelihood of stress and illness, which increases the probability of premature aging, which increases the likelihood of stress and illness. So, as with other aspects of life, people in the lower strata have less to look forward to than people in the higher strata.

Social Psychological Factors

Attitudes. One reason old age is a devalued role is that Americans tend to have *negative attitudes toward being old*. These negative attitudes are reflected in the various myths about old age, which, as we have pointed out, can become self-fulfilling prophecies. People who believe the elderly have lost the capacity to enjoy living may make life more difficult for the elderly, and may themselves plunge into despair when they become old.

Attitudes toward old age are not completely negative, of course. In one study of 1,000 children in the fifth, seventh, ninth, and eleventh grades, both positive and negative attitudes were found (Thomas and Yamamoto, 1975).

The children were asked to make up stories based on three pictures—of a young man, a middle-aged man, and an old man. They also rated the three age groups along a number of dimensions such as wise-foolish. The stories tended to be stereotypical. In the ratings, there was a tendency to ascribe more goodness and wisdom to the older than to the younger ages. But, the children saw the old as less pleasant and happy than the young. And they believed the old to be much less active and to have much less power than the young.

A study of 180 children between ages 3 and 11 reported results more negative. Some of the children described old people as wonderful or rich or friendly, but more commonly they said that the elderly are "sick, sad, ugly, and bad."[7] Also, the children tended to be negative about growing old themselves.

The Louis Harris Poll mentioned in the section on intellectual functioning reported that public perceptions of people over 65 included a number of negative ideas. We noted that the public perceptions were different from the self-perceptions of the elderly. Specifically, the public was more likely than the elderly to think of the elderly as spending a lot of time watching television, sitting and thinking, sleeping, or just doing nothing. On the other hand, the public was less likely than the elderly to think of the elderly as bright and alert, open-minded and adaptable, and good at getting things done (Riley and Waring, 1976:398).

Fortunately, the elderly do not believe so widely as the public does that the elderly spend most of their time in nonproductive, leisure pursuits or in doing nothing, and that the elderly could probably do little else even if it were available! This *conflict between the two sets of im-*

ages means that public attitude is one of the problems the elderly face as they seek to effect changes that will improve their lot. When only slightly more than one-third of the general public believe the elderly are very good at getting things done, it is not likely the public will support policies that open a wider range of activities to the aged—particularly policies that reopen the possibility of participation in the economy.

Public attitudes are important, then, for three reasons: they cast the elderly into a devalued role; they create self-fulfilling prophecies; and they influence public policy. Negative attitudes about the capabilities of the aged help maintain policies that restrict the elderly to socially devalued activities. Those negative attitudes must be altered in support of the kind of changes the elderly need.

Attitudes may already be changing to some extent. Neugarten (1973), a noted expert on aging, says that the negative attitudes about old age so firmly rooted in American society are giving way to more realistic images. In particular, more Americans are becoming aware of the diversity among old people, thereby helping to break down the stereotype of the old. Neugarten does not rule out the possibility that the status of the aged could become worse rather than better in the near future. However, if our attitudes become more realistic, which also means more positive, the status of the aged could be improved.

Values.   Our attitudes toward old age are buttressed by the *value we place on youth*. In our culture, as Lerner (1957:613) said, the elderly are treated "like the [tag] end of what was once

good material." We value youth so much that we fail to see old age may have something to offer that the young cannot offer.

> The most flattering thing you can say to an older American is that he "doesn't look his age" and "doesn't act his age"—as if it were the most damning thing in the world to look old. There is little of calm self-acceptance among the old, of the building of the resources which give inner serenity and compel an outer acceptance. There is correspondingly little cultural valuing of old people. One finds nothing like the Japanese reverence for ancestors or the valuation the Chinese set on the qualities of the old [Lerner, 1957:613].

Our value of youth is reflected in advertisements that tell us what products to buy in order to keep our skin and hair and general appearance youthful. It is reflected in the reluctance of people to tell their age. It is reflected in the fad during the 1960s and early 1970s to substitute "young" for "old" when giving one's age (such as, "I'm 72 years young"). It is reflected in the myth that an elderly individual is no longer capable of directing a corporation. It is reflected in the saying that emerged in the 1960s, You can't trust anyone over 30.

American culture manifests the value it puts on youth, and the concomitant devaluing of old age in numerous ways. Not surprisingly, the role of the elderly is a restrictive one, for this role is consistent with the dominant attitudes and values of the American people. I say "dominant" here because not all Americans value youth to the detriment of old age.

A different set of values and attitudes and a different role for the elderly are found in a West Virginia community, where there is "retirement to the porch" (Lozier and Althouse, 1975). The front porch becomes more and more important as the elderly man retires from work. At first he does occasional paid or volunteer jobs, which are normally secured by interacting with people who pass by his front porch. Eventually the man no longer does part-time or occasional jobs, and begins full retirement on the porch. He begins to draw on the "social credit" that he has accumulated. For instance, he can request a passerby to visit with him or to run an errand for him. These requests are generally not viewed as intrusive. On the contrary, the community senses a responsibility to maintain the retiree's social interaction. Say the man becomes infirm and must spend a great amount of time inside the house. Whenever his health permits, he will be brought back to the porch. The word that he is available is passed throughout the community, and many people come to visit with him.

Such community concern and responsibility for the elderly is accorded those who had good social standing for a number of years. Rather than suddenly becoming the "tag end," the aged in this West Virginia community have a definite and honored role. Age is not devalued. The dominant American value of youth, which has involved devaluing the elderly, is not universal in our society. Choosing between a value of youth and a value of old age is unnecessary. Each age category can be valued for its own sake.

What Is To Be Done?

Our analysis suggests a number of considerations we should keep in mind when addressing the problem of the aged in our society. The first consideration is the *diversity* of the aged. A good deal of private and governmental efforts to provide housing for the aged have focused on high-rise apartment buildings and *age-segregated* communities. Some of the elderly prefer such arrangements, but others prefer to avoid them. Whatever aspect of the age problem we deal with, we cannot treat the elderly as if they were all alike or all had the same needs and preferences.

Second, we must consider the need of the elderly for activity and for autonomy. The elderly need meaningful activity and some sense of control over their lives if they are to have satisfaction and fulfillment. The way to achieve this is to *involve the elderly* in making policy and planning programs. Such involvement can even occur in nursing homes. In a striking demonstration, one group of patients in an Eastern nursing home was given some responsibility for self-care, while another group in the home was made to feel that their care was the staff's responsibility. The group given responsibility for their own care made decisions about various matters, cared for plants, and made suggestions for change in the home. After eighteen months, the involved group showed more interest, more initiative, and more sociability, and the death rate was half that of the other group![8]

Third, *intergroup conflict* is likely to be involved as the aged struggle to obtain their share of those things valued in our society. This demands organization. Organization of the elderly has already begun, in the form of the *Gray Panthers,* the American Association of Retired Persons, the National Council of Senior Citizens, and other groups.

The Gray Panthers, the most militant of the groups, seek to generally improve the care and the status of the aged in America. A high priority concern of the Gray Panthers is health care, which the organization claims has been dehu-

Figure 10.7 Involvement in making policy and planning programs for themselves is important for the elderly.

manizing and little concerned with the total person (Downey, 1974). The Panthers want grievance procedures available to the elderly who receive inadequate medical care in nursing homes or hospitals.

The Gray Panthers were organized in 1970 by Maggie Kuhn, who got a group of people together in Philadelphia to discuss ways to deal with age discrimination and the victimization of the elderly. Groups of Gray Panthers are in at least nineteen cities; each group is autonomous. Local conditions for the elderly vary, and the Panthers want each local group to address its own particular problems. Some local groups include activities such as **"consciousness raising"** in small group sessions in order to encourage the elderly to assert their rights. Small group sessions can help the elderly as they help others. In fact, small group therapy has effected striking changes even in very old, disoriented, and withdrawn patients in institutions (Manaster, 1972).

More than the attitudes of the aged must be changed. Aligned against the aged are attitudes of the below-65, the intense value placed on youth, the traditional role of the elderly, the norms that reinforce the problems of the aged, and institutional arrangements that plunge the aged into poverty.

The elderly need not be the "tag end" of good material even in an advanced, industrial society. In Japan the aged tend to live with their children and to be an integral part of the household. Most men over 65 continue to work, and the aged are integrated into their communities and have a high status (Palmore, 1975). We need not duplicate the Japanese pattern, but we can learn from it that old age can be "golden years" in an advanced industrial society. To make old age "golden" in the United States, however, the organized elderly have much persuading and educating to do with respect to the rest of the citizenry, especially political leaders.

Summary

The problem of old age is more than the biological consequences of growing old. Sociocultural factors impose on the biological process to create a social problem. Even the definition of who is old is a sociocultural rather than a biological decision. In the United States the age of 65 is considered the point at which an individual is old. This is an arbitrary age, based on a political decision at the time the Social Security program was established.

By 1979 there were nearly 24.7 million elderly in America (about 11.2 percent of the population). Both the number and proportion of the aged have increased, especially in the 70-and-above age group, and especially women.

Aging can be described in biological terms as certain changes in body structure and functioning. Aging is also part of the developmental process, with certain developmental tasks for the aged to solve. Contrary to the well-known disengagement theory, the process of aging shows considerable diversity between individuals and also a high degree of continuity with an individual's lifestyle.

The diminished quality of life of the aged results from their aloneness, their loss of autonomy, myths about the elderly, and their health. Most elderly are not alone, but they all face the threat of aloneness, which means a loss of meaningful and necessary relationships. The loss of autonomy can be a result of inadequate income, lack of opportunity for meaningful activities, or

Involvement

What Do Those Old People Want, Anyway?

The Gray Panthers, according to a pamphlet published by the organization, assert that "ageism" is as destructive as racism and sexism. The focal concern of the organization is the problem of ageism—a problem that sooner or later will confront most of us. Consequently the Gray Panthers enlist the aid of people of all ages: "We are a group of people—old and young—drawn together by deeply felt common concerns for human liberation and social change."

Contact the national office of the Gray Panthers—3700 Chestnut St., Philadelphia, Pa., 19104—and request literature. The literature will identify the group nearest to you. If possible, visit a meeting of the Gray Panthers and see how you can contribute to a resolution of the problem of ageism. To what extent are the members concerned about the various aspects of the problem discussed in this chapter?

As an alternative project, volunteer to work in an institution for the aged. Many such institutions welcome volunteers. To what extent do the residents express a sense of having lost autonomy and meaning in their lives? In what ways does the institution attempt to address such problems?

institutionalization. Myths about the elderly contribute to the negative stereotype of old age and may become self-fulfilling prophecies. Typical myths attribute intellectual and sexual decline to the elderly. Medical advances cope with the illnesses that kill the young more than with the illnesses that afflict the old. Consequently, while more Americans live to a ripe old age, they are likely to have health problems that compound their devalued status.

Social structural factors impose a role on the elderly that is ambiguous at best, restricted and devalued at worst. It is a role likely to induce stress and thereby produce illness. Often, the elderly must also face transitions to even further devalued roles—widowhood and the sick role. The role problems are reinforced by norms that narrow the range of activities available to the elderly. The norm of separate residences contributes heavily to the problem of aloneness.

A disproportionate amount of poverty among the elderly is due in considerable measure to political and economic arrangements that minimize the income allowed to the aged. Poverty, in turn, implies a series of other negative consequences that further depress the quality of life. The aged are more likely to have serious health problems, to lose their autonomy, and to suffer from aloneness, and they are more likely to age at an earlier time in their lives.

Social psychological factors important to the problem include the negative attitudes of Americans toward old age. The public image of the elderly is, essentially, a group of people who spend most of their time in nonproductive or leisure pursuits or doing nothing, and who could probably do little else even if other activities or work were available. These attitudes devalue the role of the elderly, can become self-fulfilling prophecies, and influence public policy.

Negative attitudes about the aged are reinforced by the value we place on youth. In our culture the aged are considered the "tag end of what was once good material." To put high value on youth does not demand that old age be devalued, but in American culture the value on youth is so strong that the elderly have been cast into a devalued role.

Glossary

consciousness raising   the process by which people become aware of their situation as the situation is defined by some group

longevity   the length of human life, usually in years

senescence   biological aging

stereotype   an image of members of a group that standardizes them and exaggerates certain qualities

superannuate   to retire someone because of age

work ethic   notion that our sense of worth and the satisfaction of our needs are intricately related to the kind of work we do

For Further Reading

Atchley, Robert C. *The Social Forces in Later Life: An Introduction to Social Gerontology.* Belmont, Calif.: Wadsworth, 1972. A comprehensive examination of aging and the problems of America's elderly. Includes a useful bibliography.

Blau, Zena Smith. *Old Age in a Changing Society.* New York: New Viewpoints, 1973. Shows how the process of advanced industrialism tends to devalue the aged in a society. Also explores the role problems of the aged and argues that the elderly need activity rather than disengagement.

Cumming, Elaine, and William E. Henry. *Growing Old: The Process of Disengagement.* New York: Basic Books, 1961. The original statement of the disengagement theory, based on interviews with the elderly in Kansas City, Missouri.

Gross, Ronald, Beatrice Gross, and Sylvia Seidman, eds. *The New Old: Struggling for Decent Aging.* New York: Anchor Books, 1978. A large collection of articles written by a variety of authors, including social scientists, government officials, and activists. The articles generally cover the problems of aging and courses of action that can be and are being taken to address the problems.

Havighurst, Robert J., Joep M. A. Munnichs, Bernice Neugarten, and Hans Thomae, eds. *Adjustment to Retirement: A Cross-National Study.* Assen, Netherlands: Van Gorcum, 1969. Shows how people in various countries, including the United States, cope with the problem of retirement or loss of the work role. People everywhere appear to need activity rather than disengagement in retirement.

Kessler, Julia Braun. "Aging in Different Ways." *Human Behavior,* June 1976, pp. 56–60. An interesting and easy-to-read account of how people age in various societies, based on various studies by anthropologists.

Riley, Matilda White, and Anne Foner. *Aging and Society. Vol. 1: An Inventory of Research Findings.* New York: Russell Sage Foundation, 1968. Summarizes the research on aging in four broad areas: sociocultural context, the organism, personality, and roles. The research is used to present a series of propositions (for example, "morale is generally higher among men than women").

Notes

1. *St. Louis Post-Dispatch,* June 3, 1976.
2. Henry Maas and Joseph Kuypers, as quoted in Margie Casady, "Senior Syndromes," *Human Behavior,* March 1976, p. 47.
3. Figures here derived from U.S. Bureau of the Census, *Current Population Reports,* series P-60, no. 121, "Money Income in 1978 of Households in the United States" (Washington, D.C.: Government Printing Office, 1980), p. 35.
4. In *Toward a National Policy on Aging, Proceedings of the 1971 White House Conference on Aging, Volume II* (Washington, D.C.: Government Printing Office, 1972), p. 37.
5. Ibid., p. 53.
6. The results of the study are reported in *Vital and Health Statistics,* 1972, series 12, no. 17, (December), pp. 1–42.
7. The study is reported in the *St. Louis Post-Dispatch,* August 22, 1976.
8. Reported in *Human Nature,* May 1978, pp. 14–16.

Sex Inequality: The Problems of Women

1 Are women biologically programmed to be passive?

2 Are men and women equal in America?

3 How do we expect women to behave?

4 If a mother works, will her children suffer?

5 Why do some women believe that their place is in the home?

Americans agree in general that ours is a land of equal opportunity, that all citizens have the right to pursue their own happiness. In specific, there are some disagreements about what equal opportunity means. LeMasters (1975:182) found that the blue-collar workers with whom he interacted in a tavern looked with abhorrence on the women's movement. When he asked one worker if he would vote for a female candidate for the local school board—a woman who was well educated, active in community affairs, and good looking—the response was "explosive":

> "I wouldn't vote for her if she was built like Marilyn Monroe," he said. "The goddamn women are trying to take over this town— they're just like the niggers; give them an inch and they'll take a mile" [LeMasters, 1975:182].

The man's position was based on one simple point. He was opposed to women being in positions of power, regardless of their qualifications. The woman, incidentally, was elected to the office. The man's response was simply to shrug helplessly in the face of a world "going to hell."

Because women suffer discrimination as a result of an **innate** characteristic (their **gender**) as do racial minorities, women are called the "*largest minority*" in America. Actually, females are a majority because, although more male than female babies are born in the United States, the mortality rate is higher among males. As a result, the female population was 51.3 percent of the total in 1979.

As we examine this inequality between the sexes, we will ask first whether it is justified on biological grounds. The biology issue must be faced because some observers argue that sex inequalities are the necessary result of biological differences. According to this argument, we may not prefer or desire such inequalities, but we must face the fact that they are inevitable biological outcomes rather than sociocultural discrimination.

We will present evidence to support the contrary position—that the problems of women are sociocultural rather than biological. We will show how those problems affect the quality of life of women. Finally, we will examine the structural and social psychological factors that contribute to sex inequality, and suggest some ways to address the problem.

Biology or Society?

Unquestionably there are numerous differences in the attitudes and behavior of the sexes. Men and women do not perceive the same way or have the same kind of aspirations, or use the same strategies in competitive games. Research of almost any kind usually takes account of background variables such as sex, and usually some differences between the sexes are found. The crucial question is, what accounts for those differences? Are they rooted in biology or in society? Are the differences a reflection of gender or of **sex roles**?

Our attitudes today about these questions have, in many ways, not advanced beyond where they were in 1928, as described in this early text on social problems:

> Woman seems to possess less physical vigor and bodily strength. We take it for granted that women will be of more delicate build and incapable of as strenuous physical exertion. Still the peasant women of Europe work in the fields beside their men, the Indian squaw was a beast of burden, and our modern athletic girl is making records never dreamed of before. We

further take it for granted that she will be ruled more by the emotions; that she will be more "womanly," in the man-made sense of the term. But are these sex characteristics, or has woman merely lived up to what was expected of her. . . ? We used to feel that she did not have the mentality for the stern but pleasant tasks which men reserved for themselves; that she might do very well in the home, but that she was helpless in the larger world of activity outside. To-day we find her successfully competing in most of the professions and in many occupations [Gillin, Dittmer, and Colbert, 1928:267–68].

In 1928 people generally believed women were less capable than men, in spite of evidence to the contrary. And they believed that the lower capacity was an inevitable consequence of biological differences. In the 1970s people continue to believe the same things. Do we have any evidence to counter such beliefs?

One interesting piece of evidence comes from the research of Margaret Mead (1969). In the 1930s Mead studied three primitive peoples in New Guinea and concluded that *the meaning of being male or female* is largely a matter of *cultural conditioning* rather than biological demand. She said that many—perhaps all—of the traits we think of as masculine or feminine are actually "as lightly linked to sex as are the clothing, the manners, and the form of head-dress that a society at a given period assigns to either sex" (Mead, 1969:260). In fact, in one of the tribes she studied, the Tchambuli, males and females were virtually the opposite of our own ideals. The women were in command and were concerned with the practical matters of tribal life such as fishing and trading. Women also took the initiative in matters like mating. The males, on the other hand, behaved much like our women, concerning themselves with their personal appearance, their jewelry, and their rivalries and jealousies in their efforts to get female attention.

On the basis of this and other evidence, Chafetz (1974:27–28) drew a number of conclusions about the influence of biology and society on the sexes. First, the "vast majority of the behavioral and psychological characteristics" identified as masculine or feminine in a society are not innate aspects peculiar to gender. Traits defined as masculine in one society may be feminine in another, and vice versa. Second, in looking at the data on hormones and chromosomes, we find a few tendencies that are innately linked to gender. These are only *tendencies,* and sociocultural factors can virtually eliminate the effects of the tendencies. For instance, if male hormones tend to make men aggressive, sociocultural factors can neutralize the tendency and cause men to be less aggressive than women (recall the Tchambuli studied by Margaret Mead). Third, "whatever innate behavioral and psychological differences may exist between the genders, they are a matter of degree, not kind" (Chafetz, 1974:28). It is not that men are aggressive and women passive, but, if anything, that men are more *inclined* to aggressiveness. In other words, while there are some basic biological differences between males and females, and while there are certain functions that can be assumed by only one of the sexes (bearing children, for example), most of the traits we think of as masculine or feminine are sociocultural rather than biological.

Not everyone agrees with this conclusion. Sigmund Freud and the contemporary anthropologist Lionel Tiger, for example, argued that biology is critically important in sex-related behavior. Freud's arguments were summed up in his famous idea that *"anatomy is destiny."* Freud argued that as girls reach the point in their development when they recognize they are anatomically different from boys in that they lack a penis, they feel short-changed. They develop "penis-envy." Only in the act of conceiving and giving birth to a child can a woman find fulfillment for her desire for a penis. Freud also concluded from his observations that women are naturally more passive, submissive, and neurotic than men (Freud, 1949; Deckard, 1975:15–19).

Freud's arguments are based on questionable evidence at best. Essentially, he developed his psychoanalytic theories by observing middle-class behavior of his day, then explaining the relationships between the sexes in terms of his theories. There is a high degree of circularity involved. Nevertheless, many of his ideas are accepted, even by people who know little or nothing of his theories.

Tiger (1970) offered a different kind of argument and cited various kinds of evidence to support the idea of *male dominance.* For instance, he noted research that connected the hormone testosterone to aggressiveness (the hormone is at a much higher level in males than in females). He also pointed to the fact that 2-day-old female infants smile spontaneously much more than do males, suggesting that females have a tendency for that kind of behavior; since the smile is a gesture of deference and accommodation rather than assertion, females must have a tendency for the passive behavior.

Women are biologically predisposed to being subordinate, according to Tiger, and men are biologically programmed for dominance. The male, he said (Tiger, 1969), has an innate propensity to form all-male groups. *Male bonding*

 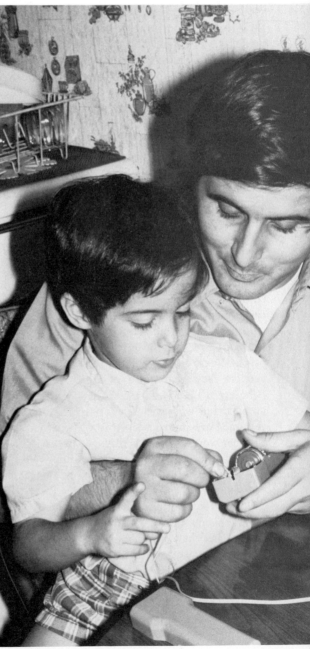

Figure 11.1 We are born with male or female gender, but we are taught sex roles by society. Some people believe that sex-role teaching in the U.S. puts down women and fosters inequality.

resulted in our ancestors' cooperative, aggressive behavior, such as hunting. In the contemporary world, the biological propensity of men to form groups means they are likely to remain dominant. Women are, by nature, unlikely to participate meaningfully in things such as political affairs. Human nature makes it "unnatural" for women to "engage in defense, police, and by implication, high politics. For human females to do so requires explicit self-conscious provision of special facilities by a concerned, sensitive and willing community" (Tiger, 1969:112).

Tiger's argument in favor of *biological bases* for behavioral differences between the sexes means that traditionally assigned sex roles do not represent female oppression. Rather, an evolutionary process has specifically equipped one sex (male) with providing for the needs of the community and the other sex (female) with the care and nurturance of the children. While few Americans would put the argument in such terms, a good many would agree that it is "natural" for men to be aggressive, to be the providers, and for women to be submissive and keepers of the children and the home.

Both Freud and Tiger relied much more on theory than on hard fact to support their arguments. Although their views support the traditional roles of the sexes in America, the bulk of evidence supports the contrary position of Chafetz, which we summarized earlier. We will proceed, therefore, on the basis that while there are important biological differences, most of the traits we think of as masculine or feminine are sociocultural rather than biological. And, whatever biological differences there are, they do not justify the kinds of discrimination and oppression we will describe in this chapter.

Sex Inequality and the Quality of Life

The similarity in justifications and implications of *sex inequality* and racial inequality was pointed out in 1951 by Helen Hacker (1951). Females and blacks, she noted, have been categorized as intellectual inferiors (on the basis of smaller brains in many cases). Both have been said to be more emotional or childlike than white men. Both are thought to have a "proper place," and are fine as long as they stay "in their place." Both have ways of subtly trying to get what they want (blacks try to outwit whites, and women use their feminine wiles). Compared with white males, both groups have fewer educational opportunities, lower-paying jobs, and a history of exclusion from the full rights of citizenship (such as voting).

All of these elements of discrimination are *contradictions between our ideology of equal opportunities and the reality of life for females.* The fact is, women lack certain basic rights that are supposed to be available to all Americans.

The Right to Equal Economic Opportunities

Trends in participation.   A growing percentage of women are *participating in the economy.* As table 11.1 shows, the proportion of employed married women (with husband present) increased from 23.8 percent in 1950 to 49.4 percent in 1979. The most dramatic increase occurred among women with children under 6 years of age. It might appear from this evidence that economic discrimination against women is diminishing, and that women are increasingly

Table 11.1   Percent of Married Women in the Labor Force (Husband Present), by Presence and Age of Children, 1950–1979

	1950	1955	1960	1965	1970	1979
All married women (husband present)	23.8	27.7	30.5	34.7	40.8	49.4
With children under 6 years of age	11.9	16.2	18.6	23.3	30.3	43.2
With children 6–17 years of age only	28.3	34.7	39.0	42.7	49.2	59.1
With no children under 18 years of age	30.3	32.7	34.7	38.3	42.2	46.7

Source: Adapted from U.S. Bureau of the Census, *Statistical Abstract of the United States, 1976 (Washington, D.C.: Government Printing Office, 1977), p. 359; and 1980 (Washington, D.C.: Government Printing Office, 1981), p. 403*

free to enter the labor force even when they have small children at home.

However, we must ask another question. How many women wanted to work during this period? It is possible that there are more women who want to work and cannot find a job today than in 1950. Some evidence on this matter can be seen in table 11.2, which shows *unemployment rates*. Keep in mind that the rates do not include people who do not claim to be in the labor force. The rates give us a measure of the number of people who desire employment but who are out of work. Since the end of World War II, the rates have nearly always been higher for women than for men. Furthermore, the ratio of female:male unemployment was higher in the 1970s than in the 1950s. Even though more women were working than ever before (more *want* to work than ever before), proportionately more females were out of work in 1979 than in 1950. Regarding equal opportunities for employment, sex inequality was greater in the 1970s than in the 1950s or 1960s. Clearly, this situation *contradicts our ideology of equal opportunity*. Equality means that men

and women are equally affected by the changing rates of unemployment.

Thus, the trend in female participation includes both gains and losses. There are gains in the sense that a greater number of women are working, that an increasing proportion of the labor force is female, and that females are gaining access to various kinds of work from which they were once excluded. There are losses in the sense that the unemployment rate among females is higher than before and that some of the well-publicized gains can blind people to the other kinds of inequalities, which we will now discuss.

Career discrimination.   According to our *ideology,* if you have the ability and the determination, you are on your way to success in a career. This ideology, however, is *contradicted* by the *discriminatory treatment of females in various occupations.* There is discrimination both in hiring and in promotions, including discrimination in the sense that females are often barred or discouraged from entering certain occupations. Consider, for example, the following

Table 11.2   Unemployment Rates by Sex, 1948–1979
(persons 16 years and over)

Year	Male	Female
1948	3.6	4.1
1950	5.1	5.7
1955	4.2	4.9
1960	5.4	5.9
1965	4.0	5.5
1970	4.4	5.9
1975	7.9	9.3
1979	5.1	6.8

Source: U.S. Department of Labor, *Employment and Training Report of the President* (Washington, D.C.: Government Printing Office, 1980), p. 249.

Table 11.3   Ratio of Women to Men in Selected Occupations, 1978

Occupation	Ratio of Women : Men
Total employed	0.70
Accountants	0.43
Engineers	0.03
Lawyers and judges	0.10
Librarians, archivists, and curators	4.29
Teachers, except college and university	2.45
Bank officers and financial managers	0.44
Sales managers, except retail trade	0.07
Demonstrators, hucksters, and peddlers	5.67
Sales clerks, retail trade	2.51
Bank tellers	10.82
Secretaries, stenographers, typists	62.89

Source: U.S. Bureau of the Census, *A Statistical Portrait of Women in the United States, 1978* (Washington, D.C.: Government Printing Office, 1980), p. 63.

facts. Although there are far more female than male teachers, the proportion of females in top administrative jobs in education (superintendents, assistant superintendents, principals, and assistant principals) ranged from 3 percent in Utah to 30 percent in Maryland in 1979. At the start of 1979 only 11 of 505 federal judges were female. A 1979 survey of engineering degrees showed that 9 percent of bachelor degrees and 2 percent of doctoral degrees were granted to women (and less than 1 percent of practicing engineers were women).[1] Traditionally, women have not been encouraged to enter the higher prestige, higher paying occupations. Table 11.3 reveals how, in the late 1970s, women were still disproportionately confined to particular kinds of jobs. Perfect equality would make all the ratios 0.7, which was the ratio of total employed women : men.

Females are likely to encounter discriminatory practices as they attempt to break into more desirable kinds of work. They are also likely to encounter *discrimination as they pursue advancement in their careers*. For example, a survey of psychologists in colleges and universities in the West found that, given the same quality of preparation, men were likely to get tenure and the rank of full professor sooner than women.[2] Deckard (1975:120–36) found, similarly, that women in academic life face discriminatory practices at every stage of their careers:

> In 1960 the National Academy of Sciences studied a group of men and women, all of whom got Ph.D.'s in 1935. The study found that women took 2 to 5 years longer to get to full

professor in the natural sciences and 5 to 10 years longer in the social sciences. In fact, an average of only 50 percent of women with a Ph.D. and 20 years' teaching experience are full professors, but an average of 90 percent of men Ph.D.'s with 20 years' teaching experience are full professors [Deckard, 1975:127].

Income discrimination. Slower advancement means that women tend to cluster in the lower levels of virtually all occupational categories and are, therefore, accorded less prestige and lower salaries than men. The demand of the women's movement for *equal pay for work of equivalent value* reflects the fact that women are not rewarded equally with men even when they are equally prepared, equally qualified, and equally competent. The median income of females has gone up, as it has for everyone else. But the gap between male and female earnings changed little between 1956 and 1970. During the 1970s, nonwhite females made gains relative to all males and to white females, but in 1977 white females working full time were farther from equality with white males working full time than they were in 1970 (figure 11.3) and, in fact, than they were in 1956. In 1956 the median income of white, female, full-time workers was 62.8 percent of the median income of males: in 1977, it was 57.7 percent.

We must inquire further into this inequality because there could be multiple causes. We know that income is closely related to education, to occupational category, to proportion of time worked, and so forth. Can the differences between men and women be accounted for by some of these factors? Do women earn less because they have less education, because they work fewer hours, or because they obtain lower-paying jobs?

Figure 11.2 Women protesting their lot in life. Data on employment alone provide good grounds for protest.

Figure 11.3 Median earnings of year-round, full-time workers with income, by race and sex, 1970 to 1977. (Persons 14 years and over.) (Source: U.S. Bureau of the Census, *A Statistical Portrait of Women in the United States: 1978* [Washington, D.C.: Government Printing Office, 1980], p. 97.)

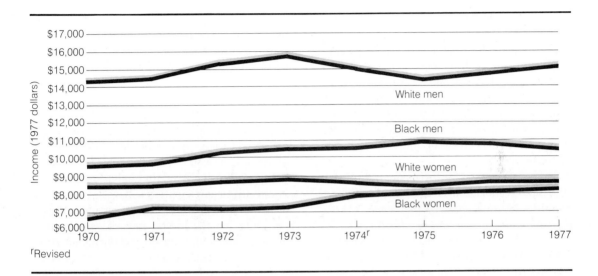

When we group the sexes by educational attainment and look at their incomes, women have lower incomes. If we look at groups of males and females with the same work experience and the same amount of time spent in working, women earn far less than men (Treiman and Terrell, 1975). If we look at male and female union members in the same kind of work, again we find that differences persist (U.S. Department of Labor, Women's Bureau, 1976:109). In fact, males tend to have higher average incomes in every single category for full-time workers—whether union or nonunion. Tsuchigane and Dodge (1974:49) made adjustments for differences in hours worked, educational attainment, job seniority, and absenteeism, and found that these factors accounted for only one-third of the difference between male and female earnings. We can conclude that the remaining two-thirds of the income gap is the result of discrimination against females.

In sum, even when we make allowances for virtually every factor that might influence the difference, women are paid less than men for equal work. The discriminatory income gap is very large: females may average as little as 50 to 60 percent of the income of their male counterparts.

Educational Attainment

Americans *value education.* Furthermore, there is a very close relationship between years of schooling and income as we have seen. In general, the greater the amount of education a person has, the better the positions he or she can obtain.

How do women fare with respect to this valuable resource? At first glance it appears that women and men have equal opportunity for education because in 1974 males and females had almost the same median years of school completed—slightly over 12. The similar median obscures the facts that at one end of the range more males completed four or more years of college, while at the other end of the range more females graduated from high school. In 1979, 20.4 percent of males and 12.9 percent of females completed four or more years of college. When we look at graduate degrees specifically, we find that in 1978, 51.8 percent of all master's degrees and 73.6 percent of all doctorates went to males.[3]

Part of the reason for the inequality in post-high school education is that *the traditional female role (as keepers of the home) contradicts our value of maximum education.*

Another part of the reason is that females are discriminated against in higher education. *Affirmative action programs* to equalize opportunities for females are having some effect, but it is still possible to practice covertly what was once done overtly. Chafetz (1974:135) gives some examples:

> Several institutions have admissions quotas: Stanford requires a 60 percent male class, Princeton three males for every female, Harvard 25 percent female. Females generally need much higher grades to get into college. They also receive substantially less in scholarship money. . . . This fact is especially important when we consider that parents are more willing to make financial sacrifices to send their sons to college than to do so for their daughters. . . . Prejudice and discrimination against female graduate students is even more severe. Thus, in one year 34 percent of the females entering graduate school at the University of Chicago had at least an A minus average, compared to only 27 percent of the males. . . . Some medical schools have even established a combined quota for "minorities," that is, females, blacks, and browns, thus setting them in direct competition with one another, without hindering the opportunities for white males to gain entrance.

Females are less likely than males to have opportunities for maximum education because traditional socialization has been reinforced by established patterns of discrimination.

Political Participation

The American ideology is that all citizens can and should *participate in the political processes* of the nation. Voter apathy is considered cause for alarm. It is believed that only through maximum citizen participation will we have the kind of nation that provides liberty, justice, and opportunity for all. In the case of women, this *ideology contradicts norms and the female role.* The most blatant example of the contradiction is the long exclusion of women from voting rights.

Political participation includes more than voting. Mary Goddard served as postmaster of Baltimore from 1775 to 1789 (Gruberg, 1968:117). Nevertheless, the number of women holding appointed or elected government positions has always been small at all levels—local, state, and national—and the positions have not been the best or more desirable ones. Gruberg (1968:131) pointed out that while the federal government employs a considerable number of women, there are "very few who do important work. . . . Women have moved into government but they have been restricted to positions of lower prestige."

In 1978, two of fifty state governors were women, and 17 of 535 members of Congress were women. Many women are active in political parties, but very few hold top positions. So, although Americans generally value political participation, women do not participate equally with men. They have never been totally excluded from political participation, but they are still a long way from being equally represented in our government. When women do participate, they tend to be deprived of the better positions in politics and in government.

The Right to Dignity as a Human Being

Certain beliefs about women and certain patterns of interaction between men and women are an affront to the dignity of women as human beings. Here again we encounter a *contradiction between our belief in the dignity of human beings and the ideology about a particular group.*

The belief that women are inferior is ancient and pervasive throughout many cultures. Confucius declared that two kinds of people are very difficult to deal with—those of low birth, and women. Women in China had a subservient role for thousands of years. In the West the disparagement of women goes back at least as far as the Greeks. Plato gave thanks that he was a Greek rather than a barbarian, a free man rather than a slave, and a man rather than a woman. Aristotle said that woman is an unfinished man, that she has been left standing on a lower plane of development. In our country the early Puritans were convinced of the inferior intellectual capacities of women. Puritan men believed that women lacked the mental capacity for higher education, and they were told to instruct their wives in religion but to make it "easy" because of their limited abilities. Until recent times, it was widely believed that the presumed inferior intellect of woman was rooted in her smaller brain capacity. When Oberlin College offered women a course of study similar to the men's, it shortened the literary work because of the belief that women could not assimilate as much as men.

The *belief in the inferiority of women,* or at least in the propriety of women's inferior status, is expressed in our language. Certain words and phrases tend to relegate women to an inferior place in our society (if not an inferior place in nature). One obvious example is the masculine orientation of the language—we use "he" and other masculine pronouns to refer to people generally. Positions of dominance typically have a masculine name, such as chairman, policeman, and congressman. Perhaps the masculine nature of English was best summed up in 1923 by the Danish linguist Otto Jespersen. He wrote that English was the most "positively and expressly masculine" of all languages, a language of "a grown-up man, with very little childish or feminine about it" (Strainchamps, 1971:349).

The belief in male dominance and female inferiority is expressed in certain patterns of interaction as well as language. Women who want to interact with men as equals may be subjected to humiliation, particularly when they move into nontraditional areas. Deckard (1975:127) related the following incident between President Nixon and reporter Helen Thomas at a public gathering in the White House:

> He said, "Helen, are you still wearing slacks? Do you prefer them actually? . . . Slacks can do something for some people and some it can't. I think you do very well—turn around. . . . Do they cost less than a gown?" "No," she replied. "Then change," the president suggested, and everyone in the room laughed. It is nice to have a humorous President.

Figure 11.4 Feminists argue that many of our traditions are sexist and dehumanizing for women.

Figure 11.4 Feminists argue that many of our traditions are sexist and dehumanizing for women.

Even when women break through the barriers of discrimination and gain entry into a field, the battle is far from won. A woman may get into graduate school only to hear a comment such as "You're so cute. I can't see you as a professor of anything" (Chafetz, 1974:136). Such experiences tell women they are not really taken seriously by males, that the road ahead includes a struggle for recognition and advancement.

Contributing Factors

Many factors contribute to the problem of sex inequality. These factors include people—both men and women—who recognize that the problem exists, as well as people—both women and men—who do not recognize that a problem exists.

If the inequality is a problem, why aren't all women, or even most women dissatisfied with their lot? The inequality clearly exists, and it bars women from areas of life that are sources of considerable reward in American society. Why do many women accept such a situation? Why don't more women protest? Some answers will emerge as we discuss the structural and social psychological factors involved.

Social Structural Factors

The normative role of the female. Understanding roles is important for understanding human behavior, for roles exist prior to and apart from particular individuals who assume those roles. If you want to be a physician, you don't decide for yourself how to relate to people or treat them; the physician-patient interaction is already defined by social roles. The roles allow for variability, of course, but they also specify certain kinds of behavior as appropriate and other kinds as inappropriate. In other words, we know what it means to be a physician or a patient, a salesperson or a customer, a teacher or a student because all are social roles. Whenever we assume one of these roles, we are likely to behave in the expected ways.

Similarly, there are *sex roles* in every society. The terms "male" and "female" have *social meanings*, and individuals are likely to function in accord with those meanings. As we have seen, the meanings in one society can contradict those in another, and most individuals will conform to the expectations of their own society. What, then, is the *traditional role for the American female?* How has that role contributed to the kinds of inequality we have discussed?

The traditional *homemaker role of women* is paralleled by the traditional role of the male as breadwinner. The woman is expected to provide a good home for her husband and children and find her own fulfillment in caring for her family. Such a role assumes that a woman will marry and have children. Within the traditional role, education is thought to be irrelevant and a career is a deviant path. In the 1960s and 1970s women's attitudes toward this traditional role changed considerably. Nevertheless, the traditional view still received considerable support, particularly with respect to the woman's responsibility for the home (Mason, Czajka, and Arber, 1976).

The extent to which women themselves continue to support the traditional role is seen in female opposition to the *Equal Rights Amendment,* in the notion of the "*total woman*", which emerged in the 1970s, and in similar courses in "fascinating womanhood." The nature of this effort can be inferred from the following newspaper feature story.

> Next time you're angry at your husband, call him names that compliment his masculinity. He's not weak, simpleminded, etc., but a "big tough brute" or a "hairy beast." Stamp your feet, beat your fists on his chest and ask, "How can a great big man like you pick on a poor little girl like me?" Threaten, "I'll tell your mother on you." This advice comes from Mrs. Helen B. Andelin, author of "Fascinating Womanhood.". . . Mrs. Andelin firmly believes that a woman's place is in the home. . . . "Nothing compares with staying at home with my eight children. When my last child was born, I held my baby in my arms, looked out my window and asked, 'What more could a woman want?' "[4]

Marabel Morgan's book *The Total Woman* and courses with the same name "celebrate male dominance and depend on guile and sauciness to get their way, but they use sex more overtly than their fascinating sisters."[5] One aim of both these movements is to get women to *stop competing* with men. According to Mrs. Andelin, a number of the women who take her course quit their jobs.

Some men support the traditional view of the female role, not surprisingly. The blue-collar workers interviewed by LeMasters (1975:84) thought that their wives should work but still had traditional notions about their wives' role. They believed their wives should be satisfied to live in a sex-segregated world. The woman must also care for her home and children adequately. A carpenter was quoted as saying that "if a woman can't take care of the house and the kids, she shouldn't get married." And, a woman must be reliable:

> When a blue-collar aristocrat spends a lot of time with his male buddies he likes to be sure that his children are being cared for properly and that his wife is home minding her business. Above all she must not be "running around" with some other man [LeMasters, 1975:84].

The traditional role obviously discourages women from pursuing higher education or a career. In a social context where being female means taking care of a home and family, it is difficult to find support for a desire to secure an advanced degree or to commit oneself to a career.

Doherty and Culver (1976) surveyed 165 female students in a suburban high school to determine the relationship between their views of their sex roles and their academic achievement and intellectual ability. The girls were classed as "traditional" or "nontraditional" according to their responses to such statements as: "a woman's place is in the home"; "the greatest contribution a wife can make to her husband's progress is her constant and watchful encouragement"; and "it is unfair that women have to give up more than men in order to have a good marriage." The researchers found that girls with nontraditional views of the female sex role (who valued personal fulfillment above marriage and family life) had higher verbal intelligence scores but ranked lower in the class than girls with traditional views.

In other words, nontraditional girls tended to have more ability but lower achievement levels than the traditionalists. The authors suggested one possible explanation for this puzzling finding: the achievement levels may reflect a tendency for teachers to reward females who conform and who are passive and dependent (traits less characteristic of the highly intelligent). In any case, something about the traditional sex role of females apparently worked to the detriment of the brighter female students in this study. One other finding of the researchers is also pertinent to our discussion. About half of the students said they would like to go to college, but only about one-third said they realistically expected to finish college.

Female aspirations and expectations about undergraduate or graduate education are affected by parental views, and many parents hold traditional notions about the female role. In a study of high school seniors in Wisconsin, Sewell and Shah (1968) found that fewer females than males perceived parental encouragement to attend college. Fewer females than males planned to attend college, therefore, and fewer actually did attend, except where both the father and mother or just the mother had a high amount of education. In those cases, boys and girls perceived about the same amount of parental encouragement, and about the same proportions planned to and actually did attend college.

These findings suggest that if females were treated the same as males, they would achieve the same levels of education, and probably the same levels of work and careers, also. We do not know how many women would like to work or pursue a career but do not because it conflicts with other role obligations (as opposed to the number who, for whatever reason, prefer "fascinating womanhood"), but some estimates indicate that there were about 1 million such women between the ages of 16 and 59 in 1974 (U.S. Department of Labor, Women's Bureau, 1976:34).

Figure 11.5 Women are assuming many new roles, although both men and women have resisted such changes.

We pointed out in chapter 5 that the *restrictive role for women can lead to illness*. Depression, for instance, is quite common among middle-aged women who are left with the "empty nest" after their children leave home. Going to work does not resolve all the problems. A woman who breaks out of the traditional constraints and goes to work may have problems of overload. Traditional obligations are not easily cast off even when nontraditional ones are assumed. Consequently, many women who go to work continue to bear the major responsibility for the home.

To have a job outside their home, in other words, often means for women "in addition to" rather than "instead of." The proof is in time-budget studies, which show how people allocate their time to various activities through the day and the week. A study of 1,318 households in New York found that while working women averaged fewer hours per day doing household work than did nonworking women, the amount of time spent by husbands on household work varied little in the two kinds of family. And, the working wife spent anywhere from two to four times as many hours as her husband on household tasks (U.S. Department of Labor, Women's Bureau, 1976:141).

American women are not unique in this regard. In a study of twelve nations, including the United States, a common pattern emerged for women (Robinson, Converse, and Szalai, 1972). Working women tend to bear the main responsibility for household chores and, therefore, have an average of ten hours less free time per week than their husbands. Many men throughout the world, like the blue-collar workers discussed by LeMasters, are willing to have their wives work but are unwilling to relieve them of their traditional responsibility for the home.

Socialization at home and school.   To understand why women tend to accept the traditional role, we must look at their *socialization*. At home and at school (and, for that matter, throughout the culture) women are taught the traditional meaning of their role. They learn it at an early age. When sixty boys and sixty girls between the ages of 2.5 and 11 years were asked to link various items of clothing, household tools, and equipment with sex roles, they were remarkably accurate, even at the age of 30 to 40 months (Vener and Snyder, 1966). The children were also asked their preferences for the various objects. Girls at all ages preferred traditionally female-appropriate items, while boys from the age of 51 months on chose mainly male-appropriate items.

Girls and boys also learn "appropriate" kinds of work at an early age. Looft (1971) asked second-grade girls what they wanted to be when they grew up and how strongly they felt they would reach those goals. Most of the girls named occupations traditionally associated with females (nurse and teacher were the most frequent). When asked if they really expected to become what they desired, some changed and said they would probably become mothers and housewives.

Another study of *occupational aspirations* among young children was conducted by Schlossberg and Goodman (1972), who worked with kindergarteners and sixth graders in two elementary schools. The children were shown a set of drawings of various work settings, half of which were traditionally male and half traditionally female. The children were asked whether a man or a woman could do each job, and were also asked about their own aspirations. The researchers found *stereotyped notions about occupations* among both the kindergarteners and the sixth graders. The children tended to accept the traditional sex-appropriate divisions of work. They also tended to believe that men can perform most of the traditionally female jobs but that women cannot perform most of the traditionally male jobs. Finally, most of their aspirations followed the traditional stereotypes.

Children learn at an early age what kinds of things and what kinds of feelings and behaviors are considered appropriate for males and for females. Because socialization rather than biology accounts for the differences, the emphasis is on "learn."

Socialization occurs at home, at school—everywhere. Hoffman (1972) showed that in innumerable ways, some subtle and some not so subtle, little *girls are taught to be dependent and passive* and boys are taught to be independent and aggressive. Boys are trained to be independent at an early age; girls are taught independence less frequently and at a later age. For instance, when mothers in one study were asked the age at which they allowed their children to do things such as cross a street alone or play away from home without telling her, the age given for girls was consistently later than that for boys. Girls are treated as if they are more fragile and less needful of achievement than boys. Parents tend to express more delight in the achievements of their sons. At an early age, when the infant is first learning to walk, the mother may watch her daughter anxiously and her son with admiration. The infant observing such reactions will develop a greater or lesser sense of self-confidence, depending on whether the infant is a boy or a girl.

Sex-role teaching is reinforced by television (McGhee and Frueh, 1980) and by picture books. Lenore Weitzman and her associates examined award-winning picture books for preschool children (Weitzman, 1972) and found that females tend to be invisible, because most of the books are about boys or men or male animals. There were approximately eleven pictures of males for every one picture of a female! When females were shown, they were often either insignificant or inconspicuous. Different kinds of activities are shown with boys being generally depicted as active and girls as passive. "Not only are boys presented in more exciting and adventuresome roles, but they engage in more varied pursuits and demand more independence" (Weitzman et al., 1972:1131). The girls are shown indoors more often than the boys, and even the youngest girls are shown in traditional female tasks such as pleasing and helping their brothers and fathers. When adults appear in the books, they too fit the stereotypes. Women had *status as wives of achieving men,* for instance, but were not engaged in their own achievements. The researchers concluded:

> The world of picture books never tells little girls that as women they might find fulfillment outside of their homes or through intellectual pursuits. Women are excluded from the world of sports, politics, and science. Their future occupational world is presented as consisting primarily of glamour and service. Ironically, many of these books are written by prize-winning female authors whose own lives are probably unlike those they advertise [Weitzman et al., 1972:1146].

If the very young child is not saturated with notions of appropriate sex-role behavior from experiences within the family, the school will do its part to teach the traditional expectations. A survey of 134 readers used in elementary schools in New Jersey showed five boy-centered for every two girl-centered stories; three times as many adult male characters as adult female characters in major roles; six times as many male as female biographies; twice as many male as female animal stories; and four times as many male as female folk and fantasy stories (Deckard, 1975:32). Again, although females are a slight majority of the population, they are a decided minority in school books.

Children learn that they live in a male-dominated world, where men are engaged in demanding, exciting activities and women are keepers of the home and family. It is not surprising, then, that when a group of fifth and sixth graders were asked to name their heroes, the boys chose on the basis of possessions or activities or power, while the girls were more likely to choose on the basis of qualities such as goodness, niceness, and honesty (Hawkes, 1973). What we learn at an early age at home and at school legitimates the restricted role traditionally assigned the female. These inequalities between the sexes cause great difficulties to women who attempt to carve out a nontraditional kind of life for themselves.

The economics of sex inequality. Any situation that continues to exist in our country is likely to be *profitable* to someone, and sex inequality is no exception. For males, the kind of sex inequalities we have discussed are profitable in a twofold sense: they increase male job opportunities and male incomes.

The history of women's participation in the labor market is a checkered affair. Just before 1941 and the entry of the U.S. into World War II, many businesses would not hire a woman who was over 35. The war caused a serious shortage of men in business and industry, and women flocked into the factories and offices. During the height of the depression of the 1930s, more than 80 percent of Americans strongly opposed employment of married women. By 1942 only 13 percent were opposed; 71 percent said the country needed more married women in jobs (Chafe, 1972:148). It appeared that American women had established a major beachhead in the labor market.

When the war ended and the men returned home, public opinion again turned against employment of women, particularly married women. Fear of another economic recession and persisting hostility toward the notion of women competing with men in the economy were two important factors among the several involved, according to Chafe (1972:176–77). Many women were fired in order to create more jobs for the vast numbers of returning servicemen. But, many women who did not want to return to their homes continued to work. Obviously, women prefer to participate in the economy to a greater extent than many men consider appropriate or desirable. Men want no additional competition for jobs.

Since sex inequality also means that women are paid less than men, on the average, this is a profitable arrangement for males. They can reserve better-paying jobs for themselves. In our economic system are a number of menial and low-paying jobs that must be done by someone if other jobs are to be highly paid and employers are to maintain high levels of profit. Who will take such jobs?

Szymanski (1976) showed that *sexism and racism are "functional substitutes"* with respect to such jobs. That is, either women or racial minorities tend to cluster in the low-paying, menial jobs. Racial minorities, where they are available, provide that labor. Where they are not available, women provide the labor. The greater the racial discrimination in an area, the less the sex discrimination, and vice versa. This does not mean that where racial minorities are available for low-paying jobs, women are equal to men in the labor market. Women are merely better off in such cases; they are next to the lowest group on the totem pole rather than the lowest.

The politics of sex inequality.   The history of women is a history of *legal subservience.* Men have dominated government and used their political power to maintain social dominance. In the early days of our country, married women had no right to sign contracts, to keep their own earnings, to have title to property even if they had inherited it, or to keep their children in the case of a legal separation from a husband. When a woman married she lost the rights she had as a single person, and those rights were not the same as a man's.

Women have made considerable legal gains since the founding of the nation, but they still suffer discrimination in some legal matters. In the few states that still have community property laws, for instance, the husband has the ex-clusive right to manage and control the property (which may include the earnings of both husband and wife). Some states have restrictive laws with regard to a woman's right to sign contracts or engage in business on her own. A woman attempting to get credit for some enterprise may find that she is treated quite differently from a man.

Discriminatory laws often have assumed or asserted the traditional, stereotyped sex roles. A 1908 decision of the United States Supreme Court justified legislation that regulated women's hours of work by the argument that "woman has always been dependent upon man," and even if the law made men and women completely equal, "it would still be true that she . . . will rest upon and look to him for protection" (Chafe, 1972:128). In this particular case the legislation benefited women. Unfortunately, the rationale used by the court is not beneficial in the long run, for it is used time and again to justify the legal subservience of women.

Men sometimes have legal recourse that is denied to women under similar circumstances. Chafe (1972:121) cited some examples with respect to sexual behavior:

> In Virginia a father could not be required to contribute to the maintenance of his illegitimate child. In Maryland a husband could divorce his wife if she had been unchaste before marriage. And in Minnesota a man whose wife was guilty of adultery could collect damages from her lover—a recourse denied the wife in a similar situation.

The laws of our land—not to mention those of other countries—have discriminated between men and women in many ways, perpetuating inequalities.

Figure 11.6 Women have made considerable legal gains since the founding of the nation, but they still suffer discrimination in some legal matters.

The religious justification. Justification of sex inequality is embedded in both the teachings and practices of all the world's religions, as Deckard (1975:5–7) showed. They all imply or assert specifically that men are superior to women and that women should be subservient.

In Christianity, for example, the teachings of St. Paul are that it is the duty of the woman to be submissive to her husband and to learn in silence in the church "with all subjection"; that woman was created for the sake of man rather than man created for the sake of woman.

The practices of religions, like the teachings, legitimate the social dominance of males. Women generally do not hold the honored positions—minister, priest, rabbi. A few groups have ordained women in recent years. But, even denominations that are very liberal in other respects may resist female leaders. In 1977 the presiding Bishop of the Episcopal Church said that his understanding of the Christian position would not allow him to believe "that women can be priests any more than they can become fathers or husbands."[6] Lay religious leaders are likely to be male also, even though females may be more numerously, regularly, and fully involved in the activities of the group. Some religious groups still segregate males and females in worship or educational gatherings, and even require females to maintain silence during worship (in the sense that females do not speak before the group). Finally, the impact of religion, and particularly of the *more conservative* religious groups, is seen in the fact that many churches are among the strongest opponents of ERA (Arrington and Kyle, 1978).

Social Psychological Factors

Attitudes and values. The structural factors we have identified that perpetuate sex inequality are themselves perpetuated by attitudes and values of both men and women. Consider the results of a number of polls. A 1977 poll showed that 41 percent of men and 47 percent of women believed that the women's movement has been a major cause of family breakdown. A 1978 poll reported that 47 percent of the respondents agreed that the notion "A woman's place is in the home" still makes sense; 39 percent completely believed and another 39 percent partially believed that a wife should put her husband and children ahead of her own career; and 22 percent completely believed and 30 percent partially believed that the wife is responsible for keeping the house clean and neat even if she works as hard as her husband. Finally, a 1980 poll reported that 42 percent of both men and women said that the most satisfying and interesting way of life would be a traditional marriage, with husband working and wife caring for the home and children.[7]

The *traditional stereotypes of the sexes* reflected in our various attitudes and values portray women as more emotional, less logical, more passive, more dependent, more fragile, and more interested in domestic matters than are men. Women are supposed to find gratification in caring for their home and family. Men are supposed to find gratification in competing in the world outside of the home.

Such stereotyped attitudes lead naturally to the notion that women require less education than men. Recall that girls reported less parental encouragement to attend college than did boys. The blue-collar respondents LeMasters (1975:114) interviewed believed that most of what their daughters needed to learn could be obtained at home from their mothers, and that if money was allocated for college, it should go to the sons. Some male college professors appear to have traditional attitudes; some of them have negative attitudes about females in graduate work, or doubt the seriousness of women who pursue higher degrees. Ann Sutherland Harris recorded statements such as the following (Chafetz, 1974:135–36):

> I know you're competent and your thesis advisor knows you're competent. The question in our minds is are you *really serious* about what you're doing.
>
> A pretty girl like you will certainly get married; why don't you stop with an M.A.?
>
> We expect women who come here to be competent, good students, but we don't expect them to be brilliant or original.
>
> Somehow I can never take women in this field seriously.

It is not surprising that female college students have been found to have lower aspirations for higher education than male students, and that they set lower goals despite their apparently equal capability for graduate education (Coates and Southern, 1972).

Even if women hurdle the barriers to a professional career, discriminatory attitudes still persist. Quadagno (1976) studied medical specialties to determine the extent of sex-typing. She found that the 6.9 percent of American physicians who were women in 1971 were not equally distributed over the several specialties.

A smaller proportion of female physicians specialized in surgery and heart disease; the larger proportion went into pediatrics, psychiatry, and public health.

How do the medical specialties themselves reflect traditional or stereotyped attitudes? Quadagno interviewed fifty-eight physicians—thirty males and twenty-eight females—who ranged from recent graduates to people nearing retirement. The physicians were asked to rate five specialties in terms of the "characteristics of specialists." The list of characteristics from which choices were made had been previously rated by other research techniques as traditionally "masculine" or "feminine." The five specialties included two that a disproportionately large number of female physicians entered, pediatrics and psychiatry; two that were "neutral," radiology and dermatology; and one that a disproportionately small number of female physicians entered, thoracic surgery.

The results showed that stereotypes are indeed attached to the specialties, and that younger physicians had even more sex-typed notions than older physicians. Young male physicians tended to see pediatrics and psychiatry as requiring traditionally feminine traits, while the young female physicians saw thoracic surgery in terms of traditionally masculine traits. These findings suggest that sex-typing of medical specialties may be increasing, and that, in the future, an even greater proportion of pediatricians and psychiatrists will be female and a greater proportion of surgeons will be male. Since surgery is the most prestigious and the best paid of all medical specialties, one might infer that women will continue to suffer from inequality even within a prestigious occupation.

In the interviews she conducted, Quadagno also found that women tend to be pressured into particular specialties, and that males have negative attitudes about women entering certain specialties, particularly surgery. One woman said that her chairman had complained when she was assigned to him because he had asked never to be given a female. Another woman reported a similar problem:

I liked surgery, but I never thought about it real seriously, I think because surgery was my first module, and I had a bunch of residents who really did not appreciate women. They just plain don't think you belong. You're a foreigner. In a way you're not even there. . . . The residents I had, they were of the opinion that women couldn't do surgery, because they didn't have the stamina, which is ridiculous. They kind of changed their minds by the time I was finished because obviously I could keep up with all of them [Quadagno, 1976:450].

Women must contend with negative attitudes about entering the better positions in medicine, just as they must confront the same attitudes in business and industry. In an experiment designed to tap the attitudes of managers, Rosen and Jerdee (1974) sent questionnaires to subscribers of a noted business journal asking the managers to make decisions about a number of problem situations involving employees. For each situation, the employee was identified as a male to some of the managers and as a female to others. A total of 1,500 managers returned the questionnaire, and they clearly expressed different attitudes toward hypothetical female and male employees.

For instance, in one situation there is a quarrel between a junior executive and his wife, or her husband, because the spouse does not want to go to a boring cocktail party where the executive feels attendance would be a plus for his or her career. When the executive was a man and the spouse a woman, almost 70 percent of the managers thought the wife should attend the party. But, when the executive was a woman and the spouse a man, less than half the managers felt that the husband should attend. The managers also indicated they would try harder to keep a male employee than a female if the spouse wanted to take a job that required a move to a different city. Similarly, managers were more willing to promote a male who said that his "first duty is to my family" than a female who made the same statement.

Attitudes of males need not be negative to express and reinforce stereotyped ideas about the sexes. A female acquaintance of the author was struggling to break into an overcrowded profession. Her children were grown, and she had gone back to school and completed her education. When she discussed with a male friend in the profession her frustrations about getting a job, he was sympathetic. He wanted her in the profession but, recognizing the shortage of jobs, he said to her, "Have you ever thought about having another baby?" Helpful though he intended to be, his attitude reflected the stereotyped view that a woman can find fulfillment in home and family and, therefore, does not need a career as a man does.

What are the attitudes and values of women? What is the effect of years of socialization in home and school and of stereotyped attitudes throughout the society? Women often have negative attitudes about their abilities and about the appropriateness of pursuing a career. They thereby help to perpetuate their own inequality. In a study designed to determine the effects of sex-role stereotypes on the way people think about themselves, seventy-four male and eighty female students were given a questionnaire that measured their ideas of the typical traits of males and females (Rosenkrantz et al., 1968). The students agreed that there are differences between the sexes. Both male and female students valued the established masculine traits more often than they did the feminine traits, and the female students did not have as high a sense of self-worth as did the male students.

Given this tendency to value masculine traits and a sense of being less worthy than the other sex, it is not surprising that women are often inhibited about trying to enter the male-dominated spheres.

Ideology and inequality.   In the nineteenth century, numerous American writers stressed two "facts" about women. First, women were said to have a "higher nature" than men, in the sense that they are more virtuous. Second, women were said to have a higher calling than men, a nobler work to perform, because they were the guardians of the nation's morality through their example and their influence on children. If a woman failed to fulfill her role, therefore, one of the guardians of society abdicated from her position of responsibility. The consequences could be nothing less than damaging. As Philip Wylie, one of the more severe writers of recent times, expressed it:

> Mom got herself out of the nursery and the kitchen. She then got out of the house. . . . She also got herself the vote, and, although politics never interested her (unless she was exceptionally naive, a hairy foghorn, or a size 40 scorpion) the damage she forthwith did to society was so enormous and so rapid that the best men lost track of things . . . political

scurviness, hoodlumism, gangsterism, labor strife, monopolistic thuggery, moral degeneration, civil corruption, smuggling, bribery, theft, murder, homosexuality, drunkenness, financial depression, chaos, and war [Deckard, 1975:3–4].

Most American men would not go to such extremes in attributing moral and social decay to the abdication of women from their domestic role. However, many Americans still believe that the woman's place is in the home, and when she leaves the home to pursue higher education or a career, she leaves her post as one of the guardians of the social order. The ideology that *abdication of women from the home* can only result in *social disorganization* was expressed by those who insisted that women return to their homes after World War II. They identified working women as a primary cause of delinquency and argued that for women to continue in the labor force would mean instability in the social institutions of the nation. A Barnard College sociologist asserted that women had "gotten out of hand" during the war "with the result that children were neglected and the very survival of the home was endangered" (Chafe, 1972:176).

Bayer (1975) reported a survey of 188,900 college freshmen that included the following statement for the students to respond to: "The activities of married women are best confined to the home and family." Those who said they "strongly agree" with the statement were categorized as sexists. A total of 23,700 made the sexist response—16 percent of the males and 8 percent of the females. Analysis of the respondents showed that they were disproportionately black, from the lower socioeconomic strata, nonurban, and male. In comparison with nonsexists, they also tended to be older than their peers, to be less academically successful, and to have lower educational aspirations.

Since an important part of the ideology asserts that a mother's working harms her children, we need to ask whether that is indeed true. Many Americans agree with the idea that a mother with small children (and, in some cases, with any children) should remain at home. Claire Etaugh (1974) made an exhaustive analysis of the research from 1963 to 1972 on the effects of maternal employment. The studies showed that the relationship between the mother and the infants or preschoolers depended on the *quality and intensity of interaction* whether or not the mother was working, not on whether the mother was available constantly. The important thing for the preschooler is that he or she have "stimulating caretaking arrangements" so that personal and cognitive development can occur while the mother is working. With respect to children of other ages, the research is summarized as follows:

> Studies of elementary school children do not reveal clearcut or consistent differences in adjustment related to maternal employment. Mothers who are satisfied with their roles— whether working or not—have the best-adjusted children. The mother's working has little effect on the adjustment of adolescents, although lower-class boys and girls may have some problems adjusting to full-time maternal employment. . . . Maternal employment appears to be unrelated to academic achievement for girls, and either unrelated or negatively related for boys. Mothers in professional occupations tend to have highly achieving children. Educational aspirations generally are higher among both sons and daughters of working mothers. Similarly, working women's daughters have higher career aspirations and more often choose male-dominated careers than do daughters of

nonworking women. Maternal employment is largely unrelated to children's perceptions of maternal behavior, but it is associated with less favorable perceptions of the father among lower-class boys [Etaugh, 1974:90].

One could argue that maternal employment has more desirable than undesirable effects. Even undesirable effects are not necessarily the result of the mother working. Woods (1972) studied a sample of fifth-grade students from a lower-class community who had working mothers. The researcher found that problems with intellectual development and school relations occurred only where the mother's working resulted in a lack of supervision of the child. The problem was not working per se. In fact, the mother's working full-time seemed to increase the adjustment of the children when they were supervised.

Various other *myths* about the consequences of women working all have the basic purpose— to justify resistance to women's entering the labor force. These myths have been identified and refuted by the U.S. Department of Labor, Women's Bureau (1974):

The Myth	The Reality
Women aren't seriously attached to the labor force; they work only for extra pocket money.	Of the nearly 34 million women in the labor force in March 1973, nearly half were working because of pressing economic need.
Women are out ill more than male workers; they cost the company more.	A recent Public Health Service study shows . . . 5.6 days a year for women compared with 5.2 for men.

Women don't work as long or as regularly as their male co-workers; their training is costly—and largely wasted.

A declining number of women leave work for marriage and children. But even among those who do leave, a majority return when their children are in school. . . . Studies on labor turnover indicate that net differences for men and women are generally small.

Married women take jobs away from men. . . .

If all the married women stayed home and unemployed men were placed in their jobs, there would be 17.3 million unfilled jobs. Moreover, most unemployed men do not have the education or the skill to qualify for many of the jobs held by women. . . .

Women don't want responsibility on the job; they don't want promotions or job changes which add to their load.

Relatively few women have been offered positions of responsibility. But when given these opportunities, women, like men, do cope with job responsibilities in addition to personal or family responsibilities.

What Is To Be Done?

The conflict between those who insist on equal rights and opportunities for women and those who insist that woman's place is in the home has been waged since the beginning of our nation. The size and strength of the former group have increased over time, but a large number of the women themselves remain in the latter group. However, efforts at "*consciousness raising*" have been helping women become aware of their situation, their potential for change and growth, and their need for concerted action.

The technique of consciousness raising was developed by radical feminists and was quickly adopted by more moderate groups of women as a valuable tool. Deckard (1975:431) described the typical group as having five to fifteen women who meet weekly for six to eighteen months. The groups encourage free discussion, and sometimes a "facilitator" tries to move the women from their personal experiences to an analysis of the society in which they live. Normally, a particular topic is set for each session, and all the women are encouraged to express their thoughts and feelings. The participants, according to Deckard (1975:431):

> . . . almost universally consider the experience not just worthwhile but one of the most important of their lives. Reexamining the notions one has held since childhood and being truly honest with oneself is painful, yet it is necessary if one is to start on the long journey toward becoming a free woman.

Consciousness raising groups have been criticized on the grounds that they too often failed to result in concrete action. It is not enough to become aware of inequality; the oppressed must take action to alter their situation. What kind of action can address the problems of women? Alice Rossi (1964) suggested three important areas that need attention: child care, residence, and education.

Child-care centers need to be established so that mothers can be free to pursue full-time careers or perhaps part-time jobs. As we have seen, the children of satisfied mothers are better adjusted, whether the mothers stay at home or work away from home. The option of working is closed to many women unless child-care centers are available. Such centers are also a part of the "bill of rights" of the National Organization of Women (NOW).

Rossi's second area of concern, residence, refers to the fact that the *suburban residential pattern* greatly restricts the opportunities of many women: "Not only does she have to do and be more things to her children, but she is confined to the limitations of the suburban community for a great many of her extrafamilial experiences" (Rossi, 1964:635). A change of residential patterns could open many opportunities for women; the central cities still contain a large number of the more prestigious and high-paying jobs.

Education is crucial in order to alter notions of the "proper" roles of the sexes and to attack the ideology that restricts women to the home. Education can help people develop new ideas about the capabilities of women and new child-rearing patterns so that females are no longer socialized into a subordinate role, and to develop new norms about women participating in all sectors of the economy.

Legal changes would be involved in or would facilitate many of the changes mentioned earlier. The *Affirmative Action program* was designed to do more than eliminate discriminatory practices. Employers are supposed to take positive steps to increase the number of women and racial minorities on their payrolls, and to insure that women and racial minorities have equal opportunities for advancement once they are hired. The program is enforced by the withholding of government funds from employers who do not comply with the guidelines (which means, of course, that the program cannot help where no government money is involved).

Another legal change that many observers feel will help is the *Equal Rights Amendment* (ERA) to the Constitution. The ERA was proposed in 1923 by the National Women's Party and was immediately opposed by some women's groups as well as by men. In its initial form, it simply said: "Men and women shall have equal rights throughout the United States and every place subject to its jurisdiction" (Chafe, 1972:112). Although introduced continually into Congress for half a century, and finally passed in 1972, the amendment still has not been adopted into the Constitution because of the opposition of state legislatures. The amendment would prohibit different treatment of anyone on the basis of sex.

The *intergroup conflict* surrounding the ERA has involved some unusual groupings. As Freeman (1975:217) noted, when the Congress passed the ERA in 1972, people could hardly decide their attitude toward it on the basis of which groups supported it and which opposed it. The initial opposition included labor, the John Birch Society, the National Council of Catholic Women, and the Communist party.

Soon after, a good part of the opposition seemed to be coming from various right-wing groups. In 1973 noted right-wing author Phyllis Schlafly gained national attention with a "Stop ERA" campaign. The arguments used against the ERA include the ideas that women need to be protected and that a whole chain of undesirable consequences will follow upon the ratification of the amendment. Among the undesirable consequences, according to the opponents, are that women would be drafted into military service; a woman's right to be supported by her husband would be lost; and things

Involvement

Getting Rid of the "Sugar and Spice" Syndrome

Some social work students at a Midwestern university put together a "Women's Awareness Workshop" as a community project required for one of their courses. It included a talk on female sexuality by a worker from Planned Parenthood, a discussion of rape, and a demonstration of assertiveness training by a psychiatric social worker. Competent, experienced leaders for the workshop were enlisted through university and community resources.

Work with a group of students to set up a similar workshop in your community. It could be concentrated in one day or weekend, or spread over a period of time, as was the program described in the illustration.

First, talk with professional and business women in the community to identify the primary needs of women in your area. Discuss the workshop with them and get suggestions for topics and workshop leaders. The women will probably be both resources and potential clientele.

As a part of the workshop, or as an alternative project, set up a "consciousness raising" group. Talk with someone who has participated in such a group, if possible, and gather literature on the topic for ideas about how to conduct it. You could also set up a mixed group of males and females to discuss the meaning of sex roles and of being a female in our society. The mixed group could identify how traditionally defined sex roles impose stress on males as well as females.

September

22

Where are we coming from?

Film: The Emerging Woman
Discussion leader: *Dr. Jean Fields, Lindenwood College*

To what extent do customs appropriate to another era fit our present way of life? The film evokes the social, economic, and cultural history of American Women from the 1800s to the present. The discussion will focus on the constants and the changes of the past two hundred years.

September

29

What are little girls made of?

Film: Girls at Twelve
Discussion leader: *Dr. Penelope Biggs, Lindenwood College*

In the film we will see three twelve-year-old girls responding to social pressures molding them into women. In the discussion we will examine some of the ideas underlying our expectations that women will behave one way, men another.

October

6

Sugar and spikes

Film: Anything You Want to Be
Videotape: Sugar and Spikes
Discussion leader: Dr. Russell McIntire, Lambuth College

Two short pictorial essays present the difficulties of breaking out of the traditional feminine mold. We will discuss what usually happens when girls and women try to enter customarily male pursuits.

Organizers of this series of programs planned everything well ahead of the event. They generated interest by announcements through the local newspaper and radio and TV stations and by distributing a brochure widely to schools, businesses, and to the mailing lists of many local organizations.

emerging women

A series of public programs featuring films and discussions about the status of women in American society.

Sponsored by the **Tennessee Committee for the Humanities** *and the Jackson chapter of the* **National Organization for Women.**

Where have we been?
Where are we now?
Where are we going?

October

13

The twenty-four hour working day

Films: Tiger on a Tight Leash
Fortunately I Need Little Sleep
Chris and Bernie
Discussion leader: Joyce Beiswenger, M.A., Center for Women's Studies, Nashville

Three short films depict working mothers talking about their life styles. Our discussion will center on the problems and rewards of mothers who work.

such as prisons and public toilets would be sexually desegregated.

Proponents of the ERA dismiss such arguments as irrelevant or nonsensical. They argue that women are not a special breed of humanity who require special legal protection (which really means legal discrimination anyway). Women are capable of doing whatever men do, and should not be prevented from doing things either by law or by custom. Women should have the same rights and privileges as men have. A woman should be able to choose for herself whether she wants to be a housewife, a professional, a factory worker, a mechanic, and there should be neither stigma nor impediment to any of those choices.

Passage of ERA can be an important victory for women. As the legal basis for equality, it could, in turn, help change attitudes and alter ideologies. The goal of sex equality can also be aided through an attack on sexism in the socialization process. So long as girls learn a subservient and restricted role through school experiences, books, and parental expectations, equality will be difficult to achieve.

Summary

Because they have suffered some of the same problems as racial minorities, women have been called our "largest minority," and, in fact, they comprise the majority of our population—over 51 percent. Until recently, much professional as well as popular opinion was that the disadvantages of women are rooted in biology rather than in society. In other words, many Americans have accepted the idea that women are less capable than men, and that what we consider feminine and masculine traits are due to biological

differences. Freud and, more recently, Lionel Tiger argued that differences between men and women have a biological basis and that the differences are justification for a subordinate position of women. But, the bulk of the evidence shows that sociocultural rather than biological factors account for most differences between men and women.

The effects of sex inequality have, in some ways, been similar to the effects of racial inequalities. Women have been denied the right to equal economic opportunities. An increasing proportion of the labor force is female, but the unemployment rate among women has also increased. There is considerable evidence of discrimination in career entry, advancement, and salary in all occupational categories. Women have also suffered discrimination in opportunities for higher education. They are less likely than men to hold desirable political positions. And, various beliefs and patterns of interaction between men and women violate women's dignity as human beings.

The normative role of women in society is one of the most important structural factors perpetuating their problems. Because their traditional role is home-centered, women are discouraged from pursuing higher education or work or a career. Parents who hold to such a role are less likely to encourage their daughters to obtain advanced degrees or follow a career. Norms about the female role are so strong that women who go to work tend to continue to assume major responsibility for the home.

Women accept the traditional role because of their socialization at home and school. They learn the traditional role at a very early age, and most aspects of the culture reinforce that learning. Men can easily accept the traditional

Figure 11.8 Evidence shows that neither children nor the social order are damaged by working women.

role for women because it maximizes their economic advantages. Our legal and religious systems are other structural factors that maintain the subordination of women.

Among social psychological factors involved in sex inequalities, certain attitudes and values reflect the traditional stereotypes of the sexes. Both men and women have tended to believe that women are more emotional, less logical, more passive, more dependent, more fragile, and more interested in domestic affairs. Such attitudes justify discrimination against women in education and work. Women themselves have often accepted the stereotype and have tended, then, to devalue themselves and to set lower goals for themselves.

Inequality is also perpetuated by the ideology that says women are more virtuous than men and therefore their high calling is to act as guardians of the nation's morality and social order. Women who choose to focus their activities outside the home are said to abdicate their responsibility, leading to inevitable damage to society. The evidence contradicts the ideology, showing that neither children nor the social order are damaged by working women. But, the ideology inhibits women who accept it from seeking higher education and participating in the economy.

Glossary

gender   sex; male or female

innate   existing in an individual from birth

sexism   prejudice or discrimination against someone because of his or her sex

sex role   the behavior that any particular society considers appropriate for each sex

For Further Reading

Abramson, Joan. *The Invisible Woman: Discrimination in the Academic Profession.* San Francisco: Jossey-Bass, 1975. An interesting, readable account of a woman's experience when she protested her denial of tenure at a large university.

Flexner, Eleanor. *Century of Struggle: The Woman's Rights Movement in the United States.* New York: Atheneum, 1972. An excellent and thorough history of the struggle of American women—both white and black—from colonial times to 1920.

Friedan, Betty. *The Feminine Mystique.* New York: Dell, 1963. The book that helped begin the current phase of the women's movement. Shows the subordinate role of women in America and the negative consequences for society.

Gornick, Vivian, and Barbara K. Moran, eds. *Woman in Sexist Society; Studies in Power and Powerlessness.* New York: Mentor Books, 1971. A collection of essays that deal with virtually every aspect of the problems of women, including myths and reality about beauty, love, and marriage; socialization; work and education; and controversies over the feminist movement.

Kirkpatrick, Jeanne J. *Political Woman.* New York: Basic Books, 1974. Based on a study of female state senators and representatives and a comparative sample of male state legislators. Relates the particular difficulties faced by women as they attempt to participate in the political process on an equal basis.

Rossi, Alice S., ed. *The Feminist Papers: From Adams to de Beauvoir.* New York: Bantam Books, 1973. A collection of essays by feminists over a span of two centuries. Includes both American and foreign writers on topics such as human freedom, sexism in politics and the economy, and the meaning of sex roles.

Notes

1. Foregoing figures taken from *The National Now Times News,* August 1979 and November 1979; and the *Newsletter* of the Engineers Joint Council, December 1979.
2. Reported in *Human Behavior,* January 1975, p. 62.
3. Data in this paragraph taken from U.S. Bureau of the Census, *Statistical Abstract of the United States, 1980* (Washington, D.C.: Government Printing Office, 1981), pp. 149 and 174.
4. *St. Louis Post-Dispatch,* July 20, 1975.
5. *Time,* March 10, 1975, p. 77.
6. Ibid., October 17, 1977, p. 80.
7. Polls reported in *Public Opinion,* January/February 1979, pp. 38, and December/January 1980, p. 34; and *St. Louis Post-Dispatch,* April 27, 1980.

Racial Minorities

1   **What are the different ways of defining "race"?**

2   **Do nonwhites in America have the same rights as whites?**

3   **Is there a superior group of people?**

4   **Is the race problem merely a matter of prejudice?**

5   **What is reverse discrimination?**

Are people with white skin biologically inferior? Are they inherently less capable, less deserving, or less willing to work to get ahead than others? For most Americans the questions sound absurd, but millions of nonwhite Americans confront such questions about themselves. Throughout our history, our racial minorities have been declared to be, and treated as if they were somehow inferior human beings.

Among both professional and lay people, there are two contrary positions about differences among people: one argues for inherent differences, while the other argues that people are basically alike, or that any average differences between one group of people and another are due to cultural and social factors (learned) more than they are **biological characteristics** (genetically transmitted).

Some social scientists argue that certain races are biologically superior, while others maintain that any racial inequalities must be accounted for by sociocultural rather than biological factors. This chapter is based upon the latter position. There are significant racial differences in a variety of matters, but the differences are basically rooted in sociocultural factors.

Before discussing the race *problem,* therefore, we need to inquire into the meaning of **race.** Then, we will discuss briefly the origin and distribution of America's racial minorities, what the "race problem" means for those groups, what factors contribute to the problem, and how the problem can be attacked.

The Meaning of Race

For many people, the meaning of the term "race" is simple: different races are people of different *skin colors*. There are problems with this simple method of distinguishing races. For one, skin coloring varies enormously. There are people whose parents are of one "race" but who could easily be classified as members of a different "race" on the basis of skin color. Furthermore, because there are so many shades of skin color, classifying a person as a member of one or another race on that basis is arbitrary.

Another problem with this simple method is that it is based on a biological characteristic, and there are other biological characteristics by which people could be classified. For example, we could classify individuals according to blood type, or according to the presence or absence of the RH factor in their blood, or according to their ability to taste the chemical phenylthiocarbamide—and in each case the groups would be composed of different people. For instance, people who can taste the chemical (as opposed to those who cannot taste it) include large numbers of Europeans, Americans, American Indians, and Chinese. The point is, any biological basis for distinguishing among people is arbitrary and results in different groupings, depending on which characteristic is used. Thus, the popular division of people into races by the skin colors of red, black, brown, yellow, and white is an arbitrary procedure that masks certain other differences as well as certain other similarities among people.

All human beings belong to one biological species—*Homo sapiens*. The breakdown of that species into subcategories is somewhat arbitrary, as evidenced by the fact that neither geneticists nor physical anthropologists agree on one particular classification scheme. A frequently used system of classification, devised by Coon, Garn, and Birdsell (1950), used geographical distributions, **morphological** characteristics, and population size to identify six major "stocks" comprising thirty races. The six stocks are: Mongoloid, White, Negroid, Australoid, American Indian, and Polynesian. Each represents a group of races that shares certain characteristics. For example, the Mongoloid category includes all races that have adapted to very severe winters; the Negroid category includes all races that have achieved special adaptation to severe light and heat.

No matter how we divide people into groups according to geographical distribution and certain biological characteristics, keep in mind that all people have far more shared than especial characteristics, and that no group is biologically superior to another. Some advocates of racial superiority argue that there are average differences in brain size from one race to another. But, brain size varies considerably within any population and is generally a function of body size and diet. Eskimos have brains that average as large as or larger than those of any other group, but advocates of racial superiority do not argue that Eskimos are among the most biologically superior people on earth. Actually, there appears to be no relationship between brain size and intelligence. Some geniuses have had relatively small brains.

Skin color cannot be used to establish biological superiority or inferiority, or even race. It is, in fact, a relatively minor biological characteristic. Nevertheless, skin color is used to identify races, and the consequences are serious. Although skin color has assumed great sociocultural importance, we need to keep in mind that differences between racial groups are the result of sociocultural factors and not biology.

Extent and Origin of the Race Problem

The 1970 census showed that blacks were the largest of America's racial minority groups (U.S. Bureau of the Census, 1973:593–95). They numbered 22,539,362 (11.1 percent of the population). The next largest group was composed of those of Spanish heritage (including Mexicans and Puerto Ricans), with 9,294,509 (4.6 percent of the population). Asians numbered 1,427,565 (0.7 percent of the population). Native Americans (Indians) numbered about 760,572 (0.4 percent). In all, over 16 percent of the population were racial minorities. By 1978 blacks numbered around 25.5 million (11.7 percent of the population), comprising about two-thirds of the racial minorities. Most of this chapter relates to blacks specifically, but we will briefly compare whites, blacks, and hispanics (Americans of Spanish heritage) to see similarities and differences among the groups. All racial minorities have endured some of the same kinds of difficulties, and each group has had some distinctive problems.

Hispanics, the second largest of the racial minorities, are the fastest growing group. There were over 12 million hispanic Americans in 1979.[1] Both blacks and hispanics have higher birth rates than whites, with hispanics having the highest and, therefore, the youngest population (median age in 1979 was 22, compared to 24.4 for blacks and 30.7 for whites). Both blacks and hispanics are more concentrated than are whites in metropolitan areas, and a somewhat greater proportion of blacks live in central cities (as opposed to the suburbs). Both racial minorities have lower educational levels than whites, hispanics having the lowest. Both have more single-parent families than do whites, and blacks have far more than hispanics. In 1979 black unemployment was higher (12.2 percent) than hispanic (8.7 percent), which was higher than white (5.1 percent). The median family income in 1979 of hispanics ($12,566) was lower than that of whites ($18,368) but higher than that of blacks ($10,879).

To fully understand the race problem, we must see it in historical perspective. A brief overview of the black experience in America illustrates the historical roots of the problem. Blacks were brought to the United States in 1619. At that point they were not *slaves*. For about three decades they had the status of indentured servants. The economic utility of slaves quickly led to hundreds of thousands of blacks being shipped from Africa to North America. Slavery as an institution did not become fully developed until the eighteenth century, however. As Jordan (1970:107) said, the total "deprivation of civil and personal rights, the legal conversion of the Negro into a chattel," was a gradual process that required about a century.

The process began soon after the first blacks were brought to this country. Laws were passed that legitimated slavery, the Virginia statutes becoming a model for those of other colonies. But, even before slavery became a legal reality, blacks suffered discriminatory treatment in the justice system. As early as 1640 a Virginia court handed down a discriminatory sentence on a runaway Negro servant. Two white servants who had also run away were ordered to serve their masters for an additional year and the colony for three years; the Negro was ordered to serve his master, or whoever the master would assign the servant to, for the rest of his life. This decision marked the beginning of the transformation of blacks *from persons into property,* a process that was completed in the eighteenth century.

Paralleling this transformation was the development of strong racial prejudice. The prejudice did not cause the slavery, and the slavery was not wholly the cause of the prejudice. Rather, "both may have been equally cause and effect, constantly reacting upon each other, dynamically joining hands to hustle the Negro down the road to complete degradation" (Jordan, 1970:112). In other words, the prejudice rose out of the process of enslavement and, in turn, tended to reinforce that process.

Human beings strive to make sense of and justify the world they live in. The only way to make sense of and justify slavery is to define the slaves as somehow deserving of their lot. Thus, various kinds of "evidence" of the inherent inferiority of blacks was accumulated during the years of black slavery.

The slavery system ultimately gave way to a castelike system. In a caste system, people are categorized into groups according to some characteristic over which they have no control, such as their race or the status of their parents. These

groups have different power, status, and access to those things which are valued. In the case of America, blacks formed one caste and whites another, with the whites having most of the power, status, and financial resources. The chances of any individual changing his or her caste position were virtually nil.

This does not mean that all whites were well off and all blacks had nothing. Actually, a class system existed within each caste. During slavery, the slaves of prominent families had a somewhat higher status than other slaves, and the small number of free blacks had a higher status than slaves. White society likewise has been stratified. The difference is that even lower-class whites have often been better off than higher-class blacks. In effect, the two races formed two separate class systems, with the black system severely underpopulated at the apex of its pyramid and overpopulated at the bottom. Not only was the proportion of upper-class blacks far less than the proportion of their white counterparts, but the black upper class was roughly equivalent to the white middle class in terms of material advantages.

While the relationships between whites and nonwhites have been undergoing almost continuous change, the *nature of black protest has been changing also, and definitions of the race problem have changed* (Meier, Rudwick, and Broderick, 1971). The philosophy of Booker T. Washington, dominant during the latter part of the nineteenth century, urged social, economic, and moral development of blacks, but also acquiesced to a segregated society. The failure of this accommodation to improve the lot of blacks facilitated the founding of the National Association for the Advancement of Colored People

(NAACP) and the subsequent era of legal protest. With the problem defined as a legal one, blacks had to take their cause to the courts to fight for their constitutionally guaranteed rights. Legal victories did not result in sufficient changes in the social order, and the age of direct nonviolent action emerged and reached a peak under the leadership of Martin Luther King, Jr. Under King's leadership the problem was defined as a moral one. That meant that white Americans had to be redeemed through the power of love and suffering. Continuing resistance to change and brutal treatment of nonviolent protesters paved the way for a period of black militancy. With protest expressed through the exercise of power, the problem was defined as a power struggle. Black militants began to reaffirm the separation that Booker T. Washington espoused and combined it with exercise of power to try to secure their rights. Finally, in the 1970s, militancy tended to give way to renewed efforts to work "through the system." Many blacks, including some who had been militants in the 1960s, emphasized the importance of running for political office and of using political means to make gains.

The changing black-white relationships have been paralleled by *changing spatial distribution of blacks*. Blacks are still concentrated in the South, but throughout this century there has been considerable migration of blacks to urban areas of the North and West. By 1979 slightly over three-fourths of blacks lived in metropolitan areas (compared to 66 percent of whites).

Figure 12.3 Bobby Seale, one of the founders of the Black Panthers, campaigning for office. By the 1970s many militant leaders of earlier protests were changing their methods.

Race and the Quality of Life

What does it mean to be nonwhite in America? How does being nonwhite affect the *quality of life*? We can get the "feel" of the race problem by looking at four areas in which all Americans are supposed to have equal *rights:* (1) certain rights as citizens; (2) equal economic opportunities; (3) the right to life, liberty and the pursuit of happiness; and (4) the right to dignity as a human being. In each of the four areas being white is a distinct advantage, although the advantage is not as great as it was earlier in the century. A number of race riots in urban areas in the summer of 1980 dramatize that black disadvantages are still severe.

The Rights of Citizenship

We are often reminded by the mass media of the *rights and privileges attached to our citizenship.*

1. Ours is a nation governed by laws rather than by individuals.
2. As citizens, we not only have the privilege but the responsibility of participating in the political process to ensure that the laws that are formulated reflect the will of the people.
3. The people, after all, do not exist to serve the government; rather, the government exists to serve the people, and to serve all equally.

All of these statements can be found at various times in the mass media, but all break down when we consider minority groups. In this section we will examine how the rights of citizenship have not been given to America's racial minorities. In particular, where the minorities

are concerned, everyone is not equal before the law; ours is not wholly a nation of law; and some groups do not even have the privilege, much less the responsibility, of participating in the political process. The quality of life is diminished by the deprivation of rights.

The right to vote.   If you don't like the way things are going, it is said that you can express your disapproval at the polls. Indeed, voting is the responsibility of every citizen because one way Americans are presumably able to change things is by exercising their right to vote. However, this right and privilege, basic as it is to our notions of our system of government, has often eluded American blacks and was long withheld from American Indians.

When the Fifteenth Amendment to the Constitution was ratified in 1870, all Americans had the right to vote, regardless of their race, creed, color, or prior condition of servitude (Rodgers and Bullock, 1972). In the latter part of the century, however, various steps were taken to keep blacks from voting. Laws that effectively **disfranchised** black voters were passed in the southern states. Some of the laws required literacy and property tests. Others imposed a poll tax. Such laws excluded poor whites as well as blacks, however, so loopholes were created. One loophole was the "understanding clause," which allowed a registrar to enroll any individual who could give a "reasonable" explanation of a part of the state constitution that was read to him. Similarly, the "grandfather clause" exempted from the literacy test those who descended from pre-1865 voters. Laws relative to primary elections allowed only whites to vote in the Democratic Party primary on the grounds that a political party is a private organization and can determine its own membership. Louisiana offers a striking example of the effectiveness of such laws because the number of its black voters declined from 130,334 in 1896 to 1,342 in 1904.

Intimidation was also used to keep blacks from registering and voting. Sometimes the threat of violence or actual violence (including even murder) discouraged blacks. The pressure of economic intimidation was also applied. Blacks faced the possibility of losing their jobs or of being refused supplies at local stores.

The efforts to deprive blacks of their right to vote have been intensive and, in some cases, blatantly illegal. Boley, Oklahoma was founded as an all-black community. In 1906, two of its residents were selected as Republican candidates for county commissioner, and they appeared certain to win the election (Toch, 1965:34–36). But, the white election board refused to certify the returns from Boley and declared the opposing candidates to be the victors. This illegal action was upheld by the state supreme court. Subsequently, the state constitution was amended to prevent the possibility of blacks winning elections in the future. Not satisfied with this maneuvering, the white farmers organized clubs to find ways of driving black farmers out of their area.

Tactics changed over time, and efforts to prevent blacks from voting became less widespread and intensive, but the black voter has faced difficulties from the latter part of the nineteenth century right up to the present. Throughout the 1950s and 1960s, renewed attempts of blacks to register were met with fierce resistance and various intimidation tactics. In Tennessee a black who registered to vote might discover that he or she could no longer buy supplies, or that the doctor was no longer available, or that other forms of help commonly available to citizens were shut off. Some blacks faced forcible and illegal eviction from their land.

When blacks could not be intimidated away from the voters' registration desk, various other measures were employed to prevent them from completing the registration process. Rodgers and Bullock (1972:21) characterized the registration of blacks as being

> much like an initiation into a letterman's club, complete with hazing and a number of trivial tasks to be completed by the applicant. Completion of the registration procedures, without assistance or advice from the registrar and in the face of open hostility on the part of the ruling whites, was often a formidable task.

Whites invariably passed the requirements for registration, while blacks failed in large numbers. In some instances blacks with graduate degrees were found to be "illiterate" by the examiners and were, therefore, forbidden to register. In 1975 the NAACP found evidence of continuing efforts in Mississippi to prevent blacks from registering. Those who sought to register were required to complete an application that asked questions about religion, place of business, and where the applicant kept his or her personal possessions. The application began with the statement, "Under penalty of perjury, write the following answers," and proceeded to request everything from the applicant's name to the location of his or her real property. As Roy Wilkins pointed out such questions have "ominous overtones" to blacks, particularly to those who know about the days when the questions really meant "What's more important—your vote or your job?"[2]

When all else failed, registered black voters were harassed when they arrived at the polls. This too continued into the 1970s. In 1971 black candidates and black and white poll watchers were beaten, and other poll watchers had to be protected with armed escorts in Mississippi. Armed bands of whites tried to frighten blacks away from the polls. Such tactics may account for the failure of most black candidates to win, even in areas where black registered voters outnumbered whites. In addition, some observers charged that white election officials failed to report an accurate count of the balloting.[3] While the battle of black citizens and other minorities to gain the vote has been largely won, it is not yet over.

The rule of law.   Another right and privilege of citizenship is to live in a land *governed by laws* rather than by individuals. The experiences of blacks recounted earlier show that whites have found numerous ways to circumvent the law in order to deprive racial minorities of their rights. Maneuverings with respect to *public accommodations* and *school desegregation* offer further examples.

Segregation in public accommodations was declared unconstitutional in 1964. Prior to that time, segregated facilities prevailed in various degrees throughout the nation. The first "Jim Crow" cars (segregated public conveyances) were in Massachusetts in 1841 (Nearing, 1969:172). In the South, not only public conveyances but things such as rest rooms and drinking fountains were segregated, with signs attached that said "white only" and "colored only." In fact, nearly all governmental services

were offered separately to the races, including hospitals and health centers. Restaurants in both the South and the North often catered to one race or the other but not both, and theaters had segregated seating.

During the 1960s, segregated facilities were challenged by the "sit-ins" at lunch counters. Blacks and their white supporters would sit at a lunch counter and refuse to move until they were served. Ultimately, such protests, combined with federal legislation and the 1964 Supreme Court decision, opened nearly all public accommodations to blacks as well as whites. Compliance with the law has been great in this area, probably because businessmen find the new situation more profitable than the old. Nevertheless, there have been some incidents of resistance, particularly in restaurants and recreational facilities. Owners would declare their establishments to be private clubs and would then allow any white to patronize the business for a very small fee. A 1968 Supreme Court decision made such practices illegal.

Segregated educational facilities were declared illegal in the now-famous 1954 Supreme Court decision in the *Brown v. Board of Education of Topeka* case. They were ruled unconstitutional because they are *inherently unequal*. At the time the decision was given, some states allowed local school districts to practice segregation, and seventeen states required segregated education. By 1975, twenty-one years after the decision, court battles were still being waged over the extent to which particular school districts have complied with the law.

One reason for these continuing legal struggles is that whites have found numerous ways to circumvent the law—just as they did with

Figure 12.4 U.S. Representatives Shirley Chisholm (D., N.Y.), John Conyers, Jr. (D., Mich.), and U.S. Ambassador to the United Nations Andrew Young signify that black political leaders became more prominent than numerous in the 1970s.

regard to voting. Blackwell (1975:105) identified nine delaying tactics the South used immediately after the 1954 decision:

(1) nullification and interposition in Virginia; (2) massive resistance throughout the South; (3) legal maneuvers; (4) threats against and intimidation of blacks and white sympathizers; (5) resistance to desegregation by white Southern congressmen as reflected in the *Southern Manifesto*; (6) violence against integrationists and their property; (7) personal intervention by respected state officials who attempted to block the entry of black children into previously all-white schools; (8) the closing down of schools to prevent desegregation; and (9) the use of state funds to establish private schools for whites.

Similar tactics were developed in the North. Although much of the literature focuses on the South, racial hostility is a problem of the entire nation. The 1960s and 1970s saw widespread urban riots and anti-busing movements in the North. The South has often been maligned about many agonizing efforts to resolve the race problem, and there is poetic justice in a group of Southern high school youth going to Boston in 1975 to try to advise the northerners on ways to facilitate school integration.

The anti-busing issue of the 1970s is complicated by a number of factors. White flight to the suburbs tipped the balance possible in any urban mix toward a higher percentage of blacks. Then the tradition of local school districts throughout the nation often made the problem an either/or matter—either integrate schools or maintain local school districts. Undoubtedly, some of the concern about maintaining local school districts had racial overtones, but concern about loss of schools is surely genuine in many cases. But, whatever may be the motivation of people opposed to busing, victory for the anti-busing forces would mean continuation of segregated schools.

The slow pace of integration of the schools is illustrated by a 1967 report of the U.S. Commission on Civil Rights (1967:4–5). The report published the extent of elementary school segregation in seventy-five different school systems. Segregation was measured by, among other things, the proportion of blacks in schools where 90 to 100 percent of the students were black. Some representative findings were: Mobile, Alabama, 99.9 percent; Little Rock, Arkansas, 95.6 percent; Miami, Florida, 91.4 percent; Indianapolis, Indiana, 70.5 percent; Flint, Michigan, 67.9 percent; St. Louis, Missouri, 90.9 percent; and Pittsburgh, Pennsylvania, 49.5 percent. In other words, there were numerous districts throughout the country that, over twelve years after the desegregation order, were still segregated or substantially segregated.

By 1978, 16.1 percent of minority-group pupils were still in schools where the student body was between 99 and 100 percent nonwhite.[4] The states showed considerable variation in the extent of segregation. In Illinois 50.7 percent of minority-group students were in schools with 99 to 100 percent nonwhite students, while in some states there were no totally segregated schools. School segregation largely reflected residential segregation in the 1970s, leading some observers to identify busing as the only solution to integration of the races in the schools.

Equality before the law.   All Americans are supposed to stand as *equals before the law*. Not only are we ruled by law rather than by men, but the law applies equally to all of us. Most people, of course, quickly recognize that not all Americans are treated equally. The wealthy are rarely accorded the harsh treatment endured by the poor. Few people are probably aware of the extent to which blacks receive unequal treatment under the law. An incident that occurred in 1968 in North Carolina illustrates how unevenly justice can be administered. Five young blacks stood before a judge to be sentenced. The day that Martin Luther King, Jr. was buried they had set fire to a building known to be a Ku Klux Klan hangout. The damages amounted to less than $100. The oldest youth was 21 and the youngest was 17. They were each sentenced to twelve years in prison.[5] The question immediately raised is, What kind of sentence would five white youths have been given under similar circumstances?

The illustration is not an isolated incident. Systematic data that has been gathered confirm discriminatory application of the law. A study of prison sentences handed out in Tennessee showed that the average sentence for white offenders was 12.8 years, while blacks received an average sentence of 22.1 years. Sentences, of course, depend on the crime involved, and a larger percentage of the crimes committed by blacks were against persons (and thus would be associated with longer sentences). But, when crimes against persons alone are examined, blacks still receive longer sentences. In Arkansas, Georgia, and Tennessee, blacks served roughly 7.5 years longer than whites for crimes against persons. Moreover, crimes committed by blacks against whites are much more severely punished than crimes committed by whites against blacks. In a study of 359 cases,

blacks received an average sentence of 28 years for committing a crime against a white, while whites received an average sentence of 20.7 years for committing a crime against a black.[6]

The same pattern of discrimination was found in the study of a specific crime in a specific area—rape in St. Louis.[7] Disposition of the cases of 105 white and 291 black defendants from 1961 to 1972 was examined. Convicted blacks spent an average 4.4 years in the penitentiary while the whites spent an average 2.5 years. Moreover, convicted blacks who had court-appointed lawyers served an average 6.95 years, while whites with court-appointed lawyers served an average 3.3 years.

Finally, a disproportionate number of blacks have been sentenced to death (figure 12.5). In fact, about 54 percent of all persons executed between 1930 and 1968 were blacks (U.S. Department of Justice, Law Enforcement Administration, 1979c:8).

In the face of such statistics, the notion of equal justice before the law must be revised. In actuality, it is far better to be a white criminal than a black criminal in the United States, in terms of potential punishment.

This is not to say that nonwhites are accorded worse treatment in the courts in all cases. Some observers dispute that nonwhites are accorded different treatment. Nevertheless, showing that there is equal treatment in some areas does not negate the kind of data presented earlier. Clearly, there are many cases where an individual is not equal before the law simply because of skin color.

414

Figure 12.5 Blacks as a percent of all persons sentenced to death, 1968 to 1978. (Source: U.S. Department of Justice, Law Enforcement Administration, *Capital Punishment: 1978* [Washington, D.C.: Government Printing Office, 1979], p. 4.)

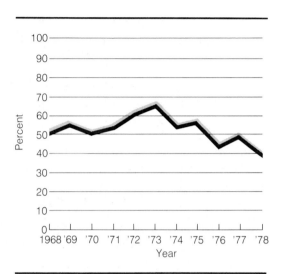

The Right to Equal Economic Opportunities

Economically, racial discrimination means, among other things, that nonwhites are more likely to be poor, unemployed, or—if they work—underemployed. Nonwhites also receive, on the average, less income than whites. Such economic inequalities are important factors in the diminished quality of life of nonwhites.

Race and employment. A group might have *unequal access to employment* in at least four ways. First, the group might have a higher rate of unemployment than does the larger society. Second, a greater proportion of the group might be *underemployed.* Third, members of the group might be clustered at the lower levels of occupational categories. That is, the proportion of blacks who are managers may be the same

as in the larger society, but they are primarily at the lower levels of management. Fourth, a disproportionate number of the group might become disillusioned and drop out of the labor market.

All four kinds of inequality apply to nonwhites in America. It is not easy, of course, to get systematic information on all of the kinds, but unemployment rates are readily available. We saw in table 9.1 that black unemployment rates have been roughly double those of whites since about 1948. Figure 12.6 shows that black males and black females are disadvantaged in the area of employment, and that the fluctuations are more severe for blacks than for whites.

The employment problem for nonwhites does not vanish in times of affluence, or even when measures are taken to provide benefits for nonwhites, as, for example, when Southern schools were desegregated. Patricia Lutterbie (1974) studied the job histories of 343 black principals in Florida from 1961 to 1972. She found that the blacks tended to be displaced by whites or demoted or dismissed as schools were integrated. In 1960, 130 of the blacks in her sample were principals of secondary schools. By 1972 only 8 retained their positions. Social change designed to enhance the quality of education for blacks had unintended and unfortunate consequences for black educators who had held leading positions in their segregated schools. Similarly, when manufacturing expanded in the South during the 1950s, the census figures showed that the number of manufacturing jobs in the South rose by 947,705 between 1950 and 1960. Although there were nearly 1 million more jobs in 1960 than there had been in 1950, the proportion of jobs held by blacks decreased

Figure 12.6 Unemployment rates, by sex and race, 1945 to 1980. (Source: U.S. Department of Labor, *Employment and Training Report of the President* [Washington, D.C.: Government Printing Office, 1980], p. 269.)

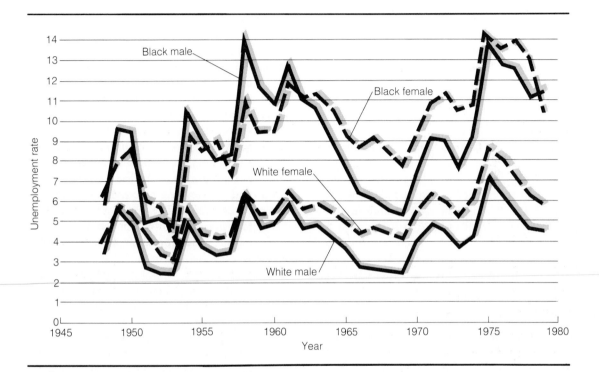

during that period. In fact, the total number of jobs held by black women increased by only 11,830 (about 1.2 percent of the total number of new jobs), while the total number held by black men increased by only 332 (about 0.035 percent of the total number of new jobs). A little over 1 percent of the jobs went to blacks, even though they were nearly 21 percent of the population in the South in 1960 (Batchelder, 1965).

To be nonwhite, then, means to suffer *discrimination in job opportunities*. This holds true in the North and the South. A comparison of a sample of white and black workers in Milwaukee, Wisconsin showed that the average job authority of the blacks was far lower than that of whites (job authority was defined as supervisory authority) (Kluegel, 1978). The discrimination occurs in all regions of the country and in all occupations except for those at the lowest level. The trade unions have been notoriously resistant to including blacks. In 1968 the president of the Negro American Labor Council said, "Our work and our activities are still not welcome in large sections of the labor movement" (Foner, 1974:400). And, in 1970 the Black Labor Leadership Conference found it necessary to issue a "Declaration of Rights of Black and Minority Group Workers," which asserted their rights to hold any jobs for which they were qualified and to hold office at any level of union leadership (Foner, 1974:424). "Black power" was making an assault on the unions.

Was that assault necessary? We need only look at the situation in the unions to understand the bitterness and militancy manifested in the 1970s. In 1970 blacks were underrepresented in virtually every union except those that represented low-status, low-paying work. Almost one-third of laborers (low-status and low pay) were black, while black membership in other unions ranged from as little as 0.2 percent for plumbers to 9.6 percent for teamsters. Such figures do not reflect the preference of blacks for type of job. On the contrary, blacks have been systematically excluded from union membership through a variety of tactics. The steam fitters' union in New York administered tests to applicants in the early 1970s. While there is no question about the potential usefulness of screening applicants through testing, we must wonder at tests that reject 66 percent of nonwhites and only 18 percent of whites. Furthermore, we must ask why applicants for steam fitter apprenticeships were questioned about the relationship of Brahms to music and Whitman to poetry.[8] The outcome of this New York test was rejection of large numbers of nonwhites.

Professions as well as unions have techniques for keeping nonwhites out. In 1972, for example, fifty-one blacks, all graduates of law schools, took the Georgia bar examination and all failed. About 54 percent of the whites taking the examination passed. The discrepancy cannot be explained on the basis of inferior black schools, because even blacks who had equal ac-

ademic records from the same schools as whites failed the Georgia test. Similar results were found in some other states (Parker and Stebman, 1973).

In every occupational category, nonwhites have had more restricted economic opportunities than whites. According to census figures for 1970, nonwhites were disproportionately represented in various occupational categories. As table 12.1 shows, nonwhites tend to be more heavily concentrated in the less desirable categories and to have lower percentages in the more desirable categories. The first two categories in table 12.1 are also those with the highest average income. The proportion of white workers in those categories was over double that of black workers and over 1.5 times that of Spanish heritage and Indian workers. On the other hand, in the category of "laborers, except farm," which represents lower income, nonwhite workers outnumbered white by a wide margin.

The clustering of nonwhites in lower-skilled occupations has tended to hold in all kinds of industries. An examination of black participation in American industry in 1970 concluded that blacks had achieved equitable participation in only nineteen of fifty-nine different industry groups (Peake, 1975). In most industries and in most occupational categories, to be nonwhite means to have a greater probability of working in a lower-status, lower-paying job.

The black worker has been at a disadvantage even in his or her own neighborhood. A study of small businesses in Boston, Chicago, and Washington, D.C. reported that the labor market in the ghettoes was dominated by white-owned businesses, and that the white owners

Table 12.1   Occupational Distribution (Percentage) of Employed Persons, by Race, 1970

Occupation	Race White	Black	Spanish Heritage	American Indian
Professional, technical, and kindred workers	15.5	8.3	9.1	9.8
Managers and administrators, except farm	9.0	2.3	5.0	5.7
Sales workers	7.7	2.3	5.1	2.3
Clerical and kindred workers	18.4	13.7	15.3	7.3
Craftsmen, foremen, and kindred workers	14.4	9.0	13.7	22.1
Operatives, including transport	16.9	23.7	24.8	23.7
Laborers, except farm	3.9	9.4	7.1	10.5
Farmers and farm managers	2.0	0.6	0.5	2.5
Farm laborers and foremen	1.1	2.4	4.2	4.2
Service workers, except private household	10.3	20.0	13.7	11.1
Private household workers	0.8	8.3	1.5	0.8
Total	100.0	100.0	100.0	100.0

Note: Figures on whites, blacks, and Spanish heritage are for employed persons 16 years old and over. For American Indians, figures are for employed heads of families.

Sources: U.S. Bureau of the Census, *Census of Population: 1970,* "General Social and Economic Characteristics," Final Report PC (1)–Cl (Washington, D.C.: Government Printing Office, 1972); and *Census of Population: 1970,* "Subject Reports, American Indian," Final Report PC (2)–1F (Washington, D.C.: Government Printing Office, 1973).

hired fewer nonwhite than white employees in proportion to nonwhites living in the area (Aldrich, 1973).

Race and income. Table 12.2, based on the 1970 census, shows the extent to which nonwhites are concentrated more heavily than whites in the lower income brackets. It shows that American Indians, as a group, are the poorest of the nonwhites. Nearly 40 percent of Indians, in contrast to 13.7 percent of the total population, were below the poverty level in 1969.

Racial minorities made some gains after the mid-1950s, but those gains were not as substantial as people believed. As table 12.3 shows, white and nonwhite income has risen rapidly. In 1955 the median income for black and other races was 55.1 percent that of whites; in 1978 it was 64.0 percent of the median for whites. In other words, in the twenty-three years after 1955, blacks and other races gained only about nine percentage points toward equality with whites. A gain was made, but it certainly was not dramatic.

Table 12.2   Income in 1969 of Families, by Race

Income	Percentage of Families			
	White	*Black*	*Spanish Heritage*	*American Indian*
Less than $1,000	2.0	6.6	4.2	7.9
$1,000 to $4,999	15.9	34.6	25.3	35.0
$5,000 to $9,999	32.3	34.9	38.3	34.7
$10,000 to $14,999	27.8	16.1	21.0	15.3
$15,000 to $24,999	16.9	6.9	9.3	6.0
$25,000 to $49,999	4.2	0.8	1.7	
$50,000 or more	0.8	0.2	0.3	1.0
Total	99.9	100.1	100.1	99.9
Median income	$9,961	$6,067	$7,534	$5,832
Mean income	$11,418	$7,114	$8,578	$6,857

Sources: U.S. Bureau of the Census, *Census of Population: 1970,* "General Social and Economic Characteristics," Final Report PC (1)–CI (Washington, D.C.: Government Printing Office, 1972); and *Census of Population: 1970,* "Subject Reports, American Indian," Final Report PC (2)–IF (Washington, D.C.: Government Printing Office, 1973).

Family income is closely dependent on education and occupation. To some extent, the differences between nonwhite and white income reflect the greater amount of education of whites and their heavier concentration in the higher-paying categories of employment. But, differences persist when we compare whites and blacks within the same occupational category. Table 12.4 shows significant differences between the mean income of whites, blacks, and hispanics within the same occupational categories.

So, to be nonwhite in America means that one probably will have a lower income even when one has the same amount of education and the same type of job as a white. It is particularly distressing to nonwhites that they have not been able to capitalize on education to the same extent as whites. The strong relationship between amount of education and income still holds, but education does not reward nonwhites with the same amount of mobility as it does whites.

The Right to Life and Happiness

The right to "life, liberty, and the pursuit of happiness" was affirmed in the Declaration of Independence. Various polls have reported *less happiness and less satisfaction among nonwhites* than among whites (Armbruster, 1972: 155–56; Clemente and Sauer, 1976). In one poll, for instance, 12 percent of nonwhites and 5 percent of whites said they were, in general, not happy; 18 percent of whites and 44 percent of nonwhites indicated they were dissatisfied with the quality of life in their communities.

Table 12.3   Median Family Income, by Race, 1947–1978

Year	White	Black and Other Races	Hispanic
1947	$ 3,157	$ 1,614	(NA)
1950	3,445	1,869	(NA)
1955	4,613	2,544	(NA)
1960	5,835	3,230	(NA)
1965	7,251	3,993	(NA)
1970	10,236	6,516	(NA)
1975	14,268	9,321	9,551
1978	18,368	11,754	12,566

Source: U.S. Bureau of the Census, *Current Population Reports,* series P–60, no. 120, "Money Income and Poverty Status of Families and Persons in the United States: 1978" (Advance Report) (Washington, D.C.: Government Printing Office, 1979), p. 12.

Table 12.4   Mean Household Income, By Race and Occupation, 1978

	White	Black	Hispanic
White collar workers	$25,100	$17,944	$19,519
Blue collar workers	19,626	16,319	15,999
Farm workers	15,839	8,247	11,944
Service workers	14,435	10,906	11,983

Source: U.S. Bureau of the Census, *Current Population Reports,* series P–60, no. 121, "Money Income in 1978 of Households in the United States" (Washington, D.C.: Government Printing Office, 1980), pp. 13–17.

This should not be surprising, since racial minorities have not had ample access to the kinds of things that make Americans happy. A *Psychology Today* survey of over 52,000 readers reported that among the more important factors in happiness were the individual's job or primary activity, recognition and success, financial situation, housing, and health.[9] We have already seen that racial minorities have been deprived in such matters. In this section, we will look at three areas closely related to life and happiness—life chances, freedom from fear, and the value of human life.

Life chances.   Insurance companies and governmental agencies compile mountains of information on **life chances,** including things such as probability of divorce, disease, suicide, and mental illness. The life chances of whites are generally better than those of nonwhites. For example, compared to whites, nonwhites tend to have: (1) a higher rate of infant deaths and deaths from tuberculosis and homicide; (2) a lower median family income; (3) lower-level jobs; (4) proportionately fewer full-time and white-collar jobs; and (5) fewer people receiving old age and survivor insurance benefits. The last point is a consequence of the shorter life expectancy of nonwhites compared to whites. The life expectancy gap has narrowed somewhat, but in 1974 the average life expectancy for whites was 72.7 years, while that for blacks and other races was 67.0 years.

Nonwhites' disadvantages with respect to life chances are related to their lower economic levels. Burma (1970:327) noted that Mexican Americans have high rates of diseases associated with poverty and inadequate medical care: "Studies of specific Mexican American communities show that over half the pre-school children did not receive immunization, that half of the families had no family doctor, and about 85 percent did not own health insurance." Similar health problems are prevalent among the poorest Americans, the Indians (Wax, 1971:225).

Their death rate from tuberculosis in 1967 was eight times as high as the overall rate for the United States (tuberculosis is one of the diseases associated with poverty). Clearly, nonwhites in America are at a disadvantage with respect to physical well-being.

Freedom from fear.   One of the four basic freedoms proclaimed by President Franklin Roosevelt was freedom from fear. No one should have to live in constant fear of offending someone who claims to be superior. Yet, for decades black mothers and fathers taught their children to fear offending the white man. Richard Wright related an incident from his own childhood that illustrates the point (Bernard, 1966:145–46). A group of white boys had thrown broken bottles at him and some of his friends, and the two groups had fought. Wright was badly cut. He went home and sat on his steps to wait for his mother to come home from work. He felt that she would understand both the pain of the cut and the hurt that was inside him. Rather than sympathy, he received a severe beating. Had a white mother treated her son in this way, we might have questioned her love. But Wright's mother was teaching him what she regarded as a most important lesson—to avoid such encounters at all costs. She was teaching him what it meant to be black in America, and that he would ultimately always be the loser in battles with whites. She wanted to save him from a future encounter that could be even more disastrous for him. Her method was severe, but so was the reality in which she knew he would have to exist.

Throughout their history in America nonwhites have feared being *victims of violence.* The news of lynchings was printed throughout the black press. Consider the chilling effect of reading the following, which appeared in 1919: "75 Negroes Lynched—One a Woman, 7 Burned Alive, 9 Burned After Being Shot or Hanged, 19 Charged With Assault on Women" (Kerlin, 1968:100). The accompanying story gave details, naming the states where the lynchings occurred.

The fear created by lynching stories is rekindled periodically by news of other kinds of violence against blacks. For example, when the news of the murders of over twenty black children in Atlanta swept across the nation in 1981, some blacks in the Georgia city tried to form armed vigilante gangs to protect themselves and their children from further violence. A prominent civil rights leader, the Rev. Jesse Jackson, said that it was "open season" on blacks, that whether the killer or killers turned out to be white or black the murders showed that black life was not as valuable as white life.[10]

In some cases, violence against property was used to threaten violence against the people. Early one New Year's Eve morning a bomb shattered the windows of a black home. A note was also sent to the family: "Nigger Be Warned. We Will Get Your First Born." The incident is not out of the distant past; it occurred in Rosedale, New York at the dawn of 1975.[11] The black family had moved into a white suburban area.

The cherished right of Americans to move about as they please and to live according to their means has not yet been fully extended to

Figure 12.7 Throughout their history in America, nonwhites have feared being victims of violence. The Ku Klux Klan has traditionally been the ultimate symbol of terror to black people.

nonwhites. Nonwhites who try to break down old barriers are still subject to threats of violence and efforts at intimidation. Freedom from fear is merely a promise rather than a reality.

The value of human life. The right to life and the pursuit of happiness means that *the life of each individual in the society is equally valuable.* But, the lives of minority groups have not been valued as highly as the lives of whites. Two situations that came to light in the 1970s testify to the lower value placed on the life of blacks. One involved medical experimentation and the other, sterilization. In the experimentation case, 425 poor and uneducated black males in Alabama were allowed to go untreated for syphilis in order to study the long-range effects of the disease on the human body. The study was made with the knowledge and approval of the U.S. Public Health Service.[12] The other situation involved several cases of *sterilization* of blacks without their full understanding of what was being done to them.[13] In one case, a black welfare recipient apparently thought the operation's effects would be only temporary. In another case, a mentally retarded girl and her sister living in a welfare home were taken to a hospital, presumably to receive shots that functioned as a contraceptive. The two nurses who picked up the girls told the mother to sign a paper, and the mother unknowingly placed an X on a surgical consent form. The girls were taken to a hospital and sterilized the next day.

The value, or lack of value, of black life was also demonstrated when schoolchildren in Florida were questioned about the assassination of Martin Luther King, Jr. soon after it occurred.

While the majority of white schoolchildren stated that the assassin should be brought to trial and punished, 17 percent thought he should be freed or even congratulated. A ninth grader, for instance, said the assassin "should get the Congressional Medal of Honor for killing a nigger" (Clarke and Soule, 1968:35–40). Only a minority held such extreme views. Nevertheless, nonwhite life is not treated as though it were as valuable as white life.

The Right to Dignity as a Human Being

Most of the material already discussed in this chapter relates to human dignity, and it shows again and again how nonwhites are directly *deprived of their dignity as human beings.* Their right to dignity has been violated indirectly also by the *myths* that justify the segregated, inferior status of racial minorities. The right to dignity includes the right to truthful representation of one's group. We will discuss three of the myths that have been more or less widely circulated and that violate this right.

The myth of success around the corner. An important American myth is that *success is "just around the corner" for anyone who is willing to work for it.* The implication is that the racial minorities can end their impoverishment merely by being willing to work as hard as other people. "If they want to get ahead," it is said, "let them work for it and earn it." A 1963 Gallup poll asked, "In general, do you think Negroes have as good a chance as white people in your community to get any kind of job for which they are qualified, or don't you

think they have as good a chance?" The responses: 43 percent thought that blacks have as good a chance as whites; 48 percent said that blacks do not have as good a chance; and 9 percent had no opinion (Gallup, 1972:1829). If nearly half the people feel that blacks have as much opportunity as anyone else, this raises the question, Why do blacks not seize those opportunities? The answer sometimes given is that something is wrong with the blacks, not that something is wrong with the society.

Another Gallup poll asked white people how they would advise blacks to achieve their goals of better jobs and community respect. In response, 44 percent advised "get more education," and 19 percent advised "work harder, try harder" (Gallup, 1972:1961). Again, the implication is that success is available if only blacks will do what whites have been doing all along. Although Gallup did not repeat the question in subsequent surveys, nothing has occurred to suggest any significant change in attitudes.

Associated with the myth that success is readily available to those willing to work for it is the notion that blacks prefer welfare to hard work. Blackwell (1975:54) identified four "misconceptions" about blacks and welfare: (1) that a disproportionate number of blacks are on relief; (2) that most blacks on welfare are able-bodied but lazy; (3) that blacks prefer loafing to working; and (4) that blacks have illegitimate children who are supported through welfare.

The myth that American blacks have the same opportunities as anyone else but prefer handouts and loafing to hard work is sometimes supported by pointing to other immigrant groups. The Irish and Italians, for instance, were able to work out of their initial poverty.

However, a number of factors are working against blacks that other ethnic groups did not have to face.[14] One is the changed nature of our economy. We are an advanced industrial society and no longer need the pool of unskilled workers supplied by other ethnic groups who poured into the cities. Second, the "visibility" of blacks does not allow them to blend into American society as an Irish immigrant, for instance, could. Third, the political system has changed. The urban political machines that offered jobs to European immigrants in exchange for votes are not functioning now for various reasons. Fourth, certain cultural factors favored the Europeans. For instance, they came from societies that were poorer than America and that had lower standards of living. The dirty, poor-paying jobs they found were not beyond their aspirations at the time, and were certainly not below the situation they had left in Europe. They were able to manage partly because their extended family system meant that a single household probably had several wage earners. We must keep in mind that when the European immigrants lived in ghettoes, they behaved as do people who live in ghettoes now. It took immigrants from rural backgrounds a number of generations to escape the ghetto. The argument that contemporary blacks can escape the ghetto and poverty because the Europeans did ignores the social situation of both groups.

The notion that blacks prefer welfare to work is also a distortion of the truth. Blacks did not appear on welfare rolls in large numbers until the late 1940s. Furthermore, as we saw in our discussion of poverty, extremely few able-bodied men of any race are receiving welfare, and there is evidence that poor blacks are willing to do anything to escape their poverty. Also, the majority of all children receiving welfare are legitimate. There is no evidence that nonwhites prefer welfare to work, or that nonwhites are failing to take advantage of work opportunities available to them. Quite simply, the notion that success is just around the corner to all nonwhites willing to work for it is a myth.

The myth of inferiority.   The insidious myth that nonwhites are *inherently inferior* and, consequently, must accept their inferior status, takes a number of different forms. One argument is that nonwhites are, and always have been biologically inferior. This has appeared in respectable scientific sources. For instance, American Indians were described as inferior on the basis of anatomy (particularly the skull) and their performance on intelligence tests (Carlson and Colburn, 1972:33–36). The 1895 edition of *Encyclopaedia Britannica* said that blacks have a "premature ossification of the skull, preventing all further development of the brain," with consequent "inherent mental inferiority" (Carlson and Colburn, 1972:98).

In more recent times, a few social scientists and others argued that blacks are intellectually inferior to whites for genetic reasons. Intense controversy over the issue began after the publication of a 1969 article by educational psychologist Arthur Jense, which attributed the gap between white and black IQ scores to *genetic differences* and not merely to environmental deprivation of blacks. According to Jensen (1972), environmental differences such as poverty and other kinds of deprivation cannot explain the consistent differences in IQ scores between blacks and whites or between the poor and nonpoor. The primary question is, What proportion of IQ is genetic and what proportion is due to environmental factors? Jensen claimed that around 80 percent of the difference in scores is due to genes. For this reason, Jensen argued, programs for the disadvantaged such as Head Start have failed to produce the expected changes in academic performance. He said that compensatory programs will always be ineffectual in the face of biologically rooted characteristics.

The English psychologist Hans Eysenck agreed with Jensen, claiming that there are group differences, including racial, and not merely individual differences in intellectual capacity (Eysenck, 1971).

The bulk of social scientists have rejected the Jensen position. They have agreed that IQ tests are culturally biased and, at the most, reflect *mental achievement* rather than *mental capacity*. They have also pointed out that Jensen has taken a position that most geneticists are unwilling to take. We simply do not know enough at present to make firm statements about the heritability of a particular trait like intelligence. Moreover, some evidence contradicts the Jensen position. Studies of identical twins (genetically the same) who have been separated and reared in different environments show that the children grow up to be quite different individuals and may have IQ scores as much as fourteen points apart. Other studies have found that blacks score better on IQ tests when the tests are administered by blacks rather than by whites. Also, there is considerable evidence that IQ scores can be altered dramatically by specific programs. A Milwaukee experiment found that children from poor families who were subjected to intense stimulation made gains in IQ scores of as many as thirty or forty points![15] Typically such gains are lost some time after the end of the experiment—a point made by Jensen to underscore the genetic argument. We do not know the long-term effects if the experiments were to be extended. After an experiment ends and the children involved must again function in the environment associated with poorer IQ scores, it is not surprising that intellectual performance declines. The fact that short-term gains can be realized suggests that the children are not bound by genetic limitations. Furthermore, IQ data on European immigrants to this country during World War I and the 1920s are quite similar to the data now being recorded for blacks. The descendents of those earlier low-IQ groups are now doing as well as other Americans on the tests.

The argument of a second form of the inferiority myth is that nonwhites are *culturally inferior*. Whatever may or may not be true biologically, it is argued, the culture of a particular people is obviously inferior and the people therefore are unfit to rise above their low status. An 1879 magazine article suggested that while we can say nothing definitive about the Chinese as a race, we *can* say

> ". . . that the Chinese have fixed habits, language, customs, and modes of life, which they do not and will not change, and that these modes of life are not so good as our own. Whether the Chinese themselves are inferior or not, there is no question that their civilization is inferior. That is what is meant when they are called barbarians" [Carlson and Colburn, 1972:176].

Figure 12.8 Most social scientists agree that IQ tests are culturally biased because they have been devised mainly by and for the white middle class. At the most, they reflect mental achievement rather than mental capacity.

Probably few people would make such a blunt statement today, but most people believe that their own culture is superior to the culture of other groups.

The idea that black culture is inferior to white is embedded in some analyses of the problems of black Americans. The difficulties blacks have are attributed to aspects of black life that are supposed to represent black culture. For instance, the widely publicized Moynihan Report (1965) suggested that a core problem of blacks is the nature of black family life, with black socialization processes tending to result in a greater amount of antisocial behavior, less effective education, and less occupational achievement. A report of research on teenagers in Illinois disputes this, asserting that there is little difference between black and white families at equivalent socioeconomic levels (Berger and Simon, 1974). In fact, one of the findings was that a *greater* proportion of nonwhites desired a college education.

Whatever differences there are among whites and nonwhites in the United States, all groups share certain goals. Most Americans, regardless of color, have always aspired to a good education, a good job, and a decent home. In a 1919 edition of a black newspaper, black aspirations were expressed in terms that are no doubt as applicable now as then:

> The Negro wants the right to earn a decent livelihood; to accumulate property according to his ability; and to have his property rights protected. The Negro wants better school facilities; a chance to educate his children; justice in the courts and executions by law instead of by lynchers [Kerlin, 1968:52].

The fact that blacks and other minorities have not achieved such aims cannot be attributed to their biological or cultural inferiority, because the notion of inherent inferiority is a myth.

The myth of mongrelization.   It has been argued that if people of different races intermarry, their children will be inferior. In other words, intermarriage is supposed to mean both biological and cultural degeneration, for inferior people can produce only an inferior civilization.

Whatever the original basis for this argument, there actually is some historical evidence suggesting the contrary. The mingling of different peoples may, if anything, produce a better nation and a higher form of civilization (for example, in the Italian city-states).

There are other myths about race and the races, but the point is that such myths deny people the right to dignity as human beings. The myths function to justify in one way or another the inferior status of certain groups and the discriminatory practices that maintain that inferior status. These myths and the purposes they serve are contrary to the ideal of a society of equality of opportunity.

It is evident why the civil rights movement encouraged *black pride* and *black power*. (There has been a similar but not nearly so strong effort to stimulate a comparable sense of red power and brown power.) To those who have been victimized the race problem means deprivation, oppression, and powerlessness. People who lost much of their sense of self-worth had to begin to perceive themselves with pride, and people who had been oppressed by a sense of their own powerlessness, among other things, had to be convinced that they could seize control of their own destiny and alter the direction.

The race problem seriously diminishes the quality of life of nonwhites because some of the most fundamental rights are denied them. How could this happen in the "land of the free"? We turn now to an examination of the multiple factors that generated and tend to perpetuate the problem.

Contributing Factors

America's race problem is well described by the title of Gunnar Myrdal's classic work, *American Dilemma* (Myrdal, 1944). The author, a Swedish social economist, came to the United States in 1938 to direct an analysis of our race problem. The book that resulted defined the problem as a moral issue and stated that the *dilemma involved a contradiction between the American creed and our racial behavior.* The creed proclaims the primacy of individual dignity, equality, and the right of all citizens to the same justice and the same opportunities, but the racial behavior systematically denies racial minorities the same rights and benefits accorded to whites.

The race problem also involves *contradictory value systems.* Some people define the segregated and deprived state of blacks as a problem, but others define efforts to "mix" the races as the real problem. The latter vigorously resist efforts of the former to alter the existing structure of segregated relationships. A fundamentalist Protestant paper carried the sermon of a minister in 1962 that included the following description of the "tragedy in Mississippi"—the entrance of a black into the University of Mississippi.

. . . the arrogant left-wing Kennedys and socialists have ridden roughshod over the people of Mississippi, spent millions of dollars of the people's money, combined with the left-wing National Association for the Advancement of Colored People against the local cultured citizenry who were for law and order and peaceful development.[16]

As with all social problems, there is no consensus about its nature. Both whites and nonwhites are found on the same as well as opposing sides of the issue, some defining the ideal as an integrated society and some defining the ideal as a segregated but equal society.

Contradictions in the social structure also have been identified. Baran and Sweezy (1966:263) argued that our economy has developed to the point where the demand for unskilled and semi-skilled labor is small, a situation that adversely affects blacks more than any other group. That means there is a contradiction between the skill structure (education, in part) of black Americans and the skill demands of the American economy.

Many contradictions are involved in America when minority races tend to interact as inferiors or subordinates with the majority race. We will examine the factors that generated and tend to perpetuate this condition.

Social Structural Factors

The tables in this chapter show that racial minorities occupy a *low position in the stratification system.* There is, of course, stratification in every society, but the important point here

Involvement

"The White Race Will Perish!"

"Racial superiority." The words create an image in many people's minds of the white bigot who believes that his own race is inherently better than others. But whites are not the only people to proclaim superiority. The late Elijah Muhammad, founder of the Black Muslims, said that nonwhites are superior to whites. Furthermore, he opposed interracial marriages because, as C. Eric Lincoln (1961:89) put it, "a further admixture of white blood will only weaken the Black Nation physically and morally. . . . The white race will soon perish, and then even a trace of white blood will automatically consign its possessor to an inferior status." Many Black Muslim teachings seem to be mirror-image counterparts of the whites' myths of superiority/inferiority and mongrelization which are discussed in this chapter.

A vast amount of literature produced by black writers expresses various other reactions to the treatment of black people in America. Since the 1920s black writers and scholars have caught the attention of white America by the power of their literary efforts. Their work stimulated, in turn, thoughtful articles and books by whites trying to gain a new understanding of blacks.

Read some of the black literature that has been produced since the 1920s. There is much to choose from—the poetry of Langston Hughes or Gwendolyn Brooks, the fiction of Ralph Ellison or Richard Wright, Alex Haley's *Roots* or his earlier *Autobiography of Malcolm X,* the essays of Eldridge Cleaver, or any of the numerous other black writers who have produced important works. Find passages that reflect the quality of life of black people in America and identify the factors that the writers feel are responsible for the situation of blacks. What social ideals are explicit or implicit in the writings?

429

is that the racial minorities are disproportionately in the lower strata, having fewer economic benefits, less power, less prestige, and less gratification. Various institutions of our society reflect this low status position of racial minorities by the way they discriminate against them.

The term **"institutional racism"** was coined to refer to the fact that established policies and practices of social institutions tend to perpetuate racial discrimination. In other words, whether or not the people involved are prejudiced or deliberate in their discriminatory behavior, the normal practices and policies themselves guarantee that racial minorities will be short-changed. The reason for this is that policies and practices are set by those in power, and the racial minorities have typically lacked the necessary power to control institutional processes. We will examine institutional racism in three important institutions—education, the economy, and government.

Education.   Two practices of our educational institution that serve to perpetuate discrimination are *so-called IQ testing* and *so-called ability-grouping of children.* A good deal of evidence shows that these practices discriminate against people in the lower socioeconomic strata. Because racial minorities are disproportionately in the lower strata, they suffer disproportionately from such practices. A child may do poorly on an IQ test, for example, because little in his or her home environment has served as preparation for tests constructed by middle-class educators. Then, when placed in a group of lower ability, a child may accept the label of mediocrity or even inferiority.

Textbooks used in schools often reflect minority-group powerlessness by discussing nonwhites in *dehumanizing* ways. A superintendent of schools who is a devout Baptist would hardly allow textbooks that slander Baptists in his school district. Yet, textbooks that handle racial minorities in ways that justify their being treated as inferiors or subordinates have been widely used in the case of blacks. For example, textbooks have tended either to ignore them and their place in American history or to reinforce notions of their inferiority. A 1949 study by the American Council on Education had the following findings (Kane 1970:77): (1) blacks in contemporary society were ignored in the average textbook; (2) any references to blacks were primarily with respect to the pre-1876 era, showing them either as slaves or as bewildered freedmen—an inferior group in either case; (3) scientific information on the nature of race was not included in the books; and (4) illustrations depicting blacks were even less adequate than the written text. Subsequent studies show that these conditions tend to persist.

The textbooks from which some children in America learn about their history have portrayed travesties such as the Ku Klux Klan's loyalty and concern for law and order and the contented lives of slaves picking cotton for their gentle masters. Even college textbooks can be faulted for their treatment of minorities. A study of major textbooks in family sociology concluded that their treatment of black families usually dealt in myth and speculation (Peters, 1974). The "typical" textbook black family was headed by a female (actually, the majority of black families have male heads of the household), and children were depicted as lacking in

Figure 12.9 Many blacks and whites attend school together, but educational opportunities are still not equal.

ambition because of the negative influence of the black father (studies of black aspirations and achievement do not support this). Some textbooks treat interracial marriage as a form of deviant behavior.

By implication as well as direct statements, textbooks have helped to perpetuate the notion that whites are superior and deserve to be dominant. Children's schoolbooks have told us that Africa needs white capitalists to show the blacks how to run plantations, and that blacks quickly follow and imitate white styles of living in Africa. It is not surprising that a child of any race taught from such materials would see race relations in America as a problem (except in the sense that "outside agitators" or unethical individuals have created a problem), and would tend to interact as though whites were superior.

The economy. Institutional racism has pervaded the economy in at least three ways: **exploitation** *of nonwhite labor; exclusion of nonwhites from full participation in the economy;* and *exploitation of nonwhite consumers* (Knowles and Prewitt, 1969:15–30). We described earlier how only the worst and lowest-paying jobs have been open to nonwhites. As for participation in the economy, no group has been more effectively excluded than Native Americans. Their exclusion is rooted in government policy:

> It is worth remembering that the lands reserved for Indians were selected because they were away from the main natural routes of travel, inhospitable for agriculture, and lacking in other visible resources (such as mineral wealth). Accordingly, most reservations have not had an adequate ecological basis for their existence as

self-sufficient communities. From their inception, the reservations have required subsidization of some sort [Wax, 1971:67].

As a result, Native Americans are one of our most impoverished groups.

Other nonwhites' marginal participation in the economy as entrepreneurs is closely related to credit practices and policies. Lending institutions traditionally demand credit history, some kind of collateral, and some evidence of potential success before they lend money to prospective businessmen, white or nonwhite. These are standard practices, defined as necessary and practical when giving credit. However, applying them to nonwhites, who may have poor credit records because of exploitation and who may have nothing to use as collateral because of poverty, means that the standard practices only insure continued white domination of the economy.

Insisting on comparable "sound" business practices when the prospective customers are nonwhite results in exploitation of the nonwhite consumer. It is true that the poor are greater credit risks and that businesses in ghetto areas must pay higher insurance premiums because of the greater probability of theft and property damage. But, it is also true that these higher costs of doing business exploit the nonwhite consumer, who must then pay more than others for the same quality of goods. Ploski and Kaiser (1971:445–46) bring to light some findings of various surveys and studies.

1. Retailers of furniture and appliances in low-income areas get double the mark-up of other retailers in nearly every large American city.

2. A Washington, D.C. study revealed that retailers of furniture and appliances in low-income areas paid on the average $37.80 for the goods for which they received $100, while other retailers in the general market paid an average of $64.50 for the goods for which they received $100.

3. A 1966 study reported that appliances that sold on the average for $159 cost an average of $255 in stores in low-income areas in Washington, D.C. Those who paid the inflated prices were mainly black laborers and people on welfare or Social Security.

The most serious exploitation may be in housing, however. Blacks are often forced to pay more than whites for the same quality of housing. In a Newark, New Jersey study, nonwhites paid from 8.1 to 16.8 percent higher rent than whites paid for the same type of housing— "a definite 'color tax' of apparently well over 10 percent on housing. This condition prevails in most racial ghettos."[17]

Economic deprivation of nonwhites has meant economic gains for whites. From an analysis of census data, George Dowdall (1974) found that in areas where blacks were kept in a subordinate position, whites benefited in the decade from 1960 to 1970 by securing higher occupational status, lower rates of unemployment, and higher family income. Similarly, the economist Walter Heller (1970) estimated the annual white gain from racial discrimination at $15 billion. He argued that the country as a whole would benefit economically if discrimination were reduced.

Government.   If nonwhites are to make headway in their efforts to achieve equality of opportunity in America, they must be able to exercise *political power* and find help in the

Figure 12.10 In recent years, efforts have been made to bring blacks back into American history by identifying the contributions they have made to that history.

IN HONOR OF
THE FIRST BLACK SLAVES
AND FREEMEN WHO FOUGHT IN
THE BATTLE OF RHODE ISLAND
AS MEMBERS OF THE
FIRST RHODE ISLAND REGIMENT

THE BLACK REGIMENT

STONE ERECTED BY
NEWPORT R.I. BRANCH N.A.A.C.P.
R.I. BICENTENNIAL COMMISSION
AND CITIZENS – MAY 2 1976

courts. In the past the government often impeded progress. Consider the effects of the decision of the U.S. Supreme Court that a black has no rights that whites must respect (in the famous Dred Scott case prior to the Civil War). Or consider the effects of being jailed for wanting to exercise the legal right to register and vote.

In their survey of the gains and lack of gains made in various areas of civil rights, Rodgers and Bullock (1972:178) observed that variable success could be attributed to the fact that "the Federal government has made fewer demands in some areas than in others." Where the federal government has pushed hardest, as in the area of voting rights, the gains have been the greatest. Government pressure is not the only tool for change, of course, but government unresponsiveness to the needs of racial minorities is a prime factor in perpetuating the race problem. That unresponsiveness, in turn, reflects the powerlessness of the racial minorities to shape government policies and practices to their benefit. The racial minorities have barely begun to infiltrate those positions of power. By 1979 there were 4,584 elected black officials in America—less than 1 percent of the total of the nation's elected officials, though still a dramatic increase over 1969, when there were 1,185 elected black officials.[18]

Thus, the social structure has tended to create and perpetuate superior/inferior patterns of interaction because of the clustering of racial minorities in low-status, low-power roles in institutions. The minorities have lacked the power to exercise control over the institutions and have, therefore, failed to receive the full benefits of *participation* in those institutions. The policies and practices of economic institutions, like government bodies, tend to maximize and perpetuate the well-being of those who are dominant. Institutions thereby work to the detriment of racial minorities independent of any individual prejudice among institutional leaders.

Social Psychological Factors

We said previously that ideology affects social interaction. Why does not the ideology of equal opportunity alter the superior/inferior kind of interaction between whites and nonwhites that results from the social structure? It might, except for the many ideologies in any society. Some of the ideologies of America have helped to shape and sustain the traditional interaction patterns between the races. In fact, some values, attitudes, and ideologies among both whites and nonwhites tend to perpetuate the race problem. We will examine those of the whites first.

Majority perspectives.   The initial low position of racial minorities in America stems from the circumstances of their arrival—as indentured servants, slaves, or unskilled laborers. The *ideology necessary to legitimate the enslavement* or *subordination of racial minorities* was present from the first. The first white settlers in America believed in their own racial superiority, and certainly considered themselves superior to the "savages" who were native to America. Similarly, the English, on first making contact with Africans, considered them very "puzzling" creatures and tried to determine why the people were black. One explanation identified them as the descendants of Ham, whom God had cursed according to the Bible.

In any case, Africans were a different kind of people, and the difference was not seen to be desirable: "From the first, Englishmen tended to set Negroes over against themselves, to stress what they conceived to be radically contrasting qualities of color, religion, and style of life, as well as animality and a peculiarly potent sexuality" (Jordan, 1968:43).

While a number of white groups entered the country in low-status, low-power positions (and were to some extent the objects of prejudice), none of them were so looked down upon as the racial minorities. A number of additional factors worked against racial minorities but not against whites; (1) the economy needed less and less unskilled labor; (2) their skin color was a "visible" disability; (3) the political system no longer offered jobs for votes so freely; and (4) their smaller households probably did not have several wage earners.

Prejudice, a "rigid, emotional attitude toward a human group" (Simpson and Yinger, 1965:15), is an attitude widely held among the white majority. Prejudice legitimates different treatment of group members and helps to perpetuate white dominance. Prejudice is an individual characteristic, but its causes lie outside the individual—no one is born with prejudice. Simpson and Yinger (1965:49–51) identified a number of sources of prejudice. The sources included personality needs; the usefulness of prejudice for certain groups (low-status whites, for instance, who have been better off than blacks in America); group tradition (children learn to hate without knowing precisely why); and certain attributes possessed by the minority group. Group attributes as a source is questionable, however. They may serve as a useful rationalization for prejudice, but they do not generally cause that prejudice. In his classic study of prejudice, Gordon Allport (1958) found that people were prejudiced against others for contradictory reasons. The same people who disliked Jews because they were "intrusive" also disliked Jews because, they said, Jews are "seclusive." In other words, they disliked Jews whatever the attributes.

Prejudice does not necessarily have so rational a basis as a consistent set of beliefs about or a well-defined image of the target group. Social psychologists have known for a long time that certain groups can be defined as undesirable even when the attributes of those groups are vague. This insight is expressed in an old poem:

I do not love thee, Dr. Fell,
   the reason why I cannot tell.
But this I know and know quite well,
   I do not love thee, Dr. Fell.

White prejudice is reflected in a series of Gallup polls in which whites expressed a preference for discrimination against blacks.[19] For example, in a 1948 poll a total of 42 percent (84 percent of the Southern respondents and 36 percent of those outside the South) affirmed their belief that blacks should be segregated in trains and buses. In 1956, two years after the U.S. Supreme Court declared segregated education unconstitutional, 31 percent overall and 67 percent in the South indicated that they disapproved of the decision. In 1958, 62 percent of those in the South and 40 percent of those outside the South said that they would definitely or possibly move if "colored people came to live next door." By 1963, 45 percent of all those polled indicated they would definitely or

possibly move under such circumstances, and by 1967 the proportion dropped to 35 percent.

The declining prejudice reflected in the polls continued into the 1970s. A 1978 Gallup survey of racial attitudes reported that only 13 percent would definitely or possibly move if blacks came to live next door. Furthermore, over 75 percent of the respondents said that they would vote for a black candidate for president (compared to 38 percent in 1958), and 36 percent said they approved of interracial marriages (compared to 20 percent in 1968).

The changing attitudes not only indicate a decline in prejudice, but also show what Hadden (1969:146–59) called the "new American dilemma"—a contradiction between an equal opportunity ideology and not so equal behavioral reality. As a result of the civil rights movement, many of the old attitudes and aspects of the old ideology were shown to be false. Furthermore, it is clear that the racial minorities have not had equal opportunities in America. Americans have become increasingly willing to affirm the right of racial minorities to have equal opportunities to participate in the life and benefits of the nation. But, Americans now face the problem of implementing these new attitudes in concrete ways, and many people are not yet prepared to take that step. It is one thing to affirm the right of a black family to buy a home wherever it chooses. It is another thing to welcome a black family to the house next door. Attitudes have changed, but there is room for more change if the race problem is to be resolved.

Prejudice, of course, is not confined to white-black relationships. We pointed out that all non-white groups have been *labeled as inferior*.

However, this prejudice varies in relation to where and against whom it is expressed. While Asians in general are disliked less than blacks, an Asian's experience in the Midwest might be quite different from his experience on the West Coast. In a study of a Western city, Pinkney (1970) found that less prejudice was expressed against Mexican Americans than against blacks: 83 percent of the respondents agreed that Mexican Americans should have the right to work side-by-side with other Americans, but only 66 percent agreed that blacks should have that right. While 45 percent approved of Mexican Americans living in the same neighborhood as whites, only 23 percent approved of blacks living in the same neighborhood.

Prejudice varies in other ways too. Many whites would approve of a black working with them but would oppose the same black moving into their neighborhood or joining an organization they belonged to. Many respondents in Pinkney's sample approved of Mexican Americans working with whites but disapproved of social mixing. The degree of prejudice may vary, but it is persistently present.

In other words, prejudice legitimates and helps to perpetuate the interaction patterns occurring in institutions. In the schools, for instance, a black child may perform poorly because, in part, he or she senses a teacher's hostility, born of prejudice. The teacher labels the child as of mediocre ability and places him or her in an appropriate group. The child may accept the teacher's definition of his or her ability, and that definition may be further reinforced through IQ tests and subsequent teachers' reactions. Thus, prejudice further reduces the chances of academic success of a poorly-prepared child, and the normal policies and practices of the school, such as IQ testing and grouping by ability, reinforce an official definition of the child's ability. Social structural factors mesh with social psychological processes to maintain a child in a subordinate and inferior role. If a child rebels against this hostile and repressive environment and becomes a "behavior problem," the teacher will conclude that his or her initial hostility is fully justified.

Minority perspectives. *Negative self-esteem* may develop among racial minorities as the outcome of socially structured interaction. Pettigrew (1964) pointed out that playing the role of "Negro" by acting like an inferior person impairs self-understanding and self-acceptance. Also, a number of studies show various degrees of self-hatred among blacks. The black power movement reacted against such tendencies to self-debasement by asserting the worth and dignity of black Americans, for the ultimate debasement is a minority group accepting the majority's definition of itself as inferior.

Again we deal with a vicious circle. By experiencing deprivation and powerlessness, members of a minority group develop attitudes of alienation and cynicism about their society, and perhaps attitudes of debasement about themselves. These attitudes lead them to adjust to their low position rather than to struggle against it. Their remaining deprived and powerless confirms their perspective.

Nonwhite perspectives on education illustrate the circularity. We already mentioned that education is crucial to upward mobility and that a greater proportion of nonwhites than whites desired a college education, according to an Illinois study. In the same study, respondents were asked how much education they actually expected to get. The proportion of lower-class nonwhite males who named a college degree was far less than the proportion of lower-class white males who expected to get a college degree. In other words, many nonwhite youth who aspire to higher education do not realistically expect to get it. Many social psychologists argue that the expectation is as important as the aspiration.

Even if there are numbers of nonwhites who value a college education, many nonwhite children, subjected to the kind of hostile and oppressive school environment described earlier, learn to detest school. As one boy in a Washington, D.C. ghetto school expressed it, "Hopin' never changed nothin! . . . *Hope* this school gonna fall down but it don't. It stand right here, ever' mornin', ugly and mean" (Fader, 1971:92).

Similarly, Heller (1969) pointed out a number of beliefs, values, and attitudes among Mexican Americans that inhibit that group from educational attainment. She noted that by the end of the 1960s the Mexican Americans were the only sizable minority group who did not show a substantial intergenerational rise in socioeconomic status. This reflects, among other things, their lack of educational attainment, which itself reflects certain attitudes.

> Somehow, the Mexican Americans have long held on to the belief that formal education was useless for *them* and did not get them anywhere. They viewed it as leading their children not toward mobility, but toward frustration and humiliation. To help their children avoid the latter, parents pointed to those Mexican Americans who received an education and yet did not hold a job appropriate to it [Heller, 1969:400].

Heller's remarks well illustrate the circularity of anti-education attitudes and values inhibiting education, thereby perpetuating a group's low socioeconomic status, which in turn legitimates the attitudes and values.

To the extent that nonwhites hold negative attitudes and values about education, they will not achieve positions of power in education, which would allow them to alter the structure of the institution. Their attitudes and values minimize their participation and in turn allow continuation of policies and practices that maintain them in subordinate positions.

What Is to be Done?

Minority groups themselves have launched an attack on the forces that discriminate against them to the detriment of their desired quality of life. The first step in their awakened militancy was to understand the disadvantages they labored under. They also had to see the possibility of social change and how the change could be brought about. Many factors contributed to the growing awareness: (1) the minorities' growing educational levels; (2) participation in American wars; (3) contact with the ideology of equal opportunity in the mass media; (4) acceptance of Christianity and its ideals of dignity and worth; (5) contact with whites who had rejected nonwhite subservience; and (6) the continual efforts of nonwhites who never accepted either slavery or subordination. The result has been *intergroup conflict* as minorities strive to alter values, attitudes, ideologies, and social structural arrangements. We mentioned the shifting mode of attack of blacks from the self-help and accommodation ideology of Booker T. Washington to the militant "black

Figure 12.11 Proponents and opponents of busing in Detroit. Efforts to resolve social problems generally involve conflict and struggle.

power" approach to the determination to infiltrate the political process and gain new positions of power and privilege. The shift has also intensified the conflict.

Resolution of the race problem requires more than the actions of the racial minorities, however. The white majority must also recognize the necessity of action. The violence and conflict associated with the issue of busing schoolchildren show that we cannot escape an agonizing struggle between opposing viewpoints as we attempt to deal with the problem. The urban riots of the 1960s demonstrated that we cannot escape violent struggle by ignoring the seriousness of the problem. What kind of actions may be taken, keeping in mind that any action will probably involve some conflict (of verbal debate at the very least)?

First, attitudes and ideologies can be changed through persistent education in schools, churches, and the mass media. Many efforts have already been initiated, of course, but there still is extensive racial prejudice throughout the country and adherence to ideologies that disparage racial minorities. Second, legislation must be continually introduced, backed up by the commitment of the federal government to enforce the law. We pointed out a number of beneficial changes that occurred in the wake of such legislation and commitment. There are those who despair of the law having any force, but they often expect too much from law. Laws *can* change attitudes and alter behavior, but by increments, not once for all time. A law is passed, people find ways to circumvent it, and a new law is passed to address the contradiction between the intended and actual results of the first law. Over time the intent of the law is increasingly realized. Burstein (1979) re-

ported that the equal opportunity laws passed in the 1960s and 1970s had a positive impact on the incomes of nonwhite males and females relative to the incomes of white males. Such results rarely come as quickly as we would like. Still, legislation can have a significant impact.

Local as well as national programs must attack institutional racism directly. The *affirmative action program* calls for positive steps to increase the participation of racial minorities in business, industry, education, and service agencies. The program has introduced a new problem, however—the charge of *reverse discrimination.* Some lawsuits claimed that white males were discriminated against in employment practices and university admission policies. In 1977 the U.S. Supreme Court heard the case of *Regents of the University of California v. Bakke.* Allan Bakke, a white male, applied for admission to the medical school and was rejected. He sued on the grounds that some minority students were admitted even though they were less qualified than he (the university reserved a number of admissions for disadvantaged applicants). Bakke won his case and was subsequently admitted. The Supreme Court agreed with the lower courts that the university's special admissions procedures were unconstitutional, though the justices were also careful to point out that this did not disallow all efforts to recruit disadvantaged or minority students.

The Bakke case did not resolve the problem. The problem may not be resolved for some time because the notion of reverse discrimination raises difficult issues. Should we start now and guarantee equal opportunities for all people from this point on? Or should there be, in effect, a period of reverse discrimination in order to erase past injustices? The author heard a black civil rights leader declare on a radio program that at least 50 percent of the work force of a large industry in the area should be blacks in order to make up for past discrimination. There are good arguments on both sides of the question.

The argument of one side is that preference must be given to blacks and others who have suffered discrimination in the past, for even if we suddenly affirm equal opportunity for all, those opportunities will not really be "equal." "Desirable candidates" for new opportunities "do not simply appear: they have to be created" (Keller, 1976:79). Moreover, as we have seen, racism is so built into the institutional arrangements of the society that merely proclaiming equal opportunity is insufficient. Positive steps must be taken to change those arrangements and insure that previously deprived groups are incorporated into privileged positions. Whatever preferential treatment may be involved is little more than just reparation for past discrimination.

The argument of the other side is that we should not hold people responsible for the actions of their forebears. Any program designed specifically to help blacks "totally ignores others who are equally deprived through no fault of their own" (Borgatta, 1976:67). Furthermore, because Americans believe that the same standards should apply to all, our goal at this point should be to insure truly equal opportunity for all by insisting that everybody meet the standards. This line of reasoning admits that preferential treatment has been accorded white males in the past. But, it holds that past grievances cannot be redressed by giving preferential treatment to women and racial minorities, and thereby punish a new generation of white males.

These arguments cannot be resolved by data, for they depend on values. The issue of reverse discrimination will undoubtedly haunt the nation's courtrooms for some years because it bears directly on one of our most cherished values—equality of opportunity.

Conflict has, and will, accompany other programs. Busing schoolchildren as a means of ending segregation in education has also been a focal point of intense conflict. (The school busing issue is discussed in the next chapter.) Members of racial minorities are being urged to seek political office and use their influence to secure minority rights. To do so will bring them into conflict with other groups and, in some cases, even portions of their own constituencies. Manpower training programs have been funded by the federal government in an effort to bring minorities into fuller participation in the economy. Conservatives have been highly critical of such programs.

One aspect of the race problem that has broad implications is *residential segregation*. The majority of Native Americans live on reservations. Most Spanish-speaking Americans live in their own segregated neighborhoods. Blacks are concentrated in the inner city of metropolitan areas. Such patterns of residential segregation virtually guarantee segregated social life and education (without busing). They also inhibit the kind of intergroup contact that can break down myths, prejudice, and racist ideologies. Consequently, a program designed to achieve residential integration could have significant influence on the race problem.

Desegregation programs that have already been tried often have been vigorously criticized as having failed in their purpose. But, we should keep in mind that any program can attack only a small part of the vast, complex problem. Reform efforts are invariably slower than desired by the advocates of reform. This does not mean that all desegregation programs are useful. Each program should be continually monitored, and efforts should be made to improve it or abandon it for a potentially more fruitful program. We should not discard programs just because they do not quickly resolve the whole problem. The present race problem is the result of processes that have been at work for 200 years. They will not be reversed overnight.

Summary

America's Black, Native American, Asian, and Spanish-heritage racial minorities comprise over 16 percent of the population. Inequalities between the majority white race and minority races are primarily the result of sociocultural factors. Skin color is a minor biological characteristic, but it is a major sociocultural factor.

The meaning of the race problem and the diminished quality of life it imposes on nonwhites may be summed up in terms of citizenship rights; economic opportunities; the right of life, liberty, and the pursuit of happiness; and the right to dignity as a human being. In each of these four areas it is a distinct advantage to be white. Nonwhites have been deprived of basic citizenship rights, such as the right to vote and the right to be governed by and be equal before the law. Economically, nonwhites have suffered discrimination in employment opportunities and income. With respect to our value on life and happiness, nonwhites have been disadvantaged in terms of life chances: they often have lived in fear, and their lives have been treated as though they were of less value than the lives of whites. Finally, nonwhites' right to dignity has been violated by a number of myths, including the myth of "success around the corner," the myth of inferiority, and the myth of mongrelization.

An important social structural factor that contributes to the race problem is institutional racism. Nonwhites are kept clustered in the lower levels of the stratification system and are exploited by the normal policies and practices of institutions such as education, the economy, and government. Social psychological factors of attitudes, values, and ideologies of both the white majority and the racial minorities compound the structural discrimination. While the social structural factors lead to devaluation of nonwhites, the social psychological factors lead to nonwhite self-devaluation and to self-defeating behavior.

Glossary

biological characteristic   an inherited in contrast to a learned characteristic

disfranchise   to deprive of the right to vote

entrepreneur   one who organizes and manages a business enterprise

exploitation   use or manipulation of people for one's own advantage or profit

genetically transmitted   biologically inherited

institutional racism   policies and practices of social institutions that tend to perpetuate racial discrimination

life chances   the probability of gaining certain advantages defined as desirable, such as long life and health

morphological   pertaining to form and structure

prejudice   a rigid, emotional attitude toward people in a group that legitimates discriminatory behavior

race   a group of people distinguished from other groups on the basis of certain biological characteristics

For Further Reading

Botkin, B. A., ed. *Lay My Burden Down*. Chicago: University of Chicago Press, 1945. The stories of former slaves, collected in the 1930s. Tells what slavery means from the point of view of the victims.

Conyers, James E., and Walter W. Wallace. *Black Elected Officials*. New York: Basic Books, 1976. A study of blacks who hold elected offices, based on a questionnaire survey. Includes background, political ideologies, and motivations of black officials.

Himes, Joseph S. *Racial and Ethnic Relations*. Dubuque: Wm. C. Brown Co., 1974. A brief but readable overview of the problems and the literature of racial and ethnic relations.

Knowles, Louis L., and Kenneth Prewitt, eds. *Institutional Racism*. Englewood Cliffs, N.J.: Prentice-Hall, 1969. Shows how racism is built into American institutions, including the economy, the system of justice, education, government, and health care.

Nearing, Scott. *Black America*. New York: Schocken Books, 1969. Illustrations and text combine effectively to convey the historical meaning of being black in America.

Tumin, Melvin M., ed. *Comparative Perspectives on Race Relations*. Boston: Little, Brown, 1969. Shows the international nature of race problems and gives insight into the wide variations in race relations. The U.S. is neither the worst nor the best in the way it treats minorities.

Notes

1. Data in this paragraph are from U.S. Bureau of the Census, *Current Population Reports,* series P-20, no. 350, "Population Profile of the United States: 1979" (Washington, D.C.: Government Printing Office, 1980), pp. 49–52.

2. Information derived from a letter sent by Roy Wilkins on April 18, 1975. The letter contained a copy of the application form.

3. *The New York Times,* November 7, 1971.

4. Data in this paragraph are from U.S. Bureau of the Census, *Statistical Abstract of the United States, 1980* (Washington, D.C.: Government Printing Office, 1981), p. 156.

5. *Time,* July 11, 1969, p. 51.

6. *Trans-Action,* October 1969, p. 11.

7. *St. Louis Post-Dispatch,* April 6, 1975.

8. *Time,* March 1, 1971, p. 10.

9. *Psychology Today,* August 1976, p. 28.

10. *Time,* May 4, 1981, p. 6.

11. *St. Louis Post-Dispatch,* June 8, 1975.

12. *Time,* February 17, 1975, p. 80.

13. Ibid., July 23, 1973, p. 50.

14. *Report of the National Advisory Commission on Civil Disorders* (New York: Bantam Books, 1968), pp. 278–81.

15. David K. Cohen, "Does I.Q. Matter?" *Commentary,* April 1972.

16. Quoted in *The Sword of the Lord,* October 19, 1962.

17. *Report of the National Advisory Commission on Civil Disorders* (Washington, D.C.: Government Printing Office, 1968), p. 471.

18. Figures taken from U.S. Bureau of the Census, *Statistical Abstract of the United States, 1976* (Washington, D.C.: Government Printing Office, 1977), p. 466; and *1979* (Washington, D.C.: Government Printing Office, 1980), p. 512.

19. Following results taken from George H. Gallup, *The Gallup Poll: Public Opinion 1935–1971* (New York: Random House, 1972), pp. 748, 1465, 1572–1973, 1824, and 2076.

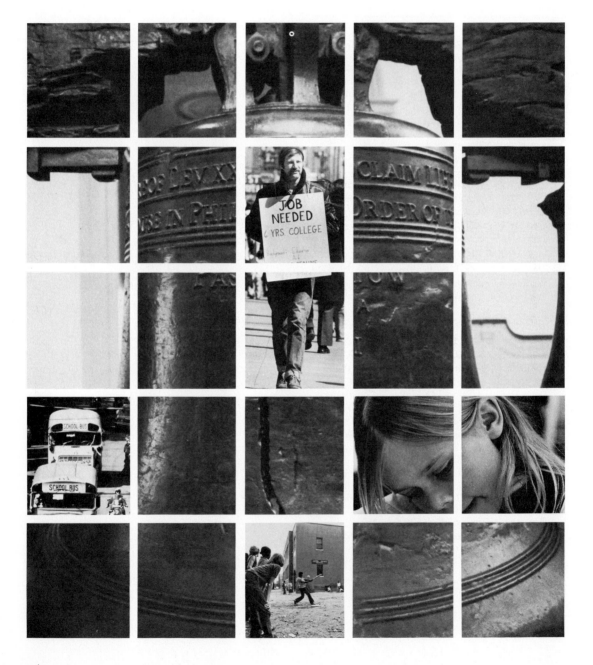

444

Education

13

1 What are the purposes of education?

2 Is the payoff of education decreasing?

3 Do pupils learn or merely survive in schools?

4 How does an individual's home life affect his or her educational career?

5 Are there racial differences in intellectual ability?

In several other chapters we point to education as an important tool in resolving social problems. A well-known writer on education suggested that we have a problem, not a solution, in education:

> America is in headlong retreat from its committment to education. Political confusion and economic uncertainty have shaken the people's faith in education as the key to financial and social success. This retreat ought to be the most pertinent issue in any examination of the country's condition in its Bicentennial year. At stake is nothing less than the survival of American democracy [Hechinger, 1976:11].

Historically, Americans have viewed education as an answer to many social ills. But, as the passage quoted above argued, quite rightly, when education is a problem, it is a very serious problem because education is the foundation of American life.

In what sense has education become a problem? In this chapter we will find the answer by first looking at the purposes Americans assign to education and the high value typically placed on education. We will also show how the high value is reflected in the continually "higher" amount of education attained by Americans.

In the light of the purposes and value of education, we will see how certain problems such as unequal opportunities bear upon the quality of life of Americans.

We will then examine some structural and social psychological factors that contribute to the problems and conclude with some examples of efforts to resolve the problems.

Why Education?

What do Americans expect their educational system to achieve for them personally and for their society? In 1787 the Northwest Ordinance included a provision for the encouragement of education on the grounds that "religion, morality, and knowledge" are "necessary to good government and the happiness of mankind." The significance of this, as Parker (1975:29) pointed out, is that "a people, not yet formed into a nation, declare education to be an essential support of free government and set aside western lands for schools and education." Similarly, Thomas Jefferson believed that education was essential to the freedom and happiness of the citizenry, for only the educated individual can see through the demagogue and avoid being taken in by those who claim to be wise.

Thus, one of the tasks of education is to create *good and effective citizens*. There is some dispute about the meaning of a good citizen, however. Some believe that education should equip the citizenry to reshape their society so that the flaws and inequities are rooted out. Others stress the conservative role of education—the need to produce citizens who will accept traditional values and protect the "American way of life" (which obviously means different things to different people). In any case, education has been held to be essential in the process of creating effective citizens in the republic.

A second task of education is to provide the individual with the *possibility for upward mobility*. For a long time Americans have associated education with good jobs. Most students in colleges and universities are there to prepare for the better-paying and more prestigious jobs, not for the love of learning. Most students believe that the primary aim of the schools is to prepare them for work rather than for effective citizenry or personal development. In a 1975 sample of junior and senior high school students, three common responses emerged to the question, "What are the overall educational goals of the school you attend?" Forty-three percent said the school was preparing them for college. Twenty-five percent said the school was preparing them for a job. Ten percent said that the school's goal was to graduate the students and get them out of school.[1] Apparently, students see their schools' aims in instrumental terms. Few of the students in the survey mentioned any of the personal development goals so often stressed by educators: that through education the individual is liberated from the bonds of ignorance and is prepared to maximize his or her intellectual, emotional, and social development.

Whatever their views of the primary aim of education, most Americans would probably agree that all three purposes we described are legitimate. The schools should produce good citizens. They should help the individual to better himself or herself. And they should prepare the individual to maximize his or her own development. Since all three purposes are related to the quality of *life* of the individual, if any person or group is not given the opportunity to secure an education that fulfills such purposes, education becomes a social problem. Quality of life is diminished when the individual lacks the tools necessary to participate effectively in political processes, or to achieve some measure of success in work or a career, or to develop his or her potential to its fullest.

Figure 13.1 Children usually start school with an eagerness to learn for the sake of learning.

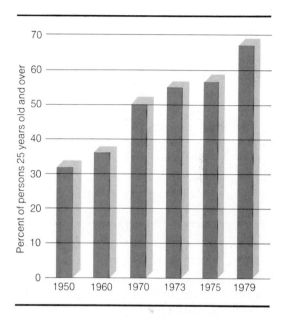

Figure 13.3 Four years of high school or more completed by adults, 1950 to 1979. (Source: Adapted from U.S. Bureau of the Census, *Statistical Abstract of the United States, 1979* [Washington, D.C.: Government Printing Office, 1980], p. 145).

Thus, it is not surprising that Americans value education highly. A 1939 survey showed that 54 percent of those under 20 who were not in college aspired to go, and several surveys since that time have shown that half or more of America's high school students aspire to college (Hauser, 1970:115).

Americans believe that education serves certain purposes that are crucial to our quality of life. They therefore aspire to high levels of education—much higher than in the past. There are differences of aspiration among different groups, of course. Nelson and Simpkins (1973) reported a survey of 40,000 high school juniors in Minnesota. They found that the children of white-collar workers were more likely to aspire to college than the children of blue-collar workers, that Protestants were more likely than Catholics to aspire to college, and that children from small families were more likely than those from large families to have college aspirations. But, even the lowest rate of aspiration reported—24.6 percent of females in a blue-collar, Protestant family of nine or larger who aspired to college—is higher than the overall rate of a few generations ago.

When people do not feel they have attained their ambitions in life, they tend to blame two things above all others—financial barriers and limited amounts of education (Campbell, Converse, and Rodgers, 1976: 384–85).

Educational Attainment and Payoff

We expect, from the earlier statements, that Americans would be securing an increasing amount of education over time. The aspirations are high, but what about the **attainment?** Once

attained, does education yield the expected payoff? Is our value on education reflected in concrete results?

Levels of Attainment

In 1870, 57 percent of the youth in the 5 to 17 age category were enrolled in school, and 1.2 percent were in high school. By 1978, 96.8 percent of those between the ages of 5 and 17 were in school, and 30.5 percent were in high school.[2] Not too long ago, completion of elementary school was considered a good *level of attainment*. Today, completion of high school is considered the appropriate minimal level of attainment, and, as figure 13.3 shows, an increasing proportion of the population has been reaching that level. By 1979, 67.7 percent of the population had completed high school and

Table 13.1   Years of School Completed, by Age, 1979
(persons 25 years old and over as of March 1979)

Age	Population (1,000)	Percent of Population Completing							Median School Years Completed
		Elementary School			High School		College		
		0–4 years	5–7 years	8 years	1–3 years	4 years	1–3 years	4 years or more	
All	125,295	3.5	6.2	8.6	14.0	36.6	14.7	16.4	12.5
25–29 years	17,940	1.0	1.8	1.7	9.9	39.3	23.2	23.1	12.9
30–34 years	16,113	1.2	2.2	2.5	10.4	39.1	20.1	24.5	12.9
35–44 years	24,611	1.6	3.4	4.1	13.7	42.0	15.5	19.6	12.6
45–54 years	22,826	2.8	5.6	7.6	16.5	40.1	12.4	15.0	12.4
55 years and over	43,806	6.7	11.3	16.6	16.0	29.9	9.9	9.7	11.9

Source: U.S. Bureau of the Census, *Statistical Abstract of the United States, 1980* (Washington, D.C.: Government Printing Office, 1981), p. 149.

over 31 percent had completed one or more years of college (table 13.1). The increasing amount of education attained by Americans is reflected in the data on different age groups in table 13.1. Note, for example, that nearly eight times as many people in the 55 years and older group completed only zero to four years of elementary school compared to people in the 25 to 29 years category. On the other end of the attainment scale, the proportion of the older group that completed four or more years of college was just a little over one-third the proportion in the younger group.

Another way to look at the increasing education attainment is to note the diminishing *dropout rate.* Students begin to drop out of school after the fifth grade. Since the 1920s the proportion dropping out, especially before completing elementary school, has greatly decreased (figure 13.4).

Overall, then, the level of educational attainment has been steadily increasing in our country. The minimum amount of education considered appropriate today is completion of high school, and the majority of Americans have reached that level. The dropout rate, which once increased steadily from the fifth grade on, now tends to remain minimal until after the eighth grade. Americans are getting more and more education. Is it yielding the expected payoff?

Attainment and Payoff

In some ways we cannot talk about the *payoff of education.* We cannot, for instance, measure the personal development of individuals and correlate that with education. We do have evidence that people with a college education report a greater degree of happiness than people with a high school education; and people with a high school education report a greater degree of happiness than people with an elementary school education (Armbruster, 1972:155). Campbell, Converse, and Rodgers (1976:128–32) found that people's satisfaction with some aspects of their lives went up with higher levels

Figure 13.4 School retention rates, 1924 to 1969, from fifth grade to high school graduation. (Source: Executive Office of the President, Office of Management and Budget, *Social Indicators, 1973* [Washington, D.C.: Government Printing Office, 1973], p. 78; and U.S. Bureau of the Census, *Statistical Abstract of the United States, 1979* [Washington, D.C.: Government Printing Office, 1980], p. 160.)

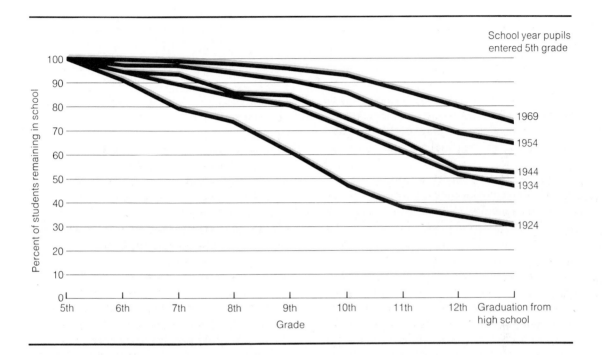

of education, while their satisfaction with other aspects was negatively correlated with educational attainment. In particular, those with some college but not a college degree expressed the greatest dissatisfaction in many areas of their lives (including their amount of education). Those with low amounts of education were the most satisfied in areas such as their friends, neighborhoods, and communities. But, these are not measures of personal development—the fulfillment of the individual's potential. At best, we can say that education creates some dissatisfactions as well as some fulfillments, and that the greater amount of happiness reported by the better educated *may* reflect a tendency toward greater fulfillment of potential.

Similarly, we have only a little evidence that education creates an effective citizenry. We do know, for instance, that there is a *direct correlation between level of education and voter participation.* For example, in national elections in 1968, 1972, and 1978 the proportion of those voting was 54.5 percent, 47.4 percent, and 34.6 percent, respectively, for those with eight years of education or less. The proportion was 81.2 percent, 78.8 percent, and 57.3 percent, respectively, for those with more than twelve years of education.[3] Evidence also indicates that education is directly correlated with democratic values and the support of democratic practices (Lipset, 1963:40). While such findings indicate positive contributions of education to citizenship, they do not tell us whether education enables people to detect and reject demagoguery and to participate meaningfully in the defense of freedom and the shaping of a just social order. Education does increase political participation and understanding. However, the more educated among us usually are the political and corporate heads who accept and maintain the institutional policies and practices that can contribute to the various social problems of the nation.

We have more evidence with respect to the third function of education—providing a means of upward mobility. We know that there is a strong relationship between levels of education and income. In 1978, people with four or more years of college averaged nearly three times as much annual income as people with less than eight years of education, and one and a half times as much annual income, as those with a high school education (table 13.2). In 1972 a male with less than an elementary education could expect to earn around $280,000 during his lifetime. With a high school education, he could expect about $479,000. A college graduate could look forward to around $758,000.[4]

Does this mean that an individual can maximize his or her income by maximizing education? In general, yes. Does this mean that any individual, regardless of background, has an equal opportunity to attain a high level of education and of income? In general, no. We will discuss this in some detail later, but the point here is that the high correlation between education and income does not mean that education is the open road to success. Those who attain high levels of education are likely to come from homes where the parents had a relatively high

Table 13.2   Mean Household Money Income, by Education, 1978

Educational Attainment of Head	Mean Household Income
Less than 8 years	$ 9,430
8 years	11,425
1 to 3 years high school	13,697
4 years high school	17,648
1 to 3 years college	19,407
4 or more years college	27,237

Source: U.S. Bureau of the Census, *Current Population Reports*, series P-60, no. 121, "Money Income in 1978 of Households in the United States" (Washington, D.C.: Government Printing Office, 1980), p. 37.

level of education. There is mobility in the United States, but education is more useful to the privileged as a means for passing on their privileges to their children than as a means for the underdog to be upwardly mobile.

Some people argue that education is of no use in reducing inequality in America (Jencks et al., 1972); that schools do virtually nothing to help the poor be upwardly mobile; and that education has little effect on the future incomes of people. Rather, the argument goes, economic opportunities depend on the state of the economy, one's family background, and various other noneducational factors, such as the contacts one is able to make.

It is true that education alone is not sufficient to deal with economic inequality in America. And it is true that the best way to "get ahead" in America is to start from a high socioeconomic position (obviously something over which the individual has no control). This argument overstates the case, however. The advantaged child will not maintain his or her advantage without an education. And, at least some people gain new advantages through education. Education is not a cure-all, but it is not useless in the struggle for new advantages.

We may conclude, then, that while many people are upwardly mobile through educational attainment, those most likely to benefit from education are already in the middle and upper strata. As pointed out previously, there are differences in aspirations for college among various groups; there are comparable differences in attainment. The middle- and upper-class child is most likely to secure a college degree and to transform that degree into a high lifetime income. In terms of mobility, then, there is a payoff in education, but that payoff is not equally likely to be gained by all groups. The probability that any individual will get the payoff depends on his or her social background. It is precisely this aspect of education in the United States that makes education a social problem.

Education and the Quality of Life

Ideally, as we have seen, education performs a number of valued functions that enhance the quality of life of Americans. It prepares us to be good, effective citizens. It is the pathway to our social and economic betterment. It is the tool by which we develop our full potential as individuals. To perform such functions, education would have to be of high quality, equally available to all, and consistently yield the expected payoff. Education is a problem because there are inequalities, and the expected payoff does not always occur.

Inequality of Opportunity and Attainment

Besides the inequality of attainment we have touched on, there is *inequality of opportunity*— a debatable and ambiguous notion, as we will see. Such inequalities *contradict our value of education and our ideology of equal opportunities* for all. Ideally, every American ought to have equal opportunity to maximize his or her education. However, racial minorities, women, and the poor do not attain the same educational levels as white males. Is this inequality of attainment a reflection of unequal opportunities or of some characteristics of the groups themselves? We have seen in previous chapters that the answer is both, but that the characteristics of the groups do not include an inferior level of intelligence. Part of the reason a son of a poor white farmer does not go to college is his own lack of motivation, but even that lack must be seen as a social phenomenon that is rooted in a complex situation in which multiple factors work together. In other words, the unequal educational attainment of various groups does not mean that those groups with lower levels of attainment are incapable of extending their education. It is important to keep this in mind as we explore how educational opportunities and attainment are distributed in our society.

The meaning of unequal opportunities. There is a considerable amount of debate over the meaning of inequality of opportunity. Most Americans, including most social scientists, would affirm the *ideal of equal educational opportunity* for all. But what does that mean? Does it mean that a child should have the opportunity to attend a nonsegregated school?

Does it mean that all children should be schooled with equal amounts of money? Does it mean that the proportion of people of various kinds (racial minorities, women, different socioeconomic strata) in various educational levels should be the same as their proportion in the total population? Does it mean that each child should have access to the same quality and the same amount of education? Does it mean that the same amount of education should yield the same payoff in terms of income or personal development?

If we choose one of these questions as appropriate and answer it affirmatively, the other questions may be answered negatively. If, for instance, we say that equality means that all children should attend nonsegregated schools, there may still be considerable inequality of funding between various schools. If we define equality as equal funds per student, children could still attend segregated schools, or be less likely to attend college if they are black, female, or poor.

Since the meaning of unequal opportunities is debated vigorously, it is unlikely that we can settle upon a definition that will be acceptable to everyone. Nevertheless, it is important to select a meaning so that we can explore the extent of inequality in America. For our purposes, equality of educational opportunity means that every child has access to quality education and is not deterred from maximizing that education by social background or economic factors. Social background factors include race, sex, and socioeconomic status. Economic factors include the funding of education and the cost to the student. In other words, equality means that people from various races and socioeconomic

backgrounds, and the two sexes, attain fairly equal amounts of education. It also means that students attend schools that are equally funded and that the cost of education (college or graduate school) does not force some students to drop out before they have reached their goal. In these terms, how much inequality is there?

Inequality of attainment. We have given figures in previous chapters on *differences in educational attainment* among the sexes, the races, and different socioeconomic strata. A measure of inequality may be the proportion of various groups that has attained different levels of education. In 1979, as table 13.3 shows, the proportion of blacks and hispanics who had completed four or more years of college is less than half the proportion of whites who had. Similarly, less than half of all blacks and hispanics had completed high school, compared to nearly 70 percent of whites who had.

The inequalities have not remained stable over time, however. In their study of changing educational patterns among American men, Hauser and Featherman (1976) found that the differences in attainment in a particular generation tended to decline over time. There was half as much variance in educational attainment among men born during World War II as there was among men born around the time of the Spanish-American War. Moreover, the inequality associated with certain groups tended to decline—specifically affected are those from rural backgrounds, those coming from broken families, those born in the South, and blacks and Spanish-origin men. On the other hand, people from the lower socioeconomic strata or from large families continued to attain lower

Table 13.3   Educational Attainment by Race and Spanish Origin, 1979
            (numbers in thousands)

	All Races	White	Black	Spanish Origin
Total, 25 years and over	125,295	110,798	12,227	5,367
Percent high school graduates	67.7	69.7	49.4	42.0
Percent completed some college	31.1	32.2	19.4	16.4
Percent completed 4 or more years of college	16.4	17.2	7.9	6.7

Source: U.S. Bureau of the Census, *Current Population Reports,* series P-20, no. 350, "Population Profile of the United States: 1979" (Washington, D.C.: Government Printing Office, 1980), p. 51.

levels of education. Overall, the researchers found considerable inequality, though not as much as there was at the turn of the century, and not as much for particular groups of men.

Funding and costs.   The second aspect of unequal opportunities is the *funding and cost of education.* Children do not have equal educational opportunities if they attend schools with unequal resources or if they are forced to drop out at some point because they cannot pay for the cost of their education.

There are considerable inequalities of resources, among the states and among school districts within a state. In 1978 the average expenditure per pupil ranged from $1,189 in Georgia and $1,193 in Arkansas to $2,527 in New York and $3,341 in Alaska.[5] The school expenditures in a state, of course, tend to reflect the overall wealth of the state and the personal income of the residents of the state. Arkansas does not have fiscal capacity equal to New York for funding public schools. Moreover, there are regional differences in the cost of maintaining schools. A dollar in Georgia would purchase more of some things than would a dollar in Alaska. Still, the child born in Georgia or Arkansas—or South Carolina or Idaho or some other state below the national average—will have to go to a school that is probably less well funded than the schools in other regions.

We must be cautious about such figures. A particular school in a Georgia city may offer an immeasurably better education than a ghetto school in New York. Not every school in the better-funded state is better than every school in the poorer-funded state. Rather, overall, the schools in the better-funded state have an advantage in resources for educating students.

One reason the Georgia school may be better than the New York school is that funding varies considerably within states. Schools have been funded by the *property tax* (discussed in more detail later). This means that a school district populated largely by people from lower income groups who live in cheaper homes will have a low tax base. School districts that encompass affluent areas, on the other hand, may actually have a lower rate of taxation (number of dollars of school tax per assessed value of the property) but a much higher per-pupil income. An affluent school district may have double, triple, or quadruple the funds per pupil that an adjacent poor school district has. Should the funds available for a child's schooling be considerably less because of the neighborhood in which he or she happens to be born?

Similarly, we may ask whether an individual should drop out of college because of inadequate financial resources even though he or she is quite capable of doing the work. Since the mid-1960s less and less money has been available for student loans and scholarships, while the cost of attending college has risen rapidly. By 1980 the cost of an education at a private school was higher than the annual median income of American families; it was estimated that four years would cost around $24,328.[6] Millions of American families have annual incomes less than the cost of room, board, and tuition at an average private university. Obviously, then, many Americans are simply priced out of the better colleges and universities in the country, apart from any other considerations.

In sum, the quality of life for many Americans is depressed because of unequal educational opportunities at all levels of education. Many children cannot afford to go to a better college or even to any college. Their level of attainment will be less than their abilities warrant and often less than they desire. Those same children probably attended elementary and secondary schools that spent less on them than other schools could spend. Thus, the inequality of education exists from kindergarten to the university.

The Atmosphere: Learning or Surviving?

Another kind of inequality that contradicts our ideology of equal opportunity involves the **atmosphere** *of the school*. Some atmospheres are conducive to learning, and some require the student to focus on surviving, on merely getting through the institution with body and sanity intact. Some critics have argued that the bulk of America's schools require more attention to survival than to learning. Silberman (1970:10) concluded that the public schools of America "mutilate" the spirit of children:

> It is not possible to spend any prolonged period visiting public school classrooms without being appalled by the mutilation visible everywhere— mutilation of spontaneity, of joy in learning, of pleasure in creating, of sense of self. The public schools . . . are the kind of institution one cannot really dislike until one gets to know them well. Because adults take the schools so much for granted, they fail to appreciate what grim, joyless places most American schools are, how oppressive and petty are the rules by which they are governed, how intellectually sterile and esthetically barren the atmosphere, what an appalling lack of civility obtains on the part of teachers and principals, what contempt they unconsciously display for children as children.

Some schools—perhaps a distinct minority— allow flexibility for teachers and students. Others require almost total conformity to rules, rigid schedules, and approved and disapproved kinds of behavior. An example of rigidity is offered by Silberman (1970:125):

> A scholar studying curriculum reform visits a classroom using a new elementary science curriculum. Arriving a few minutes before the class was scheduled to begin, he sees a cluster of excited children examining a turtle with

enormous fascination and intensity. "Now, children, put away the turtle," the teacher insists. "We're going to have our science lesson." The lesson is on crabs.

Rigidity in schools has certain useful functions, of course. It means that everyone is treated the same and that the administration is exercising extensive control over the educational process. But equality does not demand uniformity. To say that every child should have an equal opportunity for quality education does not mean that every child should follow the same schedule and curriculum as every other child. In fact, that kind of "equality" is inequality because it ignores differences among individuals and even whole classes.

Fincher (1976) argued that the gifted, creative, intellectually superior children are among the more deprived students in our schools. We spend far more on underprivileged and handicapped children than we do on the gifted. An estimated 4 million gifted children are in America, but less than 5 percent of them have even been identified as such. In general, our approach to the gifted has been characterized by

> . . . lack of funds, lack of leadership, lack of trained personnel, lack of public understanding, lack of priority, lack of legislation, appallingly poor diagnosis of the very population it is supposed to serve, too much isolation, too little organization and a stubborn history of nonintervention and state autonomy in how federal funds should be used [Fincher, 1976:19].

It has been argued that the gifted can learn without the kind of help needed by others, so we need not expend our time and money on them as we must on others. But, Fincher pointed out, gifted children typically work beneath their abilities when they are in a conventional school atmosphere, and many of them drop out of school.

Perhaps even worse than the rigidity that precludes individual schedules of learning is the *atmosphere of fear* in which some students must function. In a 1978 Gallup poll, over half the teenagers in the sample said that classroom disturbances, student use of marijuana, theft, and vandalism were serious problems at their schools. Nearly one-third said that fighting was a serious problem.[7] In a 1977 poll, 18 percent of the students reported fear for their personal safety; 4 percent said they had been physically assaulted; 12 percent had had money stolen: and 24 percent had had other property stolen. A survey of victimization in urban schools in twenty-six cities reported a total of more than 270,000 cases of victimization, including rape, robbery, aggravated assault, and larceny (McDermott, 1979). Most of the victims were students, but tens of thousands of teachers are also assaulted and otherwise victimized each year. Both teachers and students may have to function in an atmosphere of fear where their main concern is not about the survival of interest and motivation, but about the survival of physical and emotional well-being.

Another kind of atmosphere in many American classrooms may be characterized as **ritualized deprivation.** The teacher performs in a substandard fashion, and may be with the children for only a short period of time. The building and facilities are substandard and contain little if anything to stimulate curiosity or motivate the intellect. There is a daily ritual—some of the motions of teaching and learning are present. However, the ritual occurs in such a deprived context that the student is more concerned to survive the process than to learn.

The kind of school that has an atmosphere of ritualized deprivation is most likely to be found in the urban ghetto or other dominantly low-income area. Berlowitz (1974) studied the employment of teachers in Buffalo, New York schools from 1956 to 1963 and found that the teachers assigned to the inner-city schools were likely to be young males who were unlicensed and inexperienced. The children seldom had the same teacher for an entire year, the teachers' experience could not match that of others in the city, and their competence was even more questionable.

Kozol (1967), who taught in ghetto schools in Boston, portrays what it is like when one first walks into such a school:

> You walk into a narrow and old wood-smelling classroom and you see before you thirty-five curious, cautious and untrusting children, aged 8 to 13, of whom about two-thirds are Negro. . . . Nobody seems to know how many teachers they have had. Seven of their lifetime records are missing: symptomatic and emblematic at once of the chaos that has been with them all year long. . . . Of forty desks, five have tops with no hinges. . . . The general look of the room is as of a bleak-light photograph of a mental hospital. Above the one poor blackboard, gray rather than really black, and hard to write on, hangs from one tack, lopsided, a motto attributed to Benjamin Franklin: *Well begun is half done.* Everything, or almost everything like that, seems a mockery of itself [Kozol, 1967:190–91].

The bleakness is matched by a lack of basic materials. When he taught in the "discipline school" in Boston, Kozol found no appropriate books for the pupils to read. Many of the children in the school were older but were functioning academically at a first grade level. One boy asked Kozol to get him a first grade book because

> . . . he couldn't find such a book at school and was embarrassed at his age to walk into a public place and ask for one. He wanted desperately to read. . . . Yet the school offered him nothing and he had to humble himself to plead with me. One of the saddest things on earth is the sight of a young person, already becoming adolescent, who has lost about five years in the chaos and oblivion of a school system and who still not only wants but pleads to learn, as this boy was doing [Kozol, 1967:47].

The Payoff: A Great Training Robbery?

As noted earlier, one of the expectations that Americans have about education is that it will pay off in terms of upward mobility. Most Americans pursue education in order to secure more prestigious and better-paying jobs, and we have seen the correlation between education and income is quite strong. But, in the 1970s a *contradiction* developed between education and the economy. Our value of education and our average educational attainment outstripped the capacity of the economy to absorb the graduates. There is still a close relationship between education and occupation and income, but an increasing number of college graduates in the early 1970s had difficulty finding jobs. Many who did find jobs worked at tasks that did not require the amount of education that they had. Ivar Berg (1970) argued that education in America had become the "great training robbery," offering little relationship to many aspects of work performance. We will look at this situation in more detail, beginning with the problem of too many graduates for the economy.

The problem of what Freeman (1976) called the *"overeducated American"* began with the great expansion of education in the 1950s and 1960s. During those decades the number of college students tripled, and the number receiving master's degrees and doctorates more than tripled. This increase was encouraged by data on the relationship between education and income. Advertisements in the mass media pointed out that the typical college graduate would earn $100,000 more than the typical high school graduate over a lifetime of work. By 1970 there were more workers with one or more years of college than there were blue-collar union members.

But, by the mid-1970s, graduates were having difficulty getting jobs that required college training. A massive oversupply of teachers glutted the job market, and doctorates in fields such as physics and English literature were almost worthless in terms of securing employment. At all levels of college and university education, from the bachelor's degree to the doctorate, graduates were getting less payoff than their predecessors and were entering occupations that had little to do with the training they had received.

The problem is expected to continue in the 1980s when, according to one estimate, there will be an oversupply of roughly 900,000 college graduates.[8] We should keep in mind at this point that the diminished payoff refers strictly to employment and income. Unfortunately, Americans have focused so strongly on the economic payoff that many consider their college education useless if it does not yield a desirable, well-paying job. Only in this sense can we speak of an "oversupply" of college graduates. We could argue that all or at least the majority of Americans would profit by some college because higher education can enable the individual to think more deeply and explore more widely and enjoy a greater range of experiences. But, as long as education is valued primarily for its economic payoff, the quality of life will be depressed by the failure to yield that payoff.

Ironically, employers have helped to create the oversupply of graduates by insisting on high levels of educational attainment. Employers demand too much education for the kinds of jobs they offer. For instance, an insurance company might insist on a college degree for its agents. However, studies show that the productivity of agents, as measured by the amount of insurance sold, does not correlate with years of formal education. Similarly, studies of various other occupations show that education does not necessarily correlate with productivity or lack of absenteeism or promotion. Education can even have negative consequences for workers, for those who are overeducated may be less satisfied and productive than others.

Contributing Factors

Why are there inequalities in educational opportunities and attainment? And why hasn't education yielded the expected payoff for some people? As we will see, part of the answer does lie in the structure and processes of the educational system. A greater part of the answer lies in nonschool factors. The problems of education are only partially a problem of our schools.

Social Structural Factors

Social class, family background, and educational inequality. In our discussion of poverty, we pointed out that *families in the lower strata* of society are different in a number of respects from those in the middle and upper strata. Certain characteristics of the lower-strata family tend to depress **cognitive development.** This suggests that children who come from such families enter school with an intellectual disadvantage, and various studies confirm this. In a sense, even if they attend equally good schools and receive equal treatment from teachers, children from a disadvantaged background cannot have educational opportunity equal to that of others. As Tesconi and Hurwitz (1974:22) put it:

> Children raised in an environment in which the abilities, talents, and skills fostered are not those which the school uses to measure success will not have an equal opportunity to compete for the school's rewards with those whose environment more closely matches the culture of the school. Thus, if we extend the equal treatment premise of the input view beyond tangible, measurable inputs (property tax, scope and range of the curriculum, age of building, etc.) to the child's background, and regard the

opportunities provided by that background prior to schooling as "inputs" which the child brings to school, we run into new—and major—difficulties in providing equality of educational opportunity.

Whether or not we should include what the child brings to school as an appropriate matter for consideration when we discuss equal opportunity is debatable. Equal opportunity could simply mean providing equally good schools for all, because the society cannot be responsible for deficiencies in the family background. On the other hand, it can be argued that the schools are set up—in terms of curriculum or teachers' expectations—to reward students with particular kinds of backgrounds, namely middle- and upper-class backgrounds. Equal opportunity will not be a fact until the schools are set up to deal with all children according to their background so that all have an equal chance to succeed.

In any case, the *position of the family in the stratification system has a close relationship to the educational achievement of the children* coming from that family. Children who come from disadvantaged families may find the schools an alien setting. Children from the lower strata and teachers from the middle strata of society may be totally unprepared to deal with each other. The teachers may react to the children's range of experiences with astonishment and perplexity. The children may not even be able to distinguish the various colors when they enter school, and they may appear to have little grasp of abstract qualities such as shape and length. The teacher's training did not prepare him or her for this kind of student. One elementary school teacher read her class the story of Frosty the Snowman, then found that some of her pupils assumed a snowman is a man who shovels snow from city streets; they had seen one of those, but knew of no other kind. She later found that one of her children was sure a fire engine's purpose was to bring fire. No one had ever told him otherwise.[9]

As these children progress through school, their academic problems become more rather than less serious. Learning depends more and more on the ability to deal with abstractions. What is a society? What is a nation? What happened in the past? "Suddenly it's discovered that these children are unprepared for skilled use of such basic abstract ideas as bigger and smaller, higher and lower, round and square."[10]

Such children could be looked upon as a challenge, but teachers may be more likely to react to them with despair or contempt. Albert Yee (1968) argued that one of the reasons children from poor families do not achieve in school is that their *teachers do not like them.* The poor children have, if anything, a greater need for acceptance and warmth but are less likely to receive it than are middle-class children. Yee's conclusions were based on surveys of teachers and pupils in fifty schools in California and Texas. The children were asked about their perceptions of their teachers' attitudes, and the teachers were asked about their feelings toward their pupils. Yee found that the teachers were likely to be less warm and permissive, and hold less favorable attitudes toward students when they taught in lower-class schools. In other words, the emotional and intellectual support of the teacher is more likely to be absent for the lower-class pupil.

A survey of Philadelphia schools over a number of years modifies Yee's findings somewhat (Summers and Wolfe, 1977). Teachers with

degrees from better colleges had a positive effect on both low-income and middle-income students. An examination of the years of teaching experience revealed that experienced teachers had a positive effect on above-average students but a negative effect on those well below grade level. Newer teachers may have more enthusiasm and commitment to students who perform badly.

Socioeconomic status is one of the prime factors in unequal educational **achievement.** The reason is the discrepancy between the typical cognitive development of the child in the lower-class family and the typical patterns of interaction between lower-class pupils and middle-class teachers.

This was one of the findings of the Equality of Educational Opportunity Survey carried out by the National Center for Educational Statistics. The survey resulted from the Civil Rights Act of 1964, which required the Commissioner of Education to identify any inequality of educational opportunities due to race, color, religion, or national origin and to report that inequality to the President. A total of roughly 650,000 students in 4,000 public schools throughout the nation were surveyed. The "Coleman Report" was issued in 1966 as the first analysis of the data (Coleman, Campbell, Hobson, et al., 1966). A second report appeared three years later, and concluded, among other things:

Very little of the schools' influence on their students can be separated from the influence of the latter's social background. Conversely, very little of the influence of the students' social backgrounds can be separated from the influence of the schools. The children who benefit most from their schooling are those who:

1. Come from the higher socioeconomic strata rather than from the lower socioeconomic strata.
2. Have both parents in the home rather than only one or neither parent in the home.
3. Are white or Oriental-American rather than Mexican-American, Indian American, Puerto Rican or Negro [Mayeske et al., 1973:3].

Research by Wilson and Portes (1975) also stressed the importance of socioeconomic background. They used data from a national sample of adolescent boys from eighty-seven high schools who were studied between 1966 and 1970. The researchers were concerned with attainment rather than achievement, and measured attainment by number of years of schooling completed. The attainment ranged from those who dropped out of high school to those who attended a university. They found that various social psychological factors were less important than certain structural variables in explaining attainment. One of the important structural variables was socioeconomic level of the family, which had a direct impact on attainment level independent of things such as the influence of significant others. This is not surprising in view of our previous discussion.

Generally, family background factors in addition to socioeconomic level are of crucial importance. The Coleman Report included eight different factors in the family situation: (1) urbanism (based on community in which the pupil and his or her mother grew up), (2) education of parents; (3) structural integrity of the home (whether one or both parents were present); (4) size of the family; (5) whether items such as a television, telephone, record player, refrigerator, automobile, and vacuum cleaner were in the home; (6) presence of read-

ing material in the home; (7) parental interest (whether parents discussed school matters and read to the child when he or she was small); and (8) educational desires of the parents for the child. Taking these factors plus various characteristics of the schools into account, Coleman and his associates noted the following results:

1. The great importance of family background for achievement.
2. The fact that the relation of family background to achievement does not diminish over the years of school.
3. The relatively small amount of school-to-school variation that is not accounted for by differences in family background, indicating the small independent effect of variations in school facilities, curriculum, and staff upon achievement.
4. The small amount of variance in achievement explicitly accounted for by variations in facilities and curriculum.
5. Given the fact that no school factors account for much variation in achievement, teachers' characteristics account for more than any other. . . .
6. The fact that the social composition of the student body is more highly related to achievement, independently of the student's own social background, than is any school factor.
7. The fact that attitudes such as a sense of control of the environment, or a belief in the responsiveness of the environment, are extremely highly related to achievement, but appear to be little influenced by variations in school characteristics [Coleman et al., 1966:325].

Perhaps the most startling result of the Colemen report was the relatively small impact of the school upon the child's educational achievement. As presently constituted, the schools do

Involvement

Learning for Living

A philosopher once observed that it is the struggle and not the victory that pleases us. Similarly, social psychologists have pointed out that we continually try to enlarge the range of our satisfactions. In other words, human life is an unending striving for self-development. One of the aims of education is self-development. But, as this chapter points out, personal development goals are often ignored, lost, or neglected in our educational system.

Make an inventory of your own development goals. What kinds of knowledge or skills or activities would be satisfying to you? Make a list of activities and skills that would increase your life satisfaction and aid your personal development. Then inventory the educational resources in your community that could help you achieve your goals. Keep in mind that "educational resources" include much more than formal programs of schools. You may find help in those programs or in the noncredit courses being offered at many schools. You may also find help in libraries, special-interest organizations, and individuals with particular skills. You may even want to start an educational program with a group of other people who share your goals. For instance, you might get a retired mechanic to teach auto repairing to a group, or someone from a foreign country might teach you his or her language. Any community has resources that offer numerous possibilities of education for personal development.

RAICES Y VISIONES

CONTEMPORARY HISPANIC ART IN AMERICA

National Collection of Fine Arts
8th and G Streets, N.W. Washington, D.C.
July 9 - October 2, 1977

IOWA THEATER LAB

WINTER WORKSHOP

IRON
AT THE RENWICK GALLERY

k Douglass Townhouse, Capitol Hill
A St., Northeast, Washington, D. C.

Mon.-Fri. 11:00-5:00 Sat., Sun., Holidays 12:00-5:00

Grass

Renwick Gallery
of the National Collection of Fine Arts
Smithsonian Institution
Pennsylvania Avenue at 17th Street, N.W.
Washington, D.C.
August 5, 1977—February 20, 1978

STUDIO

12 x 22 x 9 for rent by hour,
day, week, or month.
Ideal for photographers, painters,
small group rehearsals, sunset lovers,
etc. Lots of natural light. 8th floor
2 bdrm apt has a great view of D.C.
Call Jack at 387-6763 eves.

10 DOWN
TOWN
TEN YEARS
AT P.S.1

THE INSTITUTE FOR ART & URBAN RESOURCES
PRESENT AN EXHIBITION CELEBRATING THE
TEN YEARS OF 10 DOWNTOWN
INSTALLATION BY LAWRENCE ALLOWAY
PROJECTS STUDIOS ONE (P.S.1)
46-01 21 ST LONG ISLAND CITY QUEENS, N.Y.
FROM SEPT. 11 THROUGH OCT. 2 1977
HOURS 1-6 PM THURSDAY THRU SUNDAY
RECEPTION SUNDAY SEPTEMBER 11, 3-6 PM

YOGA EXERCISES

• RELIEF FROM TENSION
• PEACE OF MIND

NOON TIME AND AFTER WORK CLASSES
8 WEEKS SESSION - $27

EXPERT INSTRUCTION BY
SITA FRENKEL

FOR INFORMATION CALL:
347-3565
YOGA SCHOOL OF WASHINGTON D.C.
2000 VERMONT AVE. N.W.
SUITE 210
WASHINGTON D.C. 20005

human nature: color images off the tube
and of the natural world by

W. KRUPSAW

September 18 through October 17, 1977
Opens Sunday, September 18, 3 to 6 P.M.

INTUITIVE EYE GALLERY

THE TRAVELIN'
BLUES WORKSHOP
Lisner Auditorium/G.W.U.
BIG MAMA THORNTON
Libba Cotten, John Jackson,
Chief Ellis, Mama Yancey,
Archie Edwards & Flora Molton

Sunday September 18th
2:30 P.M. & 7:30 P.M.
Tickets $6.50, $5.50, $4.50

ON WOOD
Furniture Since the 17th Century

Renwick Gallery
of the National Collection of Fine Arts
Smithsonian Institution
Pennsylvania Avenue at 17th Street, N.W.
Washington, D.C.
March 10 through November 6, 1977

Paper Song

not exert an influence that is independent of the family and social background, according to Coleman. This "means that the inequalities imposed on children by their home, neighborhood, and peer environment are carried along to become the inequalities with which they confront adult life at the end of school" (Coleman et al., 1966:325).

Further analysis by Mayeske and his associates showed that *at the twelfth grade level, the influence of the school becomes greater than the influence of the social background* for the first time in the child's educational career. This is true only for motivation and attitudes, not for achievement. Mayeske and his associates (1973:16) found some differences among various racial and ethnic groups in the relative importance of the different family background factors, but, overall, the following conclusions can be drawn from their analysis. Achievement scores tend to be higher for those pupils

1. whose parents are in the middle and upper socioeconomic levels (as measured by their educational attainment);
2. who have both parents in the home, have not moved around very much, and whose family income derives primarily from the father;
3. who perceive that their parents and teachers want them to be one of the best students and who share that desire for themselves;
4. whose parents want them to go to college and who themselves desire to go to college and aspire to the higher occupational levels;
5. who discuss school work frequently with their parents and who were read to by their parents when they were small, and who are determined and diligent about their school work;
6. who hold the following attitudes— "that people who accept their condition in life are not necessarily happier; that hard work is more important for success than good luck; that when he tries to get ahead he doesn't encoun-

ter many obstacles; that with a good education he won't have difficulty getting a job; that he would not sacrifice anything to get ahead nor does he want to change himself; that he does not have difficulty learning nor does he feel that he would do better if his teachers went slower; and that people like him have a chance to be successful" (Mayeske et al., 1973:6).

In sum, the analyses of the survey conducted by the U.S. Office of Education stress the importance of social class and family background factors in achievement in school. Things often associated with a good education—well-equipped schools with well-trained teachers—were found to have relatively little influence compared to social class and family background. This is not to say that school facilities and quality teachers are unimportant. We have seen a number of factors that can make some difference for various kinds of pupils. In addition, the Philadelphia study noted earlier concluded that class size and school size as well as teacher education and experience affect performance (Summers and Wolfe, 1977). In particular, large classes seem to stimulate high achievers but impede the work of low achievers, and small schools benefit all students but help blacks even more than others. While such factors are important, their importance to student achievement is less than that of the nonschool factors we have identified.

The organization of education.   As pointed out previously, the gap between children from the lower socioeconomic strata and those from the middle and upper strata tends to increase with the level of school. This suggests that the schools may somehow contribute to educational inequality—children who are disadvantaged by their social background when they enter school become even more disadvantaged as they progress through school. The Coleman Report noted certain school characteristics that contributed to achievement scores. For example, variations in the facilities available and in the curriculum make little *overall* difference in achievement scores (because they do not seem to be related to differences among white students). However, such variations are of some importance to minority groups; the facilities related to differences among the minorities are those for which the schools of minority students are less equipped than the schools of whites.

The quality of teachers showed a stronger relationship than facilities to the achievement of students, and the relationship became stronger at the higher grades. Finally, the achievement of students "is strongly related to the educational backgrounds and aspirations of the other students in the school" (Coleman et al., 1966:22).

The Coleman Report pointed out that, as with facilities, quality of teachers seems to be more important for minority students than for whites. It also notes that many potentially important characteristics of teachers were not measured in the survey. Among those characteristics that were measured, the teachers' scores on verbal skills tests and their educational backgrounds were most important to the achievement of their pupils. Teachers of minority students ranked lower on both measures than teachers of white students.

The Coleman Report suggests three characteristics of the organization of education that can bear upon achievement: (1) *distribution of funds for facilities* (particularly when some schools do not have adequate funds for things such as science laboratories); (2) *assignment of teachers to schools* (some schools receive a disproportionate number of the inferior teachers); and (3) the *socioeconomic composition of the student body* (schools tend to be homogeneous so that, for example, a lower-class child is unlikely to encounter peers with high educational aspirations or a value of intellectual achievement). We will discuss distribution of funds in the next section because it is a political issue. The assignment of teachers is handled by the school district, and, as we will see below, the school district itself may be an aspect of the organization of education that is of great importance for achievement. The homogeneous socioeconomic composition of schools has been attacked, insofar as it relates to racial differences at least, by busing, which we will examine in the final section of this chapter.

Before looking at the relationship of school district characteristics to achievement, we will briefly discuss a fourth aspect of the organization of education that bears upon inequality— *bureaucratic evaluation and labeling of ability*. Wilson and Portes (1975) pointed out that in addition to socioeconomic level, the "bureaucratic evaluation of ability" was an important structural variable in explaining educational attainment. Academic performance was a major predictor in explaining level of attainment in their study. Individuals with high performance levels are selected and encouraged by the school to continue their educational careers.

It might be argued that this is precisely what should happen, that those who show they have the capacity through their performance should be encouraged to continue. The situation is not as simple as that, however. Inequality of achievement during the first years of school does not mean that the low achievers lack the capacity to attain high educational levels. Low achievement, as we have shown, tends to follow from a particular kind of social and family background. We have also seen, in previous chapters, the effects of labeling. If the low achiever is labeled as one with a low capacity, both the reaction of the teacher and the self-expectations of the child are negatively affected.

We noted in our discussion of poverty that a good deal of evidence shows that *labeling affects the achievement of children*. An experiment in an elementary school reported by Rosenthal and Jacobson (1968) showed that the expectations of teachers about the intellectual abilities of their students was reflected in the students' IQ scores. A student whom the teacher expected to do poorly tended to get low scores, and a student whom the teacher expected to do well got higher scores. The performance of people, whether children or adults, can be significantly influenced by the expectations of others and can reflect those expectations more than any innate abilities.

Labels can be effective. When the disadvantage of background is compounded by the negative consequences of bureaucratic labeling, the outcome is likely to be a low level of attainment for some children—perhaps a great many—who actually have the capacity to achieve high levels. The present organization of education tends to identify achievement with capacity. If the child has an IQ score of 100, the child is believed to have average intellectual capacity. If the score is 70, the child is believed to be a slow and limited learner. Labels are applied to children according to their achievement. Those labels can become *self-fulfilling prophecies,* retarding or stifling the achievement of able students.

Is there any evidence that the labels are inaccurate? Can't teachers detect and encourage children who are bright but who perform poorly on achievement tests? No doubt some teachers can and do. However, some children from lower socioeconomic backgrounds have a capacity that is masked by their initial disadvantage and by their subsequent experiences and performance in the school. The evidence is scattered and, in some cases, indirect. We will see some evidence when we look at the effects of desegregation in the last section of this chapter.

We don't know exactly how many students there are in our schools whose capacity or actual achievement is well above the official achievement. We do know, however, that the official achievement is closely related to ultimate attainment and to the manner in which teachers interact with students. So long as we rely on such measures as achievement scores to label students, a great deal of potential will go undetected.

The final aspect of the organization of education that we will discuss is the *division of the student population into school districts*. In their examination of 104 school districts in Colorado, Bidwell and Kasarda (1975) found that some of the conclusions of the Coleman Report had to be modified. When we look at differences between districts and not merely between and within individual schools, we find some of the factors that appeared to be of little importance in the Coleman Report take on greater significance. The crucial importance of the family and social background is not denied by the research of Bidwell and Kasarda. Rather, certain factors such as pupil-teacher ratios emerge as more important than the Coleman Report findings suggest. In other words, the organization of education may contribute more to educational achievement than the Coleman Report indicated.

Bidwell and Kasarda analyzed data from 104 districts in Colorado for the 1969–70 school year. Over 90 percent of all public school students in the state were in those districts. Student achievement was measured by median levels of reading and mathematics scores on standardized tests. The researchers looked at the relationships between achievement on the one hand, and certain environmental and organizational factors on the other hand. The environmental factors included the size of the school district (in terms of average daily attendance); fiscal resources per pupil; proportion of students from poverty-level families; and educational level of adults in the district (measured by the proportion who had at least a high school education). The organizational factors included the pupil-teacher ratio; administrative intensity (ratio of administrators to classroom teachers); professional support (ratio of support staff to classroom teachers); and certified staff qualifications (proportion of all the certified staff who had at least a master's degree).

Achievement levels were found to be related to most of these factors. The median achievement scores tended to be higher in those school districts where: the pupil-teacher ratio was lower; administrative intensity was lower; and the certified staff was more qualified (the relationship was not statistically significant for mathematics scores, however). The effects of professional staff support were not significant. The environmental factors—size, fiscal resources, proportion of disadvantaged students, and educational level within the district—were

related to achievement to the extent that they influenced the staffing.

> Our Colorado findings give clear evidence of the simple but important fact that as school districts command more income they buy more and better-qualified front-line staff, investing in both teachers and supporting professional specialists. Therefore at the district level, at least so far as investment in teachers is concerned, the availability of revenues has important consequences for student achievement [Bidwell and Kasarda, 1975:69].

Unequal fiscal resources are associated with inequalities of achievement. That leads us directly into what became a hotly-debated political issue in the 1970s.

The politics of school financing. If fiscal resources prevent some districts from having an adequate or high-quality staff, one way to deal with educational inequality would be to *equalize the money available* to various districts. According to a Gallup poll, there is public support for equalizing within a state the funds available to various school districts.[11] When asked about an amendment to equalize amounts spent on school children within a state, 66 percent of the respondents said they favored such a change. Equalizing fiscal resources is a political matter, however, and up to now the government has not acted on the matter.

The reason pupils in wealthier districts have more money available for their education is that the public education is financed largely by the property tax. As noted earlier, this can result in gross inequalities. Those who have opposed this method of financing have argued that no child should be denied a quality education simply because of the socioeconomic status of his or her parents. This is not an unusual argument in America. As Perlman (1973:116) noted:

> There is nothing new in considering wealth a discriminating determinant where fundamental interest is involved. The poll tax was banned on just that basis. Similarly in ordering reapportionment of voting districts in line with population densities, the Supreme Court held that voting power should not be determined by location of residence, if the rights of individuals to equal protection under the law are to be upheld.

This logic was followed by the California Supreme Court in 1971, in the *Serrano vs. Priest* case, to declare the property tax system unconstitutional:

> We have determined that this funding scheme invidiously discriminates against the poor because it makes the quality of a child's education a function of the wealth of his parents and his neighbors . . . the right to an education in our public schools is a fundamental interest which cannot be conditioned on wealth. . . . We have concluded, therefore, that such a system . . . must fall before the Equal Protection Clause [Tesconi and Hurwitz, 1974:57].

The *Serrano* case was not supported by subsequent decisions of the U.S. Supreme Court, which denied that the property tax system of financing education was a violation of the Equal Protection Clause of the Fourteenth Amendment. The advocates of equality must renew their struggle in the political arena. Changes must occur in state legislatures, which have the power to alter the system of financing. It appears that until state governments can be influenced to act, inequality of fiscal resources will continue to characterize the nation's school districts.

The economics of education.   As with so many important areas of American life, *education is affected by the ups and downs of the economy.* Recessions cause political leaders to look with jaundiced eyes at the costs of education and to resist any kinds of change that will involve more money. Inflation may rapidly outstrip the fiscal resources of schools, with resulting problems regarding salaries and the purchase of supplies. In the 1970s the nation suffered from a combination of recession and inflation, and the schools—from the elementary level to the university—often found themselves in precarious situations. The resources of many colleges and universities were severely cut. A survey in 1972–74 concluded that about one of every seven institutions of higher learning was "financially unhealthy"—so unhealthy that their "long-term survival is problematic unless some major external intervention occurs."[12] The schools were rated on a scale from unhealthy to healthy, and only one-fourth were considered in a healthy financial state, while nearly half were either unhealthy or "relatively unhealthy." The schools most likely to have serious financial problems were small and private, and the single-sex and church-related schools.

Public schools were also in financial difficulties. In 1977 the University of Cincinnati lost its effort to maintain its independence as a municipal institution and became part of the Ohio state university network. In 1976 the City University of New York closed for a brief period because it was out of money. A number of state universities in the 1970s reduced the size of their faculties and cut back on various supportive services (including even crucial things such as the purchase of books for the library).

Elementary and secondary schools also faced serious fiscal problems. The urban school systems in particular were caught between declining tax bases on the one hand and increasing inflation on the other hand. In the fall of 1976, urban schools were showing various effects of the economic squeeze.[13] New York City had 5,000 fewer teachers than it had in the previous fall. Some Los Angeles classes had to be cancelled because there was no money to fix leaking roofs. Athletic programs in a number of cities were cut back, and in some cases could be continued only because of private gifts. Teachers went on strike in many areas because of inadequate salary increases or none at all. In Chicago the teachers accepted no increase in order to keep the schools open for the entire school year.

To some extent, the *economic problems are also political problems.* Not everything suffers equally in times of economic difficulty—political leaders make decisions that bear upon the resources available. The governor of a state must decide whether education, mental health, highway maintenance, or a number of other areas will receive priority consideration when budgets must be cut (or not increased, which amounts to a cut in time of inflation). Obviously, the problems of education cannot be separated from other problems in a time of national economic difficulty. When resources are scarce, the decision to fund one area—such as education—more fully is a decision *not* to adequately fund another area—such as health programs. A faltering economy, therefore, inevitably means an intensification of at least some of our social problems.

Social Psychological Factors

Attitudes. We have already noted some *attitudes that contribute to educational problems.* The attitudes of children in the lower strata, for example, tend to inhibit them from aspiring to higher levels of attainment. We also pointed to the attitudes of the teachers of such children, noting that the teachers typically expect little and often hold negative feelings toward the children. Kozol (1967:44) told how one teacher advised him to get out of a particular school if he was really interested in teaching: "This place isn't a school. It's a zoo. And those are the animals," he said, motioning toward the pupils.

We expect that the attitudes of students toward school and schoolwork relate to achievement, and the Coleman Report supported this. The researchers looked at three attitudes and their relationship to achievement: the *student's interest in school and in reading* outside of school; the *student's self-concept,* specifically the view of the student toward his or her learning and success in school; and the *student's sense of control over the environment.* The self-concept was measured by the amount of agreement or disagreement with statements such as "I sometimes feel I just can't learn" and "I would do better in school work if teachers didn't go so fast." The sense of control over the environment was measured by agreement or disagreement with statements such as "People like me don't have much of a chance to be successful in life" and "Every time I try to get ahead, something or somebody stops me."

The three attitudes, as measured by various statements and questions, had the strongest relation to achievement of any of the factors measured in the survey. The different attitudes were not equally important for all ethnic and racial groups, however, and some interesting variations appeared. Of the three attitudes, the self-concept had the weakest relationship to achievement, particularly among minority groups. For all groups except whites and Oriental Americans, the sense of control was more strongly related to achievement than was self-concept. This result was interpreted as follows:

> The special importance of a sense of control of environment for achievement of minority-group children and perhaps for disadvantaged whites as well suggests a different set of predispositional factors operating to create low or high achievement of children from disadvantaged groups than for children from advantaged groups. For children from advantaged groups, achievement or lack of it appears closely related to their self-concept: what they believe about themselves. For children from disadvantaged groups, achievement or lack of achievement appears closely related to what they believe about their environment: whether they believe the environment will respond to reasonable efforts, or whether they believe it is instead merely random or immovable [Coleman et al., 1966:320–21].

It seems that the sense of powerlessness that tends to characterize those in the lower socioeconomic strata inhibits educational achievement. Perhaps the child makes minimal efforts because those efforts are viewed as largely fruitless in any case.

The value of education. We have emphasized the high value that Americans place on education, but that value is largely *instrumental.* Education is valued because it has been the path to upward mobility, to better-paying jobs. The goals shared by most educators—the development of the individual and of an effective citizenry—are not often shared by others.

Fred Hechinger pointed out that many Americans in the mid-1970s were asking if too many young people were going to college. "The unmistakable implication is that one should not waste the time and money when college can't deliver a lucrative job and a promising career" (Hechinger, 1976:12). It is not surprising that one of the contemporary problems of education is frustration over the failure to yield the payoff. With an increasingly well-educated citizenry, we will have increasing levels of frustration unless the bases upon which education is valued are broadened.

A Concluding Note on the Inequality in Education

We implied above that if the various factors we have identified are all taken into account, then children of different racial, ethnic, and socioeconomic backgrounds should be able to show about the same levels of achievement. Research sponsored by the Office of Education supports this. Figure 13.7 shows the achievement scores for sixth graders when various factors in their backgrounds are taken into account. If we look only at the scores of unequalized whites, Orientals, Indians, Negroes, Mexicans, and Puerto Ricans in the United States, we see considerable differences in their achievement (far left of the figure). The Puerto Rican students had the lowest average score and the white students the highest, about 50 percent higher.

Suppose we control for socioeconomic background? What will the differences be for children of different racial and ethnic groups but the same socioeconomic level? The answer is in the second set of points in figure 13.7, labeled "Equalized for socioeconomic status." The spread narrows considerably, showing that a good part of the differences we observed among the groups were really rooted in different socioeconomic backgrounds. As we continue to move to the right in the figure, each set of points takes progressively more background factors into account, and the differences in scores diminish correspondingly. The third set of points adjusts the scores to equalize for socioeconomic status *plus* degree of family structure and stability. The next set of points adds the students' attitude to life (as described previously). The fifth set of points takes in the students' expectations for excellence, educational desires, and study habits. The sixth adds to those factors the area of residence. The last set includes the achievement-motivational mix of fellow students, which means if the students were to come from the same socioeconomic background, have the same family experiences, and exhibit the same social psychological processes, what would be the differences between the scores of the various racial and ethnic groups? The answer, as shown in figure 13.7, is about 1 percent. Unequal educational achievement in the United States is a sociocultural, not a racial-genetic matter.

What Is To Be Done?

A variety of ways have been tried to attack the various problems of education—inequalities of achievement and attainment, inadequate learning atmospheres, and lack of the expected payoff. We will look at three of these ways: **compensatory programs** and other innovative

474

Figure 13.7 Racial-ethnic group achievement means of sixth grade pupils adjusted for social background conditions. (Source: Adapted from George W. Mayeske et al., *A Study of Achievement of Our Nation's Schools* [Washington, D.C.: Government Printing Office, 1973], p. 137.)

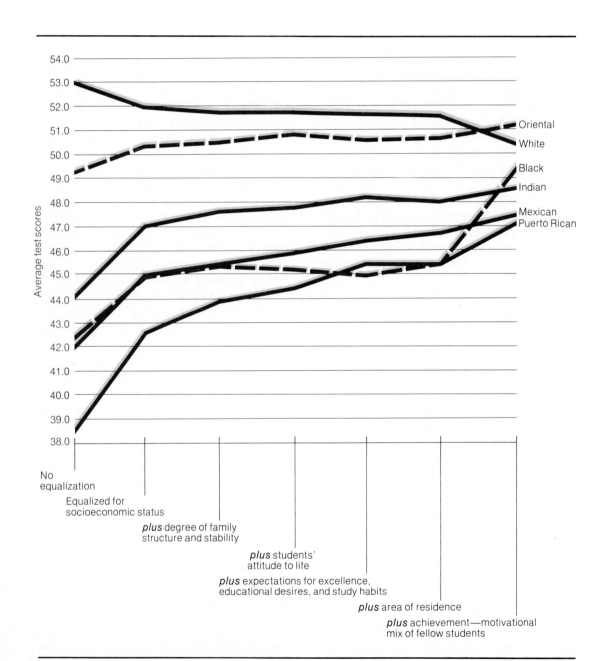

approaches; the **"deschooling"** movement; and *desegregation efforts,* including *busing.* Our analysis suggested some other steps that could be taken: teaching the public to value education as a means to self-development and not merely as a door to a career; maintaining a healthy economy and effectively dealing with the problem of poverty; and equalizing the money per pupil in various school districts. Rather than discuss these points, however, we will look at efforts already under way, including some that are highly controversial. We will begin with an approach that has been in the forefront of public concern and the focus of considerable *inter-group conflict*—desegregation, including busing.

The Desegregation Process

In 1954 in the now-famous case *Brown vs. Board of Education of Topeka, Kansas,* the U.S. Supreme Court ruled that segregated education imposed by governments was no longer legal. This reversed a nineteenth century decision that argued "separate but equal" facilities may be provided by states. The 1954 decision declared that separate facilities are inherently unequal and, therefore, unconstitutional. The process of desegregating the schools began. It has been a slow process—painfully slow in many cases. By 1978, 16.1 percent of minority-group pupils in public elementary and secondary schools were still attending schools with minority-group enrollment of 99 to 100 percent.[14] There is also concern about resegregation due to the "white flight" to the suburbs to escape school desegregation. This, in turn, provided a basis for the pro-busing argument.

Before looking at the busing question, we may ask whether segregation indeed means inequality in education. *What happens to children in desegregated schools* that would not happen in segregated schools? The evidence is that levels of achievement of black children are raised by desegregating the schools. The Coleman Report noted that black children from lower socioeconomic strata brought into schools with middle-class white children showed higher achievement levels than black children in segregated schools. In Hartford, Connecticut, children from ghetto areas were sent to various suburban schools, beginning in 1966. A study of the effects made a few years later showed that black fourth graders who were bused to the suburbs were reading at a level four months behind their white peers but nine months ahead of their black peers who remained in the city schools (Eitzen, 1974:328). The Philadelphia study showed that blacks and whites benefited when they were in schools with 40 to 60 percent blacks rather than in more segregated schools (Summers and Wolfe, 1977). Desegregation is not always beneficial to students, but it is more likely than not to be beneficial. A review of seventy-three studies of desegregation by the National Review Panel on School Desegregation Research found that black achievement increased in forty cases, was unaffected in twenty-one cases, and declined in the other twelve cases.[15]

Despite such findings, intense *conflict over busing* as a means of achieving integration did arise. Gallup polls in the 1970s showed an increase in the proportion of people favoring busing, but by 1978 only 21 percent favored it.

To compound the matter of busing, various studies have yielded contradictory results. Ac-

cording to some, busing brings about definite gains in achievement for black children, and in some cases for white children as well (Pettigrew, Useem, Normand, and Smith, 1973). According to others, black children who are bused not only fail to show achievement gains, they may show some losses both academically and socially (Armor, 1973; Miller and Gerard, 1976). James Coleman, the main author of the Coleman Report, created something of a stir in 1975 when he publicly stated that busing has not worked because it increased the flight of whites out of the cities and thereby reinforced patterns of segregation. Coleman was accused ˙ of virtually being a traitor to the cause of integration and black development, but in an interview he explained that he strongly favored integration. Busing, he argued, was not a desirable or effective way to achieve that integration:

> Fundamentally, it's a matter of finding ways to make the central city attractive for middle-class whites, to make the suburbs available to middle-class blacks, and to provide jobs for lower-class blacks. . . . I'd propose that each central-city child should have an entitlement from the state to attend any school in the metropolitan area outside his own district—with per-pupil funds going with him. . . . If an integrated school had one-and-a-half times the budget of a nonintegrated school and could remain open from the time parents went to work until they got back, that would attract a lot of people.[16]

One reason for the contradictory results of studies of busing may be that where an atmosphere of tension and conflict is created by severe parental opposition, the children are simply inhibited from learning. In the same interview just mentioned, Coleman argued that if children learn to read more quickly and are happy and not threatened by physical harm at their schools, the parents will not care about the racial composition. But, where busing is an emotionally charged issue and is accompanied by overt opposition, it is less likely that children will be happy about school or feel unthreatened. The intensity of the opposition may become a self-fulfilling prophecy. As parents create an atmosphere in which their children are unable to learn well, opposition to busing is reinforced.

This line of reasoning is supported by the extensive review of the problem offered by Orfield (1978). Orfield used court cases, various research data, newspaper stories, and interviews in an effort to sort out the contradictory views about busing. He concluded that many of the objections are based on myth. There is no evidence, for instance, that busing per se has any negative consequences. Generally, violence does not increase and may even decrease if the school district has made appropriate plans. Furthermore, busing is not necessarily a financial drain on a district. A good deal of evidence has accumulated about students who have been helped as a result of busing, and a good number of cases prove that integration can be achieved with relative ease through busing. According to Orfield, busing is not only largely beneficial—apart, of course, from the deleterious consequences of mishandling the process—it is also the only way urban schools can be desegregated.

Compensatory and Other Innovative Programs

Compensatory programs are aimed at the *disadvantaged pupils.* They focus on skills such as reading and speech and attempt to offer an intensive program of help so that the disadvantaged pupil can approach the level of others in the school. Some compensatory programs are remedial and attempt, among other things, to reduce the number of students per teacher, to provide the student with extra help (including after school hours), and to use special teaching materials. The Head Start program attempts to stimulate learning of verbal and social skills among preschool disadvantaged children.

Compensatory programs have not produced the hoped-for results in most cases. It may be, as Kniker (1975) pointed out, that such programs have been inadequately funded and also have been evaluated before their effects had ample time to appear. We should recall that our analysis above indicates that the family background of the child is a crucial factor in educational achievement and attainment, and any program that aims only at the child's skill deficiencies will have limited success.

Other programs have focused on things such as *dropouts* and education of *special students*. With regard to dropouts, the Congress passed legislation in 1968 to authorize dropout-prevention projects. Local public educational agencies were allowed to develop programs in target schools that "would interest and allow the potential dropout to stay in school and to increase his or her capacity to be a productive citizen upon graduating from high school."[17] After four years the number of dropouts in the target schools has been reduced by 52 percent. The success of this program suggests that sufficient commitment plus agreement about the desirability of the program can resolve or at least ameliorate some of our educational problems. Even the "special" student can learn to some extent. In an experimental program at Washington University in St. Louis, Hamblin and his associates (1969) reported the following results:

Extraordinarily aggressive boys, who had not previously responded to therapy, have been tamed. Two-year-olds have learned to read about as fast and as well as their 5-year-old classmates. Four ghetto children, too shy, too withdrawn to talk, have become better than average talkers. Several autistic children, who were either mute or could only parrot sounds, have developed functional speech, have lost their bizarre and disruptive behavior patterns, and their relationships with parents and other children have improved. All of these children are on the road to normality [Hamblin et al., 1969:20].

The Deschooling Movement

The *deschooling movement* has aimed at eliminating the "grim, joyless" atmosphere we described earlier and providing to students a situation in which they will maximize their learning. In all cases, the movement emphasizes the necessity of a break with the existing educational structure and the creation of new schools where children can be free to learn. One facet of the movement involves the *"free schools,"* which assume that children are naturally curious and that, given an appropriate atmosphere, they will be highly motivated to learn in accord with their own interests. Many of the free schools do not last long, but three types have tended to survive: (1) the storefront academy in a black ghetto that gives "the rigorous college preparation that few minorities get in city public schools"; (2) the rural school where counterculture whites teach "agrarian survival skills"; and (3) the middle-class schools that try to develop emotional as well as intellectual skills.[18]

The most radical advocate of deschooling is Ivan Illich, who argued that learning has become a commodity and that the existing schools monopolize the market. The educational establishment, according to Illich, is an oppressive institution. If educational institutions are needed at all, they should "ideally take the form of facility centers where one can get a roof of the right size over his head, access to a piano or a kiln, and to records, books, or slides" (Illich, 1975:89). Thus, compulsory education should be abolished, and each individual should be free to pursue his or her own education (much of which could be gained by contract with people who have the desired knowledge and skills) in accord with his or her goals in life.

The various efforts to "deschool" society and establish free schools or a system of individuals in pursuit of their own education is not likely to be accepted by many Americans. The educational problems of some pupils may be resolved through free schools, and the deschooling advocates may influence some of the practices and policies of the educational establishment. The struggle for equality and quality must take place within the educational establishment however. The bulk of Americans will continue to pursue their educational aspirations in the existing school system.

Summary

Education is a problem when it fails to achieve the expected purposes—creating good and effective citizens; providing the possibility for upward mobility; and facilitating individual development. For these purposes education is highly valued by Americans. Lack of education is frequently associated with failure to achieve one's ambitions in life.

America has become an increasingly educated society. By 1978, 70.2 percent of the population had completed high school, and nearly 30 percent of all Americans 25 years or older had completed one or more years of college. Whether this education has yielded the expected payoffs is not always clear. The greater degree of happiness reported by the highly educated may reflect a tendency toward greater fulfillment of individual potential. Education increases political participation and understanding. There is a strong relationship between education and income, but those most likely to benefit from education are already in the middle and upper strata.

Education is a problem because there are inequalities, and the expected payoff does not always occur. Educational attainment is unequally distributed among the sexes, the races, and the different socioeconomic strata. Educational funding is unequally distributed among states and school districts within states. The cost of education prices many Americans out of the better colleges and universities. The learning atmosphere of some schools (critics would say nearly all schools) is rigid and joyless and precludes individual schedules of learning; sometimes students suffer an atmosphere of fear and threat or ritualized deprivation.

During the 1970s an oversupply of educated people developed, reducing the career and income payoff of education for increasing numbers of people.

Among the social structural factors that contribute to the problems of education, social class and family background are particularly important. The social background of the student has more to do with his or her academic achievement than any characteristic of the school. The organization of education also makes a difference in students' achievement and attainment. Particularly important are the distribution of funds, the assignment of teachers, the socioeconomic composition of the student body, the bureaucratic evaluation and labeling of ability, and the division of the student population into school districts. The inequitable distribution of funds is a political issue that must be resolved by political action. Finally, the quality of education varies with the economy. Recessions and inflation both drain the resources available to schools.

Attitudes of both teachers and students are important social psychological factors that contribute to the problems of education. The attitudes of students toward school and intellectual activities, toward themselves, and toward their control of the environment are strongly related to achievement. Teacher attitudes can inhibit or facilitate student achievement.

The lack of expected payoff is partly rooted in our value of education as instrumental. Generally, Americans value education because it leads to upward mobility, not because it leads to self-fulfillment and enrichment.

Our analysis implies that, when the various contributing factors are taken into account, children of different social backgrounds have the same capacity for achievement. The Office of Education survey supports this position. Given the same socioeconomic background, family background, attitudes, and the like, there is only about a 1 percent difference in the achievement scores of the various racial and ethnic groups.

Glossary

achievement   as distinguished from educational "attainment," the level the student has reached as measured by scores on various verbal and nonverbal tests

atmosphere   the general mood and social influences in a situation or place

attainment   as distinguished from educational "achievement," the number of years of education completed by a student

cognitive development   growth in the ability to perform increasingly complex intellectual activities, particularly abstract relationships

compensatory programs   programs designed to give intensive help to disadvantaged pupils and increase their academic skills

deschooling   process of removing education from the existing school system and creating a new system in which students can maximize their learning

ritualized deprivation   a school atmosphere in which the motions of teaching and learning continue while the students are more concerned to survive than to learn

For Further Reading

Fantini, Mario, et al. *Community Control and the Urban School*. New York: Praeger, 1970. A description of the conflict between those who advocate local control of education and those who insist that education must be controlled by professional educators.

Freeman, Richard B. *The Over-educated American*. New York: Academic Press, 1976. A discussion of the failure of education to yield a payoff of income and career: discusses particularly the oversupply of college graduates that arose during the 1970s.

Harrison, Bennett. *Education, Training and the Urban Ghetto*. Baltimore: John Hopkins University Press, 1972. Based upon studies made by the Department of Labor, the author analyzes the relationship between education and the employment, income, and occupational status and mobility of ghetto workers.

Hart, Harold H., ed. *Summerhill: For and Against*. New York: Hart Publishing Co., 1970. Various articles discuss the pros and cons of the famous Summerhill school, a radical educational innovation created by A. S. Neill in England.

Rosenthal, Robert, and Lenore Jacobson. *Pygmalion in the Classroom*. New York: Holt, Rinehart & Winston, 1968. Describes a well-known experiment in an actual school setting, showing the consequences of teacher expectations for pupil performance.

Tesconi, Charles A., Jr., and Emanuel Hurwitz, Jr. *Education for Whom? The Question of Equal Educational Opportunity*. New York: Dodd, Mead & Company, 1974. A readable discussion of the problem and meaning of equal educational opportunity. Includes numerous readings by people of various perspectives.

Notes

1. Reported in *The Gallup Opinion Index,* no. 119, May 1975, p. 24.
2. U.S. Bureau of the Census, *Current Population Reports,* series P-20, no. 346, "School Enrollment—Social and Economic Characteristics of Students: October 1978," (Washington, D.C.: Government Printing Office, 1979), p. 21.
3. Figures found in the U.S. Bureau of the Census, *Statistical Abstract of the United States, 1976* (Washington, D.C.: Government Printing Office, 1977), p. 467; and *1979* (Washington, D.C.: Government Printing Office, 1980), p. 514.
4. U.S. Bureau of the Census, *Statistical Abstract of the United States, 1979* (Washington, D.C.: Government Printing Office, 1980), p. 144.
5. Ibid., p. 157.
6. *St. Louis Globe-Democrat,* July 28, 1980.
7. Reported in *Public Opinion,* August/September 1979, p. 38.
8. Reported in *The Chronicle of Higher Education,* September 27, 1976, p. 4.
9. U.S. Office of Education and Office of Economic Opportunity, *Education: An Answer to Poverty* (Washington, D.C.: Government Printing Office, 1966), p. 8.
10. Ibid.
11. *The Gallup Poll Index,* no. 119, May 1975, p. 22.
12. *The Chronicle of Higher Education,* September 13, 1976, p. 2.
13. Facts in this paragraph are reported in the *St. Louis Post-Dispatch,* September 26, 1976.
14. U.S. Bureau of the Census, *Statistical Abstract of the United States, 1980* (Washington, D.C.: Government Printing Office, 1981), p. 156.
15. Reported in the *St. Louis-Post Dispatch,* August 8, 1978.
16. "Integration, Yes; Busing No, Walter Goodman interviews James S. Coleman," *The Education Digest* 41 (November 1975), p. 6.
17. U.S. Department of Health, Education, and Welfare, Office of Education, *Positive Approaches to Dropout Prevention* (Washington, D.C.: Government Printing Office, 1973), p. iii. Twelve of the projects are described in some detail in this booklet.
18. *Time,* April 26, 1971, p. 81.

Family Problems

1 **Is the family, as we know it, doomed?**

2 **What do Americans expect from their families?**

3 **How much of a generation gap is there?**

4 **What are the consequences of a one-parent family?**

5 **Who has happier families, low-income people or high-income people?**

Would we be better off without families? Or is that a moot question since the family is dying whether we wish it or not? Some observers of contemporary social life argue that the family is doomed, and some go further and say that the family as we know it now *should* be doomed because it no longer functions in a useful way. The family, according to this argument, contributes more misery than help to people because it is ill-adapted to modern social life.

Other observers argue that the family is essential and ineradicable. What is needed is help for troubled families, not radical changes or the abolition of family life. In this chapter we will look at the argument that the family as we know it is doomed. Then, taking the position that it is not doomed, we will look at the family as a problem. In previous chapters we asked how the family contributed to other problems. Now we will look at the family itself as a problem and discuss the nature and extent of family problems. We will also describe how those problems affect the quality of life. Finally, we will identify the structural and social psychological factors that contribute to family problems and inquire into ways those problems might be resolved.

Is the Family Doomed?

If prophecies could kill, the family would have been dead long ago. The popular and the professional literature continue to forecast the death of the family, at least the *death of the family as we know it now*—the **nuclear family** consisting of a husband, a wife, and their children, if any. The evidence used to support the notion that the nuclear family is dying typically includes things such as **divorce rates,** birth rates, runaway children and wives, and the growing number of youth communes and cohabitation. The last-mentioned phenomena suggest that *intimate relationships* must and will continue, say some observers. Youth are merely finding expression in alternative forms.

Alternative Forms of the Family

There are a good many alternatives to the traditional nuclear family. Some have already been explored by Americans (Otto, 1970). One alternative is *"progressive" or "serial" monogamy,* which is a legitimation of an already-existing and prominent American pattern. People have a series of spouses, one at a time, but without the stigma or difficulty of present divorce proceedings. Another alternative is group marriages, such as those that have been tried in some communes. In this arrangement, all males and females have access to each other for sex or companionship. It has also been suggested that we institute a system of trial marriages, perhaps with renewable contracts for specified periods of time, or "open marriages" where each partner has the right to sexual and companionate relationships with someone other than the spouse. Another kind of arrangement, which increased enormously in the 1970s, is cohabitation. As noted in chapter 3, there are well over a million "unmarried-couple" households in the nation today.

Some of the alternative arrangements pose problems with regard to children who might be born. Consequently, some observers have suggested that the state take a greater role in child care, or that communal arrangements like those in the Israeli kibbutzim be instituted.

It is unlikely that the bulk of Americans will pursue alternatives in the near future. Most Americans retain certain traditional values about the family. At the same time, the American family clearly is changing in a number of important ways. We need to examine both the changes and the continuities.

The Changing American Family

Among the important changes in American families in recent times are *increases* in: (1) age at first marriage; (2) proportion of young adults remaining single; (3) divorced adults; (4) adults living alone; (5) unmarried couples; (6) families maintained by adults with no spouse present; (7) children living with only one parent; (8) wives and mothers working; and (9) dual career families (both husband and wife pursue a career, with minimal, if any, interruption of the wife's career for childbearing).

While such changes may be interpreted as threatening to the traditional nuclear family, we must look at evidence on the other side of the ledger. Most men and women marry at some time. In 1977 only 6 percent of males and 4 percent of women in their early 50s had never married. Most married people have been married only once—85 percent of males and 88 percent of females.[1]

Most Americans remain *committed to the ideal of the nuclear family.* In a sample of undergraduate students given a choice of participation among twelve alternatives (including remaining single, a traditional marriage, child-free marriage, and various kinds of nontraditional sexual relationships), both males and females expressed greatest commitment to an egalitarian marriage (Strong, 1978). In a 1979 Gallup poll 91 percent of the respondents said they would welcome more emphasis on traditional family ties. A 1980 survey that asked about the most satisfying and interesting way of life reported the following results: 42 percent of both men and women opted for a traditional marriage, with the husband working and the wife caring for the home and children; 52 percent of the women and 49 percent of the men preferred an egalitarian marriage and family life; less than 8 percent preferred the other options of cohabitation, remaining single, or communal life; 2 percent said they didn't know.[2]

The major trend seems to be for a traditional nuclear family but nontraditional roles. An increasing proportion favor an egalitarian arrangement, where both husband and wife work and share responsibility for the home and children.

Functions of the Family

If we accept the continuing existence of the nuclear family in America we should consider the kinds of problems the family will face. The problems reflect not only the expectations and values we have for family life, but also the *functions of the family*. Those functions, like other aspects of the family, have changed over time. At one time the family was primarily responsible for matters such as education, religious training, recreation, and production of the necessities of life. Those functions have been largely assumed by other institutions. However, the family continues to be an important factor in *regulating sexual behavior, reproduction,* and *rearing of children*. Family arrangements vary from one society to another, but all societies use their family arrangements to regulate sex, reproduction, and the rearing of children.

Another important function of the family is to provide a *primary group* for individuals. The primary group is of enormous importance to individuals. According to Cooley (1967:158), human nature itself comes from participation in primary groups like the family: "In these, everywhere, human nature comes into existence. Man does not have it at birth; he cannot acquire it except through fellowship, and it decays in isolation." A famous study concerning the family was originally described by Anna Freud and Dorothy Burlingham (1943) and quoted by Stanton and Schwartz (1961). A children's home created "artificial" families after it was noted that the children were having developmental problems. All of the children were cared for by all of the attendants, who were careful not to become too involved with any one child in order to avoid any appearance of favoritism. Because this arrangement seemed to contribute to the children's problems, the home was divided into family groups of about four children and a "mother." The results were "astonishing":

> The need for individual attachment for the feelings which had been lying dormant came out in a rush. In the course of the one week all six families were completely and firmly established . . . the children began to develop in leaps and bounds. The most gratifying effect was that several children who had seemed hopeless as far as the training for cleanliness was concerned suddenly started to use the pot regularly and effectively [Stanton and Schwartz, 1961:236].

Primary groups are important for adults as well as children. We have a personal status in primary groups. We gain our understanding of the kind of people we are and learn the kind of norms by which we are to live. Primary groups,

"No other success can compensate for failure in the home."

The Late PRESIDENT DAVID O. McKAY

in other words, are crucial to our well-being as functioning humans. And, for most Americans, the family is a primary group *par excellence.*

When problems arise in the family, they arise in the group that is important to our well-being, in the group that provides most of us with important emotional support. This purpose, along with others, was recognized in a statement by Catholic, Protestant, and Jewish organizations in 1966. The statement reflects American ideals for the family:

> We believe and unite in affirming that family life is the cradle of personality and character for each child and creates an environment for the societal values of each succeeding generation as well as the principal source of meaningful personal relations for each adult member of our society. All children need a father and a mother firmly united in love to guide their growth into manhood or womanhood and to provide the emotional security that fosters development toward mature and responsible relationships between men and women.
>
> We believe that the family is the cornerstone of our society. It shapes the attitudes, the hopes, the ambitions, the values of every citizen. The child is usually damaged when family living collapses. When this happens on a massive scale, the community itself is crippled.[3]

The Nature and Measurement of Family Problems

Many of the other problems we have studied are problems simply because they exist. Poverty, illness, and crime, for example, are defined as inherently diminishing the quality of life. But, the family is not a problem merely because we have families. Rather, the family becomes a problem when it does not fulfill its purposes, particularly its purpose as a primary group. The American ideal, as we have seen, is that the family should be *structurally complete.* Children should have both a father and a mother in the home. The family should be a *supportive group,* providing emotional support for each member. Finally, the family should be a *learning group* in which *societal values are acquired;* the values thus can be transmitted to subsequent generations.

Incidentally, "ideal" here does not refer to the best (though an unrealistic) situation expected. Rather, the ideal is defined as realistic and expected. When the actual situation falls short of the ideal, the *quality of life* is diminished. Expectations are thwarted. Our most important primary group is disrupted. Family members experience stress. It is not surprising, then, that in a nationwide survey, marriage and family life ranked second and third in importance in predicting the life satisfaction of Americans (Campbell, Converse, and Rodgers, 1976:85).

We will look at three kinds of family problems—structural, supportive, and generational. Structural problems relate to the breaking up of husband and wife and/or parent and child. Supportive problems involve the emotional support or lack of support of each family member. Generational problems relate to value and behavioral conflicts between parents and children.

Any measurements of the extent of each of these problems can only be partial. For example, how is it possible to accurately assess whether all members of a family are receiving adequate emotional support? Some people may not even be aware of inadequacies in their own families. Nevertheless, there are data available that give us some indication of the extent of the three kinds of problems.

Structural problems can be measured by *divorce rates* and the *number of single-headed families*. Divorce does not mean continuing structural problems of course, since remarriage is common. But, divorce rates do give us some indication of how many families are subject to structural problems at some point. The data on single-headed families provide us with more information than divorce rates because they include cases where spouses are absent for some reason and where the head of the household is widowed or single.

Supportive problems are more difficult to measure. Consider, for instance, the following case of supportive failure. The college student who wrote the story says that she can discuss nearly any subject with her parents except one.

> To me there came the day that comes to almost every girl. I met a boy with whom I thought I was in love. This happened about three years ago, and although I have not seen Roger for two years, I have not yet forgotten him. Perhaps the reason for this is because he was the turning point in my life.
>
> I attempted to tell Mother and Father how I felt about Roger, hoping once again for their understanding. Instead, they said, "You don't know what love is," and laughed as they said it. I know they didn't realize at the time that that was the worst possible thing they could have done. They will never know just how small and ignorant they made me feel. . . . Since that incident, I have given them evasive answers to almost every question they have asked me concerning boys—even as to where I go and what I do on dates [Dubbé, 1965:59].

We do not know the number of such problems that occurs in families. Other kinds of supportive problems for which there are some data available involve *marital dissatisfaction* and *family violence*. Marital dissatisfaction can be

Table 14.1   Divorces, 1950–1978 (excludes Alaska and Hawaii prior to 1960)

Divorces	1950	1955	1960	1965	1970	1975	1978
Total (1,000)	385	377	393	479	708	1,026	1,122
Rate per 1,000 population	2.6	2.3	2.2	2.5	3.5	4.8	5.1
Rate per 1,000 married women, 15 years old and over	10.3	9.3	9.2	10.6	14.9	20.3	22.0
Percent divorced, 18 years and over:							
Male	1.8	1.9	2.0	2.5	2.5	3.7	4.7
Female	2.3	2.4	2.9	3.3	3.9	5.3	6.6

Source: Adapted from U.S. Bureau of the Census, *Statistical Abstract of the United States, 1979* (Washington, D.C.: Government Printing Office, 1980), p. 81.

measured through surveys. Family violence includes things such as police calls for family disturbances, homicide, fighting as a factor in divorce suits, and child abuse. Any estimate of the prevalence of family violence will be conservative. Our figures include only the reported cases.

Finally, generational problems are manifested in the so-called **generation gap.** As we will see, generational differences are inevitable but do not necessarily constitute problems. However, when parents define their basic purpose of defending and transmitting cultural values as thwarted, we have a problem. Subsequent generations may define the children's values and behavior as preferable to those of the parents. Nevertheless, a social problem exists when the parents feel that the quality of their life is diminished by the contradictions between their children's values and behavior and their own. We can measure the generation gap by surveying the values of the different generations.

The Extent of Family Problems

Three kinds of evidence convince many Americans that families are not fulfilling their purposes: the number of broken and single-headed families, family violence, and the generation gap. How extensive are these problems in American society today?

Broken and Single-Headed Families

Divorce rates have fluctuated somewhat in our country, but the general *trend has been upward.* The rates are affected by business cycles and special circumstances such as war. Since 1860 there has been a general increase in the number of divorces per 1,000 population. Since 1965 the rate has increased dramatically (table 14.1). By 1974 the United States had the highest divorce rate in the West (Glick, 1975).

Divorce rates are also calculated as the number of divorces per 1,000 marriages. In those terms, there were 424 divorces for every 1,000 marriages in 1974, which means nearly one divorce for every two marriages. In 1979, nearly 9 million Americans reported themselves as di-

Table 14.2   Families Not Headed by a Married Couple, 1960–1979 (in thousands)

Characteristic	1960*	1970	1974	1979
Number of family units (1,000)	5,727	6,778	8,211	10,074
Male head	1,233	1,211	1,423	1,641
Married, wife absent	166	200	236	252
Widowed	465	414	407	384
Divorced	115	180	292	460
Single	487	416	489	545
Female head	4,494	5,567	6,788	8,433
Married, husband absent	1,099	1,321	1,558	1,769
Widowed	2,325	2,389	2,505	2,465
Divorced	694	1,258	1,881	2,807
Single	376	599	843	1,392

*Persons 14 years old and over.

Source: Adapted from U.S. Bureau of the Census, *Statistical Abstract of the United States, 1980* (Washington, D.C.: Government Printing Office, 1981), p. 51.

vorced. Moreover, both the number and the proportion of children affected by divorce are increasing. The number of children under 18 involved in parents' divorce increased from 361,000 in 1956 to 1.12 million in 1976.[4]

Single-headed families, another indication of structural problems, have also been increasing (table 14.2). In 1979 there were over 10 million such families. Fewer than half of these family heads were unmarried or widowed; the remainder involved either divorce or absence of a spouse.

Family Violence

It is difficult to get information on the amount of *violence in families,* but the data we have indicate that it is not a rare phenomenon. A sample of 150 recently divorced people revealed 15 percent who reported violence within the family (O'Brien, 1971). In most cases it was the husband who had behaved violently. Another indication of the amount of violence within families is the fact that family fights comprise the largest single category of police calls (Steinmetz and Straus, 1973). Furthermore, a significant proportion of all murders are committed within families. Various studies and data indicate that anywhere from one-fourth to nearly one-third of all murders involve people who are relatives. Family members comprise the largest single category of murder victims.

In the 1960s and 1970s a number of studies of *spouse abuse* and *child abuse* were undertaken. One of the more extensive studies involved interviews with over 2,000 American couples who comprised a representative sample of the nation (Gelles and Straus, 1979; Straus, Gelles, and Steinmetz, 1979). The researchers measured violent acts, not just abuse (which implies a destructive outcome of a violent act). They found that 16 percent of the couples admitted that they had engaged in at least one violent act against a spouse during the preceding year. About one of every eight couples said that they attack their spouses at least annually. The researchers concluded that at least 1.8 million women and 2.0 million men are abused each year by their spouses. The numbers are undoubtedly higher than that, the researchers acknowledge. Other researchers estimate that tens of millions of cases of spouse abuse occur every year (Langley and Levey, 1977).

Child abuse is another form of family violence. Estimates of the amount of child abuse in the nation vary widely. As one survey of the literature concluded, estimates vary from about 40,000 abused children to 1.5 million children who are vulnerable to physical injury (Eskin, 1980:14). One problem with getting reliable figures is that mandatory reporting laws were not passed in the states until the 1960s. In the national survey noted earlier, 58 percent of the couples said they had used some form of violence (which ranged from very mild forms such as spanking to severe forms such as biting, beating, and threatening with a weapon) during the preceding year, and 71 percent had done so at some time in past years (Gelles and Straus, 1979:22). About 3 percent of the children had been kicked, bitten, or punched by their parents during the preceding year, and 8 percent had been similarly treated at some time. Four percent of the children were beaten at least one time while growing up, and 3 percent had been assaulted with a gun or knife. The researchers said that "these data are truly astonishing when we remember that these numbers are based on parents' *own* testimony" (Gelles and Straus, 1979:23). The actual numbers are probably much higher.

Whatever the actual number of cases of abuse in families, the numbers reported are sufficiently high to justify the assertion by Gelles and Straus (1979:15) that, next to the police and the military, the family is the most violent group in American society.

The physical harm resulting from abuse can be severe. Children may be battered by their parents—both fathers and mothers. In one survey of 302 battered children who were brought to hospitals, 33 died and 55 suffered permanent brain injuries (Raffalli, 1970). When we speak of violence against children, we are dealing with more than a "sound thrashing." The emotional harm resulting from abuse is more difficult to measure. Perhaps one of the better indicators of emotional harm is the large number of battered children who grow up to become parents who, in turn, abuse their own children.

Despite the amount of supportive failure as evidenced by family violence, the majority of Americans indicate satisfaction with their marriages. In their survey of the quality of American life, Campbell, Converse, and Rodgers (1976:324) found that 64 percent of the women and 71 percent of the men said that the thought of getting a divorce had *never* crossed their minds. And 56 percent of the women and 60 percent of the men reported that they were "completely satisfied" with their marriages. There was somewhat less satisfaction expressed about "family life," but many of the respondents may have taken this to mean more than the nuclear family—including at least the mothers- and fathers-in-law.

Besides the observable and measurable supportive problems in the form of family violence, there is a considerable amount of supportive failure that we cannot measure—intense conflict or alienation within families. But, considerable satisfaction is also expressed with family life and particularly with marriages. Supportive problems probably occur in most families some of the time, and they occur in a few families most of the time.

The Generation Gap

To what extent do youth reject the values of their parents? Bengtson (1970) pointed out that the mass media have emphasized generational differences and stress the view that they confront us with an increasingly serious problem. On the other hand, he noted, the professional literature holds to one of three positions: (1) that the gap is serious and large; (2) that there is really no gap; or (3) that there are both continuities and differences between the generations.

Those who argue that the gap is serious and large claim that a vast psychological gulf exists between parents and their children. Young people are said to be "so radically disaffiliated from the mainstream assumptions of our society" that they have taken on the "alarming appearance of a barbaric intrusion" (Roszak, 1969:42). The contrasting typical, middle-class belief about the ideal relationship between parents and children—that the parent should be a "pal" to the child (Bell, 1963:363)—implies that the family should be a close-knit unit in which people share like experiences and values.

Not all professionals agree that the generation gap is large. Some claim that it is an illusion, that whatever differences may exist are insignificant compared to the *continuities between the generations.* Those continuities reflect continuing and significant parental influence (Lubell, 1968:58–59). A third position is that there are both continuities and differences. The behavior of even the student activists of the 1960s is said to have reflected the values of their parents, although their parents would not have carried their commitment that far (Block, Haan, and Smith, 1970).

Just how big is the generation gap? One reason for the contradictory positions is that those who say there is a large gap often think of student radicals as one of the polarities. Of course, the radicals are a minority. When we look at surveys of both college and noncollege youth, we find differences and continuities between the generations. There is a generation gap—it is no illusion, but the gap is not as large as many people have been led to believe.

Contrary to the popular image of youth as radical, or at least liberal, there is considerable *conservatism* among America's young. This basic conservatism was shown in a 1973 national survey of 6,000 college and noncollege youth between 16 and 25 years old (Yankelovich, 1974). Only 21 percent of those in college and 25 percent of those not in college said that the nation needs radical change.

Surveys of college students from the 1940s to the 1970s show three trends.[5] First, younger generations are typically more liberal than older generations. Second, except on a few issues, college youth are more liberal than noncollege youth of the same age. And, third, the 1960s college generation was disproportionately liberal on various issues. Students in the 1970s were more conservative on most issues than were their counterparts in the 1960s.

On many issues there is little difference in the attitudes of youth and the attitudes of adults. Kalish and Johnson (1972) examined value similarities and differences in a sample that consisted of three generations—fifty-three young women, their mothers, and their maternal grandmothers. Values relating to social and political issues, religion, student behavior, aging, and death were examined. While the younger women were more liberal, secular, and permissive toward students than were their mothers (who were more liberal, secular, and permissive than were the grandmothers), it was found that "family members most definitely hold relatively similar values" (Kalish and Johnson, 1972:53). In other words, in general, no radical shifts in values were found from one generation to the next, or even from grandmother to granddaughter.

Another way to look at the generation gap is to determine whether the individual orients his or her thinking *to peers or to parents*. Floyd and South (1972) investigated the extent to which young people select parents or peers as a frame of reference for their behavior. They found that 27 percent were peer-oriented, 30 percent were parent-oriented, and 43 percent had a mixed orientation. When 259 students 14 to 19 years old were asked who they preferred to discuss various subjects with, it was found that they preferred to discuss career and family problems with adults and things such as sex and dating with their peers (Lauer, 1973b). Also, three different patterns emerged among the youth. Some preferred adults. Others preferred their peers. A third group showed preference for both adult and peers, depending on the topic.

A survey of Pennsylvania high school students found that only three topics were sources of major disagreement between youth and their parents: hairstyles, homework, and spending money (Losciuto and Karlin, 1972). What makes the study particularly interesting is the similarity in attitudes between the generations on the topics of premarital sex, marijuana use, and war.

What can we conclude from all this? Generally, the studies show both similarities and differences between the generations. Those similarities and differences appear to vary over time and from one locale to another. The generations may differ on sex in one area but not in another area, and they may differ about war at one period of time but not at another. Finally, there are differences among the youth themselves, particularly between college and noncollege youth, that are often as great as the differences between the generations. It is apparent that the generation gap is not as widespread or as broad as some observers have claimed. Nevertheless, all studies seem to show a gap in the sense that no generation ever fully accepted the values of the preceding generation.

To the extent that a gap is detrimental to the quality of life (perhaps because of the conflict and alienation involved), generational problems are social problems of the family. A gap means that there is always the potential for *conflict*, for *alienated relationships*, and for the *stress* that can result from the alienation.

Family Problems and the Quality of Life

How the family problems discussed previously affect the *quality of life* is sometimes obvious and sometimes not so obvious. Physical violence against an individual by someone in his or her primary group produces emotional trauma as well as physical pain. Alienation from those in one's primary group is emotionally traumatic. And where generational conflict is acute, alienation and stress can also be acute.

Less obvious is the effect of a broken home on a child. Is it really important for a child to have both a father and mother while growing up? Supportive problems mean, by definition, that family members endure some degree of stress. A generation gap means, by definition, that there is a potential for conflict and alienation. But, the meaning of structural problems is less clear. Consequently, much of this section will be an examination of structural problems. We will discover that supportive and generational problems also have some not-so-obvious consequences for the quality of life.

Most of the effects that we will discuss later in this section involve a *contradiction between interaction patterns and American values.* Supportive problems mean that interaction patterns within the family contradict our value on emotional and physical health. Structural problems result in interaction patterns that contradict our value on social adjustment. Because children who grow up in broken homes lack experience with either a mother or a father, they have various problems of adjustment and have to cope more than others with things such as illness, poverty, and deviant behavior. Such interaction patterns diminish the quality of their lives.

Physical and Emotional Difficulties

In chapter 5 we noted that both physical and mental illness are rooted, in part, in family arrangements. Broken homes (structural failure) and homes in which parents frequently quarrel (supportive failure) have been linked to stress in children, and stress often results in physical or emotional illness. In this section we will explore the relationships a little further. We will deal with stressful emotions as well as actual illnesses.

One common observation in studies of family problems is the *similarity between bereavement and divorce.* That is, the individual's adjustment to divorce has some striking similarities to the bereavement process. The Social Readjustment Rating Scale (discussed in chapter 5), which measures the amount of stress likely to be created by various life events, ranks death of a spouse first and divorce second in degree of difficulty of adjustment.

Contrary to a popular notion that divorce may be an avenue to freedom and therefore an exhilarating experience (at least once the legal procedure has been completed), divorced people typically face a process of painful adjustment not unlike that which occurs after a death in the family. In both death and divorce, *a primary relationship has been disrupted,* and the disruption of a primary relationship is always traumatic. A sense of loss, of bewilderment, of uncertainty, and of deprivation is likely to follow. According to Burns (1958:45), the typical pattern for the first six to twelve months is as follows:

> Most divorcees experience, during these months, attacks of easily recognized physical symptoms which usually last fifteen minutes or more. The attacks are characterized by dryness in the mouth and throat, difficulty in breathing, a mild nauseous feeling in the stomach, generalized weakness, and the all-pervasive sense of mental and physical misery. . . . These feelings are so painful that divorced persons usually attempt to protect themselves by limiting drastically the number of places they go, things they do, and people they see. A vast majority of divorced persons find that during these early months of their long-sought freedom their five senses seem to play strange tricks on them. Disturbance of the senses of taste and smell added to a generalized lack of interest may lead them to faulty eating habits. . . . On the other hand, some divorced persons will stuff food in their mouths in an absentminded way. Even though the food has no satisfying taste for them they continue eating merely to be doing something.

In the first months, divorce is more likely to bring emotional and physical disturbances than the anticipated sense of freedom. In one study, 139 divorcees were compared with 61 control subjects who were married or widowed. The former group had a much higher incidence of illness—three-fourths of the divorced women and two-thirds of the divorced men had had, or did have, some kind of psychiatric disorder such as depression, an antisocial personality, or hysteria (Briscoe, Smith, Robins *et al.,* 1973).

Many observers believe that children suffer the most in divorce, that their emotional problems may become acute if the parents become involved in a divorce. Actually, we do not know the extent of emotional trauma endured by children in divorces. We do know that children from a divorced background are more likely to have a variety of negative consequences in their lives, as we will see later. And, there are certain *problems of adjustment that the children must face.* They will be confronted by questions from peers, particularly when they are in elementary school, about why they have only one parent. They will have to adjust to a change in a primary relationship, with restricted interaction with one of the parents (generally, the father). They may have to cope with parental conflict, which may continue after the divorce, and with attempts by each parent to gain the child's loyalty and affection at the expense of the other parent. It is not surprising, then, that children whose parents are divorced report a greater number of psychosomatic symptoms than do children who come from intact homes (Rosenberg, 1965:86).

Nevertheless, the discord that led to the divorce was probably more stressful than the divorce itself for the child. Parents who stay together "for the children's sake" may actually harm the children more than if they were to separate. A home with continual conflict or emotional coldness can be more damaging to the children than a home that is broken. We must not, as we discuss the negative consequences of the broken home, make the wrong conclusion that the intact home is always better than the one that is broken. The intact home may have supportive problems that are far more damaging to the child or to the spouses than a structural problem would be. In other words, while structural problems of broken homes are associated with various kinds of physical and emotional problems, this does not mean that the intact home is free of such problems (as we will see later).

Once a home is broken because of divorce, separation, or death, the problems are not all resolved. The most acute stress tends to occur around the time of dissolution, but serious physical and emotional difficulties can precede and follow the dissolution. Many difficulties appear to be more intense in the case of divorce or separation than in the case of death, probably because divorce and separation tend to occur in the context of a good deal of family discord. Adversity, such as death, can strengthen a family, even though the remaining family members will have some problems of adjustment.

In a five-year study of *one-parent families* in Baltimore, four problems were frequently found: (1) a sense of incompleteness and frustration; (2) a sense of failure; (3) feelings of guilt; and (4) some degree of ambivalent feelings between the parent and child or children (Freudenthal, 1959). For instance, the parent would forego his or her own desires in order to be with the child, and then would battle feelings of resentment toward the child for having made the sacrifice. Child and parent are very important to each other in such families, but the parent tends to feel weighed down by the responsibility of rearing the child alone. The difficulty of being the only parent in the home may be part of the problem faced by unwed mothers, who report a greater amount of stress and more physical illness than married mothers (Berkman, 1969). This interpretation is also supported by the fact that unwed mothers who keep their children encounter more difficulties and have more problems than those who give the children up (Jones, Meyer, and Borgatta, 1962). Other studies have shown that children in broken homes suffer more from *anxiety,* particularly in homes where the father is absent (McCord, McCord, and Thurber, 1964).

Anxiety is also associated with supportive failure. Parents who reject their children create anxiety in them. If, for example, a mother continually disapproves of her infant's need for tenderness, the infant will display anxiety (Bowlby, 1961). *Rejection,* of course, does not necessarily imply overt hostility; it can occur through indifference and neglect. Whatever form the rejection takes, the result for the child is likely to be anxiety. And, the child may attempt to cope with that anxiety through some kind of deviant behavior such as drug use (as we noted in chapter 4).

In the most serious cases, family problems lead to negative emotions and to *physical and mental illness.* All three types of problems have been associated with psychiatric disorders. In contrast to normal people, schizophrenics report a higher proportion of divorce, separation, and desertion among their parents (Oltman, McGarry, and Friedman, 1952). Mentally disturbed children tend to come from families in which they are caught up in problems between their parents (Spiegel, 1960). Schizophrenic adolescents are more likely than normal adolescents to be caught between the contradictory values of their peers and their parents (Weinberg, 1952). Clearly, family problems can contribute to serious physical and mental illness.

Poverty

We have pointed out that *female-headed families* are more likely to be in *poverty* than male-headed families. Since most single-headed families have a female head, the broken home has a higher probability of being in poverty than do other homes. In part, the poverty of female-headed families reflects the *contradiction between two American values*—that of the *mother being in the home* and that of *work.* Americans tend to believe that the mother's place is in the home. We encourage her to stay there by discriminating against females in the economy (as detailed in chapter 11). On the other hand, we believe that people should work for what they get, so welfare payments are low enough to insure poverty for the recipients. The woman is caught in a bind—whether she works or stays home and receives welfare, she may find herself and her family living in poverty.

Urie Bronfenbrenner described the problem before the Senate Subcommittee on Children and Youth:

In 1970, 10 percent of all children under 6—2.2 million of them—were living in single parent families with no father present in the home. This is almost double the rate for a decade ago. . . . In 1970, the average income for a single-parent family with children under 6 was $3,100—well below the poverty line. Even when

Figure 14.3 Female-headed families are more likely to be in poverty than others, and are more likely to perpetuate that poverty.

the mother worked, her average income of $4,200 barely exceeded the poverty level. Among families in poverty, 45 percent of all children under 6 are living in single-parent households; in non-poverty families, the corresponding figure is only 3.5 percent.[6]

Bronfenbrenner estimated that in 1970 there were about 4.5 million children under 6 years of age whose "families need some help if normal family life is to be sustained."

Because there is a correlation between the *absence of the father and lower academic achievement* (recall that education is vital to upward mobility), poverty tends to be perpetuated by the absence of the father from the home. In a study of 300 elementary children from mother-headed homes and 773 elementary children from two-parent homes, the children without a father had significantly lower reading achievement scores than those with both parents (Sciara and Jantz, 1974). In another study, 286 junior high school students were surveyed to determine the state of their homes when they were in elementary school (Santrock, 1972). Records on I Q and achievement test scores were obtained from the elementary schools, and students who had been in mother-headed homes were compared with those who had been in two-parent homes. Those with the father absent scored lower than the others on the tests (and, interestingly, divorce, desertion, or separation had a more negative effect than the death of the father).

Deviant Behavior

Sexual deviance, drug and alcohol abuse, and juvenile delinquency have been associated with disturbed family life. We have already pointed out in earlier chapters that homosexuals, prostitutes, and drug and alcohol abusers often have a background of disturbed relationships with their parents. Broken homes particularly have been associated with deviant behavior, and supportive failure is also involved. For instance, alcoholism has been associated with a cold and dominating father and rejection by the mother (McCord and McCord, 1960).

Broken homes are more likely to produce delinquents than are intact homes, and homes broken by divorce, desertion, or separation are more likely to produce delinquents than are homes broken by death. Supportive problems are no less serious than structural problems; children from intact but unhappy homes are far more likely to become delinquent than are children from intact and happy homes (Goode, 1964:102). There is some evidence that juvenile delinquency, as well as schizophrenia, is associated with contradictory expectations of peers and parents.

A study of fifteen victims of *father-daughter incest* adds further evidence of the deleterious consequences of supportive failure (Herman and Hirschman, 1977). The girls tended to have strained or hostile relationships with their mothers, which may have facilitated the incestuous relationship. The girls also tended to be alienated from other people and to get involved with violent, abusive men when they became adults.

Maladjustment

People who come from disturbed families tend to have various difficulties that we can subsume under the category of **maladjustment.** The kinds of maladjustment include antisocial behavior (such as aggression and bullying), insecurity, over-conformity to one's peers, a tendency to withdraw from relationships, difficulties in relating to others, and problems with one's personal identity (Ackerman, 1970). For example, girls without fathers have been found to have problems relating to males. There are interesting differences, though, depending on whether the father is dead or absent because of divorce, desertion or separation. In observing girls at a community recreation center, Hetherington (1973:49–50) pointed out a number of differences:

> Girls whose parents had been divorced sought more attention from the male adults at the center than did girls in the other two groups. They often struck up conversations or exhibited their handicrafts such as beadwork, pottery and ceramics to the male recreation directors in order to get praise and attention. In addition, these girls spent much of their time hanging around the . . . male areas of the center. However, they did not participate more in male activities. They were there to be near the boys. . . . In contrast, we found that girls whose fathers had died avoided the male areas of the centers; they spent most of their time in the female areas.

The girls whose parents were divorced appeared hungry for male attention and approval. But, the girls whose fathers had died revealed sexual anxiety, shyness, and general uneasiness around males. In both cases there were problems in relating to the opposite sex.

Research has also focused on boys without fathers. The first studies concluded that boys tend to be feminized by the lack of a father. Subsequent work indicates that the tendency to feminine behavior (as traditionally defined) diminishes with age as the boys learn what it means to be male from their peers and their culture.

We mentioned earlier that parents can *reject their children* in various ways. It follows that different kinds of supportive problems result. A parent who is hostile toward a child fails to support the child, and the result can be maladjustment in the child's attempts to relate to others. Inconsistency in how the parent treats the child can also be viewed as a form of supportive failure. Inconsistency means that the child lives in a capricious environment, and people do not function well with chronic uncertainty. Inconsistent discipline, consequently, leads to various kinds of maladjustment, including hostility, truancy, and interpersonal difficulties at home and school (Rosenthal, 1962; Clark and van Sommers, 1961).

The *child's sense of self-esteem,* so important in his or her social functioning, is crucially related to family experiences. Low self-esteem is associated with emotional and interpersonal problems (Lauer and Handel, 1977:189–90). Rosenberg (1965) measured the self-esteem of over 5,000 high school students in New York and found that high self-esteem was more prevalent among those who reported close relationships with their fathers and reported other indications of parental interest, such as the mother knowing most of the child's friends, or concern about school grades, or conversations with the parents at meal time. In an eight-year project on self-esteem, Coopersmith (1967) also found that parents' warmth, respectful treatment of their children, and other expressions of concern for their children's well-being were extremely important elements in development of self-esteem. Supportive failure is related to low self-esteem.

Structural problems are also a factor in self-esteem. Rosenberg (1965) found that more children from homes broken by divorce or separation had lower self-esteem than those coming from intact homes. This was particularly likely to happen when the child was Catholic or Jewish rather than Protestant, or when the mother was very young, or when the child was 4 years or older at the time the home was broken.

Children who come from disturbed families have more interpersonal difficulties than children who come from intact and happy homes.

Contributing Factors

The factors we will examine in this section contribute in various ways to the three basic kinds of problems we have identified—structural, supportive, and generational. The three types of problems can be independent, and some families may suffer from one, some from two, and some from all three kinds of problems. On the other hand, the three types of problems tend to be interrelated. Structural problems, for instance, may either make supportive failure more likely or reflect supportive failure in the past.

Social Structural Factors

Social Norms.   As we have noted, the divorce rate has shown a general upward trend since at least the middle of the nineteenth century. At first it appears (and some have so argued) that the continually increasing divorce rate reflects the breakdown of the family in America or increasing unhappiness in marriages. But, another very important factor is that divorce is more respectable now than it was in the past. In other words, the *norms about divorce have changed*. In the past, religion and the law both said in effect, "You should not get a divorce. You should make every effort to work it out and stay together." Today the norms about divorce reflect loosening of the laws (including the recent "no-fault" kind of divorce) and a greater tolerance even among religious groups. In contrast to the *stigma* formerly attached to divorce and the divorcee, by 1967 a national magazine could write that the divorced woman in America "is often professionally successful, almost never overtly scorned. . . . Indeed, divorce may be evolving into something of a status symbol—at least in the fashion and society pages."[7]

Divorce is much more likely if people marry at a young age (15 to 19 years old), and if there is a short or no engagement period. Bumpass and Sweet (1972) examined national data on white women under 45 years of age and found age at marriage to be one of the most important factors in marital instability. Regardless of such factors as education and premarital pregnancy, women who marry before they are 20 years old have a significantly higher rate of disruption (divorce or separation) than do those who marry at 21 years and older. Those who marry at 30 and above have very low rates of disruption.

There is evidence that both structural and supportive problems are more common among the very young. Not only is the marriage likely to break up, but problems of child-rearing are likely to be serious. Indeed, adolescent marriage and parenthood have been called a case of "children who attempt to raise children." A three-year study of young families in rural and small town settings found serious financial problems, considerable disillusionment, and a good deal of intolerance, impatience, insensitivity, and irritability toward the children (de Lissovoy, 1975).

Figure 14.4 Early marriages, especially when early parenthood is involved also, have significantly higher rates of failure than later marriages.

Why do adolescents marry at a young age? Social norms define the appropriate time for marriage. For most Americans, that time has been soon after high school graduation or, at the latest, soon after college. In the past, females in our society who were not married by the time they were 20 could develop a sense of panic that they would become old maids. Males who waited until their late 20s or after to get married were suspected of having homosexual tendencies or, at least, of having an inadequate sex drive, which is an affront to one's manhood. To some extent the norm about marital age is changing. In 1950 the median age at first marriage for brides was 20.3 years and for grooms 22.8. By 1977 the figures were 21.1 for brides and 23.0 for grooms.[8] The "swinging single" is now an acceptable individual. But, the average age for marriage is still quite young, and the swinging single may not be acceptable to many businesses and corporations who still prefer their young executives to be married. Consequently, we can expect continuing structural and supportive problems due to young age at marriage. The median age at marriage will have to rise much more than it has over the past twenty-five years in order to moderate the extent of those problems.

Norms also contribute to the amount of family violence in the nation. A common norm in families is that hitting someone who is misbehaving and who does not respond to reason is proper. One-fourth of American wives and about one-third of American husbands accept slapping one's spouse as somewhat necessary or even good. Hitting is even more acceptable in parent-child relationships. Many Americans consider use of physical punishment in the rearing of children virtually an obligation (Gelles

and Straus, 1979). Recall the old saying "Spare the rod and spoil the child." In some cases it is applied with a vengeance.

Role problems.   A number of *role problems* have been identified as important in marital dissatisfaction, for they can contribute to both structural and supportive problems.

Couples who disagree on *role obligations* of husband and wife are more prone to divorce than those who agree. What the obligations are is not as important as whether the couple agree on them and on whether each feels that the other is fulfilling them (Tharp, 1963). When there is a gap between the expectations and the perceived behavior, dissatisfaction will be high (Burr, 1971).

One qualification to the general principle is that it is more important for the wife to conform to the husband's expectations than vice versa. In other words, "wives seem more accepting of disappointment or noncompliance with their expectations" (Laws, 1971:500). On the other hand, the husband's fulfillment of expectations is particularly important in one area—his role as provider. Fulfillment of the male's role as provider is a critical predictor of marital happiness (Hicks and Platt, 1970).

As the impact of the women's movement increases, and as women become more firmly entrenched in the labor force in all occupational categories, role obligations will change. There will be less expectation that the husband will be the main provider and the wife primarily the homemaker. Still, the principle that consensus on role obligations is important for marital satisfaction will still hold true.

By 1963 women were already reporting more happiness in their marriages to the extent that their own *roles were flexible* (Orden and Norman, 1969). The respondents in the survey were located in three metropolitan areas. One-fourth worked full-time, another 9 percent worked part-time. An important predictor of happiness for the women was their freedom to choose work in the home, work outside the home, or leisure activities. Both men and women rated their marriages lower in happiness when the wife felt compelled to work because of family finances (supporting the research that showed the importance at the time of the male provider role). When the woman could choose how to fulfill her role, marital happiness was greater, whatever the choice. When a woman chooses to work, and her husband supports her choice, the wife is likely to be more satisfied with her life, and neither marital adjustment nor companionship will suffer (Locksley, 1980). This assumes, of course, that the couple agrees on role obligations. Agreement may not always be easy, particularly in dual-career couples. How much responsibility does each have for housework, for meals, or for child care? The woman who is pursuing a career, as opposed to merely holding a job, may want different answers to those questions than other women. Nevertheless, role restrictions are much more likely to have deleterious consequences than role flexibility. Whether or not such restrictions lead to disruption of the marriage, they virtually insure a certain amount of supportive failure.

Family continuity.   There is a tendency for those who are reared in problem families to perpetuate the problems in their own families. Bumpass and Sweet (1972:758) reported this tendency with respect to divorce. They found that women who came from families in which one or both parents had died had rates of marital disruption that were little different from women who came from intact families. However, women who came from families in which the parents were divorced or separated had much higher disruption rates than those coming from intact families.

Similarly, family violence tends to be continued from one generation to the next. A number of studies have pointed out that parents who abuse their children were often abused by their parents. In turn, the battered child of today is likely to become the battering parent of tomorrow, perpetuating the problem of family violence. (See, for example, Fontana, 1971; Gelles and Straus, 1979:29).

A family can perpetuate its own problems into the next generation simply because the family is such an important factor in the *socialization* of the child. The family is an important place for learning what it means to be a male or a female, how to function as a parent, and generally how to relate to others. There is some continuity in parent-child relationships and husband-wife relationships from generation to generation, therefore. As the parents relate to each other and to the child, so the child learns how to relate to his or her spouse and children of the future. The child may reject some of the patterns in the home, but the tendency is to follow those patterns.

Stratification and family problems.   As with all problems, there are differences among families depending on the socioeconomic level. For one, *divorce is more common in the lower strata than in the middle and upper.* This may seem contrary to common sense, for surely the well-to-do can afford the costs of divorce more easily than can the poor. Actually, there are a number of reasons why divorce and socioeconomic position are inversely rather than directly related. Certain aspects of middle- and upper-class life decrease the likelihood that families will break up.

Financial problems put an enormous strain on marital and family relationships. We pointed out that a husband's adequate fulfillment of the provider role is an important factor in the wife's satisfaction with the marriage. In fact, income is one of the best predictors of family stability. Structural failure is increasingly probable as we go down the socioeconomic ladder. It appears that the lower incomes imply greater potential for financial difficulties and thereby help produce interpersonal problems that lead to marital disruption.

Another aspect of life that probably bears upon the divorce rate is jointly owned property and financial investments, which are more likely to be held by people in the middle and upper income levels. Divorce is more difficult and expensive when division of assets is involved. Middle and upper income people are also more likely to have a network of friends and relations who will resist their divorce (and who may support them as they try to work through their problems). They may, under these circumstances, be willing to have an "open" marriage, or at least remain in the same home while tolerating each other's infidelity. In short, divorce may be ruled out because of the economic and social costs even when there is no intention of continuing a satisfying marital relationship.

This suggests that we might find a greater degree of supportive failure in middle- and upper-class families, but the evidence seems to indicate the contrary. Rosenberg (1965) found that middle-class fathers are more supportive of their children, particularly their sons, than are working-class fathers. Similarly, middle-class mothers show more affection, less rejection, and are more supportive of their children than are mothers in the lower strata (Sears, Maccoby, and Levin, 1957). An experiment involving middle- and lower-class mothers and their children found that middle-class mothers interacted more with their children by "Contacting, Directing, Helping, Interfering by Structurizing, Observing Attentively, and Playing Interactively" (Zunich, 1969:77). "Contacting" referred to either verbal or physical contact. "Directing" involved telling the child the course of action the mother preferred for him or her. "Helping" was physical aid, such as pounding a nail or fixing a toy for the child. "Interfering by structurizing" involved telling the child why certain behavior was undesirable. "Observing attentively" meant that the mother gave the child her attention in a noticeable, though not verbal way. "Playing interactively" was playing with the child as though the mother too were a child. Middle-class mothers tended to do all these things more than did the lower-class mothers. And, the children from middle-class homes perceive a greater degree of parental interest than do children from lower-class homes (Kerckhoff, 1972:123–24).

As one moves down the socioeconomic scale, there appears to be less and less interaction with children. When we reach the poverty scale, as we noted in chapter 8, the interaction with adults is minimal and the parent-child relationships tend to exhibit serious problems. Not only does interaction decrease, but the interaction there is tends to be less supportive.

Supportive failure is also suggested by the data on spouse and child abuse. We know that a certain amount of abuse occurs in middle-class families. But, the abuse seems to be more prevalent in the lower strata than in the middle or upper strata (Gil, 1970; Elmer, 1971; Gelles and Straus, 1979). Battered wives are more likely to have husbands with lower levels of education and lower incomes (Carlson, 1977; Gaquin, 1977/1978). Goode (1956) found that married couples in the higher socioeconomic strata were more likely to look to each other for help and to communicate their emotional problems to each other. Similarly, they were less likely to take out negative feelings on each other than were couples in the lower socioeconomic strata.

Among the less-educated and lower-income blue-collar workers, marital relationships are characterized by a considerable amount of separateness and *isolation of the spouses from each other.* As summarized by Shostak (1969: 128):

> Personal relations are often strained in the early years. Frequently the couples are dissatisfied with the boredom of their marriage, its overall meagerness of communication, its mutual misunderstandings, and the real or suspected indiscretions of the mate (almost always of the husband). Blue-collar wives are by far . . . more dissatisfied . . .; many of them conveyed to . . . Komarovsky and her interviewers their yearnings for reassurance, counsel, appreciation, encouragement, and sharing for its own sake. . . . Family members are constrained from reaching out to one another by a host of taboos and folk prescriptions based on a common fear of loss of identity in the absence of role restrictions.

Even among upper-income blue-collar workers, marriage is not generally seen in terms of companionship and sharing. LeMasters (1975:37) reported a conversation with a blue-collar worker who described his wife as "not a bad kid, but she's a goddam woman and they get under my skin." The man, commented LeMasters, was not really complaining about his wife so much as about marriage. He preferred the company of men. Except for sexual relations, he found women "dull and uninteresting."

The family in a changing structure.   As we have seen, rapid change of the social structure creates its own problems, including some problems for families. Certain kinds of change can affect the divorce rate. If roles are in a state of flux, the potential for conflict within the family is increased and the probability of divorce becomes greater. If rapid change involves confusion and ambiguity about what it means to be a husband or a wife or a parent, then we would expect more stress, more conflict, and more structural and supportive problems.

Rapid change influences family problems primarily because of effects on generational relationships. It was Davis (1940) who first argued that rapid change tends to increase *generational conflict* between parents and children because the children are reared in virtually a different world from that of their parents. The parents are "old-fashioned," and the children rebel because they recognize that their parents' ways are outmoded and of little use in their own adaptation. Other writers have accepted and, in some cases, elaborated upon this thesis. The basic idea is that change makes the ways of the parents unsuited to the world of the children. The children must reject those ways if they are to adapt to their environment. If the parents insist that their ways are appropriate, conflict is inevitable. Furthermore, over the past two centuries parents and children have spent an increasing amount of time with peers rather than with each other (Bernstein, 1978), so it has become easier for children to adhere to a different set of values. This *changing pattern of interaction* results in *differential association,* which, as we have seen, facilitates in-group behavior. While the argument is logical, we really do not have much evidence at present to support or reject it.

Social Psychological Factors

Values and homogamy.   When you marry, you undoubtedly hope that the relationship will last and be rewarding to both you and your spouse. Is that more likely to happen if you and your spouse have similar or dissimilar backgrounds? The question has been debated by social scientists. Some have argued that those with *dissimilar backgrounds* (**heterogamy**) will be attracted to each other and will *complement* each other so that the marriage is more rewarding and successful. Others have argued that similar backgrounds and *shared rather than different values* (**homogamy**) are more likely to produce a rewarding and lasting marriage.

Research generally supports the view that homogamy is more conducive to a lasting marriage. While homogamy does not mean that the couple must have similar backgrounds in every respect, it appears that the greater the similarity, the greater the likelihood of a satisfactory marriage. Various studies show that a satisfactory marital relationship is more likely to result when there is similarity in family background, in socioeconomic background, in cultural back-

ground, in personality traits, and in religion. For example, in a study of fifty married couples, Blazer (1963) found homogamy to be positively correlated with marital happiness. Pickford (1966) and his associates studied three groups. Thirty-five married couples were in each group. The couples in one group were happily married, in another were having troubles, and in the third were on the verge of separation. Again, homogamy was correlated with happiness. Perhaps the more similarity between spouses, the fewer the areas of conflict. In any case, shared rather than dissimilar values are important in maintaining a satisfactory marriage. Structural and supportive problems are more likely to occur when the couple come from dissimilar backgrounds and hold diverse values.[9]

The value of success.   The American *value of success* can lead to supportive failure in the family. Merton (1957:136f) showed how the "goal of monetary success" pervades our society, so that Americans "are bombarded on every side by precepts which affirm the right or, often, the duty of retaining the goal even in the face of repeated frustration." In our families, our schools, and the mass media we are urged to pursue the goal with unrelenting diligence. Most Americans share this value of success. Even in the lower socioeconomic strata, where people often do not *expect* it, they still share it in the sense of *wishing* for it (Han, 1969).

Success in monetary terms often means long hours spent at work and minimal contact with the family. Some upper-middle-class wives are isolated from their husbands as much as the blue-collar wives are isolated from their husbands, as described earlier.

What are the consequences for the family? We do not have systematic data with which to answer the question, but a number of illustrations in the literature suggest that supportive failure can result. As one ambitious man put it, "I'm working so hard that I'm killing myself and wrecking my family, but I'm making so much money that I can afford it" (Schelling, 1973:627). Whyte (1956:162) described the sales manager who was looking forward to the time when his children would be grown so that he would no longer "have to have such a guilty conscience about neglecting them."

Ideology of the good family.   We have seen that unfulfilled expectations about role obligations can lead to marital dissatisfaction and dissolution. Our expectations about the behavior of others may or may not be realistic, but they are important to our sense of satisfaction with interaction. The *American ideology of the "good" family* generates a set of *expectations,* and when those expectations are not met, the result may be stress and dissatisfaction. Because neither an ideology nor the consequent expectations may be realistic, an ideology may contribute to family problems by generating stress in the wake of shattered expectations.

This kind of process may be involved in the overly romanticized view of marriage that Americans have held. Today it is also involved in two rather different ideas about the "good" family.

One idea is that a *good family is a happy family* and that *happy families are harmonious* and free of conflict. Furthermore, the family is believed to be a kind of miniature society in which all the important human relationships and feelings can be experienced. Each individual can find within the family a complete range of experiences in the context of harmony and happiness.

Sennett (1970) found this kind of ideology among middle-class urban families and said that it led to a *"guilt-over-conflict syndrome"* in the families. When there is conflict within the home, those who hold to the ideology can only conclude that their family and each of its members have failed to maintain a good home:

> . . . people look, for example, at conflicts between generations as an evil, revealing some sort of rottenness in the familial social fabric, rather than as an inevitable and natural process of historical change. Sharp personality differences between the children's generation, leading to estrangements between brothers and sisters, are viewed as a sign of bad parental upbringing, and so on. Put another way, anxiety and guilt over family conflict really express the wish that for the sake of social order, diversity and ineradicable differences should not exist in the home [Sennett, 1970:34].

Such a view of family life is unrealistic, and the result is a higher rate of emotional stress when conflict is suppressed because of the ideology. The ideology, rather than resolving any problems, leads to supportive failure and emotional stress.

Another ideology about family life that has emerged in recent years recognizes the need to express feelings and engage in creative conflict. This ideology has grown out of small group work and says, in effect, that the good family maintains *healthy relationships* and that healthy relations can be obtained only where people are able to give *free expression to their feelings.* We should "level" with each other and accept each other.

Involvement

One Big Happy Family

Some utopian communities that have arisen in the United States have considered the traditional family arrangements detrimental to human well-being. The nineteenth century Oneida community, for instance, was founded on the notion of "Bible communism." Private property was abolished, including the private property of a spouse or child. The entire community was a family. Every adult was expected to have sex relations with a great variety of others. Women who bore children cared for them for the first fifteen months, then placed them in the children's house where they were raised communally and taught to regard all adults in the community as their parents.

Secure some literature about utopian communities of the present or past. For example, you might investigate Bethel, Brook Farm, Oneida, Ephrata, the Icarians, the Rappites, the Shakers, or any one of numerous contemporary communes. Consider what kinds of family arrangements they have created. Do any of these arrangements solve the kinds of problems discussed in this chapter? Why or why not? Do the utopian arrangements appear to create other kinds of problems? Would the utopian arrangement be practical for an entire society? What is your own ideal after reading about the utopian alternatives and some of the alternatives mentioned early in this chapter?

The Oneida Perfectionists practiced "complex marriage" in which every man was married to every woman and every woman to every man. Children belonged to and were raised by the community.

If the first ideology errs by condemning conflict in the family, this one errs by encouraging too much *aggression* in the home. In a review of research, Straus (1974) found that venting aggression does not, as the theorists presume, lead to reduction of further aggressive behavior. Rather, encouraging people to give free expression to their aggressive feelings may result in increased aggressive behavior. Straus found in his own study of 385 couples that the more verbal aggression, the more physical aggression there was. Giving free expression to one's feelings may provide one with a sense of release and relief, but it does not necessarily enhance the quality of interpersonal relationships. Freud (1961:44) argued that civilization is built upon a "renunciation of instinct," which means some degree of nonsatisfaction of things such as our aggressive and sexual instincts. We could paraphrase him and say that a good family is built upon some degree of nonexpression of aggression. Some balance must be struck between complete openness and freedom of expression on the one hand, and suppression and guilt on the other hand. Neither extreme appears to be conducive to a healthy, satisfying family life.

What Is To Be Done?

As with all problems, *both therapeutic and preventive measures* can be applied. Therapeutic measures include the more traditional counseling services as well as the newer efforts that involve discussion and interaction in small group settings. These measures, of course, attempt to resolve problems that have already begun.

What kind of preventive measures could be taken? What measures, that is, might minimize the number of family problems in the nation?

We could *experiment more with new forms.* For instance, we could legalize a system of trial marriage in which couples would contract to marry for a specific period of time and would then have the option of renewing the contract. We should be aware, however, of the nature of experiments. They are searches—often blind gropings—for answers, and not firm guidelines. That means that if we are willing to experiment, we must also be willing to have the experiments fail (and perhaps even make a problem worse). But, some of the experiments may show us a new way that works.

Good *family life education,* at all stages of the life cycle, through the schools and the mass media, could break down the harmful ideologies about the "good" family. Family life education might change our norms about young marriages and persuade males to allow greater role freedom for their wives. A great many false and/or counterproductive ideas can be attacked through educational programs.

Family problems, like others we have examined, are more intense in the lower socioeconomic strata. At least some of the problems of family life are intertwined with the problem of poverty. Solving the poverty problem will not completely resolve family problems, but without addressing poverty we cannot adequately deal with the troubles of families.

Figure 14.5 Sensory awareness training is one of a variety of therapeutic and educational methods used to enrich marital relationships.

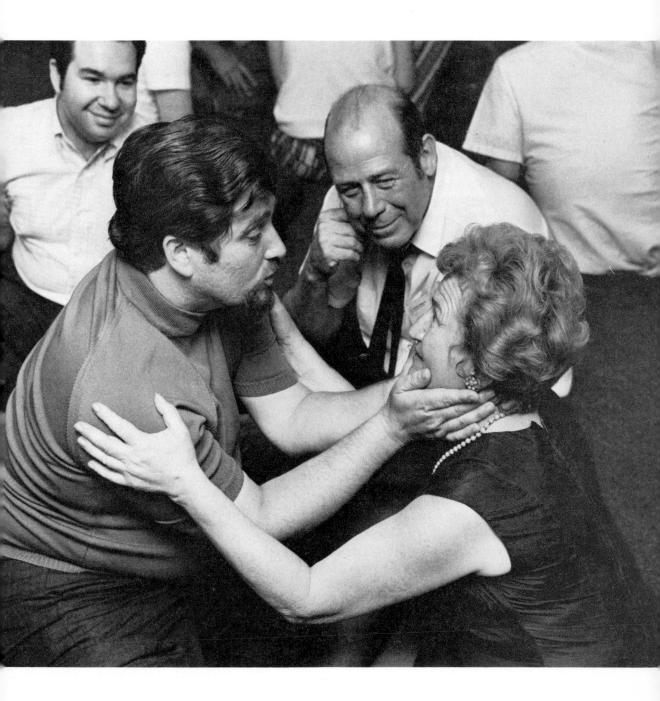

Summary

Family problems are so common that some observers have argued that the family, as we know it, is doomed. Those who predict the end of the present type of family suggest a number of alternatives, such as progressive monogamy, group marriages, trial marriage, or cohabitation. But, the bulk of Americans continue to marry and establish homes, so the family will continue for at least the near future.

The problems of the family stem from the fact that it is one of our most important primary groups. Americans believe the family to be the cornerstone of society, and that an ideal family provides stability, support, and continuity for American values. We can identify three basic types of problems: structural (one-parent families); supportive (lack of emotional support); and generational (the generation gap).

Several kinds of data suggest the extent and the seriousness of family problems. Structural problems may be measured by the divorce rate, which has risen dramatically since 1965, and by the number of single-headed families, which has also been increasing. Supportive problems are evident in the amount of family violence, including child abuse. Generational problems may be indicated by measurements of the generation gap.

All family problems diminish the quality of life. Physical and emotional difficulties follow family conflict and the additional problems of adjusting to a broken home follow divorce or separation. Poverty is more frequently associated with a female-headed than a two-parent family, and the poverty tends to be perpetuated because the child from a single-headed family does not perform as well academically as others. Several kinds of deviant behavior have been associated with disturbed family life—sexual deviance, drug and alcohol abuse, and juvenile delinquency. People who come from families with problems tend to have a variety of difficulties that we can call madadjustment—antisocial behavior, interpersonal problems, and low self-esteem.

Norms that are now more permissive about divorce and that encourage very young marriages are two social structural factors that contribute to family problems. Role problems contribute to marital dissatisfaction and thereby lead to both structural and supportive failure. Family problems are especially likely to occur when there is disagreement on role obligations, or when the wife does not live up to her husband's expectations for her role behavior, or when the husband does not adequately fulfill his role as provider. The family itself also contributes to future family problems because children learn patterns that will create future problems.

Family problems are generally more prevalent in the lower social strata, partly because of financial strains and partly because of different norms and roles. Rapid social change is yet another structural cause of family problems because it intensifies the generation gap.

Among the social psychological factors, values are important, and a couple with similar values based on similar backgrounds is more likely to have a satisfactory marriage. The value of success in American culture, on the other hand, puts a strain on marriages and family life because certain occupations consume those who are striving for that success.

Two ideologies generate expectations and behavior that strain marriage and family relationships. The ideology that says the good family is happy and free of conflict leads to a suppression of conflict and guilt. The ideology that says that in the good family people can freely express their feelings, including aggression, can perpetuate debilitating conflict. Both ideologies tend to result in supportive problems. Families need a balance between excessive openness and free expression of feelings, on the one hand, and suppression and guilt, on the other hand.

Glossary

divorce rate   typically, the number of divorces per 1,000 marriages

generation gap   differences in values and behavior between parents and their children

heterogamy   marriage between those with diverse values and backgrounds

homogamy   marriage between those with similar values and backgrounds

maladjustment   poor adjustment to one's social environment

nuclear family   husband, wife, and children, if any

For Further Reading

Clark, Shirley M., and John P. Clark, eds. *Youth in Modern Society.* New York: Holt, Rinehart & Winston, 1972. Deals with generational differences and conflict, including a number of institutional areas.

Epstein, Joseph. *Divorced in America: Marriage in an Age of Possibility.* New York: E. P. Dutton, 1974. An account of a man's experience of divorce, including both the personal and social factors that led to the disruption of a ten-year marriage and the various problems and difficulties encountered in the divorce proceedings and the post-divorce adjustment.

Fuchs, Lawrence H. *Family Matters.* New York: Random House, 1972. Argues that the contemporary tension in family life is rooted in our values on personal independence and individualism; that a healthy family life can be secured only by a change in the role of the father.

Goode, William J. *The Family.* Englewood Cliffs: Prentice-Hall, Inc., 1964. A brief, readable overview of marriage and the family by one of the foremost experts in the field. An excellent introduction to the sociology of the family.

Kephart, William M. *Extraordinary Groups.* New York: St. Martin's Press, 1976. A study of utopian communities of the past and present by a family expert.

LeMasters, E. E. *Parents in Modern America.* Homewood, Ill.: Dorsey Press, 1970. An analysis of the meaning of parenthood in America, in both single-parent and two-parent families. Includes some of our folklore about parenthood.

Scanzoni, Letha, and John Scanzoni. *Men, Women, and Change: A Sociology of Marriage and Family.* New York: McGraw-Hill, 1976. Examines the meaning of marriage and family life in the context of changing roles in contemporary America. Also includes cross cultural and historical materials.

Notes

1. These figures reported in Stephen Rawlings, *Perspectives on American Husbands and Wives* (Washington, D.C.: Government Printing Office, 1978), p. 1.

2. Reported in the *St. Louis Post-Dispatch,* April 27, 1980.

3. U.S. Congress, Senate, Subcommittee of the Committee on Labor and Public Welfare, *American Families: Trends and Pressures, 1973: Hearing on Children and Youth,* September 24, 25, and 26, 1973, p. 278.

4. U.S. Bureau of the Census, *Divorce, Child Custody, and Child Support* (Washington, D.C.: Government Printing Office, 1979), p. 8.

5. "Gaping at the Generation Gap," *Public Opinion,* February/March, 1980, pp. 38–39.

6. U.S. Congress, Senate, Subcommittee of the Committee on Labor and Public Welfare, *American Families: Trends and Pressures, 1973: Hearings on Children and Youth,* September 24, 25, and 26, 1973, pp. 148–49.

7. *Newsweek,* February 13, 1967, p. 64.

8. U.S. Bureau of the Census, *Statistical Abstract of the United States, 1979* (Washington, D.C.: Government Printing Office, 1980), p. 81.

9. This relationship may no longer hold true, according to the research of Jorgensen and Klein (1979). Because their sample was small and nonrandom, we must withhold judgment until additional research is conducted.

Part 4

Global Social Problems

Is there any hope for mankind? In the present time, according to Heilbroner (1975:13), this is a question that "is in the air, more sensed than seen, like the invisible approach of a distant storm. . . ." We are an anxious people, living in an uncertain world. And what are the causes of our anxiety and of our question about hope for the future? Heilbroner (1975:31-53) identified three problems that are the "external" causes of our mood: population growth, war, and environmental problems. All three pose a serious threat to the very existence of the human race.

   In this final part, we will examine these three problems. They are global problems. They cannot be discussed meaningfully without our seeing them in their global context. The threat they pose goes beyond us, but inevitably includes us. We will first examine war. The problems of population and the environment will be combined in the last chapter because they are closely related: population growth is a major contributing factor to environmental problems. Although we are dealing with them last, they are perhaps the most important of all problems. They threaten not only the quality, but the existence of life on earth, also.

War

1 How concerned are Americans
   about the problem of war?

2 How does war affect people
   psychologically?

3 How much does it cost us to keep
   prepared for war?

4 In what sense are we a "garrison"
   society?

5 Is disarmament possible?

Many people agree that war is a senseless and brutal way for nations to attempt to resolve their problems. No nation has ever gone to war with the full support of all of its citizens. Most Americans regarded World War II as unfortunate but necessary, and as a crusade against evil. But even in that war some Americans refused to fight.

The concern of Americans with the problem of war is reflected in the series of Gallup polls taken since 1935, which asked about the "most important problem" facing the nation. The question was asked twenty-nine times between 1935 and 1975, and the problem of war and peace was named twenty-seven times (Lauer, 1976:126). The next most frequently named problem was the high cost of living (including inflation). War has been named more often than any other problem, including economic problems, taxes, crime and delinquency, and poverty.

In this chapter we will examine this problem of great concern to Americans. We will begin by looking at the extent of the problem. We will show the many ways war detracts from the quality of life. We will identify the sociocultural factors that contribute to the problem. Finally, we will discuss some proposals for minimizing or eliminating war.

Extent of the Problem of War

Some observers have claimed that the human bloodshed and human agony resulting from war has intensified rather than diminished over the course of human history. Pitirim Sorokin (1942:216), writing before the end of World War II, called ours the "bloodiest and most belligerent of all the twenty-five centuries" in

Figure 15.1 American soldiers on Buna Beach, South Pacific theatre, World War II.

the West from the fifth century B.C. to the twentieth century A.D. This does not take into account, however, the growth of population and nations. As we try to measure the extent of the problem or war, we need to know more than the absolute number of wars and the total casualties; we need to know the number of wars per nation and the number of casualties per unit of population.

One effort to measure the extent of the problem took account of such factors. A study of wars between 1816 and 1965 throughout the world by Singer and Small (1972) covered 93 international wars and 29 million deaths of military personnel. Among the findings were the following:

1. An international war was being fought in 126 of the 150 years from 1816 to 1965.
2. On the average, an interstate war broke out every three years.
3. The years 1914 and 1939 were the bloodiest in terms of military deaths, with over 8 million and over 15 million, respectively.
4. When we take into account factors such as the growth of population and the number of nations, there does not appear to be any increase in the number or intensity of wars during the 150-year period (intensity refers to casualty rates).
5. There seems to be no level of losses that causes a nation to concede defeat. Nor does the victorious side necessarily have a smaller ratio of battle deaths. In about one-third of the wars the victors lost as many or more men as did the losers.

The research of Singer and Small emphasized that war is a frequent phenomenon in the modern era. They remind us that tens of millions of people have been killed since the beginning of the nineteenth century, the victorious nation sometimes having as heavy losses as the nation that is defeated. However, wars do not appear to be occurring more frequently and they are not proportionately more destructive of human life in relation to population figures.

The United States was not the most war-prone of all nations in the Singer and Small study; France and England each had 19 wars during the period. American involvement and American casualties have been heavy however. In our first 200 years we have been directly involved in nine official wars (official in the sense that we sent troops and publicly acknowledged our involvement). These wars, as we will see later, have not just taken a great toll of lives; they have affected most living Americans in one way or another.

War and the Quality of Life

War is violence on an international level. As with violence at the interpersonal and intergroup levels, it is not possible to fully capture its impact in writing. We will look at some of the reports of those who have experienced war in order to get a sense of what people are doing to each other through warfare. It has been remarked that we should have an international law to the effect that no new wars will be allowed until everyone has read about the last one. The following paragraphs illustrate the basis for such a statement. War destroys and dehumanizes. Let us hope that the more we know about those effects, the less we will be willing to support and engage in war.

Human Destruction and Injury

Human destruction reaches a peak in war. More people have died from war in the twentieth century than in any other century in history. In addition to deaths, there are massive numbers of *injuries* during war, both physical and psychological.

One reason for the increasing number of people killed in war in the modern era is the *changed nature of war*. In the past, wars were fought primarily between armies of professional soldiers. In more recent times, civilian populations have been involved on a large scale. Furthermore, nations have increased their skill in killing. Technological advances have made it possible to kill people in numbers that are staggering. In World War I, fewer than 3 people per 100,000 were killed by bombs in England and Germany. In World War II, nearly 300 people per 100,000 were killed by bombs (Hart, 1957:44).

The amount of human destruction as a result of war may be seen in the figures for American casualties in various wars (table 15.1). From the Civil War to the present at least 641,000 Americans have died in battle and nearly 500,000 more have died in related noncombat incidents. In addition over 1.4 million military personnel have been wounded in the wars.

Occasionally, nations have plunged into wars that virtually decimated their population. In the middle of the nineteenth century, Paraguay went to war against the combined forces of Argentina, Brazil, and Uruguay. The Paraguayan army was outnumbered by ten to one. The consequences for Paraguay were disastrous. Her

Table 15.1   War Casualties of American Military Personnel
(in thousands)

War	Battle Deaths	Nonbattle Deaths	Wounded
Civil War	215	283	282
Spanish-American War	*	2	2
World War I	53	63	204
World War II	292	115	671
Korean War	34	21	103
Vietnam War	47	10	304

*Less than 500

Source: Adopted from U.S. Bureau of the Census, *Statistical Abstract of the United States, 1980* (Washington, D.C.: Government Printing Office, 1981), p. 377; and *The World Almanac and Book of Facts* (New York: Newspaper Enterprise Association, Inc., 1975), p. 364.

population was reduced from 525,000 in 1865 to 221,000 in 1871. Fewer than 29,000 men were among the survivors. The dictator of Paraguay, Francisco Lopez, had ordered boys as young as twelve and men who were grandfathers to be drafted in a desperate attempt to win a war that was utterly hopeless and largely of his own making (Herring, 1957:674–75). The war, one of the bloodiest in Latin American history, brought the nation of Paraguay to the edge of extinction.

Today, in the nuclear age, the destruction experienced by Paraguay in the nineteenth century could be surpassed within a matter of hours. The combined explosive power of U.S. and Soviet warheads in the late 1970s was equivalent to about 1.3 million Hiroshima-size bombs (Lineberry, 1979:13). According to one estimate, if the Soviet Union initiated a "limited" attack on the U.S. by striking at seventy-one of our largest metropolitan areas, the attack would kill half of all Americans within thirty days and would injure tens of millions more. Ninety-eight percent of our key industries would be destroyed. And, the Russians would have used only about 10 percent of their arsenal (Knox, 1980:33)!

The destruction is not limited to the duration of the war. An examination of fifty nation-wars showed *increased homicide rates in the postwar years.* The increases occurred in both the victorious and the defeated nations, and in those with improved as well as those with worsened economic conditions (Archer and Gartner, 1976). The legitimation of violence that occurs during war apparently carries over into postwar years.

Psychological Disruption and Dehumanization

In war, *psychological disruption and dehumanization* occur on a massive scale. War is disruptive for military and civilian personnel, particularly for those who are directly engaged in battle conditions. People dehumanize others and are themselves dehumanized by the experience of war. In part, these effects result from the sheer horror of battle conditions. During the latter days of World War II, the American Air Force launched a massive air attack on German positions near Saint Lo, France. The famous war correspondent Ernie Pyle was there to record his reaction as the planes began to come:

> . . . they came in a constant procession and I thought it would never end. . . . I've never known a storm, or a machine, or any resolve of man that had about it the aura of such a ghastly relentlessness. . . . It seems incredible to me that any German could have come out of the bombardment with his sanity. When it was over I was grateful, in a chastened way that I had never before experienced, for just being alive [Commager, 1945:441, 444].

Even more horrendous than the European bombings was the atomic bombing of the Japanese cities of Hiroshima and Nagaski in World War II. Hiroshima was a city accustomed to crises, having experienced periodic disastrous floods. Nevertheless, the social order of the city collapsed after the atomic bomb was dropped. The city was rebuilt mainly through the work of migrants from the hinterland rather than by the efforts of the surviving residents. The survivors

> suffered from extreme shock and fatigue that lingered for a year. . . . Demoralization was so extreme that industrial alcohol was sold as a substitute for saki; many citizens died or went blind from drinking it [Dentler and Cutright, 1965:420].

Drugs were used to escape reality. Children who survived had a *fear* of becoming attached to others and of having their own children when they became adults. Crimes of violence and theft of precious water and other scarce goods were common. Four months after the bomb had been dropped, the number of reported *crimes* for one month was as high as all reported crime throughout the entire war. Years later, a psychiatrist who studied the survivors reported that they were not capable of leading normal, happy lives. Most of them still carried a deep sense of *guilt,* including the guilt of surviving when so many others had died.

Hiroshima became a city of chaos, pain, crime, anxiety, and deep-rooted fear. So many people continued to feel sick a month after the bomb fell that a rumor spread saying the bomb had left some kind of poison that would give off deadly fumes for seven years (Hersey, 1946:94). Such rumors, of course, intensified the already pervasive anxiety and fear of the people and contributed to an atmosphere that drained people of the necessary psychological strength to function normally and proceed with the work of rebuilding.

Not just victims are dehumanized and psychologically traumatized by the effects of war. The perpetrators of violence in war are themselves dehumanized by their own acts. During World War II, acts such as mass extermination of and "medical" experiments on Jewish people seemed beyond the capacity of human beings to perform. Some of the worst acts of the war were committed at the infamous *concentration camps,* especially Dachau (Gellhorn, 1959:235–42). The Germans wanted to know how long one of their pilots could survive without oxygen. At Dachau they put prisoners into a car and pumped the oxygen out. Some prisoners survived as long as fifteen minutes. They also wanted to see how long pilots could survive in cold water. To determine how long a German pilot shot down over the English Channel or some other body of water might survive, prisoners were placed in vats of ice water that reached to their necks. Some subjects were able

to survive for two and one-half hours. In both experiments the outcome was a painful death for all the subjects.

Inhuman punishments were meted out to prisoners at Dachau who violated rules such as standing at attention with hat off when an SS trooper passed within six feet. Prisoners were lashed with a bullwhip, hung by bound hands from a hook, or placed in a box that prevented them from sitting, kneeling, or lying.

Perhaps the most disquieting aspect of all was the crematorium. A reporter who was in Dachau after it had been captured by the Allies wrote her reaction on seeing piles of dead bodies:

> They were everywhere. There were piles of them inside the oven room, but the SS had not had time to burn them. . . . the bodies were dumped like garbage, rotting in the sun, yellow and nothing but bones, bones grown huge because there was no flesh to cover them, hideous, terrible, agonizing bones, and the unendurable smell of death . . . Nothing about war was ever as insanely wicked as these starved and outraged, naked, nameless dead [Gellhorn, 1959:240].

Dehumanizing acts are not confined to any one people. Americans learned during the Vietnam War that we too are capable of atrocities. That war was particularly vicious for soldiers because there were no "lines" in the usual sense of the word. The enemy was everywhere and could not be distinguished from allies. Americans and some Vietnamese were fighting other Vietnamese. A Vietnam veteran expressed the situation this way: "After a while you get so sick of the trouble that you start killing everyone. . . . it gets so you don't feel so bad about shooting at a 6-year-old kid because the kids are throwing hand grenades at you." The South

Figure 15.2 It is difficult to carry on our usual tasks under the dehumanizing conditions of war.

Koreans who fought with the Americans and South Vietnamese reportedly wiped out entire villages, including men, women, and children when they suspected that enemy forces dominated a village.

As part of their training, American soldiers were told that they were fighting to insure democracy in Asia. The fact that the soldiers were told that they were fighting for a principle, in a war that used both conventional and guerrilla tactics, no doubt helped cause such atrocities. The My Lai massacre, which resulted in courts-martial, was another atrocity. An American soldier wrote to his parents:

> Today we went on a mission and I am not very proud of myself, my friends or my country. We burned every hut in sight! It was a small rural network of villages and the people were incredibly poor. My unit burned and plundered their meager possessions [Hampden-Turner, 1970:100].

The soldier went on to relate another incident. One of his friends had called for anyone in a hut to come out. An old man emerged, and the soldier prepared to throw a hand grenade into the hut. The old man talked furiously, and ran toward the soldier but was restrained by another soldier. Just after the grenade was thrown a crying baby was heard. A mother and three children were killed in the blast.

Soldiers who perform such actions may have *serious psychological problems* when they reflect on what they have done. They have treated other human beings as objects, dehumanizing them, and they are appalled at their own actions. In a study of dehumanization during wartime, three researchers found that dehumanizing reflects back on the perpetrator as well as outward toward the victim. A soldier experiences a diminished sense of his own humanness as well as that of others (Bernard, Ottenberg, and Redl, 1968:17–34).

The researchers pointed out a number of aspects of the "maladaptive" dehumanization that occurs in war:

1. *Increase in emotional distance* from others. Any concern for another is suppressed.
2. *Decreased sense of responsibility for one's own actions.* The feeling that one is fighting for principle rather than for any personal advantage facilitates this attitude, as noted earlier.
3. *Increased concern with procedures rather than with human needs.* Military training facilitates this attitude. The author asked an ROTC student how he thought he would have reacted at the My Lai massacre. The student said he would have obeyed orders, killed the people, and asked questions later.
4. *Lack of resistance to group attitudes and pressures.* Some soldiers have reflected on acts of killing and recognized that they acted, at times, contrary to their own values and desires but were impelled by the expectations of their comrades. If your comrades expect you to kill a helpless, wounded enemy soldier, you may do so regardless of how repulsive the idea would be to you if you were alone.
5. *Feelings of helplessness and alienation.* The individual soldier may feel powerless (and rightly so) to halt a massacre of civilians. That powerlessness is heightened by the notion that a superior officer has knowledge which the soldier does not, making the officer's orders mandatory.

The overwhelming disruption and dehumanization during war reach far beyond the victims and perpetrators of violence. The family and friends of those killed or injured suffer psychological disruption, too. Whatever may be the value of war in settling political disputes, the human cost is enormous.

Environmental Destruction

As we will see in the discussion of ecology in the last chapter, a precarious balance exists between natural resources and the growing demand for energy. This means that *conservation* of natural resources throughout the world is essential. But, there is a *contradiction between this need and the willingness of people to engage in war,* which always involves a certain amount of **environmental destruction.** Increasing sophistication in weaponry and increasing power of destructiveness have made wars more disastrous for the land on which people must live.

As of this writing, full details of ecological damage from America's involvement in Vietnam are not available or, for that matter, even determinable. A few years before the war ended, however, the Stanford Biology Study Group (1970) published a report of a number of known consequences. Over 12 percent of South Vietnam had been sprayed with defoliating chemicals, the effects of which can last for years if not decades. The defoliation program was designed to cut off food for the Viet Cong (the Communist group seeking to overthrow the South Vietnamese government) and to prevent ambushes in dense areas. It also reduced rice production to the point where the "rice bowl of Asia" had to import 850,000 tons in 1968. Also,

the yield of rubber dropped about 45 percent. Other crops decreased between 10 and 40 percent. Some of the chemicals used for defoliation may have caused an increase in the number of birth defects and deformed babies.

The bombing of Vietnam created a land of craters, and each crater was as large as 30 feet deep and 45 feet in radius. More bombs fell on Vietnam than were dropped by all the Allied forces in World War II. By 1972 one estimate placed the number of craters at 20 million! The *long-range effects of the bombing and the defoliation* are uncertain, but they are likely to be severe, and they could be disastrous for the well-being of the Vietnamese people. Two scientists who visited Vietnam in 1971 made this assessment of the impact of the craters:

> . . . those cultivated areas hit heavily with conventional high explosives will be very difficult, if not impossible, to recultivate. They can perhaps be used as a fish-rearing ponds or, in certain situations, as sources of fresh water for irrigation. They may provide additional breeding areas for insect vectors of disease . . . the immediate problem of greatest concern is the vast number of unexploded mines, bombs, rockets, and so forth, that must be removed if the land is to be resettled. Since the Department of Defense reports that approximately 1 to 2 percent of our air and ground munitions fail to explode, there are several hundred thousand of these randomly buried through Indochina [Pfeiffer and Westing, 1974:257].

The actions of modern warfare are doubly perilous, for they involve environmental as well as human destruction. Ironically, intensive bombing contributes little to winning a war. A study of strategic bombing of Germany during World War II concluded that at least 300,000 Germans were killed (including adults and children) and 780,000 injured, and 155,546 British and American airmen died. But, "the slaughter made little contribution to victory" (Wilensky, 1967:25).

The Economic Costs

War is *one of the greatest devourers of economic resources*. An enormous amount of the world's resources is being channeled into paying for past wars and preparing for future wars.

There is an absurdity in present preparations for future wars, according to some observers. An individual or a community can be destroyed only once, but the United States is spending enough money on weaponry to kill every human being on earth and to do so more than once (Seymour Melman, 1970:485). In 1965 America's strategic aircraft and missiles had the capacity for "19 billion tons of TNT-equivalent, or about 6 tons for each human being on earth." Another way of dramatizing our "preparedness" is to point out that if a bomb the size of the one dropped on Hiroshima had been exploded every day from the birth of Christ until 1965, the combined force would be slightly more than 14,000 megatons. That would be "only 70 percent of the destructive capability now encased in the U.S. long-range bombers and missiles alone" (Melman, 1970:486).

All of this, of course, represents an enormous economic investment. According to some estimates, the assets of the military in the U.S. are over three times the combined assets of five of the largest American corporations. Well over half of all federal employees, the armed forces included, work for the Defense Department. By 1978, over $105 billion was allocated for national defense functions, the military employed

over 3.1 million people, and the Department of Defense owned hundreds of billions of dollars worth of property.

One reason for the *high cost of preparedness* is the technological advances made in weaponry, for sophisticated weapons cost considerably more than weapons of the past. According to one estimate, each military death cost $.75 during the Roman wars, $3,000 during the Napoleonic wars, $5,000 during the Civil War, $21,000 during World War I, and $50,000 during World War II (Bossard, 1941).

Another way to compare escalating costs is to look at particular weapons. The cost, in 1977 dollars, of 1 late-model tank equalled the cost of about 3.5 World War II tanks; the cost of 1 bomber equalled the cost of 27 World War II bombers; and the cost of 1 submarine equalled the cost of 39 World War II submarines.[1]

In the late 1960s the cost of world armaments was increasing faster than either world population or the world's economic product (Alexander, 1969). The world's military budget amounted to about $53 for every person on earth, a figure higher than the per capita **gross national product** of some nations. By 1977 the world's military budget was well over $100 per person. In fact, military spending in the world was as large as the annual income of nearly two billion people in the thirty-six poorest nations of the world, and was more than six times the amount spent on energy research (Sivard, 1977:5). In the 1970s the world's military budget was higher than any other budget category, including education, health, and international peacekeeping. The United States and the Soviet Union are not the only nations caught up in heavy investments in war. Most segments

Figure 15.3 A student at the University of Wisconsin yells "Fascist" at the police who were breaking up a protest demonstration against the Vietnam War.

of the human race are caught up in the costly, frantic efforts to gain **military parity.**

Our political leaders often stress that we cannot afford to lag behind in military preparedness and must, therefore, be willing to sacrifice whatever is necessary to remain the world's strongest nation. Critics of that policy stress the undesirable economic and social effects of massive military spending, including inflation, the diversion of resources from enterprises that enhance people's well-being, the lack of balanced growth in the economy, and the waste of both human and material resources.

In a world where one-fourth of the adults are illiterate, where health problems reduce the average life span in Africa by twenty-five years compared to Europe, and where over half a billion people are chronically hungry, the nations of the world continue to give *priority to military preparedness.*

Sivard (1977:19) pointed out that only 5 percent of the world's annual military budget is sufficient to:

1. vaccinate the 5 million children in developing nations who die each year from preventable, contagious diseases;
2. extend literacy to all the world's adults by the end of the century;
3. sharply increase the number of medical auxiliaries in areas where people have no access to professional health services;
4. increase aid to Third World nations to develop their agriculture so that the hundreds of millions of people suffering from malnutrition might be helped;
5. begin a program of help for the hundreds of millions of people living in urban slums and shanty towns;

6. provide food for the 200 million malnourished children of the world who may otherwise suffer permanent mental and/or physical disability;

7. provide additional food for 60 million malnourished pregnant and lactating women, enhancing maternal health and reducing the rate of infant mortality;

8. build schools for half of the world's children who now cannot attend school;

9. begin a program to provide safe, clean water for the hundreds of millions who do not now have it, thereby reducing or eliminating the 25,000 deaths per day from diseases carried in the water people use.

The trade-off between human needs and the military budget is real, not hypothetical. Melman (1974) analyzed the 1974 national budget. In the budget, support of elementary and secondary education was cut by $1.5 billion, while $1.2 billion was put into the military budget for one Trident submarine. The budget for construction of hospitals and health facilities was cut by $36 million, while $39.5 million was allocated to increased research into manned space flights. Approximately the same amount was cut from the program for child nutrition for the schools ($200 million) as was allocated for the **SAM-D missile** ($194.2 million).

It would be hard to disagree with the conclusion that our war-oriented economy results in "a tremendous waste of human, monetary, and natural resources" (Eitzen, 1974:129). In addition to the costs just discussed are subtle consequences such as the domestic "brain drain" of scientists diverted from socially beneficial to military projects. We could ponder what the quality of life might be today if we had taken but half of all the resources poured into military projects and used them for enhancing the well-being of people. This is not to ignore that benefits have been associated with military spending—employment, new technological developments, the support of various kinds of research, and so forth. The argument is that we could have all of these plus more if the resources had been committed to social progress rather than military buildup.

War and Civil Liberties

The *right of free speech* is a long-standing American value. However, there is a *contradiction between this value and the perceived need for consensus during a war*. Political leaders and many citizens become disturbed when some people protest and resist involvement in a declared war. During World War I there was mob violence against dissenters and numerous prosecutions of people who spoke out against our involvement. In the later years of the Vietnam War there were similar cases of mob violence against war protestors, mass protests against the war, massive arrests of demonstrators, and resultant court cases in which the issue of civil liberties was fought.

Violations of civil liberties were less severe for most Americans during World War II, but one group, the Japanese Americans, were almost totally deprived of their civil rights. In 1942 over 100,000 Japanese Americans were relocated from their homes into detention camps in isolated areas. They had committed no crimes. There was no evidence that any of them supported Japan rather than the United States in the war, but they were defined as a potential source of subversion. Long-standing

Figure 15.4 Even though there was no evidence of any lack of loyalty, many Japanese Americans were put into relocation camps during World War II.

prejudice against the Japanese Americans and jealousy of their land holdings, on the West Coast especially, played into this decision. The relocations caused serious economic and psychological problems for many of the Japanese Americans. This wholesale deprivation of civil liberties was upheld as legal by the U.S. Supreme Court, which ruled that the government did not have to respect traditional rights during a national emergency.

Contributing Factors

War is a complex phenomenon. As with violence, some thinkers have tried to make war a simple outgrowth of a *human need for aggression.* But war, like aggression and violence, is linked with *cultural values and patterns.* Some societies have no notions of organized warfare. The Hopi Indians traditionally had no place for offensive warfare and did not idealize the warrior as did some other tribes. Furthermore, the Hopi conceived of the universe as a harmonious whole, with gods, nature, people, animals, and plants all working together for their common well-being.

Why do people support wars, then? In particular, why do they support wars in view of the consequences that we have described earlier? In the following sections we will look primarily at those factors within nations that contribute to the likelihood of war. International factors—political, territorial, and economic disputes—are also important. But, the concerned individual is likely to feel helpless in the face of international forces. We will, therefore, concentrate on factors over which we feel that we as a nation have some control—those within the nation itself.

Social Structural Factors

The economics of war. The idea that wars have an *economic cause* is an ancient one. The Greek philosophers Plato and Aristotle both argued that economic factors are fundamental in the outbreak of war (Wells, 1967:201–202). Plato believed that the quest for unlimited wealth brings on not only war but a number of other human problems. Aristotle saw economic competition as the root of wars. In particular, poverty is the "parent" of both revolution and crime. The same economic inequality that leads to revolution within a nation results in wars between nations.

In modern times Marxists argue that war has an economic basis. The **Marxist** view is that war is a *mechanism for maintaining inequalities* in a struggle for control of raw materials and markets. The inequalities are necessary because **capitalism** requires an ever-expanding market in order to endure. One way to insure that a nation will have control over adequate resources and an expanding market is warfare. Consequently, war is an inevitable outcome of capitalism.

The Marxist argument is not a complete explanation of war, however. For one thing, war is not confined to capitalist nations or to the capitalist era of history. Also, a number of wars (some analysts would even say the majority of wars) have not had economic factors as the primary cause. Bronfenbrenner (1969:35) pointed out that two major expansionist efforts of Japan—the war with Russia in 1904–05 and the "China Incident" of 1937—occurred in periods of general prosperity in the nation "with little or no economic distress to be alleviated by overseas adventure."

On the other hand, economic factors are probably always at work in war to some degree. We pointed out that high military budgets always mean the sacrifice of certain social needs. High military budgets also mean considerable profits to a number of industries. In the trade-off between social needs and military demands, someone always gains and someone always loses. Unfortunately, those who gain from high military budgets tend to exercise the most *power* in the government. In 1979 the total military procurement in the United States amounted to 69.3 billion.[2] Without these orders for military supplies, some industries would face financial crisis. Consequently, there are intense lobbying efforts in the Congress to maintain and increase military expenditures. Costly though they are in terms of social programs, they are lucrative in terms of business profits. Even if the arms buildup should lead to war, some businessmen will reap considerable financial gains.

As this line of thought suggests, economics and militarism are intertwined. But, the relationships are even more involved. The government is also a part of the so-called military-industrial complex. We will turn, therefore, to a consideration of the political aspect of preparations for war and peace.

The politics of war: militarism.   In America the *military influence* is pervasive, and perhaps even more dangerous than in some other countries where it is more obvious. Few Americans realize the extent to which the military infiltrates American life. It has operated in such insidious ways as to increase purchase of grapes during a national boycott on grapes to support unionization of California farm workers.

So pervasive is the military influence in our country that Vernon Dibble (1967) labeled us a "*garrison society*." In a garrison society the boundaries between the military and civilian areas have broken down. The breakdown occurs, in part, because of the enormous size and economic power of the military. The breakdown involves linkage of the military, the government, and the corporations into a group with *common goals* and *shared interests*. The principle of restraint by means of civilian control of the military dissolves because the civilians who have the authority to exercise control share goals and interests with the military.

Some examples of shared interests are provided by Muller (1970:114–15). A senator from a western state has been a noted champion of the military-industrial complex and its demands. The senator's state has received more than half its income from government orders. An important member of the House of Representatives has also taken up the cause of the military and has, in return, brought a good deal of business into his home district. Congressional committees that review requests for funding by the Pentagon have tended to call in as witnesses mainly people from the Pentagon.

The power of the military-industrial complex is such that expenditures were made even when the evidence and testimony presented by scientists indicated that the money would be wasted. Muller noted that one secretary of defense agreed to a $5 billion missile-defense system even though he pointed out that the defense it offered was not adequate and scientific advisers of the president argued against it.

Some observers have argued that describing the United States as a garrison society overstates the case. They have pointed out that *defense spending* consumed an increasingly smaller proportion of the federal budget from

Figure 15.5 Weapons for sale in a French catalogue. Considerable profits are involved in the international arms market, and governments, like the military, and industry are linked together in an effort to exploit that market.

1960 to 1978. However, the total amount for 1978 was larger than the total for 1960.

The arms race continues throughout the world, not merely in the United States and Soviet Union (see fig. 15.5). In 1975 the developed countries, which represented 25.9 percent of the world's population, accounted for 81.5 percent of all military expenditures. The United States expended $85.9 billion and the Soviet Union expended $84.0 billion for military purposes. In 1974 the United States gave $3.4 billion in foreign economic aid (the Soviet Union gave $0.67 billion) and spent $80.3 billion for public education and $38.6 billion for public health (Sivard, 1977:20–21).

Perhaps the most dangerous manifestation of a combined military-industrial interest and influence is the continuing *arms race* and the continuing production of arms for sale to other countries:

> Although almost all arms in the West are manufactured by private companies, governments are deeply involved at nearly every step of the high-stakes operation. Pentagon and Commerce Department officials, for example, aid sales teams from U.S. arms manufacturers at the biennial Paris Air Show, where hundreds of millions of dollars of weapons business is transacted. . . . Usually . . . it is the military attaché, stationed in nearly every embassy around the world, who spots a potential customer and makes preliminary contacts. Having ingratiated himself with senior officers of the host country's armed forces, the attaché might gradually convince them that they need a new-model helicopter or a more powerful tank.[3]

Together the U.S., the Soviet Union, Britain, and France supply about 90 percent of all weapons for the world. In 1974, eight American corporations sold more than $100 million each of

Figure 15.6 Worldwide military expenditures in current dollars, 1970 to 1980. (Source: U.S. Bureau of the Census. *Statistical Abstract of the United States* [Washington, D.C.: Government Printing Office, 1980], p. 365.)

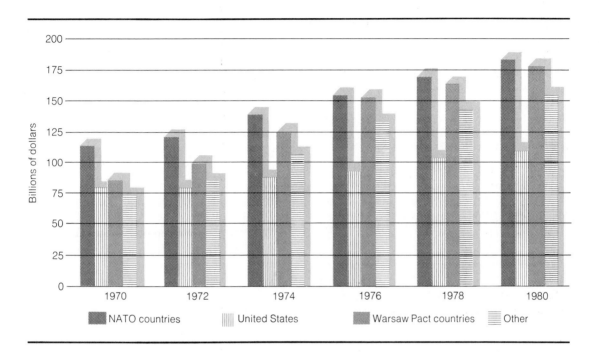

NATO countries   United States   Warsaw Pact countries   Other

arms to foreign nations, ranging from $119.7 million for McDonnell Douglas (for aircraft) to $271.8 million for FMC Corporation (for armored personnel carriers).[4]

Both the United States and the Soviet Union have attempted to settle diplomatically the dispute between Israel and the Arab nations. At the same time, both nations have supplied the two adversaries with the necessary weapons to continue the conflict. All wars in the last two decades have been fought in less developed areas of the world, but the weapons used for the wars have been supplied primarily by the developed nations. As this suggests, the significance of the military expenditures is that they virtually insure the continuation of war.

Rathjens (1969) wrote about the "*action-re-action phenomenon*" associated with the arms race, a process in which each nation responds to the developments occurring in the other by attempting to equal or better the other's achievements. Rathjens provided a number of examples of developments in both American and Soviet weaponry that were responses to the developments of the other nation.

An arms race tends to be self-perpetuating because each side views developments of the other with alarm and responds with its own efforts, which then become a stimulus to the other side to make further advances. It seems reasonable to argue that we cannot maintain peace unless we are strong enough to dissuade any enemy attack. The military stresses such an argument. However, a military buildup that keeps pace with our potential enemies is likely to bring us to war. The historical evidence shows that an arms race is more likely to end in war than to maintain peace.

Social Psychological Factors

Attitudes. Militarism and war are legitimated by a number of attitudes. By the end of the Vietnam War, most Americans had anti-militaristic attitudes, but by the late 1970s attitudes were changing. In 1971 only 11 percent of the respondents in a national poll favored increased defense spending. By 1979 the proportion had risen to 60 percent.[5] In the early 1970s the draft was abolished and the nation accepted the notion of an all-volunteer force. By 1980 many observers were complaining that volunteerism would not be sufficient. There was, according to some, a serious shortage of personnel in the armed forces. In the wake of problems with Iran and the Soviet invasion of Afghanistan, the nation reinstituted registration for the draft in 1980. The move was favored by the public. A Gallup poll that asked whether we should return to the military draft found 59 percent affirmative responses.

In other words, public attitudes in the late 1970s and early 1980s favored a turn toward greater militarism.

Our attitudes may also legitimate war, particularly the set of attitudes that comprise *international misperception.* C. Wright Mills (1958) dealt with these attitudes in his discussion of *"crackpot realism."* He said that men of power take what they define as hard-headed and realistic approaches and laud each other for their realism. But, they are wrong in their appraisals of situations and so behave in accord with a "crackpot realism," which includes ideas such as: war is more natural than peace; the other side is eager to see us fail; it is easier and more realistic to prepare for war than for peace; and military leaders must be left free to deal with military problems. Because both sides operate with these attitudes, crackpot realism characterizes all leaders, not just ours.

Other observers provided support for Mills's argument, showing that leaders and people on each side of hot and cold wars have typically misperceived other countries in ways that facilitate military buildups and legitimate war. White (1966) identified six different forms of misperception that recur in cases of international wars:

1. *The diabolical enemy-image* imputes flagrant evil to the enemy, who is conceived to be thoroughly criminal in behavior.
2. *The virile self-image* implies preoccupation with one's own strength and courage and the need to avoid humiliation by determined fighting.
3. *The moral self-image* affirms our goodness as well as our strength; we are the people of God and the enemy is of the devil.
4. *Selective inattention* means that only the worst aspects of the enemy are noticed; at the same time we attend to the best aspects of ourselves, reinforcing the idea of the war as a conflict between black and white, good and evil.
5. *Absence of empathy* means inability to understand how the situation looks from the other's viewpoint. An American might wonder, for example, how any German could fight in behalf of Hitler, or how any South Vietnamese could not welcome the American effort to save Vietnam from Communism. People on both sides of a war fail to understand how the war could be justified by those on the other side.

6. *Military overconfidence* refers to the conviction that our side can win. Perhaps the supreme example of such overconfidence was the willingness of Lopez to lead the Paraguayans against the combined armies of Argentina, Brazil, and Uruguay.

These attitudes are found on both sides of a conflict and are encouraged by the opposing leaders. People support war to the extent that they accept these attitudes. Since both sides have the same attitudes, the attitudes obviously cannot reflect reality. Nevertheless, they have typically been defined as valid and have served to legitimate international violence.

War and ideology.   Militarism and the attitudes discussed above are supported by *ideologies*. There is, for example, the ideology that asserts that Americans are the *policemen of the world*. This ideology says that we maintain the kind of democratic society that is best for all people and that it is our duty to protect and extend that kind of society. Communism anywhere is a threat to us and to our way of life, and it may be necessary (even though we would prefer to avoid it) to engage in small wars wherever communists are attempting to take over a nation. We are, thereby, only protecting people from an evil system, according to this ideology.

A different ideology has been employed to support and extend defense spending. Melman (1974:287–90) called it the *"ideology of no way out."* Essentially, the ideology argued that a war economy is necessary for the well-being of the United States. A book-length report presenting the Pentagon as an economic boon to the nation was issued by the Department of Defense in 1972—in time, Melman noted, to be used for opposing the presidential aspirations of

George McGovern, who proposed large cutbacks in military spending.

It is interesting that this ideology is accepted by those on the left as well as those on the right. Conservatives use the ideology to gain support for military spending, which they feel is necessary to maintain a strong nation and neutralize the threat of communism. Leftist thinkers, on the other hand, use the ideology to argue that capitalism inherently leads to warfare. They assert that without wars a capitalist society would crumble from within; that wars and preparation for future wars are the main stimuli to economic growth in capitalist nations.

In any case, the acceptance of the ideology leads to continuation of the militaristic trends in our society, and militarism tends to lead ultimately to war. The ideology may not reflect reality. Melman argued convincingly that in many ways there are *contradictions between reality and the ideology*. For instance, the ideology says that military spending creates jobs and bolsters the economy. During the 1972 presidential campaign, Vice-President Agnew exploited this notion by telling people that the Democratic candidate, George McGovern, was "apparently oblivious to the fact that his defense cutback proposals would throw an estimated *1.8 million* Americans out of work" (Melman, 1974:130).

Reality, argued Melman, contradicts this aspect of the ideology. Increased defense spending obviously helps those industries engaged in the production of war materials, but other industries inevitably lose because of the trade-off between military expenditures and other needs. We do not gain anything in national income by pouring money into the military. We only enhance national income in a particular sector of

Involvement

"What a Great War That Was"

A friend of the author served as a navigator in the Air Force during World War II. "Those," he says, "were some of the best days of my life." He recalls his days in the military as a time of adventure. He does not desire war, but neither does he think of it in terms of the detrimental consequences that we discussed in this chapter.

Interview a number of armed forces veterans. If possible, find veterans who served in different wars, and include people who did and people who did not have combat experience. How do they describe the experience of war? Do they mention any of the consequences discussed in this chapter? Would they be willing to serve in another war or to have their children serve? Note if there are differences based on service in different wars or on combat versus noncombat experience. If everyone felt like your respondents about war, would the probability of future wars be greater or less?

the economy at the expense of other sectors. Furthermore, a high level of defense spending "induces reductions in the productivity of capital, which holds down productivity and hence job growth for the civilian economy as a whole into a far future" (Melman, 1974:130). He argued that there are sufficient needs and demands among the American people for an expanding economy and job market without the heavy investment in defense spending. In the past the American economy did not rest on military spending. Except for the two years we were in World War I, our nation used an average of less than 1 percent of the gross national product for military purposes between 1900 and 1930. There is no reason to believe that the economy needs to rest on military spending now.

Melman mentioned the belief that we could not shift funds into other programs even if we wished to because military spending is supported by Congress and the majority of the people. He referred to a poll reported by *Time* magazine in 1972 that asked a national sample of Americans whether they supported increased, maintained, or reduced federal spending for various purposes. Sixteen programs received considerably greater support than defense spending. By contrast, there was considerable support for maintained or increased spending for programs to combat crime, help the aged, prevent drug abuse, deal with pollution, improve the education of low-income children, improve medical and health care, and expand Medicaid for low-income families (Melman, 1974:136). In effect, by the 1970s, contrary to ideology, Americans were willing to change our war economy into an economy that addressed social needs and social problems.

Even in the late 1970s, when attitudes toward defense spending became more positive, the majority of people indicated that the government spends too little on attacking crime, improving health, and improving education.

What Is To Be Done?

Inequalities of wealth and power among nations, political and ideological conflicts, and economic factors all contribute to the likelihood of war. However, one important step toward solving the problem of war would be to reverse the pattern of increasing militarism by stopping the arms race and the increasingly heavy investment in military resources.

The "enemy" may indeed attack the nation that begins to *demilitarize,* but there is some evidence to suggest that the risk is minimal. In the process called *Graduated Reciprocation In Tension-reduction* (GRIT), one nation imitates an action that visibly reduces the way it threatens the other nation without at the same time endangering its own security. The action is an invitation to the other side to reciprocate (Elms, 1972:370–71). Will such reciprocation occur? Following the 1962 Cuban missile crisis, President Kennedy announced that we would stop atmospheric nuclear tests and resume them only if another country's action compelled us to do so. The next day the Soviet Union agreed to a Western-backed proposal in the United Nations to send observers to Yemen (a proposal they had been blocking). America reciprocated by agreeing to restore the Hungarian delegation to full status in the United Nations. A few days later Khrushchev announced that Russia would stop producing strategic bombers. Shortly thereafter the "hot line" between the White

House and the Kremlin was installed (Etzioni, 1967). This series of concessions was the result of each side taking a step that led the other to reciprocate.

Despite such evidence, and despite a general agreement that a nuclear war would be a catastrophe for victor and vanquished alike, efforts to bring about disarmament or even *arms control* have been frustrating at best and dismal failures at worst. The difficulties of getting nations to reverse their arms buildup are illustrated by the *Strategic Arms Limitation Talks* (SALT) between the United States and the Soviet Union. The goals of the talks, which began about 1970, were to prevent a nuclear war between the two nations and eventually reduce the costly investment in armaments so that each nation could put more of its resources into social needs.

How successful have the negotiations been? After two years of talks, the SALT I agreement was signed by leaders of the two nations. One part of the agreement limited the construction and installation of defensive anti-ballistic missiles—missiles that destroy offensive missiles of an enemy before they can strike their target. Such an agreement seems to allow both sides to continue to have the opportunity to destroy the other side! A second part of the SALT I agreement put limits on the strategic arsenals of the two nations. The Soviets were given a higher limit than the United States on the grounds that the U.S. arsenal of weaponry used more sophisticated technology and was, therefore, more deadly than that of the Soviets. The limitation on offensive weapons, however, was set to expire in 1977 unless a new agreement was reached or the deadline was extended.

Meanwhile, in the years after SALT I was signed, negotiators worked on SALT II, an agreement that would, among other things, place more permanent limits on offensive weapons. In 1974 a tentative agreement was reached between the Soviet leader Brezhnev and the American president, Ford. For ten years neither country was to construct and install more than 2,400 strategic missile launchers (intercontinental bombers were defined as missile launchers in the agreement).

The agreement between the leaders appeared to be the breakthrough that was needed to reach a formal agreement. However, as of this writing the agreement has not been ratified by the U.S. Senate, which has opposed it on various grounds. Among some of the problems (in addition to the notion that you can never trust the Russians, and that the Russians benefit from the terms far more than the U.S.), the leaders did not define with sufficient precision the meaning of certain terms used. "Strategic" and "missile" can mean different things to different people. The United States maintained that the agreed-upon limits do not apply to its new "cruise missile." The cruise missile is relatively small (about twenty feet long) and inexpensive (less than $1 million each!) but incredibly accurate. The missile is guided by a miniature computer. It can travel over 1,500 miles with a warhead that equals about ten Hiroshima bombs and strike within 100 feet of its preprogrammed target. We argued that the cruise missile is not technically a missile because it is self-propelled and it does not follow the same path as a ballistic missile. The Soviets, by the same token, argued that a new bomber they developed does not qualify as a "strategic" weapon because it cannot fly to our country and return home without refueling.

Both sides are attempting to circumvent the agreement and maximize their respective positions by excluding certain weapons from the agreement. As a result, defense spending in both countries continues to rise, and arms control is a hope rather than a reality. The further step of disarmament is a faint hope for the future.

In spite of the difficulties and agonizingly slow pace of negotiating arms control, the work must continue. There is little likelihood of peace in a world armed to the teeth. And there is little likelihood of having the resources to deal with other social problems when militarism consumes so much.

Along with efforts to control and, ultimately, reduce arms, some kind of *political arrangements at an international level* may reduce the incidence of wars. As Wells (1967:232) put it:

> Our greatest hope for emerging from the anarchy in which world affairs are carried out doubtless rests on some form of political cooperation or organization. The alternatives to war lie in the areas of international law, international diplomacy, and international organization.

This does not mean that we must immediately create a world government or world judicial system or world army. Even if these were done, there would still be the possibility of wars between segments of the world system, analogous to a civil war within a nation.

But, certain kinds of political arrangements can minimize the possibility of war. Deutsch (1957) called such an arrangement a "*security-community*." In a security-community, members settle their disputes by nonviolent means.

There are two kinds of security-communities: the "amalgamated" and the "pluralistic." An amalgamated security-community has a common government. Two or more independent units merge into a larger unit and become a single governmental unit. The United States today is an example of this kind of security-community. A pluralistic security-community is one in which members retain their independence and their own governments. The combined area of the United States and Canada is a pluralistic security-community.

There are a number of examples in the world of both kinds of security-communities, but Deutsch (1957:30–31) believed that the pluralistic type was the "more promising approach to the elimination of war over large areas. . . ." The task for those who desire peace is to research more thoroughly the political arrangements between nations that appear to have minimized the probability of war and to suggest how those political arrangements might be adapted to the world as a whole.

The effort to avoid war and reduce the costs of preparing for war entails considerable frustration and confronts us with perplexities. But, as with the other problems we have studied, the alternatives to making the effort are grim. The noted man of peace Martin Luther King, Jr. put it this way:

> "In a day when sputniks dash through outer space and guided ballistic missiles are carving highways of death through the stratosphere, nobody can win a war. The choice today is no longer between violence and nonviolence. It is either nonviolence or nonexistence" [Weinberg and Weinberg, 1963:74].

Summary

Americans have been greatly concerned about war, mentioning it more frequently than any other problem in Gallup polls between 1935 and 1975. Tens of millions of people have died in wars since the beginning of the nineteenth century. Americans have been involved in nine official wars during our history.

War diminishes the quality of life for most people and destroys the lives of many. Since the Civil War at least 640,000 Americans have died in battles alone. War causes psychological disruption and the dehumanization of everyone involved. Much environmental destruction occurs during war, some of which may be irreversible. The economic costs of war and of preparation for possible wars are staggering. Military spending inevitably means that certain social needs will be neglected. And, war always poses a threat to our civil liberties, as illustrated by sanctions against dissenters and the detention of Japanese Americans in isolated camps during World War II.

Social structural and social psychological factors help bring about war and motivate people to support war. Some analysts have said that wars are economic phenomena. Military spending is highly profitable to some industries, and people who profit from such spending tend to exercise the most power in the government. Thus, economic factors, while present to some extent in all wars, are not the primary cause of every war.

The military influence in America is pervasive. We have been called a "garrison society" because the military, the government, and the corporations have common goals and shared interests. This military-industrial-governmental linkage maintains the arms race and high levels of defense spending. The arms race tends to be self-perpetuating because each side views developments of the other with alarm and responds with its own efforts, which then become the stimuli to the other side to make further advances.

Militarism and war are justified by a number of attitudes, including favorable attitudes toward the draft and toward increased defense spending, and the set of attitudes called "international misperception." These attitudes are held by both sides of the conflict. They include notions such as: the enemy is evil; we are strong and moral; this is a struggle between good and evil, black and white; and it is inconceivable to us that the enemy could justify its behavior.

A number of ideologies support the attitudes and the militarism of our society. One ideology argues that Americans must be the policemen of the world. Another, called the "ideology of no way out," argues that a war economy is necessary for the well-being of the United States because military spending creates jobs and bolsters the economy. Even if we wished to cut back on military spending and channel our resources into social needs, we could not do so because neither Congress nor the general public would approve social programs so readily as they approve military spending. There are a number of contradictions between this ideology and the reality of our situation. Nevertheless, to the extent that the ideology is accepted, it helps perpetuate the problem of war and militarism.

Glossary

capitalism   an economic system in which there is private, rather than state, ownership of wealth and control of the production and distribution of goods; people are motivated by profit, and compete with each other for maximum shares of profit

environmental destruction   alterations in the environment that make it less habitable or useful for people or other living things

gross national product   the total value, usually in dollars, of all goods and services produced by a nation during a year

Marxist   pertaining to the system of thought developed by Karl Marx and Friedrich Engels, particularly emphasizing materialism, class struggle, and the progress of humanity toward communism

military parity   equality or equivalence in military strength

SAM-D missile   one of the American surface-to-air missiles designed to intercept airplanes or other missiles

For Further Reading

Bramson, Leon, and George W. Goethals, eds. *War: Studies from Psychology, Sociology, and Anthropology.* New York: Basic Books, Inc. 1964. Essays representing different disciplines and, therefore, various perspectives on the causes of war.

Deutsch, Karl. "Changing Images of International Conflict." *Journal of Social Issues* 23 (January 1967):91–107. A readable journal article that describes seven major ways of looking at war that make war appear sensible and also increase the likelihood of war.

Dougherty, James E., and Robert L. Pfaltzgraff, Jr. *Contending Theories of International Relations.* Philadelphia: J. B. Lippincott, 1971. An overview and synthesis of international relations theory, including various theories on conflict and war.

Hersey, John. *Hiroshima.* New York: Alfred A. Knopf, 1946. An account of the confusion, turmoil, and suffering in Hiroshima when the atomic bomb was dropped.

Melman, Seymour. *The Permanent War Economy.* New York: Simon & Schuster, 1974. A convincing argument that defense spending is detrimental rather than beneficial to the American economy and American people.

Wright, Quincy. *A Study of War.* Chicago: University of Chicago Press, 1964. A classic work that investigates virtually every aspect of war, including the history of and changes in war; the causes of war; the relationship between war and nationalism, cultural factors, public opinion, and so forth; and the prediction and control of war.

Notes

1. *Time,* May 23, 1977, p. 18.
2. U.S. Bureau of the Census, *Statistical Abstract of the United States, 1980* (Washington, D.C.: Government Printing Office, 1981), p. 372.
3. *Time,* March 3, 1975, p. 34.
4. Ibid., p. 36.
5. Reported in *Public Opinion,* December/January 1980, p. 22.

Ecology and Population

16

1 Why must humans learn to live
within the ecosystem?

2 What kinds of pollution and
depletion of resources threaten us?

3 Is America's population growth a
problem?

4 Can we survive industrialism?

5 Will we have to give up our
affluence?

Some observers say that mankind is a threatened species, that the future of the human population is in serious jeopardy. Others argue that
even if the survival of our species on earth is not
threatened, we nevertheless face a crisis:

> The word "crisis" is not to be used lightly. But
> we have surely reached one. By any other name,
> the situation is the same—the relationship
> between man and the earth's natural resources
> has reached a critical juncture. Unless action is
> taken soon to reduce the waste of our dwindling
> natural resources, unless we recycle and reuse
> more of the products we consume, and unless we
> carefully protect the environment in doing so,
> America will no longer be beautiful or bountiful
> [Citizens' Advisory Committee on Environment
> Quality, 1975:12].

The message is clear: we can no longer assume that we have unlimited resources or that
we can continue to expand our production and
consumption without regard to the land on
which we live. The complex set of interrelationships between the earth and its inhabitants is
threatened, and we are slowly becoming aware
that ignoring those interrelationships can mean
self-destruction.

The problem has not arisen overnight. In ancient Rome, Seneca complained about the
heavy air of the city and the odors coming from
the sooty chimneys. In the Middle Ages, London's air was already offensive, and at least one
man was hanged for burning coal. By the nineteenth century, Shelley wrote that Hell was a
populous and smoky city like London (Revelle,
1971:390). Today the problems of the environment are seen to be more complex and more
serious than anyone thought in the past.

Ecological problems constitute a social problem because they affect our quality of life and because they are the result of social factors as well as purely technical factors.

We will first look at the **"ecosystem"** to set the stage for an understanding of ecological problems. Then we will look at the various kinds of ecological problems we face and their extent throughout the contemporary world. We will see how the problems affect the quality of life and what structural and social psychological factors contribute to them. Some of the ways to attack ecological problems require us to choose between undesirable alternatives. We will examine some proposed as well as some actual efforts at resolving these problems.

The Ecosystem

The ecosystem refers to a set of living things and their environment—which means all the interrelationships among the things and the environment. The emphasis is on the _interdependence of all things_—people, land, animals, vegetation, atmosphere, and social processes. In an ecosystem, anything that one element does or anything that happens to one element of the system has consequences for all other elements. Commoner (1971:16–17) called the ecosystem of the earth a "machine" and described some of the crucial interrelationships:

> Without the photosynthetic activity of green plants, there would be no oxygen for our engines, smelters, and furnaces, let alone support for human and animal life. Without the action of the plants, animals, and microorganisms that live in them, we could have no pure water in our lakes and rivers. Without the biological processes that have gone on in the

soil for thousands of years, we would have neither food crops, oil, nor coal. This machine is our biological capital, the basic apparatus on which our total productivity depends. If we destroy it, our most advanced technology will become useless and any economic and political system that depends on it will founder. The environmental crisis is a signal of this approaching catastrophe.

Nature is not "out there" to be conquered for human benefits. Rather, people and nature and the earth form a delicately balanced system. What we do at one place can have serious consequences for the system at other places. Ecological consequences of our behavior are well illustrated in two current problems: "_acid rain_" and the threat to the _ozone layer_. Some observers consider acid rain to be one of the most important of our ecological problems. The problem is caused by sulfur dioxide emissions from coal-burning plants and factories and by nitrogen oxides from automobile exhaust and some industries. As they rise, the chemicals mix with water vapor to form sulfuric and nitric acids, which then fall to the earth as rain or snow. While the effects are not yet completely known, acid rains have killed fish in lakes, reduced crop yields, and caused damage to buildings and monuments.

Ozone is a rare form of oxygen that is poisonous to humans at ground level but is necessary in the upper atmosphere in order to absorb the deadly ultraviolet radiation of the sun. Ozone is distributed from ground level to the stratosphere with a natural balance. Human activity disturbs that natural balance. Higher than normal concentrations at ground level pose health problems to the eyes, throat, and lungs. High-voltage electrical equipment creates ground level ozone. Ironically, electrostatic air cleaners, which have been used to reduce other kinds of air pollution, are another kind of equipment that generates ozone. The ecosystem is so complex that sometimes our apparent victories come back to haunt us.

The ozone in the upper atmosphere is reduced as a result of a number of human activities, including the use of nitrogen fertilizers, supersonic airplanes, fluorocarbons from aerosol spray cans (now banned in the U.S.) and nuclear explosions in the atmosphere. The effects of a depleted ozone layer are wide-reaching, involving changes in the earth's climate, destruction of some plant and animal life, reduced crop yields, increased incidence of skin cancer, possible genetic damage to plants and to humans, and an impact on the food chain of the oceans (Brodeur, 1979:18).

Our ecological problems involve everything on earth, and virtually everything can be affected by our action. A poet once wrote that one cannot stir a flower without troubling a star. It is imperative that we make every effort to evaluate all the implications of human action for our delicately balanced ecosystem. We must try to understand the chain of consequences of our behavior, for the sake of long-term effects on our environment as well as short-term effects on our comfort.

Our Ecological Problems Defined

We may divide our ecological problems into three types—**environmental pollution, environmental depletion,** and **overpopulation.** "Pollution" refers to degradation of air, land, water, aesthetic environment (eye pollution), and sound environment (noise pollution). "Depletion" refers to the diminishing supply of natural resources, which we are particularly aware of in the face of increasing demand for energy, for instance. "Overpopulation" occurs when the human population puts stress on the ecological balance, or when the population is too large for people to attain a desired quality of life. All three types of problems are intricately linked.

Environmental Pollution

"Pollution is the *harmful alteration of our environment by our own actions*. **Pollutants** are either unwanted by-products of our activities or the obnoxious residues of things we have made, used, and thrown away" (Revelle, 1971:382). There are numerous kinds of pollution and pollutants, as we will see later. We must always remember that we are dealing with an ecosystem, so the overall impact of pollutants is greater than the impact of particular pollutants in particular places.

Air pollution. Millions of tons of *pollutants are thrown into the air* every year in the United States. Not all the results are as dramatically visible as urban smog. Much pollution is not visible to the naked eye because it is due to discharge of gases and tiny particulate matter into the air. Winds may blow the pollutants away from a populated area where they are generated, but this does not mean that there is no damage. In some areas, atmospheric conditions tend to concentrate pollutants in the air.

The Council on Environmental Quality has compiled a list of the major air pollutants and their characteristics, sources, principal effects, and ways they can be controlled (figure 16.2). Most air pollution is caused by the burning of fossil fuels—oil, natural gas, and coal. Air pollution is associated primarily with the produc-

Figure 16.1 A factory pouring pollutants into the air is obvious. Not all pollutants are visible, however, so the absence of smoke does not necessarily mean clean air.

tion of energy, with industrial processes, and with the internal combustion engines of the motor vehicles that clog our streets and highways.

Water pollution. Revelle (1971:396–401) identified eight different kinds of *water pollution* in the United States. First is organic sewage, which requires dissolved oxygen in order to be transformed into carbon dioxide, water, phosphates, nitrates, and certain plant nutrients. Less oxygen is needed if the sewage is treated, but the amount of treatment varies from place to place, and in some cases there is no treatment at all.

"Eutrophication," a second kind of water pollution, is overfertilization of water from excess nutrients, leading to algae growth and oxygen depletion. Eutrophication threatens aquatic life. Great numbers of fish in the United States and in other nations have already been killed by it.

A third type of water pollution results from infectious agents. Many water-borne bacteria that cause disease have been eliminated in the United States, but there is still some danger from infectious viruses such as hepatitis.

Organic chemicals such as insecticides, pesticides, and detergents cause a fourth kind of water pollution. These too may be highly toxic to aquatic life and to the creatures that use the water and the aquatic life in it.

Inorganic and miscellaneous chemicals constitute a fifth category of water pollutants. These can alter the life of a body of water, kill fish, and create unpleasant tastes when the water is used as a drinking supply.

Sixth, sediments from land erosion may cause pollution. These sediments can "reduce a stream's ability to assimilate oxygen-demanding wastes and prevent sunlight required by aquatic plants from penetrating the water" (Revelle, 1971:400).

Radioactive substances, a seventh kind of pollutant, are likely to become more serious if nuclear power plants to generate electricity become more common.

The eighth kind of water pollution is waste heat from power plants and industry. Overheated water holds less oxygen, and fish and other aquatic life are generally very sensititve to temperature changes.

Not only our lakes and rivers are being polluted, but our oceans as well. *Oil spills* and the *dumping of waste into the oceans* have made some beaches unsafe for swimming. An estimated 22 million barrels of oil are poured into the ocean each year just from the cleaning of the bilges of tankers. When Thor Heyerdahl sailed across the Atlantic in 1970, he reported seeing oil clots in the water on forty-three of the fifty-seven days of his voyage. American scientists in 1971 discovered "massive globs of oil and clots of plastic in the Atlantic Ocean from Cape Cod to the Caribbean Sea. The pollution covered 700,000 square miles, an area more than 2½ times as large as Texas" (Freeman, 1974:53). The seriousness of this problem is increasing because Americans throw millions of tons of waste into the ocean every year.

Land pollution. Soil, as well as air and water, may be polluted. **Pesticides, herbicides,** chemical wastes, radioactive fallout, and garbage can all *infect the soil.* Some of the chemicals used in pesticides are hazardous to both humans and the soil. Unfortunately, these chemicals are also

Figure 16.2 Major air pollutants for which national ambient air quality standards have been established.

(Source: *Sixth Annual Report of the Council on Environmental Quality* [Washington, D.C.: Government Printing Office, 1975], p. 300–303.)

Pollutant	Total suspended particulates (TSP)	Sulfur dioxide (SO₂)	Carbon monoxide (CO)
Characteristics	Any solid or liquid particles dispersed in the atmosphere, such as dust, pollen, ash, soot, metals, and various chemicals; the particles are often classified according to size as settleable particles: larger than 50 microns; aerosols: smaller than 50 microns; and fine particulates: smaller than 3 microns	A colorless gas with a pungent odor; SO_2 can oxidize to form sulfur trioxide (SO_3), which forms sulfuric acid with water	A colorless, odorless gas with a strong chemical affinity for hemoglobin in blood
Principal sources	Natural events such as forest fires, wind erosion, volcanic eruptions; stationary combustion, especially of solid fuels; construction activities; industrial processes; atmospheric chemical reactions	Combustion of sulfur-containing fossil fuels, smelting of sulfur-bearing metal ores, industrial processes, natural events such as volcanic eruptions	Incomplete combustion of fuels and other carbon-containing substances, such as in motor vehicle exhausts; natural events such as forest fires or decomposition of organic matter
Principal effects	Health: Directly toxic effects or aggravation of the effects of gaseous pollutants; aggravation of asthma or other respiratory or cardiorespiratory symptoms; increased cough and chest discomfort; increased mortality Other: Soiling and deterioration of building materials and other surfaces, impairment of visibility, cloud formation, interference with plant photosynthesis	Health: Aggravation of respiratory diseases, including asthma, chronic bronchitis, and emphysema; reduced lung function; irritation of eyes and respiratory tract; increased mortality Other: Corrosion of metals; deterioration of electrical contacts, paper, textiles, leather, finishes and coatings, and building stone; formation of acid rain; leaf injury and reduced growth in plants	Health: Reduced tolerance for exercise, impairment of mental function, impairment of fetal development, aggravation of cardiovascular diseases Other: Unknown
Controls	Cleaning of flue gases with inertial separators, fabric filters, scrubbers, or electrostatic precipitators; alternative means for solid waste reduction; improved control procedures for construction and industrial processes	Use of low-sulfur fuels; removal of sulfur from fuels before use; scrubbing of flue gases with lime or catalytic conversion	Automobile engine modifications (proper tuning, exhaust gas recirculation, redesign of combustion chamber); control of automobile exhaust gases (catalytic or thermal devices); improved design, operation, and maintenance of stationary furnaces (use of finely dispersed fuels, proper mixing with air, high combustion temperature)

Photochemical oxidants (Ox)	Nitrogen dioxide (NO₂)	Hydrocarbons (HC)
Colorless, gaseous compounds which can comprise photochemical smog, e.g., ozone (O_3), peroxyacetyl nitrate (PAN), aldehydes, and other compounds	A brownish-red gas with a pungent odor, often formed from oxidation of nitric oxide (NO)	Organic compounds in gaseous or particulate form, e.g., methane, ethylene, and acetylene
Atmospheric reactions of chemical precursors under the influence of sunlight	Motor vehicle exhausts, high-temperature stationary combustion, atmospheric reactions	Incomplete combustion of fuels and other carbon-containing substances, such as in motor vehicle exhausts; processing, distribution, and use of petroleum compounds, such as gasoline and organic solvents; natural events such as forest fires and plant metabolism; atmospheric reactions
Health: Aggravation of respiratory and cardiovascular illnesses, irritation of eyes and respiratory tract, impairment of cardiopulmonary function Other: Deterioration of rubber, textiles, and paints; impairment of visibility; leaf injury, reduced growth, and premature fruit and leaf drop in plants	Health: Aggravation of respiratory and cardiovascular illnesses and chronic nephritis Other: Fading of paints and dyes, impairment of visibility, reduced growth and premature leaf drop in plants	Health: Suspected contribution to cancer Other: Major precursors in the formation of photochemical oxidants through atmospheric reactions
Reduced emissions of nitrogen oxides, hydrocarbons, possibly sulfur oxides	Catalytic control of automobile exhaust gases, modification of automobile engines to reduce combustion temperature, scrubbing flue gases with caustic substances or urea	Automobile engine modifications (proper tuning, crankcase ventilation, exhaust gas recirculation, redesign of combustion chamber); control of automobile exhaust gases (catalytic or thermal devices); improved design, operation, and maintenance of stationary furnaces (use of finely dispersed fuels, proper mixing with air, high combustion temperature); improved control procedures in processing and handling petroleum compounds

554

Figure 16.3 A Long Island beach closed because of pollution of the ocean.

relatively stable in soil; residues have been found years after the chemicals were banned.

Pests tend to develop a resistance to pesticides, so increased quantities of the pesticides are necessary. If the natural enemies of a particular pest disappear, a pest control program may require monstrous increases in dosage. "The resistance of the bollworm in the Texas Rio Grande Valley to insecticides used in its control increased 30,000 times between 1960 and 1965" (Brubaker, 1972:80).

Noise pollution. Prolonged exposure to noise of sufficient intensity can damage our hearing. At lower levels, noise can increase our irritability and can prevent sleep. Some sources of noise in our society are shown in figure 16.4. It shows that a noise level of eighty decibels is "annoying." The noise level in a third-floor apartment next to a Los Angeles freeway is about eighty-seven decibels (Sixth Annual Report of the Council on Environmental Quality, 1975:378).

Aesthetic damage. Pollution involves *deterioration of the beauty of the environment* as well as actual physical damage. Air pollution, for instance, leads to the deterioration, and therefore to aesthetic damage, of things such as buildings, statues, and paintings. Air pollution may also inhibit visibility, obscure scenic views, and produce noxious odors. Such aesthetic damage has economic costs and may also have a depressing psychological effect on people. Brubaker (1972:51) noted that this aesthetic damage is the first effect on the environment that most of us recognize. It may result from air pollution, water pollution, or simply from litter. Whatever the source, it means that our environment is less pleasing, that the beauty of the natural world has been scarred by human activity.

Environmental Depletion

Our dwindling natural resources. Air and water and land can be restored, but the problem of *dwindling resources* is another matter. If we clean up the air, it may become just as useful as it was before it was polluted. But, once a mine has been exhausted or an oil well has been pumped dry or a patch of soil has been ruined for farming, we have lost a resource that cannot be reclaimed, at least not within the next few hundred years.

For a long time Americans tended to think that our country had virtually unlimited natural resources. In 1973 a group of Arab nations temporarily suspended the sale of oil to other nations. Americans were suddenly confronted by the fact that no nation in the modern world can be self-sufficient by virtue of its own natural resources. Oil is not the only valuable resource that makes the United States interdependent with other nations. Our own resources are dwindling. In 1978 we imported 100 percent of the mica, 93 percent of the bauxite and alumina, 81 percent of the tin, and 29 percent of the iron ore that we used.[1]

Energy production and consumption. An integral part of the pollution problem and the dwindling of our resources is the *production and consumption of energy*. In producing and using energy of various kinds we pollute our environment and, at the same time, further deplete our natural resources. Energy consumption in the

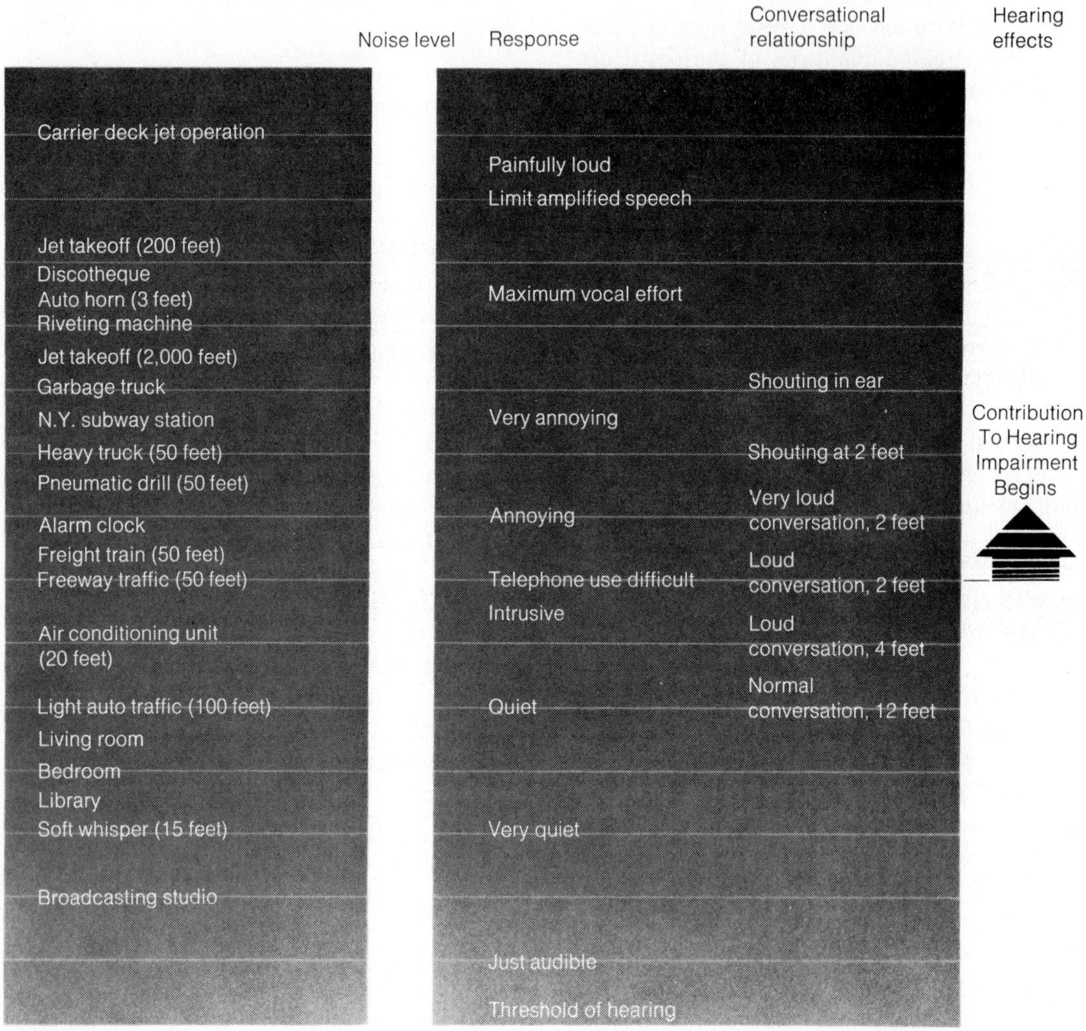

556

Figure 16.4 Sound levels and human response. (Source: *Sixth Annual Report of the Council on Environmental Quality* [Washington, D.C.: Government Printing Office, 1975], p. 85.)

Noise level	Response	Conversational relationship	Hearing effects
Carrier deck jet operation			
	Painfully loud		
	Limit amplified speech		
Jet takeoff (200 feet)			
Discotheque			
Auto horn (3 feet)	Maximum vocal effort		
Riveting machine			
Jet takeoff (2,000 feet)			
Garbage truck		Shouting in ear	
N.Y. subway station	Very annoying		Contribution To Hearing Impairment Begins
Heavy truck (50 feet)		Shouting at 2 feet	
Pneumatic drill (50 feet)			
Alarm clock	Annoying	Very loud conversation, 2 feet	
Freight train (50 feet)		Loud conversation, 2 feet	
Freeway traffic (50 feet)	Telephone use difficult		
	Intrusive	Loud conversation, 4 feet	
Air conditioning unit (20 feet)			
Light auto traffic (100 feet)	Quiet	Normal conversation, 12 feet	
Living room			
Bedroom			
Library			
Soft whisper (15 feet)	Very quiet		
Broadcasting studio			
	Just audible		
	Threshold of hearing		

Figure 16.5 Aesthetic damage is widespread in America, even in the very shadow of a sign warning of penalties.

Figure 16.6 U.S. gross energy consumption, 1900 to 1980, in QBtu's per year (1 QBtu = 10^{15} Btu's). (Source: *Ninth Annual Report of the Council on Environmental Quality* [Washington, D.C.: Government Printing Office, 1981], p. 346.)

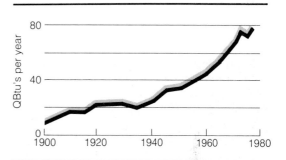

U.S. has risen rapidly and almost continuously since the turn of the century (figure 16.6). This increase is not due to an expanding population; the per capita consumption of energy in the United States has risen almost continuously. Per capita consumption is higher in the United States than in any other nation in the world.

Why do we need so much energy? Every aspect of our lives involves the use of energy. We use it for heating and air conditioning, for cooking, for refrigeration, for transportation, and for all the industrial processes in the nation.

Overpopulation

Some Americans do not believe that overpopulation is a problem in our country. But, overpopulation can be defined as a problem in two ways that are relevant to our situation: when the population is too large to be adequately supported by the available resources: and when the population size or distribution detracts from people's desired quality of life. We will discuss our situation in these terms.

How Big Are Our Ecological Problems?

Now that we have identified the kinds of ecological problems we face, we will examine just how serious those problems are. Using the same three categories—environmental pollution, environmental depletion, and overpopulation—let us see what the data can tell us.

Environmental Pollution

The federal Environmental Protection Agency (EPA) established standards for five "criteria" air pollutants—sulfur oxides, suspended particulates, carbon monoxide, photochemical oxidants, and nitrogen dioxide. Many states and cities have adopted the Pollutant Standards Index (PSI), which indicates when any of the five criteria pollutants are at a level considered to be adverse to human health.

Enforcement of *air pollution standards* has been reducing the amount of these pollutants which are thrust into the air each year, but by the late 1970s most urban areas had not yet achieved the standards. A survey of forty-three cities showed that four, Los Angeles, Denver, Cleveland, and St. Louis, were in the unhealthy range at least half the year in 1976, and all forty-three had unhealthy air quality for at least twenty-seven days of the year (Ninth Annual Report of the Council on Environmental Quality, 1978:13). However, progress in meeting EPA standards has been considerable. Among 23,000 "major" sources (which each emitted more than 100 tons of pollutants per year), 94 percent were either in compliance with EPA standards by 1977 or were meeting a schedule leading to full compliance. In other cases a good

deal remains to be done. Among power plants, which are responsible for nearly two-thirds of the sulfur oxide emissions, about 74 percent were in compliance with the standards (Ninth Annual Report of the Council on Environmental Quality, 1978:72). Efforts to control the amount of pollution must be continued if we are to achieve our goal—clean air.

Some advances have been made in *water pollution control* also. Some of the worst water quality problems may be resolved in the near future, but, like air pollution, water pollution remains a very serious problem. A 1977 EPA report said that of the 246 hydrological drainage basins in the United States 95 percent were affected by water pollution and 72 percent by industrial discharges (Ninth Annual Report of the Council on Environmental Quality, 1978:91, 98).

Industrial wastes are growing at the rate of 3 percent each year. Solid wastes from residential and commercial sources, estimated at 130 million metric tons in 1976, would fill the New Orleans Superdome from floor to ceiling twice every day of the year. Toxic substances contaminate some consumer products. Toxic wastes lie buried in soil and in thousands of dumps throughout the nation. Noise levels often range from uncomfortable to hazardous. Aesthetic damage is pervasive across the country. It is difficult to estimate the seriousness of some of these and other kinds of pollution, partly because measurement techniques have not been developed, and partly because the potential hazards involved have only recently been recognized.

Table 16.1   Energy Consumption—Total and Per Capita, 1920–1979
(total in trillions, per capita in millions, of British thermal units)

Year	All Energy[a]		Natural Gas[b]		Coal[c]		Crude Petroleum[d]	
	Total	Per Capita	Total	Per Capita	Total	Per Capita	Total	Per Capita
1920	19.8	186	0.8	8	15.5	146	2.6	25
1930	22.3	181	2.0	16	13.6	111	5.7	46
1940	23.9	181	2.7	21	12.5	95	7.5	57
1950	34.0	223	6.1	40	12.9	85	13.5	88
1960	44.6	247	12.7	70	10.1	56	20.1	111
1970	67.1	328	22.0	108	12.7	62	29.5	144
1979[b]	78.0	354	19.9	90	15.1	72	37.0	168

[a]Includes hydropower, nuclear power, geothermal and other energy, not shown separately.
[b]Preliminary figures.
[b]Dry gas only. Marketed production minus shrinkage caused by liquids extraction (34 cubic feet per gallon produced).
[c]Includes bituminous coal and lignite and anthracite coal.
[d]Includes petroleum products and, beginning 1950, natural gas liquids.

Source: U.S. Bureau of the Census, *Statistical Abstract of the United States, 1976* (Washington, D.C.: Government Printing Office, 1977), p. 549; and 1980 (Washington, D.C.: Government Printing Office, 1981), p. 604.

Environmental Depletion

We are consuming natural resources at a breathtaking pace, which many experts now feel threatens the resource capacity of the earth. We mentioned earlier that we are already importing the bulk of what we use of several important minerals, and in the future we will import even more. Based on a computer analysis of the future implications of present trends, Mesarovic and Pestel (1974:26–27) made the following observation: "The United States, which up to the 1940s was a net exporter of materials, will depend by the year 2000 on imports of around 80 percent for all ferrous metals, excluding iron, and 70 percent for all non-ferrous metals."

We use more energy than other countries not because we have more people, but because energy use per person is greater. Until the last few years, our per capita consumption was increasing. Table 16.1 shows how per capita consumption of energy nearly doubled between 1920 and 1979.

In 1979 we used roughly 28 percent of our total energy for industries, 19 percent for transportation, about 24 percent to generate electricity, and the remaining 29 percent for residential and commercial purposes.[2] The energy demands of an affluent, industrial civilization are increasingly difficult to supply. The search for new energy sources that became intense during the 1970s continues today.

Our total energy use on the highways of the nation is staggering. In 1976 Americans traveled over 1.4 trillion miles and consumed nearly 105 billion gallons of gasoline (Ninth Annual Report of the Council on Environmental Quality, 1978:359). As noted above, about 19 percent of the energy and over half of the oil we use is for transportation. The thirty years following World War II saw an automobile population explosion in the U.S. The number of cars increased by over 300 percent, a much greater rate of increase than the human population. Nineteen seventy-eight was the first year in our history that we spent more on automobiles than we did for food.

Our demand for electrical power has also increased rapidly. Consumption in the mid-1970s was over three times that in 1940.

How can we keep up with our voracious appetite for energy? Some experts believe nuclear sources are the hope for the future. Mesarovic and Pestel (1974:132) pointed out some limitations to that hope so far as energy needs of the world are concerned:

> The largest nuclear reactors presently in operation convert about 1 million kilowatts (electric), but we will give progress the benefit of the doubt and assume that our 24,000 worldwide reactors are capable of converting 5 million kilowatts each. In order to produce the world's energy in one hundred years, then, we will merely have to build, in each and every year between now and then, *four reactors per week!* And that figure does not take into account the lifespan of nuclear reactors. If our future nuclear reactors last an average of thirty years, we shall eventually have to build about *two reactors per day* simply to replace those that have worn out.

Overpopulation

In his famous 1968 book *The Population Bomb,* Paul Ehrlich expressed an alarm felt by many observers—that humans were on a suicidal course. In 1970 the world's population was growing at a rate that would have meant a doubling of the number of people in thirty-five years! But, by the mid-1970s the rate began to slow down, allowing some hope that total disaster could be averted. This is not to say that the problem is no longer severe. There are now over 4 billion people on earth, with 150,000 to 200,000 more people being born every single day. Even if the birth rate were to decline dramatically, the population would continue to increase because of the huge numbers of people coming into the child-bearing years in the near future.

An estimated 1 billion people go to bed hungry each night. One billion was approximately the total population of the earth in 1850 (Ehrlich and Ehrlich, 1979:91). Overpopulation is a frightening problem, and one that ultimately involves every individual on earth.

Ecological Problems and the Quality of Life

Our environmental problems involve a four-cornered relationship of prices, supplies, control of pollution, and our foreign policy (Freeman, 1974:12–13). The federal government has the responsibility of making decisions that require trade-offs among the four factors. For example, if the government subsidizes energy in order to keep the price low for consumers, wasteful consumption patterns will continue. Problems of limited supplies and pollution will then be intensified. We will also be required to import increasing amounts of our energy sources, which will increase the significance of international relationships and problems. Clearly, Freeman concluded, the federal government must make massive allocations to research and development so that we can get adequate amounts of clean energy. But, the allocations must take into account the need for safeguards against pollution and the need for "freedom of action in foreign policy."

It is apparent that there are *inherent contradictions among some of our values*—our value on growth and progress; our value on freedom to choose the size of family we want; our desire for abundant energy; our value on a clean environment; our preference for reasonably low prices for our energy; and our value on independence in the world arena. It is impossible to have all of these. We face, instead, a time when we must decide between various *trade-offs*. There will be trade-offs between cost and abundance, between national independence and abundance, between abundance and quality of the environment, and the like.

These contradictions are manifested in various ways that are considered incompatible with the desired quality of life. Before discussing the meaning of ecological problems for that quality of life, however, we should note that our knowledge of this area is limited. For example, the burning of fossil fuels releases carbon dioxide into the atmosphere. Since 1958 the amount of carbon dioxide has been increasing by about 0.2 percent per year. Some experts have estimated that the amount of carbon dioxide will increase by about 20 percent by the year 2000. The problem is that carbon dioxide acts as a barrier to heat, so the earth's average temperature could

grow warmer. The result might be long-term warming of the planet, melting of the polar ice cap, and flooding of the earth's coastal regions. These possibilities are speculative—we really do not know the long-term consequences of increased carbon dioxide in the air. Still the potential consequences are so serious, as one report concluded, "that much more must be learned about future trends of climate change" (Report of the Study of Critical Environmental Problems, 1970:12).

Another example of a potential hazard about which we know too little involves the tires on our automobiles. As those tires wear down from use, they leave about 700,000 tons of material on streets and highways, and about 10 percent of that material is blown up into the air (Freeman, 1974:47). The rubber particles contain carbon black, which can be carcinogenic. As we discuss some of the known ways ecological problems detract from the desired quality of life, we should not lose sight of these many potential threats. They could make the problems of ecology far more serious than we now know them to be.

The Hazards of Overpopulation

Most of the problems discussed in this book are affected by population characteristics. Here we will briefly note the "22 dimensions" of the population problem identified by Brown, McGrath, and Stokes (1976). Population growth contributes in some way to each of the following situations:

1. literacy (the number of illiterates is growing)
2. world fish catch (it has declined)

3. recreation (areas are getting glutted with people)

4. pollution (which we will discuss in more detail later)

5. inflation (the more people, the greater the demand for goods and the higher the prices)

6. illness (health problems may intensify with increased population)

7. hunger (world food supplies are critically low)

8. housing (it may be impossible to keep up with the need)

9. change in the climate (as already happens in densely populated areas)

10. overgrazing of cropland (from increased numbers of cattle)

11. crowding (people are living too close together and are moving into undesirable locations in order to have a home)

12. income (on the average, it may go down)

13. urbanization

14. deforestation (the earth's forests have actually receded as the population expanded)

15. conflict within and between nations

16. depletion of minerals

17. inadequate health services (population can grow too quickly for a nation to afford the necessary health care)

18. inadequate or unclean water

19. unemployment

20. extinction of some plant and animal species

21. energy shortage

22. threat to individual freedom (which may have to be sacrificed to the common good because of population pressures)

The Environmental Threat to Life and Health

Environmental pollution is a *threat to our physical and mental well-being.* This fact is grimly dramatized by the effects of toxic wastes in Love Canal, New York. Love Canal, which is located near Niagara Falls, was a dump for toxic wastes from a chemical company for a number of years. The company filled in the dump and gave the land to the local school district in 1953. Soon after, homes were being built on the land. In the late 1970s, national attention focused on consequences of living over a toxic dump: noxious odors penetrating houses; strange sludge seeping into basements; unusually high rates of miscarriages; birth defects; and cancer and other diseases involving the nervous system, the respiratory system, the liver, and the kidneys. Many residents were found to have chromosome abnormalities also.

Pollutants of all kinds are hazardous to both animals and humans. Eutrophication in waterways can kill massive numbers of fish. The killing of fish means less food available for a world in which millions of people are starving. Ironically, some of the eutrophication problem arises from our efforts to produce an adequate food supply. Roughly 60 percent of the phosphorus that overfertilizes water comes from municipal wastes, while "urban and rural land runoff contribute the remainder. A major contributor to the latter is runoff from feedlots, manured lands, and eroding soil" (Report of the Study of Critical Environmental Problems, 1970: 27–28). As we continue to apply fertilizer in increasing quantities in order to improve the yield of needed agricultural products, we also increase the likelihood of eutrophication of waterways and the consequent destruction of needed fish.

Air pollution can cause illness and even death. Air pollution is correlated with alcoholism, certain mental illnesses, and increased mortality rates.[3] The National Academy of Sciences has estimated that as many as 15,000 Americans die each year from air pollution and that Americans spend 7 million days in bed each year because their chronic illnesses are aggravated by air pollution. Some of the known detrimental effects of air pollution were summarized by Freeman (1974:46):

> The medical experts have linked air pollution to bronchitis, emphysema, asthma and lung cancer. It is not surprising that pollutants capable of disintegrating stone, corroding metal and dissolving nylon stockings also can damage delicate pink lung tissue. . . . We know that the aged and those already suffering from lung or heart diseases are especially vulnerable. The deaths that occurred during air pollution episodes in Donora, Pennsylvania (20 deaths in 1948), London (1600 deaths in 1952), and New York City (165 deaths in 1966) have proved that air pollution can be a killer.

Freeman also cited a study that indicated that a 50 percent decrease in air pollution would result in a 4.5 percent decrease in mortality rates.

Noise pollution, on the other hand, may be regarded primarily as a nuisance. However, working in a noisy environment can lead to increased errors, higher rates of accidents, more absenteeism, and psychosomatic symptoms (McLean and Tarnopolsky, 1977). Exposure to a noisy environment may also lead some people to be more aggressive, to experience learning problems, to have a diminished sense of enjoy-

ment, and to do less well at some tasks even after the noise has stopped (Singer, 1976).

There is no question that pollution of all kinds threatens our health and even our lives. Whether pollutants cause the minor but annoying effects of inducing irritability or the major effects of illness and death, they detract from the quality of life.

Threat to the Ecological Balance

Many of the examples given here show that a whole *chain of consequences can follow from human action on the environment.* One of the consequences can be an upsetting of the *ecological balance.* Paul Ehrlich argued that our lust for more affluence and our unrestrained population growth are ravaging our environment. But, he wrote,

> make no mistake about it, *the imbalance will be redressed.* . . . *Man is not only running out of food, he is also destroying the life support systems of the Spaceship Earth. The situation was recently summarized very succinctly: "It is the top of the ninth inning. Man, always a threat at the plate, has been hitting Nature hard. It is important to remember, however, that NATURE BATS LAST"* [Ehrlich, 1971:364].

One way the ecological system has been altered is by the *disappearance of a number of species of animals and plants* as a result of human activity. Of the approximately 20,000 different species, subspecies, and varieties of plants native to the United States, 100 (0.5 percent) are already extinct. Nearly 2,000 more (10 percent) are classified as either "endangered" or "threatened." ("Endangered" means that the plant is in danger of becoming extinct in all or a significant portion of its natural range,

564

while "threatened" means that it is likely to become endangered in the future.) The situation is similar with respect to animals. About 10 percent of all animals native to the United States may be endangered or threatened, according to surveys by the Department of the Interior's Office of Endangered Species. This is true of both the higher and lower classes of animals—the mammals, birds, and fishes as well as the crustaceans, clams, and snails (Sixth Annual Report of the Council on Environmental Quality, 1975:408).

We should be cautious in evaluating such data, however. Ecosystems are dynamic, not static. Some species would disappear regardless of whether or not they were affected by human activity. But, many more species have become extinct because of human activity, and there is some concern that the ecological balance might thereby be upset, starting a chain of consequences that would be deleterious for human life.

Perhaps more important than the balance among the species is the possibility that we will "damage in the largest way the entire web of life" (Brubaker, 1972:56). Continuation of life demands certain processes, including reproduction, **photosynthesis,** and the recycling of minerals. We know that the reproduction of some species has been affected by certain pollutants. For instance, the use of DDT caused the eggshells of some birds to become thinner and to crack before the young hatched, thus threatening the reproductive capacity. DDT has also affected the reproductive capacity of some fish. Other pesticides and herbicides may also impair reproduction.

Photosynthesis may be adversely affected by air pollution, by pesticides and herbicides, and, above all, by the spread of human population, which destroys the habitat of many other species. Brubaker (1972:56) pointed out that air pollution inhibits the plant life in which photosynthesis occurs, while human activity such as urbanization destroys the plants by destroying their habitat. A good deal of photosynthesis occurs in the sea, but it is possible that the pesticides and herbicides that are accumulating in the oceans will disrupt the process. Photosynthesis is essential in the production of oxygen, it helps maintain the carbon dioxide balance in our atmosphere, and it is of fundamental importance in producing the organic material needed for supporting life. Brubaker concluded that "it is hard to imagine a total cessation of photosynthesis; if it occurred it would be the ultimate catastrophe." Whether or not the process could cease totally, it is clearly affected adversely by certain human activities.

Human activity is also interfering with the natural recycling of minerals that occurs as rocks decompose, as soil microbes fix nitrogen, and as photosynthesis and decay release carbon:

> Modern agriculture overdraws the natural supply of minerals and nitrogen, and it is feared that artifical applications contaminate water, impair the action of soil microbes, and reduce the tilth of the soil, leaving us vulnerable to unspecified agricultural disasters [Brubaker, 1972:56].

While we are not certain of the actual consequences of our interference with natural recycling, we must be prepared to deal with them as threats to our basic life-sustaining processes. And, we must remember that the consequences are threats directly attributable to our abuse of our environment.

The Economic Costs

It is difficult to place a price tag on our ecological problems. To fully assess the cost, we would have to include an enormous number of items: damage to livestock and trees and crops; the death of wildlife; the expense of pollution control measures; the cost of medical care for those whose health is adversely affected; the lost work time because of ill health; the expense of maintaining and refurbishing buildings and other structures that deteriorate because of pollution; the cost of restoring the quality of the air and of waterways; and the like. The public is barely aware of the *innumerable ways our economic resources are consumed by our ecological problems*. For instance, between 1952 and 1967 the New York City Public Library spent $900,000 to microfilm books that "were in an advanced state of deterioration largely as the result of air pollution" (U.S. Environmental Protection Agency, 1973:45).

Consider the stages involved in trying to analyze and estimate these economic costs. First, the pollutants are emitted at some particular time and place. Second, they affect the environmental quality; for example, the amount of sulfur oxide in the air at a particular time and place may increase. Third, the altered quality of the environment results in certain damages, such as an increase in the number of people with respiratory problems. Finally, a dollar cost must be assigned to the damages.

Every stage of this process is marked by uncertainty. We are not yet aware of all the amounts and kinds of pollutants being emitted. We do not yet know how all the pollutants act and interact on our environment. Identifying actual damages is extremely problematic. Some

kinds of damage are relatively easy to assign a dollar value to, while others are extremely difficult. We can estimate the cost of painting a building marred by air pollution or the cost of replacing damaged crops, but what is the dollar value "of a human life or of a clear sky, or of a place for recreation, or of a species which contributes to the diversity, complexity, and stability of an ecosystem. . . ?" (Sixth Annual Report of the Council on Environmental Quality, 1975:498).

Keeping these difficulties in mind—for they emphasize the fact that the dollar costs we come up with do not fully reflect our losses—we can still compute some estimates of the economic costs of pollution. The 1968 costs of air pollution were computed in terms of damages in four areas: to residential property, $5.2 billion; to materials (corrosion of metals, deterioration of paint, fading of dyes), $4.7 billion; to health, $6.1 billion; and to vegetation, $0.1 billion. The total comes to $16.1 billion for the national cost of air pollution for that year alone (U.S. Environmental Protection Agency, 1973:viii).

Other studies have attempted to assess the economic cost of air and other kinds of pollution to health, materials, and vegetation. For example, the costs of death and illness resulting from diseases carried in drinking water have been estimated to amount to $644 million per year. The deterioration of rubber products due to ozone in the air costs $226 million per year. The nationwide damage to ornamental flowers and shrubs amounts to around $46.2 million per year (Sixth Annual Report of the Council on Environmental Quality, 1975:504–507).

The economic costs of pollution are staggering, to say the least. The $16.1 billion figure, the cost of air pollution alone in the year 1968, is greater than the amount the federal government spent on general science, space, and technology; or on agriculture; or on environment and energy; or on community and regional development; or, for that matter, on all four of those areas combined.

All of the dollar figures must be revised to account for inflation and also for increased knowledge about pollution and its costs, which means that the total costs are now far higher. For example by 1977 the health costs alone of air pollution were estimated at $10 billion or more per year (Ninth Annual Report of the Council of Environmental Quality, 1978:420). We should also keep in mind that the costs of combating pollution are enormous. In 1978 about $42.3 billion was spent on pollution abatement and control, with the government absorbing about 29 percent of the total cost. Estimates predict that between 1977 and 1986 consumers will directly pay $71.4 billion of the cumulative costs of pollution control (Ninth Annual Report of the Council on Environmental Quality, 1978:428).

Threat to World Peace

The contradictions between the demand for energy, the desire for a clean environment, the desire for reasonably low prices for energy, and the value on political independence are manifested on the international scene in the form of a *threat to world peace*. The developing nations of the world are demanding to share in the affluence enjoyed by the West and by Japan. Inequality among nations has become a matter of international concern. On May 1, 1974 the General Assembly of the United Nations adopted a "Declaration on the Establishment of a New International Order," which asserted a determination to work for a new and more equitable international economic order, one that will eliminate the widening gap between the developed and the developing nations. If the widening gap is not eliminated, many observers fear that the result will be a world war between the relatively few rich and the far more numerous poor nations.

There is some debate about the possibilities of narrowing the gap in living standard between the developing and the developed nations. In 1968, a group of Europeans met at Rome to discuss world problems and inequalities. The group eventually became known as the "Club of Rome." Its aims are to gain a better understanding of the world system and to use that understanding to deal with critical international problems. A study sponsored by the Club of Rome used a computer simulation to look at the future outcome of present trends in things such as population growth, use of natural resources, environmental pollution, food, and standard of living. The study concluded that there are limits to the size of population that can be sustained by the earth; that there is no possibility of bringing the developing countries up to the standard of living now realized in the developed nations; and that there is a strong probability that the nations of the West will suffer a decline in their standard of living within the next few decades (Meadows, Meadows, Randers and Behrens, 1972).

A second study sponsored by the Club of Rome, also using a computer simulation, took a slightly different approach. The outcome was still pessimistic, though not as pessimistic as the first study. The authors (Mesarovic and Pestel, 1974) argued that the gap between the rich and poor nations must be narrowed if world peace is to prevail. However, if present trends continue, the income gap between those in the rich nations and those in the poor nations will widen considerably by the year 2025. One way to narrow (though not close) the gap would be to provide massive aid to South Asia, Tropical Africa, and Latin America. Some economic sacrifices on the part of the rich nations would be required. The cost would be about $3,000 per person per year if we had started in 1975. The longer we wait, the greater the cost will be to the rich nations. An important factor in the additional cost is population growth. Even if effective birth control should cause the worldwide fertility rate to decline, there may be an *increase* in the population density in South Asia, which is over 60 percent higher than the *present* population density in "overpopulated" Western Europe.

Furthermore, as the standards of poor nations rise, the problems of environmental pollution and depletion will become more extensive and, in all probability, more serious. It appears that the contradictions inherent in our ecological problems will continue to plague us in the future.

Contributing Factors

Before looking at the sociocultural factors that contribute to ecological problems, we should note two points. First, as suggested earlier, the problems of ecology are closely linked to *population growth*. As population increases, our ecological problems also increase. All of the factors that contribute to the population problem also contribute indirectly to our ecological problems.

Second, we will probably have to live with some ecological problems that are caused by *ignorance and accidents* as well as sociocultural factors. Ignorance is involved in the sense that we often do not know and generally cannot anticipate the environmental consequences of our behavior. DDT, for instance, seemed beneficial because it controlled many pests, including the carriers of malaria. We did not know it would impair the reproductive capacity of some fish and birds.

Accidents such as explosions and spills have ecological repercussions. In 1976 a stuck safety valve in an Italian chemical plant resulted in an explosion that released over four pounds of a deadly poison into the atmosphere. In less than a week, numerous animals died, fourteen children were hospitalized for burns and pains, and adults began complaining about liver and kidney problems. Over 700 people were evacuated from villages in the area of the plant. Some of the area is still closed to humans.

Social Structural Factors

The causes of population growth. Certain norms help maintain high birth rates—in particular *norms relating to age at marriage and size of the family*. Where early marriage is the norm, family size tends to be larger. In the United States, women who marry at an early age have more children than those who marry later. There may also be a norm about the desired family size, independent of the normative age for marriage. In traditional African societies, large families were desired for both prestige and economic gain. In the United States, Mormons and Catholics have expected large families on religious grounds.

The *nature of the female role* also has a significant effect on birth rates. Where the role prescribes marriage and motherhood ("the woman's place is in the home"), birth rates are likely to be high. Where women have a variety of roles open to them, including various occupational roles, birth rates are lower. In Latin America, where the birth rate is generally very high, women's participation rates in the labor force are among the lowest in the world (Beller, 1970:4). Those who do work have a number of legal benefits that seem to encourage pregnancies, but their birth rates are lower than those of nonworking women (Kinzer, 1973:304–5).

Technological developments constitute another structural factor that influences population growth. The population explosion of the last two centuries is largely the result of lowered death rates (rather than high birth rates). The lowered death rates, in turn, are a direct result of better living standards, better sanitation and hygiene, and better health care. It is ironic that these benefits which have so greatly improved the quality of life have also created a backlash in the present population crisis.

The effects of population growth.   The impact of population growth on the environment is evident in both the highly industrialized and the developing nations of the world. In industrial Japan, for example, some cities have emergency procedures for evacuation of the population when the pollution levels become intolerably high. Similarly, cities in the United States monitor air quality and warn people with respiratory problems to remain indoors when the quality deteriorates to a point that is hazardous to health.

The problems of population expansion in developing nations tend to be of a different order. An expanding population in the Middle East has resulted in land erosion because of efforts to expand farming into areas previously used only for grazing. The ecosystem in which we live is more delicately balanced than we realized in the past, and a great increase in population may well upset that balance.

Rapid population growth also accelerates the consumption of the earth's natural resources to the point where oil, natural gas, and certain minerals may be exhausted within a few generations.

The effects of increased population are more than additive. As Ehrlich and Holdren (1971) argued, one more person does not simply mean one more polluting unit. A 1 percent increase in population has more than a 1 percent impact on the environment. As the demand for resources increases, the cost of recovering resources also increases: "As the richest supplies of these resources and those nearest to centers of use are consumed, we are obliged to use lower-grade ores, drill deeper, and extend our supply networks" (Ehrlich and Holdren, 1971:1213). We get smaller returns from the same investment of money and energy because we have depleted the most accessible stores.

A second reason why a growing population has more than an additive impact on the environment is the so-called *"threshold effect."* Vegetation in an area may be able to survive a certain size population and the air pollution created by that population. But a small addition to the population can create just enough additional pollution to kill the vegetation. It becomes the straw that breaks the camel's back. Birch (1973:38) said that this is probably what happened in Sydney, Australia when all the Norfolk Island pines along the seashore died very suddenly. "The suspected cause is detergent in the air. It blows in from the sewer outlets into the Pacific Ocean and apparently kills trees." At a certain point the pollution passes the threshold and kills vegetation, and that point may be the result of a slight addition in the population.

The same effect can occur with other kinds of environmental problems. As Ehrlich and Holdren (1971:1213) argued:

> Five hundred people may be able to live around a lake and dump their raw sewage into the lake, and the natural systems of the lake will be able to break down the sewage and keep the lake from undergoing rapid ecological change. Five hundred and five people may overload the system and result in a "polluted" or eutrophic lake.

The effects of population may be additive to a point, and beyond that point the *increasing quantitative changes become a qualitative change.*

Discussion of problems of overpopulation is more likely to evoke images of India or Southeast Asia than a picture of the United States. But, a 1 percent increase in the population of the United States has a far more detrimental effect upon the environment than, say, a 1 percent increase in the population of India or Indonesia. The issue was dramatically described by Davis (1970:13–14):

> The average Indian eats his daily few cups of rice (or perhaps wheat, whose production on American farms contributed to our 1 percent per year drain in quality of our active farmland), draws his bucket of water from the communal well and sleeps in a mud hut. In his daily rounds to gather cow dung to burn to cook his rice and warm his feet, his footsteps . . . help bring about a slow deterioration of the ability of the land to support people. His contribution to the destruction of the land is minimal.

> An American, on the other hand, can be expected to destroy a piece of land on which he builds a home, garage and driveway. He will contribute his share to the 142 million tons of smoke and fumes, 7 million junked cars, 20 million tons of paper, 48 billion cans, and 26 billion bottles the overburdened environment must absorb each year. To run his air conditioner we will strip-mine a Kentucky hillside, push the dirt and slate down into the stream, and burn coal in a power generator, whose smokestack contributes to a plume of smoke massive enough to cause cloud seeding and premature precipitation from Gulf winds which should be irrigating the wheat farms of Minnesota.

In addition, the American may personally consume thousands of gallons of gasoline, hundreds of pounds of meat, and enormous quantities of many other products. On such grounds, Davis proposed that we speak of population and ecology in terms of "Indian equivalents," which is the number of Indians required to consume the same and pollute the same as the average American. In those terms, he argued the U.S. population is the equivalent of at least four billion Indians—an "Indian equivalent" of approximately twenty for each American.

The point here is not to deny the appeal of the American standard of living, nor to suggest that Americans ought to live as simply as Indians. Rather, the point is that a slight increase in American population has a far greater impact on the environment than a similar increase in the number of Indians or Indonesians or Africans. According to one report, Americans consumed more of the world's resources during

1959–68 than the entire population of the world consumed throughout all previous history (Birch, 1973:30). Each additional American, therefore, puts a considerable strain on the environment. And, the most optimistic projections of our own population trend indicate increases for at least the next fifty years.

The industrial economy.   Both pollution and depletion of the environment are rooted in our industrial economy. Air pollution is a by-product of generating electrical power and producing the extraordinary variety of industrial products we use. Industrial fuel combustion accounts for a good deal of the air pollution, and about eighty other industrial processes contribute more than half the particulates and an important fraction of the sulfur dioxide, carbon monoxide, and hydrocarbon emissions into the atmosphere (Sixth Annual Report of the Council on Environmental Quality, 1975: 307–308). Water pollution is also a by-product of industrial processes. This includes some thermal pollution, which occurs when water is taken from a waterway in large quantities and used for cooling. The heated water can raise the temperature of the river or lake it is dumped back into to a point that is dangerous for aquatic life.

A major cause of air pollution in the United States is the *extensive use of the automobile.* The automobile also bears heavy responsibility for the rapid depletion of the world's oil reserves. The case of the automobile illustrates the dilemmas of our ecological problems. As the Citizens' Advisory Committee on Environmental Quality (1975: 15, 17) pointed out:

> The automobile is a prime target for conservation. It consumes nearly 30 percent of the total oil supply in the United States and

more than 12 percent of the Nation's total energy. It is a very major contributor to our air pollution problem. It consumes 28 percent of the average household energy budget. At the same time, the automobile business plays a very important role in the national economy. One of every six workers in the Nation is dependent on the manufacture, distribution, service, and commercial use of motor vehicles. More than 800,000 businesses hinge on motor vehicles, and 24 percent of retail sales are for automotive-related purchases. Motor vehicle users paid almost $19 billion in special State and Federal taxes in 1973.

This prime factor in environmental pollution and depletion, the automobile, is also an integral part of our affluent economy. Severe cutbacks on the use of the automobile would resolve at least a part of the ecological problem. But, at the same time, there would be serious, perhaps disastrous economic effects in the short run and uncertain effects in the long run.

Our industrial economy operates at a pace that outstrips our ability to counteract ecological problems it creates. The sheer numbers of automobiles added to the roads each year reduce or negate the effectiveness of pollution-control devices placed on those automobiles. Or, consider the chemical industry. Cancer is to a large extent an environmental problem often caused by *carcinogenic chemicals* we have produced. There are approximately 2 million known chemical compounds, and the industry is discovering thousands more each year. We can assume that some of the new compounds will be carcinogenic, but we are not taking steps to determine which ones. We simply do not have the facilities to properly test them all:

> Unfortunately, industry's capacity to develop new chemical compounds far exceeds the ability of medical and scientific investigators to

Figure 16.8 The internal combustion engines of our automobiles contribute heavily to air pollution. Automobiles, however, are a crucial part of our affluent economy.

determine the carcinogenic potential of a chemical. In the past 10 years, the production of synthetic organic chemicals has expanded by 225 percent; relatively few of the new compounds have been studied for their cancer-causing potential. Because of the typical latency period of 15–40 years for cancer, we must assume that much of the cancer from recent industrial development is not yet observable [Citizen's Advisory Committee on Environmental Quality, 1975:23].

The potential carcinogenic effect of chemicals we produce is, in a sense, just one more ecological hazard. We must add it to the list along with the effects of pesticides and herbicides, the eutrophication of waterways caused in part by the use of fertilizers, and the damage and threat of damage to fish, wildlife, and vegetation.

Virtually any useful product has undesirable ecological side effects—if for no other reason than because the economy is set up to take advantage of our great capacity for production. Because industrial technology can produce enormous quantities of any single product and an enormous range of products, and because *our economy is set up to maximize growth,* the whole situation is *self-sustaining*. Continual expansion is the goal. That goal is facilitated by (1) massive advertising; (2) the proliferation of products, many competing for the same market; (3) the "planned obsolescence" of products; and (4) lobbying at various levels of government to insure that governmental decisions will be favorable to business and industry. "Planned obsolescence" refers to the fact that many products are specifically designed to last only a limited time. In fact, some are designed and advertised as throw-away products—clothing, pots and pans, and safety razors are to be used

once or twice and then discarded. The consequences of planned obsolescence are the production of more trash that must be disposed of, the use or more resources, and the creation of more pollutants from industries that make such products.

Business and industry not only lobby for industrial growth, they vigorously oppose pollution-control proposals and, in some cases, have managed to defeat those proposals either by lobbying or by influencing public opinion. A good example is the defeat in 1970 of a proposal to control pollution from automobile exhaust in the state of California, where the problem is serious (Whitt, 1973). The relatively mild measure, known as Proposition 18, had two provisions: "that an unspecified amount of the revenue from gasoline taxes and license fees would go to control environmental pollution caused by motor vehicles; and that local voters could use up to 25 percent of their county's revenues for improving mass transit systems" (Whitt, 1973:30). Environmental groups strongly favored the measure. However, the Automobile Club of Southern California, the Teamsters Union, the California State Chamber of Commerce, and a number of oil companies all actively opposed Proposition 18. The money available for opposing the measure was far more abundant than the money available for supporting it, and the opposition succeeded.

The politics of ecology. Ecological problems generally have not been considered high-priority items. Miller (1972) conducted a survey in Boston, New York, Philadelphia, Baltimore, and Washington, D.C. of leaders selected from business, labor, political, religious, and civic and civil rights groups. When they were asked how much they were interested in and then how much they were working on various problems, *environmental problems were low-priority* for both interest and activity. Leaders were more concerned about race relations, unemployment and poverty, housing and urban renewal, education, crime, and other problems than they were about the environment.

What creates interest and activity in a particular problem? The dominant factor among the people Miller questioned was "appointment to positions." He found that both paid and voluntary positions draw people into situations where they have responsibility for urban problems. A number of the leaders specifically identified a new position as the source of their interest and activity in some urban problem:

> My interest and activity changed with my appointment to the Justice Coordinating Board last year. That has focused my efforts on control of lawlessness and crime. . . . My work in race relations began when I accepted a regional chairmanship for the National Alliance of Businessmen. The immediate demand is to find a meaningful program and result. . . . As I learn more through my activity as chairman of the League of Women Voters in my city, I have become more interested in transportation [Miller, 1972:315–16].

Apparently, the way to get something done about environmental problems is to *create positions* that have specific responsibility for those problems. People become interested in something when they have a specific responsibility for it. In the case of environmental problems, that means governmental positions. Americans dislike the creation of new governmental positions, but without them very little may be done. There is little incentive for private industry to take the lead in addressing our ecological problems.

Pollution is a national problem that requires federal action. In the past the federal government either ignored the problem or delegated responsibility to the states. Creation, in recent years, of the federal Environmental Protection Agency and Council on Environmental Quality suggests that we are beginning to recognize the scope and the political nature of our ecological problems.

Social Psychological Factors

The social psychology of population growth. Some societies *idealize or romanticize large families,* and these attitudes and values facilitate population growth. In addition, some religious groups have an *"ideology of the Divine way,"* which opposes the use of contraceptives and/or places a high value on large families. Catholics and Mormons are included in this category. We should note, however, that in a study of Catholic birth rates throughout the world, Day (1968) found that Catholics have higher birth rates only in countries that are economically developed, in which birth control is possible, and in which they are a minority of the population. Mormons are a minority in every society where they are found. They emphasize the importance of large families on religious grounds (preexistent spirits are seeking to be born into good Mormon families). The birth rates of American Mormons are significantly higher than those of other Americans (Spicer and Gustavus, 1974).

Attitudes and the environment. Means (1972) identified a number of attitudes that bear upon and intensify our ecological problems. First, there is an *exploitative attitude.* Americans have tended to value nature for what can be taken from it. The environment represents resources, and the quantity of those resources is what matters. Our attitude toward the environment is to assess its worth in terms of "production statistics, board feet, metric tons, gallons of liquid" and not in qualitative terms such as the relationship of the environment to "man's life, his health, his longevity, his peace of mind. . ." (Means, 1972:204).

Attitudes that support continued population growth in this country contribute to an increasingly serious environmental problem. A little over 5 percent of the world's population consumes over half of the natural gas, silver, tin, tungsten, and many other resources taken from the earth each year. Contrary to the common attitude, the size of the American population growth is as serious as that of any other nation.

Another problem attitude involves a distinction we make between city and country. The city has seemed removed from problems that can confront people in rural areas. There is a mistaken attitude that the city can "transcend the environment" and separate us "from the grim realities of the biological world of peasant or aboriginal culture where man traditionally struggled for survival against the natural world" (Means, 1972:206). We know now, of course, that cities only intensify our problems. We know that people who live in cities are more rather than less vulnerable to undesirable consequences. We do not escape the ecosystem by huddling together in cities, we only tend to magnify the problems within the ecosystem.

Values and the environment. Our value of growth, "the more the better," has been a theme of American life. Sorokin (1942:255) called this aspect of our culture "quantitative colossalism":

> The best business firms are those which are hugest. The society leaders are those who are richest. . . . The greatest university is that which is largest. The masterpieces of literature or art, philosophy or science, religion or politics are the best sellers bought by millions. "The biggest firm," "the largest circulation," "the biggest market of second-hand tires in the world" is our highest recommendation. Anything which is not big quantitatively, but is merely the finest in quality, tends to pass unnoticed.

Sorokin overstated the case, but his point is valid. In an examination of major value orientations in America, Robin Williams (1954:394) pointed out that our culture has had a value on action and mastery of nature, and that

> its whole history has been, in the main, an experience of expansionism and mastery: increasing population, increasing territory, increased levels of living, and so on indefinitely. Given the definition of such things as good, respect for quantity directly follows.

Sorokin argued that we define things as good simply because they are large and growing. Williams argued that the things we define as good we keep expanding in quantity, so that quantity itself gains respect. In any case, we value growth and size, pursue expansion, and thereby intensify our ecological problems.

Growth is also facilitated by our value of materialism and material comfort. (Williams, 1954:406–409). Our popular magazines focus on people who indulge in leisure or in high consumption. Our value on comfort and convenience is reflected in a 1979 Gallup poll that asked people what, if anything, they were doing to reduce their use of energy. Less than half said they had turned down their thermostats. Only about one-third said they had reduced driving. And only 3 percent said they had joined a car pool.

Our value of individualism contributes to political inaction and thus to our ecological problems. As Hardin (1971) put it, our individualism involves us in the *"tragedy of the commons."* In the middle ages the "commons" was the pasture land of a village. It was owned by no one person because it was available for use by all the people of the village. The "commons" today are the world's resources, and the "tragedy" is that it is advantageous for individuals to exploit those resources but disadvantageous to all of us when too many individuals pursue their own advantage. Yet, with our value on individualism (rather than on group well-being), we are likely to do precisely that—to pursue our individual advantage and add to the general problem. We are, said Hardin (1971:247) "locked into a system of 'fouling our own nest,' so long as we behave only as independent, rational, free-enterprisers." That same value of individualism makes Americans reluctant to yield power to government. For many Americans, political inaction is the soul of good government, but in the realm of ecology, political inaction is the harbinger of disaster.

Ideology: the purpose of nature. The attitudes and values just discussed are supported by an *ideology of the purpose of nature* that emerged in the West and was accepted by Americans. This ideology emerged with the victory of Christianity over paganism (White, 1971). Christianity provided a unique approach to nature and had a unique message to people about their relationship with the environment. In contrast to most other religions, Christianity "not only established a dualism of man and nature but also insisted that it is God's will that man exploit nature for his proper ends" (White, 1971:27). For many ancient peoples nature was filled with guardian spirits. If someone were to cut down a tree or extract ore from the earth or dam up a stream, the spirit or spirits involved had to be placated. In destroying this pagan belief "Christianity made it possible to exploit nature in a mood of indifference to the feelings of natural objects" (White, 1971:28). An ideology of Christianity placed human beings directly below God in the order of creation with the implication that nature was created for the benefit of human beings. Human beings could therefore conquer and exploit nature to provide good things for themselves.

This ideology is further demonstrated by the early scientists' consistent affirmation of their Christian faith and belief that they were doing the work of God. It is no exaggeration to say that "modern Western science was cast in a matrix of Christian theology" (White, 1971:29).

The old ideology wrought havoc. Now, a new ideology emerging among some people stresses the need for understanding and cooperating with nature.

What Is To Be Done?

A number of courses of action are suggested by the analysis presented in this chapter. First, population control will have to be brought about by a reduction of birth rates. This requirement unfortunately conflicts with religious beliefs of some people and with a value of others who want freedom to choose their family size. Historically, the most effective way to reduce birth rates has been to educate women and incorporate them into the labor force. The women's movement, a worldwide movement that insists upon full educational and career options for women, may greatly aid the population problem. Indirectly, the movement may also ease our ecological problems by slowing population growth which intensifies those problems.

People need to be educated about the seriousness of environmental pollution and depletion in order to change the attitudes and values we have discussed. People could be educated to conserve energy in many ways. Only minor changes in our life styles would add up to substantial national savings. If one-third of the families in the nation would switch from a car getting 13.5 miles per gallon to one getting 19.5 miles per gallon, we would save more than 330,000 barrels of oil per day. If the number of people riding in car pools would double, we could save around 700,000 barrels of oil per day. If families would plan and combine errands so that one auto trip per week could be eliminated, we might save 180,000 barrels of oil per day. With all three measures, we would save around 1.2 million barrels of crude oil every day (Citizens' Advisory Committee on Environment Quality, 1975:17). We should remember that reducing our oil consumption automatically means that we are dealing to some extent with environmental pollution and depletion.

In addition to such efforts, however, there is a critical need for *political action* and for certain *changes in our industrial economy*. This action and these changes must occur in the context of a new ideology that would affirm the fact that we live in an ecosystem. The new ideology would stress cooperation with nature rather than conquest of nature.

The government can address our ecological problems in many ways. It can take measures to diminish or eliminate pollution caused by its own operations and by operations supported by government funds. Legislation can impose sanctions on polluters and control the extraction of natural resources. Tax incentives can stimulate research into pollution-control measures and alternative energy sources. Direct financing by government of research on our ecological problems must also be increased.

The government must both compel enforcement of certain standards and encourage the search for solutions. Governmental sanctions do work in the area of ecology. The nationwide reduction in the severity of air pollution is attributable to federal action.

As for the needed changes in our industrial economy, we must reassess our emphasis on growth. We must learn how to balance growth with ecological considerations, and we must search for *alternative, clean sources of energy* upon which to base the economy. A number of alternatives are already being studied. Some people advocate nuclear power, but we have already seen that a total conversion to nuclear power is not feasible. Furthermore, nuclear power confronts us with the very difficult questions of how to dispose of radioactive waste and how to insure against leaks and accidents that can release radioactivity into the atmosphere. Other possible alternatives are harnessing solar energy (the light and heat from the sun) and geothermal energy (the water and hot rock beneath the earth's surface).

Involvement

Help! They're Ruining Our Land!

In the March 2, 1977 issue of *Time,* the Bethlehem Steel Corporation had a two-page advertisement about the energy problem. One page talked about the need for conserving energy and some of the alternative sources of energy that might be used. The other page was largely blank; the ad encouraged readers to use the blank to write messages to Congressmen to let them know what we all feel about the problem. Our messages, the ad assured us, "won't go unheeded."

Is that true? Does it do any good to write a letter to a Congressman? Does the government actually pay any attention to what the people think about a particular matter? Some people answer with a cynical "no," while others have a naive faith that whatever they do will command attention. Studies have shown that public opinion can influence governmental policy in some cases, though not in all. Your letter, therefore, *may* have an impact.

Either use the materials in this chapter or get in touch with a local Sierra Club or environmental group and inquire about the ecological problems in your area. Then formulate a letter and send it to a number of officials—U.S., state, or local officials who might be able to exercise some influence over the problem. Try to persuade others who share your concern to write their own letters (remember that a number of individual letters is more impressive than one letter with many signatures). Meet together to discuss the responses to your letters and what, if any, further action you should take.

The advantages and disadvantages of each of these alternatives must be explored carefully but quickly, for the supply of fossil fuels is being rapidly depleted while the demand for energy is increasing throughout the world. It is imperative that we recognize the seriousness of our ecological situation and commit the necessary funds and effort to the search for solutions.

Summary

What we variously call environmental or ecological problems have reached a state of crisis. The problems come down to maintaining a balanced ecosystem on our planet—a balance between people and their natural environment. Human activity can disrupt this ecosystem to the point of destruction.

Our ecological problems may be broadly classified as environmental pollution, environmental depletion, and overpopulation. The first category includes air pollution, water pollution, land pollution, noise pollution, and aesthetic damage. The second category involves our dwindling natural resources, including those that yield energy. The third problem involves a population size that detracts from the desired quality of life, or that is too large to be adequately supported by the available resources.

It is difficult to measure the extent of our ecological problems, but certain facts are known. They show that some progress has been made in all three problem areas, but also that the problems remain serious.

Ecological problems involve inherent contradictions among a number of our values. We do not fully understand how these contradictions are being manifested in social life, but we do know that they diminish the quality of life in a number of ways. Population growth contributes to a great many problems, including educational opportunities, food supplies, recreational facilities, economic difficulties, and health problems. Pollutants threaten the health and life of humans and animals. The ecological balance itself is threatened by the potential destruction of certain processes that are necessary to sustain life on earth. The economic costs of both pollution damage and pollution control are enormous.

Among the causes of population growth are norms relating to age at marriage and to size of the family, the nature of the female role, and technological developments. Population growth, in turn, intensifies the problems of the environment. The effects of population growth are more than additive, as evidenced by diminishing returns and the threshold effect. In addition to population growth, our industrial economy is at the root of environmental problems. The products, by-products, and continuing growth in the economy of our industrial society create serious ecological problems. The problems are intensified by the tendency of the government to ignore them or to set up ineffective programs and policies. Federal action is imperative if we are to seriously attack the problems of our environment.

Among social psychological factors, attitudes and values may facilitate population growth by idealizing or romanticizing the large family. The ideology of the Divine way contributes to high birth rates among certain religious groups. An ideology that emerged from Christianity set human beings above nature and contributed to an exploitative attitude toward nature. We thereby legitimated a lack of concern for the environment. Our values of growth, materialism, and individualism have supported the economic and political arrangements that contribute to the problems.

Glossary

ecosystem   a set of living things, their environment, and the interrelationships within and between them

environmental depletion   increasing scarcity of natural resources, including those used for generating energy

environmental pollution   harmful alterations in our environment, including air, land, and water

eutrophication   overfertilization of water due to excess nutrients, leading to algae growth and oxygen depletion

herbicide   a chemical used to kill plant life, particularly weeds

pesticide   a chemical used to kill insects defined as pests

photosynthesis   a natural process essential to life, resulting in the production of oxygen and organic materials

pollutant   anything that results in environmental pollution

For Further Reading

Carson, Rachel. *Silent Spring.* Boston: Houghton Mifflin, 1962. A pioneering book that called attention to the environmental consequences of using pesticides.

Commoner, Barry. *The Closing Circle.* New York: Alfred A. Knopf, 1971. A prominent biologist and environmentalist argues that our "counter ecological" technology is a more important factor in our ecological problems than is population growth.

Foley, Gerald, with Charlotte Nassim and Gerald Leach. *The Energy Question.* New York: Penguin Books, 1976. A survey of the energy resources in the world, the potential for developing those resources, and the way in which industrialism and energy consumption are linked together.

Neuschatz, Alan. *Managing the Environment.* Washington, D.C.: Environmental Protection Agency, 1973. A collection of papers that explore the ways in which the government and citizenry can be involved in environmental action, including such matters as information systems in the management of the environment.

Oltmans, Willem L., ed. *On Growth: The Crisis of Exploding Population and Resource Depletion.* New York: Capricorn Books, 1974. Discussions by seventy intellectuals from the social and natural sciences, the arts, humanities, and business concerning various aspects of the crisis of population growth and the depletion of our natural resources.

Opie, John, ed. *Americans and Environment: The Controversy Over Ecology.* Lexington, Mass.: D. C. Heath, 1971. A collection of readings representing conflicting opinions about nature, the controversy over ecological problems, the nature of environmental problems, and some possible alternative solutions.

————. *Population and the American Future: The Report of the Commission on Population Growth and the American Future.* Washington, D.C.: Government Printing Office, 1972. The report of a presidential commission that looked at all aspects of the population problem in the United States. A number of recommendations are included.

Notes

1. *St. Louis Post-Dispatch,* July 27, 1980.

2. U.S. Bureau of the Census, *Statistical Abstract of the United States, 1980* (Washington, D.C.: Government Printing Office, 1981, p. 604.

3. Results reported in *Psychology Today,* June 1979, pp. 32, 35, and Horst Siebert, and Ariane Berthoin Antal, *The Political Economy of Environmental Protection* (Greenwich, Conn.: JAI Press, Inc., 1979), p. 31.

4. U.S. Bureau of the Census, *Statistical Abstract of the United States, 1980* (Washington, D.C.: Government Printing Office, 1981), p. 214.

Glossary

abuse   improper use of drugs or alcohol to the degree that the consequences are defined as detrimental to the user and/or the society

achievement   as distinguished from educational "attainment," the level the student has reached as measured by scores on various verbal and nonverbal tests

addiction   repeated use of a drug or alcohol to the point of periodic or chronic intoxication that is detrimental to the user and/or the society

adjudication   making a judgment; settling a judicial matter

aggression   forceful, offensive, or hostile behavior toward another person or society

alienation   a sense of estrangement from one's social environment, typically measured by one's feelings of powerlessness, normlessness, isolation, meaninglessness, and self-estrangement

anomie   literally, normlessness; as used by Merton, it refers to a structural breakdown characterized by incompatibility between cultural goals and the legitimate means of reaching those goals

appeal to prejudice   argument by appealing to popular prejudices or passions

atmosphere   the general mood and social influences in a situation or place

attainment   as distinguished from educational "achievement," the number of years of education completed by a student

attitude   a predisposition about something in one's environment

autonomy   the ability or opportunity to govern oneself

biological characteristic   an inherited in contrast to a learned characteristic

bisexual   having sex relations with either sex or both together

capitalism   an economic system in which there is private, rather than state, ownership of wealth and control of the production and distribution of goods; people are motivated by profit, and compete with each other for maximum shares of profit

carcinogenic   causing cancer

caste   social category of a closed stratification system; that is, an individual's position throughout life is completely determined by his or her father's social rank (caste membership)

catharsis   discharging socially unacceptable emotions in a socially acceptable way

circular reasoning   using conclusions to support the assumptions that were necessary to make the conclusions

class   social category of a relatively open stratification system; that is, in spite of inequalities of property, power, and prestige, individuals have some degree of opportunity to change their class position

cognitive development   growth in the ability to perform increasingly complex intellectual activities, particularly abstract relationships

cohabit   live together without getting married

compensatory programs   programs designed to give intensive help to disadvantaged pupils and increase their academic skills

consciousness raising   the process by which people become aware of their situation as the situation is defined by some group

consumer price index   a measure of the average change in prices of all types of consumer goods and services purchased by urban wage earners and clerical workers

contradiction   opposing phenomena within the same social system

correlate   ascertain the degree of relatedness, from 0 to 100 percent, between two events or phenomena

culture refers to the way of life of a people, including both material products (such as technology) and nonmaterial characteristics (such as values, norms, language and beliefs)

cunnilingus oral stimulation of the female genitalia

decile one of ten equal categories of some variable

dehumanization the process by which an individual is deprived of qualities or traits of a human being

dependent variable the variable in an experiment that is influenced by an independent variable

deschooling process of removing education from the existing school system and creating a new system in which students can maximize their learning

detoxification supervised withdrawal from dependence on a drug

deviance behavior that violates norms

differential association the theory that illegal behavior is due to preponderance of definitions favorable to such behavior

discrimination arbitrary, unfavorable treatment of the members of some social group

disfranchise to deprive of the right to vote

division of labor the separation of work into specialized tasks

divorce rate typically, the number of divorces per 1,000 marriages

dramatic instance the fallacy of overgeneralizing

ecosystem a set of living things, their environment, and the interrelationships within and between them

entrepreneur one who organizes and manages a business enterprise

environmental depletion increasing scarcity of natural resources, including those used for generating energy

environmental destruction alterations in the environment that make it less habitable or useful for people or other living things

environmental pollution harmful alterations in our environment, including air, land, and water

epidemiology study of the factors that affect the incidence, prevalence, and distribution of illnesses

etiology causes of a disease

eutrophication overfertilization of water due to excess nutrients, leading to algae growth and oxygen depletion

exploitation use or manipulation of people for one's own advantage or profit

fallacy of authority argument by an illegitimate appeal to authority

fallacy of composition the assertion that what is true of the part is necessarily true of the whole

fallacy of personal attack argument by attacking the opponent personally rather than dealing with the issue

fallacy of sequence-equals-cause the argument that if one event follows another, the first caused the second

fellatio oral stimulation of the male genitalia

forcible rape actual or attempted sexual intercourse through the use of force or the threat of force

frequency distribution the organization of data to show the number of times each item occurs

gender sex; male or female

generation gap differences in values and behavior between parents and their children

genetically transmitted biologically inherited

ghetto an area in which a certain group is segregated from the rest of society; often used today to refer to the impoverished area of the inner city

gross national product the total value, usually in dollars, of all goods and services produced by a nation during a year

herbicide a chemical used to kill plant life, particularly weeds

heterogamy marriage between those with diverse values and backgrounds

heterosexual having sexual preference for persons of the opposite sex

homogamy marriage between those with similar values and backgrounds

homosexual having sexual preference for persons of the same sex; someone who privately or overtly considers himself or herself a homosexual

ideology a set of ideas to explain or justify some aspect of social reality

incidence the number of new cases of an illness that occur during a particular period of time

independent variable the variable in an experiment that is manipulated in order to see how it effects changes in the dependent variable

innate existing in an individual from birth

institution a collective pattern of dealing with a basic social function; typical institutions identified by sociologists are the government, economy, education, family and marriage, and religion

institutional racism policies and practices of social institutions that tend to perpetuate racial discrimination

interaction reciprocally influenced behavior on the part of two or more people

labeling theory the theory that deviant behavior is the result of individuals being defined and treated as deviants—a form of self-fulfilling prophecy

labor force all civilians who are employed or unemployed but able and desirous of work

lesbian a female homosexual

life chances the probability of gaining certain advantages defined as desirable, such as long life and health

longevity the length of human life, usually in years

maladjustment poor adjustment to one's social environment

malnutrition inadequate food, in amount and/or type

manic-depressive reaction a disorder involving fluctuation between emotional extremes

Marxist pertaining to the system of thought developed by Karl Marx and Friedrich Engels, particularly emphasizing materialism, class struggle, and the progress of humanity toward communism

mean the average

median the score below which are half of the scores and above which are the other half

military parity equality or equivalence in military strength

misplaced concreteness the fallacy of making something abstract into something concrete

morbidity the prevalence of a specified illness in a specified area

morphological pertaining to form and structure

neurosis a disorder that involves anxiety which is sufficiently intense to impair the individual's functioning in some way

non sequitur something that does not follow logically from what has preceded it

norm shared expectations about behavior

nuclear family husband, wife, and children, if any

participant observation a method of research in whch one directly participates and observes the social reality being studied

personal problem a problem that can be explained in terms of the qualities of the individual

pesticide a chemical used to kill insects defined as pests

photosynthesis a natural process essential to life, resulting in the production of oxygen and organic materials

pica a craving for unnatural substances

pimp one who earns all or part of his living by acting as a manager or procurer for a prostitute

placebo any substance having no physiological effect that is given to a subject who believes it to be a drug that does have effect

pollutant anything that results in environmental pollution

post hoc   the argument that if one event follows another, the first is the cause of the second

poverty level   defined as the minimum income level at which Americans should have to live, it is based on the Department of Agriculture's calculations of the cost of a basic diet they called "the economy food plan"

predatory crime   acts that have victims who suffer loss of property or some kind of physical harm

prejudice   a rigid, emotional attitude toward people in a group that legitimates discriminatory behavior

prevalence   the number of cases of an illness that exists at any particular time

primary deviance   deviant behavior of an individual who still considers himself or herself as a conforming member of society

primary group   the people with whom we have intimate, face-to-face interaction on a recurring basis, such as parents, spouse, children, and close friends

productivity   output per worker-hour

promiscuity   undiscriminating, casual sexual relationships with many people

prostitution   having sexual relations for remuneration, usually to provide part or all of one's livelihood

psychosis   a disorder in which the individual fails to distinguish between internal and external stimuli

psychosomatic disorder   an impairment in physiological functioning that results from the individual's emotional state

race   a group of people distinguished from other groups on the basis of certain biological characteristics

rehabilitation   resocializing a criminal and returning him or her to full participation in society

reification   defining what is abstract as something concrete

relative deprivation   a sense of deprivation based on some standard used by the individual who feels deprived

retributiveness   paying people back for their socially unacceptable behavior

retrospective determinism   the argument that things could not have worked out any other way than they did

ritualized deprivation   a school atmosphere in which the motions of teaching and learning continue while the students are more concerned to survive than to learn

role   the behavior associated with a particular position in the social structure

role conflict   a person's perception that two or more of his or her roles are contradictory, or that the same role has contradictory expectations, or that the expectations of the role are unacceptable or excessive

SAM-D missile   one of the American surface-to-air missiles designed to intercept airplanes or other missiles

sanctions   mechanism of social control for enforcing a society's standards

schizophrenia   a psychosis that involves a thinking disorder, particularly hallucinations and fantasies

secondary deviance   deviant behavior by an individual who regards himself or herself as deviant

self-fulfilling prophecy   a belief that has consequences (and may become true) simply because it is believed

senescence   biological aging

sexism   prejudice or discrimination against someone because of his or her sex

sex role   the behavior that any particular society considers appropriate for each sex

social change   alterations in interaction patterns or in such aspects of culture as norms, values, and technology

social control regulation of people's behavior, feelings, and beliefs in any society by any means acceptable in that society

social disorganization a state of society in which consensus about norms has broken down

socialization the process by which an individual learns to participate in a group

social problem related to the fact that human beings live together in organized societies; i.e., a condition or pattern of behavior caused by social factors

socioeconomic status categories of people based on similar economic resources, power, education, prestige, and style of life

sodomy intercourse that is defined as "unnatural"; particularly used to refer to anal intercourse

stagflation a combination of economic stagnation, including high unemployment rates, and inflation

statutory rape sexual intercourse with a female who is below the legal age for consenting

stereotype an image of members of a group that standardizes them and exaggerates certain qualities

stigma that which symbolizes disrepute or disgrace

subculture a group within a society that shares much of the culture of the larger society while maintaining certain distinctive cultural elements of its own

subsidy a government grant to a private person or company to assist an enterprise deemed advantageous to the public

superannuate to retire someone because of age

survey a method of research in which a sample of people are interviewed or given questionnaires in order to get data on some phenomenon

swinging exchange of mates among couples for sexual purposes

test of significance a statistical method for determining the probability that research findings occurred by chance

trauma physical or emotional injury

underemployment working full time for poverty wages, or working part time when full time work is desired, or working at a job below the worker's skill level

unemployment rate proportion of the labor force that is not working but is available for work and has made specific efforts to find work

variable any trait or characteristic that varies in value or magnitude

violence use of force to kill, injure, or abuse others

white-collar crime crimes committed by respectable citizens in the course of their work

work ethic notion that our sense of worth and the satisfaction of our needs are intricately related to the kind of work we do

References

Ackerman, Nathan W.
1970 "Adolescent problems: a symptom of family disorder." In *Family Process,* ed. N. W. Ackerman, pp. 80–91. New York: Basic Books.

Akers, R. L., M. D. Krohn, L. Lanza-Kaduce, and M. Radosevich
1979 "Social learning and deviant behavior: a specific test of a general theory." *American Sociological Review* 44 (August):636–55.

Aldrich, H. E.
1973 "Employment opportunities for blacks in the black ghetto: the role of white-owned businesses." *American Journal of Sociology* 78 (May):1403–25.

Alexander, A. S.
1969 "The cost of world armaments." *Scientific American* 221 (October):21–27.

Allport, Gordon W.
1955 *Becoming: Basic Considerations for a Psychology of Personality.* New Haven: Yale University Press.
1958 *The Nature of Prejudice.* Garden City: Anchor Books.

Amir, Menachem
1971 *Patterns in Forcible Rape.* Chicago: University of Chicago Press.

Anthony, E. J.
1969 "The mutative impact on family life of serious mental and physical illness." *Canadian Psychiatric Association Journal* 14 (no. 5): 433–53.
1970 "The impact of mental and physical illness on family life." *American Journal of Psychiatry* 127 (August):138–46.

Armbruster, Frank E.
1972 *The Forgotten Americans: A Survey of Values, Beliefs, and Concerns of the Majority.* New Rochelle: Arlington House.

Armor, D. J.
1973 "The double double standard: a reply." *The Public Interest* 30 (Winter):119–31.

Armstrong, E. G.
1978 "Massage parlors and their customers." *Archives of Sexual Behavior* 7 (March):117–25.

Arrington, T. S., and P. A. Kyle
1978 "Equal rights amendment activists in North Carolina." *Signs* 3 (Spring):666–80.

Atchley, R. C.
1975 "Dimensions of widowhood in later life." *The Gerontologist* 15 (April):176–78.

Aurelius, Marcus
1961 *Meditations.* Trans. A. S. L. Farquharson. London: J. M. Dent & Sons.

Bachman, J. G., and L. D. Johnston
1979 "The freshmen, 1979." *Psychology Today,* September, 79–87.

Baker, Robert K., and Sandra J. Ball
1969 *Mass Media and Violence. A Report to the National Commission on the Causes and Prevention of Violence.* Vol. 9. Washington, D.C.: Government Printing Office.

Ball-Rokeach, S. J.
1973 "Values and violence: a test of the subculture of violence thesis." *American Sociological Review* 38 (December):736–49.

Bandura, A., D. Ross, and S. A. Ross
1963 "Imitation of film-mediated aggressive models." *Journal of Abnormal and Social Psychology* 66(no. 1):3–11.

Bane, M. J.
1977 "Children, divorce, and welfare." *The Wilson Quarterly* 1 (Winter):89–94.

Baran, Paul A., and Paul M. Sweezy
1966 *Monopoly Capital.* New York: Monthly Review Press.

Barlow, Hugh D.
1978 *Introduction to Criminology.* Boston: Little, Brown & Company.

Barnett, Walter
1973 *Sexual Freedom and the Constitution.* Albuquerque: University of New Mexico Press.

Barr, J. W.
1969 "Tax reform: the time is now." *Saturday Review,* March 22, pp. 22–25.

Bassin, A.
1975 "Psychology in action: red, white, and blue poker chips; an AA behavior modification technique." *American Psychologist* 30 (June):695–96.

Batchelder, A.
1965 "Poverty: the special case of the Negro." *American Economic Review* 55(May):530–40.

Bayer, A. E.
1975 "Sexist students in American colleges: a descriptive note." *Journal of Marriage and the Family* 37(May):391–97.

Beauchamp, D. E.
1975 "The alcohol alibi: blaming alcoholics." *Society* 12(September/October):12–17.

Becker, Howard S.
1952 "Social-class variations in the teacher-pupil relationship." *Journal of Educational Sociology* 25(April):451–65.
1953 "Becoming a marihuana user." *American Journal of Sociology* 59 (November):235–42.
1963 *Outsiders: Studies in the Sociology of Deviance.* New York: Free Press.

Beiser, M.
1965 "Poverty, social disintegration, and personality." *Journal of Social Issues* 21(January):56–78.

Bell, Alan P., and Martin S. Weinberg
1978 *Homosexualities: A Study of Diversity Among Men and Women.* New York: Simon & Schuster.

Bell, Daniel
1960 *The End of Ideology.* New York: Free Press.

Bell, L. N.
1958 "Delinquency—there is a cause." *Christianity Today,* February 3, 19+.

Bell, Robert R.
1963 *Marriage and Family Interaction.* Homewood, Ill.: Dorsey Press.

Beller, I.
1970 "Latin America's unemployment problem." *Monthly Labor Review* 93 (November):3–10.

Bellwood, L. R.
1975 "Grief work in alcoholism treatment." *Alcohol Health Research World,* Spring, 1975, pp. 8–11.

Benet, Sula
1976 "Why they live to be 100, or even older, in Abkhasia." In *Aging in America: Readings in Social Gerontology,* eds. C. S. Kart and B. B. Manard, pp. 213–26. Port Washington, N.Y.: Alfred.

Bengis, I.
1977 "The world of the secretary." *Mother Jones,* February/March, 47–55.

Bengtson, V. L.
1970 "The generation gap: a review and typology of social-psychological perspectives." *Youth & Society* 2 (September):7–32.

Berg, Ivar
1970 *Education and Jobs: The Great Training Robbery.* New York: Praeger.

Berg, J. M., and M. Zappella
1964 "Lead poisoning in childhood with particular reference to pica and mental sequelae." *Journal of Mental Deficiency Research* 8(no. 1):44–53.

Berger, A. S., and W. Simon
1974 "Black families and the Moynihan report: a research evaluation." *Social Problems* 22(December):145–61.

Bergner, L., and A. S. Yerby
1968 "Low income and barriers to use of health services." *New England Journal of Medicine* 278(March):541–46.

Berkman, P. L.
1969 "Spouseless motherhood, psychological stress, and physical morbidity." *Journal of Health and Social Behavior* 10(December):323–34.
1971 "Life stress and psychological well-being *Journal of Health and Social Behavior* 12(March):35–45.

Berlowitz, M. J.
1974 "Institutional racism and school staffing in an urban area." *Journal of Negro Education* 43(Winter):25–29.

Berman, D. M.
1977 "Why work kills: a brief history of occupational safety and health in the United States." *International Journal of Health Services* 7 (no. 1):63–87.

Bernard, Jessie
1966 *Marriage and Family Among Negroes.* Englewood Cliffs, N.J.: Prentice-Hall.

Bernard, Viola W., Perry Ottenberg, and Fritz Redl
1968 "Dehumanization: a composite psychological defense in relation to modern war." In *The Triple Revolution,* eds. R. Perrucci and M. Pilisuk, pp. 17–34. Boston: Little, Brown.

Bernstein, B. E.
1978 "Generational conflict and the family." *Adolescence* 13 (Winter):751–54.

Bethards, J. M.
1973 "Parental support and the use of drugs." *Humboldt Journal of Social Relations* 1 (Fall):26–28.

Bidwell, C. E., and J. D. Kasarda
1975 "School district organization and student achievement." *American Sociological Review* 40(February):55–70.

Birch, C.
1973 "Three facts, eight fallacies and three axioms about population and environment." *Ecumenical Review* 25 (January):29–40.

Black, D. J.
1970 "Production of crime rates." *American Sociological Review* 35 (August):733–48.

Blackwell, James E.
1975 *The Black Community.* New York: Dodd, Mead.

Blake, W.
1973 "The influence of race on diagnosis." *Smith College Studies in Social Work* 43(June):184–92.

Blazer, J. A.
1963 "Complementary needs and marital happiness." *Marriage and Family Living* 25 (February):60–68.

Block J., N. Haan, and M. B. Smith
1970 "Socialization correlates of student activism." *Journal of Social Issues* 26(January):25–38.

Bluestone, B.
1969 "Low-wage industries and the working poor." *Poverty and Human Resource Abstracts* 3(March/April):1–14.

Blumenthal, Monica D., Robert L. Kahn, Frank M. Andrews, and Kendra B. Head
1972 *Justifying Violence: Attitudes of American Men.* Ann Arbor, Mich.: University of Michigan, Institute for Social Research.

Blusewicz, M. J., R. E. Dustman, T. Schenkenberg, and E. C. Beck
1977 "Neuropsychological correlates of chronic alcoholism and aging." *Journal of Nervous and Mental Disease* 165 (no. 5):348–55.

Boisen, Anton T.
1936 *The Exploration of the Inner World.* New York: Harper & Bros.

Borgatta, E. G.
1976 "The concept of reverse discrimination and equality of opportunity." *The American Sociologist* 11(May):62–72.

Bossard, J. H. S.
1941 "War and the family." *American Sociological Review* 6(June):330–44.

Botwinick, Jack, and Larry W. Thompson
1970 "Age difference in reaction time: an artifact?" In *Normal Aging,* ed. E. Palmore, pp. 186–93. Durham, N.C.: Duke University Press.

Bowlby, J.
1961 "Separation anxiety: a critical review of the literature." *Journal of Child Psychology and Psychiatry* 1(February):251–69.

Brenner, M. Harvey
1973 *Mental Illness and the Economy.* Cambridge, Mass.: Harvard University Press.
1978 "The social costs of economic distress." In *Consultation on the Social Impact of Economic Distress,* pp. 3–6. New York: The American Jewish Committee, Institute of Human Relations.

Briscoe, C. W., J. B. Smith, E. Robins, S. Marten, and F. Gaskin
1973 "Divorce and psychiatric disease." *Archives of General Psychiatry* 29(July):119–25.

Brodeur, P.
1979 "Aerosol sprays: a planetary time bomb." *National Parks and Conservation Magazine,* February, 15–21.

Brodsky, C. M.
1977 "Suicide attributed to work." *Suicide & Life-Threatening Behavior* 7 (Winter):216–29.

Bronfenbrenner, M.
1969 "The Japanese 'howdunit.' " *Trans-Action* 6(January):32–36.

Brotman, R., and F. Suffet
1975 "The concept of prevention and its limitations." *Annals of the American Academy of Political and Social Science* 417(January):53–65.

Brown, J. S.
1952 "A comparative study of deviations from sexual mores." *American Sociological Review* 17(April):135–46.

Brown, J. S., and B. G. Gilmartin
1969 "Sociology today: lacunae, emphasis and surfeits." *American Sociologist* 4(November):283–91.

Brown, L. R., P. L. McGrath, and B. Stokes
1976 "The population problem in 22 dimensions." *The Futurist,* October, 238–44.

Brownmiller, Susan
1975 *Against Our Will.* New York: Simon & Schuster.

Brubaker, Sterling
1972 *To Live On Earth: Man and His Environment in Perspective.* Baltimore: Johns Hopkins Press.

Bryant, C. D., and C. E. Palmer
1975 "Massage parlors and 'hand whores': some sociological observations." *Journal of Sex Research* 11(August):227–41.

Buchholz, R. A.
1978 "The work ethic reconsidered." *Industrial & Labor Relations Review* 31(July):450–59.

Bumpass, L. L., and J. A. Sweet
1972 "Differentials in marital instability: 1970." *American Sociological Review* 37(December):754–66.

Burgess, A. W., and L. L. Holmstrom
1974 "Rape trauma syndrome." *American Journal of Psychiatry* 131(September):981–86.

Burma, John H., ed.
1970 *Mexican-Americans in the United States.* Cambridge, Mass.: Schenkman.

Burns, J. H.
1958 "What it means to be divorced." *Pastoral Psychology* 9 (September):45–52.

Burr, W. R.
1971 "An expansion and test of a role theory of marital satisfaction." *Journal of Marriage and the Family* 33(May):368–72.

Burstein, P.
1979 "Equal employment opportunity legislation and the income of women and nonwhites." *American Sociological Review* 44(June):367–91.

Busse, Ewald W.
1970 "A physiological, psychological, and sociological study of aging." In *Normal Aging,* ed. E. Palmore, pp. 7–17. Durham, N.C.: Duke University Press.

Butler, R. N.
1973 "Public interest report no. 9: how to grow old and poor in an affluent society." *International Journal of Aging and Human Development* 4 (no. 3): 277–79.

Butterfield, Herbert
1949 *Christianity and History*. London: Fontana Books.

Cahalan, Don
1970 *Problem Drinking*. San Francisco: Jossey-Bass.

Cahalan, Don, and Robin Room
1974 *Problem Drinking Among American Men*. New Brunswick, N.J.: Rutgers Center of Alcohol Studies.

Camp, W. L.
1973 "We are told marihuana is harmless, except . . . ." *Personnel and Guidance Journal* 52(September):9–15.

Campbell, Angus, Philip E. Converse, and Willard L. Rodgers
1976 *The Quality of American Life*. New York: Russell Sage Foundation.

Cantril, Hadley
1965 *The Pattern of Human Concerns*. New Brunswick, N.J.: Rutgers University Press.

Caplovitz, David
1967 *The Poor Pay More*. New York: Free Press.

Carlson, B. E.
1977 "Battered women and their assailants." *Social Work* 22(November):455–60.

Carlson, Lewis H., and George A. Colburn, eds.
1972 *In Their Place: White America Defines Her Minorities, 1850–1950*. New York: John Wiley & Sons.

Carlson, R. J.
1972 "Health in America." *The Center Magazine* 5(November/December):43–47.

Carr, R.
1976 "The pot vote." *Human Behavior*, May, 56–60.
1978 "What marijuana does (and doesn't do)." *Human Behavior*, January, 20–25.

Cernkovich, S. A.
1978 "Evaluating two models of delinquency causation." *Criminology* 16(November):335–52.

Chafe, William H.
1972 *The American Woman: Her Changing Social, Economic, and Political Roles, 1920–1970*. New York: Oxford University Press.

Chafetz, Janet Saltzman
1974 *Masculine/Feminine or Human?* Itaska, Ill.: F. E. Peacock.

Chafetz, J. S., P. Sampson, P. Beck, and J. West
1974 "A study of homosexual women." *Social Work* 19(November):714–23.

Chaneles, S.
1976 "Prisoners can be rehabilitated—now." *Psychology Today* 10(October):129–34.

Chase, Stuart
1956 *Guides to Straight Thinking*. New York: Harper & Bros.

Chilton, R. J., and G. E. Markle
1972 "Family disruption, delinquent conduct and the effect of subclassification." *American Sociological Review* 37(February):93–99.

Chiricos, T. G., P. D. Jackson, and G. P. Waldo
1972 "Inequality in the imposition of a criminal label." *Social Problems* 19(Spring):553–72.

Chudacoff, H. P., and T. K. Hareven
1979 "From the empty nest to family dissolution: life course transition into old age." *Journal of Family History* 4(Spring):69–83.

Citizens' Advisory Committee on Environmental Quality
1975 *Report to the President and to the Council on Environmental Quality*. Washington, D.C.: Government Printing Office.

Clark, A. W., and P. van Sommers
1961 "Contradictory demands in family relations and adjustment to school and home." *Human Relations* 14(May):97–111.

Clark, Margaret, and Barbara Gallatin Anderson
1967 *Culture and Aging.* Springfield, Ill.: Charles
C Thomas.

Clarke, J. W., and J. W. Soule
1968 "How southern children felt about King's
death." *Trans-Action* 5(October):35–40.

Clausen, John A.
1976 "Mental disorders." In *Contemporary Social
Problems*, 4th ed., eds. R. K. Merton and
R. Nisbet, pp. 105–39. New York: Harcourt
Brace Jovanovich.

Clausen, J. A., and C. L. Huffine
1975 "Sociocultural and social-psychological
factors affecting social responses to mental
disorders." *Journal of Health and Social
Behavior* 16(December):405–20.

Clemente, F., and W. J. Sauer
1976 "Life satisfaction in the United States."
Social Forces 54(March):621–31.

Clinard, M. B., and L. F. Fannin
1965 "Differences in the conception of self as a
male among lower and middle class
delinquents." *Social Problems*
13(Fall):205–14.

Cloward, Richard A., and Lloyd E. Ohlin
1960 *Delinquency and Opportunity.* Glencoe: Free
Press.

Coates, T. J., and M. L. Southern
1972 "Differential educational aspiration levels of
men and women undergraduate students."
Journal of Psychology 81(May):125–28.

Coburn, D.
1975 "Job-worker incongruence: consequences for
health." *Journal of Health and Social
Behavior* 16(June):198–212.

Coe, Rodney M.
1970 *Sociology of Medicine.* New York:
McGraw-Hill.

Cohen, Albert K.
1955 *Delinquent Boys.* New York: Macmillan.

Cole, S., and R. Lejeune
1972 "Illness and the legitimation of failure."
American Sociological Review
37(June):347–56.

Cole, William E., and Charles H. Miller
1965 *Social Problems: A Sociological
Interpretation.* New York: David McKay.

Coleman, James S.
1961 *The Adolescent Society.* New York: Free
Press.

Coleman, James S., Ernest Q. Campbell, Carol J.
Hobson et al.
1966 *Equality of Educational Opportunity*, 2
vols. Washington, D.C.: Government
Printing Office.

Coles, R.
1968 "Life in Appalachia—the case of Hugh
McCaslin." *Trans-Action* 5(June):23–33.
1969 *Still Hungry in America.* New York: World
Publishing Co.

Commager, Henry Steele, ed.
1945 *The Pocket History of the Second World
War.* New York: Pocket Books.

Commoner, Barry
1971 *The Closing Circle.* New York: Alfred A.
Knopf.

Conklin, John E.
1975 *The Impact of Crime.* New York:
Macmillan.

Conot, R.
1970 "The Slum Merchant." In *Where It's At:
Radical Perspectives in Sociology*, eds. S. E.
Deutsch and J. Howard, pp. 412–14. New
York: Harper & Row.

Constantini, E., and K. H. Craik
1972 "Women as politicians: the social
background, personality and political careers
of female party leaders." *Journal of Social
Issues* 28 (no. 2):217–35.

Cooley, Charles Horton
1967 "Primary group and human nature." In
*Symbolic Interaction: A Reader in Social
Psychology*, eds. J. G. Manis and B. N.
Meltzer, pp. 156–58. Boston: Allyn &
Bacon.

Coon, Carleton S., Stanley M. Garn, and Joseph B. Birdsell
1950 *Races.* Springfield, Ill.: Charles C Thomas.

Cooper, B. S., and D. P. Rice
1976 "The economic cost of illness revisited." *Social Security Bulletin* 39(February):21–36.

Cooper, Cary L., and Judi Marshall
1978 "Sources of managerial and white collar stress." In *Stress At Work,* eds., C. L. Cooper and R. Payne, pp. 81–105. New York: John Wiley.

Coopersmith, Stanley
1967 *The Antecedents of Self-Esteem.* San Francisco: Freeman.

Cornacchia, Harold J.
1976 *Consumer Health.* St. Louis: C. V. Mosby.

Cottrell, Fred
1974 *Aging and the Aged.* Dubuque, Iowa: Wm. C. Brown Co.

Craig, S. R., and B. S. Brown
1975 "Comparison of youthful heroin users and nonusers from one urban community." *International Journal of the Addictions* 10 (no. 1):53–63.

Crawford, T., and M. Naditch
1970 "Relative deprivation, powerlessness, and militancy: the psychology of social protest." *Psychiatry* 33(May):208–23.

Cumming, Elaine
1976 "Further thoughts on the theory of disengagement." In *Aging in America: Readings in Social Gerontology,* eds. C. S. Kart and B. B. Manard, pp. 19–41. Port Washington, N.Y.: Alfred.

Cumming, Elaine, and William E. Henry
1961 *Growing Old.* New York: Basic Books.

Cummings, T. G., and S. L. Manring
1977 "The relationship between worker alienation and work-related behavior." *Journal of Vocational Behavior* 10(April):167–79.

Cuskey, W. R., L. H. Berger, and A. H. Richardson
1978 "The effects of marijuana decriminalization on drug use patterns: a literature review and research critique." *Contemporary Drug Problems* 7(Winter):491–532.

Darby, W. J.
1978 "The benefits of drink." *Human Nature,* November, 31–37.

Davidson, C., and C. M. Gaitz
1974 " 'Are the poor different?' A comparison of work behavior among the urban poor and nonpoor." *Social Problems* 22 (December):229–45.

Davies, J. C.
1962 "Toward a theory of revolution." *American Sociological Review* 27(February):5–19.

Davis, A. J.
1968 "Sexual assaults in the Philadelphia prison system and sheriff's vans." *Trans-Action* 6 (December):8–16.

Davis, J. H.
1975 "Alcohol as a precursor to violent death." *Journal of Drug Issues* 5:270–75.

Davis, Kingsley
1940 "The sociology of parent-youth conflict." *American Sociological Review* 5 (August):523–35.
1976 "Sexual behavior." In *Contemporary Social Problems,* 4th ed., eds. R. K. Merton and R. Nisbet, pp. 220–61. New York: Harcourt Brace Jovanovich, Inc.

Davis, W. H.
1970 "Overpopulated America." *New Republic* 162(January 10):13–15.

Day, L.
1968 "Natality and ethnocentrism: some relationships suggested by an analysis of Catholic-Protestant differentials." *Population Studies* 22 (March):27–50.

Dean, S. R.
1974 "Geriatric sexuality: normal, needed, and neglected." *Geriatrics* 29 (July):134–37.

Deckard, Barbara Sinclair
1975 *The Women's Movement*. New York: Harper & Row.

de Lissovoy, V.
1975 "Concerns of rural adolescent parents." *Child Welfare* 54 (March):167–74.

Denfeld, D.
1974 "Dropouts from swinging." *Family Coordinator* 23 (January):45–49.

Dentler, Robert A.
1972 *Major Social Problems*. 2nd ed. Chicago: Rand McNally.

Dentler, Robert A., and Phillips Cutright
1965 "Social effects of nuclear war." In *The New Sociology*, ed. I. L. Horowitz, pp. 409–26. New York: Oxford University Press.

de Tocqueville, Alexis
1955 *The Old Regime and the French Revolution*. New York: Anchor Books.

Deutsch, Karl W., Sidney A. Burrell, Robert A. Kann, Maurice Lee, Jr., Martin Lichterman, Raymond E. Lindgren, Francis L. Loewenheim, and Richard W. Van Wagenen
1957 *Political Community and the North Atlantic Area*. Princeton, N.J.: Princeton University Press.

Dibble, V. K.
1967 "The garrison society," *New University Thought* (Spring):106–155.

Doerner, W. G.
1978 "The Index of Southernness revisited: the influence of wherefrom and whodunnit." *Criminology* 16 (May):47–56.

Doherty, E. G., and C. Culver
1976 "Sex-role identification, ability, and achievement among high school girls." *Sociology of Education* 49 (January):1–3.

Dohrenwend, Bruce P.
1974 "Problems in defining and sampling the relevant population of stressful life events." In *Stressful Life Events: Their Nature and Effects*, ed. B. S. Dohrenwend and B. P. Dohrenwend, pp. 275–310. New York: John Wiley & Sons.

1975 "Sociocultural and social-psychological factors in the genesis of mental disorders." *Journal of Health and Social Behavior* 16 (December):365–92.

Dohrenwend, Bruce P., and Barbara S. Dohrenwend
1969 *Social Status and Psychological Disorder*. New York: John Wiley & Sons, pp. 275–310.

Dowdall, G. W.
1974 "White gains from black subordination in 1960 and 1970." *Social Problems* 22 (December):162–83.

Downey, G.W.
1974 "Panthers striking for power." *Modern Health Care* 2 (no. 2):65–69.

Drabman, R. S., and M. H. Thomas
1977 "Children's imitation of aggressive and prosocial behavior when viewing alone and in pairs." *Journal of Communication* 27 (Summer):199–205.

Dubbé, M. C.
1965 "What parents are not told may hurt." *The Family Life Coordinator* 14 (April):51–118.

Dubeck, P. J.
1976 "Women and access to political office: a comparison of female and male state legislators." *The Sociological Quarterly* 17(Winter):42–52.

Dulles, Foster Rhea
1966 *Labor in America: A History*. 3rd ed. Northbrook, Ill.: AHM Publishing Corp.

Durkheim, Emile
1938 *The Rules of Sociological Method*. 8th ed. Translated by S. A. Solovay and J. H. Mueller. Glencoe, Ill.: Free Press.
1951 *Suicide*. Translated by J. A. Spaulding and G. Simpson, New York: Free Press.

Dutton, D. B.
1978 "Explaining the low use of health services by the poor: costs, attitudes, or delivery systems?" *American Sociological Review* 43(June):348–68.

Eaton, Joseph W., and Robert J. Weil
1955 *Culture and Mental Disorders.* New York: Free Press.

Edwards, P., C. Harvey, and P. C. Whitehead
1970 "Wives of alcoholics: a critical review and analysis." *Quarterly Journal of Studies on Alcohol* 34(no. 1):112–32.

Ehrlich, Paul R.
1968 *The Population Bomb.* New York: Ballantine Books.
1971 "Eco-catastrophe!" In *The Survival Equation: Man, Resources, and His Environment,* eds. R. Revelle, A. Khosla, and M. Vinovskis, pp. 352–64. Boston: Houghton Mifflin.

Ehrlich, P. R., and A. H. Ehrlich
1979 "What happened to the population bomb?" *Human Nature,* January, 88–92.

Ehrlich, P. R., and J. P. Holdren
1971 "Impact of population growth." *Science* 171 (March 26):1212–17.

Eitzen, D. Stanley
1974 *Social Structure and Social Problems in America.* Boston: Allyn & Bacon.

Elliott, Mabel A., and Francis E. Merrill
1934 *Social Disorganization,* New York: Harper & Brothers.

Elmer, Elizabeth
1971 "Studies of child abuse and infant accidents." In *The Mental Health of the Child,* ed. National Institute of Mental Health, pp. 343–70. Washington, D.C.: Government Printing Office.

Elms, Alan C.
1972 *Social Psychology and Social Relevance.* Boston: Little, Brown.

Ennis, P. H.
1967 "Crime victims, and the police." *Trans-Action* 4(June):36–44.

Epstein, S. E.
1976 "The political and economic basis of cancer." *Technology Review* 78(July/August):35–43.

Erikson, Erik H.
1950 *Childhood and Society.* Middlesex, England: Penguin Books.

Erlanger, H. S.
1974 "The empirical status of the subculture of violence thesis." *Social Problems* 22 (December):280–92.

Eskin, Marian
1980 *Child Abuse and Neglect: A Literature Review and Selected Bibliography.* Washington, D.C.: U.S. Department of Justice.

Etaugh, C.
1974 "Effects of maternal employment on children: a review of recent research." *Merrill-Palmer Quarterly* 20 (April):71–98.

Etzioni, A.
1967 "The Kennedy Experiment." *Western Political Quarterly* 20 (June):361–80.

Eysenck, Hans J.
1952 "The effects of psychotherapy: an evaluation." *Journal of Consulting Psychology* 16:319–24.
1971 *The I.Q. Argument: Race, Intelligence, and Education.* New York: Library Press.

Fader, Daniel
1971 *The Naked Children.* New York: Macmillan.

Fang, B.
1976 "Swinging: in retrospect." *The Journal of Sex Research* 12 (August):220–37.

Farina, A., and K. Ring
1965 "The influence of perceived mental illness on interpersonal relationships." *Journal of Abnormal Psychology* 70 (no. 1):47–51.

Faunce, W. A.
1958 "Automation in the automobile industry: some consequences for in-plant social structure." *American Sociological Review* 23 (August):401–407.

Feldman, Harvey W.
1970 "Ideological supports to becoming and remaining a heroin addict." In *Youth and Drugs,* eds. J. H. McGrath and F. R. Scarpitti, pp. 87–97. Glenview, Ill.: Scott, Foresman.

Ferriss, Abbott L.
1970 *Indicators of Change in the American Family.* New York: Russell Sage Foundation.

Fey, Harold E., and Margaret Frankes, eds.
1962 *The Christian Century Reader.* New York: Association Press.

Fields, R. M.
1975 "Psychological genocide." *History of Childhood Quarterly* 3 (Fall):201–22.

Filstead, William J.
1972 *An Introduction to Deviance.* Chicago: Markham.

Fincher, J.
1976 "Depriving the best and the brightest." *Human Behavior,* April, pp. 17–21.

Fitzpatrick, Blanche
1975 "Economics of aging." In *Understanding Aging: A Multidisciplinary Approach,* eds. M. G. Spencer and C. J. Dorr, pp. 105–33. New York: Appleton-Century-Crofts.

Floyd, H. H., Jr., and D. R. South
1972 "Dilemma of youth: the choice of parents or peers as a frame of reference for behavior." *Journal of Marriage and the Family* 34 (November):627–34.

Foner, Philip S.
1974 *Organized Labor and the Black Worker: 1619–1973.* New York: Praeger.

Fontana, V. J.
1971 "Which parents abuse children?" *Medical Insight* 3 (no. 10):16–21.

Ford, Clellan S., and Frank A. Beach
1951 *Patterns of Sexual Behavior.* New York: Harper & Row.

Form, W. H.
1973 "Auto workers and their machines: a study of work, factory, and job satisfaction in four countries." *Social Forces* 52 (September):1–14.

Fornwalt, R. J.
1959 "For they have sown the wind." *Christianity Today,* July 6, pp. 8–10.

Fort, Joel
1974 "The marijuana abuser and the abuser of psychedelic-hallucinogens." In *Types of Drug Abusers and their Abuses,* eds. J. G. Cull and R. E. Hardy, pp. 134–45. Springfield, Ill.: Charles C Thomas.

Frantz, Joe B.
1969 "The frontier tradition: an invitation to violence." In *The History of Violence in America,* eds. H. D. Graham and T. R. Gurr, pp. 127–54. New York: Bantam Books.

Frederick, C. J., H. L. P. Resnik, and B. J. Wittlin
1973 "Self-destructive aspects of hard-core addiction." *Archives of General Psychiatry* 28 (April):579–85.

Freeberg, N. E., and D. T. Payne
1967 "Dimensions of parental practice concerned with cognitive development in the preschool child." *Journal of Genetic Psychology* 111 (December):245–61.

Freedman, Robert, ed.
1968 *Marxist Social Thought.* New York: Harcourt, Brace & World.

Freeman, Jo
1975 *The Politics of Women's Liberation.* New York: David McKay.

Freeman, Richard B.
1976 *The Over-Educated American.* New York: Academic Press.

Freeman, S. David
1974 *Energy: The New Era.* New York: Vintage Books.

Freud, Anna, and Dorothy Burlingham
1943 *War and Children.* New York: International Universities Press.

Freud, Sigmund
1949 *Three Essays on the Theory of Sexuality.* Translated by James Strachey. London: Imago Publishing Company.

1961 *Civilization and its Discontents.* Translated and edited by James Strachey. New York: W. W. Norton.

Freudenthal, K.
1959 "Problems of the one-parent family." *Social Work* 4 (January):44–48.

Fried, Marc
1966 "Effects of social change on mental health." In *Issues and Problems in Social Psychiatry,* eds. B. J. Bergen and C. S. Thomas, pp. 358–99. Springfield, Ill.: Charles C Thomas.

Friedenberg, Edgar Z.
1972 "The revolt against democracy." In *The Prospect of Youth,* ed. T. J. Cottle, pp. 147–56. Boston: Little, Brown.

Friedman, J. J.
1973 "Structural constraints on community action: the case of infant mortality rates." *Social Problems* 21 (Fall):230–45.

Fuchs, E.
1968 "How teachers learn to help children fail." *Trans-Action* 5 (September):45–49.

Fuller, R. C.
1938 "The problem of teaching social problems." *American Journal of Sociology* 44 (November):415–25.

Furnas, J. C.
1965 *The Life and Times of the Late Demon Rum.* New York: Capricorn Books.

Gagnon, John H.
1977 *Human Sexualities.* Glenview, Ill..: Scott, Foresman.

Gallup, George H.
1972 *The Gallup Poll: Public Opinion 1935–1971.* 3 vols. New York: Random House.

Gaquin, D. A.
1977–1978 "Spouse abuse—data from the National Crime Survey." *Victimology* 2 (no. 3): 632–43.

Garson, Barbara
1975 *All the Livelong Day: The Meaning and Demeaning of Routine Work.* New York: Penguin Books.

Geis, Gilbert
1972 *Not the Law's Business?* Rockville, Md.: National Institute of Mental Health.

Gelles, R. J.
1977 "Power, sex, and violence: the case of marital rape." *The Family Coordinator* 26 (October):339–47.

Gelles, R. J., and M. A. Straus
1979 "Violence in the American family." *Journal of Social Issues* 35 (no. 2):15–39.

Gellhorn, Martha
1959 *The Face of War.* New York: Simon & Schuster.

Gil, David G.
1970 *Violence Against Children.* Cambridge, Mass.: Harvard University Press.

Gilbert, J. G.
1973 "Thirty-five-year follow-up study of intellectual functioning." *Journal of Gerontology* 28 (no. 1):68–72.

Gillin, John Lewis, Clarence G. Dittmer, and Roy J. Colbert
1928 *Social Problems.* New York: Century Company.

Gist, Noel P., and Sylvia Fleis Fava
1964 *Urban Society.* 5th ed. New York: Thomas Y. Crowell.

Givens, H., Jr.
1978 "An evaluation of mandatory retirement." *Annals of the American Academy of Political and Social Science* 438 (July):50–58.

Glaser, Daniel
1969 "National Goals and Indicators for the Reduction of Crime and Delinquency." In *Social Intelligence for America's Future: Explorations in Social Problems,* ed. B. M. Gross, pp. 405–33. Boston: Allyn & Bacon.

Glenn, N. D.
1974 "Aging and conservatism." *Annals of the American Academy of Political and Social Science* 415 (September):176–86.

Glick, P. C.
1975 "A demographer looks at American families." *Journal of Marriage and the Family* 37 (February):15–26.

Gliner, Robert
1973 *American Society as a Social Problem.* New York: Free Press.

Goode, Erich
1970 "Marijuana and the politics of reality." In *The New Social Drug,* ed. D. E. Smith, pp. 168–86. Englewood Cliffs, N.J.: Prentice-Hall.

Goode, William J.
1956 *After Divorce.* Glencoe, Ill.: Free Press.
1964 *The Family.* Englewood Cliffs, N.J.: Prentice-Hall.

Goro, Herb
1970 *The Block.* New York: Vintage Books.

Gove, W. R.
1972 "The relationship between sex roles, marital status, and mental illness." *Social Forces* 51 (November):34–44.

Graham, Hugh Davis, and Ted Robert Gurr, eds.
1969 *The History of Violence in America.* New York: Bantam Books.

Graham, Neill
1976 *The Mind Tool.* St. Paul, Minn.: West Publishing Co.

Graney, M. J.
1975 "Happiness and social participation in aging." *Journal of Gerontology* 30 (November):701–6.

Gray D.
1973 "Turning-out: a study of teenage prostitution." *Urban Life & Culture* 1 (January):401–25.

Green, Gil
1971 *The New Radicalism: Anarchist or Marxist?* New York: International Publishers.

Greenberg, Selig
1965 *The Troubled Calling.* New York: Macmillan.

Grey, Alan L., ed.
1969 *Class and Personality in Society.* New York: Atherton Press.

Groth, A. Nicholas
1979 *Men Who Rape: The Psychology of the Offender.* New York: Plenum Press.

Gruberg, Martin
1968 *Women in American Politics.* Oshkosh, Wisc.: Academia Press.

Gubrium, Jaber F.
1975 *Living and Dying at Murray Manor.* New York: St. Martin's Press.

Gurr, Ted Robert
1969 "A comparative study of civil strife." In *The History of Violence in America,* ed. H. D. Graham and T. R. Gurr, pp. 572–632. New York: Bantam Books.

Guttmacher, Manfred S.
1951 *Sex Offenses.* New York: W. W. Norton.

Haberman, P. W., and M. M. Baden
1974 "Alcoholism and violent death." *Quarterly Journal of Studies on Alcohol* 35 (March, Part A):221–31.

Hacker, H. M.
1951 "Women as a minority group." *Social Forces* 30 (October):60–69.

Hadden, Jeffrey K.
1969 *The Gathering Storm in the Churches.* Garden City: Doubleday.

Hamblin, R. L., David Buckholdt, Donald Bushell, Desmond Ellis, and Daniel Ferritor
1969 "Changing the game from 'get the teacher' to 'learn.'" *Trans-Action* 6 (January):20–31.

Hammersmith, S. K., and M. S. Weinberg
1973 "Homosexual identity: commitment, adjustment, and significant others." *Sociometry* 36 (March):56–79.

Hampden-Turner, Charles
1970 *Radical Man,* Cambridge, Mass., Schenkman.

Han, Wan Sang
1969 "Two conflicting themes: common values versus class differential values." *American Sociological Review* 34 (October):679–90.

Hardin, Garrett
1971 "The tragedy of the commons." In *Man and the Environment,* ed. W. Jackson, pp. 243–54. Dubuque, Iowa: Wm. C. Brown Co.

Harrington, Michael
1962 *The Other America.* Baltimore: Penguin
      Books.

Hart, Hornell
1957 "Acceleration in social change." In
      Technology and Social Change, eds. F. R.
      Allen et al., pp. 27–55. New York:
      Appleton-Century-Crofts.

Hauser, Robert M.
1970 "Educational Stratification in the United
      States." In *Social Stratification,* ed. E. O.
      Laumann, pp. 102–29. Indianapolis, Ind.,
      Bobbs-Merrill.

Hauser, R. M., and D. L. Featherman
1976 "Equality of schooling: trends and
      prospects." *Sociology of Education* 49
      (April):99–120.

Hawkes, T. H.
1973 "Ideals of upper elementary school
      children." *Psychology in the Schools* 10
      (October):447–57.

Hechinger, F. M.
1976 "Murder in academe: the demise of
      education." *Saturday Review,* March 20, pp.
      11–18.

Hedblom, J. H.
1973 "Dimensions of lesbian sexual experience."
      Archives of Sexual Behavior 2
      (December):329–41.

Heilbroner, Robert L.
1975 *An Inquiry into the Human Prospect.* New
      York: W. W. Norton.

Heller, Celia Stopnicka
1969 *Structured Social Inequality.* London:
      Macmillan.

Heller, W. W.
1970 "Economics of the race problem." *Social
      Research* 37 (Winter):495–510.

Henslin, James M.
1975 *Introducing Sociology.* New York: Free
      Press.

Herman, J., and L. Hirschman
1977 "Father-daughter incest." *Signs* 2
      (Summer):735–56.

Herring, Hubert
1957 *A History of Latin America.* New York:
      Alfred A. Knopf.

Hersey, John
1946 *Hiroshima.* New York: Alfred A. Knopf.

Hertzler, Joyce O.
1965 *A Sociology of Language.* New York:
      Random House.

Herzberg, F.
1968 "One more time: how do you motivate
      employees?" *Harvard Business Review* 46
      (January/February):53–62.

Hess, R. D., and V. C. Shipman
1965 "Early experience and the socialization of
      cognitive modes in children." *Child
      Development* 36 (December):869–86.

Hetherington, E. Mavis
1973 "Girls without fathers." *Psychology Today,*
      February, pp. 47–52.

Hicks, N. W., and M. Platt
1970 "Marital happiness and stability: a review of
      the research in the sixties." *Journal of
      Marriage and the Family* 32
      (November):553–74.

Hills, Stuart L.
1980 *Demystifying Social Deviance.* New York:
      McGraw-Hill.

Himmelsbach, Clifton K.
1974 "Opiate addiction." In *Types of Drug
      Abusers and Their Abuses,* eds. J. G. Cull
      and R. E. Hardy, pp. 21–30. Springfield, Ill.:
      Charles C Thomas.

Hoffman, L. W.
1972 "Early childhood experiences and women's
      achievement motives." *Journal of Social
      Issues* 28 (no. 2):129–55.

Hoffman, Martin
1967 "Homosexuality and social evil." In *Change:
      Readings in Society & Human Behavior,*
      pp. 48–51. Del Mar, Calif.: CRM.

Hofstadter, Richard, and Michael Wallace, eds.
1970 *American Violence.* New York: Vintage
      Books.

Hogan, R. A., A. N. Fox, and J. H. Kirchner
1977 "Attitudes, opinions, and sexual development of 205 homosexual women." *Journal of Homosexuality* 3 (Winter):123–36.

Hollingshead, August B.
1949 *Elmtown's Youth*. New York: John Wiley & Sons.

Hollingshead, August B., and Frederick C. Redlich
1958 *Social Class and Mental Illness*. New York: John Wiley & Sons.

Holmes, Thomas H., and Minoru Masuda
1974 "Life change and illness susceptibility." In *Stressful Life Events,* eds. B. S. Dohrenwend and B. P. Dohrenwend, pp. 45–72. New York: John Wiley & Sons.

Hooker, Evelyn
1961 "Homosexuality." In *Sex Ways—In Fact and Faith,* eds. E. M. Duvall and S. M. Duvall, pp. 166–83. New York: Association Press.
1972 "Homosexuality." In *National Institute of Mental Health Task Force on Homosexuality: Final Report and Background Papers,* ed. J. M. Livingood, pp. 11–21. Rockville, Md.: National Institute of Mental Health.

Horney, Karen
1937 *The Neurotic Personality of Our Time*. London: Routledge & Kegan Paul.

Horos, Carol V.
1974 *Rape*. New Canaan, Conn.: Tobey Publishing Co.

Horton, D.
1943 "The functions of alcohol in primitive societies: a cross-cultural study." *Quarterly Journal of Studies on Alcohol* 4 (September):199–320.

Horwitz, A., and M. Wasserman
1979 "The effect of social control on delinquent behavior: a longitudinal test." *Sociological Focus* 12 (January):53–70.

Hoult, Thomas Ford
1975 *Social Justice and its Enemies*. Cambridge, Mass: Schenkman.

House, J. S.
1974 "Occupational stress and coronary heart disease: a review and theoretical integration." *Journal of Health and Social Behavior* 15 (March):12–27.

House, J. S., et al.
1979 "Occupational stress and health among factory workers." *Journal of Health and Social Behavior* 20 (June):139–60.

Huber, Joan, and William H. Form
1973 *Income and Ideology*. New York: Free Press.

Hunt, Morton
1974 *Sexual Behavior in the 1970s*. New York: Playboy Press.

Ilfield, F. W.
1977 "Current social stressors and symptoms of depression." *American Journal of Psychiatry* 134 (February):161–66.

Illich, Ivan
1975 "The alternative to schooling." In *Myth and Reality,* eds. G. Smith and C. R. Kniker, pp. 82–94, 2nd edition. Boston: Allyn & Bacon.
1976 *Medical Nemesis*. New York: Pantheon.

Ivancevich, J. M., and J. H. Donnelly, Jr.
1975 "Relation of organizational structure to job satisfaction, anxiety-stress, and performance." *Administrative Science Quarterly* 20 (June):272–80.

Jacob, T., A. Favorini, S. Meisel, and C. M. Anderson
1978 "The alcoholic's spouse, children and family interactions: substantive findings and methodological issues." *Journal of Studies on Alcohol* 39 (July):1231–51.

Jacobs, J. B.
1974 "Street gangs behind bars." *Social Problems* 21 (no. 3):395–408.

Jacobs, Paul
1966 "Man with a hoe, 1964." In *Poverty in the Affluent Society,* ed. H. H. Meissner, pp. 116–25. New York: Harper & Row.

James, Dorothy B.
1972 *Poverty, Politics, and Change.* Englewood Cliffs, N.J.: Prentice-Hall.

James, M. E., and M. Goldman
1971 "Behavior trends of wives of alcoholics." *Quarterly Journal of Studies on Alcohol* 32 (no. 2):373–81.

James, William
1890 *The Principles of Psychology.* Vol. 1. Reprint. New York: Dover, 1950.

Jencks, Christopher, Marshall Smith, Henry AcLand, Mary Jo Bane, David Cohen, Herbert Gintis, Barbara Heyns, and Stephen Michelson
1972 *Inequality: A Reassessment of the Effect of Family and Schooling in America.* New York: Basic Books.

Jensen, Arthur R.
1968 "Social class and verbal learning." In *Social Class, Race, and Psychological Development,* eds. M. Deutsch, I. Katz, and A. R. Jensen, pp. 115–74. New York: Holt, Rinehart & Winston.
1972 *Genetics and Education.* New York: Harper & Row.

Johnson, Elmer H.
1973 *Social Problems of Urban Man.* Homewood, Ill.: Dorsey Press.

Johnson, Lloyd D., Jerald G. Bachman, and Patrick M. O'Malley
1979 *1979 Highlights: Drugs and the Nation's High School Students.* Washington, D.C.: Government Printing Office.

Jones, W. C., H. J. Meyer, and E. F. Borgatta
1962 "Social and psychological factors in status decisions of unmarried mothers." *Marriage and Family Living* 24 (August):224–30.

Jordan, Winthrop D.
1968 *White Over Black.* Baltimore: Penguin Books.
1970 "Modern tensions and the origins of American slavery." In *Slavery and Its Aftermath,* ed. P. I. Rose, pp. 103–15. Chicago: Aldine Atherton.

Jorgensen, S. R., and D. M. Klein
1979 "Sociocultural heterogamy, dissensus, and conflict in marriage." *Pacific Sociological Review* 22 (January):51–75.

Joyce, Frank
1969 "Racism in the United States: An Introduction." In *The New Left: A Collection of Essays,* ed. P. Long, pp. 128–50. Boston: Porter Sargent.

Kagan, Aubrey
1971 "Epidemiology and society, stress and disease." In *Society, Stress and Disease,* ed. L. Levi, pp. 36–48. Vol. 1. London: Oxford University Press.

Kahn, Robert L.
1972 "The meaning of work: interpretation and proposals for measurement." In *The Human Meaning of Social Change,* eds. A. Campbell and P. E. Converse, pp. 159–203. New York: Russell Sage Foundation.

Kalish, R. A., and A. I. Johnson
1972 "Value similarities and differences in three generations of women." *Journal of Marriage and the Family* 34 (February):49–54.

Kane, Michael B.
1970 *Minorities in Textbooks.* Chicago: Quadrangle Books.

Kanter, R. M.
1976 "Why bosses turn bitchy." *Psychology Today,* May, pp. 56–59+.
1978 "Work in a new America." *Daedalus* 107 (Winter):47–78.

Kart, Cary S.
1976 "Some biological aspects of aging." In *Aging in America: Readings in Social Gerontology,* eds. C. S. Kart and B. B. Manard, pp. 179–83. Port Washington, N.Y.: Alfred.

Kasl, Stanislav V.
1978 "Epidemiological contributions to the study of work stress." In *Stress At Work,* eds., C. L. Cooper and R. Payne, pp. 3–48. New York: John Wiley & Sons.

Kasl, S., S. Gore, and S. Cobb
1975 "The experience of losing a job: reported changes in health symptoms and illness behavior." *Psychosomatic Medicine* 37 (March–April):106–22.

Kastenbaum, Robert, and Sandra E. Candy
1976 "The 4% fallacy: a methodological and empirical critique of extended care facility population statistics." In *Aging in America: Readings in Social Gerontology,* eds. C. S. Kart and B. B. Manard, pp. 166–74. Port Washington, N.Y.: Alfred.

Keen, S.
1978 "Eating our way to enlightenment." *Psychology Today,* October, pp. 62–66+.

Keller, S.
1963 "The social world of the urban slum child: some early findings." *American Journal of Orthopsychiatry* 33 (October):823–31.
1976 "Reply to Borgatta's 'the concept of reverse discrimination and equality of opportunity.' " *The American Sociologist* 11 (May):79–82.

Kerckhoff, Alan C.
1972 *Socialization and Social Class.* Englewood Cliffs, N.J.: Prentice-Hall.

Kerlin, Robert T.
1968 *The Voice of the Negro: 1919.* New York: Arno Press.

Kinzer, N. S.
1973 "Priests, machos and babies: or, Latin American women and the manichaean heresy." *Journal of Marriage and the Family* 35 (May):300–312.

Kleinman, P. H., I. F. Lukoff, and B. L. Kail
1977 "The magic fix: a critical analysis of methadone maintenance treatment." *Social Problems* 25 (December):208–14.

Kluegel, J. R.
1978 "The causes and cost of racial exclusion from job authority." *American Sociological Review* 43 (June):285–301.

Knight, R. C., J. P. Sheposh, and J. B. Bryson
1974 "College student marijuana use and societal alienation." *Journal of Health and Social Behavior* 15 (March):28–35.

Kniker, Charles R.
1975 "The search for equal educational opportunities." In *Myth and Reality,* eds. G. Smith and C. R. Kniker, pp. 210–26. 2nd edition. Boston: Allyn & Bacon.

Knowles, Louis L., and Kenneth Prewitt, eds.
1969 *Institutional Racism in America.* Englewood Cliffs, N.J.: Prentice-Hall.

Knox, R.
1980 "Nuclear war: what if . . .?" *Science 80,* May/June, pp. 32–34.

Kohn, M. L.
1959 "Social class and parental values." *American Journal of Sociology* 64 (January):337–51.

Komarovsky, Mirra
1940 *The Unemployed Man and His Family.* New York: Dryden Press.

Kornhauser, Arthur
1965 *Mental Health of the Industrial Worker: A Detroit Study.* New York: John Wiley & Sons.

Kosberg, J. I.
1973 "Differences in proprietary institutions caring for affluent and nonaffluent elderly." *Gerontologist* 13 (Autumn):299–304.

Kottak, Conrad Phillip
1974 *Anthropology.* New York: Random House.

Kozol, Jonathan
1967 *Death at an Early Age.* New York: Bantam Books.

Langer, Elinor
1975 "The shame of American medicine." In *Contemporary Social Issues,* ed. R. Giallombardo, 330–38. Santa Barbara, Calif.: Hamilton Publishing Co.

Langley, Roger, and Richard C. Levy
1977 *Wife Beating—The Silent Crisis.* New York: E. P. Dutton.

Langner, Thomas S., Joseph H. Helson, Edward L.
Greene, Jean D. Jameson, and Jeanne A. Goff
1970 "Children of the city: affluence, poverty, and
mental health." In *Psychological Factors in
Poverty,* ed. V. L. Allen, pp. 185–209.
Chicago: Markham.

Lasch, C.
1973 "Inequality and education." *New York
Review of Books,* May 17, pp. 19–25.

Lauer, Robert H.
1971 "The middle class looks at poverty." *Urban
and Social Change Review* 5 (Fall):8–10.
1972 "Unemployment: hard-core or hard shell?"
Urban and Social Change Review 6 (Fall):
7–10.
1973a *Perspectives on Social Change.* Boston:
Allyn & Bacon.
1973b "The generation gap as sociometric choice."
Youth & Society 5 (December):227–41.
1974 "Rate of change and stress: a test of the
'future shock' thesis." *Social Forces* 52
(June):510–16.
1976 "Defining social problems: public opinion
and textbook practice." *Social Problems* 24
(October):122–30.

Lauer, R. H., and D. E. Crismon
1972 "Social change in the valley of despair."
Growth and Change 3 (October):9–14.

Lauer, Robert H., and Warren H. Handel
1977 *Social Psychology: The Theory and
Application of Symbolic Interactionism.*
Boston: Houghton Mifflin.

Law, William
1906 *A Serious Call To a Devout and Holy Life.*
New York: E. P. Dutton.

Lawler, E. E.
1977 "Workers can set their own wages—
responsibly." *Psychology Today,* February,
pp. 109–12.

Lawrence, T. S., and J. D. Velleman
1974 "Correlates of student drug use in a
suburban high school." *Psychiatry* 37
(May):129–36.

Laws, J. L.
1971 "A feminist review of marital adjustment
literature: the rape of the Locke." *Journal of
Marriage and the Family* 33
(August):483–516.

Leach, Barry
1973 "Does Alcoholics Anonymous really work?"
In *Alcoholism: Progress in Research and
Treatment,* eds. P. G. Bourne and R. Fox,
pp. 260–76. New York: Academic Press.

LeBlanc, R., and J. LeBlanc
1979 "The case of the deadly doctors." *Human
Behavior,* May, pp. 43–47.

Lefkowitz, Bernard
1979 *Breaktime: Living Without Work in a Nine-
To-Five World.* New York: Penguin Books.

Lefkowitz, Monroe M., Leonard D. Eron, Leopold
O. Walder, and L. Rowell Huesmann
1972 "Television violence and child aggression: a
followup study." In *Television and Social
Behavior,* eds. G. A. Comstock and E. A.
Rubinstein, pp. 35–135. Vol. 3. Rockville,
Md.: National Institute of Mental Health.

LeMasters, E. E.
1975 *Blue-collar Aristocrats,* Madison, Wisc.:
University of Wisconsin Press.

Lemert, Edwin M.
1951 *Social Pathology.* New York: McGraw-Hill.

Lennard, H. L., L. J. Epstein, and M. S. Rosenthal
1972 "The methadone illusion." *Science* 176
(May 26):881–84.

Lerner, Max
1957 *America as a Civilization.* New York:
Simon & Schuster.

Levin, Tom
1974 *American Health.* New York: Praeger.

Levine, Robert A.
1970 *The Poor Ye Need Not Have With You.*
Cambridge, Mass.: MIT Press.

Levine, Sol, and Norman A. Scotch, eds.
1970 *Social Stress.* Chicago: Aldine.

Levy, Sheldon G.
1969 "A 150-year study of political violence in the
       United States." In *The History of Violence
       in America*, eds. H. D. Graham and T. R.
       Gurr, pp. 84–100. New York: Bantam
       Books.

Lewis, Oscar
1966 *La Vida*. New York: Random House.
1969 "A Puerto Rican boy." In *Culture Change,
       Mental Health, and Poverty*, ed. J. C.
       Finney, pp. 149–54. New York: Simon &
       Schuster.

Lewis, R. A. et al.
1977 "Commitment in married and unmarried
       cohabitation." *Sociological Focus* 10
       (October):367–74.

Lewis, R. A., and W. R. Burr
1975 "Premarital coitus and commitment among
       college students." *Archives of Sexual
       Behavior* 4 (January):73–79.

Leznoff, Maurice, and William A. Westley
1967 "The homosexual community." In *Sexual
       Deviance*, eds. J. H. Gagnon and W. Simon,
       pp. 184–96. New York: Harper & Row.

Lieberson, S., and A. R. Silverman
1965 "The precipitants and underlying conditions
       of race riots." *American Sociological Review*
       30 (December):887–98.

Lin, Nan
1976 *Foundations of Social Research*. New York:
       McGraw-Hill.

Lincoln, C. Eric
1961 *The Black Muslims in America*. Boston:
       Beacon Press.

Lineberry, William P.
1979 *Arms Control*. New York: The H. W.
       Wilson Company.

Lipset, Seymour Martin
1963 *Political Man*. Garden City: Anchor Books.

Little, Craig Brooks
1973 *Stress Responses Among Unemployed
       Technical-Professionals*. Unpublished Ph.D.
       dissertation, University of New Hampshire.

Locksley, A.
1980 "On the effects of wives' employment on
       marital adjustment and companionship."
       Journal of Marriage and the Family 42
       (May):337–46.

Looft, W. R.
1971 "Vocational aspirations of second-grade
       girls." *Psychological Reports* 28
       (February):241–42.

Losciuto, L. A., and R. M. Karlin
1972 "Correlates of the generation gap." *Journal
       of Psychology* 81 (July, Second
       Half):253–62.

Lozier, J., and R. Althouse
1975 "Retirement to the porch in rural
       Appalachia." *International Journal of Aging
       and Human Development* 6 (no. 1):7–15.

Lubell, Samuel
1968 "The 'generation gap'." In *Confrontation*,
       eds. D. Bell and I. Kristol, pp. 58–66. New
       York: Basic Books.

Lutterbie, P. H.
1974 "Black administrators: winners and losers."
       Integrated Education 12 (May/June):42–45.

McCall, George J., and J. L. Simmons, eds.
1969 *Issues in Participant Observation*. Reading,
       Mass.: Addison-Wesley.

McCord, J., W. McCord, and E. Thurber
1964 "Some effects of paternal absence on male
       children." *Journal of Abnormal and Social
       Psychology* 64 (May):361–69.

McCord, William, and Joan McCord
1960 *Origins of Alcoholism*. Stanford, Calif.:
       Stanford University Press.

McCracken, J. A.
1976 "The company tells me I'm old." *Saturday
       Review*, August 7, pp. 21–23.

McDermott, M. Joan
1979 *Criminal Victimization in Urban Schools*.
       Washington, D.C.: Government Printing
       Office.

McGhee, P. E., and T. Frueh
1980 "Television viewing and the learning of sex-role stereotypes." *Sex Roles* 6 (no. 2):179–88.

McLean, E. K., and A. Tarnopolsky
1977 "Noise, discomfort and mental health." *Psychological Medicine* 7 (February):19–62.

McLeish, John
1969 *The Theory of Social Change.* London: Routledge & Kegan Paul.

Macmillan, Allister, and Alexander H. Leighton
1952 "People of the hinterland: community interrelations in a maritime province of Canada." In *Human Problems in Technological Change,* ed. E. H. Spicer, pp. 225–43. New York: Russell Sage Foundation.

McQuade, Walter, and Ann Aikman
1974 *Stress.* New York: E. P. Dutton.

Madge, John
1962 *The Origins of Scientific Sociology.* New York: Free Press.

Manaster, A.
1972 "Therapy with the 'senile' geriatric patient." *International Journal of Group Psychotherapy* 22 (April):250–57.

Marble, Beula B., and M. Isabel Patterson
1975 "Nutrition and aging." In *Understanding Aging: A Multidisciplinary Approach,* eds. M. G. Spencer and C. J. Dorr, pp. 195–208. New York: Appleton-Century-Crofts.

Marmor, Theodore R., ed.
1971 *Poverty Policy.* Chicago: Aldine Atherton.

Martindale, Don, and Edith Martindale
1971 *The Social Dimensions of Mental Illness, Alcoholism, and Drug Dependence.* Westport, Conn.: Greenwood Press.

Mason, K. O., J. L., Czajka, and S. Arber
1976 "Change in U.S. women's sex-role attitudes: 1964–1974." *American Sociological Review* 41 (August):573–96.

Matza, David
1966 "The disreputable poor." In *Class, Status, and Power,* eds. R. Bendix and S. M. Lipset, pp. 289–302. 2nd edition. New York: Free Press.

Mayeske, George W., Carl E. Whisler, Albert E. Beaton, Jr., Frederic D. Weinfeld, Wallace M. Cohen, Tetsuo Okada, John M. Proshek, and Kenneth A. Tabler
1973 *A Study of the Achievement of Our Nation's Schools.* Washington, D.C.: Government Printing Office.

Mead, Margaret
1969 *Sex and Temperament in Three Primitive Societies.* New York: Dell.

Meadows, Donella, Dennis L. Meadows, Jorgen Randers, and William W. Behrens III
1972 *The Limits to Growth.* New York: Universe Books.

Means, Richard L.
1972 "Public opinion and planned changes in social behavior: the ecological crisis." In *Social Behavior, Natural Resources, and the Environment,* eds. W. R. Burch, Jr., N. H. Cheek, Jr., and L. Taylor, pp. 203–13. New York: Harper & Row.

Medea, Andra, and Kathleen Thompson
1974 *Against Rape.* New York: Farrar, Straus and Giroux.

Medley, M. L.
1976 "Satisfaction with life among persons sixty-five years and older." Journal of Gerontology 31 (July):448–55.

Meier, August, Elliott Rudwick, and Francis E. Broderick, eds.
1971 *Black Protest Thought in the Twentieth Century.* 2nd edition. Indianapolis, Ind.: Bobbs-Merrill.

Melman, Seymour
1970 "Overkill: the drain on America." In *Where It's At,* eds. S. E. Deutsch and J. Howard, pp. 485–94. New York: Harper & Row.
1974 *The Permanent War Economy.* New York: Simon & Schuster.

Merton, Robert K.
1939 "Social structure and anomie." *American Sociological Review* 3 (October):672–82.
1957 *Social Theory and Social Structure.* New York: Free Press.

Mes, G. M.
1964 *Now-Men and Tomorrow-Men.* Johannesburg: Afrikaanse Pers-Boekhandel.

Mesarovic, Mihajlo, and Eduard Pestel
1974 *Mankind at the Turning Point.* New York: Signet.

Miller, Delbert C.
1972 "The allocation of priorities to urban and environmental problems by powerful leaders and organizations." In *Social Behavior, Natural Resources, and the Environment,* eds. W. R. Burch, Jr., N. H. Cheek, Jr., and L. Taylor, pp. 306–31. New York: Harper & Row.

Miller, N. and H. B. Gerard
1976 "How busing failed in Riverside." *Psychology Today,* June, pp. 66–70+.

Miller, Stephen J.
1976 "The social dilemma of the aging leisure participant." In *Aging in America,* eds. C. S. Kart and B. B. Manard, pp. 264–85. Port Washington, N.Y.: Alfred.

Millett, Kate
1971 "Prostitution: a quartet of female voices." In *Woman in Sexist Society,* eds. V. Gornick and B. K. Moran, pp. 60–125. New York: Mentor Books.

Mills, C. Wright
1958 *The Causes of World War III.* New York: Simon & Schuster.
1959 *The Sociological Imagination.* New York: Oxford University Press.

Minturn, Leigh, and William W. Lambert
1964 *Mothers of Six Cultures.* New York: John Wiley & Sons.

Mitchell, Roger S.
1969 *The Homosexual and the Law.* New York: Arco Publishing Co.

Modlin, Herbert C.
1974 "The medical profession addict." In *Types of Drug Abusers and Their Abuses,* eds. J. G. Cull and R. E. Hardy, pp. 3–16. Springfield, Ill.: Charles C Thomas.

Morgan, W. R., and T. N. Clark
1973 "The causes of racial disorders: a grievance-level explanation." *American Sociological Review* 38 (October):611–24.

Moriwaki, S. Y.
1973 "Self-disclosure, significant others and psychological well-being in old age." *Journal of Health and Social Behavior* 14 (September):226–32.

Mott, Paul E.
1972 *The Characteristics of Effective Organizations.* New York: Harper & Row.

Moynihan, Daniel Patrick
1965 *The Negro Family: The Case for National Action.* Washington, D.C.: Government Printing Office.

Muller, Herbert J.
1970 *The Children of Frankenstein: A Primer on Modern Technology and Human Values.* Bloomington: Indiana University Press.

Mulvihill, Donald J., and Melvin M. Tumin
1969 *Crimes of Violence. A Staff Report Submitted to the National Commission on the Causes & Prevention of Violence.* Vol. 11. Washington, D.C.: Government Printing Office.

Murphy, J. M.
1976 "Psychiatric labeling in cross-cultural perspective." *Science* 191 (March 12):1019–28.

Mushkin, S.
1975 "Politics and economics of government response to drug abuse." *Annals of the American Academy of Political and Social Science* 417 (January):27–40.

Mutter, Arthur Z., and Maxwell J. Schleifer
1969 "The role of psychological and social factors in the onset of somatic illness in children." In *Research in Family Interaction,* eds. W. D. Winter and A. J. Ferreira, pp. 76–86. Palo Alto, Calif.: Science and Behavior Books.

Myers, P.
1971 "Caution: Congress may be hazardous to your health." *City* 5 (March/April):27–29.

Myrdal, Gunnar
1944 *An American Dilemma.* New York: Harper & Bros.

Nash, J.
1973 "The cost of violence." *Journal of Black Studies* 4 (December):153–83.

Nathanson, C. A.
1975 "Illness and the feminine role: a theoretical review." *Social Science and Medicine* 9 (February):57–62.

National Advisory Commission on Criminal Justice Standards and Goals
1973 *A National Strategy to Reduce Crime.* Washington, D.C.: Government Printing Office.

National Center for Health Statistics
1973 "Current estimates from the health interview survey." *Vital and Health Statistics,* Series 10, no. 85, September.

National Commission on Marihuana and Drug Abuse
1973 *Drug Use in America.* Washington, D.C.: Government Printing Office.

National Institute of Law Enforcement and Criminal Justice
1978 *Forcible Rape: Final Project Report.* Washington, D.C.: Government Printing Office.

National Institute on Alcohol Abuse and Alcoholism
1975 *Facts about Alcohol and Alcoholism.* Rockville, Md.: National Institute on Alcohol Abuse and Alcoholism.

Nearing, Scott
1969 *Black America.* New York: Schocken Books.

Nelson, J. I. and C. Simpkins
1973 "Family size and college aspirations: a note on Catholic-Protestant differences." *The Sociological Quarterly* 14 (Autumn):544–55.

Neugarten, B. L.
1973 "Patterns of aging: past, present, and future." *The Social Service Review* 47 (December):571–80.

Newman, Gustave, and Claude R. Nichols
1970 "Sexual activities and attitudes in older persons." In *Normal Aging,* ed. E. Palmore, pp. 277–81. Durham, N.C.: Duke University Press.

Newport News Community Development Program
1973 *Social Conditions and Services: Interim Report Eight.* Newport News (February).

O'Brien, J. E.
1971 "Violence in divorce prone families." *Journal of Marriage and the Family* 33 (November):692–98.

O'Connor, J. F., and A. Lizotte
1978 "The 'Southern subculture of violence' thesis and patterns of gun ownership." *Social Problems* 25 (April):420–29.

Ogburn, William Fielding
1938 *Social Change.* New York: Viking Press.

Olmstead, D. W. and K. Durham
1976 "Stability of mental health attitudes: a semantic differential study." *Journal of Health and Social Behavior* 17 (March):35–44.

Olsen, D., and R. Parker
1977 "Why prices go up when jobs go down." *Mother Jones,* February/March, pp. 11–12.

Oltman, J. E., J. J. McGarry, and S. Friedman
1952 "Parental deprivation and the 'broken home' in dementia praecox and other mental disorders." *American Journal of Psychiatry* 108 (March):685–94.

Orden, S. R., and M. B. Norman
1969 "Working wives and marriage happiness."
     American Journal of Sociology 74
     (January):392–407.

Orfield, Gary
1978 *Must We Bus? Segregated Schools and
     National Policy.* Washington, D.C.:
     Brookings Institution.

Orshansky, M.
1965 "Counting the poor: another look at the
     poverty level." *Social Security Bulletin* 28
     (January):3–29.

Orshansky, M., and J. S. Bretz
1976 "Born to be poor: birthplace and number of
     brothers and sisters as factors in adult
     poverty." *Social Security Bulletin* 39
     (January):21–37.

Otto, Herbert A., ed.
1970 *The Family in Search of a Future.* New
     York: Appleton-Century-Crofts.

Owens, W. A.
1966 "Age and mental abilities: a second adult
     follow-up." *Journal of Educational
     Psychology* 57 (December):311–25.

Ozarin, L. D., and M. J. Witkin
1975 "Halfway houses for the mentally ill and
     alcoholics: a 1973 survey." *Hospital and
     Community Psychiatry* 26
     (February):101–3.

Paige, J. M.
1971 "Political orientation and riot participation."
     American Sociological Review 36
     (October):810–20.

Palmore, E.
1969 "Predicting longevity: a follow-up controlling
     for age." *The Gerontologist* 9
     (Winter):247–50.
1975 "The status and integration of the aged in
     Japanese society." *Journal of Gerontology*
     30 (March):199–208.
1976 "The effects of aging on activities and
     attitudes." In *Aging in America: Readings in
     Social Gerontology,* eds. C. S. Kart and
     B. B. Manard, pp. 252–63. Port
     Washington, N.Y.: Alfred.

Palson, C., and R. Palson
1972 "Swinging in wedlock." *Society* 9
     (February):28–37.

Parker, Franklin
1975 "What's right with American education." In
     Myth and Reality, eds. G. Smith and C. R.
     Kniker, pp. 29–36. 2nd edition. Boston: Allyn &
     Bacon.

Parker, K. E., and B. J. Stebman
1973 "The development of the black bar." *Annals
     of the American Academy of Political and
     Social Science* 407 (May):144–55.

Parker, R.
1970 "The myth of middle America." *The Center
     Magazine,* March/April, 61–70.

Pascal, Blaise
1941 *Pensees.* Translated by W. F. Trotter. New
     York: Modern Library.

Pavenstedt, E.
1965 "A comparison of the child-rearing
     environment of upper-lower and very low-
     lower class families." *American Journal of
     Orthopsychiatry* 35 (January):89–98.

Peake, C. F.
1975 "Negro occupation-employment participation
     in American industry." *American Journal of
     Economics and Sociology* 34
     (January):67–86.

Perlman, Richard
1973 *The Economics of Education: Conceptual
     Problems and Policy Issues.* New York:
     McGraw-Hill.

Perrow, Charles
1970 *Organizational Analysis: A Sociological
     View.* Belmont, Calif.: Brooks/Cole
     Publishing Co.

Peters, M. F.
1974 "The black family—perpetuating the myths:
     an analysis of family sociology textbook
     treatment of black families." *Family
     Coordinator* 23 (October):349–57.

Pettigrew, Thomas
1964 *A Profile of the Negro American.* Princeton,
     N.J.: D. Van Nostrand.

Pettigrew, T. F., E. L. Useem, C. Normand, and M. S. Smith
1973 "Busing: a review of 'the evidence.' " *The Public Interest* 30 (Winter):88–118.

Pfeiffer, E.
1974 "Sexuality in the aging individual." *Journal of the American Geriatrics Society* 22 (November):481–84.

Pfeiffer, E. W., and A. W. Westing
1974 "Land War." In *Science, Technology, and Freedom*, eds. W. H. Truitt and T. W. G. Solomons, pp. 252–64. Boston: Houghton Mifflin.

Phillips, Derek L.
1971 *Knowledge From What?* Chicago: Rand McNally.

Pickford, John, Edro I. Signori, and Henry Rempel
1966 "Similar or related personality traits as a factor in marital happiness." *Journal of Marriage and the Family* 28 (May):190–92.

Pihlblad, C. T., and D. L. Adams
1972 "Widowhood, social participation and life satisfaction." *Aging and Human Development* 3:323–30.

Pinkney, Alphonso
1970 "Prejudice toward Mexican and Negro-Americans: a comparison." In *Mexican-Americans in the United States*, ed. J. H. Burman, pp. 73–80. Cambridge: Schenkman.

Pizer, Stuart A., and Jeffrey R. Travers
1975 *Psychology and Social Change*. New York: McGraw-Hill.

Platt, Anthony
1969 *The Child Savers: The Invention of Delinquency*. Chicago: University of Chicago Press.

Ploscowe, Morris
1968 "Rape." In *Problems of Sex Behavior*, eds. E. Sagarin and D. E. J. MacNamara, pp. 203–40. New York: Thomas Y. Crowell.

Ploski, Harry A., and Ernest Kaiser, eds.
1971 *The Negro Almanac*. 2nd edition. New York: Bellwether Publishing Co.

Polak, P. R., and M. W. Kirby
1976 "A model to replace psychiatric hospitals." *Journal of Nervous and Mental Disease* 162 (January):13–22.

Pratt, L.
1972 "Conjugal organization and health." *Journal of Marriage and Family* 34 (February):85–95.
1973 "Child rearing methods and children's health behavior." *Journal of Health and Social Behavior* 14 (March):61–69.

President's Commission on Law Enforcement and Administration of Justice
1967a *The Challenge of Crime in a Free Society*. Washington, D.C.: Government Printing Office.
1967b *Task Force Report: Crime and Its Impact—An Assessment*. Washington, D.C.: Government Printing Office.

Pruger, Robert, and Charles Wilder
1974 *Poverty: Conceptions, Realities, Issues*. New York: MSS Modular Publications.

Quadagno, J.
1976 "Occupational sex-typing and internal labor market distributions: an assessment of medical specialties." *Social Problems* 23 (April):442–53.

Raffalli, H. C.
1970 "The battered child. An overview of a medical, legal, and social problem." *Crime and Delinquency* 16 (April):139–50.

Rainwater, L.
1967 "Crisis of the city: poverty and deprivation." *Washington University Magazine*, Spring, pp. 17–21.

Ransdell, Hart, and Tressa Roche
1969 "Psychosocial treatment of psychoneurosis." In *Culture Change, Mental Health, and Poverty*, ed. J. C. Finney, pp. 97–108. New York: Simon & Schuster.

Ransford, H. E.
1968 "Isolation, powerlessness, and violence: a study of attitudes and participation in the Watts riot." *American Journal of Sociology* 73 (March):581–91.

Rathjens, G. W.
1969 "The dynamics of the arms race." *Scientific American* 220 (April):15–25.

Rawlings, Stephen
1978 *Perspectives on American Husbands and Wives.* Washington, D.C.: Government Printing Office.

Reasons, C.
1974 "The politics of drugs: an inquiry in the sociology of social problems." *Sociological Quarterly* 15 (Summer):381–404.

Reich, Charles A.
1970 *The Greening of America.* New York: Random House.

Reinhardt, James M., Paul Meadows, and John M. Gillette
1952 *Social Problems and Social Policy.* New York: American Book Co.

Reiss, Albert J., Jr.
1967 "The social integration of queers and peers." In *Sexual Deviance*, eds. J. H. Gagnon and W. Simon, pp. 197–228. New York: Harper & Row.

Reissman, L.
1969 "Readiness to succeed: mobility aspirations and modernism among the poor." *Urban Affairs Quarterly* 4 (March):379–95.

Report of the Study of Critical Environmental Problems
1970 *Man's Impact on the Global Environment.* Cambridge, Mass.: MIT Press.

Revelle, Roger
1971 "Pollution and cities." In *The Survival Equation: Man, Resources, and His Environment*, eds. R. Revelle, A. Khosla, and M. Vinovskis, pp. 382–414. Boston: Houghton Mifflin.

Reynolds, R. A.
1976 "Improving access to health care among the poor—the neighborhood health center experience." *Milbank Memorial Fund Quarterly* 54 (Winter):47–82.

Richardson, Henry B.
1970 "A Family as seen in the hospital." In *Families in Crisis*, eds. P. H. Glasser and L. N. Glasser, pp. 222–41. New York: Harper & Row.

Riessman, Frank
1962 *The Culturally Deprived Child.* New York: Harper & Row.

Riley, Matilda Whiting, and Joan Waring
1976 "Age and aging." In *Contemporary Social Problems*, eds. R. K. Merton and R. Nisbet, pp. 357–410. 4th edition. New York: Harcourt Brace Jovanovich.

Rimlinger, G. V., and H. B. Steele
1963 "An economic interpretation of the spatial distribution of physicians in the United States." *Southern Economic Journal* 30 (July):1–12.

Ro, K. K.
1964 "Medical care and family income—a 30-year trend." *Progress in Health Services* 13 (November/December):1–6.

Robinson, John P., Philip E. Converse, and Alexander Szalai
1972 "Everyday life in twelve countries." In *The Use of Time: Daily Activities of Urban and Suburban Populations in Twelve Countries*, ed. A. Szalai, pp. 113–44. The Hague: Mouton.

Rockwell, D. A.
1973 "Alcohol and marijuana—social problem perspective." *British Journal of Addiction* 68 (October):209–14.

Rodgers, Harrell R., Jr., and Charles S. Bullock
1972 *Law and Social Change.* New York: McGraw-Hill.

Rodstein, M., E. Savitsky, and R. Starkman
1976 "Initial adjustment to a long-term care institution: medical and behavioral aspects." *Journal of the American Geriatrics Society* 24 (February):65–71.

Roebuck, J. B., and T. Barker
1974 "A typology of police corruption." *Social Problems* 22 (April):423–37.

Roman, P. M.
1975 "Secondary prevention of alcoholism: problems and prospects in occupational programming." *Journal of Drug Issues* 5 (Fall):327–42.

Rorabaugh, W. J.
1979 *The Alcoholic Republic: An American Tradition.* New York: Oxford University Press.

Rosen, B., and T. H. Jerdee
1974 "Sex stereotyping in the executive suite." *Harvard Business Review* 52 (March/April):45–58.

Rosenberg, Morris
1965 *Society and the Adolescent Self-Image.* Princeton: Princeton University Press.

Rosenfield, S.
1980 "Sex differences in depression: do women always have higher rates?" *Journal of Health and Social Behavior* 21 (March):33–42.

Rosenhan, D. L.
1973 "On being sane in insane places." *Science* 179 (January 19):250–58.

Rosenkrantz, Paul, Susan Vogel, Helen Bee, Inge Broverman, and Donald M. Broverman
1968 "Sex-role stereotypes and self-concepts in college students." *Journal of Consulting and Clinical Psychology* 32 (June):287–95.

Rosenthal, M. J.
1962 "The syndrome of the inconsistent mother." *American Journal of Orthopsychiatry* 32 (July):637–44.

Rosenthal, Robert, and Lenore Jacobson
1968 "Self-fulfilling prophecies in the classroom: teachers' expectations as unintended determinants of pupils' intellectual competence." In *Social Class, Race, and Psychological Development,* eds. M. Deutsch, I. Katz, and A. R. Jensen, pp. 219–53. New York: Holt, Rinehart and Winston.

Rossi, A. S.
1964 "Equality between the sexes: an immodest proposal." *Daedalus* 93 (Spring):607–52.

Roszak, Theodore
1969 *The Making of a Counter-Culture.* Garden City: Anchor Books.

Rotenberg, M.
1974 "Self-labeling: a missing link in the 'societal reaction' theory of deviance." *The Sociological Review* 22 (August):335–54.

Rothenberg, M. B.
1975 "Effect of television violence on children and youth." *Journal of the American Medical Association* 234 (December 8):1043–46.

Rothman, Jack
1974 *Planning and Organizing for Social Change.* New York: Columbia University Press.

Roy, D. F.
1959–60 " 'Banana time': job satisfaction and informal interaction." *Human Organization* 18 (Winter):158–68.

Rubenstein, A.
1973 "How China got rid of opium." *Monthly Review* 25 (October):58–63.

Ryan, William
1971 *Blaming the Victim.* New York: Pantheon Books.

Sagarin, E. R.
1973 "The good guys, the bad guys, and the gay guys." *Contemporary Sociology* 2 (January):3–13.

Saghir, M. T., and E. Robins
1971 "Male and female homosexuality: natural history." *Comprehensive Psychiatry* 12 (November):503–10.

Saghir, M. T., E. Robins, B. Walbran, and K. A. Gentry
1970 "Homosexuality. IV. Psychiatric disorders and disability in the female homosexual." *American Journal of Psychiatry* 127 (August):147–54.

Salisbury, A. J., and R. B. Berg
1969 "Health defects and need for treatment of adolescents in low income families." *Public Health Reports* 84 (August):705–11.

Santrock, J. W.
1972 "Relation of type and onset of father absence to cognitive development." *Child Development* 43 (June):455–69.

Sanua, V. D.
1961 "Sociocultural factors in families of schizophrenics." *Psychiatry* 24 (August):246–65.

Saul, Shura
1974 *Aging: An Album of People Growing Old.* New York: John Wiley & Sons.

Sayles, Leonard R., and George Strauss
1966 *Human Behavior in Organizations.* Englewood Cliffs, N.J.: Prentice-Hall.

Schachter, S., and J. E. Singer
1962 "Cognitive, social, and psychological determinants of emotional state." *Psychological Review* 69 (September):379–99.

Schatzman, Leonard, and Rue Bucher
1964 "Negotiating a division of labor among professionals in the state mental hospital." *Psychiatry* 27 (August):266–77.

Scheff, Thomas
1966 *Being Mentally Ill.* Chicago: Aldine.

Schelling, T. C.
1973 "Foreward, symposium: time in economic life." *Quarterly Journal of Economics* 87 (November):627–28.

Schlossberg, N. K., and J. Goodman
1972 "A woman's place: children's sex stereotyping of occupations." *Vocational Guidance Quarterly* 20 (June):266–70.

Schmalleger, F.
1979 "World of the career criminal." *Human Nature,* March, pp. 50–56.

Schuck, P.
1972 "Tied to the sugar lands." *Saturday Review,* May 6, pp. 36–42.

Schulz, D. A., and R. A. Wilson
1973 "Some traditional family variables and their correlations with drug use among high school students." *Journal of Marriage and the Family* 35 (November):628–31.

Schwartz, Richard D., and Jerome H. Skolnick
1964 "Two studies of legal stigma." In *The Other Side,* ed. H. S. Becker, pp. 103–17. New York: Free Press.

Schwartzman, J.
1975 "The addict, abstinence and the family." *American Journal of Psychiatry* 132 (February):154–57.

Sciara, F. J., and R. K. Jantz
1974 "Father absence and its apparent effect on the reading achievement of black children from low income families." *Journal of Negro Education* 43 (Spring):221–27.

Sears, Robert R., E. Maccoby, and H. Levin
1957 *Patterns of Child Rearing.* New York: Harper & Row.

Seidenberg, R.
1972 "The trauma of eventlessness." *Psychoanalytic Review* 59 (Spring):95–109.

Selye, Hans
1956 *The Stress of Life.* New York: McGraw-Hill.

Sennett, R.
1970 "The brutality of modern families." *Trans-Action* 7 (September):29–37.

Sennett, Richard, and Jonathan Cobb
1972 *The Hidden Injuries of Class.* New York: Vintage Books.

Sewell, W. H., and V. Shah
1968 "Parents' education and children's educational aspirations and achievements." *American Sociological Review* 33 (April):191–209.

Shapiro, R. D.
1975 "Alcohol, tobacco, and illicit drug use among adolescents." *International Journal of Addictions* 10:387–90.

Sheppard, Harold L., and Neal Q. Herrick
1972 *Where Have All the Robots Gone? Worker Dissatisfaction in the 1970s.* New York: The Free Press.

Shostak, Arthur B.
1969 *Blue-Collar Life.* New York: Random House.

Siebert, Horst, and Ariane Berthoin Antal
1979 *The Political Economy of Environmental Protection.* Greenwich, Conn.: JAI Press, Inc.

Silberman, Charles E.
1970 *Crisis in the Classroom.* New York: Random House.

Silverman, D.
1943 "Psychoses in criminals: a study of five hundred psychotic prisoners." *Journal of Clinical Psychopathology* 4 (October):703–30.

Simon, William, and John H. Gagnon
1967 "The lesbians: a preliminary overview." In *Sexual Deviance,* eds. J. H. Gagnon and W. Simon, pp. 247–82. New York: Harper & Row.

Simpson, George E., and Milton Yinger
1965 *Racial and Cultural Minorities.* New York: Harper & Row.

Simpson, M., and T. Schill
1977 "Patrons of massage parlors: some facts and figures." *Archives of Sexual Behavior* 6 (November):521–25.

Sinclair, Upton
1956 *The Cup of Fury.* Great Neck, N.Y.: Channel Press.

Singer, J. David, and Melvin Small
1972 *The Wages of War, 1816–1965.* New York: John Wiley & Sons.

Singer, J. E.
1976 "Social and Psychological Impact of Transportation Noise." Paper presented at Acoustical Society of America.

Single, E., D. Kandel, and R. Faust
1974 "Patterns of multiple drug use in high school." *Journal of Health and Social Behavior* 15 (December):344–57.

Sivard, Ruth Leger
1977 *World Military and Social Expenditures, 1977.* Leesburg, Va.: WMSE Publications.

Sixth Annual Report of the Council on Environmental Quality
1975 Washington, D.C.: Government Printing Office.

Smith, H. W.
1975 *Strategies of Social Research.* Englewood Cliffs, N.J.: Prentice-Hall.

Smith, James D.
1974 "The Concentration of Personal Wealth in America, 1969." *The Review of Income and Wealth* 20 (June):143–80.

Smith, K. J. and A. Lipman
1972 "Constraint and life satisfaction." *Journal of Gerontology* 27 (January):77–82.

Smith, R. M., and J. Walters
1978 "Delinquent and non-delinquent males' perceptions of their fathers." *Adolescence* 13 (Spring):21–28.

Sorokin, Pitirim A.
1942 *The Crisis of Our Age.* New York: E. P. Dutton.

Spicer, J. C. and S. O. Gustavus
1974 "Mormon fertility through half a century: another test of the Americanization hypothesis." *Social Biology* 21 (Spring):70–76.

Spiegel, John
1960 "The resolution of role-conflict within the family." In *Modern Introduction to the Family,* eds. N. W. Bell and E. F. Vogel, pp. 361–81. Glencoe, Ill.: Free Press.

Spreitzer, E., and E. E. Snyder
1974 "Correlates of life satisfaction among the aged." *Journal of Gerontology* 29 (July):454–58.

Srole, Leo, Thomas S. Langer, Stanley T. Michael, Marvin K. Opler, and Thomas A. C. Rennie
1962 *Mental Health in the Metropolis: The Manhatten Midtown Study.* Vol. 1, New York: McGraw-Hill.

Stanford Biology Study Group
1970   *The Destruction of Indochina.* Stanford, Cal.: n.p.

Stannard, C. I.
1973   "Old folks and dirty work: the social conditions for patient abuse in a nursing home." *Social Problems* 20 (Winter):329–42.

Stanton, Alfred H., and Morris S. Schwartz
1961   "The mental hospital and the patient." In *Complex Organizations,* ed. A. Etzioni, pp. 234–42. New York: Holt, Rinehart & Winston.

Steinmetz, S. K., and M. A. Straus
1973   "The family as cradle of violence." *Society* 10 (September/October):50–56.

Stern, John, ed.
1973   *Prototype State-of-the-Region Report for Los Angeles County.* Los Angeles: University of California.

Strainchamps, Ethel
1971   "Our sexist language." In *Woman in Sexist Society,* eds. V. Gornick and B. K. Moran, pp. 347–61. New York: Mentor Books.

Straus, M. A.
1974   "Leveling, civility and violence in the family." *Journal of Marriage and the Family* 36 (February):13–30.

Straus, M. A., R. J. Gelles, and S. K. Steinmetz
1979   *Behind Closed Doors: Violence in the American Family.* Garden City: Anchor Books.

Straus, Robert
1976   "Problem drinking in the perspective of social change, 1940–1973." In *Alcohol and Alcohol Problems,* eds. W. J. Filstead, J. J. Rossi, and M. Keller, pp. 29–56. Cambridge, Mass.: Ballinger.

Strauss, A.
1973   "Chronic illness." *Society* 10 (September/October):33–39.

Strauss, Anselm, Leonard Schatzman, Rue Bucher, Danuta Ehrlich, and Melvin Sabshin

1963   "The hospital and its negotiated order." In *The Hospital in Modern Society,* ed. E. Friedson, pp. 147–69. New York: Free Press.
1964   *Psychiatric Ideologies and Institutions.* New York: Free Press.

Streit, F., D. L. Halsted, and P. J. Pascale
1974   "Differences among youthful users and nonusers of drugs based on their perceptions of parental behavior." *International Journal of the Addictions* 9 (October):749–55.

Strong, L. D.
1978   "Alternative marital and family forms: their relative attractiveness to college students and correlates of willingness to participate in nontraditional forms." *Journal of Marriage and the Family* 40 (August):493–503.

Suchman, E. A.
1968   "The 'hang-loose' ethic and the spirit of drug use." *Journal of Health and Social Behavior* 9 (June):146–55.

Summers, A., and B. Wolfe
1977   "Do schools make a difference?" *American Economic Review* 67 (September):639–52.

Sutherland, Edwin H.
1939   *Principles of Criminology.* Philadelphia: J. B. Lippincott.
1968   "White Collar Criminality." In *Radical Perspectives on Social Problems,* ed. Frank Lindenfeld, pp. 149–60. New York: Macmillan.

Sutherland, Edwin H., and Donald R. Cressey
1955   *Principles of Criminology.* 5th edition. Philadelphia: J. B. Lippincott.

Sutter, Alan G.
1970   "Worlds of drug use on the street scene." In *Youth and Drugs,* eds. J. H. McGrath and F. R. Scarpitti, pp. 74–86. Glenview, Ill.: Scott, Foresman.

Sviland, Mary Ann P.
1974   "The ex-addict and his alternate subcultures." In *Types of Drug Abusers and Their Abuses,* eds. J. G. Cull and R. E. Hardy, pp. 56–95. Springfield, Ill.: Charles C Thomas.

Sykes, Gresham M.
1958 *The Society of Captives*. Princeton, N.J.: Princeton University Press.
1961 "The corruption of authority and rehabilitation." In *Complex Organizations*, ed. A. Etzioni, pp. 191–97. New York: Holt, Rinehart & Winston.

Symanski, R.
1974 "Prostitution in Nevada." *Annals of the Association of American Geographers* 64 (September):357–77.

Szymanski, A.
1976 "Racism and sexism as functional substitutes in the labor market." *Sociological Quarterly* 17 (Winter):67–73.

Taft, Philip, and Philip Ross
1969 "American labor violence: its causes, character, and outcome." In *The History of Violence in America*, eds. H. D. Graham and T. R. Gurr, pp. 281–395. New York: Bantam Books.

Tavris, C.
1977 "Masculinity." *Psychology Today*, January, pp. 35–42.

Taylor, D. G., L. A. Aday, and R. Andersen
1975 "A social indicator of access to medical care." *Journal of Health and Social Behavior* 16 (March):39–49.

Temerlin, M. K.
1968 "Suggestion effects in psychiatric diagnosis." *Journal of Nervous and Mental Disease* 147 (October):349–53.

Terkel, Studs
1972 *Working*. New York: Avon Books.

Tesconi, Charles A., Jr., and Emanuel Hurwitz, Jr.
1974 *Education for Whom?* New York: Dodd, Mead.

Tharp, R. G.
1963 "Psychological patterning in marriage." *Psychological Bulletin* 60 (March):97–117.

Thomas, C. W., D. M. Petersen, and M. T. Zingraff
1975 "Student drug use: a re-examination of the 'hang-loose ethic' hypothesis." *Journal of Health and Social Behavior* 16 (March):50–62.

Thomas, E. C., and K. Yamamoto
1975 "Attitudes toward age: an exploration in school-age children." *International Journal of Aging and Human Development* 6 (no. 2):117–29.

Thomas, William I., and Florian Znaniecki
1918–20 *The Polish Peasant in Europe and America*. Chicago: University of Chicago Press.

Thompson, N. L., Jr., B. R. McCandless, and B. R. Strickland
1971 "Personal adjustment of male and female homosexuals and heterosexuals." *Journal of Abnormal Psychology* 78 (October):237–40.

Thoreau, Henry David
1968 *Walden and the Essay on Civil Disobedience*. New York: Lancer Books.

Tiger, Lionel
1969 *Men In Groups*. New York: Random House.
1970 "Male dominance? Yes, alas. A sexist plot, no." *New York Times Magazine*, October 25, pp. 35–37; November 15, p. 34; November 22, p. 45.

Tissue, T.
1972 "Old age and the perception of poverty." *Sociology and Social Research* 56 (April):331–44.

Tobin, S. S., and B. L. Neugarten
1961 "Life satisfaction and social interaction in the aging." *Journal of Gerontology* 16 (October):344–46.

Toch, Hans
1965 *The Social Psychology of Social Movements*. New York: Bobbs-Merrill.

Toffler, Alvin
1970 *Future Shock*. New York: Random House.

Treiman, D. J., and K. Terrell
1975 "Sex and the process of status attainment: a comparison of working women and men." *American Sociological Review* 40 (April):174–200.

Tsuchigane, Robert, and Norton Dodge
1974 *Economic Discrimination Against Women in the United States.* Lexington, Mass.: D. C. Heath.

Tullock, Gordon
1974 "Does punishment deter crime?" *The Public Interest*, no. 36 (Summer):103–11.

United Nations
1973 *Demographic Yearbook, 1972.* New York: United Nations.

U.S. Bureau of the Census
1973 *Census of the Population: 1970, Detailed Characteristics*, Final Report PC (1)-D1. Washington, D.C.: Government Printing Office.

1976 *Current Population Reports*, series P-60, no. 102, "Characteristics of the Population Below the Poverty Level: 1974." Washington, D.C.: Government Printing Office.

1980 *Current Population Reports*, series P-20, no. 350, "Population Profile of the United States: 1979." Washington, D.C.: Government Printing Office.

U.S. Commission on Civil Rights
1967 *Racial Isolation in the Public Schools.* Washington, D.C.: Government Printing Office.

U.S. Department of Commerce
1975 *Crime in Retailing.* Washington, D.C.: Government Printing Office.

U.S. Department of Health, Education and Welfare
1973 *Work In America.* Washington, D.C.: Government Printing Office.

U.S. Department of Justice, Bureau of Justice Statistics
1980 *Intimate Victims: A Study of Violence Among Friends and Relatives.* Washington, D.C.: Government Printing Office.

U.S. Department of Justice, Drug Enforcement Administration
1973 *Fact Sheets.* Washington, D.C.: Government Printing Office.

U.S. Department of Justice, Law Enforcement Assistance Administration
1979a *Criminal Victimization in the United States: 1977.* Washington, D.C.: Government Printing Office.

1979b *Rape Victimization in 26 American Cities.* Washington, D.C.: Government Printing Office.

1979c *Capital Punishment: 1978.* Washington, D.C.: Government Printing Office.

U.S. Department of Labor
1980 *Employment and Training Report of the President.* Washington, D.C.: Government Printing Office.

U.S. Department of Labor, Bureau of Labor Statistics
1979 *Handbook of Labor Statistics, 1978.* Washington, D.C.: Government Printing Office.

U.S. Department of Labor, Women's Bureau
1974 *The Myth and the Reality.* Washington, D.C.: Government Printing Office.

1976 *The Role and Status of Women Workers in the United States and Japan.* Washington, D.C.: Government Printing Office.

U.S. Environmental Protection Agency
1973 *Cost of Air Pollution Damage: A Status Report.* Washington, D.C.: Government Printing Office.

U.S. Federal Bureau of Investigation
1976 *Crime in the United States, 1975, Uniform Crime Reports.* Washington, D.C.: Government Printing Office.

U.S. National Criminal Justice Information and Statistics Service
1975 *Criminal Victimization in the United States, 1973 Advance Report.* Washington, D.C., Government Printing Office.

U.S. Riot Commission
1968 *Report of the National Advisory Commission on Civil Disorders.* New York: Bantam Books.

Vaillant, G. E.
1973 "A 20-year follow-up of New York narcotic addicts." *Archives of General Psychiatry* 29 (no. 2):237–41.

Valentine, Charles A.
1968 *Culture and Poverty.* Chicago: University of Chicago Press.

Velie, L.
1960 "Strange case of the country slickers vs. the city rubes." *Reader's Digest,* April, 108–12.

Vener, A. M., and C. A. Snyder
1966 "The preschool child's awareness and anticipation of adult sex-roles." *Sociometry* 29 (June):159–68.

Verwoerdt, Adriaan, Eric Pfeiffer, and Hsioh-Shan Wang
1970 "Sexual behavior in senescence." In *Normal Aging,* ed. E. Palmore, pp. 282–99. Durham, N.C.: Duke University Press.

Vetri, D.
1979–80 "The legal arena: progress for gay civil rights." *Journal of Homosexuality* 5 (Fall/Winter): 25–34.

Vigderhous, G., and G. Fishman
1978 "The impact of unemployment and familial integration on changing suicide rates in the U.S.A., 1920–1969." *Social Psychiatry* 13 (no. 4):239–48.

Vinokur, A., and M. L. Selzer
1975 "Desirable versus undesirable life events: their relationship to stress and mental distress." *Journal of Personality and Social Psychology* 32 (August):329–39.

Waller, W.
1936 "Social problems and the mores." *American Sociological Review* 1:922–34.

Wallerstein, J. S., and C. J. Wyle
1947 "Our law abiding law breakers." *Probation* 25 (March/April):107–12.

Waltz, J. R., and C. R. Thigpen
1973 "Genetic screening and counseling: the legal and ethical issues." *Northwestern University Law Review* 68 (September/October):696–768.

Walz, Thomas H., and Gary Askerooth
1973 *The Upside Down Welfare State.* Minneapolis, Minn.: Advocate Services, Inc.

Warheit, G. J., C. E. Holzer, III, and J. J. Schwab
1973 "An analysis of social class and racial differences in depressive symptomatology: a community study." *Journal of Health and Social Behavior* 14 (December):291–99.

Washington Consulting Group, Inc.
1974 *Uplift: What People Themselves Can Do.* Salt Lake City: Olympus Publishing Co.

Watts, Harold W., and Albert Rees, eds.
1977 *The New Jersey Income-Maintenance Experiment.* New York: Academic Press.

Wax, Murray
1971 *Indian-Americans: Unity and Diversity.* Englewood Cliffs, N.J.: Prentice-Hall.

Wechsler, H., and D. Thum
1973 "Teen-age drinking, drug use, and social correlates." *Quarterly Journal of Studies on Alcohol* 34 (December):1220–27.

Weinberg, Arthur, and Lila Weinberg, eds.
1963 *Instead of Violence.* New York: Grossman Publishers.

Weinberg, S. Kirson
1952 *Society and Personality Disorders.* Englewood Cliffs, N.J.: Prentice-Hall.
1974 *Deviant Behavior and Social Control.* Dubuque, Iowa: Wm. C. Brown Co.

Weissman, M. M.
1972 "The depressed woman: recent research." *Social Work* 17 (September), 19–25.

Weissman, M. M., E. S. Paykel, and G. L. Klerman
1972 "The depressed woman as a mother." *Social Psychiatry* 7 (May):98–108.

Weitzman, L. J., D. Eifler, E. Hokada, and C. Ross
1972   "Sex-role socialization in picture books for preschool children." *American Journal of Sociology* 77 (May):1125–50.

Wells, Donald A.
1967   *The War Myth.* New York: Pegasus.

Welty, Paul Thomas
1970   *The Asians: Their Heritage and Their Destiny.* 3rd edition. Philadelphia: J. B. Lippincott.

Weppner, R. S., and M. H. Agar
1971   "Immediate percursors to heroin addiction." *Journal of Health and Social Behavior* 12 (March):10–17.

West, James
1945   *Plainville, U.S.A.* New York: Columbia University Press.

Whisler, Thomas L.
1970   *Information Technology and Organizational Change.* Belmont, Calif.: Wadsworth.

White, Lynn, Jr.
1971   "The historical roots of our ecologic crisis." In *Man and the Environment,* ed. W. Jackson, pp. 22–31. 2nd edition. Dubuque, Iowa: Wm. C. Brown Co.

White, R. K.
1966   "Misperception and the Vietnam war." *Journal of Social Issues* 22 (July):1–19.

Whiteman, Martin, and Martin Deutsch
1968   "Social disadvantage as related to intellective and language development." In *Social Class, Race, and Psychological Development,* eds. M. Deutsch, I. Katz, and A. R. Jensen, pp. 86–114. New York: Holt, Rinehart & Winston.

Whitt, J. A.
1973   "Californians, cars and technological death." *Society* 10 (July/August):30–38.

Whyte, William H., Jr.
1956   *The Organization Man.* Garden City: Anchor Books.

Wilcock, Richard C. and Walter H. Franke
1963   *Unwanted Workers.* New York: Free Press.

Wilensky, Harold L.
1967   *Organizational Intelligence.* New York: Basic Books
1976   "The welfare mess." *Society,* May/June, p. 12.

Wilkinson, A. Earl
1974   "The alcohol abuser." In Types of Drug Abusers and Their Abuses, eds. J. G. Cull and R. E. Hardy, pp. 146–59. Springfield, Ill.: Charles C Thomas.

Williams, Robin M., Jr.
1954   *American Society: A Sociological Interpretation.* New York: Alfred A. Knopf.

Williamson, J. B.
1974   "Beliefs about the welfare poor." *Sociology and Social Research* 58 (January):163–75.

Wilson, James Q.
1975   *Thinking About Crime.* New York: Basic Books.

Wilson, J. Q., M. H. Moore, and W. D. Wheat, Jr.
1972   "The problem of heroin." *The Public Interest* 29(Fall):3–28.

Wilson, K. L., and A. Portes
1975   "The educational attainment process: results from a national sample." *American Journal of Sociology* 81 (September):343–63.

Winick, Charles, and Paul M. Kinsie
1971   *The Lively Commerce.* Chicago: Quadrangle Books.

Wolfgang, Marvin E., and Franco Ferracuti
1967   *The Subculture of Violence.* London: Tavistock Publications.

Wolin, S. J., L. A. Bennet, D. L. Noonan, and M. A. Teitelbaum
1980   "Disrupted family rituals: a factor in the intergenerational transmission of alcoholism." *Journal of Studies on Alcohol* 41 (March):199–214.

Woodring, P.
1976   "Why 65? the case against mandatory retirement." *Saturday Review,* August 7, pp. 18–20.

Woods, M. B.
1972 "The unsupervised child of the working
       mother." *Developmental Psychology* 6
       (January):14–25.

Worthy, J. C.
1950 "Organizational structure and employee
       morale." *American Sociological Review* 15
       (April):169–79.

Wylie, R. C.
1963 "Children's estimates of their schoolwork
       ability as a function of sex, race, and
       socioeconomic level." *Journal of Personality*
       31 (June):203–24.

Yahraes, Herbert
1978 *Why Young People Become Antisocial.*
       Washington, D.C.: Government Printing
       Office.

Yankelovich, Daniel
1974 *The New Morality: A Profile of American
       Youth in the 70's.* New York: McGraw-Hill.

Yee, A. H.
1968 "Source and direction of causal influence in
       teacher-pupil relationships." *Journal of
       Educational Psychology* 59
       (August):275–82.

Zaleznik, A., M. F. R. K. de Vries, and J. Howard
1977 "Stress reactions in organizations:
       syndromes, causes, and consequences."
       Behavioral Science 22 (May):151–62.

Zborowski, M.
1952 "Cultural components in responses to pain."
       Journal of Social Issues 8 (no. 4):16–30.

Zimbardo, P. G.
1972 "Pathology of imprisonment." Society 9
       (April):4–8.

Zinberg, N. E., and R. C. Jacobson
1976 "The natural history of 'Chipping.' " *The
       American Journal of Psychiatry* 133
       (January):37–40.

Zunich, Michael
1969 "A study of relationships between child
       rearing attitudes and maternal behavior." In
       Class and Personality in Society, ed. A. L.
       Grey, pp. 70–83. New York: Atherton Press.

Credits

Part 1

2 Rick Smolan

Chapter 1

7 Clinical Center, National Institute of Mental Health / 14 Robert Maust / 20 Jean-Claude Lejeune / 28 James L. Shaffer / 36 (*top*) Julie Lauer (*bottom*) James Ballard

Chapter 2

50 Paul M. Schrock / 55 James Ballard / 61 Wide World Photos / 65 The Office of U.S. Congresswoman Lynn Martin / 68 Albert Bandura

Part 2

74 Peter Karas

Chapter 3

82 (*left*) Wide World Photos (*right top*) Jean-Claude Lejeune (*right bottom*) Mimi Forsythe, Monkmeyer Press / 85 (*top*) Bill Epperidge, Life Magazine © Time, Inc. (*bottom*) Jean-Claude Lejeune / 94 © Bernie Cleff / 97 (*top*) Jan Lukas, Editorial Photocolor Archives / 97 (*bottom left*) Dan O'Neill, Editorial Photocolor Archives (*bottom right*) Jan Lukas, Editorial Photocolor Archives / 103 Bob Eckert

Chapter 4

117 (*top*) Marilyn Silverstone, Magnum (*bottom*) M. Erwitt, Magnum / 120 Michael Hanulak / 130 Ken Regan, Camera 5 / 133 Wide World Photos / 143 National Institute on Alcohol Abuse and Alcoholism

Chapter 5

148 St. Louis Post Dispatch / 155 Arthur Tress / 161 Paolo Koch, Woodfin Camp / 166 John Robaton, Camera 5 / 174 Bob Coyle / 180 Ken Regan, Camera 5

Chapter 6

191 AP Wirephoto / 195 Julie O'Neill / 201 AP Wirephoto / 209 Historical Pictures Service, Inc. / 214 (*top*) Cornell Capa (*bottom left*) David Strickler (*right*) Paul Conklin / 219 St. Louis Post Dispatch

Chapter 7

227 UPI Photo / 230 UPI Photo / 234 Historical Pictures Service / 240 FBI Law Enforcement Bulletin / 249 Michael Keller / 253 David Strickler / 256 Cary Heinz, Nancy Palmer Agency

Part 3

260 Rick Smolan

Chapter 8

267 © Jill Krementz / 272 (*left*) David Vaughn (*right*) Rick Smolan / 276 (*top*) RNS Photo (*bottom left*) Michael Heron (*bottom right*) Tom Mosier / 282 UPI Photo / 293 Paul Conklin / 298 David Vaughn

Chapter 9

305 Library of Congress / 309 Library of Congress / 313 National Archives / 315 Library of Congress / 323 Stan Greenwood / 326 National Archives, Records of the Children's Bureau

Chapter 10

333 UPI Photo / 340 (*left*) Vernon Sigl / 340 (*right*) ACTION / VISTA / 347 Rick Smolan / 353 (*top*) Vernon Sigl (*bottom*) Rick Smolan / 355 Rick Smolan / 360 Paul Conklin

Chapter 11

370 (*left*) Bob Combs (*right*) Barbara Van Cleve / 374 Jean-Claude Lejeune / 378 UPI Photo / 381 UPI Photo / 386 Jean-Claude Lejeune / 396 Spencer Pendergrass / 397 Alan Ruid / 398 Jean-Claude Lejeune

Chapter 12

404 Paul Conklin / 406 UPI Photo / 407 Wide World Photos / 411 (*top*) Editorial Photocolor Archives (*bottom*) UPI Photo / 421 Contact Press Images / 425 (*left*) Bob Eckert (*right*) Mimi Forsythe, Monkmeyer Press / 431 David Strickler / 433 *The Crisis*, NAACP Journal / 438 (*left*) Bob Scott (*right*) Wide World Photos

Chapter 13

447 Rohn Engh / 448 John Maher, EKM Photos / 460 UPI Photo / 470 UPI Photo / 476 UPI Photo

Chapter 14

486 (*top*) James Ballard (*bottom*) Julie Lauer / 488 L. Manning, Van Cleve Photography / 497 David Vaughn / 501 Rick Smolan / 509 Bettmann Archive / 511 Richard Kalvar, Magnum

Part 4

516 Peter Karas

Chapter 15

520 George Strock, Time / Life
Picture Agency / 525 Larry
Burrows, Time / Life Picture
Agency / 529 UPI Photo / 531
(*top*) Wide World Photos
(*bottom*) UPI Photos

Chapter 16

550 Environmental Protection
Agency / 554 © The Long Island
News / 557 Bob Eckert / 564
The New York Zoological
Society / 572 (*top*) © Ted
Streshinsky (*bottom*) Wide
World Photo / 579 (*background*)
Bob Coyle (*foreground*)
H. Armstrong Roberts

Name Index

Subject Index